Learners on the
Autism Spectrum

Learners on the Autism Spectrum

Preparing Highly Qualified Educators and Related Practitioners

Second Edition

Edited by
Kari Dunn Buron and Pamela Wolfberg

Foreword by Carol Gray

AAPC
PUBLISHING
P.O. Box 23173
Shawnee Mission, Kansas 66283-0173
www.aapcpublishing.net

© 2014 AAPC Publishing
P. O. Box 23173
Shawnee Mission, Kansas 66283-0173
www.aapcpublishing.net • 913.897.1004

Publisher's Cataloging-in-Publication

Learners on the autism spectrum : preparing highly qualified educators and related practitioners / edited by Kari Dunn Buron and Pamela Wolfberg ; foreword by Carol Gray -- 2nd ed. -- Shawnee Mission, Kansas : AAPC Publishing, c2014.

p. ; cm.

ISBN: 978-1-937473-94-5
LCCN: 2014936981
Includes bibliographical references and index.
Summary: Update and expansion of the first (2008) edition of the textbook, with new chapters on self-regulation, evidence-based practice and special interests.--Publisher.

1. Children with autism spectrum disorders--Education. 2. Autistic children--Education. 3. Asperger's syndrome--Patients--Education. 4. Teachers of children with disabilities--Handbooks, manuals, etc. 5. Teaching--Aids and devices. I. Buron, Kari Dunn. II. Wolfberg, Pamela J. III. Gray, Carol, 1952- IV. Title.

LC4717.8 .L43 2014
371.94--dc23   1404

This book is designed in Minion and Adobe Garamond.

Cover Art: Original art by Kari Dunn Buron.

Printed in the United States of America.

Dedication

Dedicated to my parents, Tom and June Dunn, who possess two
of the gentlest and purest souls here on earth.
How fortunate I am to have witnessed their love of mankind.
– K.D.B.

Dedicated in loving memory of my beau-père Murray Gordon,
whose equally passionate pursuit of science and art
is an inspiration to all who teach and learn.

– P.W.

Table of Contents

About the Editors

Kari Dunn Buron, MS, worked with students on the autism spectrum in K-12 special education for over 30 years. She created an ASD certificate program for educators at Hamline University in St. Paul, MN. Kari received her master's of science degree in behavior disorders and learning disorders from Illinois State University, where she has been inducted into the Education Department Hall of Fame. Kari was one of the founding members of the MN Autism Network, a statewide group of educators, and is a past president of the Autism Society of Minnesota. She has spent over 20 years working with the Autistic Society of Trinidad and Tobago, where she continues to travel annually to volunteer in homes and schools. In 1995, Kari developed Camp Discovery, a summer camp for youth with ASD Level 1. In 2003, she received a fellowship that allowed her to study social cognition and ASD from an international perspective. Kari is the co-author of *The Incredible 5-Point Scale* and *Social Behavior and Self-Management*. She is the author of *When My Worries Get Too Big!*, *A 5 Is Against the Law!*, *A 5 Could Make Me Lose Control*, and most recently, an early chapter book for children entitled *Adalyn's Clare*. Kari serves on the professional advisory boards for the Autism Society of Minnesota, Minnesota LIFE College, and the *Autism Asperger Digest*. For more information, visit www.5pointscale.com.

Pamela Wolfberg, PhD, is professor of the Autism Spectrum Graduate Certificate and Related Studies at San Francisco State University and faculty advisor for the joint doctoral program in special education with the University of California, Berkeley. For three decades her life's work has centered on the unique needs of individuals on the autism spectrum in the areas of socialization, play and imagination, and inclusion in peer culture. As originator of the Integrated Play Groups (IPG) model and co-founder of the Autism Institute on Peer Socialization and Play, she leads research, training, and development efforts to establish inclusive peer socialization programs worldwide. She is further engaged in global outreach as a human rights advocate for the child's right to social inclusion in play, recreation, and cultural experiences. Widely published in peer-reviewed journals and books, she is the author of *Play and Imagination in Children With Autism* and *Peer Play and the Autism Spectrum: The Art of Guiding Children's Socialization and Imagination*. Pamela has an active international agenda as an invited speaker and serving in advisory roles for government and non-government organizations. She also serves as associate editor for *Autism: International Journal of Research and Practice* and as a guest reviewer for the *Journal of Autism and Developmental Disorders*. Finally, she is the recipient of several eminent awards for her scholarship, research, and service to the community. For more information, visit www.wolfberg.com

Contributors

Tony Attwood, PhD, The Asperger's Syndrome Clinic, Petrie, Queensland, Australia

Simon Baron-Cohen, PhD, professor, Autism Research Centre, Department of Psychiatry, University of Cambridge, United Kingdom

Kari Dunn Buron, MS, autism educational specialist and author, St. Paul, Minnesota

Julie Donnelly, PhD, senior autism resource specialist, Project ACCESS, Columbia, Missouri

Winnie Dunn, PhD, OTR FAOTA, professor and chair, Department of Occupational Therapy Education, University of Kansas Medical Center, Kansas

Ofer Golan, PhD, senior lecturer, Department of Psychology, Bar-Ilan University, Israel

Paula Jacobsen, LCSW, BCD, private practice and adjunct clinical professor, Department of Psychiatry and Behavioral Sciences, Stanford University School of Medicine, California

Bonnie J. McBride, PhD, associate professor, Developmental and Behavioral Pediatrics, University of Oklahoma Health Sciences Center

Heather McCracken, executive director, Friend 2 Friend Social Learning Society, Vancouver, BC, Canada

Gary B. Mesibov, PhD, professor emeritus of psychology, Departments of Psychiatry and Psychology, University of North Carolina at Chapel Hill NC

Nancy J. Minshew, MD, professor of psychiatry and neurology, University of Pittsburgh School of Medicine, Pennsylvania

Brenda Smith Myles, PhD, consultant with the Ohio Center for Autism and Low Incidence (OCALI) and the Ziggurat Group

Cathy Pratt, PhD, director, Indiana Resource Center for Autism, and board chair, Autism Society of America

Ilene S. Schwartz, PhD, professor and chair, area of special education, University of Washington

Victoria Shea, PhD, adjunct associate professor of psychology, Department of Psychiatry, University of North Carolina at Chapel Hill

Stephen Shore, EdD, professor, Adelphi University, New York

Sheila Smith, PhD, assistant director, Ohio Center for Autism and Low Incidence, Columbus, Ohio

Terri Cooper Swanson, PhD, instructor and autism certificate coordinator, Pittsburg State University, Kansas

Diane Twachtmann-Cullen, PhD, CCC-SLP, executive director, Autism and Developmental Disabilities Consultation Center, Higganum, Connecticut

Tara Tuchel, MS, CCC-SLP, autism specialist, Stillwater Area Schools, Stillwater, Minnesota

Diane L. Williams, PhD, CCC-SLP, associate professor, Department of Speech-Language Pathology, Duquesne University, Pennsylvania

Michelle Garcia Winner, MA, SLP, specialist for persons with social cognitive challenges, Michelle G. Winner's Center for Social Thinking, Inc., San Jose, California

Mary Ann Winter-Messiers, PhD, adjunct instructor and research assistant, Special Education and Clinical Sciences, University of Oregon

Pamela Wolfberg, PhD, professor, Autism Spectrum Studies, Department of Special Education and Communication Disorders, San Francisco State University, California

Chapter Reviewers

California Team

Think Tank Leaders:
Shayla Duda
Emmy Fearne
Betty Yu

Think Tanks:
Sue Brock
Seana Corona
Caitlin Cota
Julianne Hoffman
Talya Kemper
Bridgette Malatesta
Vicki McCoy
Johanna Ploude
Suchitra Thapliyal

Seenae Chong
Bert Dyer
Jessica Fink
Yvette Gonzales
Rochelle Hooks
Kiara Lopez
Miriam Nathanson
Andrew Preston
Amy Schaller

Shi Shyuan Ba
Alex Caldwallader
Leah Felson
Helen Lara-Crea
Kathleen Madden
Rachel Manfredi
Corrina McGraw
Michelle Young

Minnesota Team

Mary Kay Bachel
Cathy Banks
Patty Bowe
Sarah Boyer
Cindy Brown Polson
Tami Childs
Patricia Cretella
Anne Dudley
Joseph Falkner
Diane Gallagher
Angela Haffner
Jan Hanson
Linda Hanson
Janet Holler
Nancy Huninghake
Nancy Jackley
Trudy Kluba
Jill Kuzma
Mary Lesch
Peggy Locke
Kathleen Lund
Lyn Malone

Sandra Manns
Susan McGill
Margie Menard
Dianna Michels
Donna Miller
Cathy Milostan
Laura Moore
Lynne Patterson
Kathy Patton
Lynn Peal
Christine Rodrick
Joyce Santo
Adele Simon
Kristine Smallfield
Mary Beth Solheim
Lynn Stansberry-Bousnahan
Shelly Thomas
Theresa Urmann
Candace Vittorini
Pam Warren
Nichelle Zimmer

Foreword

This is an important textbook in the current autism renaissance. Thirty years ago the number of titles addressing autism spectrum disorders (ASD) could be counted on one hand. In the short history of autism, that was just yesterday. Today, parents and professionals have a wide variety of books to inform and guide their efforts. This book, however, isn't about autism's "yesterday" or even its "today." *Learners on the Autism Spectrum: Preparing Highly Qualified Educators and Related Practitioners* is about autism's tomorrow. It merges current thinking with insight to equip each reader with the tools he or she will need to effectively educate learners on the spectrum *in the future*. Designed specifically for university students, its purpose and quality distinguishes it from many other books in the field. In addition to university students, I believe that every educator – whether a parent of a child diagnosed with an ASD or an autism professional – will refer to this book many times for years to come.

Teaching is a social activity; to gain access to what is presented, students participate in an intricate exchange of information with their teacher. For typical students this is relatively easy. While students may occasionally divert their attention or decide not to follow a direction, most students have little difficulty understanding the meaning of what has been said or done. For learners with ASD the experience of a classroom and instruction is quite different. Meaning may be diverted, altered, or lost many times each day. On the seemingly short journey from teacher to student, peer to peer, or parent to child, words lose their intent. Gestures arrive without interpretation. Sensory information may be distorted. The result is often misunderstanding and frustration for student and teacher alike. Imagine being the educator, with a student diagnosed with an autism spectrum disorder in your care, and not knowing what to do.

Not knowing what to do is a part of autism's past. In 1977, when I was hired to teach four students with autism, I definitely did not know what to do. Sadly, my lack of knowledge was more the norm than the exception. This resource changes everything. For university students studying to work with learners with ASD, this text is a guide for their thinking and actions. The editors and authors have gathered information and gained experience over the last several years. Regardless of their titles – researcher, professional, parent, or person diagnosed with an autism spectrum disorder – they have combined their study, research, and experience to create one of the most accurate, trustworthy, and practical guides to autism and its interventions to date; the first step toward sound programming.

Information alone does not make an effective educator. It is evident that the editors and authors of *Learners on the Autism Spectrum: Preparing Highly Qualified Educators and Related Practitioners* have responded to people on the spectrum with care, creativity, and a respectful and unassuming curiosity. In between the lines of text, and directly reflected in the case examples that open each chapter and the lists of ideas that close them, is a demonstration of *how to think about* autism spectrum disorders. The result is a volume that contains a rare social competence with the potential to connect *all learners* on *or* alongside the autism spectrum – university students, professionals, parents, and learners diagnosed with ASD and their peers.

Each child has only one chance to grow and learn, a singular opportunity that is extremely critical when that child is also diagnosed with an autism spectrum disorder. There's no going back to the beginning and starting over. For years I had a short note to myself in a small frame on my desk: *These are not my children and I cannot be with them in the future.* It was a reminder to be very careful with the future of another person. In the same way, this text has a respect for the passing of time, and the importance of what educators do with it.

If I had owned this book in 1977, it would be dog-eared by now. Like a toddler's threadbare stuffed animal, its worn cover would be evidence of its continual use and timeless value. With this in mind, I bring my comments to a close with a word of caution for those still studying at university. When I was a university student, at the close of each term I would return triumphantly to the bookstore to sell my textbooks after final exams. It was a ceremony of sorts, a happy parting that brought me a step closer to graduation and "real life."

As you gather up your books at the end of the term, you may consider selling this book along with the rest. I wouldn't do that if I were you.

– Carol Gray

Acknowledgments

We wish to thank the many people who made this book possible. We are deeply indebted to our contributors who gave so generously of their precious time and immeasurable expertise. We are grateful to the many educators, therapists, students and parents whose thoughtful reviews and reflections helped us to refine this work, including our large group from Minnesota and think tank participants from San Francisco State University and the University of California, Berkeley. We would like to thank Roy and Rose Anna Peake for allowing Kari to photograph their son, Gareth, for the cover of this text. We extend our sincere gratitude to the AAPC team, and especially to Ruth Aspy for her amazing work on the support materials and to Kirsten McBride for her meticulous editing and perseverance in seeing this work through to completion. Heartfelt thanks go to our families (especially our incredibly patient spouses), friends and faithful canine companions for their unconditional support, friendship and love throughout this endeavor. And finally, our deepest appreciation goes to the many children, adults, families, and professionals who are living and learning with autism.

Preface

A Message From Kari Dunn Buron

In 1981, I was hired to develop a program for children with autism (which we now refer to as autism spectrum disorders (ASD). My secret was that I really didn't know what I was doing. I had a master's degree in learning disabilities and emotional and behavior disorders. My training had prepared me well for assessing learning disorders and using behavior modification, but many of the strategies I thought would work did not. As I began to meet with other educators working with children with autism, I was relieved to find that nobody else seemed to know what they were doing either – at least I wasn't alone.

In 1985, I attended my first Autism Society of America (ASA) conference, and thus began my formal education in autism. I continued to work with a small group of local colleagues, and we became the metropolitan area autism consultants through a Minnesota state-funded project for low-incidence disabilities (Metro SPLISE). We met once a month to discuss the issues we faced in our classrooms, consulted with other teachers, and created training opportunities. As our project grew, the MN State Autism Project was developed, including professionals from every region of Minnesota. At that point, we were able to bring in world-class speakers to help in our continued education, and our project included early childhood autism initiatives.

Over my first 10 years of working in the field of autism, I realized that many of the strategies I had learned in school were not only ineffective, but quite possibly harmful to the children I was teaching. I watched my students grow with feelings of pride for some achievements and feelings of guilt and remorse for the gains that were not realized. I struggled to understand the core issues of autism in my effort to develop more effective teaching strategies. Through my affiliation with the Autism Society of Minnesota, Metro SPLISE, and the MN Autism Project, I continued to learn and evolve with every passing year.

At the ASA annual conference in 1994, I met a group of adults with autism, who represented the increasing number of people with autism who were speaking out and writing their stories. I asked them what support they wished they had received growing up. Overwhelmingly, they told me that they wished they had known other children like themselves. This information prompted me to work with the Autism Society of Minnesota to start Camp Discovery, a summer camp for children and adolescents with ASD Level 1 (formerly known as Asperger Syndrome and high-functioning autism).

Camp Discovery has continued to grow and change as we acquire new information about the core issues of autism. Many campers have returned over the years, and some have reported that it is one of the most comfortable experiences they have ever had.

My interest in the campers at Camp Discovery led to an almost insatiable desire to learn more about what I recognized as their different form of logic. My study led me to amazing researchers and therapists who were talking about ASD as being a disorder of social thinking. It all made so much sense to me. As I continued to study, I realized that the concept was largely unrecognized in the educational setting, yet the educational setting was proving to be perhaps the most socially frustrating environment for these students. For example, I was often called to consult about a student who was being suspended from his school program for behavior that seemed to me to be directly related to an inability to understand or effectively negotiate social information. I decided that I had to find out more about this theory of autism if I was going to be able to explain it to others and successfully support and advocate for these students.

Several years later, this professional dream was realized when I was awarded a Bush Leadership Fellowship, set up by Archibald Granville Bush and his wife, Edyth Bassler Bush, of Minnesota. This fellowship made it possible for me to pursue a 12-month, self-designed study of social cognition, challenging behavior and ASD Level 1. My goal was to gather information from noted therapists, scientists, and educational researchers, from educational initiatives related to ASD Level 1, and from individuals with ASD themselves to develop some promising practices related to ASD and social cognition.

My study took the form of a "who's who" in the world of autism. Brenda Smith Myles at the University of Kansas, a leader in the field, graciously agreed to be my advisor. She supported my efforts and assisted me in reviewing current educational research. I spent time with Tony Attwood in Brisbane, Australia, where I was able to observe the use of cognitive behavioral approaches used in his clinic. I met with Ami Klin and Robert Schultz at Yale University and learned first-hand how functional Magnetic Resonance Imagery (fMRI) studies were conducted. (These are studies that look at the brain while the brain is functioning to pinpoint what part of the brain is being used.) I was able to ask them directly about their thoughts on education and how they hoped their research might impact the future of ASD education. Dr. Klin shared a paper with me explaining his learning theory called Enactive Mind. This theory implies that social learning must include active learning and doing to be truly effective. I also met with Nancy Minshew, professor of psychiatry and neurology at the University of Pittsburgh School of Medicine, and discussed her work and possible implications for understanding autism behavior. I traveled to Emory in Atlanta, Georgia, where I met with Steve Nowicki and Marshall Duke, who have done amazing work in the area of nonverbal social communication (dyssemia). Because they are social psychologists and do not study autism per se, they were able to give me insight from a completely different perspective about an issue so connected to ASD.

As my fellowship year progressed, it was my task to pull all the information together and make sense of it for the real world of public education. I was learning so much – at times it felt contradictory and at other times it fit. I continued to frame and reframe my thoughts about social cognition and what it meant for education. I then traveled to the United Kingdom, where I was able to meet with Simon Baron-Cohen at Cambridge

University and Sarah Blackford and Daniel Glaser at the Institute of Cognitive Neuroscience. Simon Baron-Cohen did a wonderful job of clarifying his thoughts about systematic learning styles as well as explaining his approach to teaching nonverbal facial communication. Daniel Glaser was perhaps the most unexpected pleasant surprise of my year-long quest. He talked with me for hours about the science-education connection and eventually mentioned mirror neurons. After listening to his explanation of mirror neurons, I set off for the British Library to investigate. Later that day I had an "a-ha" moment. The excitement was overwhelming as the puzzle pieces of enactive mind, dyssemia, relationship building vs. systematic learning, cognitive behavior therapy, teaching mind reading and, finally, mirror neurons all came together.

Finally, I traveled to California, where I spent time with friends and formidable colleagues. I met with the people from AASCEND, a group of adults with ASD Level 1, families, and professionals in the San Francisco area. I was able to visit the Orion Academy, a high school program designed specifically for students with ASD Level 1. I met with Paula Jacobsen, a therapist whose work in understanding the "ASD perspective" is inspiring. Paula introduced me to Judith Piggot, a researcher at Stanford, who met with me in the fMRI lab and shared how she was investigating the neurological basis of social cognition. I was also able to observe some of Michelle Garcia Winner's social thinking groups and discuss with her the issues involved with designing appropriate social training opportunities for students with ASD Level 1.

It was on this same trip that I had an opportunity to connect with Pamela Wolfberg, a special education professor at San Francisco State University and co-founder of the Autism Institute on Peer Socialization and Play. Pamela and I talked about the ASD certificate program I had developed at Hamline University in St. Paul, Minnesota. Pamela was developing a new interdisciplinary Autism Spectrum graduate studies program at San Francisco State University. She asked me what text I was using for the Introduction to Autism class. This immediately led to a discussion about the need for a current volume that could be used as a core text in similar university programs. The idea was a flash of brilliance experienced simultaneously between Pamela and myself. The outline for the book was created that night at a small restaurant just a few blocks from Golden Gate Park.

As with our first edition, it is our hope that this newly updated text will offer educators and related practitioners an opportunity to make connections between science, therapy, personal experience, and educational practices. The book's content and organization are designed to give the reader examples of how different issues affect diverse learners with ASD in a variety of learning environments, current information regarding theory and promising practices, combined with practical tips from fellow educators about how the information might be used to improve the quality of educational practices for individuals with ASD.

A Message From Pamela Wolfberg

When I met Kari Dunn Buron at the end of her fellowship year, it was like finding a long-lost soul mate. Having both traversed the field of special education for a number of years we quickly discovered that we shared a historical and global perspective on issues facing learners on the autism spectrum. For my own part, my special education career began in the 1980s at a time when autism was not only considered rare in terms of incidence, but was also still largely mistaken as being a psychologically-based disorder caused by poor parenting. My own education was to a large extent rooted in developmental psychology with leanings toward the psychodynamic tradition, although the behavioral tradition was also becoming prominent at the time. My first professional position was as an educational therapist in a children's psychiatric hospital, where I taught adolescents who were identified as emotionally disturbed, several of whom would surely be diagnosed with ASD today. I recall 15-year-old Lydia, who was fascinated with the popular television program "Mod Squad." Although secretly I was flattered that she associated me with the lead female character (I happened to have the same hairstyle), the psychiatric team interpreted Lydia's repeated references and rituals surrounding the show as obsessive and delusional equated with a psychotic disorder. As was common at the time, Lydia's treatment comprised a combination of heavy-duty antipsychotic medication, psychotherapy, and behavioral intervention that included the use of aversive methods (i.e., confinement in an isolation room) to subdue her when agitated. In my role as educator, I was expected to defer to the medical experts and support implementation of the treatment plan in my teaching. As a young teacher, I wrestled with my conscience and only lasted a short while in this position. Disillusioned, I took a several-year hiatus to study and work around the world, only to discover that I was being pulled back into the field at the dawn of a new awakening to autism.

Although three decades have passed, still not a day goes by that I don't wonder how things could and should be different for the many children like Lydia who fall through the cracks because they are misdiagnosed, mistreated, or simply misunderstood. Building on my own varied experiences – initially as a teacher and play therapist, later as a researcher and founding director of the Autism Institute on Peer Socialization and Play (see Chapter 8) and professor of Autism Spectrum Graduate Studies at San Francisco State University – I am immensely grateful for the knowledge that has been accumulating over these years to refine our understanding of ASD. At the same time, however, I am acutely aware that gaps remain in the knowledge and skills of many educators and related professionals to meet the unique needs of this diverse and rapidly growing population.

The complex nature and wide spectrum of variability in autism poses challenges for preparing highly qualified educators and related professionals. The result of a neurological condition, autism affects the most essential of human behaviors, including social interaction, communication, language, flexible thinking and learning, sensory processing, play, imagination, and peer relations. While changing over the lifespan, the presence of behaviors may manifest in a wide variety of combinations and degrees of intensity, ranging from mild to moderate to severe. Further, each person's capacity to learn, develop, and function in the world is naturally influenced by experiences with others, as well as the social, cultural, and societal contexts in which they participate (American Psychiatric Association, 2013).

Taking into account the multifarious and changing needs of each individual with autism, there is no single educational method or treatment approach that has been found to work for all individuals or for any single individual at any given time. Thus, knowledgeable and skilled professionals and families must carefully configure educational supports to maximize each individual's capacity to learn, develop, function independently, and participate in the full range of social, cultural, and general life experiences.

Based on the premise that successful teaching and therapy are rooted in understanding and experience, this volume responds to the critical need to prepare teachers and others with foundational knowledge and practical skills for providing competent and humanistic support to people on the autism spectrum representing diverse ages, abilities, languages, cultures, social and economic experiences.

Now in its second edition, this state-of-the art text brings together leading experts representing diverse disciplines and perspectives (i.e., researchers, therapists, educators, parents, advocates and adults on the autism spectrum) to cover a range of essential topics and themes. We hope that this collective effort will allow educators and others to translate the most up-to-date theory and research into effective and meaningful practices to ensure that every person on the autism spectrum receives the high-quality education and support that he or she deserves.

Overview of Textbook Features

The *Learners on the Autism Spectrum: Preparing Highly Qualified Educators and Related Practitioners* (2nd ed.) textbook contains the following features to help strengthen your understanding of material discussed in each chapter, as well as share this knowledge with parents and colleagues and apply it to your everyday work with children and adolescents with ASD:

- **Chapter learner objectives** – Refer to the list of learner objectives at the beginning of each chapter for a preview of the chapter's content, as well as to learn what information you are expected to understand and be able to explain after reading the chapter.

- **Vocabulary** – Note the terms included in boldface text within each chapter for at-a-glance reminders of key vocabulary. The definitions of these terms are included in the glossary in Appendix B.

- **Chapter highlights** – Review the main points listed at the end of each chapter to recall the main points discussed within the chapter.

- **Chapter review questions** – Answer the questions at the end of each chapter to check your understanding of and ability to explain the information discussed within the chapter. The review questions may also be used as a study guide when preparing for tests and/or exams.

- **Chapter review answers** – Refer to Appendix A to confirm your answers to the review questions that accompany each chapter.

- **Glossary** – Refer to Appendix B for an alphabetical listing of all vocabulary terms included in grey boldface text within the textbook.

- **Tips for Practical Application** – Refer to the final section of each chapter for Tips for Practical Application designed to provide you with information on how to effectively use the material learned in the chapter while in the classroom or otherwise working with students on the autism spectrum.

Learner Objectives

After reading this chapter, the learner should be able to:

- Discuss the historical background of the evidence-based practice (EBP) movement

- State the criteria used to determine which practices are evidence based in special education

- Discuss the positive contributions EBP efforts have made to the education of diverse learners with ASD

- Discuss some of the ongoing disparities in EBP as they impact the education of diverse learners with ASD

- Discuss ways educators and related practitioners may refine their knowledge and application of EBP with diverse learners with ASD as the field continues to evolve

Chapter 1

Perspectives on Evidence-Based Practice and Autism Spectrum Disorders: Tenets of Competent, Humanistic, and Meaningful Support

Pamela Wolfberg and Kari Dunn Buron

The educational team at Bear Lake Elementary School convened to discuss the individualized education program (IEP) for Will, a 10-year-old student with ASD Level 2. Although assessment data indicated that Will had been successfully meeting most of his goals in academic, functional, and related skill areas, he was demonstrating aggressive behavior, including hitting and scratching, towards his teachers, parents, and peers.

Six months prior to this meeting, his educational team had completed a functional behavior assessment and determined that Will's aggressive behavior was directly connected to his inability to effectively communicate his social desires, anxieties, and fears. A communication program was developed for Will to teach him to use a "break" card when he showed evidence of feeling stressed. Teacher and therapist data indicated that Will had not successfully responded to this program.

The team agreed to explore alternative approaches to support Will. Will's psychologist had recently read an article about a new intervention that she felt would be a better fit for Will's communication program. The other team members were unfamiliar with the intervention and expressed concerns that it was still experimental since the only research included a case study of three students. Will's speech-language therapist mentioned that she had attended a workshop focused on an intervention that had been widely studied and published in European journals and was now being implemented in several schools in the United States with reported success.

The team was excited about the intervention's potential for supporting not only Will's communication abilities but also his ability to engage in positive social interactions. However, the special education director said that since the intervention was not on the list of evidence-based practices provided to her by the state, she would not allocate funds for staff training. Instead, she would hire an outside consultant to help the team in making their decision about further support for Will.

———————————

The above scenario is one that educational teams throughout the world have wrestled with for decades. There are rarely easy answers to difficult problems when it comes to supporting diverse learners on the autism spectrum. Every IEP team is made up of individuals with varying backgrounds and areas of expertise. The recent focus on the use of evidence-based practices in special education attempts to add increased structure and order to the process of solving these problems.

Historical Influences

The application of **evidence-based practice (EBP)** to the education, social intervention, and clinical treatment of individuals with autism spectrum disorders (ASD) is the product of historical influences, decisively shaped by prevailing political and economic trends. Derived from the natural sciences, EBP has it origins in evidence-based medicine (EBM) (EBM Working Group, 1992). Medical schools around the world have adopted the following definition of EBM:

> Evidence-based medicine is the conscientious, explicit, and judicious use of current best evidence in making decisions about the care of individual patients. The practice of evidence-based medicine means integrating individual clinical expertise with the best available clinical evidence from systematic research. (Sackett, Rosenberg, Gray, Haynes, & Richardson, 1996, p. 71)

EBP has been applied to several fields, most recently special education and related clinical and health care professions devoted to individuals with disabilities (Gibbs, 2003). While the meaning of EBP varies across disciplines, it is generally viewed as denoting any practice that has been established as effective through scientific research following an explicit set of criteria. A number of factors have contributed to the evolution of EBP as applied to learners on the autism spectrum, as reviewed below.

Over the past two decades, the astounding rise in the number of individuals identified with ASD has had a profound impact on education and clinical practice. Prevalent in approximately 1% of the population across much of the world, as of 2013 the Centers for Disease Control estimate ASD to occur in about 1 in 88 births in the United States. However, based on a more recent government survey of parents, the number of school-age children with ASD has been reported at an even higher rate of 1 in 50 (Centers for Disease Control, 2013). Further, ASD is the fastest growing special education eligibility category in the public schools in the United States (U.S. Department of Education, 2012).

As the incidence of autism has risen, schools have faced chronic shortages of competent educators and related service providers (e.g., speech-language pathologists, behavioral interventionists, occupational therapists, school psychologists, play therapists, adaptive physical educators, transition and vocational experts, instructional assistants) to effectively serve this population in diverse settings (Scheuermann, Webber, Boutot, & Goodwin, 2003).

In 2001, the National Research Council (NRC) issued a groundbreaking report that included a comprehensive review of the scientific base for educating children on the autism spectrum. Among its key findings and recommendations, the NRC stressed the need for future research while highlighting the role of families, characteristics of effective programs (e.g., early and intensive intervention, low ratios of students and teachers), and the preparation of educational personnel.

It is pertinent to note that the NRC report was released at a time that coincided with the reauthorization of the Elementary and Secondary Education Act (ESEA), known as No Child Left Behind (NCLB). NCLB requires states to ensure that educators at the elementary and secondary school levels are capable of the following:

Accountability

- Demonstrate knowledge and skill in applying state-wide standards, assessments and alternate assessments

- Collect meaningful data to assess for instruction and monitor student progress

Scientifically based instruction

- Demonstrate knowledge and skill in applying "evidence-based practices" supported by research that applies rigorous, systematic, and objective procedures to obtain relevant knowledge

Highly qualified teachers

- Demonstrate knowledge and skill-based competencies in the design and delivery of effective educational programs

- Understand and apply core elements of effective educational practice

Both the NRC report and the NCLB Act have significantly influenced efforts focused on personnel preparation and EBP in the area of ASD. Among its reported outcomes, the NRC (2001) concluded: "Personnel preparation remains one of the weakest elements of effective programming for children with autism spectrum disorders and their families" (p. 225). Thus, with the mandate to be accountable for the design and delivery of effective and appropriate educational services for diverse learners on the autism spectrum by highly qualified personnel, the educational community has faced unprecedented challenges (Yell, Drasgow, & Lowrey, 2005).

A major challenge has been the lack of university-level special education and clinical preparation programs that include a specialization in ASD (Baker, 2012; Barnhill, Polloway, & Sumutka, 2011; Scheuermann et al., 2003). An initial reason was that autism was not included as an eligibility category for special education until the reauthorization of the Individuals with Disabilities Education Act (IDEA) in 1990. Moreover, it took more than a decade before autism became identified as a distinct category by the Council for Exceptional Children (CEC), which designates standards (i.e., professional competencies) for teacher training that are aligned with state teacher credentialing agencies (CEC, 2009).

However, at the time, there was no universally agreed-upon set of standards for autism. As a result, the handful of universities beginning to offer specializations in ASD attempted to create their own standards, which often did not align with standards for state credentials (Baker, 2012). Thus, teachers lacking the requisite knowledge and skills filled the vast majority of special education positions serving students with ASD. These included interns who were earning their credentials and teachers who had earned credentials in generic or cross-categorical training programs with little or no preparation in the area of ASD (Center for the Future of Teaching and Learning, 2004).

With the influx of students with ASD into the system, school districts carried much of the burden of compensating for the gap in the knowledge and skill of teachers and related staff. To counteract this problem, many districts hired outside contractors to provide services at premium costs. In addition, they often went to great lengths to patch together their own inservice training programs. Not surprisingly, the training content tended to be piecemeal and fragmented, focusing on a single approach without presenting the larger picture of how it might fit (or not fit) to guide educators in meeting the unique needs of diverse learners with ASD and their families (Iovannone, Dunlap, Huber, & Kincaid, 2003; Scheuermann et al., 2003).

Advances in the Field

Spurred on by the historical influences noted above, noteworthy research and policy have led to significant advances for determining standards for professional competency and EBP related to ASD. Following the NRC report, Iovannone and colleagues (2003) published a seminal review of the scientific research base focused on effective practices aimed at students with ASD. Drawing on the literature, the authors identified a number of specific strategies and approaches (most are aimed at young children but are also relevant for older students) that correspond to essential elements of effective educational practice.

1. Individualized supports and services

2. Systematic, carefully planned instruction

3. Comprehensible and structured learning environments

4. Specialized curricula focused on core challenges (social/communication)

5. Functional approach to problem behavior

6. Family involvement. (p. 153)

Reviewing a similar literature base, Scheuermann and colleagues (2003) focused on issues related to personnel preparation, resulting in a set of recommendations for competency areas for educators of students with ASD, including 13 areas that mirrored and expanded Iovannone et al.'s (2003) findings. Both of these articles have been highly quoted and formative in efforts to establish professional competency and EBP guidelines within and across states.

In 2009 the National Autism Center released the National Standards Project (NSP) report, the result of a five-year project designed to address the need for EBP guidelines for ASD. The project assembled a panel of experts to serve as conceptual reviewers while developing a systematic process for determining EBP. Evaluation criteria included (a) a minimum number of studies focused on a select intervention published in peer-reviewed journals in the English language; (b) conducted in an early-intervention, school, home, and/or community setting; (c) focused on children, adolescents, and adults up to age 22; and (d) corresponding to the conventions of an experimental or quasi-experimental research design (e.g., randomized control design for large groups, single-case design for small groups).

A scientific merit rating scale (SMRS) was developed to guide the analysis. Studies were rated for scientific rigor based on adherence to conventions accepted within the arena of social science, including controlling for measurement of dependent variables, measurement of independent variables (treatment fidelity), ascertaining participant diagnosis, and generalization. Based on the ratings, the interventions were sorted into categories that yielded 11 established treatments, 22 emerging treatments, and 5 unestablished treatments. Table 1 provides an overview of categories that met the NSP's criteria for an established EBP.

At the same time the NSP was convened, the National Professional Development Center on Autism Spectrum Disorders (NPDC, 2009) carried out a similar project, which involved a comprehensive review of the literature to establish EBP for individuals with ASD up to age 22 years. Commensurate with the process carried out by the NSP, the NPDC established a systematic set of criteria to evaluate the scientific rigor of studies to determine the efficacy of a given practice. Their criteria included a hierarchy rating based on the number of peer-reviewed studies, number and type of research design, and the number of different investigators for a respective practice. The review yielded 24 interventions that met criteria for EBP. As noted in Table 1.1, there is much overlap between the practices identified by both the NSP and the NPDC while some differences were also noted in light of terminology and the application of somewhat different criteria.

Table 1.1
Comparative Summary of Evidence-Based Practices Identified by the NSP (2009) and NPDC (2009) Projects

National Standards Project (NSP)	National Professional Development Center on ASD
1. Antecedent Package	1. Antecedent-Based Intervention
2. Behavioral Package	2. Prompting 3. Time Delay 4. Reinforcement 5. Extinction 6. Task Analysis 7. Discrete Trial Training 8. Functional Behavior Analysis 9. Functional Communication Training 10. Response Interruption/Redirection 11. Differential Reinforcement
3. Comprehensive Behavioral Treatment	*Not Reviewed*
4. Pivotal Response Treatment	12. Pivotal Response Training
5. Story-Based Intervention Package	13. Social Narratives
6. Modeling	14. Video Modeling
7. Naturalistic Interventions	15. Naturalistic Teaching Strategies
8. Joint Attention Intervention	*Not Reviewed*
9. Peer Training Package	16. Peer-Mediated Intervention
10. Visual Supports	17. Schedules 18. Structured Work Systems
11. Self-Management	19. Self-Management
12. Parent-Implemented Intervention	20. Parent-Implemented Intervention

Social Skills Training Package (Emerging)	21. Social Skills Training Groups
Augmentative Alternative Communication (AAC) (Emerging)	22. Speech-Generating Devices
Technology and Treatment (Emerging)	23. Computer-Aided Instruction
Picture Exchange Communication (Emerging)	24. Picture Exchange Communication

It was also in 2009 that the Council for Exceptional Children adopted professional standards for teaching students with ASD as the result of a three-year grant involving collaboration with the Autism Society of America (ASA) (CEC, 2009). A workgroup comprising researchers, educators, therapists, family members, and adults on the autism spectrum was integral to the competency development process. Among the members were those engaged in developing ASD specializations at universities with the support of state and federal funding and those involved in the NSP and NPDC workgroups. This allowed for cross-fertilization of the parallel works in progress.

To guide the process, information was initially gathered from existing guides, standards, and competencies, including the CEC Division on Developmental Disabilities, Project Mosaic at San Francisco State University (Wolfberg, 2011), University of Iowa, West Midlands Regional Partnership Autism Spectrum Disorders Training Policy and Framework, and the National Autistic Society of the United Kingdom. An extensive review resulted in two sets of professional competencies (beginning and advanced level) comprising the knowledge and skill educators would need to acquire to effectively work with students across the autism spectrum from early development through 22 years. The final sets of competencies that were adopted by CEC and approved by the National Council for the Accreditation of Teacher Education (NCATE) may be found at https://www.cec.sped.org/~/media/Files/Standards/News%20and%20Reports/Redbook%202009.pdf/.

Table 1.2 provides a summary of core professional competencies in autism-related knowledge and skill adopted at the university level for preparing special educators, speech-language-pathologists, and related professionals (Wolfberg, 2011; Yu & Wolfberg, 2011-2016).

Table 1.2
Core Professional Competencies in Autism-Related Knowledge and Skill Adopted at the University Level

ASD Core Competency Area		ASD-Related Knowledge and Skill
1	Nature of ASD in Theory and Practice	1.1 Historical and theoretical foundation 1.2 Current definitions (state, federal) 1.3 Early indicators, etiology, prevalence 1.4 Diagnostic tools, criteria (DSM-5) and differential diagnosis 1.5 Characteristics associated with ASD 1.6 Current and emerging practices and service delivery models
2	Family Support and Partnerships	2.1 Supports parents and family members as active participants in all aspects of child's education 2.2 Responsive to family culture, language, values, parenting styles and personal perspectives 2.3 Facilitates communication between school, home and community 2.4 Provides family with timely information, education and resources pertinent to child's needs 2.5 Assists family in accessing community supports and services 2.6 Collaborates with family to improve professional practices
3	School and Community Partnerships	3.1 Links with community agencies and organizations serving diverse learners with ASD across the lifespan 3.2 Interdisciplinary team collaboration within and across systems 3.3 Accesses community supports and services for children and adults with ASD and their families 3.4 Facilitates communication between school, home and community

4	Individualized Educational Services and Supports	4.1	Develops IEP/IFSP in collaboration with family and professionals across disciplines
		4.2	Responsive to social, cultural and linguistic backgrounds of each individual and family with consideration of family preferences
		4.3	Degree of structure and level of intensity adapted to child's strengths, challenges and emergent potentials
		4.4	Incorporates child's preferences and special interests in program goals and methods
		4.5	Incorporates environmental and instructional adaptations and accommodations
5	Assessment Frameworks and Procedures	5.1	Typical and atypical learning and development across the lifespan
		5.2	Formal and informal assessment tools and techniques
		5.3	Systematically collects and analyzes multiple sources of data across settings to assess and monitor individual learning, development and overall progress
		5.4	Constructs profiles of strengths, challenges and emergent potential across core domains of learning and development
		5.5	Uses results to set realistic and meaningful goals and plan instruction and intervention
6	Curriculum and Instruction	6.1	Balanced functional, developmental and academic curriculum aligned with standards, cross cultural and English Language Learning
		6.2	Well-planned, systematic and differentiated instruction adapted to range of ages, abilities, interests and learning styles
		6.3	Instructional activities provide multiple opportunities to practice skills across natural learning contexts within home, school and community
		6.4	Varied instructional formats through multiple modes of one-to-one, small group, large-group, adult-directed, child-centered, and peer mediated instruction geared to individual
		6.5	Supports maintenance of learned skills over time and generalization of skills to natural settings
		6.6	Trains and manages paraeducators/program staff
7	Structuring Learning Environments	7.1	Clearly organized and comprehensible learning environments
		7.2	Use of visual cues and supports to maximize engagement and learning
		7.3	Incorporates predictable routines, rituals, schedules for activities and events
		7.4	Structures materials and work tasks
		7.5	Defines physical space with clear boundaries
		7.6	Facilitates transitions, flexibility and change
8	Addressing Challenging Behaviors	8.1	Functional approach through Positive Behavior Supports
		8.2	Responsive to unique modes of communication, social-emotional regulation and sensory processing
		8.3	Data-based functional behavioral assessments (FBA) and behavior supports plans consistent with state and federal guidelines
		8.4	Application of a variety of empirically validated behavioral intervention strategies (ABA, cognitive behavior, developmental, sensory-based)
		8.5	Crisis intervention techniques
9	Supporting Communicative Competence	9.1	Patterns of speech, language and communication in ASD
		9.2	Continuum of approaches to assessment and intervention (discrete trial, traditional behavioral, developmental, social-pragmatic)
		9.3	Supports intentional and spontaneous communication across partners, activities and settings
		9.4	Functional expressive and receptive communication for mute, preverbal and verbal children
		9.5	Augmentative and alternative communication (AAC) strategies
		9.6	Integrating verbal and nonverbal forms of communication
10	Supporting Social Competence	10.1	Patterns of socialization with adults and peers
		10.2	Supports spontaneous joint attention, imitation, initiations and social reciprocity across partners, activities and setting
		10.3	Adult-directed social skills training (ABA/direct instruction/ social-cognitive approaches); child-centered approaches (developmental, relationship-based, transactional)
		10.4	Socio-Cultural (peer social inclusion, autism demystification)
11	Supporting Play/ Recreation and Imagination	11.1	Patterns of play and imagination in ASD
		11.2	Supports spontaneous engagement in a range of developmentally and age-appropriate play/ leisure activities across independent and social contexts
		11.3	Incorporating play materials, activities and themes varying in degree of symbolic representation
		11.4	Adult-directed approaches (ABA, social-cognitive)
		11.5	Child-centered approaches (developmental, relationship)
		11.6	Socio-cultural approaches (social inclusion in play, recreation cultural experiences, autism demystification)

12	Inclusion With Typical Peers	12.1 Facilitates inclusion across natural contexts within school, home and community settings 12.2 Explicit guidance for both children with autism and typical peers 12.3 Creates culture of inclusion via awareness activities that promote understanding, empathy and acceptance 12.4 Consistent opportunities to form social relationships and mutual friendships 12.5 Guided participation in mutually enjoyed activities that are a natural part of the peer culture (play and recreation) 12.6 Designs inviting play spaces and selects play materials with high interactive potential
13	Transition, Vocational and Independent Learning	13.1 Promotes adaptive behaviors to foster independence at all age and ability levels 13.2 Plans transitions from one classroom, program, or service delivery system to another 13.3 Supports transition to self-determined careers and post-secondary education and community living 13.4 Training in vocational and independent living skills 13.5 Interagency collaboration 13.6 Self-advocacy and disclosure perspectives of adults with ASD
14	Professional Literacy and Leadership	14.1 Peer-reviewed journals and publications on research and practice in ASD 14.2 Professional and parent organizations (local, national, and international) 14.3 Current trends and controversies in the field of ASD 14.4 Judges quality and efficacy of educational program models, services and practices 14.5 Engages in reflective practice via multiple modes of field-based systematic inquiry 14.6 Uses multimedia technology to produce and present educational tools and techniques

Disparities in the Field

While lauding the many important efforts to date, it is essential to acknowledge disparities in the field's perception and practical application of EBP. A first consideration is with respect to building consensus on EBP standards. Critics within and across disciplines have widely debated whether it is feasible or even justifiable to reach such a goal (Mullen & Streiner, 2004). A number of limitations bring this issue into focus. Specifically, there are pitfalls with the methodologies used for conducting systematic reviews of the research to determine what does and does not constitute EBP. This is consistent with Marks' (2012) insightful analysis of EBP in related healthcare professions:

> [To] be judged 'sound,' evidence must pass through [a number of] filters, all operated in the context of an establishment that is predisposed to preserve existing practices, traditions and myths. Undeniably, this evidence selection procedure is systematic and the evidence derived from it may well be judged 'sound' (at least by narrowly defined criteria). But is it not supremely wasteful of evidence? And does it not give too high a weighting to the beliefs and values of those in the knowledge establishment with the greatest stake in regulating and controlling our health and education systems? (pp. 32-33)

A related issue is the lack of a coherent, consistent evidence base for the many diverse practices studied and applied in the field. With respect to ASD, there is an overrepresentation of EBP based on applied behavior analysis (ABA) compared to practices that are developmentally or socio-culturally based. This is largely because ABA is rooted in reductionist scientific principles that easily allow for the measurement of observable behavior using research methodologies that are more heavily weighted. By contrast, interventions rooted in scientific traditions that address the process and nature of development in a broader cultural context are more difficult to study using the same methodologies.

Similarly, there are drawbacks to determining the validity of interventions that reduce development and socio-cultural experience to a discrete set of skills or behaviors in an effort to apply the dominant research paradigm. For instance, interventions designed to foster developmental capacities such as spontaneous initiation, imitation, mutual engagement, play, and imagination are not readily assessed using common measures such as percentage of correct responses. It is, therefore, an artifact that interventions that conform to the dominant research paradigm more readily meet the criteria for EBP.

Critics also argue that EBP does not consider the realities of individualized, contextualized practice and the values and preferences of those being served (Marks, 2012; Mullen & Streiner, 2004). The omission of **social validation** among the rating criteria in systematic reviews of intervention studies is a serious limitation. Social validation measures have long been established as fundamental to applied research involving vulnerable populations, including persons with disabilities, as a means to tie the research results to social context while ensuring that the goals, procedures, target behaviors, and effects are deemed socially relevant and important (Schwartz & Baer, 1991). Often these measures elicit feedback from key stakeholders, including family members, the individuals themselves, as well as others who serve and care for them.

Another critical concern is the need to integrate practitioner expertise with the best available evidence from the scientific research base. Burns and Ysseldyke (2009) noted a gap between research and practice in light of educators' perceptions that they (a) do not have ready access to research, (b) experience difficulty drawing causal connections from research, and (c) lack trust in the research results and claims being made. According to Baker (2012),

> In order for students with ASD to fully benefit from the provisions of IDEA, it is essential that their teachers receive training in evidence-based autism interventions. Colleges of Education in Institutes of Higher Education must determine which interventions should be presented within the different teacher preparation programs so that all teachers and related service providers are prepared to collaborate in providing an appropriate education to the students with ASD. (p. 1)

The reality is that there continues to be a pressing need for professionals who are fully competent in the design and delivery of effective practices that support individuals with ASD and their families. While professional competency standards have been established, there continues to be great variability with respect to the preparation of both pre- and inservice professionals. This variability likely reflects the range of teacher credentialing requirements adopted by states as they interface with personnel preparation programs.

Based on a 2011 survey conducted by Barnhill and colleagues, 41% of reporting institutions of higher education did not offer any ASD-specific coursework toward completion of a special education degree. As opposed to covering ASD in depth through an integration of coursework and field-based experience, preparation is often relegated to existing courses as part of a generic or cross-categorical special education program. Even among institutions that offer specialized ASD studies, typically at the graduate-degree level, the content and approaches to fulfilling professional competencies may differ vastly.

To address teacher shortages, some states require the bare minimum, authorizing teachers as "highly qualified" to work with students with ASD after they have attended a weekend workshop or online courses. Moreover, in some cases the courses or trainings are delivered by professionals who themselves lack the requisite knowledge, skill, and experience.

Future Directions

As we contemplate future directions for research, training, and practice in the field of ASD, it is essential to deepen and broaden our understanding of EBP within the context of a dynamic and ever-developing field. Consistent with this text, this requires drawing on complementary perspectives to help guide professionals in making decisions about which practices are best matched to and valued by individuals with ASD and those closest to them. According to Baker (2012),

> In order to develop appropriate preparation models for teachers who will teach students with ASD, it is imperative that preparation programs infuse evidence-based practices into the coursework. Yet, there needs to be agreement among experts concerning the different skill sets needed by general education teachers, special education teachers who provide inclusive supports, and special education teachers who provide full instructional programs and related service providers … Even though the professional literature contains a comprehensive set of evidence-based practices for individuals with ASD, not all teachers need to be fluent with all of the strategies. (p. 4)

Given the range and variability in the development and socio-cultural experience of individuals with ASD, a closer understanding of the different layers and configurations of contextualized support must be carefully weighed and considered in the selection and application of EBP. EBP not only needs to be carefully selected and matched to the individual, it also needs to be implemented with fidelity across diverse learning contexts (Fixsen, Blasé, Horner, & Sugai, 2009). To optimize the benefits requires a person- and family-centered approach to ensure social validation of selected practices. This includes collaborating as an interdisciplinary team to craft a unique "mosaic" or collection of specialized practices for each individual (Wolfberg, 2011; Yu & Wolfberg, 2011-2016).

When we first conceived of *Learners on the Autism Spectrum,* we were responding to the urgent need to prepare educators with specialized knowledge and skill grounded in the most up-to-date theory and research-based practices. Edging forward with new developments in EBP, this revised edition of the text confidently expands on our previous work.

This textbook offers an essential foundation that is optimized when delivered as part of a competency-based personnel preparation program. The content may be streamlined to programs that integrate specialized courses with highly relevant field experiences in multiple settings and contexts and that include school, family, and community partnerships. Commensurate with ASD professional competencies, this volume is a cornerstone for addressing a number of key areas, including the role of families, culture and language, diagnosis and assessment, goals for and characteristics of effective education and intervention, interdisciplinary team collaboration and integrated services, public policies that ensure individuals and families access to appropriate education and services, and research to further efforts to validate and expand knowledge and practice.

As standards of EBP will inevitably continue to evolve, we hope that readers will embrace the need for and privilege of life-long learning. This will ensure that educators are prepared to provide competent, humanistic, and meaningful support by applying sound practices that are contextually relevant and socially validated by families and others who are important in the lives of individuals with ASD.

Tips for Practical Application

✓ Review the historical influences of evidence-based practice (EBP) as it applies to education so that educational teams can maintain the original intent of the movement.

✓ Develop your own systems for evaluating interventions being used, as well as new interventions.

✓ With the educational team, agree upon measuring tools to monitor the success or lack of success of the strategies chosen.

✓ Recognize that a scientific understanding of ASD is still evolving and that with new information come new ideas and innovations for teaching students on the spectrum.

✓ Dedicate resources to ongoing staff training, as well as access to journals and periodicals that carry articles specific to teaching practices related to ASD.

✓ Exercise caution when considering EBP to prevent creating a "one-size-fits-all" plan.

Chapter Highlights

• While there have been many advances in research and policy, many critical concerns related to EBP remain.

• ASD is the fastest growing special education eligibility category in the public schools in the United States.

• As the incidence of autism has risen, schools have faced chronic shortages of competent educators and related service providers.

• The Elementary and Secondary Education Act (ESEA), known as No Child Left Behind (NCLB), requires states to ensure that educators at the elementary and secondary school levels: demonstrate accountability, provide scientifically based instruction, and are highly qualified.

• As we contemplate future directions for research, training, and practice related to ASD, it is essential to deepen and broaden our understanding of EBP within the context of a dynamic and ever-developing field.

• With the influx of students with ASD into the system, school districts have had to carry much of the burden of compensating for the gap in the knowledge and skill of teachers and related staff. To deal with this challenge, many districts hired outside contractors to provide services at premium costs. In addition, they often went to great lengths to patch together their own inservice training programs.

• With respect to ASD, there is an overrepresentation of EBP based on applied behavior analysis (ABA) compared to practices that are developmentally or socio-culturally based. This is largely because ABA is rooted in reductionist scientific principles that easily allow for the measurement of observable behavior using research methodologies that are more heavily weighted. By contrast, interventions rooted in scientific traditions that address the process and nature of development in a broader cultural context are more difficult to study using the same methodologies.

• There are drawbacks to determining the validity of interventions that reduce development and socio-cultural experience to a discrete set of skills or behaviors in an effort to apply the dominant research paradigm. For instance, interventions designed to foster developmental capacities such as spontaneous initiation, imitation, mutual engagement, play, and imagination are not readily assessed using common measures such as percentage of correct responses.

Chapter Review Questions

- List and explain three factors that have contributed to the evolution of EBP as applied to learners on the autism spectrum.

- Discuss the challenges that school districts have faced in preparing personnel in the area of ASD.

- Explain the following statement, "It is, therefore, an artifact that interventions that conform to the dominant research paradigm more readily meet the criteria for EBP."

References

Baker, C. (2012). Preparing teachers for students with autism. *New Horizons for Learning, 10*(2). Retrieved from http://education.jhu.edu/PD/newhorizons/Journals/specialedjournal/BakerC

Barnhill, G., Polloway, E., & Sumutka, B. (2011). A survey of personnel preparation practices in autism spectrum disorders. *Focus on Autism and other Developmental Disabilities, 26*(2), 75-86.

Burns, M. K., & Ysseldyke, J. E. (2009). Reported prevalence of evidence-based instructional practices in special education. *The Journal of Special Education, 43*, 3-11.

Center for the Future of Teaching and Learning. (2004). *Special education – Not so special for some: Qualified teachers in short supply for special education students.* Santa Cruz, CA: Author.

Centers for Disease Control and Prevention. (2013). Prevalence of autism spectrum disorders. *Autism and Developmental Disabilities Monitoring Network, United States, 2006, 58*(SS-10), 1-10.

Council for Exceptional Children. (2009). *Advanced knowledge and skill set: Developmental disabilities/autism specialist.* Retrieved from https://www.cec.sped.org/

Evidence-Based Medicine Working Group. (1992). Evidence-based medicine. A new approach to teaching the practice of medicine. *Journal of the American Medical Association, 268*(17), 2420-2425.

Fixen, D. L., Blasé, K. A., Horner, R., & Sugai, G. (2009). *Scaling up evidence-based practices in education* (Scaling-Up Brief #1). Chapel Hill, NC: The University of North Carolina. Retrieved from http://fpg.unc.edu/sites/fpg.unc.edu/files/resources/reports-and-policy-briefs/SISEP-Brief1-ScalingUpEBPInEducation-02-2009

Gibbs, L. E. (2003). *Evidence-based practice for the helping professions: A practical guide with integrated multimedia.* Pacific Grove, CA: Brooks/Cole-Thompson Learning.

Iovannone, R., Dunlap, G., Huber, H., & Kincaid, D. (2003). Effective educational practices for students with autism spectrum disorder. *Focus on Autism and Other Developmental Disabilities, 18*, 150-165.

Marks, D. F. (2012). *Perspectives on evidence-based practice* (HAD Contract no 02/042, Project 0047). London, UK: Health Department Agency Public Health Evidence Steering Group.

McGee, J., Menolascino, F., Hobbs, D., & Menousek, P. (1987). *Gentle teaching: A non-aversive approach to helping persons with mental retardation.* New York, NY: Human Sciences Press.

Mullen, E. J., & Streiner, D. L. (2004). The evidence for and against evidence-based practice. *Brief Treatment and Crisis Intervention, 4*(2), 111-121.

National Autism Center. (2009). *National standards project: Findings and conclusions: Addressing the need for evidence-based practice guidelines for autism spectrum disorders.* Retrieved from www.nationalautismcenter.org

National Professional Development Center on Autism Spectrum Disorders. (2009). *Evidence-based practices for children and youth with ASD.* Retrieved from http://autismpdc.fpg.unc.edu/content/briefs

National Research Council. (2001). *Educating children with autism.* Committee on Educational Interventions for Children With Autism. Washington, DC: National Academy Press.

Sackett, D. L., Rosenberg, W. M., Gray, J. A., Haynes, R. B., & Richardson, W. S. (1996). Evidence based medicine: What it is and what it isn't. *British Medical Journal, 312,* 71-72.

Scheuermann, B., Webber, J., Boutot, E. A., & Goodwin, M. (2003). Problems with personnel preparation in autism spectrum disorders. *Focus on Autism and Other Developmental Disabilities, 18,* 197-206.

Schwartz, I. S., & Baer, D. M. (1991). Social validity assessments: Is current practice state of the art? *Journal of Applied Behavior Analysis, 24*(2), 189-204.

United States Department of Education. (2012). *Individuals With Disabilities Education Act (IDEA) data. Number of children served under IDEA by disability and age group.* Washington, DC: Office of Special Education Programs. Retrieved from www.ideadata.org

Wolfberg, P. J. (2011). *Project mosaic: Preparing highly qualified educators to meet the unique need of learners on the autism spectrum in diverse settings.* Final report personnel preparation project. United States Department of Education, OSERS (#H325K060211).

Yell, M. L., Drasgow, E., & Lowrey. K. A. (2005). No Child Left Behind and students with autism spectrum disorders. *Focus on Autism and Other Developmental Disorders, 20,* 130-139.

Yu, B., & Wolfberg, P. J. (2011-2016). *Project common ground: Preparing highly qualified speech-language pathologists to meet the communication needs of children with autism spectrum disorders in diverse settings.* Personnel Preparation Grant, United States Department of Education, OSERS (#H325K110326).

Learner Objectives

After reading this chapter, the learner should be able to:

- State the meaning of autism spectrum disorders (ASD)

- State signs of ASD in both early and late onset

- State and describe three specifiers under the heading of ASD

- State the two areas used in the diagnostic criteria for determining ASD

- State the differences between the DSM IV and the DSM-5 definitions of ASD

- State the six aspects characterizing ASD

- Discuss why the dimensions of ASD can be considered a continuum

- Discuss the causes of ASD, both historical and current

- Discuss the psychological theories of ASD

- State gender differences in ASD

- Discuss why increasing numbers of children are being identified as having ASD

Chapter 2

An Overview of
Autism Spectrum Disorders

Tony Attwood

Colton is an 8-year-old with a diagnosis of an autism spectrum disorder. He was nonverbal until age 7, when he began to speak using echoed speech, usually repeating phrases from popular cartoons on television. Colton avoids eye contact with others and has not established any friendships. He appears to be interested in books, but often looks at them upside down and seems to study the page numbers with as much interest as the pictures. He is particularly interested in the weather and spends time looking at the daily calendar in his classroom that shows the day's weather. Colton has difficulty when having to change clothing from one season to the next and often insists on wearing shorts far into the fall season. He has difficulty each winter when boots and coats are required for going outside to recess. Colton has demonstrated disruptive and tantrum behaviors during his school day, most often during schedule changes or even daily activity changes. He is mainstreamed for part of his day, but does not participate in the academic activities of his mainstreamed classroom. During recess, Colton typically walks around the boundaries of the playground, avoiding crowded areas and interactive play activities.

Nic is a 10-year-old with a recent diagnosis of autism spectrum disorder. He has done well in school, but has recently had difficulty with reading tests that require him to predict or empathize with a character's position. Nic prefers to read nonfiction and has an above-grade-level knowledge of history and science facts. He seems to have some friends at school, but his parents report that he has never invited anyone to his house nor been invited to a birthday party. Nic seems to prefer to interact with adults and has a precocious vocabulary, sounding a bit like a little professor. Although he has not demonstrated problem behavior at school, Nic is often withdrawn at family functions and asks his parents to be excused from such events as Thanksgiving and 4th of July parties where his family typically gathers with extended family members for a large party.

These two students illustrate the broad nature of the autism spectrum and the varying levels of support required to benefit from education. This chapter offers a comprehensive introduction to autism spectrum disorder (ASD), the various levels of severity associated with ASD, and some possible causes. The section titled The Autism Spectrum is separated into six aspects of autism: social reasoning, language, special interests, cognition, sensory sensitivity, and emotion expression and management, with illustrations of how these dimensions might look at each end of the spectrum.

What Is an Autism Spectrum Disorder?

Autism spectrum disorder is a neurodevelopmental condition that is complex to define and diagnose. According to the recently updated *Diagnostic and Statistical Manual of Mental Disorders, 5th Edition* (DSM-5) diagnostic criteria of the American Psychiatric Association (APA, 2013, pp. 50-51), an autism spectrum disorder is diagnosed when the following are present:

A. Persistent deficits in social communication and social interaction across multiple contexts.

B. Restricted, repetitive patterns of behavior, interests, or activities.

C. The symptoms are present in the early developmental period and

D. Cause clinically significant impairment in social, occupational or other important areas of current functioning.

E. These disturbances are not better explained by intellectual disability or global developmental delay. Social communication should be below that expected for general developmental level.

The full diagnostic criteria are provided in Table 2.1.

Table 2.1
Autism Spectrum Disorder Diagnostic Criteria

A. Persistent deficits in social communication and social interaction across multiple contexts, as manifested by the following, currently or by history (examples are illustrative, not exhaustive):

   1. Deficits in social-emotional reciprocity, ranging, for example, from abnormal social approach and failure of normal back-and-forth conversation; to reduced sharing of interests, emotions, or affect; to failure to initiate or respond to social interactions.

   2. Deficits in nonverbal communicative behaviors used for social interaction, ranging for example, from poorly integrated verbal and nonverbal communication; to abnormalities in eye contact and body language or deficits in understanding and use of gestures; to a total lack of facial expressions and nonverbal communication.

   3. Deficits in developing, maintaining, and understanding relationships, ranging, for example, from difficulties adjusting behavior to suit various social contexts; to difficulties in sharing imaginative play or in making friends; to absence of interest in peers.

   Specify current severity:

   Severity is based on social communication impairments and restricted, repetitive patterns of behavior (see Table 2.2).

B. Restricted, repetitive patterns of behavior, interests, or activities, as manifested by at least two or the following, currently or by history (examples are illustrative, not exhaustive; see text):

   1. Stereotyped or repetitive motor movements, use of objects, or speech (e.g., simple motor stereotypies, lining up toys or flipping objects, echolalia, idiosyncratic phrases).

   2. Insistence on sameness, inflexible adherence to routines, or ritualized patterns of verbal or nonverbal behavior (e.g., extreme distress at small changes, difficulties with transitions, rigid thinking patterns, greeting rituals, need to take some route or eat same food every day).

   3. Highly restricted, fixated interests that are abnormal in intensity or focus (e.g., strong attachment to or preoccupation with unusual objects, excessively circumscribed or perseverative interests).

   4. Hyper- or hypo-reactivity to sensory input or unusual interest in sensory aspects of the environment (e.g., apparent indifference to pain/temperature, adverse response to specific sounds or textures, excessive smelling or touching of objects, visual fascination with lights or movement).

   Specify current severity:

   Severity is based on social communication impairments and restricted, repetitive patterns of behavior (see Table 2.2).

C. Symptoms must be present in the early developmental period (but may not become fully manifest until social demands exceed limited capacities, or may be masked by learned strategies in later life).

D. Symptoms cause clinically significant impairment in social, occupational, or other important areas of current functioning.

E. These disturbances are not better explained by intellectual disability (intellectual developmental disorder) or global developmental delay. Intellectual disability and autism spectrum disorder frequently co-occur; to make comorbid diagnoses of autism spectrum disorder and intellectual disability, social communication should be below that expected for general developmental level.

From *Diagnostic and Statistical Manual of Mental Disorders, 5th Edition* (APA, 2013, pp. 50-51).

Specifiers

The DSM-5 criteria for ASD require further information from the multidisciplinary team conducting the diagnostic assessment to more precisely describe any associated developmental disabilities, medical and psychiatric factors, and level of expression. A new term, *specifiers,* has been created to describe additional information relevant to the diagnosis, in particular:

- With or without accompanying intellectual and/or language impairment

- Association with a known medical, genetic condition, or environmental factor

- Association with another neurodevelopmental, mental, or behavior disorder or catatonia

- Severity of expression from Level 1 to Level 3 based on the level of support needed for social communication and restricted, repetitive behaviors (see Table 2.2)

The following is an example of the diagnostic profile for an ASD using the specifiers:

James is a teenager who has an ASD at Level 3 for both social communication and restricted, repetitive behaviors, with accompanying severe intellectual disability and language impairment, in association with fragile X syndrome, epilepsy, and attention deficit hyperactivity disorder, and generalized anxiety disorder.

> The DSM-5 text clearly states that the level of severity should not be used to determine eligibility for and provision of services as these can only be developed at an individual level and through discussion of personal priorities and targets.

Table 2.2
Severity Levels for Autism Spectrum Disorder

Severity Level	Social Communication	Restricted, Repetitive Behaviors
Level 3 "Requiring very substantial support"	Severe deficits in verbal and nonverbal social communication skills cause severe impairments in functioning, very limited initiation of social interactions, and minimal response to social overtures from others. For example, a person with few words of intelligible speech who rarely initiates interaction and, when he or she does, makes unusual approaches to meet needs only and responds to only very direct social approaches.	Inflexibility of behavior, extreme difficulty coping with change, or other restricted/repetitive behaviors markedly interfere with functioning in all spheres. Great distress/difficulty changing focus or action.
Level 2 "Requiring substantial support"	Marked deficits in verbal and nonverbal social communication skills; social impairments apparent even with supports in place; limited initiation of social interactions; and reduced or abnormal responses to social overtures from others. For example, a person who speaks simple sentences, whose interaction is limited to narrow special interests, and who has markedly odd nonverbal communication.	Inflexibility of behavior, difficulty coping with change, or other restricted/repetitive behaviors appear frequently enough to be obvious to the casual observer and interfere with functioning in a variety of contexts. Distress and/or difficulty changing focus or action.
Level 1 "Requiring support"	Without supports in place, deficits in social communication cause noticeable impairments. Difficulty initiating social interactions and clear examples of atypical or unsuccessful responses to social overtures of others. May appear to have decreased interest in social interactions. For example, a person who is able to speak in full sentences and engages in communication but whose to-and-fro conversation with others fails, and whose attempts to make friends are odd and typically unsuccessful.	Inflexibility of behavior causes significant interference with functioning in one or more contexts. Difficulty switching between activities. Problems of organization and planning hamper independence.

From *Diagnostic and Statistical Manual of Mental Disorders, 5th Edition* (APA, 2013, pp. ??).

Changes in DSM-5 vs. DSM IV

When comparing the changes in diagnostic criteria from the DSM IV to the present DSM-5, a major change is that the APA has dispensed with the term ***pervasive developmental disorder*** and replaced it with ***autism spectrum disorder***. This change is in accordance with the preference of clinicians and academics throughout the world.

Another noticeable change is dispensing with the DSM IV diagnostic categories of Rett's disorder, childhood disintegrative disorder, pervasive developmental disorder-not otherwise specified (PDD-NOS), and Asperger's disorder. The rationale for using a dimensional rather than a categorical concept of ASD is that a single umbrella term of ASD, with specific information about the level of expression, is more accurate and consistent with the research literature and clinical experience.

Asperger Syndrome

Even though not included in the DSM-5, clinicians, therapists, teachers, parents, and those with an ASD Level 1 can still use the term Asperger Syndrome, which has been in general usage for over two decades. The concept of Asperger Syndrome has not suddenly disappeared; it has been replaced with the new diagnostic term – ASD Level 1 without language or intellectual impairment – and according to the authors of DSM-5, all children and adults who had a previous diagnosis of Asperger Syndrome or PDD-NOS should be given the diagnosis of ASD.

In my own clinical practice, I use DSM-5 diagnostic criteria and state that a child has ASD Level 1 but also use the term Asperger Syndrome so that parents, teachers, and therapists will be able to use a term that is often understood by the general public. Asperger Syndrome is also a term that can be used to seek further information from the Internet and published books and research articles published prior to 2013. Thus, the term will still be legitimately used by clinicians, parents, teachers, therapists, those with an ASD, and the general public in conversations and as the basis for seeking further information on how to understand and help a child.

Hyper- or Hypo-Reactivity to Sensory Input

A significant improvement in the diagnostic criteria of DSM-5 is the inclusion of hyper- and hypo-reactivity to sensory input or unusual interest in sensory aspects of the environment. This has been a characteristic of ASD that has been clearly and consistently described by those who have an ASD and recognized by parents and teachers. Sensory sensitivity is also a dimension of autism previously examined in the published diagnostic assessment scales and interviews for autism and we now have several research studies confirming the presence and nature of sensory sensitivity within the spectrum of autism.

The DSM-5 diagnostic criteria include hyper- and hypo-reactivity to sensory input as an example of "restricted, repetitive patterns of behavior, interests, or activities." However, the rationale for inclusion in this diagnostic category is not obvious or explained in the text accompanying the criteria. Future research may establish why this is a characteristic of ASD and whether it is an example of restricted or repetitive behavior or a separate and independent characteristic of ASD.

Collapsing Three Diagnostic Dimensions Into Two

DSM IV listed three diagnostic dimensions: a qualitative impairment in social interaction, a qualitative impairment in communication, and restricted and repetitive behavior. DSM-5 combines the social and communication dimensions into one; namely, deficits in social communication. This is consistent with the profile of social and communication abilities recognized by clinicians and speech-language pathologists and confirmed by research.

Social (Pragmatic) Communication Disorder

The DSM-5 includes a diagnostic category for children who have marked deficits in social communication but do not have restricted or repetitive behavior, interest, or activities. The diagnostic criteria for social (pragmatic) communication disorder (SCD) describe a deficit related to the pragmatic aspects or social use of language without section B of the diagnostic criteria for ASD. It is a new differential diagnosis for ASD.

Catatonia

One of the specifiers for ASD is catatonia. Recent research has identified an association between catatonia and ASD. During adolescence, a teenager or young adult who has an ASD may demonstrate a marked deterioration in movement abilities with a slowing and "freezing" of movement mid-action accompanied by symptoms of mutism, posturing, grimacing, and waxy flexibility. Should a deterioration in movement abilities occur, an assessment is warranted by a specialist in the movements disorders associated with ASD.

Stricter Diagnostic Criteria

DSM-5 uses stricter diagnostic criteria than DSM IV, which will have an impact on the number of children diagnosed with an ASD. Several research studies have compared the two diagnostic criteria (DSM IV vs. DSM-5), and all have indicated that with the DSM-5, fewer children will receive a diagnosis of ASD, with reductions ranging from 75% to 10% (Gibbs, Aldridge, Chaler, Witzlsperger, & Smith, 2012; Huerta, Bishop, Duncan, Hus, & Lord, 2012; Matson, Belva, Horovitz, & Bamburg, 2012; Matson, Kozlowski, Hattier, Horovitz, & Sipes, 2012; McPartland, Reichow, & Volkmar, 2012; Taheri & Perry, 2012). It is too early to tell in late 2013 when this chapter is being written how the diagnostic landscape will change, but it appears that there may be a future decrease in the number of children receiving a diagnosis of ASD.[1]

Early Signs of Autism

The first medical signs of autism, such as sleep disturbance and feeding problems, may go unnoticed, as they are typical of many children in their first year. However, parents may become concerned that they have difficulty comforting the child, who also may not be drawn towards social activities, preferring to play alone, and who does not point to interesting objects he or she wants them to notice and share the experience.

---

[1] My personal opinion is that the DSM-5 criteria are an improvement on the old criteria and consistent with advances in clinical wisdom and academic research. Although I lament the removal of the term Asperger Syndrome from the DSM, I agree with the rationale and know that the term will remain in common usage. I commend the American Psychiatric Association's work group in neurodevelopmental disorders for its improvements in the conceptualization and diagnostic criteria for autism in DSM-5.

The very young child with an ASD appears not to consider people as the most important aspects of daily life, preferring instead to explore and play with objects and enjoy sensory experiences. Indeed, sometimes the child appears to treat a person as an object, a "climbing frame," with fascinating sensory or perceptual experiences such as sparkling jewelry, long strands of hair, or reflections in a pair of glasses. The child may be fascinated and delighted by natural sensory experiences, such as the feeling of the wind on her face, or be mesmerized by the spinning of the wheel of a toy truck. When excited, the child may literally jump for joy or express pleasure in an unusual way such as hand flapping and a contorted facial expression. The child may shun the approaches of a peer or adult to share the experience or switch the interest to another activity.

Parents may also notice that the child does not imitate their actions or domestic chores, or repeat an activity that caused a parent to smile, laugh, or show approval. Eye contact is fleeting in greetings, in seeking approval or reassurance from a parent, and in noticing and being interested in what somebody else is looking at. The typical "look at me" or "look at this" actions may be rare, and the child is often content with long periods of solitude. The child clearly prefers consistency and routines in his daily life. Variety is not the "spice of life," and surprises and changes are not enjoyed.

Based on these behaviors, parents, and especially mothers, develop an intuitive feeling that something is wrong with the child's ability to relate to others and describe the child "as being on a different wavelength," "as if we have borrowed him, as if he isn't ours," or "as looking through me when I try to make her smile, as if I am in the way of what she wants to look at." Finally, the child may demonstrate a delay in speech and shared imaginative play and express extreme distress associated with specific sensory experiences.

A variety of therapists and specialists in developmental disorders may become involved at this point. The delay in the development of communication abilities, such as the use of speech and gestures, may lead parents to suspect that the child is deaf (since often the child does not respond when his name is called and fails to orientate to the speech of another person), and consequently seek a referral to a speech-language pathologist or an audiologist. Delays in self-care skills, such as toilet training, and acute sensitivity to sensory experiences, such as sudden noises or various tactile sensations, may lead to a referral to an occupational therapist. Also, challenges with specific aspects of play, learning, behavior, and emotion management often necessitate a referral to a developmental psychologist.

Further, parents may seek a medical examination by a developmental pediatrician, especially if the child has an unusual growth pattern, such as a larger head circumference and being much taller than expected of a child of that age, or demonstrates neurological problems such as epilepsy. These multidisciplinary professionals may be the first to confirm the signs of an autism spectrum disorder when they conduct a thorough assessment of a range of abilities and behavior and review the child's developmental history.

Regressive or Late-Onset Autism

We can now reliably identify the signs of autism in some children prior to one year old, but many children with an ASD demonstrate few behaviors and abilities of concern to their parents until they are well into the latter part of their second year (Moore & Goodson, 2003). Such children achieve the typical developmental milestones in motor, linguistic, and cognitive abilities, and develop a reasonable spoken vocabulary, take an interest in others, and develop early symbolic and imaginative play. However, over a very short period, sometimes just a few weeks, between the age of one and two years (with a peak at 18 months), the child who otherwise demonstrated no conspicuous signs of autism, very quickly, over several weeks or even days, has significant deterioration or regression in abilities. Speech development stagnates or age-typical vocabulary disappears, the child becomes socially isolated and self-absorbed, and play abilities deteriorate. However, motor and self-care skills are usually not affected. By the age of 3 years, there may be no distinguishing features in behavior and abilities between a child whose onset of autism was apparent in her first year and a child who appeared to be developing normally but whose signs of autism became dramatically apparent between the ages of 1 and 3 years. Regressive or late-onset autism is variably reported to be present in 20% to 40% of cases (Siperstein & Volkmar, 2004).

Six Aspects of the Autism Spectrum

When the diagnosis of ASD is confirmed, therapists, teachers, and psychologists examine six aspects of ASD to determine the child's unique profile of abilities and behavior and then go on to design remedial programs for each aspect. The six aspects of ASD consist of social reasoning, language, cognition, special interests, sensory sensitivity, and the expression and management of emotions.

Social Reasoning

At one end of the spectrum or dimension of difficulties in social interaction and social reasoning is the aloof child, who actively avoids social interactions; next is the child described as passive, who can tolerate social interaction with encouragement and can initiate social contact, but primarily to achieve access to something he or she wants. The next stage on this dimension is the "active but odd" child, who actively wants to interact with others, usually adults, but, despite a motivation to socialize, appears odd due to a lack of social understanding and limited range of social abilities. Interactions may not commence with conventional greetings, and may continue as if the child has a limited social script or repertoire of social behavior, such as a reliance on repetitive questions (Wing & Gould, 1979). At the upper end of the social continuum is the child who wants friends but appears to have a significant delay in social maturity, has conspicuous problems with theory-of-mind abilities, such as reading facial expressions, body language, tone of voice, and contextual cues to know what someone is thinking or feeling (Baron-Cohen, 1995), and may interact more as a miniature adult (or teacher) than a child (Wing & Attwood, 1987). This part of the dimension was previously known as Asperger's disorder but has become ASD Level 1 using the DSM-5. We now have programs specifically designed to improve social reasoning and friendship skills (see Chapters 8 and 9).

Language Abilities

The severest expression of impaired communication or language abilities for children who have an ASD is the silent child who has a vocabulary of sounds, but not of words. This child may have a greater comprehension of language than expression but does not easily replace a lack of speech with the development of a natural spontaneous gestural language. Parents may notice that the child tries to speak but appears unable to connect thought to the oral-motor abilities required to do so. This is a description of the classic silent and aloof child first described by Leo Kanner in 1943.

In the next area of the communication spectrum, vocalizations can occur, but speech often requires an external prompt; for example, immediately echoing the utterance of someone (**echolalia**), seeing an object and being able to say the name of the object, or using sentences "borrowed" and repeated verbatim from a favorite TV program. The words may be appropriate for the context and often said in the voice or accent of the original utterance.

In the next area on the spectrum, ASD Level 1 according to DSM-5, the child has a remarkable verbal fluency and vocabulary but encounters significant problems with the pragmatic aspects of language (i.e., the "art" of conversation), sometimes an unusual prosody, and a tendency to be very pedantic, often making a literal interpretation of someone's comments. There may also be challenges with **auditory discrimination** and **auditory processing**. Strategies to encourage the development of speech and language abilities are described in Chapter 4.

Cognition

The cognitive spectrum starts with the child who has profound learning difficulties and a significant intellectual impairment as assessed on a standardized intelligence scale. The child's natural play may be within the very early or infantile stages of development. This child is interested in the sensory rather than the functional or symbolic qualities of objects. She explores the world by touch and taste and is fascinated by perspective, symmetry and order, arranging items in lines and examining objects from unusual angles.

The next stage on the cognitive skills spectrum is the child who is familiar with and has relatively advanced skills in such activities as construction toys or jigsaw puzzles. He is fascinated by shapes and patterns and the functional as opposed to the symbolic use of objects. The child may display natural engineering skills with construction blocks or produce drawings with photographic realism.

When the child starts school, a formal test of intellectual abilities usually identifies an uneven profile of cognitive development. This indicates that the child has an unusual learning style. Academic abilities such as reading or mathematics may be self-taught, and sometimes the child is precocious in these areas. In contrast, some children with ASD have significant difficulties with reading and number skills, despite an IQ that suggests that such abilities are within their intellectual capacity. There can also be problems with organizational skills, working memory, and time management (Adreon & Duroucher, 2007; Verte, Geurts, Roeyersd, Oosterlaan, & Sergeant, 2006; Williams, Goldstein, & Minshew, 2006).

Although autism is considered a **neurodevelopmental disorder**, not all aspects of the brain functioning are necessarily adversely affected (Herbert, 2005a). Approximately 10% of children with autism develop **savant** characteristics; that is, remarkable abilities compared to the child's overall level of ability (Hermelin, 2001). This can involve abilities in mathematics, music, drawing, mechanics, and information technology. Examples include rapid completion of mathematical computations; the ability to listen to music and to immediately play the music on another instrument – note perfect; or a very young child acquiring the ability to draw in perspective or to design machines or learn computer languages. Some children develop visual reasoning abilities that are in remarkable contrast to their verbal abilities, such as being able to solve visual puzzles or learn to read despite having very limited speech.

While teachers and therapists are concerned about cognitive abilities that are significantly below the abilities expected of a typical child of the same age, we must also consider programs to improve particular talents and work on the child's relative strengths. For those who are visualizers, that is, having relatively good visual reasoning abilities, it is important to remember that "a picture is worth a thousand words" when trying to help them understand an educational concept. Developing a talent can lead to increased self-esteem and the possibility that a specific ability can be used constructively in the classroom and may become a successful career path (Grandin & Duffy, 2009).

Special Interests

Children with ASD are known for having a wide range of intense or special interests that can change in focus and complexity over the years (see Chapter 12). The spectrum of interests may include those enjoyed by typical children, although often at a younger age, as well as some that are quite eccentric.

The first stage is a preoccupation with parts of objects. This interest may include spinning the wheels of a toy tractor or manipulating electrical switches. The next stage is a fascination with a specific category of objects and accumulating as many examples as possible. Sometimes collections comprise items typically acquired by other children, such as unusual stones, but some can be quite unique, such as drain covers or batteries. In this stage, the child's play may also be somewhat unusual in that he may pretend to be the special interest. For example, a child rocked from side to side pretending to be windshield wipers. His fascination with windshield wipers led to his eagerly approaching cars waiting at red traffic lights and examining the wiper blades. This caused great confusion and distress for the driver, but the child was exceptionally happy.

The next stage is acquisition of information and remembering facts about a topic or concept. Common topics or concepts include transport, animals, and electronics. Some of the interests are developmentally appropriate and typical of same-aged peers, such as Thomas the Tank Engine, dinosaurs, castles, and computer games, but other interests are unusual, such as vacuum cleaners and alarm systems. The reason for the interest is usually idiosyncratic, and not because the topic is popular with peers or the "currency" between friends (Attwood, 2006).

The focus of the interest invariably changes, but at a time dictated by the child, and is replaced by another special interest that is also the choice of the child, not a parent or teacher. The complexity and number of interests vary according to the child's developmental level and intellectual capacity. Over time there is a progression to multiple and more abstract or complex interests, such as periods of history or specific countries or cultures (Attwood, 2003b). This is the domain of the child with ASD Level 1 according to DSM-5. Chapter 12 describes ways to support individuals with ASD using their special interests.

Sensory Sensitivity

The spectrum of sensory sensitivity is the dimension of ASD that we know least about empirically. However, the autobiographies of adults with an ASD vividly describe a sensory perception that is different (Barron & Barron, 2002; Grandin, 1995; Shore, 2003). In the severest expression of sensory sensitivity, the child appears to be living in a "war zone" with sudden explosions of excruciating noises, visual sensations that are "blinding," and touch and aromas that are perceived as extremely aversive and frightening. The child might be hyper-vigilant in anticipation of the next sensory bombardment or sensory overload and demonstrate a startle response that is extremely difficult to inhibit and does not attenuate through repeated experience or desensitization programs (Baranek, 2002). For example, the noise of a chair scraping the classroom floor, a dog barking, or the sound of small electric motors can cause the child to cover her ears, try to escape the situation, or somehow stop the sensory experience. There can also be sensitivity to the degree of natural light intensity or artificial light, especially fluorescent light and down lights. The aromas of perfumes and smell of cleaning products can be overpowering, and the smell of certain foods can cause the child to retch or vomit. Further, the taste and texture of food may be perceived as extremely unpleasant, leading to a severely restricted self-imposed diet.

The continuum of sensory sensitivity can also include a lack of visible response to certain sensory experiences; for example, the child may not communicate pain when injured or indicate medical problems as severe as a fracture. Some children do not appear to experience any discomfort at being cold, and are able, for example, to walk into a lake in sub-zero temperatures.

When the sensory sensitivity is a dominant characteristic of ASD, the child may develop maladaptive strategies to control her environment in order to avoid specific sensory experiences, such as running from a supermarket because of the noise of the refrigeration units or refusing to use the bathroom at school due to the automatic flushers and aroma. Sensory sensitivity can also lead to increased anxiety, as the child can never be sure when a potentially terrifying sensory experience will occur (Bellini, 2006; Goldsmith, Van Hulle, Arneson, Schreiber, & Gernsbacher, 2006). We use the term **sensory meltdown** when sensory experiences have been overwhelming and unavoidable (Lipsky, 2011) Support strategies are described in Chapter 6.

Expression and Management of Emotions

The DSM-5 diagnostic criteria refer to a deficit in social-emotional reciprocity. As a result, a thorough assessment of a child with an ASD should include an evaluation of the child's ability to express reciprocal emotions as well as to label and describe emotions in others and himself and to express and manage intense emotions, especially anxiety, despair, and anger. Some individuals with ASD have difficulty expressing and enjoying affection (Attwood & Garnett, 2013).

We now have theoretical and neurological models of why ASD is associated with impairments in the communication of emotions (see Chapter 10), and psychologists have modified cognitive behavior therapy (CBT) to treat mood disorders in children who have an ASD (Scarpa, Williams White, & Attwood 2013). In fact, CBT programs have been developed for children with ASD Level 1 as young as 5 to 7 years old (Scarpa, Wells, & Attwood, 2013). Chapter 10 describes these and other support strategies for regulating emotions.

Progression Through the Autism Spectrum

When conducting a diagnostic assessment or annual educational review of a child with ASD, it is important to establish a baseline and subsequently assess progress along each of the six aspects of ASD. One way of understanding the autism spectrum is to imagine a recording studio and the recording console with six sliding knobs, or for those who are interested in home audio entertainment, a graphic equalizer. During the assessment or review, the child's level of expression of each of the six aspects of autism is evaluated, and an explanation is given that autism itself is a spectrum, such that the expression of autism may change over time. At one point in a child's early development, autism may be the correct diagnosis, but some children with an ASD show a remarkable improvement in abilities, moving across the spectrum and levels of ASD towards, and potentially within, the normal range. Current research and clinical experience suggest that in the adult years, around 10% of those diagnosed with ASD Level 1 in childhood can progress to the subclinical level of expression. That is, the symptoms do not cause a clinically significant impairment in social, occupational, or other important areas of function (Criterion D of DSM-5; Cederlund et al., 2008; Farley et al., 2009).

Causes of Autism Spectrum Disorder

When first described from the late 1940s to the early 1970s, autism was considered to be an expression of schizophrenia or psychosis in childhood, and the cause to be due to a mother not loving her child. The term ***refrigerator mother*** is commonly attributed to Leo Kanner and was propagated by Bruno Bettelheim to describe an emotionally unavailable and emotionally "cold" and detached mother. The cause of autism was considered to be **psychogenic**: a reaction to rejection. The only treatment was prolonged psychoanalysis for both mother and child.

Scientific research has established that the cause of autism is not faulty parenting as there is clear evidence of neurological impairment (Bauman & Kemper, 2003). We now consider autism a neurodevelopmental disorder, with specific structures of the brain not functioning as we would expect. As a result, there is a trend towards conducting research on the possible causes of autism and examining factors that can affect brain development and functioning from conception to very early childhood.

Genetics

The original studies to suggest a genetic cause of autism used identical and nonidentical twins (Hallmayer et al., 2002). The rate of autism among identical twins is between 70 and 90%, while in nonidentical twins, the rate is about 0 to 5% (Bailey et al., 1995). If a family has a child with autism, the chances of having another child with autism range from 18-22% and an estimated recurrence rate of 26% if the subsequent child is a boy (Constantino, Zhang, Frazier, Abbacchi, & Law, 2010; Ozonoff et al., 2010). Recent research suggests that a similar profile of abilities, although to a lesser degree, may be identified in the relatives of a child with ASD (Bailey, Palferman, Heavey, & LeCouteur, 1998; Cederlund & Gillberg, 2004; Volkmar, Klin, & Pauls, 1998). Geneticists use the term *broader autism phenotype* to describe such individuals, and the presence of a number of the characteristics in some relatives has been one of the reasons why genetic factors have been considered as having a significant role in the etiology of ASD.

Some specific chromosomal abnormalities have been associated with the development of the characteristics of ASD, such as fragile X syndrome (Zafeiriou, Ververi, & Vargiami, 2007). Research studies have also identified individuals with autism who have chromosomal abnormalities on one of the following chromosomes: 2, 7, 15, 16 and 19 (Rutter, 2005). These rare chromosomal abnormalities may not be inherited but affect genetic material or the "genetic blueprint" for specific aspects of brain development.

We also now recognize that the risk of having a child with an ASD increase significantly with advancing parental age, low birth weight, and fetal exposure to psychotropic medication, especially valproate (Lundstrom et al., 2010).

Neurology

Neurological studies of autism have focused on **neurochemistry**, **neuropathology** (i.e., the various structures of the brain), and **functional neuroimaging** (i.e., the way parts of the brain function during specific thoughts, emotions, or behavior) (Barnea-Gorlay & Manzelli, 2014;). Findings of studies of neurochemistry suggest a dysfunction of two chemicals within the brain, the neurotransmitters serotonin and dopamine. As a result, many of the medications prescribed for children and adolescents with ASD modify the levels of serotonin and dopamine. While such medication does not provide a cure, it may have a beneficial effect on mood and emotion management.

Neuropathological studies have indicated that approximately 10% of young children with autism and 25% of young children with ASD Level 1 have a heavier and larger brain and head circumference than typical, known as **macrocephaly** (Chawarska & Volkmar, 2005; Gillberg & de Souza, 2002). The young brain is often enlarged by as much as 10% in volume. However, by later childhood, the brain size may be within the normal range. There appears to be a rapid but short-lived acceleration in the growth of the brain; typical children attain the same brain size, but later in their development (Herbert, 2005b).

Neuropathological studies have also identified structural abnormalities of the limbic system and especially the Amygdala (Nordahl et al., 2012) within the brain, which is associated with emotions, with reduced neuron size and increased neuron density. Further, there also appear to be structural abnormalities of the cerebellum and inferior olive (Bauman & Kemper, 1994).

Several structural **magnetic resonance imaging (MRI)** studies have also identified larger brain volumes in young children with ASD, with increased amounts of white matter in the cerebellum and cerebral cortex, and increased amounts of grey matter in the cortex (Courchesne et al., 2001; Rojas et al., 2006). Having a larger and faster growing brain in early childhood with more nerve cells may not be beneficial to the development of specific abilities, such as socialization and communication skills and cognition. Something appears to have gone wrong with early brain development such that there is too much development rather than too little.

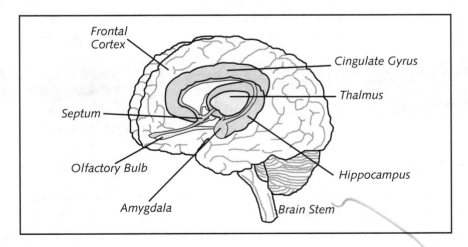

Figure 2.1. Labeled brain showing the location of the amygdala and the frontal cortex.

Studies using functional neuroimaging have suggested that in children with autism the amygdala and orbitofrontal cortex (see Figure 2.1) areas of the brain, associated with emotion regulation and social reasoning, are not functioning as we would expect (Baron-Cohen et al., 1999). Thus, we now have a neurological explanation for our observations over many decades of these children's impaired ability to understand complex social situations and to manage emotions.

Possible Errors of Metabolism

Children born with **phenylketonuria (PKN)** have a deficiency in the enzyme that converts the amino acid phenylalanine to tyrosine. A deficiency of this enzyme leads to a toxic accumulation of phenylalanine, resulting in damage to brain function that leads to intellectual disability and a behavioral profile in some children that is similar to autism. Treatment for phenylketonuria is a phenylalanine-free diet, typically involving the elimination of meat or milk, which prevents the development of intellectual disability and behavioral signs of autism (Batshaw & Tuchman, 2002). Thus, we have some evidence that one of the causes of the behaviors associated with autism is an error of metabolism.

A current debate between scientists and parents is whether ASD may be caused by an error in the metabolism of gluten, which occurs in certain cereals, and casein, which occurs in dairy products. While casein- and gluten-free diets have become popular with many parents, we do not have any independent and objective studies that clearly establish the value of such diets, though there is anecdotal clinical support (Elder et al., 2006).

Infections in Pregnancy and Early Childhood

Certain viral infections have been suggested as a cause of autism. In the 1970s, it was suggested that autism might be caused by congenital rubella, but a recent study has not found supportive evidence (Fombonne, 2003). Some studies have suggested that a mother contracting the herpes virus during pregnancy might be another cause of autism, and post-measles encephalitis and herpes encephalitis in early childhood have also been cited as potential causes (Beversdorf et al., 2005). One interesting theory is that immigrants may be at greater risk of having a child with autism (Gillberg & Gillberg, 1996). To date, few studies have examined the theory that moving culture and climate may affect a mother's immune system and increase the likelihood of having a child with autism, and those who have investigated this hypothesis have relied on small population samples.

Finally, the issue of immunizations causing autism has been discussed widely in the media. At present, no research study has established a consistent link between the MMR (measles, mumps, rubella) vaccination in which mercury has been used as a preservative and the development of autism (DeStefano, Price, & Weintraub, 2013; Honda, Shimizu, & Rutter, 2005; Hornig et al., 2008; Price et al., 2010; Richler et al., 2006; Tozzi et al., 2009).

Autoimmune Disorders

Recent research (e.g., Chen et al., 2013) has indicated an association between autism and a history of autoimmune disorders in the family of children with an ASD. The autoimmune disorders include Type 1 diabetes, rheumatoid arthritis, asthma, Crohn's disease, and increased level of celiac disease, especially in mothers of a child with an ASD.

Gender Differences

ASD is diagnosed four times more often in males than in females. However, the ratio can be 2:1 when comparing boys and girls with ASD Level 1. Girls have the same clinical profile and depth of ASD characteristics but are often more creative in camouflaging social confusion by strategies such as imitation, and may have less conspicuous restricted and repetitive patterns of behavior. Girls may not come to the attention of clinicians until their adolescent years with the development of a secondary mood, eating or personality disorder (Attwood, 2007).

Psychological Theories of Autism Spectrum Disorder

Three psychological theories explain some of the characteristics of ASD, impaired theory of mind, weak central coherence, and impaired executive function.

Impaired Theory of Mind

The psychological term *theory of mind* refers to the ability to recognize and understand the thoughts, beliefs, desires, and intentions of other people in order to make sense of their behavior and predict what they are going to do next. It has also been described as "mind reading" (see Chapter 13). Impaired theory of mind is often referred to as "**mind blindness**" (Baron-Cohen, 1995) or, colloquially, difficulty in "putting oneself in another person's shoes." The child with an ASD typically does not recognize or understand the cues that indicate the thoughts or feelings of another person at a level expected for someone of his age. However, we are developing strategies to teach theory of mind abilities (Attwood, 2006; Kerr & Drukin, 2004).

Weak Central Coherence

Children with autism can be remarkably good at attending to detail but appear to have considerable difficulty perceiving and understanding the overall picture or gist of something (Frith & Happé, 1994). A useful metaphor is to imagine rolling a piece of paper into a tube, closing one eye and placing the tube against the open eye like a telescope and looking at the world through the tube; details are visible, but the context is not perceived.

Typical children have a broader cognitive perspective than the child with autism. When learning in the classroom, the problem may not be attention, but focus. Some activities are difficult to complete on time because the child with autism has become preoccupied with the detail, focusing on parts rather than wholes (Schlooz et al., 2006). A teacher or parent sometimes needs to explain to the child where to look and what is relevant in the situation.

Impaired Executive Function

The psychological term *executive function* includes:

- organizational and planning abilities
- working memory
- inhibition and impulse control
- time management and prioritizing
- using new strategies

Children with ASD have been recognized as having problems with executive function (Russell, 1997; Yerys, Hepburn, & Pennington, 2007). The teacher of a child with autism will soon become familiar with these characteristics and have to make adjustments to the school curriculum. In the early school years, the main signs of impaired executive function include difficulties with inhibiting a response (i.e., being impulsive), working memory, and using new strategies. Many children with autism are notorious for being impulsive in schoolwork and in social situations, appearing to respond without thinking of the context, consequences, and previous experience (Bower & Parsons, 2003; Happé, Booth, Charlton, & Hughes, 2006; Raymaekers, van der Meere, & Roeyers, 2006).

By the age of 8, a typical child is able to "switch on" and use his or her frontal lobe to inhibit a response and think before deciding what to do or say (Diamond, Kirkham, & Amso, 2002). The child with ASD may be capable of thoughtful deliberation before responding, but under conditions of stress, or if feeling overwhelmed or confused, is often impulsive. It is important to encourage the child to relax and consider other options before responding and to recognize that being impulsive can be a sign of confusion and stress.

ASD in Association With Other Disorders

ASD frequently co-occurs with other disabilities (Filipek, 2005). For example, it can occur in children with Down syndrome and children with movement disorders, such as cerebral palsy and muscular dystrophy. A high percentage of children with ASD also have signs of an attention deficit disorder (Lecavalier, 2006). Further, we have recently become more aware that some children with autism develop involuntary movements such as motor and vocal tics associated with Tourette syndrome and adolescents may develop the signs of catatonia. Some children with tuberous sclerosis or neurofibromatosis show signs of ASD that may be due to the effects of specific brain lesions, particularly in the temporal lobes. Finally, there is an association between autism and epilepsy, with bimodal peaks of onset in early childhood and the start of puberty. Up to 30% of children with severe autism have epilepsy (Nordin & Gillberg, 1998), which can lead to epileptic seizures.

Can the Child With ASD Develop a Secondary Disorder?

Having autism means that the child has difficulty with social integration, communication, sensory experiences, and cognition. This inevitably leads to stress and the possibility of developing a mood or conduct disorder (Attwood, 2003a; Bradley, Summers, Wood, & Bryson, 2004). We do not know if the development of an anxiety disorder or depression is a psychological reaction to having autism or if it is a constitutional characteristic. Research studies have confirmed that families in which there is a child with autism have a higher incidence of mood disorders. However, this is not always simply a parental reaction to having a child with autism, since treatment for a mood disorder may have occurred before the child was born. Thus, the child may have inherited a predisposition for strong emotional responses (Bolton, Pickles, Murphy, & Rutter, 1998; DeLong, 1994; Micali, Chakrabarti, & Fombonne, 2004).

Difficulties in developing socialization skills, coping with change, and frustration due to impaired communication and cognitive skills can lead to problems with anger management and the development of conduct problems such as oppositional and defiant behavior (Attwood, 2003a; Gadow, DeVincent, Pomeroy, & Azizian, 2004; Tantam, 2000). These secondary disorders also need to be considered when conducting a diagnostic assessment and developing special education programs.

Is There an Autism Epidemic?

Throughout the world, the number of children with a diagnosis of ASD is increasing. In epidemiological studies published between 1966 and 1991, the rate of ASD was, on average, 4.4 children in every 10,000. In studies published in the 1990s, the rate increased to 12.7 in every 10,000. In 2007, estimates of the occurrence of autism spectrum disorders ranged from one in one thousand to as high as 1 in 150 births, and more recently, 1 in 88 births with as many as 1 in 50, reported by parents of school-age children (Baio, 2012).

Why are we diagnosing more children with ASD than we used to?

There are several explanations. The first is that we have widened the diagnostic goal posts. We have changed our conceptualization and broadened our definition of ASD to include ASD Level 1. Also, we accept that children may have more than one disorder: We no longer consider some disorders as discrete and mutually exclusive. That is, a child may have several developmental disorders, including ASD. Second, we have become better at diagnosing autism, especially in younger children. We are improving our ability to detect autism and to ensure fewer children escape detection. Third, in the past a child may have received a diagnosis of intellectual disability with no further diagnostic assessments conducted to determine if she also had signs of autism. These children are now becoming more accurately diagnosed with a more specific developmental disorder (Fombonne, 2005).

While we may be able to state that more children are being diagnosed because we are getting better at diagnosing them, there remains the problem of access to resources, specific educational programs for ASD and therapy. Government agencies have faced challenges in providing funding based on accurate prevalence rates. Services for children with autism have been experiencing a threefold increase in genuine referrals but without the proportional increase in funding. This is particularly agonizing for parents who are becoming increasingly knowledgeable about the range and success of various treatment options from information available on the Internet and literature written for parents. Policies are needed to make adjustments in funding for individuals with autism.

Summary and Conclusions

We know that the outcome or prognosis for individuals with an ASD is much better today than in the past. We also have a better understanding of ASD and how to engineer autism-friendly environments that can enable the person to achieve greater self-reliance and reduce the impact of autism on his or her quality of life. Finally, we are achieving more success in the areas of employment, independence, and relationships.

The practices presented in the following chapters work. They do not propose to present a miracle cure but outline strategies to achieve progress along the autism continuum. For many on the autism spectrum, the best outcomes would be a full-time job, leaving home, living independently, and having a lifelong relationship with a partner. A diagnosis of ASD does not automatically preclude these kinds of outcomes. Any or all of these may be the eventual outcomes for many children. Although outcomes will inevitably vary with appropriate supports, it is possible for every child to meet his or her potential and live a happy and fulfilling life.

Tips for Practical Application

✓ In the early stages of identifying ASD, it is important for educators and other professionals to listen to what parents have felt intuitively about their child regarding social interaction and communication.

✓ It is important to recognize that our understanding of ASD is still evolving.

✓ Educators need to understand the history of ASD and the impact that history has had and can continue to have on families.

✓ It is important for educators to understand new developments in neuroscience and how those findings can help us understand the social disorder as well as the emotional issues observed in children with ASD.

✓ It is important that educators understand the implications of current psychological theories of ASD as they relate to effective teaching methods.

✓ Students with ASD can have associated disorders that may complicate their learning profiles and subsequently their needs.

✓ It is important that educators understand that special interests of a student with autism can be a window into understanding how to motivate the student to engage in educational activities.

✓ Since ASD is a disorder of social relatedness, educators must make deliberate efforts to establish meaningful and mutually respectful relationships with students on the autism spectrum.

Chapter Highlights

• Autism spectrum disorder (ASD) is a lifelong condition.

• A major change in the present DSM-5 is that the American Psychiatric Association has dispensed with the term *pervasive developmental disorder* and replaced it with *autism spectrum disorder*.

• The DSM-5 also dispensed with the DSM IV diagnostic categories of Rett's disorder, childhood disintegrative disorder, pervasive developmental disorder-not otherwise specified (PDD-NOS), and Asperger's disorder.

• The term *Asperger Syndrome* will still be legitimately used by clinicians, parents, teachers, therapists, those with an ASD, and the general public in conversations and as the basis for seeking further information on how to understand and help a child.

• A significant improvement in the diagnostic criteria of DSM-5 is the inclusion of hyper- and hypo-reactivity to sensory input or unusual interest in sensory aspects of the environment.

• The DSM IV listed three diagnostic dimensions: a qualitative impairment in social interaction, a qualitative impairment in communication, and restricted and repetitive behavior. DSM-5 combines the social and communication dimensions into one; namely, deficits in social communication.

- The DSM-5 includes a diagnostic category for children who have marked deficits in social communication but do not demonstrate restricted or repetitive behavior, interest, or activities.

- One of the specifiers for ASD is catatonia.

- First signs of autism include sleep disturbance, lack of eye contact and pointing toward objects, preference for consistency, focus on objects rather than people, reluctance to share activities with others, possible fascination with sensory experiences, and failure to imitate others' actions.

- Late-onset autism is when children demonstrate no behaviors of concern until into their second year after otherwise having achieved typical developmental milestones. Reported in 20-40% of cases, children with late-onset autism lose abilities already developed, often over a short period of time, and, by age 3, present the same as a child whose onset was early.

- The six aspects of ASD are social reasoning, language abilities, cognition, special interests, sensory sensitivity, and expression and management of emotions.

- From the 1940s to the 1970s, autism was thought to be an expression of schizophrenia or psychosis caused by mothers not loving their children/being emotionally unavailable. The term *refrigerator mother* was used to describe these mothers, and autism was seen as a response to this rejection.

- Autism is now considered a neurodevelopmental disorder in which specific structures of the brain do not function as expected.

- Research into the causes of autism has investigated: genetics, neurology, possible errors of metabolism, and infections in pregnancy and early childhood.

- To date, no research study has established a consistent link between immunizations and autism.

- Psychological theories of autism include impaired theory of mind, weak central coherence, and impaired executive function.

- Autism can co-occur with other disorders.

- Children with ASD may develop secondary disorders such as mood and conduct disorders.

- ASD is diagnosed four times more often in males than in females. However, the ratio can be 2:1 when comparing boys and girls with ASD Level 1.

- There are several possible explanations for why more children are being diagnosed with ASD in recent years. These include a broader definition of ASD, realization that ASD may co-occur with other disorders, and better diagnostic procedures.

Chapter Review Questions

1. Give examples of signs of autism in early and late onset.

2. List the specifiers relevant to ASD that are included in the DSM-5.

3. What are the two diagnostic dimensions criteria for ASD in the DSM-5?

4. What are the six aspects of ASD? List and describe.

5. What was meant by "refrigerator mother"?

6. What are currently considered to be possible causes of autism?

7. State and describe the three psychological theories of autism.

8. What are the gender differences in ASD?

9. Why does the number of children identified with ASD seem to be increasing?

References

Adreon, D., & Duroucher, J. (2007). Evaluating the college transition needs of individuals with high-functioning autism spectrum disorders. *Intervention in School and Clinic, 42(5)*, 271-279.

American Psychiatric Association. (2000). *Diagnostic and statistical manual of mental disorders. 4th edition, text revision.* Washington, DC: Author.

American Psychiatric Association. (2013). *Diagnostic and statistical manual of mental disorders. 5th edition.* Washington, DC: Author.

Attwood, T. (2003a). Frameworks for behavioural interventions. *Child and Adolescent Psychiatric Clinics, 12*, 65-86.

Attwood, T. (2003b). Understanding and managing circumscribed interests. In M. Prior (Ed.), *Learning and behavior problems in Asperger Syndrome* (pp. 126-147). New York, NY: The Guilford Press.

Attwood, T. (2006). *The complete guide to Asperger's Syndrome.* London, UK: Jessica Kingsley Publishers.

Attwood, T. (2007). *The complete guide to Asperger's Syndrome* (2nd ed.). London, UK: Jessica Kingsley Publishers.

Attwood, T., & Garnett, M. (2013). *CBT to help young people with Asperger's Syndrome (autism spectrum disorder) to understand and express affection.* London, UK: Jessica Kingsley Publishers.

Bailey, A., Palferman, S., Heavey, L., & LeCouteur, A. (1998). Autism: The phenotype in relatives. *Journal of Autism and Developmental Disorders, 28*, 369-392.

Bailey, A., Le Couteur, A., Gottesman, I., Bolton, P., Simonoff, E., Yuzda, F., et al. (1995). Autism as a strongly genetic disorder: Evidence from a British twin study. *Psychological Medicine, 25*, 63-77.

Baio, J. (2012). Prevalence of ASD. *Autism and Developmental Disabilities Monitoring Network, 14 Sites, United States, 2008. Surveillance Summaries (SS03)*, 1-19.

Baranek, G. T. (2002). Efficacy of sensory and motor interventions for children with autism. *Journal of Autism and Developmental Disorders, 5*(32), 397-422.

Barnea-Gorlay, N., & Manzelli, M. (2014). Introduction to neuro-imaging in autism spectrum disorders. In V. B. Patel, V. Preedy, & C. Martin (Eds.), *Comprehensive guide to autism.* New York, NY: Springer.

Baron-Cohen, S. (1995). *Mind blindness: An essay on autism and theory of mind.* Cambridge, MA: MIT Press.

Baron-Cohen, S. (2004). *Mind reading: The interactive guide to emotions.* London, UK: Jessica Kingsley Publishers.

Baron-Cohen, S., Ring, H. A., Wheelwright, S., Bullmore, E. T., Brammer, M. J., Simmons, A., & William, S.C.R.,(1999). Social intelligence in the normal autistic brain: An FMRI study. *European Journal of Neuroscience, 11,* 1891-1898.

Barron, J., & Barron, S. (2002). *There's a boy in here: Emerging from the bonds of autism.* Arlington, TX: Future Horizons.

Batshaw, M. L., & Tuchman, M. (2002). PKU and other inborn errors of metabolism. In M. L. Batshaw (Ed.), *Children with disabilities* (5th ed., pp. 333-345). Baltimore, MD: Paul Brookes Publishing.

Bauman, M. L., & Kemper, T. L. (1994). Neuroanatomic observations of the brain in autism. In M. L. Bauman & T. L. Kemper (Eds.), *The neurobiology of autism* (pp. 119-145). Baltimore, MD: Johns Hopkins University Press.

Bauman, M., & Kemper, T. (2003). The neuropathology of the autism spectrum disorders: what have we learned? *Novartis Foundation Symp*osium, *251,* 112-122.

Bellini, S. (2006). The development of social anxiety in adolescents with autism spectrum disorders. *Focus on Autism and Other Developmental Disabilities, 21*(3), 138-145.

Beversdorf, D., Manning, S., Hillier, A., Anderson, S., Nordgren, R., Walters, S., et al. (2005). Timing of prenatal stressors and autism. *Journal of Autism and Developmental Disorders, 35*(4), 471-478.

Bolton, P., Pickles, A., Murphy, M., & Rutter, M. (1998). Autism, affective and other psychiatric disorders: Patterns of familial aggregation. *Psychological Medicine, 28,* 385-395.

Bolton, P. F., Murphy, M., Macdonald, H., Whitlock, B., Pickles, A., & Rutter, M. (1997). Obstetric complications in autism. Consequences or causes of the condition? *Journal of the American Academy of Child and Adolescent Psychiatry, 36,* 272-281.

Bower, J., & Parsons, L. (2003). Rethinking the "lesser brain." *Scientific American, 289*(2), 50-57.

Bradley, E., Summers, J., Wood, H., & Bryson, S. (2004). Comparing rates of psychiatric and behavior disorders in adolescents and young adults with severe intellectual disability with and without autism. *Journal of Autism and Developmental Disorder, 34*(2), 151-161.

Canitano, R., & Vivanti, G. (2007). Tics and Tourette syndrome in autism spectrum disorders. *Autism: The International Journal of Research and Practice, 11*(2), 19-28.

Cederlund, M., & Gillberg, C. (2004). One hundred males with Asperger syndrome: A clinical study of background and associated factors. *Developmental Medicine and Child Neurology, 46,* 652-661.

Cederlund, M., Hagberg, B., Billstedt, E., Gillberg, C., & Gillberg, C. (2008). Asperger Syndrome and autism: A comparative longitudinal follow-up study more than five years after the original diagnosis. *Journal of Autism and Developmental Disorders, 38,* 72-85.

Chawarska, K., Campbell, D., Chen, L., Shic, F., Klin, A., & Chang J. (2011). Early generalized overgrowth in boys with autism. *Archives of General Psychiatry, 68,* 1021-1031.

Chawarska, K., & Volkmar, F. (2005). Autism in infancy and early childhood. In F. R. Volkmar, R. Paul, A. Klin, & D. Cohen (Eds.), *Handbook of autism and pervasive developmental disorders* (3rd ed., pp. 223-246). New York, NY: Wiley.

Chen, M., Su, T., Chen Y., Hsu, Y., Huang, K., Chang, W., Chen, T., & Bai, Y. (2013). Comorbidity of allergic & autoimmune diseases in patients with autism spectrum disorder: A nationwide population-based study. *Research in Autism Spectrum Disorders, 7,* 205-212.

Constantino, J. N., Zhang, Y., Frazier, T., Abbacchi, A. M., & Law, P. (2010). Sibling recurrence & the genetic epidemiology of autism. *American Journal of Psychiatry, 167,* 1349-1365.

Courchesne, E., Karns, C., Davis, H., Ziccardi, R., Carper, R., Tigue, Z., et al. (2001). Unusual brain growth patterns in early life in patients with autistic disorder: An MRI study. *Neurology, 57,* 245-254.

DeLong, G. (1994). Children with autistic spectrum disorder and a family history of affective disorder. *Developmental Medicine and Child Neurology, 36,* 647-688.

DeStefano, F., Price, C., & Weintraub, E. (2013). Increasing exposure to antibody-stimulating proteins and polysaccharides in vaccines is not associated with risk of Autism. *Journal of Pediatrics.*

Diamond, A., Kirkham, N. Z., & Amso, D. (2002). Conditions under which young children CAN hold two rules in mind and inhibit a prepotent response. *Developmental Psychology, 38,* 352-362.

Elder, J., Shankar, M., Shuster, J., Theriaque, D., Burns, S., & Sherrill, L. (2006). The gluten-free, casein-free diet in autism: Results of a preliminary double blind clinical trial. *Journal of Autism and Developmental Disorders, 36*(3), 413-420.

Farley, M. A., McMahon, W. M., Fombonne, E. J., Enson, W. R., Miller, J., Gardner, M., Block, H., Pingree, C. B., Ritvo, E. R., Ritvo, R. A., & Coon, H. (2009). Twenty-year outcome for individuals with autism & average or near-average cognitive abilities. *Autism Research, 2,* 109-118.

Filipek, P. A. (2005). Medical aspects of autism. In F. R. Volkmar, R. Paul, A. Klin, & D. Cohen (Eds.), *Handbook of autism and pervasive developmental disorders* (3rd ed., pp. 534-578). New York, NY: Wiley.

Fombonne, E. (2003). Epidemiological surveys of autism and other pervasive developmental disorders: An update. *Journal of Autism and Developmental Disorders, 33,* 365-382.

Fombonne, E. (2005). Epidemiological studies of pervasive developmental disorders. In F. R. Volkmar, R. Paul, A. Klin, & D. Cohen (Eds.), *Handbook of autism and pervasive developmental disorders* (3rd ed., pp. 42-69). New York, NY: Wiley.

Frith, U. (Ed.). 1991. *Autism and Asperger Syndrome.* Cambridge, UK: Cambridge University Press.

Frith, U., & Happé, F. (1994). Autism: Beyond "theory of mind." *Cognition, 50,* 115-132.

Gadow, K., DeVincent, C., Pomeroy, J., & Azizian, A. (2004). Psychiatric symptoms in preschool children with PDD and clinic and comparison samples. *Journal of Autism and Developmental Disorders, 34*(4), 379-393.

Gibbs, V., Aldridge, F., Chaler, F., Witzlsperger, E., & Smith, K. (2012). An exploratory study comparing diagnostic outcomes for autism spectrum disorders under DSM-IV-TR with the proposed DSM-5 revisions. *Journal of Autism and Developmental Disorders, 42,* 1750-1756.

Gillberg, C., & de Souza, L. (2002). Head circumference in autism, Asperger syndrome, and ADHD: A comparative study. *Developmental Medicine and Child Neurology, 44,* 296-300.

Gillberg, I. C., & Gillberg, C. (1996). Autism in immigrants: A population-based study from Swedish rural and urban areas. *Journal of Intellectual Disability Research, 40,* 24-31.

Goldsmith, H., Van Hulle, C., Arneson, C., Schreiber, J., & Gernsbacher, M. (2006). Population-based twin study of parentally reported tactile and auditory defensiveness in young children. *Journal of Abnormal Child Psychology, 34*(3), 378-392.

Grandin, T. (1995). *Thinking in pictures and other reports from my life with autism.* New York: Doubleday.

Grandin, T., & Duffy, K. (2009). *Developing talents – Careers for individuals with Asperger Syndrome and high-functioning autism* (2nd ed.). Shawnee Mission, KS: AAPC Publishing.

Hallmayer, J., Glasson, E., Bower, C., Petterson, B., Croen, L., Grether, J., & Risch, N. (2002). On the twin risk in autism. *American Journal of Human Genetics, 71*(4), 941-946.

Happé, F., Booth, R., Charlton, R., & Hughes, C. (2006). Executive function deficits in autism spectrum disorders and attention-deficit/hyperactivity disorder: Examining profiles across domains and ages. *Brain and Cognition, 61*(1), 25-39.

Herbert, M. (2005a). A brain disorder or a disorder that affects the brain. *Clinical Neuropsychology, 2*(6), 354-379.

Herbert, M. (2005b). Large brains in autism: the challenge of pervasive abnormality. *Neuroscientist, 11,* 417-440.

Hermelin, B. (2001). *Bright splinters of the mind.* London: Jessica Kingsley Publishers.

Honda, H., Shimizu, Y., & Rutter, M. (2005). No effect of MMR withdrawal on the incidence of autism: A total population study. *Journal of Child Psychiatry and Psychology, 46*(6), 572-579.

Hornig, M., et al. (2008). Lack of association between measles virus vaccine and autism with enteropathy: A case-control study. *PLoS One.* E3140. doi: 10. 1371/journal.pone.0003140.

Huerta, M., Bishop, S., Duncan, A., Hus, V., & Lord, C. (2012). Application of DSM-5 criteria for autism spectrum disorder to three samples of children with DSM-IV diagnoses of pervasive developmental disorders. *American Journal of Psychiatry, 169,* 1056-1064.

Kanner, L. (1943). Autistic disturbances of affective contact. *Nervous Child, 2,* 217-250.

Kerr, S., & Drukin, K. (2004). Understanding of thought bubbles as mental representations in children with autism: Implications for theory of mind. *Journal of Autism and Developmental Disorders, 34*(6), 637-648.

Lecavalier L. (2006). Behavioral and emotional problems in young people with pervasive developmental disorders: Relative prevalence, effects of subject characteristics and empirical classification. *Journal of Autism and Developmental Disorders, 36,* 1101-1114.

Lipsky, B. (2011). *From anxiety to meltdown.* London, UK: Jessica Kingsley Publishers.

Lundstrom, S., Haworth, C., Carlstrom, E., Gillberg, C., Mill, J., Rastam, M., Hultman, C., Ronald, A., Anckarsater, H., Plomin. R., Lichtenstein, P., & Reichenberg A. (2010). Trajectories leading to autism spectrum disorders are affected by paternal age: findings from two nationally representative twin studies. *Journal of Child Psychology and Psychiatry, 51,* 850-856.

Matson, J. L., Belva, B. C., Horovitz, M., & Bamburg, J. (2012). Comparing symptoms of autism spectrum disorders in a developmentally disabled adult population using the current DSM-IV-TR diagnostic criteria & the proposed DSM-5 diagnostic criteria. *Journal of Developmental and Physical Disabilities, 24,* 403-414.

Matson, J. L., Kozlowski, L., Hattier, M. A., Horovitz, M., & Sipes, M. (2012). DSM-IV versus DSM-5 diagnostic criteria for toddlers with autism. *Developmental Neurorehabilitation, 15,* 185-190.

McPartland, J. C., Reichow, B., & Volkmar, F. (2012). Sensitivity and specificity of proposed DSM-5 diagnostic criteria for autism spectrum disorder. *Journal of the American Academy of Child and Adolescent Psychiatry, 51*(4), 368-383.

Micali, N., Chakrabarti, S., & Fombonne, E. (2004). The broad autism phenotype: Findings from an epidemiological survey. *Autism, 8,* 21-37.

Moore, V., & Goodson, S. (2003). How well does early diagnosis of autism stand the test of time? Follow up study of children assessed for autism at age 2 and development of an early diagnostic service. *Autism: International Journal of Research and Practice, 7*(1), 47-63.

Nordahl, C. W., Scholz, R., Yang, X., Buonocore, M., Simon, T., Rogers, S., & Amaral, D. (2012). Increased role of amygdala growth in children aged 2-4 years with autism spectrum disorder: A longitudinal study. *Archives of General Psychiatry, 69,* 55-61.

Nordin, V., & Gillberg, C. (1998). The long-term course of autistic disorders: Update on follow-up studies. *Acta Psychiatrica Scandinavica, 97,* 99-108.

Orsmond, G. I., Krauss, M. W., & Seltzer, M. M. (2004). Peer relationships and social and recreational activities among adolescents and adults with autism. *Journal of Autism and Developmental Disabilities, 34*(3), 245-246

Ozonoff, S., Josif, A., Baguio, F., Cook, I. C., Moore Hill, M., Hutman, T., Rogers, S. J., Rozga, A., Sangha, S., Sigman, M., Steinfield, M., & Young, G. S. (2010). A prospective study of the emergence of early behavioral signs of autism. *Journal of the American Academy of Child and Adolescent Psychiatry, 49,* 256-266.

Price, C., et al. (2010). Prenatal and infant exposure to thimerosal from vaccines and immunoglobulins and risk of autism. *Pediatrics, 126*(4), 656-664.

Raymaekers, R., van der Meere, J., & Roeyers, H. (2006). Response inhibition and immediate arousal in children with high-functioning autism. *Child Neuropsychology, 12*(4-5), 349-359.

Richler, et al. (2006). Is there a "regressive phenotype" of autism spectrum disorder associated with the measles-mumps-rubella vaccine? A CPEA Study. *Journal of Autism and Developmental Disorders, 36*(3), 299-316.

Rojas, D., Peterson, E., Winterrowd, E., Reite, M., Rogers, S., & Tregellas, J. (2006). Regional gray matter volumetric changes in autism associated with social and repetitive behavior symptoms. *BMC Psychiatry, 6,* 56.

Russell, J. (1997). *Autism as an executive disorder.* Oxford, UK: Oxford University Press.

Rutter, M. (2005). Genetic influences and autism. In F. R. Volkmar, R. Paul, A. Klin, & D. Cohen (Eds.), *Handbook of autism and pervasive developmental disorders* (3rd ed., pp. 425-452). New York, NY: Wiley.

Scarpa, A., Wells, A., & Attwood, T. (2013). *Exploring feelings for young children with high-functioning autism or Asperger's disorder.* London, UK: Jessica Kingsley Publishers.

Scarpa, A., Williams White, S., & Attwood, T. (2013). *CBT for children and adolescents with high-functioning autism spectrum disorders.* New York, NY: The Guilford Press.

Schlooz, W., Hulstijn, W., van den Broek, P., van der Pijll, A., Gabreels, F., van der Gaag, R., et al. (2006). Fragmented visuospatial processing in children with pervasive developmental disorder. *Journal of Autism and Developmental Disorders, 36*(8), 1025-1037.

Shore, S. (2003). *Beyond the wall – Personal experiences with autism and Asperger Syndrome*. Shawnee Mission, KS: AAPC Publishing.

Siperstein, R., & Volkmar, F. R. (2004). Parental reporting of regression in children with pervasive developmental disorders. *Journal of Autism and Developmental Disorders, 34*(6), 731-734.

Stanfield, A. C., McIntosh, A. M., Spencer, M. D., Philip, R., Gaur, S., & Lawrie, S. (2008). Towards a neuroanatomy of autism: A systematic review & meta-analysis of structural magnetic resonance imaging studies. *European Psychiatry, 23*, 289-299.

Taheri, A., & Perry, A. (2012). Exploring the proposed DSM-5 criteria in a clinical sample. *Journal of Autism and Developmental Disorders, 42*, 1810-1817.

Tantam, D. (2000). Psychological disorders in adolescents and adults with Asperger Syndrome. *Autism. The International Journal of Research and Practice, 4*, 47-62.

Tozzi, A., et al. (2009). Neuropsychological performance 10 years after immunization in infancy with thimerosal-containing vaccines. *Pediatrics, 123*(2), 475-482.

Verte, S., Geurts, H., Roeyersd, H., Oosterlaan, J., & Sergeant, J. (2006). The relationship of working memory, inhibition, and response variability in child psychopathology. *Journal of Neuroscientific Methods, 151*(1), 5-14.

Volkmar, F., Klin, A., & Pauls, D. (1998). Nosological and genetic aspects of Asperger syndrome. *Journal of Autism and Developmental Disorders, 28*, 457-463.

Williams, D., Goldstein, G., & Minshew, N. (2006). The profile of memory function in children with autism. *Neuropsychology, 20*(1), 21-29.

Wing, L., & Attwood, A. (1987). Syndromes of autism and atypical development. In D. Cohen & A. Donnellan (Eds.), *Handbook of autism and pervasive developmental disorders* (pp. 3-19). New York, NY: John Wiley and Sons.

Wing, L., & Gould, J. (1979). Severe impairments of social interaction and associated abnormalities in children: Epidemiology and classification. *Journal of Autism and Developmental Disorders, 9*, 11-29.

Yerys, B., Hepburn, S., & Pennington, B. (2007). Executive function in preschoolers with autism: Evidence consistent with a secondary deficit. *Journal of Autism and Developmental Disorders, 37*(6), 1068-1079.

Zafeiriou, D., Ververi, A., & Vargiami, E. (2007). Childhood autism and associated comorbidities. *Brain and Development, 29*(5), 257-272.

Learner Objectives

After reading this chapter, the learner should be able to:

- State the meaning of core deficit in understanding ASD

- State the current most popular theories related to what are the primary impairments in ASD

- Describe why ASD can be referred to as a disorder of information processing

- Discuss what is meant by "hidden information demands"

- State the value of the complex information processing concept

- Demonstrate an understanding of what is meant by the term *complexity*

- Define the term *central coherence*

- Define *information processing*

- State how the development of new imaging technology, specifically the fMRI, is important to the understanding of ASD

- State what is different about the brains of individuals with ASD that leads to differences in how they think and perceive things

- Demonstrate an understanding of compensatory strategies used by individuals with ASD

- State why the chapter authors believe the diagnostic criteria of ASD should be extended beyond social interaction and restricted and repetitive behaviors

- Discuss why the chapter authors believe intellectual disability in autism cannot be considered a separate diagnosis

- Discuss implications of the brain basis of ASD

Chapter 3

Brain-Behavior
Connections in Autism

Nancy J. Minshew • Diane L. Williams

Evan, a fifth-grade student, was extremely agitated. "They don't belong there. Make them go away," he said, pointing toward the three construction trailers taking up half of the school playground. His teacher calmly explained, "The construction men put the trailers there this summer. They needed them to put their work things in. The men will come to pick them up as soon as they have a chance." "They don't belong there. Make them go away," Evan repeated with an increasingly high pitch. His teacher once again tried to reason with him, explaining the purpose of the trailers and why they weren't moved yet. Finally, Evan threw himself onto the floor and began screaming, "They don't belong there." The teaching assistant then removed him from the room.

Evan's response might at first seem out of proportion to the problem of the construction trailers being left on the playground, but his perception of the problem was very different from that of his teacher because Evan has autism.

This chapter is about the cognitive and brain basis of autism, or what is different about the brain of individuals with autism that leads to differences in how they think and perceive things. Studies of the brains of individuals with autism provide evidence of differences in how the brain is organized, in how it functions, and even in its size. Thinking differently is not a choice in autism, but a consequence of very real differences in the brain. Understanding how people with autism think is the foundation for effective and appropriate intervention. Intervention based on an understanding of the neurocognitive aspects will help individuals with autism maximize their functioning and overall happiness.

Autism as a Disorder of Information Processing

Previously considered a psychological or behavioral disorder, autism was accepted to be of neurologic origin in the 1960s (Minshew, Sweeney, Bauman, & Webb, 2005). The search then focused on **cognition** and parts of the brain that caused the behavior that is called autism. By cause, what was meant was the deficit or alteration in thinking and in the brain that led to the abnormal behavior. Two approaches to understanding autism were subsequently pursued.

Approaches to Understanding Autism

The first approach focused on individual deficits based on the hypothesis that a single deficit causes a cascade, which results in the entire constellation of deficits in autism. The specific deficit hypothesized as "the **core deficit**" in autism has varied over the decades and from investigator to investigator. Eventually, it became apparent from accumulated research that there was evidence in autism of many such deficits. As a result, the focus shifted to emphasizing the temporal primacy of specific deficits. That is, theorists emphasized that one of the deficits preceded all others with an onset in infancy. Such hypotheses are difficult to test, and no evidence has yet substantiated the pre-existence of a single deficit in the absence of other deficits. The most popular of such theories now propose a primary impairment in the disengagement of attention (Keehn, Muller, & Townsend, 2013), in **representational** capacity (Meltzoff & Decety, 2003), or in **social motivation** or orienting to **social stimuli** (Dawson, Webb, & McPartland, 2005; Chevallier, Kohls, Troiani, Brodkin, & Schultz, 2012).

An alternative approach is to investigate the evidence of all simultaneously occurring impairments and intact abilities. The purpose of this line of investigation is to identify a common denominator of impairments and abilities that illuminates fundamental principles about cognition and the brain in autism. This is the traditional approach of neurologists, based on the recognition that brain abnormalities rarely result in a single impairment but rather a constellation, the pattern of which reflects the nature of the biologic disturbance. For example, the constellation of deficits resulting from acquired insults to the brain may reflect the distribution of a blood vessel, the coup-counter-coup[1] pattern of a traumatic injury, or the vulnerability profile of a metabolic insult. Similarly, the constellation of deficits resulting from a developmental disturbance may reflect the pattern of a first-trimester abnormality in the formation of the brain, a second-trimester disturbance in neuronal proliferation (increase or decrease in brain cell numbers) or migration (movement of brain cells from place of origin to final destination), or a third-trimester disturbance in neuronal organization (development of the elaborate connections of the human brain). A developmental disturbance might also reflect the impact of fetal exposure to a virus or a toxin.

Based on the perspective that many domains would be impacted by a **developmental disorder**, we approached the investigation of the cognitive basis of autism by simultaneously assessing all the common domains of neuropsychologic functioning in samples of children, adolescents, and adults with ASD Level 1 (those with Full Scale and Verbal IQ scores of 70 and above). Individuals with ASD Level 1 were selected because they had all the features specific to autism without the potential nonspecific features associated with intellectual disability; they could be IQ matched to a normal control group; and they could cooperate for a comprehensive battery of tests.

---

1 An injury in which the brain is damaged on impact with the inside of the skull at the site of impact and then suffers additional damage when the brain moves back and forth, hitting the inside of the bony skull.

Subgroup Studies of the Cognitive Basis of Autism

The principle of subgroup studies is that the subgroup is a proxy for the entire group of people with autism, even though they are not representative of the entire group. That is, even though they do not have intellectual disability with autism, they have the same disorder as individuals with autism who have intellectual disability. Therefore, principles or characteristics identified in this subgroup can be considered to be true of people with autism as a whole. Extrapolation of these characteristics or principles to more impaired individuals with autism requires consideration of their expression in a more severe form. However, the specific qualities of the disorder would remain the same, regardless of the functioning level of the affected individual.

To date, three studies, two involving adult samples and one involving children, have been completed.

Study 1 – Adolescents and adults. The first study included 33 individually matched pairs of adolescents and adults with autism compared to individually matched normal controls, all of whom had Full Scale and Verbal IQ scores of 80 and above (Minshew, Goldstein, & Siegel, 1997). The diagnosis of autism was established using the ***Autism Diagnostic Interview-Revised*** (**ADI-R**; Le Couteur et al., 1989; Lord, Rutter, & Le Couteur, 1994), a two-hour structured interview developed for research to standardize the early developmental history and current functioning in the areas of social, communication, and restricted interests and repetitive behavior relevant to the diagnosis of autism; and the one-hour ***Autism Diagnostic Observation Schedule*** (**ADOS**; Lord et al., 1989; Lord et al., 2000), a direct observation of the individual composed of a number of tasks designed to elicit social, communication, and play abilities relevant to the diagnosis of autism. All items were scored using set ratings, and the items were then scored according to the *Diagnostic and Statistical Manual, 4th Edition* (DSM-IV) criteria for autism (American Psychiatric Association, 1994).[2] The diagnosis of autism made in this way was confirmed by expert clinical opinion. Individuals with autism with fragile X syndrome, tuberous sclerosis, or some other identifiable cause of autism were excluded from participation in the study.

This study revealed a unique profile of impaired and intact abilities, as displayed in Table 3.1. The first principle apparent from this profile is that the acquisition of information in autism was intact. That is, the capacity to attend to (attention), perceive (elementary sensory perception), and remember (basic memory abilities) information was not impaired relative to the controls. In addition, basic or elementary skills in the other domains tested were also intact. Formal language abilities (spelling, reading words and nonwords, speaking words) were superior to those of the age- and IQ-matched controls. The capacity for learning the attributes or characteristics of objects and rules was also intact.

---

2   In Europe, this would be ICD-10 criteria (World Health Organization, 1992).

Table 3.1
Intact or Enhanced Abilities and Deficits in Adults With ASD Level 1

Intact or Enhanced	Cognitive Weaknesses
Attention **Sensory** **Perception** **Elementary Motor** **Simple Memory** Formal Language Rule Learning **Visuospatial Processing**	**Complex Motor** Complex Memory **Complex Language** **Concept Formation** Face Recognition

Relative impairments were present in higher cortical sensory perception (What is the object in your hand? Are you being touched at two analogous spots on opposites sides of your body? What is the number being drawn on your fingertip?); skilled motor movements (handwriting, tying shoes, skipping); memory for complex material (a large amount of the same type of material, like word lists or material that is inherently complex like scenes or stories); higher-order language (idioms, metaphors, inferences, paragraph comprehension); flexibility (shifting strategies when one does not work); and concept formation (problem solving when there are no set rules; associated skills are insight and judgment).

The overriding principles of this pattern, other than the integrity of information acquisition, were not immediately apparent. It was not a pattern that had been seen before in other diseases. The principles to emerge were the following. First, the acquisition of information was intact in autism. However, information-processing capacity was reduced or constrained. This constraint disproportionately impacted higher-order information processing or the capacity to process information or material when the demands of the task or situation are high. This processing constraint occurred at a lower level than would be expected based on the individual's age and IQ.

Second, the predominance of symptoms across domains appeared to reflect the complexity of the information-processing demands. This complexity explained the preponderance of symptoms in the social, communication, and reasoning domains. However, the presence of impairments not part of the diagnostic triad and even not predicted (e.g., in memory and in motor) strongly suggested that the neurobiology or brain basis of this disorder involved a mechanism that was general to the development of brain architecture and, therefore, was not confined to the three neural systems underlying the traditional diagnostic triad (social, language, and reasoning).

Study 2 – Children. The second study involved 56 children with ASD level 1 and 56 typically developing children between the ages of 8 and 15 years with Full Scale and Verbal IQ scores above 80 and between 80 and 120 (Williams, Goldstein, & Minshew, 2006). These findings replicated the major principles of the initial adult study with minor differences. One particularly interesting difference was the more prominent sensory symptoms in the children with autism than in the adults, suggesting some amelioration or lessening in sensory symptoms over time.

Another difference was that the impairments in concept formation appeared more prominent in the adult study. One possible explanation for this finding is that neither the children with autism nor the typically developing controls may have reached the level of development that allowed manifestation of the reasoning impairments in autism. It is clear from our studies and the literature that abstraction abilities dependent on the frontal lobe mature in the second decade of life in typically developing children. However, adolescents with autism do not acquire these skills, and between-group differences emerge on more and more tests in the concept-formation domain (Luna, Doll, Hegedus, Minshew, & Sweeney 2006; Minshew, Meyer, & Goldstein, 2002).

Study 3 – Adults. The third study involving a second sample of adults replicated the first set of results (Minshew & Goldstein, unpublished data). Therefore, there is consistent evidence across a large age range of constraints on information processing that disproportionately impact higher-order or integrative processing. These constraints transcend domains to involve sensorimotor and memory abilities not previously appreciated to be integral elements of this syndrome. The traditional diagnostic conception of autism, therefore, needs to be expanded, and the notion that this is merely or predominantly a disorder of social function or interactions must be set aside. Indeed, the difficulties with restricted and repetitive behavior, common sense, insight, and judgment are as impairing as the social impairment. These have been referred to as the non-social or cognitive aspects of autism (Minshew, Meyer, & Goldstein, 2002).

Independent Validation of the Constraints on Information Processing

One of the first concerns of a researcher upon completing a study that suggests a new principle is whether there is independent validation – a different method from a different investigator – that provides confirmation that the conclusion is correct. For example, if it is agreed that autism is a disorder characterized by a reduced capacity for information processing, then one would expect to find a decline in performance during a dual task (one that requires simultaneous processing of two types of incoming information).

A study of dual-task processing with individuals with autism was found in the literature (Garcia-Villamisar & Della Sala, 2002). This study involved 16 participants with autism with average IQ scores compared to 16 normal controls. Each group performed two tasks individually and then simultaneously. The tasks were digit recall (similar to remembering a phone number) and motor tracking (like moving a pen to keep up with a moving dot). These tasks were not demanding. When each task was performed individually, the autism group performed similarly to the control group. When the control group performed both tasks simultaneously, their performance rate on the individual tasks was unchanged from when they performed the tasks individually. However, when the autism group performed the tasks simultaneously, their performance declined about 40%. This is a dramatic example of the constraints on information processing in individuals with autism. That is, these were very simple tasks, and yet the autism group could not do them at the same time without their performance suffering substantially.

Most of everyday life entails **multitasking**. The teacher talks while she writes on the board. People speak words in combination with the tone of their voice, their facial expressions, their gaze, their gestures, and other body language. You listen to the person walking next to you while watching for the traffic in the street ahead. We are constantly managing large amounts of information and the associated allocation of processing resources. Individuals with autism have difficulty managing all of this incoming information. What we do almost without thinking about it, individuals with autism find incredibly challenging.

Though not directly tested in the dual-task study, **speed of processing** is also a variable that constrains the ability of individuals with autism to process information. That is, information-processing capacity is restricted by the amount of information presented, its complexity, and time constraints. Individuals with autism are renowned for having "one gear" that has a slower pace than others. This is another manifestation of constrained information-processing capacity in this group.

A Lesson in Hidden Information-Processing Demands

One of the first tests of language comprehension we administered was the Oral Directions subtest from the *Detroit Tests of Learning Aptitude* (**DTLA-2**; Hammill, 1985; Minshew, Goldstein, & Siegel, 1997). It begins with simple instructions such as "Touch the yellow circle," and then becomes steadily more complex: "Before you touch the blue square, touch the green triangle," then "Before you touch the red square, touch the purple circle, then touch the black triangle," and so on. Although individuals with ASD Level 1 could readily comprehend sentences of the same length or longer that had simple grammatical construction, they had substantial difficulty understanding sentences with complex grammatical construction.

Why was there a difference when the number of words was the same? The answer is that the information processing demands were far greater when there were clauses and phrases. When there is a clause, the brain must process the meaning of the first part of the sentence and hold it in **working memory**, then process the meaning of the second part of the sentence, and then process the meaning of the first part in relation to the second part. The information-processing demands are much higher for **complex sentences**. The language of daily life uses complex grammatical construction. Therefore, when individuals with autism are having difficulty complying with instructions, a shift to simple grammar may improve their comprehension and, in turn, compliance.

Even though the individuals with autism who participated in our studies spoke in complex sentences, they did not necessarily comprehend them when they spoke them or heard them spoken by others. And why was that? The reason was that clauses and phrases were often a single word to them. For example, in the movie *Rain Man*, when Raymond refers to the seats in his deceased father's antique car as "pitiful red," this is a stereotyped phrase that is one piece to him, not two separate words. For individuals with ASD Level 1, longer phrases and even sentences become single encoded units that they do not fully understand. Hence, it is important to assess what individuals with autism understand by how they act – the demonstration of their understanding – and not take their words at face value. Many parents have complained, "I know he knows the rule. He says the rule while he is doing what the rule says not to do." In other words, his actions demonstrate that although he says the words, he does not know what those words mean. The parent has made the mistake of thinking that saying equals understanding. In reality, however, "doing" is the test of understanding, not saying.

The effect of increased processing demands can also be evident when individuals with autism are using expressive language. They may fail to integrate the intended message with the words and sentences that would clearly express their idea. When language is stored in chunks, those chunks must be used for spoken language, too.

The teachers were becoming very frustrated with Amanda. Day after day, she would repeatedly say, "Go swimming? Go swimming? Go swimming?" The teachers patiently told her that Tuesday was swimming day, and today was not Tuesday. They showed her the weekly picture schedule with swimming clearly indicated under Tuesday, but nothing seemed to satisfy Amanda. She persisted, "Go swimming? Go swimming? Go swimming?"

I[3] was called in to try to find a way to get Amanda to understand what her teachers were trying to communicate to her. After observing the classroom routine, I had an idea of what the problem might be. I told the teachers that the next time Amanda began saying, "Go swimming," they should answer as if she had said, "What's next?" The teachers did as instructed, and Amanda ceased her repetitive questioning. Swimming was Amanda's favorite activity. Therefore, it had strong retrieval strength for her. Whenever Amanda tried to compose a message about a school activity, the language that came "on-line" was "Go swimming?" What she really intended to say was, "What are we doing next?"

As illustrated, Amanda's language had to be analyzed according to its context rather than by its content.

People with autism do not always say what they mean and are dependent on their communication partners to carry the burden of interpreting their meaning.

Utility of the Complex Information-Processing Concept

The complex information-processing concept is only of value to the extent it is of help with intervention and understanding of behavior. Table 3.1, which lists the intact and impaired abilities, is an extremely useful guide for intervention in autism. Individuals with autism are generally operating on facts and rules. As a result, they need information conveyed succinctly with the fewest words possible. The bottom line needs to be stated; that is, numerous examples should not be given in hopes that they will figure out the concept or bottom line.

One case makes the application of the utility of this profile immediately apparent:

Adam was a 27-year-old young man who had been given a diagnosis of schizophrenia in early childhood, although he had never shown any signs of psychosis.[4] He lived in a rural area and had a job in a department store that he had held for 10 years. One day Adam was fired when a comment he made to a female was interpreted as sexually harassing in nature. With no job, Adam stayed in his apartment without any activities or supervision. Because he came from a religious family, he began watching evangelical shows and became preoccupied with sin and going to hell.

Adam was found by his caseworker agitated, carrying a Bible, quoting passages about going to hell. He was admitted to a psychiatric unit. The psychiatric residents were concerned that Adam was manic and thought he

---

3 DLW.
4 This is a common misdiagnosis in adults with ASD Level 1.

should be put on Lithium, but Adam refused to comply. For Adam, Lithium was associated with an unpleasant experience: He had taken Lithium on June 7, 1978 (17 years prior) and had gotten a stomachache. He went to the mental health clinic quite afraid that he had been poisoned and was reprimanded for coming without an appointment. He grew more agitated and soon was in physical management on the floor with several men sitting on him. No wonder he would not take Lithium again after that experience!

My advice[5] was asked, and I used what I knew of Adam's thinking. Knowing he had autism, not schizophrenia, I told the resident, "There are two forms of the medicine. One is pink, and the other is blue. Put one in each of your hands and ask which one Adam took before. When he tells you, say 'oh you took the bad pink/blue before, and now you can take the good pink/blue.'" The psychiatric resident tried this, and Adam agreed immediately to the medication. Earlier the resident had tried insight and reasoning, which Adam did not understand. Adam thinks simply in facts and concretely (show and tell).

Let's look at another case.

Stephen, a man weighing 85 lbs and near starvation, was admitted to the psychiatric unit. The resident had tried every method to persuade him to eat, but to no avail. Persuasion involves insight and higher-order language. When I met Stephen, it was 10:30 in the morning. He still had his breakfast tray and was staring at it and not eating. Through his ramblings, I gathered that his mother had told him 40 years earlier that he was getting pudgy and had better watch what he ate. So he did, by staring at it. Then someone told him that "watching what you ate" meant that he should not eat too much. However, Stephen was now depressed and had reverted to the earlier rule of watching what he ate by staring at his food. Understanding this, we established rules of the same type to restore his eating.

More About Complexity

Complexity is a general term or concept just like learning disability or intellectual disability. It does not refer to one specific thing. Hence, a learning disability such as dyslexia is not defined absolutely as the inability to read a book, sentences, or particular words. Reading ability or disability is defined relative to a person's age and general level of function. Age-appropriate tests and norms have been developed to make such determinations. At this point in research, we have defined impairments in information processing that disproportionately impact complex abilities as resulting in poorer performance relative to age- and IQ-matched peers and below standardized norms. For example, the motor impairment in the adult profile study was not only significantly worse than in the control group but was in the moderately severe range of impairment, according to clinical norms.

The term *complexity* can be articulated further. Various types of information can be complex. Information can be complex by virtue of its amount – small units but many of them, such as a word list or branch points to be

---

5 NJM.

learned in a maze. Further, information can be complex because of its inherent structure – a complex visual scene or a story with a theme. Information can be complex because it is of multiple types and must be integrated. A good example is the need to integrate visual, vestibular, and position sense to maintain postural control. Another example of this type of complex information is skilled motor movements, where individual motor actions must be integrated into a complex sequence that is greater than the individual parts. Finally, information processing may become complex because of time constraints, multiple simultaneous processing demands, or stress or anxiety. These factors are true for all of us, but since individuals with autism have a lower capacity for information processing, these factors become limiting far sooner than for age- and IQ-matched peers.

What Is in a Name?

Once the results of the cognitive and neurologic profile studies indicated an inherent deficit in autism with the processing of complex information, the question became what to call this profile – how to characterize it?

Uta Frith (1989) had coined the term *central coherence* for a similar constellation of impairments in high-order cognitive and language abilities and strengths on tasks that required perception of details, primarily visuospatial in nature. However, this term did not accommodate the sensory, motor, or memory impairments of individuals with autism, nor did it consider the expressive deficits. Central coherence was suited to explaining the problems with comprehension – the failure to make sense of things – but individuals with autism have equal difficulty with expression, including prosody, facial expression, telling a logical story, detecting the inherent structure in material to be able to remember it, or forming signs for sign language. They also have trouble with motor skills and disturbances in sensory perception. In addition, from a brain perspective, there was no central "coherer." Therefore, we chose a descriptive terminology that was applicable to all the impairments and the intact abilities and that was standard to neurology and cognitive neuroscience: *information processing*.

The developmental neurobiologic analogue of these higher-order human abilities is well known. It is referred to as neuronal organization, or the refinement in brain circuitry that produces the abilities that are unique to human beings. Like the term *autism spectrum disorder, information-processing disorder* has little meaning without a detailed explanation. It fundamentally means the processes whereby the brain attaches meaning to information. The distinction between simple and complex information processing was based on the observation that within domains, it was the highest-order abilities that were impacted, whereas the basic abilities were spared.

This pattern was unusual. If both simple and complex abilities had been equally affected, the result would have been a general deficit syndrome or general intellectual disability. If only simple information processing would have been affected, the result would have been a selective language impairment or learning disability such as dyslexia; however, social skills, communication, eye contact, facial expression, insight, and judgment would have been intact. Instead, unlike the general child neurology population, individuals with autism spectrum disorders (ASD) have problems with higher-order skills across domains but do not have the visuospatial deficits or dyslexia common to the general child neurology patient group.

Once the concept of the selective impact on more demanding information with intact simple information is understood, the complex information-processing construct becomes a functional foundation for intervention.

It is important to keep in mind that the typical predictions regarding the status of higher-order abilities based on the status of basic abilities do not hold true in ASD. Hence, it is common to overestimate the language comprehension of individuals with autism and to use reasoning rather than facts when attempting to change their behavior, as we have seen in the earlier cases studies.

The Brain Basis of Thinking in Autism

Until magnetic resonance imaging (MRI) and functional magnetic resonance imaging (fMRI) methods became available, the techniques for studying the brain in children with autism and for repeated studies were extremely limited. **Computerized axial tomography (CAT)** scans or **positron emission tomography (PET)** scans used to investigate brain disorders in adults involved radiation; thus, they could not be used in children or for repeated studies. Except for **EEG (electroencephalographic)** techniques, which yielded brain waves but not brain images, the study of the brain in autism had to wait for the emergence of magnetic resonance imaging technology.

The first application of this technology was for examining the area or two-dimensional measurements of specific brain structures (Cody, Pelphrey, & Piven, 2002). With time, computer programs and analyses were developed for three-dimensional measurements that led to more accurate volume measurements (e.g., Aylward, Minshew, Field, Sparks, & Singh, 2002; Courchesne et al., 2001; Sparks et al., 2002). The next breakthrough, and the most significant for autism, was the development of functional MRI (fMRI) methods, by which the activity of the brain during performance of cognitive or language tasks could be recorded. This became the first true window on the thinking brain in autism.

An fMRI study of sentence comprehension in 17 adolescents and young adults with ASD Level 1 and 17 normal controls found the first of many important differences in brain function in autism (Just, Cherkassky, Keller, & Minshew, 2004). Compared to the control group, the autism group displayed: (a) increased brain activation in the word region of the surface gray matter; (b) reduced brain activation in the surface gray matter area that processes the meaning of sentences; (c) reduced functional connections or correlations among 10 pairs of cortical regions that participate in language function; and (d) reduced synchrony between the activity of the region pairs. This pattern means that the brain regions were not working together to support language function. When the functional connectivity was plotted for all region pairs for the autism group and the control group, the line joining the points for the autism group was parallel to, but below, the line joining the points for the control group. This suggests that the brain was organized in the same way but did not achieve the same degree of connectivity in the autism group as in the control group.

This type of fMRI study of individuals with ASD Level 1 has been repeated using tasks that involve problem solving (Just, Keller, Cherkassky, Kana, & Minshew, 2007); social thinking (Kana, Keller, Cherkassky, Minshew, & Just, 2009); inhibiting context inappropriate behavior (Kana, Keller, Minshew, & Just, 2007); and coordinating the language and theory-of-mind networks (Mason, Williams, Kana, Minshew, & Just, 2008). The results in all cases have been similar, suggesting a common principle of underdevelopment of the **connectivity** of the neural systems for autism, especially in the communication between the frontal and posterior regions of the brain that are concurrently performing a task (see review in Schipul, Keller, & Just, 2011).

In the brain, higher-order abilities are supported by neural systems or the collaboration of many brain regions to enable a more complex ability or function to occur. This is analogous to the collaboration that must occur between the driver, the steering mechanism, the engine, the drive train, and the axel to accomplish driving a car. The fMRI studies completed to date suggest that the neural systems of individuals with autism have fewer and smaller centers to call upon and less flexibility in doing so. Hence, when the environmental demands change and different abilities are needed to address these demands, the brain in autism has less flexibility and fewer and smaller resources to draw upon. In addition, the brain regions are not working in **synchrony** or harmony.

In summary, fMRI studies are making a substantial contribution to our understanding of the brain basis of thinking, its differences, and its limitations in autism. These can be used to guide intervention. For example, intervention might focus on alternative approaches and strategy development rather than facts and rote learning of responses.

Revealing Differences in Cognitive Processing

The fMRI studies have also revealed that individuals with autism use different cognitive approaches to tasks – differences that are not apparent from their behavioral performance. Their alternate approach ultimately impacts their capacity, imposing limits or raising them, depending on the nature of the task. For example, in the sentence comprehension study (Just et al., 2004) described above, it was clear that individuals with autism focused on the words of the sentences rather than the meaning of the entire sentence. However, their behavioral performance was the same as controls, so it was not apparent from looking at the behavioral results that they were processing language differently.

A second fMRI study with a different type of task demonstrated the use of another type of strategy by the participants with autism even though their behavioral performance was equivalent to that of the participants with typical development. The task was a classic measure of working memory, called an *n*-back task. In this task, the individual is asked to monitor a string of letters presented one at a time for those that are the same when they appear two in a row (1-back) or separated by one different letter (2-back). The fMRI results suggested that the autism group viewed the letters as graphic figures and did not automatically recode them into letter names as the control group appeared to have done (Koshino et al., 2005). Hence, the control group displayed brain activation in the left executive and left language areas of the brain, whereas the autism group displayed brain activation in both posterior visual areas and the right executive area. In essence, these results indicate that individuals with autism rely on lower-level visual abilities rather than higher-level abilities to perform certain tasks. Had this task involved Russian letters rather than English letters, the controls would likely have performed very poorly, and the autism group would have performed much better because the strategic use of language would not have been as readily available.

The lack of automatic recoding of visual information into language was also found in an fMRI study with children with autism compared to children with typical development (Carter, Williams, Minshew, & Lehman, 2012). In this study, the children were shown pictures of socially appropriate and inappropriate behavior and asked to indicate in which of the pictures the blond-haired boy was being "bad." The children with autism performed the task as accurately as the children with typical development; however, the brain activation pattern differed between the two groups. Even though no language was required for the task, the control children activated a language network whereas the children with autism did not. The lack of automatic recoding of knowledge into language may explain why behavioral studies have found that children with autism can recognize socially inappropriate behavior but cannot always put that knowledge into words (see, for example, Nah & Poon, 2010).

Another study added further insight into this issue. This study involved the use of mental imagery during sentence reading (Kana, Keller, Cherkassky, Minshew, & Just, 2006). Individuals with ASD Level 1 and matched control groups were presented with low-imagery sentences (Addition and subtraction are mathematical operations.) and high-imagery sentences (There was a rainbow over the corn field.). The fMRI study showed that the control group activated the imagery area of the brain only for the high-visual imagery sentences. In contrast, the autism group activated the imagery area of the brain for both low- and high-visual imagery sentences. Hence, the latter appeared to think in visual pictures, possibly to enhance comprehension.

This tendency to rely heavily on visual processing may not be true of all individuals with autism, however. Some may think in words rather than pictures. Studies like this of a much larger number of individuals with autism are needed to determine if there are different types of thinkers, as Dr. Temple Grandin (1995) suggests.

What happens when material cannot be visualized? For example, how do people with autism visualize words that are abstract, like justice or honor? Temple Grandin has written about her experiences with **visual thinking** (thinking in pictures). For abstract words like justice, she thinks of episodes of the TV program *Law and Order.* This dependence on already experienced situations or visual pictures (e.g., concrete examples) for comprehension highlights the limitations of comprehension even in individuals with ASD Level 1. It also highlights the compensatory use of visual strategies for performance of many tasks that are typically performed with language or executive processes.

The implications of the results of the fMRI studies (suggesting that individuals with autism do not automatically recode visual information into verbal information and tend to use visual imagery when it is not necessarily needed) are that this tendency can be either a strength or a limitation, depending on the task. This knowledge is useful when considering career options. For example, jobs involving analyzing satellite surveillance maps or screening luggage or import containers coming into the country might be potential matches for individuals with ASD that would draw on their tendency to process information visually and to perceive details without creating a narrative about what they are viewing.

Using visual strategies, either pictures or written words, to communicate instructions or messages to individuals with autism serves to reduce the amount of content and compress the content to essential information. The format of these instructions should be written like the directions on a soup can – brief and to the point. As seen above, clauses and phrases add processing demands that individuals with autism may not be able to negotiate. Unnecessary words should be eliminated, and only essential facts should be included. For example, individuals with autism would greatly benefit from the software programs that extract key points from textbooks and class notes and eliminate nonessential information, clauses, and phrases. However, it is important to remember that not all individuals with autism are visual thinkers and that some think in words.

Origin of the Brain Differences

Neuroimaging studies are providing increasing evidence of the brain differences in individuals with autism, but where do these brain differences come from? Autism is currently thought to have multiple levels of causation that are assumed to originate in abnormalities in the genetic code that controls what will happen later in brain development (Rutter, 2005). Autism is a disorder that starts in utero but is only identified as development unfolds during the first years of life. The abnormal mechanisms of brain development are realized as structural and functional abnormalities of the brain. They are seen as cognitive and neurological abnormalities that are ultimately manifested as behavioral differences.

Thus, the behavioral differences that characterize the disorder we call autism result from underlying biological differences. Individuals with autism learn and act differently because their brains function differently. While the environment can influence their learning, it cannot change the underlying neurophysiological differences (not yet, at any rate). Thus, although individuals with autism cannot control the way they think about the world, we can understand better how their brains handle information. Such understanding will help us to design interventions that assist the brains of individuals with autism in handling processing challenges of increasing load and complexity of task.

Memory and Learning

Impairments of memory and learning are not included in the list of diagnostic criteria for ASD but have been documented in autism in profiles of neuropsychologic functioning (Minshew, Goldstein, & Siegel, 1997). Such impairments have significant implications for the way in which individuals with autism learn and, by inference, for identifying the teaching strategies that are most appropriate for this population.

In a comprehensive study of verbal and visual information of a wide range of complexity in 52 adolescents and adults with ASD Level 1 and 40 group-matched normal controls, Minshew and Goldstein (2001) found that the basic memory abilities were intact, but the capacity to learn and remember deteriorated as the complexity of the information increased. Impairments were found (a) if the amount of information of a single type was large or (b) if the inherent structure of the visual or verbal information was complex. A maze learning task documented the relationship between increasing complexity of the material and progressively worse memory impairments in the autism group. As the mazes became increasingly complex, the performance of the autism group became progressively worse relative to the controls.

In essence, the autism group had memory difficulty in both the auditory and the visual domains. Thus, the predictive factor for difficulty was not whether it was auditory or visual. Rather, difficulty occurred in both modalities if the material to be learned or remembered required a cognitive organizing structure or required the detection of organizational principles inherent in the material (Minshew & Goldstein, 2001). The flip side of this impairment was that learning and memory could be improved by presenting material to be learned or remembered in small chunks or by simplifying it (pre-processing it by providing the bottom line rather than examples from which the principle was to be extracted). In addition, memory and learning could be improved if increased time was provided, or if the material remained in sight for rehearsal at the individual's own pace.

There are two major implications of these findings. The first is, again, that the involvement of the brain in autism extends beyond problems with social interaction and restricted, repetitive behaviors. The second is that the brain involvement in autism extends not just to the underdevelopment of connections *within* neural systems but also to connections *between* neural systems. The observed impairment in memory and learning relates to the use of concepts and language in the service of memory and, thus, depends on interactions and connections between the memory, language, and reasoning systems of the brain.

Generalization of the Construct to Individuals With ASD Levels 2 and 3

The findings presented in this chapter are based on the study of verbal individuals with IQ scores primarily above 80 who were between 8 and 55 years old. The requirements for the participants to be verbal, over the age of 8, and to be without intellectual disability were based on the need for participants to be able to complete a large number of tests to reveal the pattern of intact abilities and impairments and be able to cooperate during functional imaging. We also wanted to match the participants with autism with a typically developing or normal IQ group. An IQ score below 80 made it impossible to find typically developing children or normal adults who matched. Intellectual disability has a variety of causes each with its own cognitive signature. Thus, the presence of intellectual disability presents a confound when looking for group differences unique to autism. Further, using mental age-matched younger children creates age disparities that present another confound when studying a developmental disorder. In brief, the use of individuals with autism with IQ scores in the average range allowed us to identify the cognitive and brain features that were unique to autism and not attributable to intellectual disability.

The study of a subgroup rather than a representative sample of the entire population of individuals with a disorder is a well-accepted scientific approach to establishing the essential features of a disorder that apply to the entire disorder. The justifications for the extrapolation to the entire disorder are based on the assumptions that all individuals have the disorder in question and that the disorder has a common **pathophysiology**.[6]

All evidence to date supports autism as being a single disorder of wide severity. Severity in and of itself has never been a justification for dividing a disorder into different conditions. Perhaps the most striking evidence of the commonality between the three levels of ASD (see Table 2.2) is the co-occurrence of ASD Levels 1, 2, and 3 cases within the same families and even within twin pairs (Le Couteur et al., 1996). Other evidence is the shared neuropathology, family history, and severity of presentation in the early years (Rutter, 2005).

How do the findings apply to those with autism who were not tested (e.g., those with ASD Levels 2 or 3 by virtue of age or IQ)? We cannot directly answer that question because those individuals were not tested since they cannot consistently cooperate for formal neuropsychological or fMRI procedures. Theoretically, as described in the following section, the information-processing capacity is progressively truncated to the point that no meaning is attached to sensory information, and there is no functional connectivity within the brain to attach meaning to sensory information.

Intellectual Disability in Autism Is Not a Separate Diagnosis

It is common practice for low-functioning individuals with autism also to receive a diagnosis of intellectual disability, as though there were two co-occurring diagnoses rather than a modifier to indicate level of function. As the severity

---

6 It is important to distinguish pathophysiology etiology. Pathophysiology refers to the mechanism of expression within the brain – the brain structures affected and the way in which they are affected. Etiology refers to the way in which this pathophysiology is triggered. There can be many different triggers for the same pathophysiology. If ASD was not assumed to have a common pathophysiology, there would be no justification for any of the scientific studies conducted. That is, if every case of autism has a totally different brain basis, there would be no rationale for studies of groups of participants that look for a common finding or difference between those with autism and those without.

of autism increases, information-processing capacity falls rapidly. The predicted consequence is intellectual disability bearing the hallmarks of the cognitive profile in autism – disproportionate impairments in higher-order sensory, motor, memory and learning, language, and abstraction abilities with preservation of elementary abilities in the same domains. When autism is at its most severe, there is essentially no capacity to attach meaning to sensory information. This progressive reduction in information-processing capacity with preservation of the autism profile (disproportionate impact on higher-order abilities and preserved simpler abilities) presents as intellectual disability. But in actuality, it is part and parcel of the cognitive impairment typical of autism. The profile is present at all levels of function in autism – in verbal individuals, it may be characterized as a learning disability, whereas in individuals with ASD Level 3, it is characterized as intellectual disability. The brain basis of this cognitive profile is a reduction in the functional connections between the brain regions needed to perform tasks. In general, as we have seen, the brain in autism has fewer processing subregions and deploys them less flexibly to address task demands than typical controls.

Implications of the Brain Basis of Autism

Expectations for an individual with autism cannot be based on an "intelligence score." There is a disconnection between IQ score and adaptive functioning in autism. In other words, IQ does not predict adaptive functioning. Individuals with autism will not demonstrate the same level of common sense or problem-solving ability as age peers of a similar level of intelligence. They cannot "act their age." Therefore, more immature behaviors should be expected, regardless of the overall cognitive functioning level.

A child with autism may be placed in a classroom with other fifth-graders because he can do fifth-grade-level academic work. However, his social behavior may be more like that of a kindergarten-age child. This should not be cause for alarm among the teaching staff, but should be an expected and planned-for consequence of the developmental disorder of autism. We see severe social and emotional immaturity persist into the adult years. For example, we know a middle-age woman with autism with an above-average IQ. She speaks of buildings as if they are "hunks" and talks about going on dates with them. If you close your eyes, you would think you were talking to a preadolescent with a crush on members of the latest boy band. She has combined her obsession with buildings with an adolescent or younger crush.

If individuals with autism are not doing something, such as following through on an assignment, it does not necessarily mean that they are being "uncooperative." They are just reacting to the biological response of their body. As human beings, we do the things we are good at and feel comfortable with and resist doing things we find difficult. However, typical people use executive functions to override this basic tendency. "If we don't do this, we are going to get fired, and if we get fired, we can't make our house payment." We talk ourselves into doing what we would otherwise resist.

Individuals with autism do not necessarily have the executive function, the decision-making process to override their initial tendency to resist doing a hard or unpleasant task. Besides, they do not respond to social consequences in the same way that individuals without autism do. Consequently, they are very unlikely to do something they judge to be difficult. It doesn't matter if this judgment is an accurate assessment or not. The fact that the individual with autism is resistant means that he perceives the behavior as being hard or unpleasant. The challenge is to figure out why he thinks the task is hard and to change the task so that he is able to do it.

Because individuals with autism cannot change the way they think and perceive the world, changes have to be made to accommodate them. Previously, autism was considered a "psychological" problem. Underlying this label was the notion that it had no connection to the brain; that it was in the "mind." Individuals with psychological problems are assumed to have some control over their actions (i.e., if you wanted to act differently, you could). As discussed above, we now have a much better understanding of the brain-behavior connection in autism.

Unfortunately, many people still hold to the idea that autism is a psychological problem that individuals choose to give into. For example, if a child with autism has already done a task and refuses to do it again, a teacher is likely to say, "He can do it. He just won't." However, the reason for the child's inaction may be that the environment has changed so that he doesn't recognize it as the same task. It may be that he does not understand what is expected of him. It may also be that he is thinking, "I've already done it, why should I do it again?" The child reacts in a certain way because of the information his brain gives him about the situation. He does not do it to be uncooperative or to create problems for the teacher. To get the child to do the task, the teacher must use her perceptive skills to try to determine what is a likely interpretation of the child's behavior and make changes so that the child will respond.

Summary and Conclusions:
The Future in Intervention for Individuals With ASD

The current work in neuropsychological and neuroimaging research is greatly advancing our understanding of the brain-behavior connection in autism. The motivation for continuing this work is the eventual development of cognitive interventions that will promote the growth of underdeveloped brain circuitry and higher-level skills in individuals with autism. While such interventions are yet to be developed, it is our hope that teachers will use the current level of knowledge as the basis for creating intervention programs that accommodate but also challenge the brain development of their students with autism.

Tips for Practical Application

✓ Because students with autism cannot process large amounts of information efficiently, the amount of information presented to them must be reduced. Rather than expecting the student to learn large amounts of detail (something he may do at the expense of learning the main idea of the material), ask, "What are the main points he needs to learn from a lesson?" and focus on that material instead. Another example would be the use of a visual work task, as outlined in Chapter 11.

✓ Because students with autism have difficulty organizing material or recognizing an implicit organization, it is important to "pre-process" the information for them by highlighting and presenting it with an explicit organization.

✓ Because students with autism process language/information differently, they do better with language/information that is clear and concise as this reduces the processing load. They also do better when given more time to process language/information.

✓ Be careful about asking a student with autism to do several demanding tasks at once. For example, he cannot think of what to write and how to write it at the same time. Writing in stages may go smoother; that is, brainstorm the idea, write the key words needed to express the idea, and then put the key words into sentences. Visual task lists are excellent ways to break down information. A good example to remember is the soup can analogy. The label on the soup can contains very specific and precise directions (add water, heat).

✓ You can't use the level of expressive language of a student with autism to gauge the level of language input. Expressive output may represent unanalyzed language that has been learned and stored as large chunks. Therefore, gauge the appropriateness of your language level by the response of the child or adult. This can be particularly confusing when working with students with ASD Level 1 because they often use very sophisticated language but have a poor grasp of social and emotional concepts. This leads many teachers to expect more social understanding from these students.

✓ Even though a student with autism may be able to do a task, you don't know what cognitive resources she is using. Therefore, she may not be able to do a task if you increase its complexity. Remember: What is complex is defined individually and situationally.

✓ Persons with autism can do some visual processing better than auditory processing because it is reduced dynamically. However, they may have difficulty with visual processing if it is dynamic or complex, demanding more than one cognitive process or coordination of different processing areas across the cortex.

✓ Persons with autism can have difficulty with new situations and environments and demanding or socially stressful situations due to inflexible problem-solving skills. Viewing inflexibility as a neurological issue can be helpful when considering what adaptations and supports are needed. Labels like *oppositional* do little to help educational teams understand the neurological nature of inflexible thought. Inflexibility also indicates the need for skill practice in multiple environments to assist in generalization.

✓ Students with ASD Level 1 may perform well in school in the early grades, but have increased difficulty in their teens. This may be due to the higher-level concepts used in secondary education. This confounded problem may also be seen in social interactions as the nature of social relationships change in the teenage years.

✓ Repetitive practice of learning routines can increase both competence and motivation in students with autism. For example, if a student refuses to participate in an activity, you can assume that something about the activity is frustrating or overwhelming to him. If you can create learning routines, the student is more likely to recognize expectations early on and consequently be more willing to participate. The use of repetitive routines is also helpful in social interactions and activities.

✓ Always consider adaptive behavior scores when assessing the needs of students with autism. This is often missed, particularly if the student performs well on academic tasks.

✓ Proactively plan to support students with autism in social environments. Misinformed educators may place unreasonable expectations for "appropriate social behavior" on students who have significant delays in social maturity. For example, a student who does well in the third-grade classroom may require support from a paraprofessional or aide on the playground where social interaction is unstructured.

✓ It is important for all educators to understand the current research on social thinking and learning. Problems in this area of learning often lead to challenging behaviors in the school setting. Recognition that challenging behaviors are the result of a differently wired brain can lead parents and teachers towards more innovative and ultimately more effective long-term interventions and supports.

Chapter Highlights

- Studies of the brains of individuals with autism provide evidence of differences in how their brains are organized and function.

- In the 1960s, it was accepted that autism was of a psychological or behavioral disorder, rather than of neurologic origin.

- Once autism was seen as brain-based, the focus shifted to cognition and parts of the brain involved in autism; specifically, the deficit or alteration in the brain and thinking.

- The brain-based and cognitive view of autism led to two different approaches to understanding autism: (a) the core deficit hypothesis/primary deficit and (b) a hypothesis that looks at all simultaneously occurring impairments and intact abilities in an attempt to come up with a common denominator or regarding thinking and the brain in ASD.

- The chapter authors discuss several studies of the cognitive basis of autism using individuals with ASD Level 1 (IQ score over 70). Various intact and impaired abilities were found, demonstrating that these individuals with ASD Level 1 appeared to acquire information on par with neurotypical controls; however, impairments were apparent in more complex processes (see Table 2.1 for specifics).

- The pattern of impairments across domains in individuals ASD Level 1 in the studies is indicative of a reduced capability in the area of information processing, with increasing difficulties as the complexity of the task increases.

- In addition to impairments in the social, communication, and reasoning domains typical of the standard diagnostic profile in ASD, the studies also showed impairments in memory and motor domains.

- Tasks requiring multitasking and increased speed of processing put constraints on the information-processing abilities of individuals with ASD.

- Hidden information-processing demands refer to the ability to understand complex sentences or work with tasks that require holding multiple steps in working memory (multitasking).

- Individuals with ASD may store verbal information in chunks and use it in expressive language; sometimes they appear to have greater understanding than they do. Observing actions rather than spoken words may give a better picture of actual abilities.

- The complex information-process concept is of value for intervention purposes by reminding those working with individuals with ASD that it is necessary to convey information clearly and succinctly and recognize that individuals on the spectrum are generally operating in a world governed by facts and rules.

- Complexity as a concept refers to the difficulty of processing information. This difficulty can be caused by certain aspects of the task requirement, such as amount of information, structure of information, time constraints on completing task, or multiple simultaneous processing demands.

- Complexity interferes with efficiency in completing tasks for everyone, but the lower capacity for information processing in individuals with ASD means they become limited in this area long before age- and IQ-matched peers.

- *Central coherence* is a term coined in 1989 by Uta Frith to refer to impairments in high-order cognitive and language abilities along with strengths in detail perception and visuospatial abilities in individuals with ASD. Essentially, these individuals have difficulty integrating parts into a whole.

- While the profile of central coherence is similar to the profile found by the chapter authors with regard to information processing, it does not include the sensory, motor, memory impairments, or expressive deficits. Thus, the authors determined that the difficulty for individuals with ASD is better termed information processing so as to address all intact and impaired structures in brain and cognition.

- Functional magnetic resonance imaging (fMRI) allows for recording of brain activity during the performance of cognitive and language tasks. fMRI studies have allowed investigators to observe what occurs in the brains of individuals with autism during different tasks and compare that to what occurs in the brains of neurotypical counterparts.

- fMRI studies have shown that the brains of individuals with ASD have underdeveloped neural pathways (also known as connectivity), less flexibility in changing and meeting different demands, fewer resources to draw on, and less synchrony or harmony in regions working together.

- fMRI studies have also found that individuals with ASD appear to use alternative strategies, or different cognitive approaches, to completing tasks. These strategies may assist or interfere with task completion, depending on the strategy and the task.

- Studies have shown impairments in memory and learning exist in individuals with ASD. As in previous studies, the basic abilities appear intact but, as demands and information become increasingly complex, the capacity of individuals with ASD to learn and remember deteriorated.

- Based on studies involving learning and memory, the chapter authors believe that the effects of autism go beyond problems with social interaction and restricted and repetitive behaviors to involve other interactive brain systems, particularly those involving language and reasoning.

- While the studies cited in the chapter involved individuals with autism who had IQ scores above 80 and were verbal, the chapter authors believe the findings can be generalized to those with more significant impairments based on the belief that the basis for ASD lies in deficits related to information processing. The progressive reduction in the ability to process information leads to increased severity in functioning, thus creating an intellectual disability.

- This intellectual disability represents what is true for all individuals with ASD: reduced information-processing capacity; a specific cognitive profile. What differentiates low-functioning from high-functioning individuals on the spectrum is level of impairment in connectivity and higher order abilities.

- Implications of the brain basis for ASD involve realizing that individuals with ASD think and perceive the world differently. It is important that interventionists take this into account when working with such students.

Chapter Review Questions

1. What is meant by "core deficit"? Is this approach still considered applicable to identifying the cause of autism?

2. What are the most popular theories with respect to the primary impairments in ASD?

3. According to the chapter authors, what is different about the brains of people with autism that leads to differences in how they think or perceive things?

4. Why is ASD seen as an information-processing deficit?

5. What are "hidden information-processing demands"?

6. What is the value of the complex information-processing concept?

7. What is meant by the term *complexity*?

8. What is "central coherence"?

9. Define information processing in terms of persons with ASD.

10. What is fMRI and why is it important to understanding ASD?

11. How are the brains of individuals with ASD different from those of neurotypical individuals?

12. What are alternative strategies used by individuals with ASD?

13. Why do the chapter authors believe that the diagnostic criteria for ASD should extend beyond problems with social interaction and restricted and repetitive behaviors?

14. Why do the chapter authors state that intellectual disability in autism is not a separate diagnosis?

15. Give three implications of the brain basis of autism.

References

American Psychiatric Association. (1994). *Diagnostic and statistical manual of mental disorders, 4th edition* (DSM-IV). Washington, DC: Author.

Aylward, E. H., Minshew, N. J., Field, K., Sparks, B. F., & Singh, N. (2002). Effects of age on brain volume and head circumference in autism. *Neurology, 59,* 175-183.

Carter, E. J., Williams, D. L., Minshew, N. J., & Lehman, J. (2012). Is he being bad? Social and language brain networks during social judgment in children with autism. *PLOS One, 7*(10), e47241. doi:10.1371/journal. pone.0047241

Chevallier, C., Kohls, G., Troiani, V., Brodkin, E. S., & Schultz, R. T. (2012). The social motivation theory of autism. *Trends in Cognitive Sciences, 16,* 231-239.

Cody, H., Pelphrey, K., & Piven, J. (2002). Structural and functional magnetic resonance imaging of autism. *International Journal of Developmental Neuroscience, 20,* 421-431.

Courchesne, E., Karns, C. M., Davis, H. R., Ziccardi, R., Carper, R. A., Tigue, Z. D., et al. (2001). Unusual brain growth patterns in early life in patients with autistic disorder. *Neurology, 57,* 245-254.

Dawson, G., Webb, S., & McPartland, J. (2005). Understanding the nature of face processing impairment in autism: Insights from behavioral and electrophysiological studies. *Developmental Neuropsychology, 27,* 403-424.

Frith, U. (1989). *Autism: Explaining the enigma.* Oxford, UK: Blackwell Publishers.

Garcia-Villamisar, D., & Della Sala, S. (2002). Dual-task performance in adults with autism. *Cognitive Neuropsychology, 7,* 63-74.

Grandin, T. (1995). *Thinking in pictures: And other reports from my life with autism.* New York, NY: Vintage Books.

Hammill, D. D. (1985). *DTLA-2: Detroit Tests of Learning Aptitude.* Austin, TX: Pro-Ed.

Just, M. A., Cherkassky, V. L., Keller, T. A., & Minshew, N. J. (2004). Cortical activation and synchronization during sentence comprehension in high-functioning autism: Evidence of underconnectivity. *Brain, 127,* 1811-1821.

Just, M. A., Keller, T. A., Cherkassky V., Kana R. K., & Minshew, N. J. (2007). Functional and anatomical cortical underconnectivity in autism: Evidence from an fMRI study of an executive function task and corpus callosum morphometry. *Cerebral Cortex, 17,* 951-961.

Kana, R., Keller, T., Cherkassky, V., Minshew, N., & Just, M. A. (2006). Sentence comprehension in autism: Thinking in pictures with decreased functional connectivity. *Brain, 129,* 2484-2493.

Kana, R. K., Keller, T. A., Minshew, N. J., & Just, M. A. (2007). Inhibitory control in high-functioning autism: Decreased activation and underconnectivity in inhibition networks. Manuscript submitted for publication. *Biological Psychiatry, 62,* 198-206.

Kana, R., Keller, T., Cherkassky, V., Minshew, N. J., & Just, M. A. (2009). Atypical frontal-posterior synchronization of theory of mind regions in autism during mental states attribution. *Social Neuroscience, 4,* 135-152.

Keehn, B., Muller, R.-A., & Townsend, J. (2013). Atypical attentional networks and the emergence of autism. *Neuroscience and Biobehavioral Reviews, 37,* 164-183.

Koshino, H., Carpenter, P. A., Minshew, N. J., Cherkassky, V. L., Keller, T. A., & Just, M. A. (2005). Functional connectivity in an fMRI working memory task with high-functioning autism. *NeuroImage, 24,* 810-821.

Le Couteur, A., Bailey, A., Goode, S., Pickles, A., Robertson, S., Gottesman, I., & Rutter, M. (1996). A broader phenotype of autism: The clinical spectrum in twins. *Journal of Child Psychology and Psychiatry, 37,* 785-801.

Le Couteur, A., Rutter, M., Lord, C., Rios, P., Robertson, S., Holdgrafer, M., et al. (1989). Autism Diagnostic Interview: A standardized investigator-based instrument. *Journal of Autism and Developmental Disorders, 19,* 363-387.

Lord, C., Risi, S., Lambrecht, L., Cook, E. H., Jr., Leventhal, B. L., DiLavore, P. C., et al. (2000). The Autism Diagnostic Observation Schedule – Generic: A standard measure of social and communication deficits associated with the spectrum of autism. *Journal of Autism and Developmental Disorders, 30,* 205-223.

Lord, C., Rutter, M., Goode, S., Heemsbergen, J., Jordan, H., Mawhood, L., et al. (1989). Autism Diagnostic Observation Schedule: A standardized observation of communicative and social behavior. *Journal of Autism and Developmental Disorders, 19,* 185-212.

Lord, C., Rutter, M., & Le Couteur, A. (1994). Autism Diagnostic Interview – Revised: A revised version of a diagnostic interview for caregivers of individuals with possible pervasive developmental disorders. *Journal of Autism and Developmental Disorders, 24,* 659-685.

Luna, B., Doll, S. K., Hegedus, S. J., Minshew, N. J., & Sweeney, J. A. (2006). Maturation of executive function in autism. *Biol Psychiatry, 61,* 474-481.

Mason, R. A., Williams, D. L., Kana, R. K., Minshew, N. J., & Just, M. A. (2008). Theory of mind disruption and recruitment of the right hemisphere during narrative comprehension in autism. *Neuropsychologia, 46,* 269-280.

Meltzoff, A., & Decety, J. (2003). What imitation tells us about social cognition: A rapprochement between developmental psychology and cognitive neuroscience. *Philosophical Transactions of the Royal Society Biological Sciences, 358,* 491-500.

Minshew, N. J., & Goldstein, G. (2001). The pattern of intact and impaired memory functions in autism. *Journal of Child Psychology and Psychiatry, 42,* 1095-1101.

Minshew, N. J., Goldstein, G., & Siegel, D. (1997). Neuropsychologic functioning in autism: Profile of a complex information processing disorder. *Journal of the International Neuropsychological Society, 3,* 303-316.

Minshew, N. J., Williams, D. L., & Goldstein, G. (2007). [Replication study of neuropsychologic functioning of adults with autism.] Unpublished raw data.

Minshew, N. J., Meyer, J., & Goldstein, G. (2002). Abstract reasoning in autism: A dissociation between concept formation and concept identification. *Neuropsychology, 16,* 327-334.

Minshew, N. J., Sweeney, J. A., Bauman, M. L., & Webb, S. J. (2005). Neurologic aspects of autism. In F. R. Volkmar, R. Paul, A.

Klin, & D. Cohen (Eds.), *Handbook of autism and pervasive developmental disorders: Volume one: Diagnosis, development, neurobiology, and behavior* (3rd ed., pp. 473-514). Hoboken, NJ: John Wiley & Sons.

Nah, Y.-H., & Poon, K. K. (2010). The perception of social situations by children with autism spectrum disorders. *Autism, 15,* 185-203.

Rutter, M. (2005). Genetic influences and autism. In F. R. Volkmar, R. Paul, A. Klin, & D. Cohen (Eds.), *Handbook of autism and pervasive developmental disorders: Volume one, Diagnosis, development, neurobiology, and behavior* (3rd ed., pp. 425-452). Hoboken, NJ: John Wiley & Sons.

Schipul, S. E., Keller, T. A., & Just, M. A. (2011). Inter-regional brain communication and its disturbance in autism. *Frontiers in System Neuroscience, 5,* 1-11.

Schultz, R. T. (2005). Developmental deficits in social perception in autism: The role of the amygdala and fusiform face area. *Developmental Neuroscience, 23,* 125-141.

Sparks, B. F., Friedman, S. D., Shaw, D. W., Aylward, E. H., Echelard, D., Artru, A. A., et al. (2002). Brain structural abnormalities in young children with autism spectrum disorder. *Neurology, 59,* 184-192.

Williams, D. L., Goldstein, G., & Minshew, N. J. (2006). Neuropsychologic functioning in children with autism: Further evidence for disordered complex information processing. *Child Neuropsychology, 12,* 279-298.

World Health Organization. (1992). *International classification of diseases and related health problems* (10th ed.). Geneva, Switzerland: Author.

Learner Objectives

After reading this chapter, the learner should be able to:

- Explain what is meant by a "spectrum disorder"

- Discuss the importance of early intervention for children diagnosed with ASD

- Explain issues surrounding early identification of ASD, including early diagnosis and referral

- State the developmental red flags that may indicate ASD in infants and toddlers

- Discuss the importance of providing families with non-jargon laden information about assessment, intervention, and community supports

- Understand the importance of providing feedback to families that includes accessible community resources as part of the assessment process

- Provide families with strategies to facilitate improved interaction with their child that they can begin immediately

- List and describe the key features of effective programs for young children with ASD

- State the types of questions families need to ask when selecting intervention programs for their young children with ASD

- Describe what is meant by the term *outcome-oriented framework*

- Discuss ways in which families may decide on meaningful outcomes for their child with ASD

- Explain what a curriculum-based assessment (CBA) is and why such a tool is useful

- List and describe the components of Project DATA

Chapter 4

Getting a Good Start: Effective Practices in Early Intervention

Ilene S. Schwartz • Bonnie J. McBride

Eric is 2-1/2 years old and has sparkling blue eyes. He does not talk yet, but if he wants something, he pulls an adult by the hand over to what he wants and then stands and waits. Sometimes it is easy for his mother or his teacher to guess what he wants, but lately he has started crying, screaming, and falling to the ground if the adult is not able to get him what he wants right away. He will keep screaming until the adult figures out what he wants. It is getting harder because once he starts screaming, it is difficult to calm him down even if he gets what he wants. Caregivers are beginning to avoid interacting with him because they don't want to be the ones who "start" his screaming.

Jamal is 3 years old and can climb higher and faster than any other 3-year-old around. He is already reading and can answer any question about team statistics or the starting lineup of his local baseball team. However, he cannot consistently answer simple questions from adults, interact with children his own age, or tolerate changes to his routine. His parents are extremely concerned because he and his mother have been asked to stop coming to music lessons at the local community center and to find a "more appropriate" placement than the local co-op preschool. His grandparents wonder if there is anything really "wrong" with him or whether his parents simply are overindulgent.

Serena is 30 months old and has a head full of brown ringlets. Her parents report that she used to walk around the house, point to objects, label them, and laugh. She does not do that any more. In fact, these days she rarely speaks except to request certain videos, books, or preferred foods. She hardly ever looks at people or things, unless she can find something that is spinning. Then she is totally mesmerized. Her parents cannot remember the last time they heard her laugh.

These young children are some of the faces of autism spectrum disorders (ASD). The number of children with ASD is increasing dramatically. ASD is a spectrum disorder, which means that children who receive this diagnosis differ dramatically in their abilities, preferences, needs, and areas of delay. As Eric, Jamal, and Serena remind us, there is no "typical" child with ASD, and there is no one "right" way of educating a child with ASD. Every child and family brings a unique story to the early intervention process, and that story must be woven into the fabric of intervention and support for the process to be successful.

The importance of early intervention in treating children with ASD has become axiomatic in the autism community. In fact, in the often confusing and contradictory world of autism, it is one of the few things that we know for sure and on which professionals, parents, and advocates agree. There is overwhelming evidence that earlier is better, both in terms of autism diagnosis and intervention (National Research Council [NRC], 2001; Reichow, Barton, Boyd, & Hume, 2012; Rogers, 1999). In this chapter we provide evidence of the importance of early intervention, identify recommended practices for providing intervention services, and give examples of how to translate these recommendations into classroom practice.

Many educational and behavioral interventions have demonstrated effectiveness in improving developmental outcomes for children with ASD (e.g., Boulware, Schwartz, Sandall, & McBride, 2006; Dawson et al., 2010; Lovaas, 1987; Schwartz, Sandall, McBride, & Boulware, 2004; Schwartz, Thomas, McBride, & Sandall, 2013; Smith, Groen, & Wynn, 2000; Strain & Bovy, 2011). While many of these interventions are effective for children of any age, there is increasing agreement that intervention has a greater impact in younger children (Harris & Handelman, 2000; Lord, 1995; Volkmar, Lord, Bailey, Schultz, & Klin, 2004) and that the gains made in level of independence, cognitive functioning, and communication associated with early intervention can result in considerable cost savings to the family and systems that provide services for children with ASD (Jacobson, 2000).

The first step towards providing high-quality early intervention to all children with ASD and their families is to accurately identify children at the earliest age possible, regardless of cultural and linguistic diversity, class, or geography. In the following, we will look at the process of early diagnosis.

The Who, What, and Where of Early Diagnosis

ASD is a lifelong neurodevelopmental disability characterized by a complex compilation of learning differences and delays in social interaction, communication, and perseverative or repetitive behaviors. Early and accurate detection is critical for early intervention. Despite leading research and advocacy groups stating that ASD can be reliably diagnosed in the first 2 years of life, the average age for diagnosis in the United States is much later, averaging 4-5 years (Lord et al., 2006; Moore & Goodson, 2003; Pinto-Martin & Levy, 2004; Zwaigenbaum et al., 2009). For children who are culturally and linguistically diverse, the diagnostic picture is grimmer, with diagnosis coming later and after many more visits to professionals (Mandell, et al., 2009). Clearly, the first step to high-quality early intervention is improved early detection and diagnosis.

Work on early detection and assessment must occur on at least two fronts: improving the accuracy of the screening and diagnostic tools used and influencing policy and practice to get these tools implemented. Some of the best examples of integrating the two strands may be found in the work of organizations such as Autism Speaks (http://www.autismspeaks.org), the web site **First Signs** (www.firstsigns.org.), and the Centers for Disease Control and Prevention (CDC), Learn the signs. Act Early Campaign (http://www.cdc.gov/ncbddd/actearly/). These organizations have been instrumental in efforts to work with local medical education groups to disseminate the most up-to-date information to pediatricians, family practitioners, and other medical professionals. In addition, these organizations have developed Internet resources, public service announcements, and other media information to raise awareness about the importance of early detection of ASD and the developmental red flags (see Table 4.1) associated with an increased risk of ASD. Since the diagnosis of ASD is complex and cannot be tied to any individual behavior at any age, this approach encourages parents, child care providers, and others to be aware of social and communication milestones and, if concerns exist, referring children to a medical practitioner right away.

Table 4.1
Warning Signs of Autism Spectrum Disorders in Early Childhood

---

Social
- Has poor eye contact
- Lacks sharing interest and enjoyment with others
- Fails to respond to his or her name
- Appears disinterested in or unaware of others

Communication
- Lacks gestures – pointing, reaching, waving, showing
- Doesn't appear to understand simple questions or directions
- Speaks in an abnormal tone of voice or with an odd rhythm
- May repeat words or phrases exactly as heard but doesn't understand how to use them

Behavior
- Repeats the same actions or movements over and over again
- Develops specific routines and rituals and becomes upset at the slightest change
- Is preoccupied with a narrow topic of interest

To Whom Should a Child Be Referred?

One of the many confusing issues families face once they or a caregiver notice any of the red flags listed above is "What do we do now?" Most families seek initial advice from their pediatrician or primary care physician. For very young children, most pediatricians, healthcare providers, or community programs refer families to a psychologist, developmental pediatrician, psychiatrist, or neurologist for a full evaluation to determine if a child has an ASD.

The most common classification system used to diagnose ASD is the *Diagnostic and Statistical Manual of Mental Disorders, 5th Edition*; American Psychiatric Association [APA], 2013). As discussed in Chapter 2, the fifth edition of the DSM represents major revisions to the classification system used to diagnosis ASD. One of the primary changes was to merge the subtypes of pervasive developmental disorders into the one category of autism spectrum disorder (ASD). Another major change was to move from three symptom domains – social impairment, communication deficits, and repetitive/restricted behaviors – to two domains – social communication impairment and repetitive/restricted behaviors. These changes were made to increase the reliability of diagnosis.

A professional licensed to provide diagnoses, who has experience with ASD and is trained in administering assessments designed to detect an ASD, is the most qualified person to provide an accurate diagnosis, especially in very young children. Unfortunately, in many communities there continues to be shortage of professionals with these credentials. It is important for parents and professionals, such as teachers, speech-language therapists, or occupational therapists, who suspect a young child is at risk for ASD to be actively involved in the diagnostic process and to be encouraged to ask questions regarding the procedures used to arrive at a diagnosis.

Another avenue for a child to be identified as having an ASD is through the educational system. Included in the amendments to the Individuals With Disabilities Education Act (IDEA) is the category of autism, which qualifies a child for educational services. While the educational criteria have some similarities to those of the DSM-5, there are important differences, particularly for young children. The classification of "autism" may not be used for children under the age of 6 or 9, depending on state law, so a younger child suspected of having an ASD may have to qualify for services under a broader category such as "developmentally delayed." Also, an educational classification of "autism" may not be accepted by many health or social service agencies that control access to potential services for children with ASD. As is the case for a clinical diagnosis of an ASD, there are shortages of professionals in school systems who have the expertise to identify ASD, particularly in very young children. Further, the instruments used by a given school district to determine eligibility for special education services may not be appropriate for detecting the kind of difficulties children with ASD experience (Dahle, 2003).

Why It Is Important to Make a Referral and Get a Diagnosis Early

The National Research Council (NRC, 2001), in a report summarizing the state of knowledge and making recommendations for practice, recommended that children begin to receive specialized, intensive early intervention as soon as they receive a diagnosis or a suspected diagnosis of an ASD. Even if a child has not received a formal evaluation or diagnosis but is suspected to be at risk for an ASD, intervention focusing on social development and communication should begin right away. This means that rather than taking a wait-and-see approach to screening and referral, parents, caregivers, the medical community, and the educational/early intervention community should refer children who demonstrate the red flag behaviors listed above as early as possible. The research is clear that early intervention is effective and can have a profound impact on the quality of the lives of children with ASD and their families. Less clear is how to determine the right amount of intervention and how to match treatment approaches to individual children and families.

Making the Transition From Assessment to Intervention – What Families Need to Know and Should Not Be Afraid to Ask

Many parents walk away from the assessment process scared and confused. One parent told us that he and his wife went home, curled up in bed with their beautiful little boy, and cried for 24 hours. Other parents decide that they are going to become ASD experts and hit the Internet, only to be stymied by 66,400,000 hits on a Google search about autism, conflicting reports in the scientific and popular press, and long waiting lists for services in their communities.

Part of the assessment process must include helping families make the transition into services in their local community. This process should include helping families identify potential service providers and providing temporary support to the family until they can enlist support and technical assistance from other professional sources.

The first referral for every child should be to the publicly funded services available in the local community. These services vary by state, but include early intervention (for children under 3) or public school services (for children 3 and above) in every state. They may also include a range of other services, such as respite care, specialized funding for intensive home programming, and wraparound services that provide support to children with ASD and their families. Information should also be provided about the characteristics of effective programming for young children with ASD (NRC, 2001); local educational programs for parents of children who have been recently diagnosed with ASD; local and national parent support groups; and web sites or books that contain clear, reliable, and accurate information. Most important, any information provided to parents at the time of diagnosis should be accompanied with written materials and followed up by a phone call or visit within two weeks to see if families have additional questions.

Another important outcome of the initial assessment and diagnosis is a clear identification of a child's strengths and challenges. For example, Eric, Jamal, and Serena, the children you met at the beginning of this chapter, have different strengths and needs. As a result, the constellation of intervention services may look very different for these three children.

Something that should *not* be part of the initial assessment is a statement of the child's predicted long-term prognosis. Although we know that all children will benefit from intensive early intervention, and that for some children it may mitigate many of the symptoms of ASD, families need to know that ASD is a lifelong disorder and that there is no way of predicting how an individual child will respond to intervention. Given that more children identified now with ASD are within the normal range of intelligence than previous statistics indicated, and that our intervention techniques continue to improve, there is no way to know what the future holds for a specific child with ASD and his family (Chakrabarti & Fombonne, 2001; Howlin, 2000; Tsatsanis, 2003).

What Does the Research Say About Intervention for Young Children With ASD?

In the last 25 years, we have learned an amazing amount about intervention for young children with ASD (Strain, Schwartz, & Barton, 2011). We have learned that early intensive behavioral intervention (EIBI) is effective in producing important behavioral, social, and cognitive changes in many children with ASD (Reichow et al., 2012). We have also learned that some children do not make significant gains as a result of EIBI, and we do not know, before intervention begins, how to predict which children will be good responders and which children will not be (Sandall et al., 2011). Although EIBI has a more robust evidence base than any other single approach to intervention, we have also learned that there are a number of other promising intensive early intervention programs for young children with ASD that share some elements with EIBI but differ based on the location of the intervention (e.g., school vs. home), age of participants (e.g., toddlers vs. preschoolers), and theoretical orientation (behavioral vs. developmental) (see Chapter 1).

In a review of comprehensive treatment models (CTM) for children with ASD, Odom and his colleagues (Odom, Boyd, Hall, & Hume, 2010) identified 30 programs that met their criteria, including publication of a manual and program description, intensity, comprehensiveness of curricula, and a theoretical or conceptual framework. These researchers concluded that although as a group these models are well defined operationally, there is an urgent need for well-designed experiments to both address the efficacy of these models and to attempt to answer the more difficult question: What intervention will be most effective for a specific child and family?

In addition to establishing the effectiveness of CTMs, a great deal of work has focused on identifying evidence-based instructional strategies for children with ASD. Both the National Autism Center (http://www. nationalautismcenter.org) and the National Professional Development Center on ASD (http://autismpdc. fpg.unc.edu/) have published literature reviews evaluating and identifying instructional strategies that can be considered to be evidence-based. This work is important for parents, practitioners, and researchers and provides a useful place to begin when developing a treatment program for a child with ASD.

But it is important to remember that an effective comprehensive program for young children with ASD is more than a collection of evidence-based instructional practices or implementation of a program described in a manual. It is a cohesive approach to assessment and intervention that is flexible enough to meet the needs of individual children and their families but is grounded in a theoretical framework that helps to drive programming and treatment decisions. An effective program must be a good match for the child and family, be responsive to family concerns and beliefs, use data-based decision making to modify the program based on child progress, and help the child make meaningful progress towards important developmental outcomes.

What Are the Key Features of Effective Programs for Young Children With ASD?

Although there is no definitive answer to the question above, guidelines exist that can help intervention teams, including families, address this issue. In 2001, the National Research Council, as part of a comprehensive review of the research and proposed recommendations, set the benchmark of 25 hours a week of intervention for young children with ASD. These hours of intervention may be made up of a combination of center-, home-, and community-based services that provide multidisciplinary instruction in the core deficit areas associated with ASD. Other sources that may be useful in determining the level of intensity needed include information from model programs that have produced good outcomes for toddlers and/or preschoolers with ASD (e.g., Boulware et al., 2006; Dawson et al., 2010; Reichow et al., 2012; Schwartz et al., 2013; Stahmer & Ingersoll, 2004; Strain & Bovey, 2011). In these programs the number of hours of intervention range from 16 to 40 hours per week. Examining the individual child's and family's strengths and needs determines the appropriate level of intensity. If family priorities change, or if the child is not making progress, the level of intensity should be reevaluated.

A number of educational interventions for children with ASD have demonstrated improved outcomes for children and families. The majority of both specific interventions and comprehensive programs for ASD come from the field of applied behavior analysis (ABA); however, there is growing agreement among professionals and researchers that there is no single educational strategy that is best for all children with ASD (Odom et al., 2010; Stahmer, Schreibman, & Cunningham, 2011).

Instead of focusing the debate on what are the "best" approaches or techniques for children with ASD, some researchers have focused on what elements of programming need to be in place, regardless of the educational or treatment approach used. The key features of an effective program for young children with autism have been outlined by organizations such as the NRC and other professionals with extensive backgrounds in autism.

In addition to beginning intervention as early as possible, the following are key elements in effective programs for young children with ASD:

1. Sufficient number of hours and intensity of services
2. Comprehensible environments with access to typical peers
3. Specialized curriculum with an appropriate scope and sequence
4. Family involvement
5. Problem-solving approach to challenging behaviors
6. Appropriate evaluation tools to monitor progress

Sufficient Number of Hours and Intensity of Services

As highlighted above, the NRC Report (2001) recommends 25 hours per week of intervention for a child with ASD. In addition to the number of hours, other dimensions of intensity are also important. These include the amount of individualized or small-group instruction that is available (some 1:1 instruction is recommended), the training and expertise of the professionals implementing the program, and the child's level of engagement in the instructional tasks (Dunlap, 1999; Schwartz et al., 2013; Strain & Bovey, 2011; Wolery & Garfinkle, 2002).

Comprehensible Environments With Access to Typical Peers

Environments must be understandable to the children (comprehensible), and children with ASD need to have access to typical peers. The physical setting must be considered when determining if the environment is understandable to the child with ASD. This includes how the physical space is arranged, how and what materials are used, and how activities are scheduled and arranged. All of these will influence a child's level of independence, opportunities for peer interaction, and child-initiated communication. For example, if a classroom is organized with distinctly defined play areas and clear traffic patterns, children are more likely to be independent at initiating play (Schwartz, Garfinkle, & Davis, 2002).

The ability to engage in meaningful interaction with typically developing peers is another important component of a comprehensive program for children with ASD (Wolfberg, 2004; see Chapter 8). Since the primary area of difficulty for young children with ASD is social-relatedness skills, having responsive peers to interact with becomes particularly critical. However, there is strong evidence to indicate that placing children in environments with other children is not sufficient for children with autism to benefit (Strain et al., 2011). Planned opportunities for peer interaction must be provided that include adequate support from trained adults.

Specialized Curriculum With an Appropriate Scope and Sequence

An appropriate curriculum for a young child with ASD would include instruction in the core deficit areas of communication, social interaction, and play. Children with ASD have difficulty in a variety of skill areas that affect relationships and learning. For example, many young children have not learned to imitate others, either for social purposes or as a learning strategy. For children who have not mastered imitation, this should be addressed as part of the curriculum. Another important area where focused teaching should occur is communication. Many children with ASD have not developed language and may not have adequate ways to communicate their wants and needs.

Family Involvement

Family members are the most consistent influence in a child's life (Wang, Mannan, Poston, Turnbull, & Summers, 2004). When a child is first diagnosed with ASD, parents often experience grief and confusion over what the future will hold for their child. Family members are bombarded with new treatments and promises of a cure. It is critical that professionals actively engage parents in the intervention planning process so that family priorities can be addressed and parents have an avenue for discussing treatments they may have questions about (Braiden, Bothwell, & Duffy, 2010).

Family involvement also enhances **generalization** of skills. Children with ASD often show difficulties in the ability to use skills learned in one context or with one person in other contexts or with other people. A collaborative partnership with families enhances the effectiveness of intervention by ensuring that strategies are implemented in a variety of contexts, including the home and the community. Indeed, in a recent survey conducted by the Indiana Resource Center for Autism (IRCA; www.iidc.indiana.edu/irca), families rated their own participation as the single most effective service received. In particular, they cited how important family impact is on their child's growth (Hume, Bellini, & Pratt, 2005).

Problem-Solving Approach to Challenging Behaviors

Many young children with ASD demonstrate challenging behaviors that are more intense and pervasive than what is typical for a young child. The intensity and frequency of behaviors, such as crying, screaming, or aggression, can result in these children being excluded from childcare settings and other community activities. Often addressing these behaviors is the number-one challenge faced by schools and parents.

Fortunately, research over the past 25 years has changed the focus of how we approach these challenging behaviors (Carr & Durrand, 1985; Carr et al., 2002). Instead of addressing only how to eliminate the behavior of concern, the focus of intervention is now on understanding what **communicative *function*** the behavior has for the child. That information is then used to target proactive behaviors that can be taught to replace the challenging behavior (i.e., a problem-solving approach). For instance, if a child screams every time he sees something he wants, teaching him to ask for something instead is a proactive approach to addressing the problem behavior (screaming) (see Chapter 7).

Appropriate Evaluation Tools for Monitoring Progress

The purpose of evaluation tools is not to determine if a child has ASD or to determine how the child is progressing compared to other children. Rather, evaluation tools are designed to determine how much the child is learning; in other words, to compare the child's progress at Time 1 to his progress at Time 2 on a specific set of behaviors and skills.

Systematic and repeated monitoring of a child's progress is an essential component of every high-quality intervention program. Progress monitoring should be done frequently and in a manner that allows for changes to occur in the child's program, if that is needed. A variety of strategies are used to monitor progress, such as recording each occurrence of the target behavior when it is observed during teaching, video taping and then recording the occurrence of target behavior from the video-tape, a skills checklist, or a rating scale.

Several factors should be considered when selecting an evaluation tool. First, it is important to ensure that the evaluation tool adequately identifies if the child is making progress or if a change in the program is necessary. For instance, if a child with ASD is learning to use an **augmentative communication** device (i.e., pictures or a computerized system) but is not using it to initiate communication across the day, choosing an evaluation method such as an observation tool will identify what is occurring in the environment that may be interfering with the child's use of the device (e.g., it is only available at certain times of the day). This, in turn, allows for making changes that will enable the child to communicate his wants and needs and continue to make progress. Second, the ease of use of the evaluation tool is important to ensure it will be used consistently to monitor progress. In summary, the important criterion for selecting an evaluation tool is whether or not it will provide the information that is needed to make changes to the child's program in a timely manner.

Translating Recommendations Into Comprehensive Programs for Children with ASD

Once a child has received a diagnosis, families are often put in the position of trying to piece together services – some publicly funded and others funded through private insurance or out of pocket – to create a comprehensive program for their preschooler with ASD. Although the literature suggests a number of "brand name" intervention approaches (e.g., UCLA Young Autism Project, **Lovaas**, 1987; TEACCH, Schopler & Van Bourgondien, 1991; see Chapter 11; Early Start Denver Model, Dawson et al., 2010; LEAP, Strain & Bovey, 2011), most families do not have the opportunity to implement a pure intervention. Instead, they combine service providers in their community, often with different theoretical and practical orientations, to provide an eclectic program for their child that may or may not include the program characteristics described above (Hume et al., 2005).

When we counsel parents about enrolling their child in intervention programs, we urge them to consider the following questions:

- What are your primary concerns for your child?

- Does the intervention or collection of interventions you are considering address those concerns?

- Are the procedures of the intervention acceptable to you?

- Are you convinced that these interventions are a good match for your child and your family?

- What types of evidence about the effectiveness of the intervention have you seen? Is this evidence convincing to you?

- How will the interventionists communicate with you and demonstrate the progress your child is making? Is that acceptable to you?

By asking these questions, we encourage parents to identify the desired outcome at the beginning of intervention so that appropriate methods or strategies can be built into the program. An optimal time to begin this process is when the educational team or the intervention team is developing a child's **individualized education program (IEP)** or **individualized family service plan (IFSP)**.

Adopting an **outcome-oriented framework** is not a one-time endeavor; it is a problem-solving process and should be updated as often as priorities change or as often as the child's needs change. Given the diverse needs of children on the autism spectrum and the lifelong nature of the disability, it is not unreasonable to expect that one child and family will experience many types of interventions during early childhood. For example, a family may decide to implement an intensive behavioral early intervention program to supplement an inclusive preschool program upon receiving the diagnosis, and after a year decide that their child needs less one-on-one intervention. Then, they may decrease or discontinue the intensive program and enroll their child in social skills groups supplemented by supported play dates at home after preschool. Another family may make a different choice. There is no "right" choice; there is no one right way. The only way to determine if an intervention is working is to document, through frequent data collection and ongoing data analysis, that the child is making meaningful progress towards the educational outcomes that the parents and other team members think are important.

What Are Meaningful Outcomes for Young Children With ASD?

Determining what to teach young children with ASD is an important part of planning and implementing effective early intervention programs. Almost all professionals agree on certain pivotal, fundamental skills: Young children need to learn to follow simple directions, imitate, communicate their wants and needs, and perform basic self-care skills, such as becoming toilet trained.

After that, opinions tend to diverge. Should the early intervention program focus on discrete cognitive concepts or emphasize social skills? Is it more important to help children develop friendships or conduct intensive discrete trial training? There is no easy or data-based answer to these questions. Families and other members of intervention teams must look at the strengths and needs of an individual student, the priorities of the families, and existing data to decide what is meaningful for a specific child with ASD and his or her family.

A meaningful outcome is one that adds significance or purpose to somebody's life. That is, it helps the child be more independent and achieve a better **quality of life** (Carr, 2007). Carr (2007) defined quality of life as subjective well-being consisting of "meaningful gains in the areas of material well-being, health and safety, social well-being, leisure and recreation, and autonomy" (p. 4). Although this way of looking at outcomes may be too abstract when discussing program planning for young children, it is important for families to begin early to think about the scope of intervention and the life goals and dreams they have for their children. Even when children are very young, it is important to help families consider the important outcomes (e.g., belonging, having friends, happiness, good health) that they want for their child, rather than becoming overly focused on the types of discrete skills often addressed by early, intensive behavioral intervention programs.

Identification of potential skills or outcomes for a child starts with a sound assessment to determine what the child needs to learn. A **curriculum-based assessment (CBA)** provides the type of information needed to develop a comprehensive program. A CBA identifies functional skills across multiple developmental domains (i.e., adaptive, communication, cognitive, social, and motor) that are necessary for activities common in early childhood (Bagnato, Neisworth, & Munson, 1997). Several commercially available assessments include an evaluation component that is criterion-referenced and also linked to a curriculum. An example of a CBA is the *Assessment, Evaluation, and Programming System* (AEPS; Bricker, 2002).

The use of a CBA will allow the intervention team to identify skills that are useful and immediately relevant to the child's life (Macy, Bricker, & Squires, 2005). Although CBAs exist that are developed specifically for use with students with ASD and related disorders (e.g., ABLLS; Partington & Sundberg, 1998), it is possible to use an assessment developed for a more general population as the core assessment and supplement with checklists designed to assess core deficit areas for students with ASD (e.g., Schwartz et al., 2004).

Project DATA: An Example of a High-Quality Early Intervention Program for Children With ASD

In 1997, at the University of Washington, we opened the doors to Project DATA (Developmentally Appropriate Treatment for Autism) with the help of a Department of Education, Office of Special Education, model demonstration grant. We have been running continually since and are now funded by a combination of school district tuition and private contributions (Schwartz et al., 2004; Schwartz et al., 2013).

Project DATA was designed to meet a need that we had noticed in our community: How could we help school districts meet the needs of young children with ASD and their families in a manner that was effective, acceptable to all parties, and sustainable? The project was developed to combine the best practices from ABA behavior analysis and early childhood special education into a program that recognized the unique learning characteristics and support needs of children with ASD and also recognized that children with ASD are children first.

Integrated Early Childhood Program

Project DATA consists of five components, as illustrated in Figure 4.1. The core component is an integrated early childhood program. We want every child with ASD to have opportunities to interact successfully with typically developing children. To be successful, the interactions may need to be planned and supported systematically. This component is not just about being with typically developing children; it is about interacting with and developing relationships with typically developing children. To achieve this, preschoolers in Project DATA attend an integrated preschool classroom for about 12 hours a week.

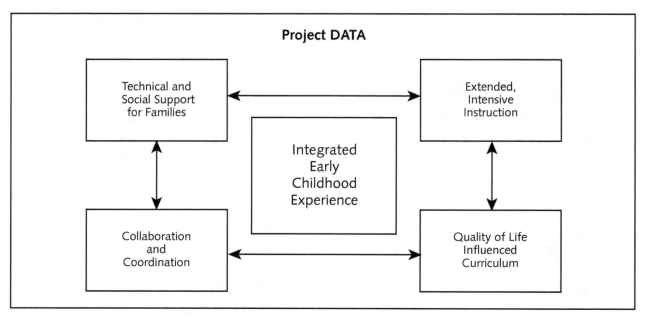

Figure 4.1. Components of project DATA.

In order to provide opportunities for the children with ASD to interact successfully with their typically developing peers, the preschool environments pay special attention to:

- Structuring the classroom environment to promote independence, participation, and successful interactions with typically developing peers

- Developing a consistent schedule and using it

- Creating the need to communicate with adults and peers

- Using children's preferred materials and activities to promote engagement

- Providing embedded and explicit instruction on valued skills

- Providing frequent reinforcement and developing effective motivation systems

Structuring the classroom environment to promote independence, participation, and successful interactions with typically developing peers. One of the primary considerations of an effective program for young children with ASD is to design the environment so as to prevent problem behaviors, promote engagement and participation, and facilitate successful interactions with typically developing peers. Because children with ASD are children first, the first step in structuring a high-quality environment is to ensure attention to the overall classroom environment, for all children.

Recommended practices for early childhood environments highlight the importance of the physical aspects of a learning environment, including the availability of developmentally and age-appropriate materials, the use of a consistent schedule of routines, and the presence of responsive adults and peers (Bredekamp & Copple, 1997; Sandall, McLean, & Smith, 2005). However, the components that comprise a high-quality early childhood environment for all young children may not be sufficient for children with ASD. Therefore, it is also important to take into consideration high-quality environments, as defined by early childhood professional groups (e.g., National Association for the Education of Young Children [www.naeyc.org] and the Division of Early Childhood of the Council for Exceptional Children [www.dec-sped.org]).

Some key characteristics of environmental design that are integrated into these classrooms include clearly defined areas of the classroom that reflect the activity to be conducted and that can be observed from everywhere in the classroom; a well-designed traffic pattern with no obvious obstacles; centers and activities that are interesting, relevant, and engaging; centers with adequate, age-appropriate materials; activities that promote and perhaps even require peer interaction; materials that are well organized and in good working order; and materials that are rotated frequently (Schwartz et al., 2002).

Developing a consistent schedule and following it. Many classrooms or intervention settings use schedules that outline the different activities children will participate in each day. In order to provide a child with ASD a comprehensible environment, a schedule of daily activities should be available in a format that is understandable to the child. For example, using pictures and symbols in addition to words may increase a child's understanding. Also, for a younger child, showing him an object that he or she associates with a common activity or routine can facilitate comprehension of what is coming next.

A schedule alone may not be meaningful to a child with ASD if the child is not taught to use it. Teachers need to refer to the schedule frequently and consistently and use it to teach the classroom routine, cue transitions, and teach children to understand changes to the routine. A variety of strategies are useful for **cueing** a child that a change is about to occur (i.e., timers, counting, singing songs, etc.). Again, whatever strategy is utilized will only be effective if the child is taught the purpose and meaning of the transition cue.

It is important to remember that schedules are not panaceas and that, used incorrectly, a schedule may end up making a child with ASD more rigid. Schedules must be used to help children navigate the environment and be independent. Children need to learn that changes to the schedule will occur and how to handle them. For example, a teacher can use a schedule to help children with ASD understand that specific activities will not be occurring on a given day (e.g., mark those activities with the international "no" symbol of a circle with a line through it) or that activities will be occurring in a different order. Schedules are instructional tools. That is, they are as useful as the instruction that accompanies them.

Creating the need to communicate with adults and peers. The classroom environment can promote opportunities and motivation to communicate. The number of opportunities that are available to help a child with ASD learn how to ask for things he wants, reject something he does not want, or initiate or respond to others is dependent on how the environment supports and, perhaps, demands those communicative behaviors.

All children who participate in Project DATA use a functional communication system. While our goal is to help all children develop functional speech, children who are not yet verbal are taught to use the Picture Exchange Communication System (PECS) (Frost & Bondy, 1994) across all school, home, and community settings. We view every classroom activity as a language-learning and -using opportunity. For instance, snack time provides an excellent opportunity for a child to learn how to ask for something he wants (i.e., favorite food), reject something she does not want (i.e., food she dislikes), and respond to the request of a peer. This can be accomplished by the use of certain strategies, such as an adult or peer regulating access to certain food items, or by providing small portions of a preferred food so that a child will have multiple opportunities to ask for what she wants. Children with ASD are also put in charge of snack items, a wonderful opportunity to work on receptive language when the child must respond to his classmates who are asking for orange slices or other snack items. Finally, across all activities, students are required to use communicative behavior to request preferred materials and activities and to control their environment. These communicative opportunities add up across the day to provide multiple opportunities to respond, which is essential in language acquisition (Hart & Risley, 1995).

Using preferred materials and activities to promote engagement. Systematically teaching children with ASD to engage in play or learning activities independently is an important goal of the preschool portion of Project DATA. To achieve this outcome, we identify materials and activities that children find interesting and make them available as part of classroom activities (McGee, Daly, Izeman, Mann, & Risley, 1991). Within the classroom, we ensure that there are preferred items for every child, and that within every activity center there is a range of materials that will engage the child with the most severe disabilities and that will challenge the most capable child.

Providing embedded and explicit instruction on valued skills. Recommended practices for young children with ASD emphasize the importance of systematic instruction on core areas of need related to autism (NRC, 2001). To promote the most optimal and generalized outcomes, such instruction needs to take place across settings, activities, people, and materials. It requires that teachers and interventionists have knowledge of different techniques to teach specific skills and are able to assess whether or not the child is making adequate progress using the selected technique so that changes can be made if progress is not sufficient.

Teachers in the preschool must plan what is going to be taught, where and how the instruction will occur, and how the child's progress will be assessed. To achieve such high frequency of instruction and data collection, teachers in the Project DATA classrooms develop an activity matrix that outlines the instructional needs for all the students in their classroom (Sandall & Schwartz, 2008). The purpose of an activity matrix is to use a grid to plan when specially designed instruction will be provided and when data collection on specific targeted skills and behaviors will occur.

Providing frequent reinforcement and developing effective motivation systems. A common characteristic of children with ASD is that they do not take advantage of the social rewards that are available to others for behaving in certain ways (Myles, 2005). They often fail to pick up important information that is communicated by adults and peers through a variety of unstated social cues or rules, and even if aware of the social rules, they may not be motivated by the social contingencies present to follow the rules. However, children with ASD respond extremely well to positive reinforcement. Therefore, systematic selection of reinforcers (i.e., reinforcer assessment) and contingent application of reinforcement to change behavior or teach new skills are necessary (Horner, Carr, Strain, Todd, & Reed, 2002).

Reinforcers come in many forms, but they always serve the same function: increasing the probability of a behavior happening again. For example, if a child with ASD points to a cup of juice, looks at the adult, and vocalizes, and the adult gives him juice, the behaviors of looking, pointing, and vocalizing are being reinforced and are more likely to happen again. However, if the child asks for juice, one teacher says no, the child begins to cry, and another teacher presents the child with juice to "help him calm down," crying is being reinforced.

When starting out in a preschool classroom, the items or activities that function as reinforcers for a child may be limited. (Remember, if an item or activity does not increase the probability of the behavior happening again, it is not a reinforcer, even if teachers think it is a preferred item.) Therefore, early in a child's preschool career, we are more likely to use more artificial (e.g., items that are unrelated to the task) reinforcers. These may include a favorite toy, stickers, bubbles, or food.

As children learn to participate in more activities and are reinforced by more items and social praise from the teacher, we attempt to use more natural reinforcers. **Natural reinforcers** are those that are logically related to the task at hand. For example, if a child wants to go outside and is standing at a closed door and says "open," opening the door and letting the child go outside is a natural reinforcer. Natural reinforcers are often the most powerful type of reinforcer because the child's motivation is high at that moment to achieve that specific outcome. Although natural reinforcers may be more acceptable in preschool classrooms, the rule in the Project DATA classroom is to use whatever type and amount of reinforcement that is needed to promote skill development and appropriate behavior.

Extended, Intensive Instruction

The second component of our program is extended, intensive instruction. Three days a week, Project DATA has extended school days. During this time children receive additional, explicit instruction on IEP objectives and on other behaviors that will help them be successful in the classroom, home, and the community. Instruction may be provided one-on-one or in small groups. The size of instructional groups and the instructional strategies used depend on the child, the objective being worked on, and the child's progress as measured by daily data collection. This component adds approximately 12 hours a week of time at school for every child. In addition, we ask parents to work with their child at home for a minimum of five hours a week.

Technical and Social Support

The third component of Project DATA is technical and social support for families. All families receive a monthly home visit and are required to participate in at least six hours of educational programming every year. Also, the first year children are in the program, parents are required to participate in a class on teaching basic skills. In subsequent years parents can participate in Project DATA-run educational classes on specific topics (e.g., play or teaching communication skills) or participate in other educational opportunities available in the community (e.g., the Autism Society of Washington conference).

Collaboration and Coordination of Services

The next component is collaboration and coordination across services. Almost every family with whom we work receives some type of family-negotiated service for their child with ASD. A family-negotiated service is defined as a therapeutic service that the school district does not pay for. Services may include speech therapy, home-based behavioral programming, or horseback-riding therapy. Once a year we attempt to hold a meeting of all the therapeutic providers for the child and the parents. The purpose of these meetings is to foster communication and collaboration, not to do joint planning or evaluation. During the planning meeting we also address issues of transition for children moving out of our program. Transitions are difficult for all children and families, but they can be especially stressful for children with ASD and their families. Therefore, we work with the school district, the preschool, and the family to ensure that adequate planning occurs to facilitate a smooth transition. This may include teaching skills specific to the new environment (e.g., carrying lunch on a tray), transferring visual supports, and providing an opportunity for the child to visit the new school and meet his new teacher a few days before school starts.

Quality-of-Life Influenced Curriculum

The final component of Project DATA is planning for and implementing a Quality-of-Life Influenced Curriculum. This part of the model acknowledges that children with ASD are children first, and that the primary outcome for any child who participates in Project DATA should be an improved quality of life. **Quality of life** is defined differently by every family and includes skills and behaviors from every developmental domain. In Project DATA, we are committed to working with families to help them and their children acquire the skills and behaviors that they need to participate fully in their family and community.

Summary and Conclusions

This chapter focused on the importance of early intervention. We specifically highlighted a range of recommended intervention services and examples of how to translate these recommendations into classroom practice. Project DATA is only one example of what effective early intervention services can look like for children with ASD. Project DATA has been extremely successful. Over 50% of the children leave our program and are placed in inclusive kindergarten programs (Schwartz et al., 2013). In addition, parents and school officials have been extremely satisfied with the program, and many school districts in the state are implementing local versions of an extended-day program. The important thing to remember is that there is no one right way to educate children with ASD, and a program is only successful if a child is making progress.

Tips for Practical Application

✓ Early and accurate identification is the first step towards providing high-quality early intervention to all children with ASD and their families, regardless of cultural and linguistic diversity, social class, or geography.

✓ Know the early signs or red flags of ASD and don't hesitate to make a referral for assessment. Some helpful resources are firstsigns.org, autismspeaks.org, and cdc.gov/ncbddd/autism/actearly/.

✓ Educators who suspect a child has ASD should be actively involved with parents in the diagnostic process and be encouraged to ask questions regarding the procedures used to arrive at a diagnosis.

✓ Help families make the transition to services in their local community by identifying potential service providers and providing temporary support to the family until they can enlist support and technical assistance from other professional sources.

✓ Even if a child has not received a formal evaluation or diagnosis but is suspected to be at risk for an ASD, intervention focusing on social development and communication should begin right away.

✓ An effective early intervention program for young children with ASD must include the following key elements:

- Sufficient hours and intensity of services

- Comprehensible environments with access to typical peers

- Specialized curriculum with an appropriate scope and sequence that addresses the core areas of ASD

- Family involvement

- Problem-solving approach to challenging behaviors

- Appropriate evaluation tools to monitor progress through systematic data keeping

- Planned opportunities for peer socialization

✓ Fundamental skills to address in an early intervention program include teaching young children to follow simple directions, imitate, communicate their wants and needs, and perform basic self-care skills.

✓ Other skills or meaningful outcomes to address must take into consideration the individual child's strengths and challenges, priorities of the family, and existing data based on a careful assessment of learning and development across multiple domains (i.e., communication, social, cognitive, adaptive, and motor).

✓ There is no one best approach to teaching all children with ASD. However, there are many educational and behavioral interventions that have demonstrated effectiveness in improving developmental outcomes for children with ASD.

Chapter Highlights

- There is no "typical" child with ASD; there can be dramatic differences in abilities, preferences, needs, and delays.

- There is overwhelming evidence of the effectiveness and importance of early detection and intervention for children with ASD.

- While research indicates ASD can be reliably diagnosed at 2 years of age, the current average age of diagnosis in the United States is 4-5 years of age. For children who are culturally and linguistically different, diagnosis may be even later.

- Some of the best examples of integrating the two strands (improving the accuracy of the screening and diagnostic tools used and influencing policy and practice to get these tools implemented) may be found in the work of organizations such as Autism Speaks (http://www.autismspeaks.org), the web site **First Signs** (www.firstsigns.org.), and the Centers for Disease Control and Prevention (CDC), Learn the signs. Act Early Campaign (http://www.cdc.gov/ncbddd/actearly/).

- For diagnosis at an early age, most families are referred to a psychologist, developmental pediatrician, psychiatrist, or neurologist for a full evaluation; however, finding professionals who are trained and experienced in diagnosing ASD is difficult in many communities.

- Another avenue for diagnosis is the educational system; however, in many cases children are classified as having a developmental delay rather than ASD.

- It is important to provide families with information on intervention services and community supports after a diagnosis of ASD.

- Parents need to be made aware that ASD is a life-long disorder and that there is no way to predict how an individual child will respond to intervention.

- The authors suggest that, rather than focusing on what program is the "best," the focus should be on what is known about the essential elements of effective programs, including:
  o Sufficient hours and intensity of services
  o Comprehensible environments with access to typical peers
  o Specialized curriculum with an appropriate scope and sequence
  o Family involvement
  o Problem-solving approach to challenging behaviors
  o Appropriate evaluation tools for monitoring progress

- Families need to ask questions before enrolling their children in early intervention programs to ensure the program matches what they see as outcomes for the child, addresses family desires for the child, matches family comfort levels, and has proof of effectiveness.

- Outcome-oriented frameworks of intervention refer to a problem-solving process that is ongoing and based on the child's needs at any given time.

- Meaningful outcomes for children with ASD should improve the child's quality of life.

- Curriculum-based assessment (CBA) is one means of identifying potential skills or outcomes for young children.

- Project DATA, an early intervention program at the University of Washington, is an example of a high-quality early intervention program for children with ASD.

- The core component of Project DATA is an integrated early childhood program with planned and systematic interactions between children with ASD and their typically developing peers. The program emphasizes:
  - Structuring the classroom environment to promote independence, participation, and successful interactions with typically developing peers
  - Developing a consistent schedule and following it
  - Creating the need to communicate with adults and peers
  - Using preferred materials and activities to promote engagement
  - Providing embedded and explicit instruction on valued skills
  - Providing frequent reinforcement and developing effective motivation systems

- Other foundational components of Project DATA are as follows:
  - Extended intensive instruction
  - Technical and social support
  - Collaboration and coordination of services
  - A quality of life-influenced curriculum

Chapter Review Questions

1. What is meant by a "spectrum disorder"?

2. Why is early intervention so important for children diagnosed with ASD?

3. What are some of the major issues surrounding early identification of ASD (including early diagnosis and referral)?

4. What are the developmental red flags that may indicate ASD in early childhood?

5. Why is it important to provide families with information on intervention services and community supports as part of the assessment process? What type of information should be shared?

6. What are the key features of effective programs for young children with ASD?

7. What types of questions do families need to ask when selecting intervention programs for their young children with ASD?

8. What is meant by the term "outcome-oriented framework"?

9. How might a family decide on meaningful outcomes for their child with ASD?

10. What is a curriculum-based assessment (CBA) and why is it useful?

11. What are the five components of Project DATA?

12. What are the areas to which Project DATA preschool environments pay particular attention?

References

American Psychiatric Association. (2013). *Diagnostic and statistical manual for mental disorders* (5th ed.). Washington, DC: Author.

Bagnato, S. J., Neisworth, J. T., & Munson, S. M. (1997). *Linking assessment and early intervention.* Baltimore: Paul H. Brookes. Boulware, G., Schwartz, I. S., Sandall, S. R., & McBride, B. J. (2006). Project DATA for toddlers: An inclusive approach to very young children with ASD. *Topics in Early Childhood Special Education, 26*(2), 94-105.

Braiden, H., Bothwell, J. & Duffy, J. (2010). Parents' experience of the diagnostic process for autistic spectrum disorders. *Child Care in Practice, 16*(4), 377-389.

Bredekamp, S., & Copple, C. (1997). *Appropriate practice in early childhood programs* (rev. ed.). Washington, DC: National Association for the Education of Young Children.

Bricker, D. (2002). *Assessment, evaluation, and programming system for infants and young children: AEPS measurement from birth to six years.* Baltimore, MD: Paul H. Brookes.

Carr, E. G. (2007). The expanding vision of positive behavior support: Research perspectives on happiness, helpfulness, and hopefulness. *Journal of Positive Behavior Interventions, 9,* 3-14.

Carr, E. G., Dunlap, G., Horner, R. H., Koegel, R. L., Turnbull, A. P., Sailor, W., et al. (2002). Positive behavior support: Evolution of an applied science. *Journal of Positive Behavior Interventions, 4,* 16-20.

Carr, E. G., & Durrand, V. M. (1985). Reducing behavior problems through functional communication training. *Journal of Applied Behavior Analysis, 18,* 111-126.

Centers for Disease Control and Prevention (CDC). http://www.cdc.gov/ncbddd/actearly/.

Chakrabarti, S., & Fombonne, E. (2001). Pervasive developmental disorders in preschool children. *Journal of the American Medical Association, 285,* 3093-3099.

Dahle, K. B. (2003). The clinical and educational systems: Differences and similarities. *Focus on Autism and Other Developmental Disabilities, 18*(4), 238-246.

Dawson, G., Rogers, S., Munson, J., Smith, M., Winter, J., Greenson, J., & Varley, J. (2010). Randomized, controlled trial of an intervention for toddlers with autism: The Early Start Denver Model. *Pediatrics, 125*(1), e17-e23.

Dunlap, G. (1999). Consensus, engagement, and family involvement for young children with autism. *The Journal of the Association for Persons with Severe Handicaps, 24,* 222-225.

Frost, I., & Bondy, A. (1994). *The Picture Exchange Communication System training manual.* Cherry Hill, NJ: PECS.

Harris, S. L., & Handelman, J. S. (2000). Age and IQ at intake as predictors of placement for young children with autism: A four-to-six-year follow-up. *Journal of Autism and Developmental Disorders, 30,* 137-142.

Hart, B., & Risley, T. R. (1995). *Meaningful differences in the everyday experience of young American children.* Baltimore, MD: Paul H. Brookes.

Horner, R. H., Carr, E. G., Strain, P. S., Todd, A. W., & Reed, H. K. (2002). Problem behavior interventions for young children with autism: A research synthesis. *Journal of Autism and Developmental Disorders, 32(5),* 423-446.

Howlin, P. (2000). Outcome in adult life for more able individuals with autism or Asperger syndrome. *Autism, 4*, 63-83.

Hume, K., Bellini, S., & Pratt, C. (2005). The usage and perceived outcomes of early intervention and early childhood programs for young children with autism spectrum disorder. *Topics in Early Childhood Special Education, 25*(4), 195-207.

Jacobson, J. (2000). System and cost research issues in treatments for people with autistic disorders. *Journal of Autism and Developmental Disorders, 30*, 585-593.

Lord, C. (1995). Follow-up of two-year-olds referred for possible autism. *Journal of Child Psychology and Psychiatry, 36*, 1365-1382.

Lovaas, O. I. (1987). Behavioral treatment and normal educational and intellectual functioning in young autistic children. *Journal of Consulting and Clinical Psychology, 55*, 3-9.

Mandell, D. S., Wiggins, L. D., Carpenter, L. A., Daniels, J., DiGuiseppi, C., Durkin, M. S., et al. (2009). Racial/ethnic disparities in the identification of children with autism spectrum disorders. *American Journal of Public Health, 99*, 493-498.

Macy, M. G., Bricker, D. D., & Squires, J. K. (2005). Validity and reliability of a curriculum-based assessment approach to determine eligibility for Part C Services. *Journal of Early Intervention, 28*, 1-16.

McGee, G. G., Daly, T., Izeman, S. G., Mann, L., & Risley, T. R. (1991). Use of classroom materials to promote preschool engagement. *Teaching Exceptional Children, 23*, 44-47.

Moore, V., & Goodson, S. (2003). How well does early diagnosis of autism stand the test of time. Follow-up study of children assessed for autism at age 2 and development of an early diagnostic service. *Autism, 7*, 47-63.

Myles, B. S. (2005). *Children and youth with Asperger Syndrome: Strategies for success in inclusive settings.* Thousand Oaks, CA: Corwin Press.

National Autism Center. http://www.nationalautismcenter.org/nsp/history.php

National Professional Development Center on ASD. http://autismpdc.fpg.unc.edu/

National Research Council. (2001). *Educating children with autism.* Committee on Educational Interventions for Children with Autism. Catherine Lord and James P. McGee (Eds.). Division of Behavioral and Social Sciences and Education. Washington, DC: National Academy Press.

Odom, S. L., Boyd, B. A., Hall, L. J., & Hume, K. (2010). Evaluation of comprehensive treatment models for individuals with autism spectrum disorders. *Journal of Autism and Developmental Disorders, 40*(4), 425-436.

Partington, J., & Sundberg, M. (1998). *The Assessment of Basic Language and Learning Skills: An assessment, curriculum guide, and tracking system for children with autism or other developmental disabilities.* Danville, CA: Behavior Analysts.

Pinto-Martin, J., & Levy, S. E. (2004). Early diagnosis of autism spectrum disorders. *Current Treatment Options in Neurology, 6*, 391-400.

Reichow, B., Barton, E. E., Boyd, B. A., & Hume, K. (2012). Early intensive behavioral intervention (EIBI) for young children with autism spectrum disorders (ASD). *Cochrane Database Syst Rev.* Oct 17;10:CD009260

Rogers, S. (1999). Intervention for young children with autism: From research to practice. *Infants and Young Children, 12*, 1-16.

Sanndall, S. R., Ashmun, J. W., Schwartz, I. S., Davis, C. A., Williams, P., Leon-Guerrero, R., ... & McBride, B. J. (2011). Differential response to a school-based program for young children with ASD. *Topics in Early Childhood Special Education, 33,* doi:10.1177/0271121411403166

Sandall, S. R., McLean, M. E., & Smith, B. J. (2005). *DEC recommended practices in early intervention/early childhood special education.* Longmont, CO: Sopris West.

Sandall, S., & Schwartz, I. S. (2008). *Building blocks for teaching preschoolers with special needs.* Baltimore, MD: Brookes Publishing.

Schopler, E., & Van Bourgondien, M. (1991). Treatment and Education of Autistic and related Communication-handicapped CHildren (TEACCH). In N. Giddan & J. Giddan (Eds.), *Autistic adults at Bittersweet Farms* (pp. 85-94). Binghamton, NY: Haworth.

Schwartz, I. S., Garfinkle, A., & Davis, C. (2002). Arranging preschool environments to facilitate valued social and educational outcomes. In M. Shinn, H. Walker, & G. Stoner (Eds.), *Interventions for academic and behavior problems II: Preventive and remedial approaches* (pp. 455-468). Bethesda, MD: National Association of School Psychologists.

Schwartz, I. S., Sandall, S. R., McBride, B. J., & Boulware, G. L. (2004). Project DATA (Developmentally appropriate treatment for autism): An inclusive, school-based approach to educating children with autism. *Topics in Early Childhood Special Education, 24,* 156-168.

Schwartz, I. S., Thomas, C. J., McBride, B., & Sandall, S. R. (2013). A school-based preschool program for children with ASD: A quasi-experimental assessment of child change in Project DATA. *School Mental Health.* doi: 10.1007/s12310-013-9103-7.

Smith, T., Groen, A. D., & Wynn, J. W. (2000). Randomized trial of intensive early intervention for children with pervasive developmental disorder. *American Journal on Mental Retardation, 105*(4), 269-285.

Stahmer, A., Schreibman, L., & Cunningham, A. (2011). Toward a technology of treatment individualization for young children with autism spectrum disorders. *Brain Research, 1380,* 229-239.

Stahmer, A. C., & Ingersoll, B. (2004). Inclusive programming for toddlers with autism spectrum disorders: Outcomes from the Children's Toddler School. *Journal of Positive Behavior Interventions, 6*(2), 67-82.

Stone, W. L., Lee, E. B., Ashford, L., Brissie, J., Hepburn, S. L., Coonrod, E. E., et al. (1999). Can autism be diagnosed accurately in children under 3 years? *Journal of Child Psychiatry, 40,* 219-226.

Strain, P. S., & Bovey, E. (2011). Randomized controlled trial of the LEAP model of early intervention for young children with autism spectrum disorders. *Topics in Early Childhood Special Education,* 133-154.

Strain, P. S., Schwartz, I. S., & Barton, E. (2011). Providing interventions for young children with ASD: what we still need to accomplish. *Topics in Early Childhood Special Education, 33,* 321-332. doi: 10.1177/1053815111429970.

Tsatsanis, K. D. (2003). Outcome research in Asperger syndrome and autism. *Child and Adolescent Psychiatric Clinics of North America, 12,* 47-63.

Volkmar, F. R., Lord, C., Bailey, A., Schultz, R. T., & Klin, A. (2004). Autism and pervasive developmental disorders. *Journal of Child Psychology and Psychiatry, 45,* 135-170.

Wang, M., Mannan, H., Poston, D., Turnbull, A. P., & Summers, J. A. (2004). Parents' perceptions of advocacy activities and their impact on family quality of life. *Research and Practice for Persons with Severe Disabilities, 29*(2), 144-155.

Wolery, M., & Garfinkle, A. N. (2002). Measures in intervention research with young children who have autism. *Journal of Autism and Developmental Disorders, 32*, 463-478.

Wolfberg, P. J. (2004). Guiding children on the autism spectrum in peer play: Translating theory and research into effective and meaningful practice. *The Journal of Developmental and Learning Disorders, 8*, 7-25.

Zwaigenbaum, L., Bryson, S., Lord, C., Rogers, S., Carter, A., Carver L., et al. (2009). Clinical assessment and management of toddlers with suspected autism spectrum disorder: Insights from studies of high-risk infants. *Pediatrics, 123*, 1383-1391.

Learner Objectives

After reading this chapter, the learner should be able to:

- Describe what is meant by "social communication"

- State how theory of mind is involved in social language learning

- Explain what the chapter author believes can cause ineffective language intervention for individuals with autism

- Explain how interactive games assist infants in developing social communication

- Discuss why experiential learning is critical for brain development

- Describe the impact of autism on infants in terms of experiential learning and later brain development

- Define joint attention and explain its importance in developing social communication

- Explain the importance of intention reading to social-pragmatic theory

- Discuss how social-pragmatic theory provides an understanding of what goes wrong in the language acquisition process in autism

- Explain the importance of pragmatics in the acquisition of language

- Explain why social-pragmatic theory may be considered the "rule" in typical language development

- Provide examples of different pragmatic functions of words based on speaker intentions

- Define presuppositional knowledge and state how this area of pragmatics relates to communication

- List and describe the four conversational maxims

- Explain word-learning differences

- List and describe general considerations related to assessment of language development in terms of social pragmatics

- List and explain the ten principles of language intervention in autism

Chapter 5

Symbolic Communication: Common Pathways and Points of Departure

Diane Twachtman-Cullen

Several years ago I was consulting with a school district regarding a preschool child with ASD Level 1. Michael was not only very bright; he was also hyperlexic. He had a love of words for their own sake that was underscored by his favorite activity – writing strings of unrelated words on the chalkboard, which he would engage in obsessively if left on his own.

Despite his extensive vocabulary and the ability to speak, Michael rarely used his words to express his needs and desires. This prompted me to ask his teacher how he typically let her know if he wanted something. The teacher informed me that he would simply obtain whatever he wanted without asking, even if it meant having to climb on a chair to fetch something from a high shelf. Upon hearing this, a red flag immediately went up! Did Michael have a problem with obtaining attention or requesting, or both? Since these are important pragmatic functions of communication, I decided to investigate what he would do if we moved an enticing item from a lower shelf to a higher one and told him that he couldn't climb up to get it.

The first thing that Michael did was to walk over to the shelves and stare at the small letter board that he wanted. Next, he pointed to it. Although his teacher and I were close by, he neither tried to obtain our attention before pointing to the shelf, nor check back to see if we were looking at the place where he was pointing, both of which are important social-cognitive precursors to symbolic communication. In fact, Michael gave no indication whatsoever that he was intending to communicate with us. He simply continued to stare at and/or point to the letter board, as though those things alone would enable him to obtain it.

After a few moments, Michael tried to drag a chair over, in an effort to obtain the letter board himself. His teacher stopped him, saying that it was too dangerous to climb on the chair and adding that she would be happy

107

to get the item for him. Even though he had the ability to say the words, and was prompted several times by his teacher to use his words, Michael said nothing. On a few occasions, he walked a short distance away, only to come back to resume his vigil. Finally, he left the area in apparent despair. I thought that he had given up on the letter board, since there was nothing in his behavior to suggest otherwise. Instead, Michael walked directly over to a flip chart on the other side of the room, picked up a marker, wrote something down, and promptly walked away. His teacher and I walked across the room to see what he had written. To our amazement, Michael had written the word HELP, without the slightest regard for the people in his environment who could assist him, or even the knowledge that someone would have to read (be aware of) the word in order to act on it.

T his vignette poignantly illustrates the nature of the **communication deficit** commonly seen in autism – even when an individual has the ability to *say* words, in no way does that guarantee that he is able to *use* them to express his intentions (thoughts, feelings, wants, and needs). Stated differently, having lots of language (i.e., words) – as Michael clearly did – does not mean that the person with autism has the ability to use that language for **social communication** purposes; that is, to bring about an intended effect in the attentional and mental states of others so that they can act upon the perceived message.

If that has a decidedly **theory-of-mind** ring to it, it is precisely because communication and theory of mind are inextricably intertwined. That is, theory of mind may be thought of as the complex array of processes that constitute the social-cognitive underpinnings of **social language learning**. At its most basic level, it is the instinctive ability to know what is in another person's mind. According to Tomasello and Bates (2001),

> Linguistic communication is about discerning what other people intend for you to pay attention to or think about when they use a linguistic convention [symbol] and then, in complementary fashion, using those same conventions yourself to manipulate the intentional and mental states of other persons. (p. 4)

Michael could not do this, even though he had the ability to say and write words. He even chose an appropriate word to write on the easel – one that would have worked in his quest for the object if it had been directed at his teacher. What Michael's behavior demonstrated was that he lacked an understanding of the quintessential function of words; that is, that they are the purveyors of one's intentions (mental states) used for the purpose of influencing the mental states of others. In other words, Michael did not know that he could *use* his words as the "**symbolic currency**" (Sacks, 1989) to communicate his *intended* meaning to someone else. Indeed, Michael's pointing behavior was **proto-imperative** or self-referenced, as opposed to **proto-declarative** – that is, accompanied by social referencing behaviors intended to direct attention and/or share his focus of interest. Clearly, Michael did not have the basic *idea* of communication as a process by which to exchange meaning between two or more people who are engaged in the complementary enterprise of influencing each other's mental states.

Happé (1996) spoke eloquently to the linkage between theory of mind and communication when she stated that "to recognize and engage in ostensive (i.e., communicative) behavior it is vital to have some recognition of mental states such as intentions" (p. 76). Carter (1999) went even further, treating communication and theory of mind as one and the same entity by stating, "More than anything, autism is a defect of communication – an inability to share feelings, beliefs and knowledge with other people" (p. 141).

Michael's inability to use words is all the more dramatic because it stands in stark contrast to his impressive **lexicon**. His plight is all too common, albeit less obvious, among many children and adolescents with autism whose vocabularies are more meager. This is particularly true for individuals at the severe end of the autism continuum. Day in and day out, these individuals are told to *use their words,* as though the ability to do so is second nature. Or worse yet, suggesting that failure to use their words represents a willful or volitional act. Such exhortations make eminently clear a fundamental lack of understanding that the essence of language does not reside in the symbols themselves – that is, in merely having them – but in the *use* of those symbols for communication purposes (Kaye, 1982).

Recall that Michael, despite having a lexicon that was rich in **symbols**, lacked the knowledge to use those symbols to communicate his intent. Unfortunately, this lack of understanding of the difference between having symbols (words) in one's repertoire and using them to communicate sets up the individual for failure in language therapy, because unknowledgeable interventionists are likely to put the proverbial cart before the horse when it comes to the selection of language-learning targets. Specifically, they are likely to build the language "structure" by starting with the "roof" (i.e., vocabulary building), instead of constructing and fortifying the "foundation" by attending to the important social-cognitive precursors (e.g., joint attention) that set the stage for symbol use.

Joint attention may be thought of as a "meeting of minds." In other words, it is not merely two people simultaneously looking at the same thing, but two people sharing an understanding that they are attending to the same thing (Call & Tomasello, 2005). Hence, a major premise of this chapter is that inappropriate language intervention practices are largely the result of a lack of understanding of the language-learning process, in general, and a lack of awareness of how abnormalities in **interpersonal relatedness** and **social cognition** serve to restrict language development in children across all levels of ASD. Consequently, the goal of this chapter is to (a) examine both the relevant language-learning and autism research literature; (b) discuss the ways in which both research bases relate to one another; and (c) provide a framework for translating research into effective assessment and intervention practices that make sense for people on the autism spectrum.

The Critical Role of Experience in Communication and Language Development

It is well accepted that experience is a major player in brain development; it shapes the structure of the brain and influences connectivity (Greenough & Black, 1992; Landa, 2003; Schwartz & Begley, 2002). This, in turn, promotes learning. However, there has been a paradigmatic shift in our understanding of how experience shapes the neural architecture. Early on, the infant's brain was largely viewed as a **tabula rasa** – the so-called blank slate, as yet unaffected by the experiences that would later be etched upon it to coax brain development.

Current research into infants' brains does not support this theory, but runs in opposition to it. Specifically, it is currently held (and supported by research) that babies come into the world with an excess of **neurons** (Wingert

& Brant, 2005). This creates a dual, richly textured, and crucial role for experience that directly affects **brain connectivity**. Specifically, one's experiences (involvement in activities) promote new connections by laying down pathways in those areas of the brain that fuel the action required of the activity (Schwartz & Begley, 2002). In addition, in "use-it-or-lose-it" fashion, experience also "prunes" the brain by "allowing" unused neurons in other parts of the brain to die (Landa, 2003). Schwartz and Begley (2002) refer to this process as "survival of the busiest" to articulate the way in which environmental inputs (experience) create the refined neural architecture of the developing brain (see Chapter 2). An illustration may help to shed more light on this phenomenon.

Neurotypical infants have a very active "social life," readily engaging in the games of infancy with their parents/caregivers. The word *game* belies the importance of these activities, for they are the vehicles by which babies traverse the road to **symbolic communication**. For example, games such as peek-a-boo and pat-a-cake provide rich opportunities for attention and affect sharing. These behaviors are important social-cognitive precursors to the development of social communication, and they are major contributors to the infant's emerging capacity for joint attention (Wetherby, 2006). They also involve social reciprocity – the forerunner of mature turn taking that will eventually mark two-way, dialogic exchanges. The games of infancy also enable the infant to regulate the interaction, establish predictability, and anticipate what comes next. Most of all, these games enmesh the infant in a tapestry of **interpersonal relatedness** that primes the system to eventually engage the **subjective states** of others.

There is impressive research evidence to support the role of experience in brain development in both animal and human subjects. For example, Greenough and Black (1992) found that by putting geriatric rats into enriched environments in which they were able to interact with the stimulating accoutrements of the new milieu, it was possible to increase synaptic activity. With respect to human subjects, Bell and Fox (1994) noted a direct relationship between behavior and brain activity. Specifically, they found "an increase in metabolic activity in the areas of the brain having to do with emotional regulation, interaction, and sequencing *at the time that infants are involved* [italics added] in choice making, search behavior, and reciprocal interactions" (p. 319) such as those required in the games of infancy. Schwartz and Begley (2002) strike a cautionary note, however, stating that while "experience molds the brain, it molds only an attending brain" (p. 224). In other words, passivity – or for that matter, forced participation in activities, *without active attention* – is not sufficient for brain development.

I would take this cautionary note one step further to underscore the importance of actual participation in activities. For example, regarding the Greenough and Black (1992) study, it is difficult to imagine that the rat subjects would have had an increase in synaptic activity if they had only been allowed to watch other rats experiencing the various accoutrements of the enriched environment without engaging in the action themselves.

As the above studies demonstrate, the effects of **experiential learning** on brain development are relevant to individuals with autism, given that experience fuels social cognition and communication. Hence, the impoverishment of these experiences in children with autism is likely a key factor in their social-cognitive, communicative, and language deficits. Moreover, since problems in attention are very much at issue for individuals on the spectrum, it is not uncommon to see children with autism in language-learning situations in which they are unengaged. Worse yet, it is also not uncommon to see these children in "forced" language-learning situations that cause discomfort and promote resistance.

To more fully understand the plight of the child with autism with respect to experiential learning, it is necessary to consider the issue of quality of experience, since not all experiences are created equal. It is well known that babies with autism do not readily engage in the games of infancy as do their typically developing peers (Wolfberg, 2009). Hence, they miss out on rich opportunities to engage in **emotional regulation**, affect and attention sharing, anticipation, and reciprocity with their caregivers, all of which lead to the development of joint attention and set the stage for symbolic communication.

In contrast, given their preference for sameness, babies with autism are more apt to engage in **self-regulatory** and repetitive behaviors, such as rocking, twirling, or flapping – behaviors that are distinctly unilateral and non-social. Given that experience both powers and prunes the developing brain, it is reasonable to speculate that the neural landscape of a child with autism would likely look very different from that of a neurotypical child. Schwartz and Begley (2002) lend support to this position, stating that "the **plasticity** of the young brain is based on the overabundance of synapses, which allows only those that are used to become part of enduring circuits that underlie thinking, feeling, responding, and behaving" (p. 129). In view of the distinctly non-social behavior that fires up circuits in the brains of children with autism, and in deference to the pruning process, it is likely that the capacity for affect and attention sharing, as well as other social-cognitive behaviors, does not fare well in their brain development.

Consequently, while all of an individual's experiences have the capacity to influence brain development and learning (Schwartz & Begley, 2002), the richness and extent of that influence is related to the quality of the experience itself. For example, it is well established that when typically developing children reach early childhood and learn to play in a more sophisticated manner, children with autism lag behind (see Chapter 8). This is likely due, at least in part, to differences in the quality of their early play experiences. Consider, for example, what a neurotypical boy can take in from the simple but high-quality act of playing with a toy car. He can learn that the doors and trunk open and close; that he needs to push the car up an incline, but that he can let it go down a hill by itself. He can also learn that he can make the car go fast or slow and that he can make it bump into things or stop. Contrast these rich opportunities for brain growth and concept development with the experience of the girl with autism who turns a toy car over in her hand and repetitively spins one wheel ad infinitum. Which child do you suppose has the most appropriate brain circuits firing and the best chance for **concept development**? Or, perhaps more to the point, which child's pattern of evolving neural architecture will better prepare him or her for entry into the world of symbolic communication (Hobson, 2005)?

All in all, the interactions seen in the games of infancy involve attention and affect sharing, and provide some of the major building blocks of interpersonal relatedness. They also set the stage for joint attention and intention reading, both of which are foundational to symbol use.

The Pivotal Role of Joint Attention

Joint attention is critically important to communication and language development in typically developing children (Baldwin, 1995; Bruner, 1983; Tomasello, 2003; Tomasello & Farrar, 1986; Tomasello & Todd, 1983; Tomasello, Mannle, & Kruger, 1986). It is also well established that joint attention deficits are stable characteristics of children with autism (Leekam, 1993; Lewy & Dawson, 1992; Mundy, Sigman, & Kasari, 1990; Wetherby, Prizant, & Hutchinson, 1998). As such, there is typically either an absence or paucity of social behaviors, such as gaze following, proto-declarative (social) pointing, and showing/offering gestures in this population. Since all of these behaviors are suggestive of the child's growing awareness of the need to engage other minds, they are considered to be early behavioral indicators of the child's developing theory of mind. Hence, the absence or paucity of this type of behavior in children with autism is one of the earliest indicators of their theory-of-mind difficulty.

Recent brain research evidence supports the close relationship between joint attention and theory of mind. Specifically, Williams, Waiter, Perra, Whiten, and Perrett (2005) found that joint attention was associated with activation of an area of the brain that has consistently been shown to be activated during mental-state **attribution** tasks. This finding led these researchers to conclude that the neural substrate of joint attention also serves a mentalizing function. In other words, joint attention and the ability to read mental states (theory of mind) are housed in the same area of the brain.

Research has also revealed similarities in the way in which joint attention impacts both children with autism and those who are neurotypical. Studies of typically developing children by Tomasello and Todd (1983) and Tomasello et al. (1986) have revealed a "very high" correlation between time spent in joint attention activities with their mothers and children's vocabulary size. Further, investigating whether language and communication development in toddlers with autism was related to changes in affective and joint attention development, Landa, Holman, Sullivan, and Cleary (2005) found that not only did the children demonstrate clinically significant change in language and social domains, but the greatest language gains were observed in toddlers with the strongest pre-treatment joint attention skills. In a similar vein, Siller and Sigman (2002) noted that the presence of joint attention in children with autism in their early years had predictive value for language development in their adolescent years. According to Twachtman-Cullen and Twachtman-Reilly (2007), these findings suggest that:

> Joint attention and vocabulary size are related in children with autism in the same manner in which they are related in typically developing children, suggesting that the same principles governing language acquisition in typically developing children also govern language acquisition in children with autism. (Based on studies by Loveland & Landry, 1986; Mundy et al., 1990)

The importance of this finding cannot be overstated, since it speaks to the relevance – heretofore largely unacknowledged – of the language development literature for understanding the communication and language deficits seen in individuals with autism. Moreover, it underscores the need for intervention practices that address the crucial role of joint attention in language acquisition.

Tomasello (2003) speaks eloquently to the importance of joint attention in language development, assigning a "foundational" role to it in the establishment of **intentional communication**. According to Tomasello (2003), the joint attentional frame is the milieu within which both the child and the adult establish the "common ground" within which the child eventually learns to infer the adult's communicative intentions. (The topic of intention reading will be elaborated in the next section of this chapter.)

Hobson's (2005) affective theory of joint attention fits well with Tomasello's views, positing that joint attention involves an active process of sharing attention, rather than the passive act of simply looking at what someone else happens to be attending to at the time. Hence, the critical variable in this sharing is *awareness*. Specifically,

The infant needs to be aware of the object or event *as* the focus of the other person's attention – and in addition, for full 'jointness,' he or she should share awareness of the sharing of the focus, something that often entails *sharing an attitude* [italics added] towards the thing or event in question. (Hobson, 2005, p. 185)

Two things come to mind with respect to this description. First, joint attention evolves over time, reaching "full jointness" only when the child becomes fully aware of the **shared focus**. This would seem to be a kind of "metaawareness" or an awareness of the awareness. Second, this description by Hobson propels joint attention into the rarefied atmosphere of **intersubjective engagement**, or the ability to share and engage emotionally in the subjective (i.e., mental) states of others – hence, his reference to "sharing an attitude."

Recall once again the games of infancy and the rich opportunities they provide for attention and affect sharing, both of which are major contributors to joint attention and intersubjectivity. Consider, too, the missed opportunities for this type of engagement by children with autism when they "reject" such games as not enjoyable, or perhaps overstimulating, and hence, off-putting. Given the social-cognitive competencies that such experiences inspire, and their intimate relationship to later symbol use, the impoverishment of these types of experiences in children with autism will likely set in motion a negative cascading effect with respect to their language development.

To summarize, even though different theorists have posited contradictory interpretations of joint attention, there are many points on which there is general consensus, all of which are important regarding its critical role in language acquisition. Specifically,

- Joint attention, regardless of its origins, is fueled by experience (Leekam, 2005).

- Joint attention provides a rich milieu within which relatedness and emotional sharing may take place (Hobson, 2005).

- Intersubjectivity – that is, shared understanding – has its roots in joint attention (Rogoff, 1990; Tomasello, 2003).

- Joint attention sets the stage for intention reading and is intimately related to the development of symbolic communication (Mundy et al., 1990).

- Deficits in joint attention are among the most robust behavioral findings in autism.

Before considering the important role of intention reading in communication development, intersubjectivity – the "bridge" between joint attention and intention reading – needs further elaboration. Trevarthan (1980) acknowledged the role that the two concepts play in communication by defining intersubjectivity as "both recognition and control of cooperative intentions and joint patterns of awareness" (p. 530). Rogoff (1990) asserted that "communication presumes intersubjectivity" (p. 71), which she went on to describe as "shared understanding based on a common focus of attention and some shared presuppositions [judgments] that form the ground for communication" (p. 71). I would add that intention reading itself also presumes intersubjectivity – the shared understanding that is necessary for one to be able to read the intentions of others.

Social-Pragmatic Theory and Its Relevance in Autism

According to **social-pragmatic theory**, intention reading – that is, the ability of the child to "read" the adult's communicative intent – plays a critical role in language development. Indeed, intention reading may be understood as the gateway to symbolic communication. According to Tomasello (2001), central to social-pragmatic theory is the notion that understanding people as intentional agents is necessary for language acquisition (word learning) to take place. He further argues that "learning new words is dependent on young children's ability to perceive and comprehend adult intentions, and they do this using a wide array of social-pragmatic cues" (p. 114).

Tomasello and his colleagues carried out a number of ingenious experimental studies, all of which support his contention (Akhtar & Tomasello, 1996; Tomasello & Barton, 1994; Tomasello, Strosberg, & Akhtar, 1995). Tomasello offered the age at which first words develop as support for his position that language learning depends upon **intention reading**. For example, it is well known that in typical children, language acquisition (first words) begins around the time of, or just after, the child's first birthday. According to Tomasello (2001), the timing of this developmental milestone is highly significant, because symbol use depends upon the emergence of the following social-cognitive skills: gaze following, **social referencing**, and **imitative learning**, all of which "emerge in rough developmental synchrony" (p. 124). All of these skills are necessary for intention reading and symbol use. Thus, unlike other theories of language acquisition, social-pragmatic theory provides a compelling and eminently reasonable answer to the question of why language acquisition begins when it does, and not at an earlier time.

Social-pragmatic theory also seems to best account for all the pieces of the language-learning puzzle; that is, the social-cognitive elements that underpin communication and language development (affect and attention sharing, intersubjectivity, joint attention, and intention reading), and the way in which children typically learn language (in social-interactive, cultural contexts) (Tomasello, 2003; Tomasello & Bates, 2001). This final point is particularly important, and perhaps the defining feature that distinguishes social-pragmatic theory from all other theories of language development.

Tomasello (2001) provides the most comprehensive – indeed, compelling – view of how children learn language according to social-pragmatic theory:

> Young children are not engaged in a reflective cognitive task in which they are attempting to make correct mappings of word to world based upon adult input, but rather they are engaged in social interactions in which they are attempting to understand adult intentions – so as to make sense of the current situation. Having complied with adult instructions to experience a situation in a particular way in a given instance, children may then learn to produce the appropriate symbols for themselves when they wish for others to experience a situation in that same way – thus entering into the world of bi-directionally (intersubjectively) understood linguistic symbols. (pp. 112-113)

Social-pragmatic theory would also seem to provide a template for understanding what goes wrong in the language acquisition process in autism. Specifically, the social-cognitive deficits in the development of attention and **affect sharing**, joint attention, and intention reading likely give rise to the unique pattern of pragmatic impairments seen in individuals with autism. In addition, problems in the social-pragmatic realm also account for many of the communication and language deficits that individuals with autism exhibit; for example, literalness, which reflects difficulty with intentionality. To illustrate, if an individual with autism is asked, "Can you pass the salt?," she is likely to take the question literally and answer "Yes," missing entirely the speaker's intent, which is to obtain the salt.

Finally, of all the aspects of language that could be impaired – **semantic**, **syntactic**, or **pragmatic** – it is pragmatic impairment that constitutes the defining language deficit in autism (Lord & Paul, 1997; Wetherby, Schuler, & Prizant, 1997), cutting across age and ability levels (Tager-Flusberg, Joseph, & Folstein, 2001). Taking all of these factors into account, it seems that (a) a social-pragmatic approach to language development affords the most comprehensive understanding of the subtleties and complexities involved in the language-learning process; (b) social-pragmatic theory stands alone in offering a plausible explanation for the age of language acquisition; and (c) social-pragmatic theory has relevance for individuals with autism, given the developmental trajectory of their social-cognitive deficits and their unique pragmatic profiles. Indeed, I would argue that social-pragmatic theory fits in so well with what is known about the way in which neurotypical children acquire language that it may be construed as the "rule" in typical language development. Further, given the specific nature of the language impairment in autism – social-cognitive and pragmatically based – I would also argue that the individual with autism is the "exception" that proves the (social-pragmatic) "rule"; that is, that a social-pragmatic theory of language acquisition is a sound one for both neurotypical children and those with autism.

Pragmatics and Intention Reading in Language Acquisition

Intention reading, broadly conceived by Tomasello (2003) as theory of mind, is intimately related to pragmatics, in that there is a complementary (i.e., correlative) relationship between communicative intentions and pragmatic functions, such that when a person uses language to express a specific intent, that piece of language is said to serve a particular function (Twachtman-Cullen & Twachtman-Reilly, 2007), based upon the work of Tomasello (2003).

Function. For example, if the child intends to summon Mommy when he says "Mommy," the word would serve the pragmatic function of obtaining attention. However, if the child utters the word *Mommy* upon seeing his mother returning home from work, the intention in that situation is to take note of the event, and the function served would be that of commenting. Finally, if the child in the last situation is saying *Mommy* to someone in the room with the intent of letting that person know that Mommy is arriving home, the function would be that of either announcing or informing.

These examples illustrate some important aspects of language understanding and use. First, it is highly dependent upon the speaker's intentions with respect to his communicative goal (e.g., to comment or inform). Second, a word, in and of itself, is not sufficient to carry the intended meaning. In the examples given above, the same word (*Mommy*) was used to express three to four different intents/functions. Third, context is a critical aspect of the communicative event, particularly with respect to the derivation of intent/meaning.

Presuppositional knowledge. A second aspect of pragmatics related to theory of mind concerns **presuppositional** knowledge. This consists of the judgments that speakers must make about their listeners' needs with respect to the informational content needed and the communicative style appropriate to the situation. For example, in order to know what information to convey, the speaker must be aware of what the communicative partner already knows in addition to what information she needs to know in order to understand the message. Further, in determining which communicative style to use, one needs to make judgments related to the status of the listener. For example, one would use a different communicative style when talking to a close friend than when talking to an authority figure. One must also take context into account, since formal and informal situations require different communicative styles. The ability to make these multifaceted social judgments requires a great deal of "people knowledge," particularly an understanding that people not only have thoughts, desires, needs, and perspectives, but that they can differ from person to person (Twachtman-Cullen, 1998).

Because of the **perspective-taking** requirements and theory-of-mind knowledge involved in making assumptions about listeners' needs and situational requirements, this area of pragmatics is a veritable "mine field" even for individuals with autism who are considered more able. According to Tager-Flusberg (1997), "Even when children with autism have acquired both lexical and syntactic forms, they remain at very primitive levels of communicative competence, hampered by their inability to add new information and extend a conversational topic over several communicative turns" (p. 140). The same observation applies across age levels. With this in mind, it should be obvious that, depending upon the degree of impairment, children and adolescents with ASD Level 3 may not possess sufficient social-cognitive knowledge to enable them to make presuppositions.

Conversational maxims. The third aspect of pragmatics that shares an intimate association with theory of mind is that of conversational maxims (Grice, 1975); that is, the rules of discourse by which speakers co-operate in their conversations with one another. These, of course, apply only to verbal individuals.

The first rule is that of *quantity.* This rule requires the speaker to convey only the amount of information necessary to transmit her meaning. Saying too much or too little would violate this rule. For example, a child with ASD Level 3 is likely to violate this rule by failing to supply enough information to get his meaning across to the listener. Contrast this with the individual with ASD Level 2 who talks non-stop on a subject of interest to her, regardless of the social distress signals (e.g., looking at one's watch multiple times) emanating from the listener.

The second maxim is that of *quality.* This rule concerns the truth value of utterances. Lying and confabulation (i.e., saying something untrue that the speaker nevertheless believes to be true) constitute violations of this rule. For example, several years ago I was called in to consult on behalf of Jason, a child with ASD Level 1 who had become so enmeshed in the character Kevin from the movie *Home Alone* that he had taken on the character's persona. For example, he would not answer to his actual name, and he would confabulate by introducing himself to people as Kevin.

The third maxim has to do with the *relevance* of utterances. Off-topic comments and tangential utterances constitute violations of this rule. For example, if a child or adolescent with ASD Level 1 constantly steers conversations toward his special interest (e.g., weather phenomena), this would be a violation of the rule of relevance.

The final conversational maxim is that of *clarity.* This rule obligates the speaker to convey information in a manner that is clear and understandable to the listener. Children with autism across the spectrum violate this rule when they fail to ground the listener in the subject matter at hand, or when they use metaphoric language. I am reminded of a 14-year-old boy who violated this rule by conveying his desire to have more control over his life in the following idiosyncratic manner: "I would buy the entire school. I would grow older than my teacher."

To summarize, according to social-pragmatic theory, the social-cognitive precursors that have been discussed throughout this chapter, culminating in the theory-of-mind knowledge that fuels language acquisition, are essential elements in the development of symbolic communication. Moreover, social-pragmatic theory fits in well with the variability that is seen in autism, given that the degree of deficit in social-cognitive processes such as joint attention and intention reading is roughly proportional to the degree of pragmatic impairment seen. In other words, individuals with ASD Level 1 who have higher levels of social cognition manifest less impairment in symbol use than individuals with ASD Level 2 or 3 who tend to have lower levels of social cognition. For example, highly verbal individuals with autism may be able to express themselves relatively well in simple, straightforward situations, particularly when dealing with concrete, factual information. These same individuals typically evidence greater difficulty in expressing abstract or emotionally laden information. By contrast, depending upon the degree of deficit in social cognition, the severity of pragmatic impairment at Levels 2 or 3 of the autism continuum can vary from a complete absence of verbal language to minimal verbal ability.

Nonetheless, I contend that there is a thread of commonality running through the entire autism spectrum such that, regardless of level, individuals on the spectrum demonstrate a unique pattern of pragmatic language impairment that has its roots in social-cognitive deficits. In terms of the nonverbal individual with autism, pragmatic impairment may masquerade as aberrant behavior. Specifically, "individuals with autism who are unable to express their needs and desires in conventional ways (i.e., through language or other symbolic means) will express them in unconventional ways (i.e., through maladaptive behaviors)" (Twachtman-Cullen, 2006, p. 45). For example, an individual with autism who is unable to exercise the appropriate pragmatic function for protesting (e.g., saying or signing *no*) may express her dissatisfaction with a particular food item by throwing it across the room. Indeed, there is seminal research to support the depiction of aberrant behavior in terms of the pragmatic function it serves (Carr & Durand, 1985; Donnellan, Mirenda, Mesaros, & Fassbender, 1984).

Word-Learning Differences

As noted previously, the social-pragmatic view of language acquisition has implications for how children learn the meanings of words. According to Tomasello (2003), children learn words in a social-interactive context in which they are engaged in an active process of trying to infer adult intentions. Bloom (2000) argued, "What theory of mind does for children is enable them to establish the mapping between a word and a concept.

But this presupposes the availability of the concept" (p. 86). In other words, children need to understand the underlying meaning (Bloom, 2000). For example, a 2- or 3-year-old child may overhear his parents discussing a legal matter involving a lawyer. The child may even be able to say the word *lawyer*; however, without an understanding of the concept of lawyer, the child can hardly be said to have truly learned the word. Moreover, without an understanding of the underlying concept, the child will not be able to use the word appropriately, since saying a word and using it to express one's intentions are two different parameters. Given the importance of the underlying concept to word leaning, interventionists should take care to ensure that vocabulary targets are within the individual's conceptual grasp.

Bloom (2000) also underscored the importance of context in word learning, stating unequivocally that "nobody doubts that for children to learn words they have to be exposed to them in contexts in which they can infer their meanings: this is a truism" (pp. 8-9). Unfortunately, given the de-contextualized settings in which language development occurs for many individuals with autism, this can hardly be said to be a "truism" for this population.

Last but not least, there are several important aspects of words and word learning that need to be taken into account in language intervention, including the following:

- According to Tomasello (2003), there is what he terms a "perspectival" quality to words, since one may use several different words to refer to the same noun (*carrot, food,* or *vegetable)* or event (fighting, disagreeing, or combating). The particular word selected would depend upon the communicative goal of the speaker vis-à-vis what he or she wishes the listener to perceive.

- Children learn verbs and nouns in different ways based upon the nature of each word class (Bloom, 2000; Tomasello, 1992; Tomasello & Kruger, 1992). For example, nouns are based upon the whole object, such as *dog* and *car.* Nouns are also static, as opposed to transient. Verbs, on the other hand, are based upon an aspect of a situation. For example, consider the verb *wags,* as in *the dog wags its tail.* The verb *wag* refers to one aspect of the dog – the movement of its tail. This movement may stop at any time, which points to the transient nature of verbs.

- Based upon the studies of Tomasello and Kruger (1992) and Tomasello (1992), Bloom (2000) notes that when a novel verb is used to comment on an ongoing event, it is harder for the child to connect it to the event and hence learn it (e.g., "*You're _pushing_ the truck.*"). He goes on to state that children learn verbs better "when the verb is used immediately before the event" (p. 83). Adults typically use verbs in this manner as the following statements clearly demonstrate: _Throw_ *the ball.* _Clean_ *your room.* _Drink_ *your milk.*

As in the case of vocabulary development and conceptual knowledge discussed previously, it is important for interventionists to take into account research findings regarding the different ways in which children learn different classes of words when addressing the language needs of children with autism.

Assessment Considerations

Going Beyond Traditional Assessment Approaches

While an in-depth examination of issues related to assessment is beyond the scope of this chapter, some general remarks are in order. First, it is necessary to go beyond static, traditional approaches that are merely "snapshots in time." Some of the main reasons why traditional approaches are of limited benefit with individuals with autism are as follows: (a) It is often necessary to assess skills for which no **standardized tests** are available. (b) Since social cognition and pragmatics are inextricably intertwined with environmental events, they require dynamic assessment approaches that take into account context and other situational variables. (c) "Snapshots in time" have limited predictive value for future language performance or learning potential. (d) Standardized tests may not be appropriate for individuals at the lower end of the autistic continuum.

This is not to say that standardized tests are never appropriate for individuals with autism. Indeed, a good rule of thumb is to use standardized tests when they are available and appropriate to the client, but to supplement them with informal assessment procedures in contextually appropriate settings and situations.

Situated Pragmatics

In view of the critical importance of the social-cognitive precursors to symbolic communication, it is crucial that observation of attention and affect sharing, joint attention and social referencing behaviors, and intention reading all be a part of the assessment protocol for individuals with autism. Hewitt (2000) argued for a "situated pragmatics" approach that takes into account contextual variables, possible barriers to communication, and the contributions (negative and positive) of communicative interactants. This approach is felt to be particularly well suited to individuals with autism, since it recognizes that there is a shared responsibility for communicative breakdown that goes beyond the individual with the language impairment.

Lund (2000) defined four main features of this approach:

- Situated pragmatics looks at the entire interaction, including the relationship between interactants for clues regarding communicative breakdown.

- Situated pragmatics is competenceas opposed to deficit-based.

- Situated pragmatics focuses on the context in which the communicative event is taking place to determine the match between communicative expectations and ability level of the individual.

- Situated pragmatics is child-centered, as it "involves understanding what the child is intending to do within events and seeing how things make sense from the child's perspective." (p. 271)

Naturalistic Contexts

The pragmatic functions of communication should be assessed in **naturalistic contexts** with a view toward assessing the environmental variables that either help to facilitate or interfere with communication (Hewitt, 2000). This ideally involves assessment across several different contexts, since some contexts are more facilitative than others, and vice versa. One of the goals is to assess the range of functions in the individual's repertoire, since children and adolescents with autism often exhibit restrictions in the range of pragmatic functions at their disposal (Wetherby & Prutting, 1984). For example, individuals with ASD Level 3 typically communicate for behavioral regulation purposes, as opposed to social ends. The assessment of the pragmatic functions of communication is especially crucial for nonverbal or minimally verbal individuals, since lacking conventional symbols to express their intents (e.g., wants, needs, and desires), they often use aberrant behavior (Twachtman-Cullen, 2006).

Conversational Maxims and Presuppositional Knowledge

It is also important to assess the **conversational maxims** and to obtain information regarding presuppositional knowledge in individuals with autism who are verbal. This is particularly important for the most able on the spectrum, inasmuch as their difficulty at the higher levels of pragmatics contrasts sharply with their functioning in other areas, causing them great difficulty in the social world. Since there are no formal measures with respect to these parameters, and given that these aspects of pragmatic functioning are both subjective and difficult to assess, observation in a variety of situations over time is needed to make judgments regarding ability level.

Vocabulary Development

Vocabulary development in verbal children with autism is also an area in need of assessment. While there are several standardized vocabulary tests on the market, it is necessary to go beyond norm-referenced tests to obtain a comprehensive view of a child's word knowledge. Hence, in addition to standardized measures, diagnosticians need to obtain information regarding vocabulary development from parents/caregivers. Last, and perhaps most important with respect to this population, informal assessment procedures such as an analysis of expressive language across different situations and settings can yield information regarding vocabulary size and diversity.

Comprehension

A final area of assessment relates to comprehension. Here again, it is necessary to go beyond formal measures and comprehension at the one-word level, given recent findings about how individuals with autism process meaning. Specifically, Just, Cherkassky, Keller, and Minshew (2004) found that in sentence comprehension tasks, individuals with autism demonstrated enhanced reliance on the processing of individual words and reduced processing of sentences. This has significant implications for comprehension, since meaning is not carried by the individual words in a sentence but by the embeddedness of those words in a communicative context (Bruner & Haste, 1987). Paul's (2000) advice regarding the assessment of comprehension takes into account both real-time discourse and theory of mind. Specifically, he notes

> To fully document the child's comprehension, we would need to look also at how the child copes with the task of understanding discourse in real time, the ability to integrate with the social context, and the ability to go beyond the spoken word, to 'read the mind' of the speaker in order to form a representation of the speaker's meaning. (p. 250)

In order to do this, Paul (2000) suggests that comprehension be carried out on two levels: the *literal* level (aimed at assessing the ability to derive an understanding of words and sentences) and the *discourse* level (aimed at both intention reading and the "integration of knowledge with the social context" (p. 250).

Intervention Considerations

A comprehensive assessment of the areas noted above should provide excellent guidance for need-based intervention. Given the variability in levels that exists among individuals on the autism spectrum, extending from nonverbal or minimally verbal to highly verbal, it should be apparent that intervention needs will differ – sometimes significantly – as well. Notwithstanding, there are general principles of language intervention in autism that apply across age and levels of ASD, and that flow directly from social-pragmatic theory.

Principle One

Intervention must begin where the learner is. If individuals with autism have not yet mastered the social-cognitive precursors to language acquisition, intervention should begin at the level of attention and affect sharing, with the goal being that of establishing joint attention. In investigating joint attention in children with autism between the ages of 3 and 4, Kasari (2005) found that they could not only learn to initiate joint attention, but also to maintain and generalize these skills.

Principle Two

Experience both prunes and powers the brain (Landa, 2003; Schwartz & Begley, 2002). Consequently, language-learning activities embedded in high-quality experiences provide an excellent milieu for establishing joint attention, intention reading, and concept and vocabulary development. Furthermore, building experiential learning activities around the individual's interests will help to provide motivation and foster engagement.

Principle Three

The use of augmentative means (e.g., gestures, handwriting, picture communication symbols, and particularly sign language) to direct and facilitate the child's attention and provide an additional language input channel is backed by a considerable body of research. For example, according to Mirenda (2003), studies investigating the use of manual signs with children with autism who were either nonverbal or minimally verbal resulted in the acquisition of both receptive and expressive vocabulary at faster rates and higher levels. Similarly, Daniels (2001) noted that because "inner speech and adept hand movements" are housed in one of the language centers of the brain (Broca's area), "there is an increased opportunity for the formation of a greater number of connections and patterns in the brain" (p. 126).

Principle Four

A great deal of emphasis must be placed upon comprehension, since it is the basis for meaningful expression (Savage-Rumbaugh & Lewin, 1994; Twachtman-Cullen, 2000). For individuals with ASD Level 3 this involves a focus on *linguistic comprehension,* or the understanding of the literal meanings of words. For individuals with ASD Level 1, this will likely involve a focus on *pragmatic comprehension*, that which is rooted in the abstract and social aspects of language. Reading between the lines to get at intended meaning, making inferences, and dealing with idioms all involve pragmatic comprehension.

Principle Five

According to Bloom (2000), "It is not how often the adult says the word that matters; it is how often the child processes it" (p. 90). That is, *intake* is more important than *input*. Hence, interventionists should make every effort to ensure that the individual with autism is actively engaged in language-learning activities, since without active engagement, he or she will not be able to take in and process language input. At the same time, one is cautioned to avoid forced participation in language intervention activities, given that it can lead to anxiety and "shutdown," neither of which is conducive to learning.

Principle Six

"To learn what a word means, one needs to possess the relevant concept" (Bloom, 2000, p. 90). This is especially germane to individuals with autism, given that research has revealed a dissociation between concept formation and concept identification in this population. Consequently, they are impaired in their ability to form the concept (understand the meaning behind the word), even as they are able to identify the concept (point to the word that represents it) (Brown, Solomon, Bauminger, & Rogers, 2005; Minshew, Meyer, & Goldstein, 2002). Thus, it is important for interventionists to make sure that vocabulary targets are within the child's conceptual grasp, since true word learning requires **concept formation** as opposed to simple **concept identification**. This can best be done by (a) providing lots of "time in" with respect to basic-level words that are used to refer to things in the here and now; and (b) rooting language-learning activities in meaningful interactive experiences.

Principle Seven

Since children do not learn different classes of words (e.g., nouns/verbs/adjectives) in the same manner, intervention should not be carried out in the same manner for different classes of words (Bloom, 2000; Tomasello, 1992; Tomasello & Kruger, 1992). To illustrate, when children are asked to point to a noun (e.g., *cup*), it is the whole object that constitutes the noun. In contrast, when they are asked to point to pictures depicting verbs (e.g., "point to *running*"), they are being asked to identify a dynamic action in a static picture format in which only one aspect of the picture is relevant. Inasmuch as individuals demonstrate a predilection for stimulus over-selectivity, as well as problems determining relevance, this is a more difficult cognitive task than learning the verb in a more active and meaningful format – say, in a game of *Simon Says*.

Principle Eight

Language intervention should be carried out in a context that supports meaning, since this makes the process of inferring intent easier. Furthermore, since, as noted earlier, words have a perspectival quality, whereby one object or event can be signified by several different words (Tomasello, 2003), the context in which the word is rendered can help to disambiguate its meaning. For example, context provides an excellent way for the individual to learn that toast is something you can *eat* in the morning, and *do* in the afternoon.

Principle Nine

Given that "theory of mind underlies how children learn the entities to which words refer, intuit how words relate to one another, and understand how words can serve as communication signs" (Bloom, 2000, p. 56), theory-of-mind activities should be woven into the fabric of the language-learning activities.

Principle Ten

Appropriate language use (which implies generalization to appropriate contexts) is most appropriately addressed in contextually relevant, usage-based, interactive routines that mirror the language-learning process by providing rich opportunities for inferring communicative intent and exercising the pragmatic functions of communication (Wetherby et al., 1997).

Summary and Conclusions

This chapter has considered the child's journey toward acquiring language – from the fledgling first steps in attention and affect sharing, to the more definitive stride toward joint attention and intention reading, and finally to the child's remarkable entry into the world of two-way symbolic communication. It is a journey that *all* children begin, but only some complete.

The issues raised in this chapter are my attempt to examine the common pathways and points of departure that demarcate the journey for neurotypical children and their peers with autism. With findings from both the language and the autism research literature as the road map, common pathways in language development between neurotypical children and children with autism were found. Specifically, joint attention and intention reading loom large as foundational elements that guide the child toward the journey's end. Moreover, joint attention and vocabulary development were found to be related in the same way for both neurotypical children and those with autism, such that the greater the capacity for joint attention, the greater the size of the child's vocabulary, and vice versa. This is a critical common pathway in and of itself, but it is all the more remarkable for what it suggests: The principles governing language acquisition in neurotypical children also apply to children with autism. This finding underscores the relevance of the language research literature for this population. It also speaks to the importance of building the language structure by laying a strong (social-cognitive) foundation to support it, for it is at the juncture of joint attention and its progression toward intention reading that the pathway toward symbolic communication begins to diverge for children with autism.

This leads quite naturally to social-pragmatic theory. Given the nature of the pragmatic impairment in individuals with autism and the social-cognitive deficits that give rise to it, social-pragmatic theory provides a "good fit" for both explaining many of the language deficits and for addressing them. This is a view supported by research regarding the similarities governing language acquisition for neurotypical children and their peers with autism. It is also a view supported by the universality of the pragmatic impairment found across age and levels of ASD, beginning with the deficits in joint attention and intention reading early on. Simply stated, if a patient shows the symptoms of a heart attack, her heart would be examined. Likewise, if pragmatic deficits are the defining features of the language impairment in autism – and there is a plethora of research to support this – we should look to the social-pragmatic arena for answers.

Finally, the ability to communicate is the most difficult and remarkable feat of humankind. The fact that most people speak so effortlessly masks its complexity. Indeed, language users perform complex social-pragmatic tasks without awareness. For example, we not only make presuppositions about our listener's needs, but also the adjustments needed to accommodate them. And we do so automatically, in split-second time. It is only when something goes dramatically wrong in the development of language – as it does in autism – that we take notice of language at all.

I suggest that the ease with which most of us learn and use language blinds us to the complexities inherent in the language-acquisition process. The effect of this on intervention in autism is that many areas of language impairment slip below the "radar screen" (e.g., joint attention and intention reading), and consequently, crucial areas of pragmatic impairment go unaddressed. Worse yet, as noted early on in this chapter, a lack of understanding of the language-learning process and of the social-cognitive elements that are an integral part of it can result in language intervention practices that are ineffective and/or inappropriate. This should be kept uppermost in mind before asking the individual with autism to *use* his or her words.

In recent years, there has been an explosion of high-quality research on language development in both typically developing children and those with autism. This research can and should inform our intervention practices. I leave the reader with two thoughts: (a) In order to translate research into practice, we have to consult it and apply it; and (b) It is not enough to look only to the autism research literature for guidance when dealing with the complexities of language acquisition. We must also look to the language research literature, since one cannot deal effectively with disordered communication without some understanding of normal language development. Only by melding together relevant research findings from both literature bases will it be possible to obtain the best, most up-to-date "road map" for the crucial journey to symbolic communication.

Tips for Practical Application

✓ Remember that the communication disorder in autism affects a student's ability to form concepts and to accurately interpret concepts in the language of others. When we attempt to modify challenging behavior, we often verbalize our disapproval using complex social and emotional concepts. This can make the communication of expectations even more difficult. Using visual cues to support the intended message can make the task of comprehension much easier.

✓ To teach nonverbal social communication, either take pictures or use commercial pictures depicting different facial expressions, and then have the student practice imitating the various expressions (e.g., making a curious face while looking at a picture of a curious face). The same pictures may be used for matching similar expressions, grouping facial expressions into categories, and creating stories about what the person in the picture might be experiencing. Using a digital camera to take pictures of the students making different faces can add an element of fun to this activity.

✓ Expand on the traditional "sharing" times so that students with autism have ample opportunities to interact with others, using their special interests or talents as motivational "hooks" to engage them in the act of sharing.

✓ Use cartooning to support theory-of-mind development by helping students to visualize others' ideas, intentions, and thoughts. This can be done with picture books and using sticky notes to label what a particular character might be thinking. Commercial photographs depicting social situations may also be used.

✓ Consider another activity that supports theory-of-mind development, employing pictures of various faces (males, females, boys, girls, teens, etc.) and a set of statement cards: Students are asked to match a statement or verbal expression with the person most likely to say it. You can expand on this activity by using pictures of people who have different relationships to the student (parents, friends, teachers, strangers, the president of the United States, etc.), asking the student to match the most likely topic of conversation they might have with each of the characters. Inject some fun into this activity by using pictures of movie celebrities or cartoon characters.

✓ Allow reluctant students to observe language groups prior to participating in them. Give them the added support of visual structure to increase their chances of success and feelings of competence.

✓ Use ongoing language activities such as Idiom of the Week or Joke of the Week. Encourage families to carry out this activity at home by writing a letter to parents describing it.

✓ Use a variation on the theme of *Mad Libs* by writing a story, personalized to your student's special interests, to encourage the use of specific concepts and word categories.

✓ Using the format of the common game of charades, create cards with various emotions or social messages and have students take turns making simple gestures with hands and/or body stance to communicate the concept, emotion, or message. You can expand on this activity to work on subtlety by adding a scale of little, medium, and big so that a student might be asked to illustrate big confusion or little disappointment.

✓ During small groups, choose the person whose turn it is by just looking at him or her. This provides a predictable communication routine that requires students to attend to your face and eyes.

✓ Plan lessons jointly with the general education teacher so that she can incorporate language activities into the classroom throughout the week. For example, this is a great way to reinforce idioms, multiple meanings of words, and social concepts.

✓ A great activity to introduce the idea of "making a thinking guess" is the Magic Window, a plastic window behind which you hide pictures, gradually opening the window while students guess what the picture is. This activity can lead to making inferences. Be sure to introduce the activity by distinguishing between the concepts of "wild guess" and "thinking guess." You can add a visual element by drawing a face on a white board with many blank "thinking bubbles" to be filled in with wild guesses at first and then a big thinking guess later.

✓ Speak in a foreign language or in gibberish while giving many exaggerated nonverbal contextual clues about what you are trying to communicate. Ask the students to guess what you want or what you might do next.

✓ Teach verbs in the manner in which they are typically learned by asking students to perform actions. *Simon Says* is an ideal vehicle for this. Use a variation on this theme for older students.

✓ Encourage teachers to use manual signs for all students as prompts and (visual) attention getters. For example, the teacher can use the manual sign for *where* (shaking the index finger from side to side) to give advance notice to the student that a question about a place will be forthcoming. Similarly, he or she can use the manual sign for *who* (circling the index finger around the mouth) to indicate that a question about a person is coming next. Research shows that all students can benefit from this approach!

Chapter Highlights

- Social communication involves not only having spoken language but also having an understanding of the function of words and of what others are thinking.

- Theory of mind and communication are intertwined.

- Communication can be defined as the ability to use words to exchange meaning and influence others.

- Individuals with autism may have a rich vocabulary of words but lack an understanding of how to use them to communicate intent or meaning.

- For infants, playing games such as "peek-a-boo" provides opportunities for attention and affect sharing and social reciprocity, which helps the infant develop the interpersonal relatedness needed for later social communication.

- Experiential learning provides infants with the opportunity to develop new neural pathways and increases brain connectivity.

- Infants with autism do not engage in games as do their neurotypical peers and, therefore, miss out on opportunities for emotional regulation, attention sharing, anticipation, and reciprocity with their caregivers.

- Infants with autism tend to engage in repetitive behaviors; therefore, their opportunity to develop connectivity and the possibility that neurons are not "pruned" may lead to less capacity for social-cognitive behaviors, brain function, and concept development.

- Children with autism have deficits in "joint attention;" that is, in the behaviors suggestive of an increasing understanding of the need to engage other minds, such as gaze following, pointing, and showing/offering gestures.

- As brain research supports the relationship between joint attention and theory of mind, including that the two are located in the same region of the brain, children with autism who lack skills in the area of joint attention also have impaired ability to judge what others are thinking.

- Joint attention plays a pivotal role in establishing intentional communication as it is based on a shared awareness (intersubjectivity) and engagement.

- Research shows joint attention impacts typically developing children and those with autism in a similar way in that the amount of joint attention engaged in is highly correlated with vocabulary development and other language and social gains.

- Joint attention sets the stage for intention reading (the ability to "read" another's intent) and is related to the development of symbolic communication.

- Social-pragmatic theory holds that intention reading plays a critical role in language development.

- Social-pragmatic theory can provide a template for what goes wrong in the language acquisition process in autism; specifically, impairments in social cognition in terms of joint attention, affect sharing, and intention reading are seen as likely causes of the pragmatic impairments of individuals with autism.

- While all areas of language may be impaired in individuals with autism (semantics, syntax, pragmatics), deficits in pragmatics constitute the defining language deficit across age and ability levels.

- When a person uses language to express a specific intent, that piece of language is said to serve a particular function.

- In order to use language to serve a function, the individual must possess both pragmatic skills and intention reading.

- Presuppositional knowledge refers to making judgments about the listener such as that of an individual's prior knowledge of the topic in order to decide what information to provide and how to convey it.

- Conversational maxims refer to having an understanding of the rules of discourse.

- Word learning depends on context, knowledge of the underlying concept, the communicative goal of the speaker, word class, and level of novelty.

- Assessment of language for individuals with autism from a social-pragmatic perspective requires certain considerations, including the use of situated pragmatics and naturalistic contexts, evaluating conversational maxims and presuppositional knowledge, and assessing comprehension at both the literal and the discourse level.

- Intervention needs differ due to the variability in levels that exist among individuals with ASD; however, 10 general principles apply across age and levels of ASD. The principles include:
  o Intervention must begin where the learner is
  o Intervention should be experiential
  o The use of augmentative means for communication is important
  o Emphasis should be placed on comprehension
  o Active engagement is important
  o Vocabulary targets should be within the individual's conceptual understanding
  o Different classes of words need to be taught differently
  o Intervention should take place in context in order to support the learning of meaning
  o Theory-of-mind activities should be included within language intervention
  o Intervention that promotes generalization of language occurs in contextually relevant routines

Chapter Review Questions

1. What is "social communication"?

2. Explain how theory of mind relates to social language learning.

3. Why can autism be described as a defect in communication?

4. Why might a student with autism experience difficulties in using his or her words to communicate?

5. What do the chapter authors believe may be a cause of ineffective language intervention for individuals with autism?

6. How do interactive games assist infants in developing social communication?

7. How is experiential learning critical for brain development?

8. How does autism affect infants in terms of experiential learning and later brain development?

9. What is "joint attention" and why is it important in developing social communication?

10. How is intention reading important to social-pragmatic theory?

11. How does understanding social-pragmatic theory help account for the difficulties individuals with autism have in understanding the pragmatic aspects of language?

12. Why is pragmatics so important to the development of language?

13. Why might social-pragmatic theory be considered the "rule" in typical language development?

14. What is meant by saying that words have different pragmatic functions based on the speaker's intentions?

15. What is "presuppositional knowledge" and why is it important to communication?

16. List and explain the four conversational maxims.

17. What does research say about word-learning differences?

18. What are general considerations related to assessment of language development in terms of social pragmatics?

19. What are the principles of intervention in autism that come directly from social-pragmatic theory?

References

Akhtar, N., & Tomasello, M. (1996). Twenty-four-month-old children learn words for absent objects and actions. *British Journal of Developmental Psychology, 14,* 79-93.

Baldwin, D. A. (1995). Understanding the link between joint attention and language. In C. Moore & P. J. Dunham (Eds.), *Joint attention: Its origins and role in development* (pp. 131-58). Hillsdale, NJ: Erlbaum.

Bell, M. A., & Fox, N. A. (1994). Brain development over the first year of life: Relations between EEG frequency and coherence and cognition and affective behaviors. In G. Dawson & K. Fischer (Eds.), *Human behavior and the developing brain* (pp. 314-345). New York, NY: Guilford Press.

Bloom, P. (2000). *How children learn the meanings of words.* Cambridge, MA: The MIT Press.

Brown, J. R., Solomon, M., Bauminger, N., & Rogers, S. J. (2005). *Concept formation and concept identification in high-functioning children with autism spectrum disorder.* Paper presented at the International Conference for Autism (IMFAR), Boston, MA.

Bruner, J. (1983). *Child's talk.* New York, NY: Norton.

Bruner, J., & Haste, H. (Eds.). (1987). *Making sense: The child's construction of the world.* New York, NY: Methuen.

Call, J., & Tomasello, M. (2005). What chimpanzees know about seeing, revisited: An explanation of the third kind. In N. Eilan, C. Hoerl, T. McCormack, & J. Roessler (Eds.), *Joint attention: Communication and other minds: Issues in philosophy and psychology* (pp. 45-64). New York, NY: Oxford University Press.

Carr, E. G., & Durand, V. M. (1985). Reducing behavior problems through functional communication training. *Journal of Applied Behavior Analysis, 18,* 111-126.

Carter, R. (1999). *Mapping the mind.* London, UK: University of California Press, Ltd.

Daniels, M. (2001). *Dancing with words: Signing for hearing children's literacy.* Westport, CT: Bergin & Garvey.

Donnellan, A., Mirenda, P., Mesaros, R., & Fassbender, L. (1984). Analyzing the communicative functions of aberrant behavior. *Journal of the Association for Persons with Severe Handicaps, 9,* 202-212.

Greenough, W. T., & Black, J. E. (1992). Induction of brain structure by experience: Substrates for cognitive development. *Developmental Behavioral Neuroscience, 24,* 155-299.

Grice, H. (1975). Logic and conversation. In D. Davidson & G. Harmon (Eds.), *The logic of grammar* (pp. 41-58). Encino, CA: Dickinson.

Happé, F.G.E. (1996). *Autism: An introduction to psychological theory.* Cambridge, MA: Harvard University Press. Hewitt, L. E. (2000). Assessing communicative intents. *Seminars in Speech and Language, 21*(3), 257-266.

Hobson, R. P. (2005). What puts the jointness into joint attention? In N. Eilan, C. Hoerl, T. McCormack, & J. Roessler (Eds.), *Joint attention: Communication and other minds: Issues in philosophy and psychology* (pp. 185-204). New York, NY: Oxford University Press.

Just, M. A., Cherkassky, V. L., Keller, T. A., & Minshew, N. J. (2004). Cortical activation and synchronization during sentence comprehension in high-functioning autism: Evidence of underconnectivity. *Brain, 127,* 1811-1821.

Kasari, C. (2005). *Growth in joint attention and symbolic play.* Proceedings of the International Meeting for Autism Research, Boston, MA.

Kaye, K. (1982). *The mental and social life of babies: How parents create persons.* Chicago, IL: The University of Chicago Press. Landa, R. (2003). *Keynote address.* Presentation at the Autism Society of America national conference, Pittsburgh, PA.

Landa, R., Holman, K. C., Sullivan, M., & Cleary, J. (2005). *Language and social change in toddlers with ASD: Early intervention.* Presentation at the International Meeting for Autism Research, Boston, MA.

Leekam, S. (1993). Children's understanding of mind. In M. Bennett (Ed.), *The development of social cognition: The child as psychologist* (pp. 26-61). New York, NY: Guilford Press.

Leekam, S. (2005). Autism and joint attention impairment. In N. Eilan, C. Hoerl, T. McCormack, & J. Roessler (Eds.), *Joint attention: Communication and other minds: Issues in philosophy and psychology* (pp. 205-229). New York, NY: Oxford University Press.

Lewy, A. L., & Dawson, G. (1992). Social stimulation and joint attention in young autistic children. *Journal of Abnormal Child Psychology, 20,* 555-566.

Lord, C., & Paul, R. (1997). Language and communication in autism. In D. Cohen & F. Volkmar (Eds.), *Handbook of autism and pervasive developmental disorders* (2nd ed., pp. 195-225). New York, NY: Wiley.

Loveland, K., & Landry, S. (1986). Joint attention in autism and developmental language delay. *Journal of Autism and Developmental Disorders, 16,* 335-349.

Lund, N. J. (2000). Assessment of language structure: From syntax to event-based analysis. *Seminars in Speech and Language, 21*(3), 267-274.

Minshew, N. J., Meyer, J., & Goldstein, G. (2002). Abstract reasoning in autism: A dissociation between concept formation and concept identification. *Neuropsychology, 16*(3), 327-334.

Mirenda, P. (2003). Toward functional augmentative and alternative communication for students with autism: Manual signs, graphic symbols, and voice output communication aids. *Language, Speech, and Hearing Services in Schools, 34,* 203-216.

Mundy, P., Sigman, M., & Kasari, C. (1990). A longitudinal study of joint attention and language development in autistic children. *Journal of Autism and Developmental Disorders, 20,* 115-128.

Paul, R. (2000). Literal and discourse approaches to comprehension assessment. *Seminars in Speech and Language, 21*(3), 247-255.

Rogoff, B. (1990). *Apprenticeship in thinking: Cognitive development in social context.* New York, NY: Oxford University Press. Sacks, O. (1989). *Seeing voices: A journey into the world of the deaf.* Los Angeles, CA: University of California Press.

Savage-Rumbaugh, S., & Lewin, R. (1994). *Kanzi: The ape at the brink of the human mind.* New York, NY: John Wiley & Sons.

Schwartz, J. M., & Begley, S. (2002). *The mind and the brain: Neuroplasticity and the power of mental force.* New York, NY: Regan Books.

Siller, M., & Sigman, M. (2002). The behaviors of parents of children with autism predict the subsequent development of their children's communication skills. *Journal of Autism and Developmental Disorders, 32*(2), 77-89.

Tager-Flusberg, H. (1997). Language acquisition and theory of mind: Contributions from the study of autism. In L. B. Adamson & M. A. Romski (Eds.), *Communication and language acquisition: Discoveries from atypical development* (pp. 135-160). Baltimore, MD: Paul H. Brookes.

Tager-Flusberg, H., Joseph, R., & Folstein, S. (2001). Current directions in research on autism. *Mental Retardation and Developmental Disabilities Research Reviews, 7,* 21-29.

Tomasello, M. (1992). *First verbs: A case study of early grammatical development.* New York, NY: Cambridge University Press.

Tomasello, M. (2001). Perceiving intentions and learning words in the second year of life. In M. Tomasello & E. Bates (Eds.), *Language development: The essential readings* (pp. 11-128). Oxford, UK: Blackwell.

Tomasello, M. (2003). *Constructing a language: A usage-based theory of language acquisition.* Cambridge, MA: Harvard University Press.

Tomasello, M., & Barton, M. (1994). Learning words in non-ostensive contexts. *Developmental Psychology, 30*, 639-650. Tomasello, M., & Bates, E. (2001). General introduction. In M. Tomasello & E. Bates (Eds.), *Language development: The essential readings* (pp. 1-11). Malden, MA: Blackwell.

Tomasello, M., & Farrar, M. J. (1986). Joint attention and early language. *Child Development, 57,* 1454-1463.

Tomasello, M., & Kruger, A. (1992). Joint attention on actions: Acquiring verbs in ostensive and non-ostensive contexts. *Journal of Child Language, 19,* 311-333.

Tomasello, M., Mannle, S., & Kruger, A. (1986). Linguistic environment of one to two year old twins *Developmental Psychology, 22,* 169-176.

Tomasello, M., Strosberg, R., & Akhtar, N. (1995). Eighteen-month-old children learn words in non-ostensive contexts. *Journal of Child Language, 22,* 1-20.

Tomasello, M., & Todd, J. (1983). Joint attention and lexical acquisition style. *First Language, 4,* 197-212.

Trevarthan, C. (1980). The foundations of intersubjectivity: Development of interpersonal and cooperative understanding of infants. In D. R. Olson (Ed.), *The social foundation of language and thought: Essays in honor of Jerome S. Bruner* (pp. 316-341). New York, NY: Norton.

Twachtman-Cullen, D. (1998). Language and communication in high-functioning autism and Asperger syndrome. In E. Schopler, G. B. Mesibov, & L. Kunce (Eds.), *Asperger syndrome or high-functioning autism?* (pp. 199-225). New York, NY: Plenum.

Twachtman-Cullen, D. (2000). More able children with autism spectrum disorders: Sociocommunicative challenges and guidelines for enhancing abilities. In A. M. Wetherby & B. M. Prizant (Eds.), *Autism spectrum disorders: A transactional developmental perspective* (pp. 225-249). Baltimore, MD: Paul H. Brookes.

Twachtman-Cullen, D. (2006, Winter). Functional communication training: Where communication, behavior, and conventional wisdom meet. *Autism Spectrum Quarterly,* 42-45.

Twachtman-Cullen, D., & Twachtman-Reilly, J. (2007). Communication and language issues in less able school-age children with autism. In R. L. Gabriels & D. E. Hill (Eds.), *Growing up with autism: Working with school-age children and adolescents* (pp. 73-94). New York, NY: Guilford Press.

Wetherby, A. (2006). Understanding and measuring social communication in children with autism spectrum disorders. In T. Charman & W. Stone (Eds.), *Social and communication development in autism spectrum disorders: Early identification, diagnosis, and intervention* (pp. 3-34). New York, NY: Guilford Publications.

Wetherby, A. M., Prizant, B. M., & Hutchinson, T. A. (1998). Communicative, social/affective, and symbolic profiles of young children with autism and pervasive developmental disorders. *American Journal of Speech-Language Pathology, 7,* 79-91.

Wetherby, A. M., & Prutting, C. A. (1984). Profiles of communicative and cognitive-social abilities in autistic children. *Journal of Speech and Hearing Research, 27*(3), 364-377.

Wetherby, A., Schuler, A., & Prizant, B. (1997). Enhancing language and communication: Theoretical foundations. In D. Cohen & F. Volkmar (Eds.), *Handbook of autism and pervasive developmental disorders* (2nd ed., pp. 513-538). New York, NY: Wiley.

Williams, J., Waiter, G., Perra, O., Whiten, A., & Perrett, D. (2005). Overlap between the neural substrate for joint attention, and white and grey matter volume differences in autistic spectrum disorder. *Neuroimage, 25,* 133-140.

Wingert, P., & Brant, M. (2005, August 15). Reading your baby's mind. *Newsweek,* pp. 32-39.

Wolfberg, P. J. (2009). *Play and imagination in children with autism* (2nd ed.). New York, NY: Columbia, Teachers College Press.

Learner Objectives

After reading this chapter, the learner should be able to:

- Define sensory processing

- List and describe the systems involved in sensory processing

- State the purpose of sensory systems transmitting information to the brain

- Explain why incorporating various sensory inputs into educational programs might be useful for students with autism spectrum disorders

- Explain Dunn's model of sensory processing for understanding patterns of sensory processing

- Explain sensory processing differences in individuals with ASD as compared to peers

- Describe each of the four sensory processing patterns

- State the goal of a sensory processing framework for intervention

- Give examples of interventions that support students to participate effectively in school by considering the student's sensory patterns

Chapter 6

Sensory Processing: Identifying Patterns and Designing Support Strategies

Winnie Dunn

Bradley is a slow starter at school. His teacher says he lies all over his desk, leans on people, walls, and furniture, and is very slow at responding to questions and directions in class. Many times when the class has already begun an activity, Bradley requires additional personal attention to get him to participate. The teacher says it is like Bradley is in another world; he doesn't pick up the cues that something is about to happen. In these situations, the teacher moves toward Bradley, bends down to get in front of him, looks him directly in the eyes, and calls his name. She brings the appropriate materials with her and hands items to Bradley as she explains what the class will be doing. She has learned that tapping Bradley's shoulder to get his attention is a bad strategy. Even though he seems oblivious, when she touches him, he lurches, screams, and pushes her away. She gets his attention, but it is not the kind of attention she wants from Bradley for classroom work. She has learned that after Bradley gets upset in this way, it takes a while to get him settled back down, thus disrupting more of the school day.

*The teacher talks with the interdisciplinary team members at the school to get additional ideas about how to handle Bradley more effectively throughout the school day. They agree that the occupational therapist (OT) on the team will be the most helpful. The OT subsequently interviews the teacher and observes Bradley during the morning work session to get more detailed information about Bradley's reactions. She sends home the **Sensory Profile** (Dunn, 1999) for Bradley's parents to complete and asks the teacher to complete the Sensory Profile School Companion (Dunn, 2007a). She suspects that Bradley is responding to sensory experiences differently than classroom peers, and that this might be contributing to his challenges with participating in school activities.*

*Bradley's Sensory Profile (Dunn, 1999) and School Companion (Dunn, 2007a) results verified what the OT suspected based on her interviews and observations: Bradley is missing information and is slow to respond to stimuli in the environment (called **low registration**). Consistent with the teacher's comments about Bradley's heightened reactions to touch, the Sensory Profile measures also indicated that Bradley notices touch input much more quickly than peers and reacts negatively to this particular type of input (called **sensitivity**).*

The OT explained to the teacher about Bradley's overall need for more intensity of input (due to low registration) so that he can notice and respond to cues. The teacher and OT brainstormed ways to increase Bradley's sensory input during the school day. The teacher decided to create daily routines for Bradley to get him up and moving around the classroom more often. For example, she assigned him the task of passing out worksheets, collecting assignments from other students, refilling materials bins when they were getting low, obtaining books for reading groups, and wiping the board throughout the day. The OT suggested giving Bradley "smelly" markers for seatwork, explaining that the extra input from the fragrance would keep Bradley attentive to the worksheet for a longer time. They also discussed giving Bradley an iPod or MP3 player with earphones so he could listen to music while working, but the teacher was skeptical about the impact of this strategy on the rest of the class. She also thought this might make Bradley more oblivious to her classroom instruction. Instead, they decided to move his desk near the window so he would get more natural light at his work area and be able to hear the traffic going by during the day. The OT also created color-coded covers for books and materials so Bradley could find materials that go together for a classroom activity. This setup allowed for all of Bradley's supplies to be more noticeable, which met his need for extra visual information.

Then they turned their attention to Bradley's sensitivity to touch, which had the potential to disrupt many activities throughout the day. The teacher had been using a safe spot in the classroom for all the children. The children could go, or the teacher could prompt them to go, to the safe spot whenever they needed to regroup. The teacher and therapist talked about how to design the safe spot so that it would provide a comforting place for Bradley. They put a beanbag chair, a heavy quilt, and some extra-oversized heavy pillows in the safe spot so Bradley could bury himself. The OT explained that firm pressure on the skin provides a calming input, and thus could help Bradley calm down more quickly. When the OT showed Bradley how to create a cocoon around his body while in the safe spot, he smiled when trying it. After a few weeks, Bradley began going into the cocoon in the safe spot on his own when he got upset in the classroom.

Anyone who has a classroom of students will get to know a student like Bradley. Bradley is an above-average student academically, but his ways of responding to sensory experiences during the school day are interfering with his ability to demonstrate his knowledge and skills in the classroom.

In this chapter, we will explore an important aspect of student behavior: **sensory processing**. Sensory processing is a person's way of noticing and responding to sensory events that occur during everyday life. We know from research that there are particular patterns (Dunn, 1997a) of sensory processing (as introduced in Bradley's story), and that these patterns affect how people respond in situations. We also know that people who have autism spectrum disorders (ASD) have more intense reactions than their peers, which may be one of the contributing factors to their differences in responding in particular situations. When professionals and families understand the relationship between a student's sensory processing patterns and the behaviors he exhibits (Dunn, 1997a), we can adjust activities, directions, expectations, and other aspects of the school day to support the student's participation.

We all have sensory processing patterns. We might miss a lot of sensory cues, as Bradley was doing, yet be sensitive to certain sensory inputs (in Bradley's case, he was sensitive to touch). When you want the TV turned down, add Tabasco to your food, have a favorite lotion, only purchase one brand of undergarments, and choose yoga as your preferred exercise, you are illustrating your individual sensory processing patterns. When you find yourself in a situation in which you cannot get your **sensory needs** met (either by increasing sensory input or by decreasing it), you may become irritable or unhappy. The specific patterns identified from research are explained below in more detail.

An Introduction to Sensory Processing Concepts

The sensory systems provide information to the brain (Kandel, Schwartz, & Jessell, 2000). We learn about our bodies from touch and body position senses (called **somatosensory** and **proprioceptive** systems), and this information builds the body scheme. We learn about the environment from seeing, hearing, smelling, and tasting (i.e., visual, auditory, olfactory, and gustatory systems), thus forming maps of the world. And we learn how our bodies interact with the environment from the movement sensations (i.e., **vestibular** system) (Dunn, 1991a, 1997b). The brain holds maps that are formed from this information, and these maps guide us so we are oriented in space and time and can make accurate decisions about how to react in particular situations.

Ayres (1972, 1979) originally proposed how to apply knowledge about sensory systems and the brain to understand the behaviors of children with learning challenges. Over the last three decades, scholars in occupational therapy and other disciplines have continued to study sensory processing concepts, expanding both knowledge and application of the knowledge in service to children and adults who have challenges in everyday life (Dunn, 2001a). Today we understand that sensory processing is part of everyone's experience; teachers, parents, and students all notice and respond in everyday life based on their particular sensory patterns. Although people with various conditions such as ASD tend to experience the world more intensely than others, reactions are all on the same continuum rather than a constellation of disability markers.

This research can help us understand the behaviors and needs of children with ASD. For example, when someone touches a child, the child typically looks toward the person before deciding what to do; looking adds visual input to the touch input so that the child can respond with the most information possible, not just based on one sensation (Dunn, 1991b). Children who have ASD sometimes react too quickly in such a situation (based on the teacher's assessment of the situation), perhaps because they are responding without the benefit of multiple sensory inputs. Their reactions may seem disproportionate to the situation from a teacher's point of view; however, the students' behavior may simply indicate their level of sensitivity. When teachers understand this about their students, they can make adjustments to their classroom routines to create a "friendlier" place for learning.

An important aspect of balance in the brain is related to something called **thresholds** (the point at which the system responds). When thresholds are too low, children respond too frequently to stimuli and can consequently be distracted from everyday tasks by all the sensory input around them. Conversely, when thresholds are too high, children miss important cues about what is going on around them and may, therefore, seem oblivious or self-absorbed (Dunn, 1997b). Some children who are sensitive to many sensory inputs feel challenged to complete classroom tasks because they are distracted from their work by the countless stimuli in the room. Other children may fixate on one sensory input (e.g., the sound of rustling papers) while being oblivious to other input, such as someone calling their name, which can also interfere with the ongoing flow of the instructional day (Dunn, 1997b).

A Conceptual Model for Sensory Processing

Based on the brain knowledge summarized above, Dunn (1997a) proposed a conceptual model for understanding patterns of sensory processing. Figure 6.1 contains a diagram of this model; the vertical axis shows the **brain thresholds** and the horizontal axis shows the **self-regulation** continuum. High thresholds require a lot of sensory input, and low thresholds require very little sensory input to react. Children who have high thresholds respond infrequently, because it takes a great deal of sensory input to activate these thresholds. Children who have low thresholds, on the other hand, respond to many stimuli very easily.

The self-regulation continuum shows how the person manages input. Children with active self-regulation strategies work to control their own input, whereas children with passive self-regulation strategies let things happen and then respond to them (Dunn, 2001b). The threshold and self-regulation parts of this diagram intersect to create four patterns of sensory processing (see Dunn, 1997a, for original presentation of this work): registration, sensitivity, seeking, and avoiding.

A series of studies have validated and standardized measures of sensory processing (*Sensory Profile for Children*, SP, *Infant/Toddler Sensory Profile*, ITSP; *Adolescent/Adult Sensory Profile*, AASP; and *Sensory Profile School Companion*), and researchers have provided additional evidence regarding performance in vulnerable populations (e.g., Ashburner, Ziviani, & Rodger, 2008; Ben-Sasson et al., 2008; Brown, Tollefson, Dunn, Cromwell, & Filion, 2001; Chen, Rodgers, & McConachie, 2009; Crane, Goddard, & Pring, 2009; Dove & Dunn, 2008; Dunn & Bennett, 2002; Dunn, Myles, & Orr, 2002; Engel-Yeger & Shochat, 2012; Ermer & Dunn, 1998; Kientz & Dunn, 1997; Miller et al., 1998; Myles et al., 2004; Reike & Anderson, 2009; Rogers, Hepburn, & Wehner, 2003; Shani-Adir, Rozenman, Kessel, & Engel-Yeter, 2009; Watling, Dietz, & White, 2001).

Findings across these studies illustrate links between sensory processing and behavior (Dunn, 2001b). Further, studies across the life span support Dunn's model of sensory processing (Brown & Dunn, 2002; Dunn, 1999; Dunn & Daniels, 2001), illustrating that everyone exhibits these patterns of sensory processing.

	Self-Regulation Strategies	
Neurological thresholds	PASSIVE	ACTIVE
HIGH	Low Registration	Seeking
LOW	Sensitivity	Avoiding

Figure 6.1. Dunn's model of sensory processing.

Adapted from "The Impact of Sensory Processing Abilities on the Daily Lives of Young Children and Families: A Conceptual Model," by W. Dunn, 1997a, *Infants and Young Children, 9*(4), 23-25. Reprinted with permission.

Specifically, researchers have found that people with various conditions have unique sensory processing patterns, including people with attention deficit hyperactivity disorder (ADHD) (Dove & Dunn, 2008; Dunn & Bennett, 2002), fragile X syndrome (Miller et al., 1998), and ASD Level 1 (e.g., Ben-Sasson et al., 2008; Crane et al., 2009; Dunn et al., 2002; Kientz & Dunn, 1997; Myles et al., 2004; Watling et al., 2001).

Children with ASD are more likely to be sensitive to touch, as well as auditory and oral sensory processing (Ben-Sasson et al., 2008; Crane et al., 2009; Dunn, 1999, 2000; Ermer & Dunn, 1998; Kientz & Dunn, 1997; Watling et al., 2001). They also have significantly different scores on registration and avoiding. For example, they may have differences in both registration (i.e., fails to notice stimuli that others notice) and avoiding (i.e., detects and withdraws from stimuli) at the same time.

Further, children with ASD often seem oblivious to the environment (i.e., registration) up until a certain point. Then they notice a stimulus (e.g., a sound, a touch) and immediately become threatened or overwhelmed, withdraw, or have a tantrum (i.e., avoiding). This scenario leaves little room for adaptive responses and learning, which is a major dilemma. We learn when we notice a stimulus and interact within the experience across time. Therefore, we want to design strategies that enable the child to notice stimuli without feeling threatened or overwhelmed.

The *Sensory Profile School Companion* supports teachers and students in the school context (Dunn, 2007a). Teachers complete the School Companion to report about students' behaviors and responses in school. Findings suggest that using this tool teachers identify unique patterns of students' responsiveness to environmental stimuli and, when combined with the therapist's data from interviews and observations and parental reports about the child at home (i.e., from the *Sensory Profile*), it provides a complete picture that can be used to guide evidence-based intervention planning. As with the other *Sensory Profile* measures, students with ASD exhibit significantly different patterns of sensory processing and school behaviors than peers (i.e., they engage in behaviors more frequently than peers).

Not every child with ASD has the exact pattern of sensory processing illustrated in group research studies. Each child is unique, so we need to understand each child's personal patterns for individualized planning to be effective. Let's look at each pattern from Dunn's model of sensory processing (see Figure 6.1).

Seeking

Seeking reflects high thresholds and active self-regulation according to Dunn's model. Children who seek more than their peers add movement, touch, sound, and visual stimuli to every life event. Seekers make noises, fidget in their seats, touch everything, feel objects, touch and hang on to others, or chew on things. Each of their actions intensifies the sensory input, which, in turn, increases their chances of meeting high thresholds. Children with a seeking pattern are also creative, and can be counted on to provide innovative solutions and strategies in learning experiences. These children might lack caution in play, display excitability, and engage in impulsive behavior in an attempt to increase sensory input (Dunn, 1997a).

Registration

Registration reflects high thresholds and passive self-regulation according to Dunn's model. Children with a high score in this area do not notice what is going on around them, so they may seem easy-going and flexible because they are not affected by changes in the routines as other students might be. Some might describe these children as dull, uninterested, or oblivious (Dunn, 1997a). Further, the children may seem withdrawn, difficult to engage, or self-absorbed. Further, they may be easily exhausted and appear apathetic (National Center for Clinical Infant Programs/Zero to Three [NCCIP], 1994) when, in fact, they are just not detecting input that others notice readily. These children need highly salient sensory input to get their attention so they can participate in school activities.

Sensitivity

With sensitivity, children have low thresholds and passive self-regulation strategies according to Dunn's model. Children with sensitivity patterns detect more details than others and, therefore, may be very discerning about school supplies; for example, these students notice differences in paper quality or writing utensils. They may also be hyperactive, distracted, and easily upset because they notice more things than peers (Dunn, 1997a). Not surprisingly, children with sensitivity have difficulty completing tasks as new stimuli capture their attention repeatedly during the day. They may also have difficulty learning from their experiences because routines are disrupted so often that they cannot complete tasks and learn (NCCIP, 1994).

Avoiding

Avoiding reflects low thresholds and active self-regulation according to Dunn's model. Children in this group actively work to reduce input, which means they are quite routinized. They may seem resistant and unwilling to participate in activities, particularly unfamiliar ones. They experience discomfort quickly, and to keep from feeling discomfort, they reduce their activity and withdraw. For example, a student may feel overwhelmed during independent work time because of all the unpredictable sounds and movements around him; a student might become irritable or aggressive as a way to get someone to take him out of this setting, thereby reducing the unmanageable visual and auditory input.

Developing rituals is a predominant strategy for dealing with sensory input. Rituals provide comfort, because they stimulate a familiar sensory input pattern, reducing the possibility of triggering low thresholds. Changes in rituals, on the other hand, increase sensory stimulation, which generates anxiety, since triggering thresholds may be uncomfortable. Students with avoiding patterns appear stubborn and controlling. They might seem inattentive to some stimuli, while being preoccupied with others. These behaviors control sensory input, but may be perceived by adults as self-absorption (NCCIP, 1994). The self-absorption is related to the vigilance required to keep control over possible "assaults" from unfamiliar sensory inputs.

Designing Sensory Processing Interventions to Support Students

Our goal in serving students in schools is to improve their active participation in education. When applying a sensory processing approach, we must identify the student's sensory processing patterns from observations, interviews, and assessments. We want to determine the exact ways that sensory processing patterns might be supporting or interfering with the student's participation. Occupational therapists (OT) are the experts on sensory processing. They focus on the student's needs in school and consider how sensory processing patterns might affect learning. For example, if a student has difficulty completing seatwork, the OT can observe, interview the teacher, and conduct assessments to determine what might be supporting or interfering with seatwork time. For a student with sensitivity to sound, students in small groups creating noise as they talk may interfere with concentration. In this situation, the OT and teacher can identify ways to construct small-group work to reduce the sound, such as sending the target student to the library for resource material.

When using a sensory processing framework for intervention, the goal is to improve participation, not to change the sensory processing patterns. People with all types of sensory processing can lead successful lives. We do not want to "cure" a student of "seeking"; we want to make sure that sensation seeking works for learning.

Sensory experiences are part of every activity, so interventions take advantage of these naturally occurring opportunities during the school day. We don't create special circumstances to provide sensory processing interventions; instead, we give the student more chances to participate successfully with the sensory patterns the student has, thus improving school performance.

When possible, we incorporate strategies that capitalize on students' strengths. For example, teachers can provide students with a card or handout containing the steps to complete the day's work to take advantage of visual strengths. We also want to minimize challenging areas. To that end, teachers can provide foam earplugs or set up a removed work area for a student who is sensitive to sounds.

Ways to Support Students Whose Seeking Patterns Interfere With Learning

Seeking interferes with school when a student stops work to get sensory input another way (e.g., running, making noises). In this case, we design interventions that provide the extra sensory input during schoolwork, as suggested in Table 6.1.

When students demonstrate a seeking pattern of sensory processing, they enjoy sensory experiences. Because these students enjoy sensory input, you might observe that they move more, hum, or rub their hands on things throughout the day. They might also point out interesting sensory events throughout the day. Students' interest and pleasure in sensory events might also lead to difficulties with task completion because they may get distracted with new sensory experiences and lose track of routine or daily tasks.

Students with a seeking pattern can profit from more opportunities to have sensory experiences as part of school work so they don't have to stop working to get the extra sensory input they desire. With more opportunities for sensory input, these students can continue to pay attention to their school tasks and, therefore, stick with them for a longer time.

Some children with ASD seek movement input by rocking, running, and jumping, and these actions interfere with school work and social interactions. Therefore, we want to reconstruct school activities so the child gets high-intensity sensory input while continuing to participate and complete work. For example, for a student who needs movement input, place books and materials on the floor next to the student's desk so she has to bend down to get the items (bending moves the head upside down, which provides the vestibular system with very strong input); this same student might benefit from jungle gym play at recess. For social interactions, pair the student with a friend to erase the chalk or whiteboard. These tasks enable the student to receive movement input without having to stop ongoing interactions with peers.

Table 6.1

Activities That Can Provide Input for a Student Whose Seeking Patterns Interfere With Daily Life

Offer chewy, crunchy snacks	Allow student to chew gum or hard candy if quiet
Provide worksheets on colored paper	Change fonts on computer
Embed cues with visual interest (e.g., moving parts, colorful words, complex pictures)	Tape record stories in character voices, add sound effects within story, set script to a song
Dramatize the scenario with jumping, skipping, holding heavy objects during scenes	Videotape story or make a pop-up book
Place a textured cushion on the student's seat	Encourage the student to wear highly textured socks, shirts
Encourage student to add accessories, such as head bands, wrist bands, belts	Provide variety in texture, flavor and temperature in food options
Add textures to finger paint	Add texture to handles and other work surfaces
Allow the student to change work positions (sitting, standing, different parts of the room)	Provide a textured rug mat under the student's chair so the student can rub feet on the mat while working
Allow student to use the chalkboard for some assignments	Provide textured blankets of student's choice for safe spots
Create longer routes to recess, lunchroom, library	Send this student on errands throughout the day
Have student help with tasks such as moving furniture, pushing milk carts and erasing the board	Create recess games that require climbing, crawling, hopping, running, etc.
Color code work materials using bright colors	Put posters/other pictures up at student's eye level
Provide lively music background or in a walkman for the student's work time	Use contrasting mats on work areas so papers and supplies are easier to see
Discuss things with the student as you do them	Have student look for things as you move about the school
Provide extra, colored lighting in this student's work areas	Hum/sing to songs, make up new verses
Open windows to enable ambient sound to enter near the student's desk	Provide scented lotions so the student can come to a designated area in the room and use it on the hands
Allow the student to take shoes off during class	Allow student to use scented lip balms during class
Clean toys with scented cleaners	Have student stand up to work and eat

From *The Sensory Profile Supplement,* by W. Dunn, 2007b, San Antonio, TX: Psychological Corporation. Adapted with permission.

We must be very careful to properly determine which behaviors are actually seeking behaviors. Seeking creates pleasure from sensory experiences. Some children who have ASD engage in a high rate of certain behaviors (e.g., rocking) because they are familiar for the child. When a familiar behavior has a more "driven" quality, it is likely to be an avoiding behavior because it keeps out new sensations (see below).

Noah is a middle school student who seeks deep pressure (e.g., pressing firmly on the skin) and touch input throughout the day. When he was younger, he stopped working to rub his arms and body and then would knock things off his desk. He now wears snuggly fitting undershirts and his favorite stretchy jacket every day, which gives him extra pressure on his skin during classes; he says he pays attention better that way (VandenBerg, 2001). Now that Noah's sensory-seeking needs are being met, he gets his class work done nearly every day.

Tracey is a fourth-grader who keeps getting up from the table to run around the room. While she is getting her sensory needs met that way, this behavior keeps her from interacting with other children at the table. The teacher assigns Tracey the job of handing out the supplies. She stacks the materials on the floor in the supplies closet so Tracey has to bend down to get them, adding more movement input. These adjustments in the small-group activity provide Tracey movement input, but she is still expected to participate with peers in the activity.

Ways to Support Students Whose Registration Patterns Interfere With Learning

When children register less than their peers, they do not notice things, and, as a result, may miss directions or other cues. Because these students notice less, you might observe that they are more easy-going than other students, and are not bothered by things that bother others in the classroom. However, not noticing can also mean the students do not respond when you call them, may drift away during activities, and have a harder time getting tasks completed in a timely manner.

Students with a low registration pattern can profit from more intensity in sensory experiences, as suggested in Table 6.2. With more intensity of sensory input, these students can continue to pay attention during daily life activities and, therefore, stick with them for a longer time.

The plan for students whose registration interferes at school is to provide enough continuous and intense sensory input so that they can persist in their work. Bradley, our case study at the beginning of the chapter, registers less than we expect. For this student, place work materials on very high or very low shelves to increase reaching and bending. Construct a flow chart for more complex tasks that students like Bradley can check off as they complete task components.

We need to find ways to intensify the sensory input available within the activities and environments around the child. Some children who have ASD may seem "out of it" because their high thresholds keep them from recognizing stimuli that other children routinely notice and respond to.

To address registration needs, increase the contrast and reduce the predictability of events as this creates more opportunities for the sensory systems to meet high thresholds. Make objects weigh more, change an item's color or the background color, or add a movement to the assignment. For example, if a student like Bradley is lethargic, we might break his seatwork assignments into smaller parts so he has to get up and turn in the parts several times during the seatwork period. We might also give the student construction paper to write on (increasing the texture) and scented markers for certain assignments. Each change adds sensory input to the seatwork task (i.e., movement, touch, smell, visual inputs, respectively), and the accumulation of inputs increases the chances that the student will reach thresholds and become more responsive.

Table 6.2

Activities That Can Provide Input for a Student Whose Registration Patterns Interfere With Daily Life

Add rough and varied textures on handles, seats, and work surfaces	Have scented lotion available that the student can rub on hands and arms
Encourage the student to wear highly textured socks, shirts	Encourage variety in texture, flavor, and temperature in food options
Create opportunities for the student to play on different surfaces (e.g., linoleum, carpet)	Have student hand out books to class and move items for teacher to provide additional input to body
Arrange it so the student can bend down to obtain supplies from lower shelves	Offer a rocking chair in the back of the classroom
Provide a bin of materials the student can manipulate while working (such as a stress ball, a key ring)	Use textured paper for individual work when writing
Place classroom materials out of easy reach so the student has to reach, walk and move to get to them	Have student carry books, work materials, and other heavy items to table
Be aware of safety measures when the student is moving about (may not notice objects, stairs, changes in terrain)	Select bright mats for student's work surface
Make mirrors available at floor level	Add colored tape to edges of work areas in classroom so student can easily see the edges
Turn on bright lights, or make a more focused desk lamp available for the student's work space	Point out things you pass by so student can stay engaged as the class moves from place to place
Provide lively music background, or a walkman with lively music during seatwork time	Talk about what the student/you are doing as you do it
Talk with varying voice intonation	Point out sounds you hear and name the sounds
Clean materials for the student with scented cleaners	Use spritzer scents in designated work areas for the student
Practice a routine a lot with the student; add visual cues about what to do next	Teach the student how to get clues from watching other students
Have student stand up to eat or do seatwork	Select heavier objects for the student to play with

From *The Sensory Profile Supplement,* by W. Dunn, 2007b, San Antonio, TX: Psychological Corporation. Adapted with permission.

Ways to Support Students Whose Sensitivity Patterns Interfere With Learning

When students notice everything, the enormous amount of sensory input they take in can interfere with school work. Because these students notice more, you might observe that they are bothered by things that others might not even notice. These students pick up more details in life and may notice changes in setting or mood very quickly. However, noticing more can also mean that students are distractible and, therefore, get interrupted from getting tasks completed in a timely manner.

Students whose sensitivity patterns interfere with learning can profit from more structured patterns of sensory experiences during daily life. With more structure of sensory input, these students can continue to pay attention during daily life activities and therefore stick with them for a longer time. See Table 6.3.

Table 6.3
Activities That Can Provide Input for a Student Whose Sensitivity Patterns Interfere With Daily Life

Place a rubber mat underneath the desk that provides a steady grip for the student's feet when doing seatwork	Encourage form-fitting clothing and undergarments that do NOT have tight spots or bunching
Identify favorite food flavors, textures, and temperatures and stick with them	When the student likes/dislikes a texture, name it for him/her. Then continue to use these words
Provide a buffer space for the student to play without getting bumped easily	Identify preferred surface textures and make them available to this student
Make heavy blankets available	Remove blowing vents/fans from student's location
Use firm pressure on skin to calm	Create a comfortable seating structure for the student
Place materials at chest level in drawers/ shelves so student does not have to bend over	Provide a rocker for calming when the student gets upset
Create a blank area for individualized work	Serve foods in a compartment tray
Place sheets over shelving areas to reduce visual distractions	Remove overhead light sources from room and replace with lamps and more focused lighting
Run water before the student enters the bathroom to reduce the startle from the sound of the water	Tell student what to do, and then be quiet
Provide written or taped instructions	Allow students to place books on lap to work
Organize classroom discussions so that one person is talking at a time	Use plastic utensils and paper plates to reduce noise in lunch room
Allow student to move to a more remote location for work	Play even-tempo background music during work time
Provide ear plugs/ear muffs/earphones during work time	Give student opportunities for moving ahead of or after other students when changing rooms or activities
Limit the amount of time the student must spend in loud public places	Be careful about using scents in hair products, perfumes, and lotions; these might upset this student
Tell student name of aromas of flavors/ foods	Use unscented cleaners in the classroom for this student
Create routines and stick with them	Have student wear back pack

From *The Sensory Profile Supplement,* by W. Dunn, 2007b, San Antonio, TX: Psychological Corporation. Adapted with permission.

It is important to emphasize the organizing aspects of the sensory systems with children who have sensitivity (see Dunn, 1991a; Dunn & DeGangi, 1992) because these sensory inputs provide the brain with information without increasing arousal. When we can provide more organizing input for these children, we increase their chances of completing tasks and learning from them. Teachers, parents, and other professionals must be flexible yet systematic because these children are more sensitive to the sensory information around them than other children.

Students with ASD are often sensitive to touch. Light touch can occur many times in a day (e.g., clothing, hair, people moving around and brushing into each other) and can make the student more and more upset. We can recommend form-fitting clothing, which presses evenly on the skin. With firm pressure on the skin, it is harder to get light touch. Bradley is sensitive to touch, and the cocoon in his classroom's safe spot is very helpful to him when he is bothered.

Ways to Support Students Whose Avoiding Patterns Interfere With Learning

Some students withdraw from situations to reduce the sensory input they have to manage. When sensation avoiding interferes with school participation, identify what sensory input is O.K. and what is challenging for the student.

When avoiding patterns interfere, students notice and are bothered by things much more than others. As a result, they may be more interested in being alone or in very quiet places. When environments are too challenging, these students may withdraw and fail to complete work. Students with an avoiding pattern participate better when there is less sensory input in the environment. When the environment is "quiet," these students can continue daily life activities for a longer period of time (see Table 6.4).

Table 6.4
Activities That Can Provide Input for a Student Whose Avoiding Patterns Interfere With Daily Life

Encourage family to select form-fitted undergarments	Arrange for lunch and snacks to be served at room temperature
Guide student to select foods with even textures	Identify work and play areas with space away from other students
Keep fans or vents from blowing on the student	Allow the student to hold books on lap while working
Keep student out of crowded spaces	Gather work materials for student in one place
Select an assigned seat for the student away from traffic patterns to prevent bumping	Allow student to use the library for work and getaways
Identify routines for the class and stick with them	Remove other work materials from the work surface
Keep shades drawn or move the student to a more remote location	Allow student to have one food at a time on plate
Serve plate to student rather than having student carry own tray	Cover cubby holes to decrease distractions
Create "blinders" for the student's work area	Run fan (that does not blow on student) to create "white" background noise to drown out unpredictable noises
Find closed-in, quiet places for the student to play/rest	Limit large unstructured time for the student
Use unscented materials with the student	Remove air fresheners from this student's areas
Craft alone-time for the student and recognize it is GOOD	Use very heavy blankets for safe spots
Have student carry/wear a backpack	Braid hair to increase firm pressure and decrease light touch
Have student hold the heavy doors while others file out	Wear clothing that covers well and is fitted
Use trips to the bathroom or errands to give student a break from intense environments	Educate others to use visual cues rather than touching to gain student's attention

From *The Sensory Profile Supplement,* by W. Dunn, 2007b, San Antonio, TX: Psychological Corporation. Adapted with permission.

We have to be careful not to push students into overwhelming sensory situations. Once the student has a "fight or flight" response (i.e., the response of fear or danger in which the child will become aggressive [fight] or retreat [flight] to protect self), learning is not possible, because the brain is in a protective mode. If the student's rituals are just quirky, we can leave the behavior alone.

For example, many children with ASD only eat one or two foods, which can interfere with their health.

Sammy would only eat chicken broth (e.g., no noodles, no bits of meat). The team was concerned over his nutrition. The OT blended the chicken broth to adjust the texture a little without adding anything to it. Sammy squealed when he noticed the texture change, but then he continued to eat the broth. The OT then blended in a few flecks of parsley; Sammy immediately noticed them, picked them out, and ate the broth. If the team took the broth away, Sammy would likely not eat at all.

Sammy was persistent about what was acceptable for him. In consultation with a dietician, the team decided that Sammy was getting nutritional value from the broth. The occupational therapist collaborated with the dietician to identify other foods with similar sensory characteristics. They began presenting other foods on his plate without any pressure to eat things other than the broth. Over time, the repeated availability of other foods led to Sammy trying strained pear juice, which had a similar appearance to the broth.

We must recognize the discomfort these students experience. Through careful observation, we can identify the sensory features of their rituals (i.e., what do they include or exclude from the ritual?). Some frames of reference might suggest that we bombard these children with input so they "get used to it." However, such a strategy can lead to more and more withdrawal (Dunn, 2007b), as the children attempt to maintain some sense of control. From a sensory processing viewpoint, we recognize that ritual and control may indicate the child's need to manage input.

Some rituals can be left alone (e.g., the way a student takes off her coat, the way the student eats a sandwich); others may need to be adjusted to support the student in learning at school (e.g., managing the sounds of the classroom while continuing to work). When identifying a ritual that needs to be expanded, study the characteristics of the ritual to expand it in some small way so that there is a blending of familiar and new stimuli (Dunn & DeGangi, 1992). This enables the child to incorporate the challenging sensory inputs into a familiar ritual.

For example, as mentioned, many students with ASD have strong food preferences, including strategies for eating and preparing the food. In order to improve nutritional circumstances, it is sometimes necessary to expand the eating patterns with the student. If the student is focused on the taste of the food, we can add a color or texture to the food to broaden the sensory qualities (e.g., we can add food coloring to pudding, or we can add finely ground nuts). By doing this, we create an opportunity for the student to notice the new stimulus and perhaps accept it into her ritual, broadening the ritual without causing an aggressive or withdrawing response. If we disrupt a ritual too quickly, the student will object more strongly, which usually leads to more avoidance behaviors and further decline of functional performance (Dunn, 1997a). There is a great risk of entering into power struggles (NCCIP, 1994), and these are not helpful to learning.

Children who avoid sensation may appear disengaged, which can be confused with low registration. However, there is a difference. Children who avoid sensory experiences notice and withdraw from activities, whereas children with low registration are not aware of what is going on around them. Children with avoiding patterns display anxiety and hypervigilance, while children with low registration seem unaware and unconcerned.

Combining Educational and Sensory Processing Strategies

Interdisciplinary teams need to integrate effective educational strategies and sensory processing knowledge to best serve children who have ASD. Dunn, Saiter, and Rinner (2002) summarized this integration for students who have ASD Level 1. Using priming, working independently, social narratives, home base, and visual supports as effective educational strategies, the authors described how sensory processing knowledge can enhance the effectiveness of these teaching approaches. Please see the original reference for more detailed explanations and case studies applying these ideas within children's stories.

Summary and Conclusions

Understanding sensory processing enables us to better understand student behavior and planning school strategies. Evidence indicates that students with ASD notice less sensory input than others (i.e., registration) and withdraw more quickly than others (i.e., avoiding). Effective intervention focuses on adjusting sensory demands so the student can participate in school more effectively.

This chapter illustrated how sensory processing difficulties can lead to challenging behaviors, including work avoidance, class disruption, aggression, and even explosive outbursts. It would follow that a sensory inventory is an important tool to use in a functional behavior assessment. Many of the strategies listed in this chapter can be used to effectively reduce unwanted behaviors in the classroom while leading to increased student participation.

Tips for Practical Application

✓ A first step to addressing the sensory needs of any given student with ASD is to consult with members of the team who have expertise in this area (e.g., occupational therapist) as well as have knowledge of the particular student.

✓ Strategies that may support students who seem to seek out sensory stimulation include:
   o Provide colored worksheets or colored sheet protectors to highlight the work.
   o Have some healthy, chewy snacks available either in the student's desk or in a special container in the teacher's desk.
   o Allow the student to change work positions or stand to do his work, as needed. It may also be helpful to allow the student to do his work on the chalkboard.
   o Arrange for the student to sit on a move-n-sit cushion™ or a t-stool that will allow for movement while sitting.
   o Send the student on errands around the school, such as to the office, to get him out of the classroom and moving.
   o Have the student wear a wristband, head band, or belt.
   o Adjust the lighting in the student's work area.
   o Allow the student to take off his shoes while he is in the classroom. Make sure to establish guidelines so the student is aware that shoes are required to be worn in the hallways, the cafeteria, etc.
   o Make sure that visual materials are at eye level.

✓ Strategies that may support students who seem to have low registration of sensory information include:
   o Allow the student to have appropriately scented lotion in his desk to put on throughout the day.
   o Arrange jobs for the student, such as handing out materials and books.
   o Provide a rocking chair in the back of the classroom and allow the student to request using it between activities.
   o Provide a variety of work surfaces with different textures and density.
   o The student may not be aware of dangerous objects in the environment, so monitor his movement.
   o Use bright lighting in the student's work areas.
   o Allow the student to listen to music using an iPod during work time to help keep him alert.
   o Be sure to provide plenty of visual supports and repetitive routines when teaching this student.

✓ Strategies that may support students who seem to have sensitivity include:
   o Provide a rubber mat underneath the student's desk that can provide a steady grip for his feet while working.
   o Provide a cafeteria tray with divided areas to help the food from mixing and for easy identification.
   o Allow the student to leave the class a bit early or stand at the beginning or end of the line while leaving the room to avoid bumping into classmates.
   o Be aware that the student might startle from unexpected or sudden noises, so it is best to prepare for noises whenever possible.
   o Avoid using repetitive verbal directives. After giving a single directive, be quiet and/or display a visual support.
   o Limit the amount of time the student has to spend in loud or crowded spaces.

- o Provide ear plugs for times when you anticipate a louder environment. Prepare the student prior to the event with a story and instructions of how to use the ear plugs.
- o Directly teach the student about his sensory sensitivities. Help him to identify scents and sounds and to advocate for himself when the environment becomes unbearable.

✓ Strategies that may support students who seem to be avoiding:
- o Create predictable routines within the classroom.
- o Break down tasks using a visual sequence when teaching the steps of an activity, such as toothbrushing, to create a routine that can be followed repetitively.
- o Be aware that the student may have a very limited diet due to his sensitivity. Identify favorite foods and textures and help the student to choose these foods at lunch. In some cases, it may help to introduce new foods in a systematic and gradual way. For example, have the student work on just looking at the new food, then tolerate smelling it prior to ever actually tasting it.
- o Arrange for lunch food to be served at room temperature.
- o Be careful that fans or vents are not blowing directly on the student.
- o Have the student's desk or work space out of the main traffic areas.
- o Find quiet spaces within the school environment where the student can work without distracting the other students.
- o Arrange for the student to go on errands to other areas of the school building to give him a break from the noise of the classroom environment.
- o Be aware that the student might be highly anxious in crowded or loud assemblies as well as gym due to the movement and echoes of the gymnasium. Be sure to prepare the student in advance of these events and activities.

Chapter Highlights

- Sensory processing is a person's way of noticing and responding to sensory events that occur during daily life.

- Sensory systems provide information to the brain, which then forms maps that guide our spatial and temporal orientation, as well as how we react to different situations.

- Sensory processing systems include touch (somatosensory), body position (proprioceptive), sight (visual), hearing (auditory), smell (olfactory), taste (gustatory), and movement (vestibular).

- Many behaviors observed in children with ASD can be attributed to their particular sensory patterns.

- Thresholds, or the point at which a particular sensory system responds, can affect our reactions: When thresholds are too low, children may respond too frequently and be distracted; if too high, children may miss important cues.

- Dunn's model of sensory processing is a conceptual model for understanding patterns of sensory processing that combines brain thresholds with self-regulation to create four patterns: low registration, sensitivity, seeking, and avoiding.

- When using a sensory processing framework for intervention, the goal is to improve participation, not change the sensory processing patterns.

- For each of the four sensory processing patterns, the author provides specific information about the pattern, as well as ways educators and others can plan interventions to support student learning based on individual sensory needs.

Chapter Review Questions

1. What is sensory processing?

2. List and describe the systems involved in sensory processing.

3. Why is it useful to incorporate various sensory inputs into educational programs?

4. Explain Dunn's model of sensory processing.

5. How do individuals with ASD differ from peers in terms of sensory processing?

6. What is the goal of a sensory processing framework for intervention?

7. Give examples of sensory processing interventions that address each type of pattern and that support student learning.

References

Ashburner, J., Ziviani, J., & Rodger, S. (2008). Sensory processing and classroom emotional, behavioral, and educational outcomes in children with autism spectrum disorder. *American Journal of Occupational Therapy, 62*(5), 564-573.

Ayres, A. J. (1972). *Sensory integration and learning disorders.* Los Angeles, CA: Western Psychological Services.

Ayres, A. J. (1979). *Sensory integration and the child.* Los Angeles, CA: Western Psychological Services.

Ben-Sasson, A., Cermak, S. A., Orsmond, G. I., Tager-Flusberg, H., Kadlec, M. B., & Carter, A. S. (2008). Sensory clusters of toddlers with autism spectrum disorders: Differences in affective symptoms. *Journal of Child Psychology and Psychiatry, 49*(8), 817-825.

Brown, C., & Dunn, W. (2002). *The Adult Sensory Profile.* San Antonio, TX: Psychological Corporation.

Brown, C., Tollefson, N., Dunn, W., Cromwell, R., & Filion, D. (2001). *The Adult Sensory Profile*: Measuring patterns of sensory processing. *American Journal of Occupational Therapy, 55,* 75-82.

Chen, Y., Rodgers, J., & McConachie, H. (2009). Restricted and repetitive behaviours, sensory processing and cognitive style in children with autism spectrum disorders. *Journal of Autism and Developmental Disorders, 39*(4), 635-642.

Crane, L., Goddard, L., & Pring, L. (2009). Sensory processing in adults with autism spectrum disorders. *Autism, 13*(3), 215-228. doi: 10.1177/1362361309103794

Dove, S., & Dunn, W. (2008). Sensory processing in students with specific learning disabilities: Findings and implications for assessment and intervention planning. *Journal of Occupational Therapy, Schools and Early Intervention, 1*(2), 116-127. doi: 10.1080/19411240802312798

Dunn, W. (1991a). Assessing human performance related to brain function. Neuroscience foundations of human performance. *AOTA Self-Study Series, 12,* 3-38.

Dunn, W. (1991b). Motivation. Neuroscience foundations of human performance. *AOTA Self-Study Series, 7,* 3-36.

Dunn, W. (1991c). The sensorimotor systems: A framework for assessment and intervention. In F. P. Orelove & D. Sobsey (Eds.), *Educating children with multiple disabilities: A transdisciplinary approach* (2nd ed., pp. 35-79). Baltimore, MD: Paul H. Brookes.

Dunn, W. (1997a). The impact of sensory processing abilities on the daily lives of young children and their families: A conceptual model. *Infants and Young Children, 9*(4), 23-25.

Dunn, W. (1997b). Implementing neuroscience principles to support habilitation and recovery. In C. Christiansen & C. Baum (Eds.), *Occupational therapy: Enabling function and well-being* (pp. 182-233). Thorofare, NJ: Slack.

Dunn, W. (1999). *The Sensory Profile Manual.* San Antonio, TX: Psychological Corporation.

Dunn, W. (2000). *The Infant Toddler Sensory Profile.* San Antonio, TX: Psychological Corporation.

Dunn, W. (2001a). The sensations of everyday life: Theoretical, conceptual and pragmatic considerations. *American Journal of Occupational Therapy, 55*(6), 608-620.

Dunn, W. (2007a). *Sensory Profile School Companion.* San Antonio, TX: The Psychological Corporation.

Dunn, W. (2007b). *The Sensory Profile Supplement.* San Antonio, TX: The Psychological Corporation.

Dunn, W., & Bennett, D. (2002). Patterns of sensory processing in children with attention deficit hyperactivity disorder. *Occupational Therapy Journal of Research, 22*(1), 4-15.

Dunn, W., & Daniels, D. (2001). Initial development of the Infant Toddler Sensory Profile. *Journal of Early Intervention, 25*(1),27-41.

Dunn, W., & DeGangi, G. (1992). Sensory integration and neurodevelopmental treatment for educational programming. *AOTA Self-Study Series, 2,* 5-55.

Dunn, W., Myles, B., & Orr, S. (2002). Sensory processing issues associated with Asperger Syndrome: A preliminary investigation. *American Journal of Occupational Therapy, 56,* 97-102.

Dunn, W., Saiter, J., & Rinner, L. (2002). Asperger Syndrome and sensory processing: A conceptual model and guidance for intervention planning. *Focus on Autism and Other Developmental Disabilities, 17*(3), 172-185.

Engel-Yeger, B., & Shochat, T. (2012). The relationship between sensory processing patterns and sleep quality in healthy adults. *The Canadian Journal of Occupational Therapy, 79*(3), 134-141. doi: 10.1016/0165-1781(89)90047-4

Ermer, J., & Dunn, W. (1998). *The Sensory Profile:* A discriminant analysis of children with and without disabilities. *American Journal of Occupational Therapy, 52,* 283-290.

Kandel, E., Schwartz, J., & Jessell, T. (2000). *Principles of neural science.* New York, NY: McGraw-Hill.

Kientz, M. A., & Dunn, W. (1997). Comparison of children with and without autism on the *Sensory Profile. American Journal of Occupational Therapy, 51*(7), 530-537.

Miller, L., McIntosh, D., McGrath, J., Shyu, V., Lampe, M., Taylor, A., Tassone, F., Neitzel, K., Stackhouse, T., & Hagerman, R. (1998). Electrodermal responses to sensory stimuli in individuals with fragile X syndrome: A preliminary report. *American Journal of Medical Genetics, 83*(4), 268-279.

Myles, B. S., Hagiwara, T., Dunn, W., Rinner, L., Reese, M., Huggins, A., et al. (2004). Sensory issues in children with Asperger Syndrome and autism. *Education and Training in Developmental Disabilities, 3*(4), 283-290.

National Center for Clinical Infant Programs/Zero to Three. (1994). *Diagnostic classification of mental health and developmental disorders of infancy and early childhood.* Arlington, VA: Author.

Reike, E., & Anderson, D. (2009). *Adolescent/Adult Sensory Profile* and obsessive compulsive disorder. *American Journal of Occupational Therapy, 63*(2), 138-145.

Rogers, S., Hepburn, S., & Wehner, E. (2003). Parent report of sensory symptoms in toddlers with autism and those with other developmental disorders. *Journal of Autism and Developmental Disorders, 33*(6), 631-642.

Shani-Adir, A., Rozenman, D., Kessel, A., & Engel-Yeger, B. (2009). The relationship between sensory hypersensitivity and sleep quality of children with atopic dermatitis. *Pediatric Dermatology, 26*(2), 143-149.

VandenBerg, N. (2001). The use of a weighted vest to increase on-task behavior in children with attention difficulties. *American Journal of Occupational Therapy, 55*(6), 621-628.

Watling, R., Dietz, J., & White, O. (2001). Comparison of sensory profile scores of young children with and without autism spectrum disorders. *American Journal of Occupational Therapy, 55*(4), 416-423.

Learner Objectives

After reading this chapter, the learner should be able to:

- State the definition of a crisis management approach and the advantages and disadvantages of using such an approach

- Discuss shifting behavioral perspectives and the set of assumptions that accompany this shift in thinking, including the specifics of each assumption

- List the members of the behavioral support team and their roles

- State the components of a functional behavioral assessment

- Discuss the issues involved in defining behaviors of concern

- Provide examples of behaviors that are observable and measurable

- State the goal of a functional behavioral assessment

- Explain the importance of antecedents and consequences in maintaining or diminishing behavior

- List and describe the types of questions that must be asked to determine the true function of a behavior

- Explain why collecting information is an ongoing process in functional behavioral assessment and positive behavior support

- Explain what hypothesis statements are and what they are based on

- Discuss the importance of looking at problem behavior pathways to determine how to support appropriate behavior

- State the focus of positive behavior support approaches

- List and describe curricular, classroom management, and instructional considerations involved in implementing interventions

- Explain the role of applied behavior analysis in intervention

- Discuss why behavior support plans may not be successful and the importance of monitoring implementation and outcomes

Chapter 7

Teaching a Different Way of Behaving: Positive Behavior Supports

Cathy Pratt

Matthew is a 7-year-old child with a diagnosis of autism spectrum disorder. He was diagnosed when he was 22 months old. Up until 19 months of age, he had been developing seemingly normally but then began losing language and becoming much more introverted. When left by himself, he preferred to sit alone engaging in self-regulatory behavior. Upon diagnosis, he was enrolled in the state's early intervention program and began working with a speech clinician, an occupational therapist, and an educational therapist in his home. His parents augmented these services with private therapy focused on behavior and communication.

Today, Matthew attends a program in a public school. Matthew remains nonverbal. In the past two years, parents and staff have noticed an increase in behavioral incidents. When requested to perform certain tasks, Matthew becomes anxious and attempts to destroy instructional materials. At recess, he either wanders the playground or pushes others off the swings. When directed to return, he refuses. His parents note that he has difficulty sleeping at night and that he is a very picky eater. He also struggles with chronic diarrhea.

Aside from these behavioral difficulties, Matthew can be a very affectionate child. He loves to crawl up on the lap of adults and be hugged tightly. He is easily entertained at times, and can sit for a period of time and play with his trains. This play is somewhat inappropriate and involves ritualistic play (e.g., spinning the wheels repeatedly of the train). He has an engaging smile and infectious laugh.

In his current program, Matthew is primarily in an early intervention classroom for students with various disabilities. The focus of the program is on teaching academic, functional, communication, and social/play skills. When working on functional/academic skills, staff report that it is difficult to keep Matthew focused on the task at hand. They often have to position a staff person close by him to continually prompt him to work on a task.

*For communication, the staff and family have chosen a **Picture Exchange Communication System (PECS)** (Frost & Bondy, 1994). Matthew has access to this system three times a week during therapy sessions. PECS is used inconsistently at home and school. Staff and family state that they understand what Matthew wants by watching his gestures and facial expressions. With strangers, he has no functional way to communicate. To teach play skills, the staff work to position Matthew in close proximity to other students in hopes that he will model their behavior.*

Matthew appears to have some sensory processing challenges. He likes to lick book pages and then play with his saliva; he becomes upset at certain noises; and he prefers to wear only certain types of clothing. As a result, Matthew works with an occupational therapist weekly on sensory-based activities. At this point, no sensory activities have been embedded into his day.

While Matthew has made some progress, there is much more to do. Overall, staff will be focusing on the following areas: initiation, joint attention, play skills, toilet training, and following directions.

Students with autism spectrum disorders (ASD) who engage in challenging behaviors (e.g., aggression, self-injurious behavior, withdrawal, refusal) place a tremendous stress on the family members and professionals who support them. This stress may be unduly increased when those involved lack training or understanding of the strategies for assessing, understanding, and addressing problem behaviors.

The purpose of this chapter is to provide some basic information about **functional behavioral assessment** approaches and **positive behavior supports**. The hope is to present information that can be easily used to ensure that programs are adopted and supports utilized that can lead to long-term behavioral change by creating positive learning environments and teaching alternative behaviors.

While this is the only chapter in this book that mentions behavior specifically in the title, behavior is involved in every topic discussed. This is for two reasons. First, the outcome of a sound behavior support plan is that an individual learns more socially appropriate ways of responding. Second, behavioral challenges are automatically reduced when programming is solid and when the individual lives and learns in supportive environments.

Role of Crisis Management

Let's begin by talking about **crisis management**. When individuals on the autism spectrum engage in behavior that threatens the safety of themselves or of others, family members and professionals want to know how to implement immediate behavior change. The question is typically framed as, "What do we do when ...?" The goal is to find an approach that will have an immediate impact in a difficult or a crisis situation.

In reality, those who ask these questions in such situations will only find a short-term solution. The response is referred to as crisis management. The goal of a crisis management plan is to diffuse or interrupt a potentially dangerous situation. While it may prove effective in the immediate situation, crisis management is a quick fix with no long-term educational benefit. In other words, the individual does not learn an alternative prosocial response.

The other danger in using a crisis management approach is that our response may strengthen a given behavior. For example, if we restrain a student who loves deep pressure, she may be reinforced for her negative behavior. If we place a student in timeout who prefers to spend time alone, we may be providing him with a vacation from the stresses of the school setting. If the behavior is related to stress or anxiety, confrontation may escalate the problem and decrease the ability to think clearly. And if we respond emotionally to a problematic situation, students may enjoy the attention and excitement their behavior elicits. Thus, we continually run the risk of reinforcing behavior through our actions.

When an individual is in the midst of a behavior, this is not the time to lecture or teach. The goal is to minimize the situation. When somebody is upset, she has less capacity to learn. Lecturing or talking to her may only serve to intensify the behavior. Instead, keep words to a minimum and always respond with a neutral affect. The goal is not to have the "last word" or to make your point heard; the goal is to keep everyone safe.

At times punishment and exclusion are considered as means to control behavioral situations. Both of these approaches also have limitations. First, many students on the autism spectrum prefer to spend time at home rather than at school, so being sent home is not punishment to many of our students. Further, once they are sent home for problematic behaviors, sometimes we must struggle to convince them to return to school. In other words, what started out as a strategy to punish or make a point has become a reward for the child.

Punishment also has limitations, in that students do not learn appropriate behaviors by being told "no" or by losing privileges. While such strategies may work in the presence of someone who physically intimidates the student or who has the stature to control, this type of control does not create a relationship of trust conducive to maximum learning. We are serving as continual role models for students. Resorting to punitive approaches as the primary means of behavior change does not teach students how to respond in a more proactive fashion in the future. In other words, the focus of a behavior support plan should be on teaching alternative behaviors and creating positive learning environments, not on gaining control or punishing students.

We now realize that learning problems associated with difficulties in executive function, central coherence, and theory of mind (see Chapter 2) may impact behavior and that the old consequence-focused strategies may not be logical approaches to behavior change. In other words, simply addressing behavior change by applying powerful consequences to decrease certain behaviors is not sufficient. Specific teaching strategies that address the core deficits of ASD will need to be applied.

Despite the many disadvantages, there is still a role for a crisis management plan. We cannot allow students to harm themselves or others. The critical word here is *plan*. Each person involved with the student must know how to respond with the goal of minimizing the situation. After an event occurs, staff and/or family members should talk about how well the plan worked and what should happen next time. When the child is not in crisis, the real work of behavior change can occur. In other words, the best time to address behavior is when behavior is not occurring. This requires a shift in thinking about behavior and the role of behavior plans, as discussed below.

Shifting Behavioral Perspectives

In recent years, the focus has shifted away from solely manipulating consequences to designing positive behavior support plans. That is, instead of designing behavior support plans that focus on consequences, behavior support plans today focus on teaching individuals socially valid ways of responding. With this approach comes a set of assumptions or beliefs about behavior. These include the following:

- *Behavior is influenced by or governed by context.* This simply means that environments provide clues about expected behaviors and set an individual up for behavioral challenges or successes. It also means that students' behavior will improve or deteriorate in various settings. For example, it is not unusual for students on the autism spectrum to behave better at home than at school. In a home setting, the student typically will have more time to regroup, and more accommodations can be made. In a school setting, there are more demands, and more stimulation. The challenge becomes one of making the school setting conducive to learning without making it so sterile that the student becomes overwhelmed when out in real-world settings.

- *Behavior is functional, purposeful, and meaningful to the individual.* It may not hold meaning for us, but for the individual with ASD there may be a sound reason for a given behavior. Our challenge is to understand his or her perspective. In addition, behavior is tied to communication challenges (Reichle & Wacker, 1993). Whether a student is verbal or nonverbal, he will use behavior when his communication system does not allow him to adequately express stress, concern, confusion, anger, or other emotions.

- *Behavior is affected by internal events, including emotional states* (e.g., *anxiety, depression*) *and biological conditions* (e.g., *gastrointestinal difficulties, seizures, ear infections*). Students cannot perform at their very best when they are not healthy. For students who have chronic ear infections, gastrointestinal difficulties, or other conditions, it is important to address health issues before expecting them to learn maximally. Likewise, many students on the autism spectrum suffer from poor self-esteem, anxiety, and/or depression. These emotional states also have a dramatic impact on behavior, and hence, learning.

- *Behavior is influenced by factors outside the immediate environment, including relationships, opportunities for engaging in various activities, and lifestyle issues.* Students on the autism spectrum who have a better overall quality of life are less prone to problematic behaviors (Carr, 2007). Sometimes parents or staff make statements such as, "until Kyle behaves, we cannot let him go into the community or be around other students." That is, they make participation in a meaningful life contingent upon perfect behavior. Instead, we need to recognize that students who are in a situation that allows them a meaningful life have fewer behavioral incidents. For example, some students do better in a general education as opposed to a special education setting because the classroom provides more stimulation and excitement.

- *Behaviors will change as people mature and develop new competencies.* One only has to mention the word *puberty* to know that this statement is true. With various ages and grade levels, certain behavioral difficulties may occur or disappear.

- *Behavioral supports are guided by a strong value base.* Our values about behavior and how we were raised will impact our response. Each of us needs to engage in self-examination to determine how our values impact our reactions. Are we more focused on quality-of-life issues and teaching the person self-control, or are we more punitive in our approach and focused on controlling the situation?

The process of examining our attitudes and belief systems must be ongoing. This is important because our values and beliefs will determine our role and the contribution we make in working as members of a team involved in an individual's life.

Putting Together a Team

The goal of any behavior support approach for a student with ASD should be long-term behavior change. While there may be a need for a short-term crisis management, as mentioned, this should never be the sole or even the primary approach used. In order to effect long-term behavior change, those involved must learn to understand the function or purpose of a given behavior. This process of gathering information is referred to as a functional behavioral assessment. While conducting a functional behavioral assessment has for many years been considered "best practice," it is now articulated in federal legislation via the Individuals with Disabilities Education Improvement Act. Likewise, this strategy is tied to national school-wide discipline and positive behavior supports initiatives.

A student enters your classroom with a history of challenging behaviors. While the first few days are calm (the so-called honeymoon period), soon you begin to see behaviors occur. These behaviors are interfering with the student's learning and the education of others. Before a behavior plan is designed, the process of conducting a functional behavioral assessment must start.

The first step in conducting a functional behavioral assessment is to identify the behavior support team who will meet to problem solve, support, and guide this process. Potential participants include family members, educators, paraprofessionals, therapists, private therapists, and the student on the autism spectrum him/herself. In other words, the team should include members from all environments in which the student interacts, people who know him well, members who know about various community support options, and members who can allocate personnel and resources. Decisions impacting the student must be made within the team structure. If other professionals (e.g., physicians, private therapists) wish to make recommendations that impact the program, they should be willing to sit as a member of the team. Programming decisions made in isolation fragments a team and lead to ineffectual planning and, ultimately, poor outcomes.

Once the team has been identified, members are responsible for (a) defining the behavior of concern, (b) gathering information, (c) developing hypothesis statements, (d) creating a behavior support plan, (e) implementing interventions, and (f) monitoring implementation and outcomes. The rest of this chapter is devoted to these steps.

Step One: Defining the Behavior of Concern

Before the behavioral assessment starts, agreement must be reached on the specific behavior of concern. The behavior then must be described and written in a measurable and observable format. That is, the behavior should be described so that everybody is clear about what the behavior looks like. For example, descriptors such as the "the student tantrums" or "the student is noncompliant or aggressive" are open to interpretation. Instead, descriptors such as "the student hits, kicks, and refuses to do work presented to her" or "the student screams" are clear and easily identified by all.

Information should also be gathered on whether a specific behavior occurs with other behaviors. For example, if a student hits, can staff also expect her to use profane language? Or if the student begins to engage in self regulatory behavior or self-talk, is this an indicator of anxiety and a warning that a problematic behavior is likely to occur? Again, the behavior must be described in an observable and measurable fashion.

Using the vignette at the start of this chapter, the following represents poor and good descriptors of Matthew's behavior. You will notice that by providing an observable and measurable description of the behavior, we begin to get insight into potential contributing factors.

Poor Descriptors	Measurable/Observable Descriptors
Aggressive	Pushes others off swing on the playground
Destructive	Tears instructional materials when presented
Noncompliant	On playground, does not come when called

Before an elaborate assessment is conducted, the student's instructional team should first determine whether the behavior is truly a problem or merely an annoyance. Each of us has varying levels of tolerance for specific behaviors. Although agreement can easily be reached on behaviors such as engaging in self-abuse or attacking other students, other behaviors (e.g., chewing gum, taking off one's shoes in the classroom, engaging in self-regulatory behaviors) are more benign and may actually be accelerated by our reaction.

Measures such as **frequency**, **duration**, and **intensity** may be used to determine the significance of a behavior. However, equally important is considering the long-term impact of a behavior on a child's adult options. That is, regardless of the age of the individual, programming must keep in mind where we are ultimately aiming for. In the example of Matthew, staff may find it endearing that he crawls on their laps. However, at some stage, this behavior will not be tolerated, and staff will have to break habits they have created with Matthew. If the hope is that the individual will live and work in the community, various behaviors need to be modified and alternative behaviors need to be taught early.

Step Two: Gathering Behavioral Information

Once the target behavior is determined, we must examine the relationship between the challenging behaviors and conditions in the student's life. This process is referred to as a functional behavioral assessment. Two points are important to remember here.

First, conducting a functional behavioral assessment is a team process. No one individual can determine the function without gaining input and information from the team. While a single person may be assigned to guide the process, information should be gathered using multiple people in multiple situations. This is a team fact-finding and problem-solving process that requires each team member – family and school alike – to be honest about the behavior and their possible contribution to the situation.

Second, the goal of a functional behavioral assessment is to identify the underlying causes of the behavior exhibited by the student. Crisis management strategies typically deal with symptoms. Symptoms can include hitting, kicking, screaming, cursing, and similar behaviors. However, these are signals that something else is happening. Potential underlying causes include lack of a communication system, health issues, skill deficits, and an unsupportive environment. There are many other potential causes, and our job becomes one of digging until we can identify those causes with some degree of confidence. Specifically, our focus becomes one of identifying antecedents (what happens before) and consequences (what happens after the behavior) that maintain behavior.

Antecedents. There are two potential types of **antecedents: slow triggers** (setting events) or **fast triggers** (immediate antecedents). Typically, there is a greater focus on immediate triggers because these are immediately evident and can often be easily identified. However, setting events play a critical role in increasing the likelihood that a behavior will occur.

Slow triggers, or setting events, such as schedule changes, staff changes, medication changes, illness, irregular sleep patterns, missed meals, excessive temperatures, fights with classmates, difficulties on the bus, or skill deficits can make the student less able to cope. So, on a certain day when Michael is required to do a task, he does it perfectly. The very next day, the same request is given, and he acts out. This behavior is probably not in response to the task, but reflects the occurrence of a setting event. Setting events "chip away" at a student's tolerance and ability to perform. This is especially true for students on the autism spectrum.

In this connection, it is important to remember that much of what is bothering a student at the moment may not be apparent or related to the immediate situation. In the example at the beginning of the chapter, potential setting events for Matthew include an inconsistent communication system, a social skills deficit, sensory challenges, biomedical issues related to diarrhea, lack of sleep, and poor diet. On any given day, these factors in Matthew's life may increase the possibility of a challenging behavior occurring.

Fast triggers, or immediate antecedents, are events that are directly related to the challenging behavior or that immediately precede it. Potential fast triggers include asking a student to do a nonfavored task, a certain noise (e.g., vacuum cleaner), the behavior of others, being interrupted during preferred activities, transitions, or being bullied. Immediate antecedents are more easily identified than setting events. In the opening vignette, immediate antecedents for Matthew include lack of structure on the playground and certain instructional materials.

Consequences. **Consequences** are responses that follow a behavior and that maintain behavior. We continue to engage in behavior because it allows us to get something we want or to escape something undesirable. There are a couple of important points to remember about consequences.

First, we often use the word *consequences* in the negative. Instead, we should think of consequences in terms of those things that sustain behavior. Second, we continually reinforce behaviors, whether we realize it or not. As a result, each of us must continually examine our own behavior to determine the role we might be playing in the behavior of students on the autism spectrum. And finally, consequences must be viewed from the perspective of the individual child. For example, we may find being screamed at as punishing. However, for a student with autism, being screamed at may be entertaining and provide some source of amusement. In the vignette, a possible consequence for destroying instructional materials is that Matthew escapes doing work that is too difficult or boring to him.

Data collection. Although it is important to keep data on behaviors, traditional **data-collection** procedures can present a limited perspective of a behavior. For example, simply counting behavior incidents or determining the duration of a behavior may not provide sufficient insight into factors related to the behavior. Conditions related to problem behaviors can be very complex and difficult to detect.

Functional behavioral assessments questionnaires provide a broader insight into why a student behaves in a certain manner under specific conditions and what professionals can do to support students to behave in a way that is more socially acceptable. While there are many formal and informal instruments (e.g., *Motivation Assessment Scale* [Durand & Crimmins, 1998], *Functional Behavioral Assessment Form* [O'Neill et al., 1997]) available to uncover important information, there is no specific instrument that includes all the questions that may need to be asked to determine why a behavior is occurring.

As educators, our challenge is to begin to identify the range of questions that can lead to a better understanding of the student and issues surrounding the behavior. By asking critical questions, the educational team can begin the detective work of identifying what is happening in the student's life to maintain the problem behaviors. The questions below are based on the work of O'Neill and colleagues (1997). In determining the true function of the behavior, additional questions may be necessary.

1. **What is the history of the undesirable behavior?**

   By gathering information about the history of the student's behavior, educators can begin to determine effective and ineffective approaches. This information will also provide insight into the student's learning history. The questions to address within this category include: How long has the student engaged in the behavior? What strategies have been used in the past? Which strategies were effective? Which strategies were ineffective?

2. **Under what conditions does the student do well? During what times or activities is she most successful?**

   Often one of the questions that provide the greatest insight into programming is related to those events, interactions, situations or activities that are in place when the student with ASD is the most successful. By identifying the conditions under which an individual does her very best, the team can begin to piece together a program that has a greater opportunity for supporting the student to be successful. For example, if the student does best with staff who give exact and clear directions, then this strategy should be practiced by all. If the student does best on days when physical activity is involved, then physical activities should be infused into each day. If the student excels in math, then math should be used to build momentum for other activities and perhaps as an activity to calm the student.

3. **What are areas of strength for the student? Are these strengths being reinforced?**

   Too often, educational programs for students with ASD are based on students' deficits rather than on strengths. Instead, areas of interest and strength should be used as the foundation for teaching other skills. When meeting on behalf of a student who is exhibiting behavioral difficulties, the first questions asked should refer to areas of strength and interests. Potential questions include: What does the student seem to enjoy? In what courses does the student seem to excel? What are his fixations or intense areas of interest?

   By planning in this manner, family members and professionals can begin to determine a course of action that will promote student success. For example, if a student loves to talk about NASCAR, perhaps giving the student 5 minutes to speak on the subject could be a powerful reinforcement. If a student knows all the state capitals, perhaps a unit could be developed that requires all of his classmates to learn the capitals. That way, the student on the autism spectrum automatically becomes a key source of information for classmates, and her self-esteem is boosted as a result.

If strengths and interests are avoided, the student may become more fixated and anxious in an effort to gain access to something that is highly preferred. Instead, by building them into the day, the student can have a clear picture of when access is available and, ideally, alleviate anxiety. At the same time, it is important to ensure that the reinforcement schedule is set up so that the student can reasonably earn the reinforcer. If the student is continually denied access to a highly preferred item, behaviors may accelerate.

4. **In what type of curriculum is the student currently engaged? Does this curriculum seem to be a good match and does it engage the student in meaningful activities?**
Questions related to curriculum address the functionality or usefulness of the curriculum from the perspective of the student with ASD. Today, with the focus on accountability and state standards, the challenge is to make sure that the curriculum is relevant for the individual. Many of us are willing to take courses or to participate in curriculum that may seem to hold no real, immediate purpose because we know that the course or class is a step towards a degree, better job, higher salary, or greater job satisfaction. That is, we are able to understand the longterm results of engaging in sometimes unpleasant events. However, many students, especially those on the autism spectrum, are less engaged if they do not see the immediate utility or relevance of a course or an activity. Students are more interested in learning content that holds meaning for current life circumstances or future life goals. Therefore, making curriculum relevant requires us to relate it to current or future goals with a focus on outcomes.

5. **According to the student's schedule, is the majority of her school day spent engaged in instruction? Are there extensive periods of unstructured or downtime?**
Professionals should calculate the number of minutes students are actively engaged in instruction or other activities during the school day. Time spent waiting for instruction, transitioning between activities, or waiting for others to complete an activity can provide students with opportunities to engage in problematic behavior. Likewise, activities such as physical education, lunch, recess, music, morning circle, and other less structured activities may increase the chances that a student with ASD will engage in a difficult behavior unless these activities are structured in some fashion. The standard is that students should spend 80% of their school day engaged in instruction. For students on the autism spectrum, this time should be spent on activities related to their individualized education program (IEP) or on the typical curriculum.

6. **Are there specific activities or courses during which the student is more likely to engage in problem behavior? Are there specific instructors who are more or less successful with the student? Does the student have a tendency to engage in problem behaviors during certain times of the day?**
Answers to these and similar questions begin to determine activities or periods of the day when students may be more or less frustrated, and when they may be more or less prone to engage in challenging behaviors. Begin to look at time periods during the day in which the student is more likely to engage in challenging behaviors. You may see a pattern that begins to tell you that the student needs periodic breaks, more support when learning certain course content, or a different instructional approach.

7. **Are varied instructional approaches used in the classroom (e.g., several shortened activities within a lesson, teaching using various modalities)?**

   Students are more likely to be engaged in lessons that are varied and that accommodate various learning styles. For students on the autism spectrum, concrete and hands-on activities are often useful. Specific lessons or courses should be observed to determine whether modifications or adaptations are necessary. For example, students who are expected to sit quietly and listen to a lecture for an hour may be at greater risk for engaging in challenging behavior than if they are involved in varied and shorter tasks, including lecture, group activity, and hands-on instruction.

8. **Does the behavior serve a purpose for the student?**

   It is commonly believed (O'Neill et al., 1997) that students engage in problem behavior because there is a payoff, including attention, escape, or fulfillment of a physiological/sensory need. If the student did not get something from engaging in the problem behavior, the belief is that the behavior would diminish or stop. Questions to probe this area might include: Does he get attention, or escape an unpleasant situation by engaging in a difficult behavior? What is unpleasant about the situation that causes him to escape? For example, students who engage in challenging behaviors to garner a reaction from someone may be engaging in the same behavior to escape work that is too difficult. And for students who engage in behavior for attention, many will not care if the attention is positive or negative.

9. **What is the student's primary means of communication?**

   There appears to be a direct link between a student's ability to communicate and the occurrence (Reichle & Wacker, 1993) of problem behavior. Even if a student on the autism spectrum is highly verbal, she may not have the ability to truly express frustrations, needs, and other feelings. If nonverbal, an augmentative communication system must be in place and readily available that allows that student to communicate important messages. If highly verbal, a student may still require the opportunity to write out feelings or may need visuals to support his ability to communicate difficult topics. Often, a family member or professional who has a good rapport with the individual is able to elicit conversation. Team members should examine how students communicate across settings. For example, Matthew in the vignette is nonverbal. He may be throwing instructional materials in an effort to tell us that the work is too hard, too easy, too boring, or not preferred.

10. **Does the student have any medical problems or take any medications? If so, could this be affecting behavior? Is there a possibility of substance abuse (e.g., drugs, alcohol)?**

    Conditions such as asthma, allergies, chronic diarrhea, gastrointestinal difficulties, sinus infections, seizures, and other chronic illnesses can lead to periods of problem or off-task behaviors. Likewise, many medications can affect a student's behavior. Be sensitive to dramatic behavior changes that may be indicators of illness, adverse reactions to medications, or some form of substance abuse. Communicate with family members about sudden behavioral changes or about the impact of medication changes. Also realize that some students may be self-medicating with either drugs or alcohol.

11. **Does the student have difficulty with sleeping and/or eating? Are the student's nutritional needs being met?**

    Students who are having difficulty satisfying basic life needs may have greater problems learning and acting appropriately. Gather information from parents concerning these issues. In addition, realize that if the child is not sleeping, neither are her parents. Be aware and understanding of the stress that lack of sleep may place on the entire family.

12. **Does the student have opportunities to engage in a range of activities outside of school? In other words, what is the student's life like outside of school? Are there conditions inside the home that may be troubling the student (e.g., divorce, death, marital stress, financial difficulties, abuse)?**

The final set of questions addresses a student's home life. At times, behaviors reflect conditions at home. We must be careful not to blame parents for their child's condition or behavior. Most of us have not experienced the emotional, financial, and physical stresses that can result from having a child on the autism spectrum. The vast majority of parents would do anything to improve the quality of life for their child and family. However, diminished quality-of-life issues outside of school can have a dramatic impact on school performance and behavior. Similarly, poor school conditions can have an impact on the home.

Information about a student's life outside of school can provide valuable insight into the conditions surrounding problem behaviors. If there are financial or other difficulties in the home, outside help from various social service agencies may be needed. A student's home life should never be used as the foundation for "giving up" on a student. It is the responsibility of school personnel to ensure that all is being done to create a positive climate that is conducive to learning and to use a curriculum that is worth being taught.

When conducting a functional behavioral assessment, school personnel need to realize that collecting information is a never-ending process. As the student's life and educational circumstances change, conditions surrounding the behavior may change. For example, the onset of puberty is usually a time when behaviors shift. In addition, family members must be involved in gathering data. As the lifelong advocate for their son/daughter with autism, they can present a longitudinal picture of the behavior.

Various instruments can be used in gathering information. These include the *Motivation Assessment Scale* by Durand and Crimmins (1988), a scatter plot (Touchette, MacDonald, & Langer, 1985), and the functional behavior assessment form developed by O'Neill et al. (1997) to determine situations that may be enhancing problematic behaviors.

A **scatter plot** is a quick tool for recording the frequency of behaviors in various contexts across the school day. While a form that simply looks at the antecedent-behavior-consequence is typically suggested, this type of instrument can be difficult for educators and families to complete because it requires ongoing and intensive observation. Videotaping can be used to perform a more in-depth analysis of the sequence of activities. Videotaping also allows one to observe situations that may go unnoticed during the rush of the day.

A functional behavior assessment should be conducted whenever a student has a history of challenging behaviors. Do not relax if the student begins the year on a positive note. You may be in a honeymoon period, and the honeymoon will end. Start early in the school year. At all costs, avoid having to start the process under time constraints or in the middle of crisis. Emotions often run too high during times of intense behavior problems to gather objective information, and typically those involved want to focus solely on crisis strategies. Also, in the beginning, realize that your initial efforts may not provide the depth of information needed. Keep searching for that underlying cause.

Step 3: Developing Hypothesis Statements

A functional behavioral assessment has been accomplished when you can begin to develop some hypothesis statements about the behavior and can list potential underlying causes. In truth, a functional behavioral assessment is done when you have gathered sufficient information so that a trend in the behavior begins to emerge and a behavioral support plan logically evolves.

Hypothesis statements are informed guesses about the underlying causes of a behavior. It is based on information that has been gathered through the functional behavioral assessment process. A **problem behavior pathway** (see Figure 7.1) can be developed that outlines setting events, triggering antecedents, problem behavior, and maintaining consequences. In the opening vignette, the following behavior pathway could have occurred.

Typically, behavior support plans focus on antecedents and consequences. A common reaction may be to consider how to make the consequences more aversive to stop the behavior from occurring. However, in the diagram depicted in Figure 7.1, it becomes apparent that a skills deficit and the lack of a communication system are contributing to the problem behavior. Until these issues are addressed, manipulating consequences will not result in appropriate behaviors. So, the focus of programming should be on building a communication system that is useful at recess, on teaching the student how to play with classmates, and on teaching the student to communicate the desire for a turn.

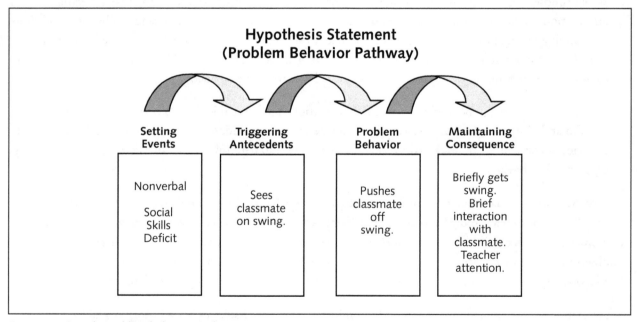

Figure 7.1. Sample problem behavior pathway.

Step 4: Creating a Behavior Support Plan

Behavior support plans should evolve from the hypotheses you develop through the functional behavioral assessment process. The type of form used in developing a behavior support plan is not important. What is important is that the plan is clearly written and that it defines how an environment will be altered in an effort to change behavior and how the student will be taught an alternative way of responding. These alternative skills should be articulated in the student's IEP.

Too often behavioral goals are written in the negative in terms of what students will stop doing; for example, the student will stop hitting, kicking, and so forth. Instead, behavioral IEP goals should be written in the positive and articulate what the student will do. Potential alternative skills relate to problem-solving skills, choice-making ability, anger control, relaxation training, self-management, communication, and social skills. Once the alternative skill is identified, it becomes important to put together a plan that includes positive behavior support approaches.

Positive behavior supports. It is important to make a distinction between positive behavior support approaches and traditional disciplinary actions or punishment procedures. As discussed earlier in this chapter, disciplinary action or punishment procedures are immediate responses to a difficult situation. In other words, they comprise short-term interventions or crisis management strategies to avoid or divert problem behavior. As such, they do not address long-term systems of support or quality-of-life issues, nor do they teach students other ways of responding in difficult or stressful situations.

Positive behavior support approaches, on the other hand, focus on creating positive learning environments and teaching students alternative ways of behaving. For some students on the autism spectrum, it may not be possible for them to generate behavioral options that have the same effect as the problem behavior or that serve the same purpose/function. For others, behaviors perceived as challenging by professionals may be appropriate or necessary for the student's survival in other settings. Our job is to expand their repertoires of acceptable options by teaching alternative behaviors.

Alternative behaviors, such as interacting with peers, waiting, participating in a conversation in a mannerly fashion, taking turns, standing at a distance from the speaker to respect personal space, and responding to adults in a positive fashion, may have to be taught. When choosing an alternative behavior, professionals and family members must consider the total person. Identify skills needed for school, home, work, and other community activities by gathering information through the functional behavioral assessment process and from conversation with family members and the student him/herself. If an appropriate alternative behavior that accomplishes the individual's purposes is not taught, she may find a replacement behavior that is less desirable than the initial behavior. Teaching alternative skills requires more effort on the part of all involved, but the beneficial outcomes will be longer lasting.

Step 5: Implementing Interventions

Once desired behavioral outcomes are identified, it becomes our job to design an instructional program that both supports and teaches the student. Below are some suggestions for creating a positive learning environment and teaching alternative behaviors, categorized under the headings of curricular considerations, classroom management and instruction, and applied behavior analysis approaches. The chapters in this book contain more information for programming or insight into autism spectrum disorders. The following are just a few ideas.

Curricular considerations. Consider the curriculum in which the student is engaged. Upon graduation, some students will attend college; others will not. Many educational programs focus on academics, rather than on career development. For many students on the autism spectrum, their high school years should be spent on preparation for employment. When choosing curriculum options and potential career paths, remember that students are more willing to learn skills and engage in activities that relate to their lives, interests, and strengths. Simply enrolling an interested student in a welding program, rather than creative writing, can begin to create an environment that attracts the student to learning. Use areas of interest to draw individuals to new situations and to ease learning activities that are challenging.

As part of the curriculum, identify alternative or replacement behaviors for the challenging behavior. Alternative behaviors should address the function of the behavior and yield the same payoff. For example, if the student engages in problem behavior as a means of gaining attention, teach a more appropriate strategy that is as effective for getting attention (and teach those involved in the student's life to listen and to respond appropriately). For example, the student may be taught to raise his hand to be called on in class instead of blurting out. If the replacement behavior is to truly replace the problem behavior, it must be as efficient and as effective as the problem behavior. In other words, when the student raises his hand, the teacher or other adult must show him proper attention.

Be specific in stating hoped-for changes. Curricular goals such as "being happy," "behaving correctly," or "being totally compliant" are open to diverse interpretations. Likewise, goals that highlight behaviors to be eliminated do not provide information about what to teach. Write goals that are specific, such as helping a student handle being teased in the hallway or moving from one class to another without an altercation. Identifying specific goals requires that those involved in the student's life examine the situation from the student's perspective and consider how best to facilitate change.

When making programming decisions, do not assume a readiness model. That is, appropriate behavior should not be a prerequisite for engaging an individual in settings or activities that may positively influence behavior.

Classroom management and instruction. Classroom structures and instructional approaches can serve as either a positive or a negative context for behavior change. Below are recommendations for structuring classroom environments and delivering instruction in the most positive and effective way.

- **Actively engage students in systematic instruction in which teaching is clearly planned.** When students have free or unstructured time, they have more opportunity to engage in difficult behaviors. Keep students busy in meaningful activities. Develop a schedule that includes varying tasks and activities to minimize fatigue, boredom, and frustration. Some students learn best when exercise or physical activity is available throughout the day. Others may need downtime to regroup.

- **Create behavioral momentum in the day.** Within the first 10 minutes of a school day or class period, we either capture or lose students' attention. When students enter an instructional situation, they need to be engaged as soon as possible. This requires instructors to be organized and prepared.

- **Intersperse easy and difficult tasks and courses to ensure that the student experiences some successes each day.** Often students who engage in problem behavior have developed a history of failures. It is critical that each student is involved in some activity in which she will be successful and be acknowledged for that success.

- **Embed opportunities for students to make choices within the context of the day.** When all control is removed, students will engage in problem behavior as a means of recapturing that control. Teaching them to control their environment in acceptable ways often results in increases in participation and skills acquisition, and contributes to decreases in the occurrence of problem behavior.

- **When a new material or a new activity is introduced, allow the student to rehearse.** Rehearsal of new materials in a classroom or resource area might involve allowing the student a sneak preview of future work. Rehearsal for a new activity might involve allowing the student to read about the activity, discuss with others, visit a new location, or view a videotape of someone else's experience. These strategies will prepare the student to be successful.

- **Clearly articulate expectations for instruction and interaction.** This assists students in knowing the expectations and helps to prevent confusion, anxiety, or anger. Clearly articulating and visually demonstrating instructions also decreases the possibility of the student engaging in inappropriate behaviors that result in negative feedback and corrective modes of interaction.

- **Assess the quality of your interactions with students.** The single most important and influential thing that school staff do in teaching students with ASD is to interact with them. At times, the majority of interactions may involve negative exchanges, such as corrective feedback or task demands. Positive exchanges should outnumber negatives. Be sure to reinforce, instruct, and converse with students in a positive fashion.

- **Establish rapport.** While this suggestion is related to the one above, it is so important that a separate bullet is necessary. If you enjoy a student and enjoy what you do, the student will read that attitude. The relationship you develop with students will promote trust and enhance their willingness and ability to learn from you.

- **Teach rules, limits, and boundaries clearly and visually and through repeated rehearsals.** Involve students in determining rules for the classroom, and for them. Behavior contracts are helpful for some. If a behavior contract is used, it should state in positive terms what you want the student to do. Once the rules have been determined, school personnel must use them consistently. You may have to teach students the rule. Do not assume that a student truly understands the rules just because he can rotely recite them verbatim. Also, students who serve as the "rule police" need to be taught flexibility and the "grayness" of situations.

- **Remember that routines are an important part of our lives.** Whether morning routines, bedtime routines, or routines when we enter the work place, routines provide comfort and ease. This is also true for students on the autism spectrum. When establishing routines, be careful not to make the student overly rigid. For example, doing the same thing every day may make the student more comfortable, but it will also make him more rigid. Build in changes periodically to help the student be more flexible. Support changes by having a visual schedule in place that highlights schedule changes and allows the student to rehearse daily events. For some students, it may be helpful to teach the routine and then gradually add variety to shape the child's tolerance for change.

- **Consider the student's learning styles.** Present prompts and instruction that acknowledge individual learning styles (e.g., kinesthetic, visual, auditory). Presenting information in a format that matches students' learning style can promote learning and ease them through uncomfortable changes. If tasks, activities, or instruction seem to be misunderstood, simplify the response requirements or present them in some other way. Allow time for students to process information. Vary the pace of instruction to meet the needs of the individual.

- **Teach strategies for coping with and negotiating the stress of daily demands.** For example, some students need to learn relaxation or other self-control strategies. The goal of self-management is to assist students in achieving greater independence and autonomy. Teaching relaxation and self-management is a long-range goal that will take time and patience, but it is well worth it.

Applied behavior analysis approaches. How does **applied behavior analysis (ABA)** fit into all of this? ABA has a long-standing and rich tradition that extends beyond the field of autism. The technology of positive behavior supports includes and is an extension of ABA. The technology of ABA should be part of any teaching situation for both students with and without ASD.

ABA approaches include discrete trial format, **chaining** and prompting procedures, shaping, and many others. **Shaping** or reinforcement of **successive approximations** of preferred behavior is particularly useful for individuals with ASD, who may become anxious if unable to perform a task with immediate perfection. Individuals may have learned inappropriate behaviors through years of practice and successful use with others in their environment. Therefore, recognize and reinforce successive approximations of the preferred behavior.

Another approach involves the use of **extinction** or **planned ignoring**. Using this strategy, professionals and family members simply ignore negative behaviors and only respond in the presence of positive behaviors. Care must be taken when using this approach, however. If you choose to ignore problem behavior, you must be prepared and able to ignore it even when the student is behaving out of control. And it must be a behavior that will not harm the student or others. If you give into the behavior after it has accelerated to a high level, you have taught the student the level she must behave at in order to get your attention in the future.

Two other approaches include redirection and consequences. Sometimes it is better to redirect students when they begin to engage in challenging behaviors. Focusing on behaviors can enhance their power and serve to intensify basically benign actions. For example, when you notice that the student is beginning to become anxious or to accelerate his behavior, redirect him to a favored activity. Consequences should be assessed in terms of what motivates a specific individual. Observe fixations as a source of uncovering potential consequences or motivators. Finally, remember that what serves as a reward may differ from person to person.

Step 6: Monitoring Implementation and Outcomes

The primary reason why a behavior support plan may not be successful is simply that it is not implemented. Behavior support plans are sabotaged when the entire team has not reached agreement about a plan, when team members refuse to implement the agreed-upon plan, when a plan is developed in isolation from the team (e.g., a consultant develops a plan without involving the team), when the plan is not doable within the various contexts in the student's life, and when the outcomes are not agreed upon by the team. So, once a plan is developed it should include a procedure for continually monitoring and improving upon the plan. As part of this monitoring process, the team must determine if there is a reduction in behavior, but more important, there needs to be a focus on enhancing positive behaviors.

Summary and Conclusions

Those who work with students on the autism spectrum who engage in difficult behavior face special challenges. There is no cookbook or recipe for handling problem behaviors. No single intervention or approach works with all students. Even if districts adopt model behavioral programs or treatment packages, many of these programs are not appropriate or effective for a student on the autism spectrum. Those involved in establishing behavior support plans must address each student individually. In other words, develop a plan based on a thorough assessment of each student's behavior. Again, the outcome of a good behavior support plan is not that students end a certain behavior, but that they begin to respond in a socially positive manner.

Learning a new way of responding takes repetition, patience, flexibility, consistency, and commitment by all. Do not give up if the student does not learn the alternative behavior quickly. The challenging behavior probably has a long history.

Finally, perhaps the hardest issue surrounding positive behavior support approaches is the realization that often it is the behavior of professionals and family members that needs to change to eliminate or decrease the student's problem behavior. For some, this realization is perceived as control being given to the student. When dealing with students with problem behaviors, thinking of behavioral reduction in terms of controlling students is a losing proposition for all involved. As educators, our goal should be to instruct. If our behavior does not change, in all likelihood, the student's behavior will not change either.

Tips for Practical Application

✓ Think prevention, rather than reaction, when it comes to dealing with problem behavior.

✓ Minimize unstructured and downtime to avoid problem situations.

✓ Consider and take into account the link between an individual's ability to communicate and the occurrence of problem behaviors.

✓ Recognize that crisis management is only a short-term solution to problem behavior.

✓ Know that in order to be maximally effective, a behavior support plan should evolve from a thorough assessment of both the problem behavior and the context in which it occurred.

✓ Bear in mind that in order for behavior support plans to work, they must be followed!

✓ Make the teaching of alternative responses an integral part of your behavior plan.

✓ Accept the fact that there is no single recipe for handling problem behavior; each individual and situation is different.

✓ Remember that behavior serves a purpose for the individual and that it is our job to figure out that purpose.

✓ Realize that effective behavioral change may require that all involved in the child's life change their behavior as well.

Chapter Highlights

• Crisis management refers to a short-term solution to immediately manage potentially dangerous behavior.

• While crisis management may play a role in terms of dealing with immediate problems, it does not teach the student a prosocial response or appropriate alternate behavior.

• Punishment, which is typically how crisis management is managed (by definition, punishment procedures decrease an undesirable behavior), does not teach appropriate behavior or create an environment of trust and learning.

• Exclusion, another way crisis situations are typically managed, also has limitations in that it may be reinforcing (and thus increase the undesired behavior) if the individual prefers not to be a part of a given activity.

• Perspectives on how to manage behavior have changed from looking at only consequences (reinforcement and punishment) to evaluating the student (including strengths, needs, desires) and the environment (including instruction, classroom management, classroom structure and routines) to design support plans to teach the individual socially valid ways of responding. The set of assumptions on which this change is based include:
  o Behavior is influenced by context
  o Behavior is functional, purposeful, and meaningful
  o Behavior is affected by external events, including emotional and biological conditions
  o Behavior is influenced by factors outside the immediate environment

- o Behaviors will change as people mature and develop new competencies
- o Behavioral supports are guided by a strong value base

- The goal of positive behavior support should be long-term behavior change based on identifying the function or purpose the behavior serves for the individual. This process is called a functional behavioral assessment (FBA).

- Before conducting an FBA, a behavior support team is created to problem solve, support, and guide the process.

- An FBA should lead to intervention to effect behavior change.

- The steps in an FBA and implementation of a behavior support plan are as follows:
  - o Defining the behavior of concern
  - o Gathering behavioral information
  - o Developing hypothesis statements
  - o Creating a behavior support plan
  - o Implementing intervention
  - o Monitoring implementation and outcomes

- When defining a behavior, the first step is to decide whether the behavior in question is a problem or merely an annoyance. Once this has been decided, it is important to describe the behavior in observable and measurable terms so that all involved are clear on what is being measured. Additionally, the behavior must be evaluated in terms of how often it occurs (frequency), how long it occurs (duration), and how strong it is (intensity).

- After the behavior has been defined, data or information about the behavior are gathered. Included in this information gathering is a quest to determine the function or cause of the behavior by examining the relationship between the behavior and conditions in the individual's life.

- Examining antecedents (what happens before the behavior) and consequences (what happens after the behavior) assists in determining what is maintaining the behavior.

- Antecedents fall into two types: *slow triggers* (setting events), which occur before the behavior but not immediately before the behavior, and *fast triggers,* which occur immediately before the behavior.

- Functional behavioral assessments must also take into account variables such as the history of the behavior, strengths of the student, reinforcement history, conditions under which the student does well, type of curriculum used and whether it is a match for the student, amount of structure in the student's day, types of instructional approaches used, occasions when the problem behavior is more likely to be exhibited, the apparent purpose served by the behavior, communication skills of the student, any medical/sleeping/ nutritional concerns, and special conditions affecting the student outside the school setting.

- After information on the behavior has been collected, a hypothesis statement is developed about what may be the underlying causes for the behavior. This statement may be based on an underlying behavior pathway, in which setting events, immediate antecedents, behavior, and consequences are outlined about the behavior of concern.

- Behavior support plans using positive support approaches are written based on the hypothesis statements.

- Positive behavior support approaches focus on creating positive learning environments and teaching alternative ways of behaving.

- Curriculum considerations in implementing interventions focus on ensuring the curriculum matches student goals, skills, and needs, and include looking at teaching alternative and pro-social behaviors to replace those that may be problematic.

- Classroom management and instructional considerations focus on ensuring the classroom environment is structured in a positive way that creates opportunities for engagement, includes systematic instruction and clearly articulated expectations, allows for rehearsal, and supports student chances for success. Included are use of routines, consideration of the student's learning style, and teaching strategies for coping with the stresses of daily demands.

- Applied behavior analysis serves as the basis for positive behavior supports. Additionally, specific techniques within applied behavior analysis such as shaping of behavior, creating behavior chains, reinforcing successive approximations, prompting, extinction, and planned ignoring have been used successfully to effect behavior change in individuals with ASD.

- Monitoring and making changes in the plan are essential to ensure its effectiveness.

Chapter Review Questions

1. What is the definition of a crisis management approach and what are the advantages and disadvantages of using such an approach?

2. What are the shifting behavioral perspectives and the set of assumptions that accompany this shift in thinking?

3. Who are the members of the behavioral support team and what are their roles?

4. What are the components of a functional behavioral assessment?

5. What are the issues involved in defining behaviors of concern?

6. What is the goal of a functional behavioral assessment?

7. What are antecedents and consequences?

8. What types of questions must be asked in determining the true function of a behavior?

9. Why is collecting information an ongoing process in functional behavioral assessment and positive behavior support?

10. What are hypothesis statements and what are they based on?

11. Why are problem behavior pathways important in determining how to support appropriate behavior?

12. What is the focus of positive behavior support approaches?

13. List and describe curricular, classroom management, and instructional considerations involved in implementing interventions.

14. What is the role of applied behavior analysis in intervention?

15. Why are behavior support plans sometimes not successful?

16. Why is it important to monitor implementation and outcomes of support plans?

References

Carr, E. G. (2007). The expanding vision of positive behavior support: Research perspectives on happiness, helpfulness, hopefulness. *Journal of Positive Behavior Interventions, 9*(1), 3-14.

Durand, V. M., & Crimmins, D. B. (1988). Identifying the variables maintaining self-injurious behaviors. *Journal of Autism and Developmental Disorder, 18*, 99-117.

Frost, L. A., & Bondy, A. S. (1994). *The Picture Exchange Communication System (PECS): Training manual.* Cherry Hill, NJ: Pyramid Educational Consultants.

O'Neill, R. E., Horner, R. H., Albin, R. W., Sprague, J. R., Storey, K., & Newton, J. S. (1997). *Functional assessment and program development for problem behavior: A practical handbook.* Pacific Grove, CA: Brooks/Cole Thomson Learning.

Reichle, J., & Wacker, D. P. (1993). *Communicative alternative to challenging behaviors: Integrating functional assessment and intervention strategies.* Baltimore, MD: Paul H. Brookes.

Touchette, P. E., MacDonald, R. F., & Langer, S. N. (1985). A scatter plot for identifying stimulus control of problem behavior. *Journal of Applied Behavior Analysis, 18*, 343-351.

Learner Objectives

After reading this chapter, the learner should be able to:

- Explain the importance of play and friendships for children's learning, development, and socio-cultural participation

- Describe the challenges faced by children with ASD in terms of play behavior and the development of friendships

- Define "peer culture" and discuss the role it plays in involving children with ASD with peers

- Define "play culture"

- State the purpose of the Friend 2 Friend (F2F) model and discuss how it is implemented

- List and describe the four steps in the F2F teaching process

- State the five key learning goals of F2F

- Explain the F2F Seven Basic Friendship Tips

- Explain the purpose of the Integrated Play Groups (IPG) model

- Describe the environmental elements of IPG

- List and describe the elements included in the IPG observational assessment of play with peers

- Explain the purpose and the components involved in the IPG intervention of guided participation in play with peers

Chapter 8

Fostering Play, Imagination and Friendships With Peers: Creating a Culture of Social Inclusion

Pamela Wolfberg • Heather McCracken • Tara Tuchel

Richie is an intriguing boy who received a diagnosis of autism spectrum disorder (ASD) in early childhood. When he first entered kindergarten, he had little interaction with his classmates and had no friends. He mostly played by himself and occasionally watched his peers from a distance. At times he tolerated playing beside his peers, but when their play became loud, he would yell, "Would you pleeeease shut up!" He didn't know how to initiate or maintain interactions with other children and had difficulty accepting invitations to play from his peers. Because he didn't have a wide repertoire of play schemes with which he was competent, he often rejected invitations to play because he didn't know what to do. Richie was able to play with toys in a functional way but used a lot of delayed echolalia, as he was re-enacting scenes from his favorite movies and cartoons.

At first, I thought, "wow ... he really is imaginative." However, after watching him closely over several sessions, I noticed that he was merely repeating and re-enacting his favorite movies and did not change his play at all. He was very rigid in his play. I realized that, for Richie, it was very difficult to let his peers into his play world because they were unpredictable and might change his carefully scripted, inflexible play routine. He was unable to handle that, so he rejected their attempts to interact and play.

Sean is a bright 27-year-old male, who was diagnosed with an autism spectrum disorder at the age of 5. Sean remained nonverbal until he was 9 years old. I met Sean at a university class on special education; he had been invited to speak to the class about his autism. Sean spoke openly and honestly about his school experiences, saying, "I hated school; it was the worst place. High school was a bit better but not much. I could not wait to get out of school; it was the most hostile environment I can imagine." During the question-and-answer portion of the class, a member of the class asked Sean, "I have a child with autism in my classroom. What could I do to help make school a better place for this child?" Sean replied, "Help him understand his autism, but just as important, help his classmates understand autism."

175

When observing children of diverse abilities in natural interactions with one another, it soon becomes apparent who is thriving and who is at risk in their development. Children with autism spectrum disorders (ASD) are among those at greatest risk, as they encounter significant challenges developing play and imagination, socializing, and forming friendships with peers (Boucher & Wolfberg, 2003). Hallmarks of autism include a lack of varied and imaginative or imitative play as well as a failure to develop peer relationships appropriate to developmental level. Further, defining features of ASD are intricately tied to characteristic impairments in reciprocal social interaction, communication and imagination (American Psychiatric Association, 2013).

A common misconception regarding children diagnosed with ASD is that they consciously choose to isolate themselves and, thus, are incapable of play and friendships with peers. Yet, there is strong evidence to suggest that they share many of the same desires and capacities for play, companionship, and peer group acceptance as typically developing children (Bauminger & Kasari, 2000; Jordan, 2003). What differs is that they express their play interests and social overtures in ways that are uniquely their own and that often set them apart from their peer group. Without appropriate support, these children are highly vulnerable to being neglected, rejected, or even bullied by peers. This, in turn, deprives them of opportunities to learn how to socialize and play in more conventional and socially accepted ways and, ultimately, to form meaningful friendships.

From both a developmental and a socio-cultural perspective, the unique and complex difficulties children with ASD face in peer relations and play pose distinct challenges to educators, therapists, and family members seeking to help them. According to the National Research Council (2001), play and social instruction with peers are rated among the top interventions that should receive priority in educational programs for children with ASD. Recent advances in our understanding of ASD and social inclusion further underscore the need for high-quality interventions that explicitly value and support children's play and friendships (Wolfberg & Schuler, 2006).

The **Integrated Play Groups®** **(IPG)** model (Wolfberg, 1994, 2003, 2004, 2009; Wolfberg & Schuler, 1993, 2006) and **Friend 2 Friend (F2F)** model (McCracken, 2004, 2005a, 2005b, 2005c, 2006, 2009, 2010) were created out of deep concern for the many children who are missing out on peer play and friendships as a vital part of their childhood experience. Drawing on current theory and empirical research, these complementary models are designed to address core challenges of socialization, communication, play, and imagination in children with autism while helping them build relationships with typical peers and siblings in inclusive social settings.

Consistent with its mission "to advance the rights of individuals on the autism spectrum to derive the joy and benefits of social inclusion in play, recreation and cultural experiences," the Autism Institute on Peer Socialization and Play (www.autisminstitute.com) was founded in 2000. Through training, research, and global outreach efforts, the focus is on establishing peer socialization programs following the Integrated Play Groups® (IPG) model. IPG aims to maximize the developmental potential and intrinsic motivation of children with autism to engage with typical peers in mutually enjoyed play experiences. Extensions of the IPG model include drama, visual arts, filmmaking, physical movement, and other culturally valued activities that are of high interest for various age groups. IPG providers include a collective of highly qualified professionals (including educators, speech-language therapists, occupational therapists, psychologists, and related care providers), who are devoted to crafting specialized programs for individuals and families to enhance full participation in social, cultural, and quality of life experiences.

Among our partners is the Friend 2 Friend Social Learning Society (www.friend2friendsociety.org), whose mission is to "enhance reciprocal social interaction, communication, imaginative play, and friendships between individuals on the autism spectrum and their typically developing peers." To meet its mandate, the F2F Society provides a variety of unique and innovative programs that not only include school- and center-based IPG programs but extends to offering the F2F Autism Demystification programs. Through the delivery of specially designed puppet presentations and simulation games, the F2F demystification programs are designed to foster mutual friendships for children and adolescents with ASD by building awareness, understanding, acceptance, and empathy in their peers. Grounded in evidence-based practices, the F2F and IPG models have shown benefits for individuals with ASD and typical peers who represent diverse ages, abilities, socio-economic groups, languages, and cultures.

This chapter translates theory and research into effective and meaningful practice by presenting the principles and practices of the F2F and IPG models. By way of introduction, we will first describe the conceptual foundation for each of these models by addressing the role of play and friendships in childhood (as it impacts children's learning, development and socio-cultural participation) and the challenges this presents for children with ASD. We will next describe and illustrate the key features of each model while drawing on first-hand experience with children of diverse ages, abilities, and backgrounds. The chapter concludes with a series of Tips for Practical Application related to demystifying autism while supporting play, imagination, and friendships with peers.

Importance of Play and Friendships

A prominent body of literature documents the importance of play and friendships for children's learning, development, and cultural participation. Thus, an abundant research base on play shows strong links to children's cognitive, language, literacy, social, emotional, creative, and sensory-motor development (for reviews, see Wolfberg, 2003, 2009).

Play

Vygotsky (1966, 1978) ascribed a most vital role to play as a primary social activity through which children develop social or interpersonal knowledge as well as symbolic capacities. In his writings he noted that play's significance is far reaching, extending beyond that of representing stages of development to actually leading development. Further, he emphasized the notion that play, like all learning and development, is mediated through social experiences with others.

When it comes to play, peers perform a distinct role in children's socialization and development by offering learning opportunities and experiences that cannot be duplicated by adults (Hartup, 1989, 1991). Thus, while playing together, children construct a peer culture that is uniquely their own (Corsaro, 1992; Wolfberg et al., 1999). It is based on active participation in the social activities that are most valued by the peer group.

"Play culture" more accurately describes that realm in which children create and live out their social and imaginary lives (Mouritsen, 1996; Wolfberg, 2009; Wolfberg et al., 1999). It is within the culture of play that children acquire many interrelated skills that are necessary for attaining social competence and, ultimately, establishing mutual friendships. Through jointly constructed activity, children refine their social communication strategies, learn to negotiate and compromise, resolve conflicts, build trust, and develop other foundation social skills. Play further provides opportunities to express intimacy and affection with peers, the core ingredients of friendship (Rubin, Fein, & Vandenberg, 1983).

Friendship

Friendships, like play, occupy a central place in children's social lives. Research suggests that friendship is not only associated with children's social, emotional, and cognitive development, but is also a determining factor for social adaptation and adjustment (Hartup, 1996; Ladd, 1990). Children with mutual friends are more socially competent and better adjusted than children without friends and tend to have higher self-esteem, be more sociable and cooperative, and better able to cope with change and manage interpersonal conflicts (Berndt, 2002; Gest, Graham-Bermann, & Hartup, 2001). Further, children with positive and stable friendships exhibit higher engagement, better adjustment, and greater achievement in school (Berndt, 1999).

In contrast, peer rejection, neglect, or bullying contributes to low aspiration in school performance (Bagwell, Schmidt, Newcomb, & Bukowski, 2001), increased problematic behaviors, withdrawn or isolative behaviors, depression, low self-esteem, and more negative expectations (Asher, Parkhurst, Hymel, & Williams, 1990; Boivin, Poulin, & Vitaro, 1994). Studies further reveal that children without close friends are decidedly lonelier than children with close friends (Parker & Asher, 1993). The presence of even one close friend has been associated with a child's happiness and sense of belonging.

Challenge of Play and Friendships for Children With ASD

Although children on the autism spectrum naturally differ from one another in distinct ways, as a group they face unique challenges in peer socialization and play. As compared to the highly interactive and creative play of typically developing children, the play of children with autism is markedly detached and impoverished.

Without any direction, these children tend to fixate on a limited number of activities, which they often repeat and carry out for long periods while alone (Frith, 2003; Wing, Gould, Yeates, & Brierly, 1977). Many children with autism are attracted to toys, activities and themes that are conventional, consistent with play preferences of peers similar in development and age. Other children are attracted to unconventional activities that include preoccupations with objects or narrowly focused interests.

Research suggests that, compared to children of a similar developmental level, children with autism engage in higher rates of manipulation or sensory exploration of objects as opposed to **representational** forms of play (Libby, Powell, Messer, & Jordan, 1998; Sigman & Ungerer, 1984; Tilton & Ottinger, 1964). In addition, they are less inclined to spontaneously engage in functional play and rarely produce pretend play (Baron-Cohen, 1987; Jarrold, 2003; Libby et al., 1998; Williams, 2003), and when they do show these capacities, their play is less diverse, flexible, and varied than that of other children. The play of children with autism often appears to be without direction or purpose as they pursue activities lacking in variations along a theme.

Socializing with peers in the context of play and other shared activities is particularly challenging for children with ASD (Jordan, 2003). Problems in both verbal and nonverbal communication (e.g., the use of eye gaze, eye contact, physical proximity, facial expression, pointing, and other conventional gestures) closely interface with underlying difficulties in joint attention, spontaneous imitation, and emotional responsiveness in social play (Baron-Cohen, 1989; Dawson & Adams, 1984; Mundy, Sigman, & Ruskin, 1999; Sigman, Ungerer, & Sherman, 1987).

With respect to social play, children with autism direct fewer obvious social initiations to peers and inconsistently respond to peers when they initiate with them. Less obvious attempts to interact with peers include initiations that may be characterized as subtle, obscure or poorly timed (Wolfberg & Schuler, 2006). Based on clinical observations, children with ASD present distinct social play styles that are consistent with Wing and Gould's (1979) early work. Some children appear "aloof," as they distance themselves from peers or act as though they are unaware of their presence. Others are "passive," as they follow along or watch what their peers are doing but rarely initiate interaction in obvious ways. Still others are "active and odd" in the sense that they attempt to engage peers, but do so in an idiosyncratic or one-sided manner, such as by talking excessively about one topic.

Addressing Peer Culture and the Social Void

The peer group, or **peer culture**, has a tremendous influence on the extent to which children with ASD are able to reap the benefits of play and friendships in childhood. Peer culture consists of those shared understandings, values, beliefs, and associated behaviors, activities, and relationship patterns that children construct out of their everyday experience with one another (Wolfberg et al., 1999). A common experience for many children with autism is that they are excluded from their peer culture because their behavior does not fit into peer perceptions of what is "normal." Consequently, a social void is likely to exist between children on the autism spectrum and typical peers when they are placed together in inclusive settings without carefully planned educational supports that demystify autism (McCracken, 2004). This social void arises in large part because typical peers lack a conceptual framework for understanding and appreciating the unique ways in which children with ASD communicate, relate, and play.

The unconventional or understated ways in which children with ASD initiate with peers are frequently mistaken for signs of deviance or limited social interest. As a result, children may be teased and taunted by intolerant peers or simply overlooked by well-meaning peers. In response, many children withdraw and cease to initiate further. Some children express feelings of alienation from their peer group. These feelings may lead to an increase in the child's anxiety and a breakdown in his or her ability to communicate. In some cases, increased anxiety manifests as negative and even aggressive behaviors. Peers seeing these behaviors are likely to continue avoiding or overtly dismissing the child with ASD, which in turn may lead to feelings of loneliness, decreased self-esteem, and the onset of depression (Bauminger & Kasari, 2000; Heinrichs, 2003). Thus, children with ASD may become caught in a cycle of exclusion, which deprives them of opportunities to learn how to socialize and play in more conventional and socially accepted ways, and ultimately to form friendships.

In order to break this cycle of exclusion, the social void must be addressed on both sides within the context of a shared peer culture. That is, effort should not only be placed on enhancing the skills and development of the children with autism, but also on educating typical peers by demystifying autism. Only by altering the skills, experiences, and perceptions of all children is it possible to narrow the gap to eliminate the social void. This will allow a new peer culture to emerge, one that is open to neurodiversity and inclusive of children with unique ways of relating, communicating, and playing.

Friend 2 Friend Model

The Friend 2 Friend Autism Demystification (F2F) model is designed to foster mutual friendships for children with ASD by building understanding, acceptance, and empathy in their peers, siblings, and classmates (McCracken, 2004, 2005a 2005b, 2005c, 2006, 2009, 2010). This model provides a framework for designing autism demystification programs for children ages 3 and up. F2F offers innovative educational programs that include puppet programs targeting younger children (ages 3-11) and simulation games targeting older children (ages 12 and up).

Grounded in current research, the model uses a systematic approach to educate both individuals with autism and their peer groups in an inclusive, fun, age-appropriate, and sensitive manner. The approach allows all children (including those on the autism spectrum) access to information about characteristics commonly associated with autism. With an emphasis on supporting typically developing peers to understand, accept, and empathize with children on the spectrum, the programs set the stage for helping children develop prosocial skills (Eisenberg & Miller, 1987), which are the basis for becoming well-adjusted and caring adults (Hartup, 1989, 1991; Ladd, 1990). Promoting these pivotal prosocial skills in typical peers is an essential part of successfully supporting children on the autism spectrum in inclusive settings. Furthermore, these skills support all children in developing to the best of their abilities through the play and socialization that friendships provide.

Teaching Process

To support the ultimate goal of fostering mutual friendships between children with ASD and their peers, the F2F model demystifies autism using a four-step process consisting of modeling, labeling, explaining, and normalizing.

Modeling. F2F programs support peers in understanding puzzling social, communicative, and self-regulating behaviors that they may see children on the autism spectrum exhibit. The first step in helping children understand the characteristics of autism is to provide a *visual model* of characteristics commonly associated with autism. This enables participants to formulate a concept of autism in their minds, one based on facts rather than personal interpretation or speculation. **Modeling** the characteristics of autism subsequently becomes the basis for fostering understanding, acceptance, and empathy for children on the autism spectrum they know and may come to know.

Labeling. The next step in the teaching model is to support children to accept the unconventional social, communicative, or self-regulating behaviors that they may see children on the autism spectrum exhibit. After providing the visual model, we *label* the characteristics that have been modeled. **Labeling** provides the children with a name for what they may otherwise not understand and helps them accept the characteristics or behaviors as genuine and real.

Explaining. Once the characteristics of autism have been modeled and labeled, the Friend 2 Friend model then *explains* the unconventional social, communicative, or self-regulating characteristics that peers may see children on the autism spectrum exhibit. Explaining the meaning or purpose behind the characteristics helps peers understand and accept children on the autism spectrum. Often typically developing peers have difficulty accepting the unique characteristics of autism because the child with autism looks "normal," making them conclude that the child "chooses" to behave in a manner that is unusual rather than realizing that the behaviors are symptoms of the autistic condition. Explaining the characteristics of autism provides children with the answers to the question, "Why does my friend do that?"

Normalizing. The final and most significant step in the F2F teaching process is to support peers in empathizing with children on the autism spectrum. Once we have modeled and labeled the characteristics of autism and explained their purpose, we link the otherwise unconventional characteristics with common characteristics that all children exhibit. Such *normalizing* of the characteristics of autism provides children with an opportunity for emotional perspective taking, which allows them to truly walk in the shoes of the child with autism. Identifying with children on the autism spectrum shifts typical peers past simply understanding and accepting to feelings of empathy. These feelings facilitate prosocial behaviors, which form the basis for fostering mutually rewarding relationships between children on the autism spectrum and their typically developing peers, siblings, and classmates (Eisenberg & Miller, 1987).

Key Learning Goals

As part of the F2F model, children are introduced to five key learning goals, which underline the learning and provide a basis for future learning when follow-up activities take place. The five key learning goals support participants to:

1. Recognize and accept differences in themselves and others by identifying and labeling their own affinities (strengths or gifts) and their own challenges (weaknesses or disabilities)

2. Recognize individuals with autism as individuals and valuable friends through the use of "people-first" language

3. Recognize that it is important to ask questions and express feelings as a means of learning new things about themselves and others

4. Empathize with what it feels like to have autism by providing an experiential learning opportunity and by modeling, labeling, explaining, and normalizing the characteristics of autism

5. Embrace all types of diversity by supporting participants to recognize the importance of peer relationships, play, and friendships

The Seven Friendship Tips

The five key learning goals set the stage for inclusion, often opening children's eyes to the differences among us all and shifting perspectives within peer groups about what it means to have autism. But changing attitudes is not enough; we need to give children concrete tools they can use to be successful in their peer relationships.

Our seven friendship tips offer prosocial communication strategies that enhance social interactions between individuals on the autism spectrum and their peers. We have found that when peers know how to communicate or interact with somebody on the spectrum they are more than willing to do so. The seven friendship tips that follow are key educational components to the Friend 2 Friend model.

1. **Get your friend's attention.** Move closer to your friend and say his or her name to get your friend's attention before you start talking.

2. **Use short sentences.** Use fewer words or shorten your sentence when speaking to your friend.

3. **Use gestures or visuals.** Use a gesture like pointing to something or a visual (i.e., picture communication symbols) to help your friend understand what you are communicating.

4. **Wait.** Give your friend extra time to think about what you are saying and then answer you.

5. **Watch your friend.** Watch your friend to learn your friend's affinities (things your friend is good at or likes to do).

6. **Give your friend choices.** When you want to play, offer your friend choices of things your friend likes to do.

7. **Use friendly words.** Use friendly words when speaking with your friend like "hi."

Friend 2 Friend Puppet Program

The comprehensive F2F puppet program is designed to teach young children by tapping into their imagination. Using child-size puppets, humor, and interactive experiences, specially trained puppeteers (F2F Program Guides) perform plays that are tailored to introduce characteristics associated with ASD. Presentations focus on modeling, labeling, explaining, and normalizing the characteristics of autism while never singling out the focus child or children on the autism spectrum. Each puppet presentation contains six learning opportunities to optimize learning for children with different learning styles or strengths. The various learning opportunities include the following.

Introduction (*opening ritual – assigned observers*). The introduction is designed to familiarize children with the program as well as to provide an overview of the presentation. The F2F Lead Program Guide begins by reviewing the steps in the lesson using specially designed picture communication symbols (PCS). The Lead Program Guide also assigns the children jobs to do. Assigning the children roles during the puppet play (*assigned observer*) increases their buy-in to what they will be learning.

Puppet play (*model or visual learning opportunity*). The puppet play provides children with a visual learning opportunity as they watch the puppets model, label, explain, and normalize the characteristics of autism. The puppets, representing a child with autism, two peers, and two teacher puppets, act out specifically designed skits that introduce children to the F2F five key learning goals and seven basic friendship tips. This provides children with a conceptual framework and language to promote further discussion and learning.

"What did Crystal learn?" (*auditory/visual learning style/performance feedback*). "What Did Crystal Learn?" is an auditory and visual review of the learning goals and friendship tips presented in the puppet play and accompanying story book. Directly following the puppet play, the Lead Program Guide reviews the learning goals and basic friendship tips with the children using the PCS as a visual support. This review offers a chance for children who are auditory and visual learners to gain additional insight into the program goals and tips. It also gives teachers an opportunity to evaluate which of the learning goals or friendship tips need to be emphasized during follow-up lessons or activities.

Pass-the-puppet circle (*role-playing and tactile learning opportunity*). The pass-the-puppet circle learning segment of the puppet presentations is a tactile learning opportunity where the children become the puppeteers while the Program Guides interact with them by role-playing with the puppets. This segment gives children an opportunity to review the learning goals and friendship tips through a tactile experience of holding and playing with the puppets.

***Questions and answers** (open dialogue)*. Once all the children have had an opportunity to interact with the puppets, the Program Guides collect the puppets and ask the children if they have any questions. Then they proceed to engage the children in open dialogue.

***Sticker time** (closing ritual/transfer training)*. Once all the children's questions have been answered, the puppet presentation concludes, and each child receives a sticker with the quote "I'm a Good Friend." The sticker serves to remind the children of the concepts introduced by the program and is a tangible reward for participating.

Follow-up materials. As part of the F2F puppet program, each educator/adult receives a coloring/story book that is adapted from the puppets and a seven friendship tips poster. The school receives a copy of the Can I Play Too? Autism Demystification packaged programs, which contains a DVD of the puppet play, implementation manual, five coloring/story books and a printable materials CD. Each child participating in the program receives an "I am a good friend" sticker.

Tim

After I had presented to two first-grade classes in a public school district, the classroom teacher approached me to tell me how much she liked the F2F program and how she felt that the typical peers had learned a great deal. She wondered if the focus child in this group (Tim) had gotten as much information or learning from the program as the other kids. She was pleased that Tim participated for the entire presentation, which is sometimes very difficult for him to do, but because Tim was nonverbal, she wondered if the messages modeled in the puppet presentation were lost on him.

As we talked, we watched Tim from the other side of the room playing with the computer prop during the pass-the-puppet circle. Tim did not want to play with any of the puppets but was fascinated by the computer. Then it was time for questions and answers, so the Program Guides began to collect the puppets. Tim's special education assistant asked him to "put the computer back" as she pointed to the puppet stage. Tim got up from the circle and went to the puppet stage. He took Min, the puppet representing the child with ASD in the puppet play, and placed him carefully on the stage. Then he put the computer in Min's lap. Tim's teacher smiled as we watched Tim arrange Min. But then Tim did the unexpected — he took Sherry (the puppet representing the typical peer in the puppet play) and sat her next to Min, leaned her over so she was looking at the computer, and placed one of her hands on the computer and the other around Min. At that point, Tim's teacher looked at me with tears in her eyes and said, "I guess he understands exactly what the puppet play was about."

Friend 2 Friend Simulation Game

This 50-minute educational program is designed to help participants understand, in an engaging manner, what it feels like to have autism while teaching the prosocial communication strategies necessary to interact successfully with their peers with autism. Each simulation game program begins with a "Simon Says" game that targets the participants' senses and their receptive communication in an effort to bring them to a state of confusion and frustration. The F2F Lead Guide gives instructions (e.g., "Simon Says touch your nose, stand up, sit down, turn around, jump up and down ...") at an extremely rapid pace while a light machine is flashing colors of light, one volunteer is blowing a whistle, and another volunteer is touching the students' faces with a feather duster.

Directly following the simulation game, the F2F Lead Guide reviews with the participants their sensory and communication experiences during the game, linking those experiences to what it feels like to have autism. Once the participants have a basic understanding of autism, the presentation continues with a lively and open discussion, "I Have the Kind of Mind," in which students are encouraged to discuss what they are good at and what they are not so good at as a way to help them understand that "everybody is different in his or her own way." This discussion also introduces participants to the concept of self-regulating behaviors.

Once the participants have had an opportunity to empathize with what it feels like to have autism, the lead guide introduces the Seven Basic Friendship Tips and the accompanying seven friendship tips animated video, which was created by Iain Robbins who is an individual on the autism spectrum. These tips include prosocial communication strategies that may support social interaction between typical peers and children with ASD. The program ends by reading a poem about friendship written by a child with ASD and a discussion about friendships.

The entire F2F simulation game program represents the perspective of a child with autism, making the concepts simple, easy-to-understand, and meaningful for all children by using sensitive language and encouraging the participation of all children. At no time during the program are references made to the focus child or to any other person with autism. The only exception is if the Lead Guide has a personal connection to an individual with ASD who gives explicit permission to share his or her experiences.

Sam

Sam's parents and teachers were stumped. For the past six years, Sam, a sensitive and creative boy with ASD had been fully integrated into his local school. These years had been happy and successful ones for Sam and his classmates. But suddenly in the fifth grade everything changed and, for no apparent reason, Sam began to have outbursts at school directed mostly at his peers.

I suggested to Sam's mother that perhaps it was time to implement an autism demystification program as a means of supporting Sam at school. Sam's mother agreed. As part of the demystification process, we implemented a series of interventions to help Sam understand his unique learning style, challenges, and gifts. For Sam's peers, we presented the F2F simulation game.

While presenting the F2F simulation game to Sam's class, I observed that only two students had ever heard the word "autism" before, and none knew what the word meant even though most of them had been in school with Sam since kindergarten. At no time during the presentation did any of the students ask any specific questions about Sam or about autism. However, it was clear that many of the students did relate the information in the presentation to Sam, because when we were finished one student whispered to me, "I know someone with autism. His name is Sam; he is in my class."

After this presentation to Sam's class, it was clear that Sam's anxiety about school, and in particular his classmates, was in direct correlation to his classmates' lack of understanding about autism and Sam's lack of knowledge about his challenges and gifts. In other words, Sam and his peers were experiencing the "social void." Sam's social situation at school continued to deteriorate to the point where he felt alienated from his classmates, which increased his anxiety and caused a breakdown in his ability to communicate. In turn, the increased anxiety and decreased communication caused Sam to exhibit aggressive behaviors. The change in Sam's behaviors caused his peers to avoid contact with him, which was exactly what Sam did not want.

Over the next few months, Sam worked very hard at home and at school to understand autism and his unique differences. At the beginning of Sam's sixth-grade year, Friend 2 Friend presented again at his school. Sam's mother felt that it might be best for Sam not to be present during the presentation, in hopes that Sam's peers might open up and begin to ask questions. When it was time for the class to come for the presentation, Sam decided he wanted to participate along with his class. Usually, Friend 2 Friend encourages the focus child with autism to be present and participate in the programs; however, the wishes of families are always respected. In this case Sam made up his own mind and participated along with his class.

When we came to the part in the presentation where I ask if anyone has ever heard the word autism, all the children raised their hands. Then I asked if anyone could tell me what the word meant. Now all the students' hands went down, except for Sam's. Sam put up his hand and said, "I know what autism means; it's a disability that is not really a disability but makes you think differently from other people; I should know because I AM AUTISTIC." For the first time, Sam spoke openly and honestly, sharing his perspective as an individual with autism, and in doing so he removed all the social barriers that had existed previously.

The F2F simulation-game presentation had helped Sam understand and accept his unique gifts and challenges and to feel safe enough to share his experience as an individual with autism. The F2F program also helped Sam's peers understand, accept, and empathize with Sam while introducing a shared vocabulary for further discussions and learning. Sam and his peers had taken the first step towards mutual friendships for Sam and all his classmates. Sam had a successful and happy sixth-grade year and continues to help others understand "I am autistic."

Integrated Play Groups Model

The following description of the Integrated Play Groups (IPG) model has been adapted from related work that offers more detailed accounts of its principles and practices (Wolfberg, 2003, 2009; Wolfberg & Schuler, 2006). The IPG model is designed to support children of diverse ages and abilities on the autism spectrum in mutually enjoyed play experiences with typical peers/siblings as playmates (Wolfberg, 1994, 2003, 2004, 2009; Wolfberg & Schuler, 1993, 2006). Influenced by the work of Vygotsky (1966, 1978), the focus of IPGs is on guiding children's participation in culturally valued activities (i.e., play) with the guidance, support, and challenge of companions who vary in skill and status (Rogoff, 1990). Originally designed for children ages 3 to 11 years old, the IPG model has been extended to older age groups with a focus on guiding participation in drama, visual arts, filmmaking, physical movement, and other high-interest activities (Bottema-Beutel, 2011; Julius, Wolfberg, Jahnke, & Neufeld, 2012; Wolfberg, Bottema-Beutel, & DeWitt, 2012). Through a carefully tailored system of support, emphasis is placed on maximizing children's developmental potential as well as intrinsic desire to play, socialize, and form meaningful relationships with peers. Consistent with the Friend 2 Friend model, of equal importance is teaching peers to be empathetic, responsive, and accepting of children's differing social, communication, and play styles. A further intent is for the children to mediate their own play activities with minimal adult guidance.

Setting the Stage for Play With Peers: IPG Program and Environmental Design

Form IPG parent-professional team. Since each IPG is customized as a part of a child's individualized education/therapy program (IEP/IFSP), it is planned as a collaborative parent-professional team process. The *Integrated Play Groups Field Manual* (Wolfberg, 2003) is designed to help support this process.

Determine if IPG program is appropriate for a child. To be eligible for an IPG, a child must be at least 3 years of age and receiving support services as part of an IFSP/IEP. An IPG may be considered appropriate if the team agrees that the child (a) presents developmental delays or differences that impact on his or her capacity to spontaneously play and socialize with peers, and (b) will potentially benefit from an intensive inclusive peer play intervention to address challenges in these areas.

Identify qualified IPG Provider. Qualified IPG Providers successfully complete a comprehensive IPG Master Guide Apprenticeship training program offered via the Autism Institute on Peer Socialization and Play. One option is to arrange for a member of the team to receive training to become an IPG Master Guide. During the training process, participants receive direct supervision from an experienced IPG Field Supervisor while implementing the IPG program. Another option is to recruit an IPG Master Guide who is already qualified to deliver the program.

Form small, stable group of compatible players. Each group includes three to five players with a higher number of expert players (typical peers and/or siblings) than novice players (children on the autism spectrum). Recruited from a child's natural social network, expert players consist of typical peers and siblings who are competent players and express an interest in participating. These may include schoolmates, family friends, and neighbors who ordinarily have contact with the novice players. It is ideal when playmates are somewhat familiar and attracted to one another in order to foster the potential of a long-lasting friendship. Different types of beneficial experiences follow when the composition of groups varies with respect to such variables as children's gender, ages, developmental status, and play interaction styles. Selecting familiar peers offer advantages from the start, but familiarity can also evolve as a part of the IPG experience.

Develop an IPG program schedule. Consistent times are designated for IPGs to run on a regular and frequent basis. IPG programs generally run for 12-week program cycles, meeting twice weekly for either 30- or 60-minute sessions. Many school programs run for 30 minutes during a natural social break (e.g., lunch/recess time) whereas many after-school, community, and home-based programs run longer. Times may vary depending upon the age and developmental level of the participating children.

Prior to the first session, the players participate in the Friend 2 Friend program and an IPG orientation that offers an opportunity for the children to meet and ask questions while gaining information about what to expect when they begin their play groups. A major focus is on preparing the expert players to be accepting of and responsive to novice players' unique ways of relating, communicating, and playing.

Choose play space and materials. Size, density, organization, and thematic arrangements are all considerations with respect to the design of the play environment. A wide range of highly motivating sensory motor, exploratory, constructive, and socio-dramatic props with high potential for interactive and imaginative play are selected as play materials. These types of materials vary in degree of structure and complexity, which affords opportunities to support children who present diverse interests, learning styles, and developmental levels. The important point is to identify play materials that are intrinsically motivating, allowing for mutual enjoyment between novice and expert players.

Develop session structure and supports. The play session follows a consistent schedule that incorporates routines and rituals while utilizing visual supports (consisting of words and/or pictures). These types of structures and supports are directed to fostering familiarity, predictability, and a cohesive group identity. From the beginning, the children are presented with basic rules that present guidelines for fair and respectful behavior and care of materials. To help children anticipate the meeting times and follow the progression of the play session, visual schedules are designed for both the individual and the group. Opening and closing rituals (e.g., greeting, song, and brief discussion of plans and strategies) begin and end each play session. Visual choice boards consist of a variety of preferred activities from which children may select to get started in play. Further, children may wear visual role tags depicting their characters or roles, such as "cashier" or "customer" while playing restaurant. Story books are also created to help children review play activities and themes as well as to teach new play schemes. Finally, group membership is established by creating play group names and associated rituals, which also serve to provide the intrinsic motivation for true peer participation.

Observing Children at Play With Peers: IPG Assessment Approach

The IPG model includes a comprehensive assessment approach that provides a basis for setting realistic and meaningful goals, identifying effective intervention strategies and documenting children's progress in a systematic fashion. These assessments include a focus on **symbolic** and **social dimensions of play**, social communication (communicative functions and means), play preferences, and diversity of play.

Symbolic dimension of play. This refers to a set of play characteristics (as opposed to mutually exclusive stages of development) that follow a relatively consistent developmental sequence. These include play acts that are directed to objects, self, or others and that signify events (adapted from McCune-Nicolich, 1981; Piaget, 1962; Smilansky, 1968). The symbolic dimension of play includes: *manipulation* play (exploring objects; e.g., spinning the wheels of a toy car); *functional play* (conventional object use and the association of two or more objects; e.g., rolling a toy car on the floor, placing a teacup on a saucer); and *symbolic-pretend play* (representing objects, people and events in imaginary ways; e.g., using a block as if it were an airplane, wiping the table as if holding an imaginary sponge, making the baby doll cry and soothing the baby doll while acting in the role of a mother).

Social dimension of play. This involves a focus on the child's distance to and involvement with one or more children (adapted from Parten, 1932). The social dimension includes *isolate* (playing alone), *onlooker-orientation* (watching peers), *parallel-proximity* (playing beside peers), *common focus* (reciprocal play with peers), and *common goal* (collaborating with peers in a highly organized way).

Communicative functions and means. This focuses on the functions of communication (i.e., what the child intends to convey; e.g., requests for objects, peer interaction, affection, protests, declarations, and comments), which may be accomplished through a variety of verbal and nonverbal *communicative means* (e.g., facial expressions, eye gaze, physical proximity, touching, gestures, intonation, vocalization, echolalia, and simple or complex speech/sign/symbol/written word). Each child's communicative attempt (as expressed through any one or combination of communicative functions and means) is recognized as a potential initiation to play with someone or something, even when expressed in a subtle or obscure form (adapted from Peck, Schuler, Tomlinson, Theimer, & Haring, 1984).

Play preferences and diversity of play. This helps to identify the number and variety of play interests in an effort to help expand the child's play repertoire. In addition, documenting play preferences offers a means to match novice and expert players based on shared play interests. Children's play preferences may take various forms, including fascinations with particular objects, actions, activities, themes and playmates. Examples include: object choices (e.g., prefers round objects, toys with moving parts, realistic replicas); action choices (e.g., prefers to spin toys, line up toys, uses toys according to function); activity choices (e.g., prefers roughhousing, quiet play, constructive play); theme choices (e.g., prefers familiar routines, invented stories, fantasy play); and playmate choices (e.g., prefers no one in particular, one or more peers).

Guided Participation in Play: Intervention Approach

The intervention approach (also referred to as ***guided participation***) involves a system of support that is tailored to each child's unique profile of learning and development. The approach is especially responsive to the child's underlying core challenges while also offering a level of intensity that taps into the child's potential. Guided participation focuses on supporting opportunities that enable novice and expert players to incorporate preferred activities into socially coordinated play while also challenging novice players to practice new and progressively complex types of play. The IPG Guide facilitates the play session in a methodical fashion, guiding novice and expert players to engage in mutually enjoyed activities that promote social interaction, communication, play and imagination; e.g., constructing, pretending, interactive games, art, music and movement. As the children demonstrate an increasing capacity to mediate play activities on their own, the adult gradually pulls out. As depicted in Figure 8.1, the practices represent the various layers that support the guided participation process.

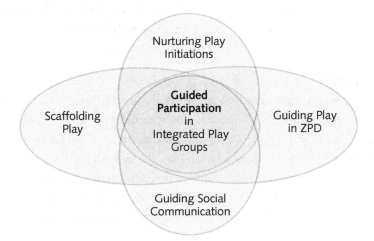

Figure 8.1. Conceptual model of guided participation in Integrated Play Groups (Wolfberg et al., 2012).

Nurturing play initiations. This focuses on uncovering novice players' meaningful attempts to socialize and play by recognizing, interpreting, and responding to the subtle and idiosyncratic ways in which they express their intentions. Play initiations may include virtually any act or display that indicates a child's interest in or desire to play in the company of peers. They may be directed to objects (e.g., toys and props), others (e.g., peers and adults), or oneself. Also, play initiations may be conventional or unconventional and conveyed through overt, subtle, or obscure means. Even acts that reflect unusual fascinations, obsessions, rituals, or idiosyncratic language are recognized as play initiations.

Play initiations are the foundation on which to build the child's social and symbolic play repertoire. They are the springboards for novice and expert players to find common ground in mutually engaging activities. The adult's capacity to recognize, interpret, and respond to play initiations is essential for delivering support that is matched to the level of comprehension and ability within the child's "zone of proximal development" (ZPD), defined by Vygotsky (1978) as "the distance between the actual developmental level as determined by independent problem solving and the level of potential development as determined through problem solving under adult guidance, or in collaboration with more capable peers" (p. 86).

Scaffolding play. The process of scaffolding play involves systematically adjusting the amount and type of support provided so that it matches or slightly exceeds the child's ability to engage independently in play with peers (i.e., within the child's *zone of proximal development).*

From a facilitation standpoint, **scaffolding** involves moving in and moving out in response to observed social, communication and play behaviors at any given point in time. At a more intensive level, the IPG Guide is much like a stage director who carefully directs and models the play by setting up the play scene with props and materials, delegating roles and play partners, performing actions and narrating lines. At a less intensive level, the

IPG Guide is much like a coach, who redirects the children to one another to set the stage for their own play. This includes standing on the sidelines and posing questions, commenting, giving suggestions, as well as offering subtle reminders using verbal and visual cues. At the least intensive level, the adult remains on the periphery and allows the children to practice the play on their own. By this point, the children exhibit a level of comfort and competency in exploring and trying out new activities. The IPG Guide serves as a secure base, ready to step in and provide support whenever needed.

Guiding social communication. The process of guiding social communication is ongoing with an emphasis on helping the children to elicit each other's attention and maintain interactions in reciprocal play. The focus is on promoting the use of verbal and nonverbal cues that are conventional with respect to children's development, age, and peer culture. The strategies used to guide social communication are directed to both the novice and expert players. They include strategies to (a) invite each other to play, (b) persist in enlisting reluctant players to play, (c) respond to each other's cues and initiations to play, and (d) sustain and expand upon interactions in play. To a large extent, the expert players learn how to interpret the cues of the novice players as having meaning and purpose. As complex social cues are broken down for the novice players, they in turn learn more conventional ways in which to initiate, respond and join peers for play.

A number of strategies are used for the purpose of guiding social communication in play. These include targeting relevant verbal and/or nonverbal social-communication cues that will serve to elicit and sustain mutual engagement in play. Visual supports have been developed for this purpose, which include posters and corresponding cue cards. The cue cards portray picture-word combinations that focus on What to Do (e.g., look, stand close, tap shoulder, take hand, point, give [toy], take turns, do what your playmate is doing) and What to Say (e.g., Say name of playmate, "Let's play," "What do you want to play?" "What are you doing?" "Can I have a turn?"). As relevant, the IPG Guide provides instruction and practice on one or more cues, which are then supported in an incidental fashion as the need arises. The idea is for the children to incorporate these cues into their natural repertoire with the visual supports gradually faded out.

Guiding play in the ZPD. Play guidance comprises a progression of strategies that are specifically geared to novice players with consideration of both their present developmental level and experience in play with peers. These strategies are designed to scaffold full immersion in play experiences that slightly exceed the child's present level or capacity within the child's ZPD (Vygotsky, 1978). This allows the child to participate with peers in more advanced play activities and themes, even if participation is initially minimal. For instance, a child who is predisposed to lining up objects might be eager to take on the task of lining up the grocery boxes on a shelf as a part of a larger play theme of shopping. With the assistance of more capable peers, the child may begin to explore and diversify existing play routines and eventually come to comprehend this role.

The progression of play guidance strategies includes *orienting* (watching peers and activities), *mirroring* (mimicking the actions of a peer), *parallel play* (playing side by side in the same play space with similar materials), and *joint focus* (active sharing and informal turn taking in the same activity) to socially coordinated activity involving *joint action* (formal turn taking), *role enactment* (portraying real-life activities through conventional actions), and *role-playing* (taking on pretend roles and creatively using objects while enacting complex scripts).

Richie had an opportunity to participate in Integrated Play Groups beginning in kindergarten. With careful scaffolding and guidance, he began to make progress in both the symbolic and social dimensions of play. The children were ready to be "coached." First, I tried to facilitate parallel play. I just wanted Richie to accept his peers playing with the same materials as he was. Rather than directly interact, I encouraged the kids to play near each other. Richie accepted this and continued to watch his peers from time to time to see what they were doing. This was important for Richie, because he has shown time and again that this is his way of learning most things: First he needs to sit back and watch for a while. Then he tends to start to understand and participate more directly.

One roadblock in the parallel play process was encountered when Richie was playing with the dollhouse and was hoarding all the dolls. He would come into the playroom, take all the dolls, and then start playing by himself. If another child asked for a doll, he would become upset and explode. I tried to coach Richie and help him understand sharing, but it was not working.

After play group was over, I brainstormed about what to do next. Do I take the dollhouse out of the playroom? Do I let Richie play alone, hoping that he'll start to share? Neither of those options seemed right. I decided that there was something Richie did not understand about sharing. That is when I thought of making visual supports for the situation. I took a digital picture of each doll from the dollhouse. Then I printed them off, laminated them, and Velcroed^{TM} them to a small choice board. I brought the choice board to Richie's next play group and showed him that each child gets to take the picture of the doll they want to play with. It worked like magic. Richie chose first and picked his favorite doll. Next, he let his friends choose a doll. Something about the visual support helped him understand what he was supposed to do in a way that verbal language had not. Sharing the dolls was never a problem again.

Richie continued to expand his repertoire of play schemes over the course of his kindergarten year. He learned to play with a vet shop, trains, cars, dollhouse, restaurant, and other activities with his friends. He got out of the habit of coming into the playroom and playing with the exact same toys every time. This was partially due to a large choice board in the playroom showing pictures of several toys/items available. This helped Richie see all the choices available, so he didn't have to try to think of something new when he came in the playroom. During this time, Richie continued to play with toys in a functional manner (i.e., used a cup to represent a cup and a phone to represent a phone). He wasn't engaging in symbolic-pretend play at this time.

When Richie was in first grade, he became more interested in his peers. During this school year, I focused a bit less on the number of play schemes he used and more on his social interaction and emerging symbolic play. He was ready to accept guidance from me as well as his peers since he was more comfortable around them. Over the course of the year, we played vet shop during several play sessions, and I encouraged his friends to try to engage him a little more. Richie usually took the role of the vet and often worked on fixing one particular stuffed animal (the lemur). He didn't want the other kids to touch the lemur, so I helped him become more flexible with his play by expanding the play scheme.

Since Richie did not want anyone else to "operate" on his lemur, I arranged for his peers to take other roles in the play scheme. One girl would use the phone to call the vet to let him know that other animals were coming into the emergency room (this expanded the number of animals he would pretend to fix), and another child would bring the animals to the "recovery center" after Richie was done fixing them.

This was the point at which the visual role tags were introduced, which subsequently helped Richie understand the different roles there are in play (in a more concrete way). He was usually able to accept his peers' roles and begin some common focus play. They started doing informal turn taking and actively sharing the materials. He still did his part, without much care for the role the others took, but he was able to accept their invitations and their play without rejecting them. He also began to accept that objects/toys may be used to represent something else. For example, when given a wooden block to represent a telephone, he was able to pretend to talk on it when one of his playmates pretended to call his vet office. These were all big advances in Richie's play during his first-grade year.

In second grade, Richie made even more advances in his play development. He still had his obstacles to overcome, one of which was sharing his favorite toys in the playroom, but he continued to improve. He loved to play with two small animal figurines (a tiger and a lion). These animals were named Shere Khan (from The Jungle Book) and Jasper the lion. However, Richie didn't want anyone else to join him in his play with these two animals and definitely did not let anyone else touch them. Session after session, Richie grabbed the animals and had an elaborate "animal fight" between them. He controlled both the animals' actions and voices. He did not let others join him.

This quickly changed when his playmate, Cameron, gathered all the other animal figurines in a semi-circle around Richie's animal fight. Richie was able to accept this from his friend, as it didn't interfere with his play scheme since the other animals were merely "watching." At this point, I facilitated the other kids in expanding the play scheme. They began to work on making tickets to the animal fight (Richie participated in this and made the best tiger drawing of all!). They also made a sign for the ticket booth and menus for the concession stand. After all of the visual supports were made, one last obstacle remained – would Richie let someone else directly participate in his play? I took a digital picture of the tiger and the lion and asked Richie to choose which one he wanted to be. He chose the tiger (his absolute favorite and always the "winner"). Next was the moment of truth – would he let his best bud, Cameron, be the lion? Again, the visual support worked like magic. Richie allowed Cameron to be the voice and to control the actions of the lion. Cameron, being a very intuitive friend, made sure that he kept the same name for the lion (Jasper) and made the same movements and noises as Richie used to do. Most important, he understood that Richie's tiger was ALWAYS the winner. Cameron was okay with that.

We were then ready for the official animal fight. There was an announcer, who made an announcement to "buy tickets now …," and a concession worker, who made an announcement that it was "last call for food." Next, the security guard announced to remain seated at all times during the fight, and finally Richie announced, "Ladies and gentlemen, welcome to the animal fight." Richie did it! He accepted Cameron's direct role in his beloved play scheme. All went off without a hitch, and Shere Khan won the fight. Then something really exciting happened: Richie tried to get his friends' attention by saying, "Hey guys, look!!! Shere Khan is sick from bubble gum!" Luckily, I was there to guide his friends in understanding that Richie was communicating to them that he wanted to change the play scheme from "animal fight" to "vet shop." Richie's peers quickly responded by pulling out the vet toys, and they all became engaged in another play scheme together. Two times in the same session, Richie engaged in common goal play with his peers. This hadn't happened in the previous two school years.

Now in third grade, Richie's growth continues to amaze me. Recently, Richie has expanded his play with the tiger and lion figurines by playing something other than the animal fight. He engages in what I call "free play," in which he doesn't rely on adult coaching or visual supports. Through the use of the visual supports in the past, he has developed the ability to understand the various roles and schemes that his animals can be involved in. He is more spontaneous and flexible. Just recently, Richie and Cameron were playing with the tiger and lion (of course, Richie still had the tiger), but the lion's name changed to Sparky. Cameron and Richie freely played with the animals, taking the dialogue and events as they unfolded. It was not scripted, and they based their play on back-and-forth interactions. Richie did not display the rigidity that he used to when he was unable to engage in play schemes other than his "movie scenarios." Over the course of this school year, Richie has also begun to play in more elaborate pretend roles with his peers without the use of toys. For example, there is an air cushion in the playroom that they pretend is a boat, and Richie likes for him and Cameron to be captains. The other two play group expert players have been "bad guys," "winter warlocks," and "crocodiles." Richie now accepts these ever-changing roles and is not upset or confused by the change. He is much more able to "go with the flow" of play rather than becoming upset by it and rejecting it.

Integrated Play Groups have made an invaluable impact on Richie's overall development. It has expanded his ability to be more flexible and has increased his social interactions and his self-confidence, which affects him throughout his school day. The benefits are enormous and have carried over into several other areas of development and education. Integrated Play Groups have given Richie the opportunity to make friends and become comfortable with his peers (and helped his peers to become comfortable with him just the way he is). He has generalized many of these skills into the mainstream classroom settings and can participate successfully in classroom plays and music concerts, which is something that used to be impossible for him.

Summary and Conclusions

The desire to play and make friends is an intrinsic need of all children. In light of their developmental differences as well as socio-cultural factors, children of diverse ages and abilities on the autism spectrum encounter unique obstacles in learning how to play and socialize with peers. In this chapter, we introduced the conceptual foundation, principles, and practices of the Friend 2 Friend and Integrated Play Groups models, which are designed to overcome these obstacles. These complementary models draw on current theory, empirical research, and evidence-based practices to address core challenges in children with ASD while fostering play, imagination, and friendships with peers within school, home, and community settings. It is our hope to provide educators and related care providers with some ideas for guiding children on the autism spectrum in mutual play and friendships with peers within a peer culture that embraces social inclusion and neurodiversity.

Tips for Practical Application

Demystifying Autism

Effective autism demystification programs provide information about the disorder in an age-appropriate, fun, and interactive manner. They are inclusive and respectful and model acceptance of diversity. The Friend 2 Friend model follows a set of guidelines to provide programs that foster understanding, acceptance and empathy. These guidelines include:

✓ **Focus on understanding and acceptance.** Autism demystification begins by supporting the child with ASD in understanding and accepting his or her own unique challenges and gifts. Supporting children in this way models a respect for individuality and diversity and empowers the child with autism. Autism demystification programs or activities should always include the focus child. This provides him with the same information made available to his peers and further models respect for diversity and a truly inclusive classroom, peer, and school culture.

✓ **Make it fun and educational.** Autism demystification should be delivered in a sensitive, age-appropriate, fun, and interactive way. Young children learn best through play and imagination; talking is often not as effective as games, story books, or fun activities. We all learn best when we are entertained and having fun.

✓ **Demystify, not identify.** Autism demystification should never single out the child with autism, nor should the child's name, diagnosis, or any personal information be discussed during the demystification process.

✓ **Model, label, explain, and normalize.** The key to demystifying autism is to provide a visual model of the characteristics of autism, label those characteristics, explain the reason behind them, and, most important, normalize the characteristics to support feelings of empathy.

✓ **Emphasize that we are all different.** Autism demystification should always include examples of various individuals with autism or role-playing to help generalize the characteristics of autism. This supports understanding and acceptance of autism as a spectrum disorder and the characteristics of autism as being real and genuine. Autism demystification should use sensitive language and encourage a shared vocabulary, such as "I have this kind of mind." "This is my self-regulating behavior, what's yours?" To promote an inclusive culture, avoid using references like "them" and "us." Instead, use "we" references such as, "We are all different in our own way."

✓ **Teach that autism is not a four-letter word.** Autism demystification should be direct and honest, while respecting individuality, diversity, and privacy. Using the word *autism* is fine. It is just a word, not a person, but it is not always necessary in providing autism demystification (especially with younger children).

Guiding Children With Autism to Socialize and Play With Peers

Effective peer socialization and play guidance is an art that requires a blend of knowledge, skill, experience, and intuition to refine and master. It requires adopting a flexible and holistic style involving many layers and levels of awareness and support. Therefore, IPG Guides must draw on a number of different sources of knowledge and insight to accommodate children with diverse developmental levels, learning styles, interests, and experiences. The following tips were adapted from Wolfberg (2003).

✓ **Understand and appreciate play.** Recognize the importance of play for children's learning, development, and cultural participation and embrace play in the lives of all children. Be sure to devote special times for your students with ASD to play with their typical peers, siblings and classmates.

✓ **Hone your skills as a good observer.** Initially, spend time observing children of diverse ages and abilities at play in a variety of natural contexts. This will provide you with a framework for understanding typical play development. Next, observe the children in Integrated Play Groups without intervening. In doing so, you will become attuned to the unique qualities of play exhibited by the children with ASD and the dynamics of the group. This will offer a starting point for identifying meaningful goals and strategies for both the novice and expert players.

✓ **Expect to wear many hats.** IPG Guides invariably take on a variety of roles while facilitating Integrated Play Groups, including model, coach, spectator, interpreter, peacemaker, theater director, entertainer, and housekeeper. In other words, expect to wear many hats to effectively support the children.

✓ **Go with the flow.** Being neither too intrusive nor laissez-faire, IPG Guides go with the flow when facilitating play groups. They must be extremely flexible and willing to follow the children's lead. This means being able to let go of control, as opposed to imposing a rigid agenda of prescribed activities.

✓ **Set the tone for the group.** IPG Guides can influence how the players treat one another without effectively taking over. It is important to set the tone for the group by modeling behavior that is respectful and inclusive of all the children. For instance, when giving an expert player a tip about a novice player, include the novice player in the discussion. Address the novice player even if she seems unable to comprehend. This will set a tone that emphasizes that all the children are competent and contributing members of the group.

✓ **Distribute attention among the players.** To ensure that every child is maximally included in the group, IPG Guides must distribute their attention and support among all the children. At times, it may be appropriate to guide a pair of players. At other times, it may be appropriate to guide the entire group. Novice players do not always need to be at center stage to receive their due share of assistance. In certain instances, it may be beneficial for the novice player to be on the periphery as the IPG Guide interacts with the expert players.

✓ **Grow into the role/find a personal style.** IPG Guides may initially feel awkward and frustrated in their roles. The best advice we can give is not to be too hard on yourself. Realize that this is a process that does get easier. Recognize that IPG Guides grow into their roles, while gaining proficiency through extended and reflective practice. Each IPG Guide must find his or her own personal style that is both effective and comfortable. Allow yourself the freedom to experiment through trial and error to figure out not only what works best for the children, but also feels right for you.

✓ **Take hold of the moment.** It is important to recognize that we all have good days and bad days. If you feel you have reached an impasse, it can be immensely helpful to step back, breathe deeply, and take hold of the moment. You may be pleasantly surprised to discover that the situation resolves itself – that you must be doing something right after all! Keep in mind that all those little moments when things are going well add up over time.

✓ **Reflect on your practice.** To evaluate the fidelity of any intervention, it is important to engage in ongoing reflective practice. A part of the reflective process is introspection – contemplating your own experience and effectiveness as a IPG Guide. IPG Guides may also engage in reflective practice with others by sharing experiences and evaluating one another in a constructive light. We have found videotapes to be especially useful for viewing oneself and others in action.

✓ **Enjoy the experience.** Perhaps one of the most vital things to keep in mind while facilitating play groups is to enjoy the experience and simply have fun. This is a lesson that we have learned from many practitioners and family members who have shared rich and amusing accounts of children's play and friendships.

Chapter Highlights

- Children with autism spectrum disorders (ASD) are among those at greatest risk, as they encounter significant challenges related to developing play and imagination, socializing, and forming friendships with peers.

- Evidence suggests that children with ASD share the same desires for play, companionship, and peer group acceptance as neurotypical peers.

- Play and social instruction with peers are viewed as a type of intervention that should receive priority in the design and delivery of educational programs for children with ASD.

- Play serves a vital role through which children develop symbolic capabilities, interpersonal skills, and social knowledge.

- Children playing together develop a peer group or "play culture" that is based on active participation in social activities leading to the development of foundational social skills.

- Friendship occupies a central place in children's social lives and serves as a determining factor for social adaptation and adjustment.

- Peer neglect, rejection, or bullying contributes to low aspiration in school performance, depression, withdrawn or isolative behaviors, low self-esteem, and loneliness.

- Many children with ASD demonstrate play that is detached and lacking in imagination.

- Children with ASD tend to stay with only a few activities that they may repeat over and over, with less inclination to engage in functional or pretend play than peers at a similar developmental age.

- While children with ASD vary in their social interaction skills, from seeming "aloof" to "passive" to "active and odd," they all demonstrate fewer interactions, inconsistency in initiating and responding, and difficulties in communication.

- Many children with ASD are excluded from their peer group or "peer culture" because their behavior lacks the culture's definition of "normal."

- Exclusion from the peer group/culture creates a social void caused by peers' lack of understanding of the behavior of children with ASD.

- Carefully planned activities and support are needed to help children with ASD and their peers develop reciprocal interaction skills.

- Friend 2 Friend (F2F) and Integrated Play Groups (IPG) are complementary models designed to address core challenges of socialization, communication, play, and imagination in children with autism while helping them build relationships with typical peers and siblings in inclusive social settings.

- The Friend 2 Friend Autism Demystification (F2F) model is designed to foster mutual friendships for children with ASD by building understanding, acceptance and, empathy in their peers, siblings, and classmates. The model provides a framework for designing autism demystification programs for children ages 3 and up.

- F2F uses a four-step teaching process consisting of modeling, labeling, explaining, and normalizing.

- Within F2F five key learning goals provide the basis for children's future learning:
  - Recognize and accept differences in themselves and others by identifying and labeling their own affinities (strengths or gifts) and their own challenges (weaknesses or disabilities)
  - Recognize individuals with autism as individuals and valuable friends through the use of "people-first" language
  - Recognize that it is important to ask questions and express feelings as a means of learning new things about themselves and others
  - Empathize with what it feels like to have autism by providing an experiential learning opportunity and by modeling, labeling, explaining, and normalizing the characteristics of autism
  - Embrace all types of diversity by supporting participants to recognize the importance of peer relationships, play, and friendships

- F2F introduces seven basic friendship tips involving prosocial communication strategies for peers to use to interact more successfully with children on the autism spectrum.

- F2F includes a puppet program designed to introduce young children to the characteristics associated with ASD. The teaching process is used while never singling out the focus child with ASD.

- The IPG model is designed to support children of diverse ages and abilities on the autism spectrum in mutually enjoyed play experiences with typical peers/siblings as playmates.

- Assessment within the IPG model focuses on systematic observation designed to analyze progress and setting realistic and meaningful goals, including evaluating the symbolic dimensions of play, the social dimensions of play, the communicative functions and means used by the children, and the play preferences and diversity of play exhibited.

- Intervention within the IPG model is based on assessment with guided participation used to implement a carefully tailored and intensive system of supports appropriate to each child's needs and abilities. The IPG Guide supports novice and expert players to engage in mutually enjoyed activities that encourage social interaction, communication, pretending, and interactive games.

- Support within the IPG model includes nurturing play initiations; scaffolding play; guiding social communication; and play guidance, in which children are supported in experiences slightly beyond their capacity.

- Play guidance strategies range from orienting to mirroring to parallel play, joint focus, joint actions, role enactment, and role-playing.

- As children become more competent and independent in play skills, the adult lessens the intensity of support provided.

Chapter Review Questions

1. Why are play and friendships integral to children's learning, development, and cultural participation?

2. What are the challenges children with ASD face in terms of developing play skills and friendships?

3. What is "peer culture" and what role does it play in terms of children with ASD developing friendships?

4. What is meant by "play culture"?

5. What is the purpose of the F2F model?

6. How is F2F implemented (include the four steps of the teaching process)?

7. What are the five key learning goals of F2F?

8. What are the F2F seven basic friendship tips and why are they important?

9. What is the purpose of the IPG model?

10. How are environmental elements important to IPG implementation?

11. Which elements are included in the IPG observational assessment of play and why?

12. What is meant by guided participation in play (include discussion of the key components)?

References

American Psychiatric Association. (2013). *Diagnostic and statistical manual of mental disorders, 5th edition.* Washington, DC: Author.

Asher, S. R., Parkhurst, J. T., Hymel, S., & Williams, G. A. (1990). Peer rejection and loneliness in childhood. *In Peer rejection in childhood* (pp. 253-273). New York, NY: Cambridge University Press.

Bagwell, C., Schmidt, M., Newcomb, A., & Bukowski, W. (2001). Friendship and peer rejection as predictors of adult adjustment. *New Directions for Child and Adolescent Development, 91,* 25-50.

Baron-Cohen, S. (1987). Autism and symbolic play. *British Journal of Developmental Psychology, 5*(2), 139-148.

Baron-Cohen, S. (1989). Joint-attention deficits in autism: Towards a cognitive analysis. *Development and Psychopathology, 1,* 185-189.

Bauminger, N., & Kasari, C. (2000). Loneliness and friendship in high-functioning children with autism. *Child Development, 71*(2), 447-456.

Berndt, T. J. (1999). Friends' influence on students' adjustment to school. *Educational Psychologist, 34,* 15-28.

Berndt, T. J. (2002). Friendship quality and social development. *Current Directions in Psychological Science, 11,* 7-10.

Boivin, M., Poulin, F., & Vitaro, F. (1994). Depressed mood and peer rejection in childhood. *Development and Psychopathology, 6,* 483-498.

Bottema-Beutel, K. (2011). The negotiation of footing and participation structure in a social group of teens with and without autism spectrum disorder. *Journal of Interactional Research in Communication Disorders. 2,*61-83.

Boucher, J., & Wolfberg, P. J. (Eds.). (2003). Special issue on play. *Autism: The International Journal of Research and Practice, 7*(4), 339-346. Corsaro, W. A. (1992). Interpretive reproduction in children's peer cultures. *Social Psychology Quarterly, 55*, 160-177.

Dawson, G., & Adams, A. (1984). Imitation and social responsiveness in autistic children. *Journal of Abnormal Child Psychology, 12*, 209-225.

Eisenberg, N., & Miller, P. A. (1987). Empathy and prosocial behavior. *Psychological Bulletin, 101*, 91-119. Frith, U. (2003). *Autism: Explaining the enigma* (2nd ed.). Oxford, UK: Blackwell Publishers.

Gest, S. D., Graham-Bermann, S. A., & Hartup, W. W. (2001). Peer experience: Common and unique features of number of friendships, social network centrality, and sociometric status. *Social Development, 10*, 23-40.

Hartup, W. W. (1989). Social relationships and their developmental significance. *American Psychologist, 44*, 120-126.

Hartup, W. W. (1991). Having friends, making and keeping friends: Relationships as education contexts. *Early Report, 19*, 1-4.

Hartup, W. W. (1996). The company they keep: Friendships and their developmental significance. *Child Development, 67*, 1-13.

Heinrichs, R. (2003). *Perfect targets: Asperger Syndrome and bullying – Practical solutions for surviving the social world.* Shawnee Mission, KS: AAPC Publishing.

Jarrold, C. (2003). A review of research into pretend play in autism. *Autism: The International Journal of Research and Practice, 7*(4), 379-390.

Jordan, R. (2003). Social play and autistic spectrum disorders. *Autism: The International Journal of Research and Practice, 7*(4), 347-360.

Julius, H., Wolfberg, P. J. Jahnke, I., & Neufeld, D. (2012). *Integrated play and drama groups for children and adolescents on the autism spectrum: Final report.* Alexander von Humboldt TransCoop Research Project, University of Rostock, Germany, with San Francisco State University, US.

Ladd, G. W. (1990). Having friends, keeping friends, making friends, and being liked by peers in the classroom: Predictors of children's early school adjustment? *Child Development, 61*, 1081-1100.

Libby, S., Powell, S., Messer, D., & Jordan, R. (1998). Spontaneous play in children with autism: A reappraisal. *Journal of Autism and Developmental Disorders, 28*, 487-497.

McCracken, H. (2004). *Enhancing peer relations in children with ASD: Friend 2 Friend model.* Presentation at the BC Association of Speech-Language Pathologists and Audiologists, Kelowna, BC, Canada.

McCracken, H. (2005a, Jan-Feb). Friend 2 Friend: Fostering mutual friendships for children with ASD. *Autism-Asperger Digest*, 6-15.

McCracken, H. (2005b). Friend 2 Friend programs help children with autism feel safe to say, "I'm autistic too." *Autism Spectrum Quarterly, 2*, 13.

McCracken, H. (2005c). *Fostering mutual friendships for children with ASD – The Friend 2 Friend model.* Presentation at the Autism Society of America national conference, Nashville, TN.

McCracken, H. (2006). *That's what's different about me – Helping children understand autism spectrum disorders.* Shawnee Mission, KS: AAPC Publishing.

McCracken, H. (2009). *Demystifying autism: The Friend 2 Friend simulation game.* Vancouver BC, Canada: Friend 2 Friend Social Learning Society Publisher.

McCracken, H. (2010). *Can I play too? Autism demystification puppet program.* Vancouver BC Canada: Friend 2 Friend Social Learning Society Publisher.

Mouritsen, F. (1996). *Play culture: Essays on child culture, play and narratives.* Odense, Denmark: Odense University.

Mundy, P., Sigman, M., Ungerer, J., & Sherman, T. (1987). Non-verbal communication and play correlates of language development in autistic children. *Journal of Autism and Developmental Disorders, 17,* 349-364.

National Research Council. (2001). *Educating children with autism.* Committee on educational interventions for children with autism, Division of Behavioral and Social Sciences and Education. Washington, DC: National Academy Press.

Parker, J. G., & Asher, S. R. (1993). Beyond group acceptance: Friendship and friendship quality as distinct dimensions of peer adjustment. In W. H. Jones & D. Perlman (Eds.), *Advances in personal relationship* (Vol. 4, pp. 261-294). London,UK: Jessica Kingsley.

Peck, C. A., Schuler, A. L., Tomlinson, C., Theimer, R. K., & Haring, T. (1984). *The social competence curriculum project: A guide to instructional communicative interactions.* Santa Barbara: University of California, Special Education Research Institute.

Rogoff, B. (1990). *Apprenticeship in thinking.* New York, NY: Oxford University Press.

Rubin, K. H., Fein, G., & Vanderberg, B. (1983). Play. In P. Mussen & E. M. Hetherington (Eds.), *Handbook of child psychology: Vol. 4, Socialization, personality, and social development* (pp. 693-774). New York, NY: Wiley.

Sigman, M., & Ruskin, E. (1999). Continuity and change in the social competence of children with autism, Down syndrome, and developmental delays. *Monographs of the Society for Research in Child Development, 64,* 1-114.

Sigman, M., & Ungerer, J. A. (1984). Cognitive and language skills in autistic, mentally retarded and normal children. *Developmental Psychology, 20,* 293-302.

Tilton, J. R., & Ottinger, D. R. (1964). Comparison of toy play behavior of autistic, retarded and normal children. *Psychological Reports, 15,* 967-975.

Vygotsky, L. S. (1966). Play and its role in the mental development of the child (translation from 1933). *Soviet Psychology, 12,* 6-18.

Vygotsky, L. S. (1978). *Mind in society: The development of higher psychological processes* (translation from 1932). Cambridge, MA: Harvard University Press.

Williams, E. (2003). A comparative review of early forms of object-directed play and parent-infant play in typical infants and young children with autism. *Autism: The International Journal of Research and Practice, 7*(4), 361-377.

Wing, L., & Gould, J. (1979). Severe impairments of social interaction and associated abnormalities in children: Epidemiology and classification. *Journal of Autism and Developmental Disorders, 9,* 11-29.

Wing, L., Gould, J., Yeates, S. R., & Brierly, L. M. (1977). Symbolic play in severely mentally retarded and autistic children. *Journal of Child Psychology and Psychiatry, 18,* 167-178.

Wolfberg, P. J. (1994). *Case illustrations of emerging social relations and symbolic activity in children with autism through supported peer play* (Doctoral dissertation, University of California at Berkeley with San Francisco State University). *Dissertation Abstracts International, #9505068.*

Wolfberg, P. J. (2003). *Peer play and the autism spectrum: The art of guiding children's socialization and imagination.* Shawnee Mission, KS: AAPC Publishing.

Wolfberg, P. J. (2004). Guiding children on the autism spectrum in peer play: Translating theory and research into effective and meaningful practice. *The Journal of Developmental and Learning Disorders, 8,* 7-25.

Wolfberg, P. J. (2009). *Play and imagination in children with autism* (2nd ed.). New York, NY: Columbia University, Teachers College Press.

Wolfberg, P., Bottema-Beutel, K. & DeWitt, M. (2012). Including children with autism in social and imaginary play with typical peers: Integrated Play Groups model, *American Journal of Play, 5*(1), 55-80.

Wolfberg, P. J., & Schuler, A. L. (1993). Integrated Play Groups: A model for promoting the social and cognitive dimensions of play in children with autism. *Journal of Autism and Developmental Disorders, 23*(3), 467-489.

Wolfberg, P. J., & Schuler, A. L. (2006). Promoting social reciprocity and symbolic representation in children with ASD: Designing quality peer play interventions. In T. Charman & W. Stone (Eds.), *Early social communication in autism spectrum disorders* (pp. 180-218). New York, NY: Guilford Publications.

Wolfberg, P. J., Zercher, C., Lieber, J., Capell, K., Matias, S. G., Hanson, M., & Odom, S. (1999). "Can I play with you?" Peer culture in inclusive preschool programs. *Journal for the Association of Persons with Severe Handicaps, 24*(2), 69-84.

Learner Objectives

After reading this chapter, the learner should be able to:

- Explain what is meant by "multiple intelligences"

- List and describe the development of skills necessary for social cognition

- Explain general intervention/treatment options for assisting students with ASD in developing social skills

- State the potential problems in defining social skills

- Identify what is meant by the term "sharing space effectively" and provide examples of skills necessary to do so in various situations

- List and describe the four steps in perspective taking identified by the chapter author

- Explain the challenges students with ASD have related to sharing space

- List and describe the components of the ILAUGH acronym

- Explain how the components of ILAUGH contribute to understanding social thinking that goes beyond social interactions and affects academics

- Explain why the demand for effective social skills increases significantly starting in grade 3 and beyond

- Discuss the differences in teaching social skills to individuals with ASD depending on their social cognitive levels

- List key concepts for teaching social skills to students demonstrating ASD Level 2

- Describe key concepts for teaching social thinking and related skills to students with ASD Level 1

- Discuss key concepts for teaching social thinking and related skills to students with ASD Level 1

- Explain how Social Stories™, Comic Strip Conversations™, Social Behavior Mapping, and the Incredible 5-Point Scale are used to teach social thinking and related skills concepts

Chapter 9

Social Thinking:
Cognition to Enhance
Communication and Learning

Michelle Garcia Winner

Doug was a cute 9-year-old boy when I first met him; he was fully included in a fourth-grade classroom with close support from his paraprofessional. He had been diagnosed with autism in his early preschool years along with his twin brother. Over the years, thanks to solid early intervention (including a discrete trial behavioral program), a focus on functional skill development, a consistent paraprofessional, and devoted parents, Doug was now referred to as having autism spectrum disorder Level 1. His twin brother, Mark, when provided with the exact same treatment program, also developed some functional language skills, but has not become as capable as Doug.

In fourth grade, Doug was able to participate at the level of the mainstream class in most activities with consistent support from his paraprofessional, Kelly. Given Doug's normal IQ and near-average language skills, as determined through language testing, his educational team, including his mother, expected that Doug would be able to continue on the same path as his peers, as long as Kelly was there to support him. Doug did an excellent job recalling facts learned from the text and had a propensity for math. He read with good fluency (decoding), but could only answer the factual questions about what he read. Doug was a very nice child with a good sense of humor, and did not cause any problems in the class. He had difficulty learning from the teacher in the context of a large group, but Kelly helped him to stay focused and provided him with explicit instructions. He lacked eye contact and was not able to engage in the type of spontaneous communication necessary to engage with his peer group. His best friend was Kelly. At recess he preferred to sit under the slide on the playground and talk to himself.

Given Doug's ability to answer the teacher's questions and Kelly's ability to work with Doug to keep him productive in the classroom, his mainstream teacher reported at his IEP meeting that he was a "good participant" and a "very smart" one. At the end of the school year, it was recommended that he continue in the mainstream classroom program in fifth grade. His mother believed that the curriculum of the full inclusion classes would provide what Doug needed to excel during adolescence and into his adult years. After all, this is the method that is touted by his parent advocacy groups as well as from the educational community. In fact, when she began the discrete trials program with her two twin boys, she was clearly told they would "outgrow" their autism by their teenage years.

I began to work with Doug and his mother when Doug was in fourth grade. I initially agreed to work with Doug only in individual sessions to help him learn more concretely about the abstract nature of social interaction and language meaning. Doug needed to learn that there were two codes of language, literal and figurative. The tricky part was (and continues to be) how to teach him to figure out what figurative and indirect language means. He also needed to learn to answer the "how" and "why" questions, which are at the heart of all real comprehension tasks.

From my vantage point, I saw a boy who had significant limitations in the development of social cognition, sensory integration, and executive function skills. A large part of his challenges stemmed from the fact that he could not understand what other people thought or felt. While he was always friendly, he had tremendous difficulty thinking about what someone else was thinking. Blessed with a lovely and compliant personality, he was happy to do what he was asked, but he did not try to interpret why he had to do it; he just did it. I began to help both his mother and his educators recognize that Doug's overall strengths and weaknesses would never be fully understood through a battery of tests, given that these tests would not be able to accurately assess the complexity of social cognition and its impact on not only his ability to develop a deeper social understanding of the people who surrounded him, but also of the curriculum that required him to use these same sets of social thinking skills.

As I worked with Doug, he learned that eye contact was used to understand what other people are thinking; until then, he had never been able to interpret how or why one would look at another's eyes. Given his strong academic intelligence, he was fairly quick to understand that we "think with our eyes" by learning that the direction in which someone's eyeballs look often provides information about what that person is thinking about. This lesson, taught in different ways over the course of a couple of years helped Doug realize that people have thoughts that are different from his own. We then began to explore what people might be thinking, based not only on what others were looking at but also on what they were doing with their bodies (e.g., if they were reaching for a cup of water, they were likely going to drink because they felt thirsty). We started to work heavily on making predictions based on what we were doing together in the therapy room, based on movie clips we watched, as well as on information from curriculum-based texts.

Given that Doug did not easily or quickly understand people's thoughts or that their thoughts were different from his, he had great difficulty interpreting what people meant by what they said. He could not read people's intentions or motives; he was not only incapable of doing this in his peer relations, but also when trying to interpret a literature passage from his classroom reading. Furthermore, he had great difficulty producing coherent written expression. His inability to read other people's minds also added to his writing challenges. Not only did he have difficulty with the task of handwriting itself, but he could not figure out what he was supposed to write, nor was he able to write paragraphs that one could easily interpret, since he was not able to write passages based on what other people needed to know. Given his social cognitive learning challenges, he struggled with narrative language – the descriptive language used to narrate our own life stories.

Doug's mother was amazed. As much as she had learned about autism, she did not understand what really made her child "act autistic." Her son was superficially friendly and compliant, yet he could not form friendships. As he aged, the classroom challenges of interpretation, group cooperation, and productivity became increasingly daunting to Doug. Kelly, Doug's paraprofessional, had to pull Doug from his classrooms with more frequency and for longer periods of time to provide him with extra lessons so he could keep trying to understand the basic lessons so many of his peers were learning intuitively. However, while school was clearly becoming more challenging academically, remarkably he was improving with his social understanding. Over the years I would explain to Doug's mom that given his more literal interpretations and weakness in understanding perspectives, the mainstream curriculum would not continue to be his friend.

Doug's mother was delighted that in middle school her son was learning to distinguish between what someone thought and what someone knew. He was learning that not all people in school were his friends; he began to see that some people he did not know were "evil" and others were "nice." He was starting to make predictions and understand that some behaviors made people have "weird thoughts," including himself. When we compared Doug to who he had been a year earlier, we saw progress; when we compared Doug to his classroom peers, we saw that with each year of school he proved to be less and less academically capable.

Doug's mother realized that Doug was not intuitively learning the skills he needed to cope in the world. He was not learning how to shop in a store or manage money, even though he was tested as having excellent money math skills. He was not able to read people's intentions well enough to avoid being tricked or possibly cheated. He could not cross a street independently, because that required him to think about what each of the drivers was thinking (e.g., Does the driver see me? Even if the driver is driving in my direction, does he plan to stop?). By the last year of middle school, she agreed to have Doug move to a self-contained or special day class to help him focus on functional academic skills as well as home and community life skills. Upon entering this class, Doug made his first set of friends; he connected with people who thought more like he did. He also began to work with more independence, since the work assigned was at the level in which he could interpret on his own.

Doug now attends a similar class at the high school. Everyone who works with him adores him. He is gentle and patient with all of his teachers, even though they don't quite understand how he thinks about the world. He is willing to work hard, and he is learning to work through tasks independently and ask for help if he needs it. He is learning to joke around with people and follow clearly established directions. However, he gets easily overwhelmed, and when this happens, he tends to "space out" rather than seek assistance. To keep Doug motivated to work and learn all the small but complex steps of life that most people take for granted, he needs a positive behavior system.

Initially, his high school special day class teachers took Doug's positive attitude for granted and forgot to reward him for doing what he does best: follow routines. Doug started to show sadness and frustration; but with a positive reward system in place, he is now willing to work through the harder tasks. He is also learning to cope with the complex array of emotions and social and community skills that can overwhelm any teen, but specifically kids like Doug, who have relatively weak social cognition development. At the same time, he is included in mainstream academic classes, where he can perform with some level of independence.

Kelly, who assisted his learning from the time he was 4 years old through middle school, was not able to transfer to the high school district with Doug. So Doug has had to deal with the challenges of training a new teacher and paraprofessional to understand him. Most professionals — medical, educational, and administrative — don't understand autism, because they fail to think more deeply about the impact of social thinking, sensory integration, and executive functioning skills across every moment of every day. They also fail to understand that simple testing is not going to get to the complex heart of this disability.

What has Doug's mom learned along the way? She has learned that at the center of autism lies a very inefficient system for interpreting the complex social information that surrounds us, even when we are not actively talking to another person. She has also learned that these same core interpretation skills are necessary to understand literature, express one's ideas on paper, and even participate as a member of a group in class. Doug's mom has also learned that many professionals don't understand the needs of students with autism.

A few weeks ago, when I was doing a rare lesson with Doug and his brother Mark, while both boys were struggling to figure out what each person knew or didn't know about a concealed picture at a table, their mom looked at me and whispered, "I thought they would be done with this by now!" I responded by saying, "Be done with what?" She said, "Be done with autism!" "Who told you that?" I asked. "The behavioral intervention team back when the boys were doing their discrete trial treatment. They told me the boys would be cured by the time they were teenagers!" She looked as if she was going to cry. Even with good interventions for all these years, in large part because Doug's mother learned she had to fight to get them, her boys still have a lot to learn to survive in the "real world."

Doug's mother has begun to trust that the most important thing to teach Doug and his brother is how to cope in the world outside of the classroom, since that is the real world that awaits her sons on the day that they graduate from high school. She understands that rather than keeping students tied to one curriculum in school, we need to figure out what each child needs to learn to help him be as productive and happy as possible in their adult years. This is the same wish all parents have for their child's elementary and secondary school years. Yet, Doug's mom had to learn that the path to making that wish come closer to being true was, in large part, based on learning about the complexity of social thinking and what we can all do to bolster it at home, at school, and in the community.

Typical social development is difficult to study given the intuitive pathways through which it develops. In this chapter, we will explore how **social learning** for people with autism spectrum disorders (ASD) tends to be a cognitive rather than an intuitive experience. Specifically, we will address the complex nature of social learning and factors that complicate social responses, such as understanding the unstated rules of social interaction and the perspectives of others. Since reading comprehension of literature, written expression, and organizational skills are often quite weak for students with ASD, the impact of social development on academic development will also be discussed. The **ILAUGH** model of social cognition (Winner, 2000) will be reviewed to help illuminate specific social learning challenges that affect social and academic learning. In the last section of the chapter, current promising evidence-based practices will be introduced. This will help to provide a foundation on which to more deeply teach our students to become better social thinkers, while producing more accurately related social skills.

The Evolution of Social Development and Social Teaching

Teaching social skills is one of the primary goals of any treatment program for students with ASD. While this sounds fairly simple, its scope and complexity rival the most complicated of sciences. In fact, we ought to view it as if we were teaching our students "social algebra." Determining how to interpret and use our body, eyes, facial expressions, words, and so on, in synchrony at the right time and the right place requires a socially algebraic equation.

Multiple Intelligences

To respect the challenges of students with social skill challenges, it is helpful to consider the contribution of social cognition to our overall intelligence. Levine (2002) describes eight types of cognition that can be explored to better understand how to evaluate and develop treatment programs for all types of students, including those with learning disabilities. While the validity of multiple intelligences (Gardner, 1993) may have sounded "funky" 20 years ago, it is now a popularly accepted part of our understanding of the whole child. That is, some students are predisposed to perform well in athletics, music, math, or social skills because, in large part, their neurological wiring provides stronger abilities in sports, music, math, or social skills. By the same token, students who do not do well in math, spelling, memorizing facts, or social skills likely have relative weaknesses in their cognitive abilities for these areas.

The importance of developing good social cognition, self-regulation, and problem-solving skills for promoting achievement, both academically and socially across our lifetime, was first explored in the research on early childhood development. Hirsh-Pasek, Golinkoff, and Eyer (2003) reviewed a multitude of research studies to demonstrate the importance of developing social relations and problem solving to help students gain access to broader learning, while also tracking the early developmental milestones contributing to our social development across our lives.

Joint Attention

During the first days of life, babies start to imitate the faces of the people around them. By the end of their first year, neurotypical babies have evolved to the point where they can follow the direction of another person's eye gaze, anticipate what the other person is thinking about, and then seek more information about where the person is looking by looking there themselves. This critical skill is called joint attention – the ability to direct attention to where someone else is looking. Joint attention is one of the first abstract social skills we engage in that shows we are tracking the mind and perspective of others around us, even if we are not directly and actively communicating with them at the time. How often do you follow the eyes of strangers you see at a store? How many times has that led you to explore a product that you might not have thought about if it wasn't for this other person's interest in it?

The ability to attend to others is critical for the development of expressive and receptive language (Murray et al., 2008). Klin and colleagues' (2000) groundbreaking research demonstrated that people who spent more time observing a situation demonstrated more social competence. Joint attention also appears to be critical for the more elaborate development of the social mind's ability to think about our own and others' thoughts and emotions which is referred to as theory of mind (ToM). The more sophisticated our development of ToM is, the more sophisticated our language development is (Hale & Tager-Flusberg, 2005).

Early Symbolic Communication

Language emerges through the synergistic acquisition of a range of concepts and skills not typically taught but acquired through the natural development of the social mind. Shortly after babies start to establish joint attention with others, early in their second year of life, they usually begin to use their index finger to point to objects or things that they are interested in, while looking from where they are pointing to the person they are trying to communicate with and then back to the object of their interest. This critical skill is the beginning of symbolic communication; that is, the baby uses the symbol (her index finger point) to encode her interest in a specific thing. While neurotypical babies are rapidly developing these skills of preverbal communication (looking, pointing, grunting, and thinking about what other people are thinking about), they are simultaneously developing the ability to consider other people's intentions. For example, when a baby watches his mom walk to the refrigerator and open the refrigerator door, he anticipates that he is about to get food delivered. While this may seem relatively unimportant given all a baby has to learn (words, language, crawling, walking, feeding oneself, etc.), the ability to anticipate another's actions is at the core of social intelligence and what is referred to as "we cooperation" (Tomasello, Carpenter, Call, Behne, & Moll, 2005). This skill lays the foundation for much of the ability to "read" people's intentions, whether physically or linguistically based, as children grow into more sophisticated communicative patterns. Over the next few years, babies will continue to develop their understanding of others. It is important for them to learn that people have different thoughts and preferences. As the ability to read people's intentions emerges, young children also start to get better at predicting what is happening in their environment, they begin to offer help to others through their actions and, eventually, begin to predict what people mean by what they say.

Imitation of Movement

It is also critical for the child to learn to imitate others' movements, first gross-motor and then fine-motor movements, to allow the brain to develop pathways to make learning more efficient. Imitation first of adults' actions and then of their peers' transitions into "parallel play," where children sit near each other and imitate different aspects of play that each child engages in (Nadel & Aouka, 2006; Parten, 1932). Parallel play, in turn, evolves into cooperative play, where children begin to share a single concept and practice sharing, taking turns and working through basic problem solving. The continuing development of expressive and receptive language allows for play to become more elaborate. More detailed ideas are expressed, and the children share a single imaginary concept that they can better manipulate and explore through actions, the use of toys, and language. By the fourth year of life, most children engage in complex interactions that allow them to anticipate the actions of others, read other people's thoughts and emotions, share an imagination, and initiate language – not only to get their needs met but also to share their own thoughts and ideas about the world.

Continued Development of Social Cognition

Children acquire social thinking systems, which consist of concept and skill development, without much notice. While these social cognitive concepts serve as the basis of children's expression of social skills that will evolve in nuance and sophistication across much of their lives, they do not appear to be important since they are not "showy" and do not appear as milestones but instead emerge somewhat quietly. As babies develop, more social interactive abilities gradually emerge. Thus, as parents we celebrate the development of children's walking and talking, but we do not celebrate the more subtle development of social thinking. While neurotypical children's social cognition evolves seamlessly, the skills that get the notice and reward are ones that impress people, such as a child who learns to count or read, build complex Lego™ towers, or play the piano at an unusually early age. Ironically, by adulthood, it is the social skills that are crucial for learning to live independently by forging solid relationships, solving personal problems, networking, organizing workload, and performing life's chores that matter.

By 6 years old at the latest, neurotypical children are also learning that one person can try to deceive another by lying, cheating, stealing, and so on (Baron-Cohen, 1995). Children are learning that not all people's intentions are good at all times, thus becoming more sophisticated at trying to "read" people's plans encoded verbally and nonverbally. Therefore, it is critical that we are socially alert to who is around us, what they are doing, and why they are doing it. This is also part of our social thinking package.

Bronson (2000) explored this topic by suggesting that the development of social competence in the early elementary school years is positively correlated with higher levels of functioning in school and life as the child grows up. Thus, the children who we might think of as "intellectual stars" based on their precocious learning of patterns with regard to academics (science concepts, music, etc.), but who do not develop good play skills, may not be as "successful" as adults (Barnhill, 2007).

Our clinical experience suggests that this is often the pattern of those with higher levels of ASD and similar disorders. Despite developing strong language and academic skills in the preschool years, in the preadolescent and adolescent years their critical thinking, problem solving, and the subtle but significant skills that lead to social sophistication are weaker, making it much harder for them to cope in adulthood. The good news is that with new treatments available to persons with social cognitive learning challenges, we hope to lessen the impact of their neurological developmental challenges.

Cognitive Behavior Intervention

To help teach strategies related to fostering further social competence, **cognitive behavioral interventions** are showing great promise for higher-functioning students with ASD, those who have a language system and can use **metacognitive strategies** for exploring their own behavior (Lopata, Thomeer, Volker, & Nida, 2006; Simpson,

2005). Cognitive behavioral strategies are defined as strategies that encourage the student to think more deeply about the concept being explored and learn how we respond with our behavior to adapt to the situations we are thinking about. Teaching children through suggestion, explanation, and reasoning rather than coercive controls such as external rewards, punishments, and so on, has been demonstrated to help children develop systems of internal controls (Hoffman, 1970) that can foster generalization of lessons learned across environments.

Cognitive behavior therapy (CBT) teaches people to monitor their thoughts and perceptions with the intention that they will become more aware of their own interpretive errors (Gaus, 2007). CBT was pioneered by Dr. Aaron Beck in the 1960s, and is considered a form of psychotherapy. Metacognition, the ability to think about one's thinking and behavior, is critical for using CBT strategies to achieve improved self-reflection and self-regulation (Sodian & Frith, 2008). The ability to develop self-regulatory skills also evolves synergistically, as typically developing children acquire not only ToM but also central coherence and executive functioning.

In a nutshell, central coherence is the ability to see the forest for the trees by integrating information into concepts rather than focusing only on the details (each tree). Central coherence is required not only for social interaction but also for reading information for deeper meaning and forming our ideas to write paragraphs and essays. Executive functioning relates to the ability to set a goal and then establish and carry out plans related to helping oneself achieve those goals. Social communication requires social executive functioning; in fact, EF has been shown to be critical for the development of ToM (Pelicano, 2010).

Generalization of Concepts and Skills

Generalization of skills learned by those who have ASD and similar disorders must be planned for in any treatment program (Klin, Volkmar, & Sparrow, 2000; Simpson, 2005). Failure to teach generalization of skills to students with autism is of concern (Gaylord-Ross, Haring, Breen, & Pitts-Conway, 1984; Ihrig & Wolchik, 1988), as many of our students tend to learn to use a specific skill in the environment where it is taught but fail to "generalize" it to other similar contexts or environments (Happé & Frith, 2006).

We are learning that we can do more to help during the critical preschool years, and our help continues throughout the adult years (Gaus, 2007; Wolfberg & Schuler, 2006). However, persons with ASD and related social learning challenges, while sharing similar symptoms in that we describe this group as having social skills problems, will not benefit from the exact same treatments nor will they all have the same prognosis. Before we investigate this further, it is important to define what the concept of "being social" means in terms of developing treatment programs. This includes exploring how we share space together, interact, and use the same core social knowledge to develop critical thinking, reading comprehension, and skills for written expression.

What Are Social Skills? Don't Kids Just Learn Them by Watching Others and Memorizing What People Do?

With all this talk about social cognition, it is important that we agree on what it means to be "social." When discussing what "effective social skills" means, the immediate response is that it is when "people interact in a reciprocal manner." When encouraged to offer other responses to the question, people usually realize that being social also means considering a given situation and who is present in it and what we know about them to help figure out how we are expected to behave to encourage them to have "normal" if not good thoughts about us. When teaching more advanced students on the autism spectrum, those who are language-based learners (i.e., they comprehend and use language spontaneously in order to continue to learn about the world), we teach them about social thinking.

The definition of social thinking is that a person considers the situation and what he knows about his own and others' thoughts, emotions, beliefs, desires, motives, prior knowledge, and experiences in that situation in order to help interpret and possibly respond to others. We use social thinking even when we are not intending to interact with another person. For example, every time you pick up a novel you are attempting to understand characters in context by figuring out what you know about them as their character evolves across the book. You also use social thinking when thinking about another person even if you are not physically sharing space with her. An example of this might be interpreting the intentions or meaning of characters playing a role on a sitcom or analyzing why anyone would participate on certain reality TV shows.

When we use our social thinking for the purpose of social interaction or sharing space, we need to be aware of our social skills in addition to our social thinking. "Social skills" are defined as social behaviors we produce based upon our related social thinking. By the time a child is 3 years old, he is beginning to adapt his social behavior based on the situation and the people within the situation, which is why we consider him ready to participate in something as complicated as group teaching activities and group play so popular in preschool. In spite of what we may have been led to believe, social skills are not simply memorized behaviors produced on cue but are a result of the social mind's intricate social reasoning, which leads us to choose how to adapt our behavior in context. While we know that 3-year-olds are not consistently good at this, it is impressive how well they can participate socially, and their social thinking and related social skills continue to snowball in development and refinement well into the adult years. In fact, it can be argued that our social abilities continue to refine across our lifetime. This is good news for parents of kids with social learning differences because it means that their children will not have to have this all figured out by the time they graduate from high school.

When you stop to analyze all the thinking and social behavioral regulation needed to produce good social skills, it is a wonder that any of us bother to work so hard at this. Which begs the next question, why bother to focus so much on social teaching? The answer is fairly simple but may surprise you. The entire reason we do engage in such intricate social thinking and monitor our social skills is that our social behaviors impact how others feel about us, which can directly impact how people treat us and how we then feel about ourselves. Consider that most people define social skills as "being polite." Now consider what it means to "*be polite*." Ultimately, this means you behave in a manner that helps others to feel good about you. If others think you are *rude* or *impolite*, this means they feel negatively about your behavior in that situation. Unfortunately what this means for our students who we describe as having *poor social skills* is that their social behaviors make people uncomfortable on a regular basis. Our social selves impact the emotions of others, which can impact our own emotions. The whole purpose of being social is to help regulate our own and others' emotions. After all, a friendship is an emotional experience. Your friends are people who make you feel good about yourself; if someone doesn't make you feel good on a regular basis, you may call them all kinds of names, but "friend" is not typically one of them!

Sharing Space Effectively

As we think of our social experiences as being those times when we actively interact with others, the truth is that we spend the bulk of our time engaging in social thinking and monitoring our social skills as we share space with others when we are not interacting with them. As I write this paragraph, I am sitting on an airplane. The hidden rules, or what Myles, Trautman, and Schelvan (2012) refer to as the "hidden curriculum," on an airplane is that you are not expected to talk to the people around you unless they are your traveling companion(s) or the flight attendant. As I look around, I notice that even though relatively few people are interacting, everybody appears to be using appropriate social skills. That is, they have "read" the situation and adapted their behavior accordingly in order to co-exist and have comfortable thoughts about each other. The same thing happens every day of school as students sit and learn together in classrooms; they adapt their social skills to share space effectively rather than focus on socially interacting.

Sharing space with others requires us to be aware of others and what they are possibly thinking about us. Classrooms are ideal environments to study this, since children are gathered in a room with the intention to learn a specific subject (e.g., math, English, science). However, teachers intuitively realize that they cannot teach the curriculum of any of these topics if their students do not share space well. Thus, the challenge in a classroom is not the curriculum itself, but teaching the curriculum to 20 or 30 different students' brains, each of which has its own idea of how to relate in the classroom. Students whose teachers feel the calmest teaching are those who understand and abide by the hidden curriculum/hidden rules of this environment. All students in a classroom are expected to intuitively think about all the others in the class and then regulate their behavior around the group's need. When a student does this well, we say she is *taking perspective* of the others around her. Both fellow students and teachers notice. They may not say anything, since we often do not acknowledge when people are sharing space well, but they will almost immediately say something when a student does not do this well, since he or she disrupts the class by not being able to regulate his or her behaviors around the intentions of the group.

Those who cannot sit quietly and listen to the teacher talk or allow their peers to respond to the teacher's questions are often considered to have "behavior problems," yet their problem may be that they don't know how to work in a group. We struggle to talk about this since we typically think of "social" as an interaction-based experience. For this reason, I encourage you to explore how a person shares space with others and how that is different from interacting with others. Both of these concepts need to be worked on in treatment with students exhibiting social learning challenges, These students may be referred to as having ASD Level 1 or 2 or social communication disorders according to the *Diagnostic and Statistical Manual of Mental Disorders, 5th Edition*; American Psychiatric Association, 2013).

Very often a teacher refers this type of student to be evaluated due to "behavior problems" or to participate in a social skills group. Once put in a social skills group, the student is taught better conversational skills, but this was not the problem the teacher was concerned about. For example, Brad was a third grader who had Level 1 ASD and was gifted and talented. He raised his hand often to answer his teacher's questions as he was good at specific types of classroom learning; however, when the teacher did not call on him, Brad was known to get out of his chair and go hit the child who answered the question. When I was asked to consult with the teacher regarding Brad's behavior problem, I asked Brad, "Why are you hitting those kids when they answer the question?" Brad replied very matter-of-factly, "Those kids are stealing my answers!" Clearly, Brad did not understand how to learn in a group, which resulted in him not sharing space well.

I developed the Four Steps of Perspective Taking (Winner, 2007a) to help all of us (adults and students) understand the process through which we share space effectively. While you think of each of these steps, imagine you are in an elevator by yourself and consider how your behavior changes as soon as somebody enters this space.

Four Steps of Perspective Taking

Step 1: When you come into my space, I have a little thought about you, and you have a little thought about me.

Step 2: I wonder "Why are you near me?" "What is your purpose for being near me?" "Is it because you are just sharing the space or do you intend to talk to me or do you intend to harm me?" I have to consider all these things in order to keep me safe around people as well as to predict what will happen next.

Step 3: Since we have thoughts about each other, I wonder what you are thinking about me.

Step 4: To keep you thinking about me the way I would like you to think about me, I monitor and possibly modify my behavior.

The "thoughts" we are having about each other are often tiny thoughts that are almost at the unconscious level. However, it is the always-present, very active thought processes of those around us, when we are neurotypical, that allow us to constantly regulate our behavior to make sure that most people have "normal" thoughts about us most of the time.

Many students with social learning challenges who have solid language skills have a clear sense of some of the hidden rules in a situation, and they expect everyone else to follow the rules (these students frequently get upset when others are not behaving appropriately), but they often do not realize that this thinking is reciprocal. Thus, they don't understand that people have very strong social expectations of them as well. For example, it is not uncommon to have a third-grade student with social learning challenges get very upset at seeing someone getting to go first during a game as he insists on going first every single time. This is not only important to help us take perspective of how students with social learning weaknesses process the world, it also helps us to learn that one of the first steps in educating these students is to teach them that other people have thoughts, feelings, and expectations (which we refer to as "expected behaviors") just like they have social thoughts, feelings, and expectations. Understanding how to be flexible when sharing space with others by considering and responding to others' perspectives, and not just your own, is what we refer to as *cooperation*, which we consider a prosocial behavior (meaning we feel good about this behavior).

Exploring the ILAUGH Model of Social Cognition: Social and Academic Ramifications

The ILAUGH Model of Social Cognition was developed from studying both the research related to social development and observing real-life experiences with persons on the autism spectrum and with related social learning challenges. For example, we observed that many of our students, even as they grew towards adulthood, failed to establish good patterns for social initiation or initiating communication when they needed help. We also noticed that the majority of our students were weak listeners, failing to "think with their eyes" to sustain active attention when listening. Furthermore, the majority had difficulty taking the perspective of others. Not coincidentally, these same students had difficulty interpreting more abstract information and making relevant inferences, while also having problems summarizing information and/or conceptualizing main ideas. Yet, in spite of these weaknesses, we also consistently observed that our students had a good sense of humor, which, if used appropriately when teaching, can help them stay calm and focused to work on these more challenging concepts.

The ILAUGH Model of Social Thinking© is as an acronym that represents six points to help further explain what constitutes social cognitive functioning. When I worked in the schools, I found that it was difficult to articulate treatment needs for my students if I did not have a more refined structure for evaluating how they process and respond to social information. The acronym recognizes that social cognition includes components that include (but are not limited to) (I) initiating communication, (L) listening actively with eyes and brain, (A) abstract and inferential thinking, (U) understanding perspective, (G) getting the gist, and (H) humor and human relatedness. As you study these six components, you will start to realize that social thinking also helps us to interpret socially abstract concepts, which include personal problem solving, effective communication (asking for help, discussions around a topic in a class as well as more social conversational skills), and interpreting curriculum that requires us to think through socially abstract thoughts (e.g., reading comprehension of literature, social studies, history; written expression; working as part of a group).

As you explore the ILAUGH model, you realize that all these concepts and related skills have developed at a basic level by the preschool years and continue to develop across the life span; therefore, the expectation is that all children have acquired these skills and are ready to fully participate in classrooms by kindergarten. Teachers often do not expect that their job is to teach students information they did not naturally acquire through their social learning prior to their school years. In addition, not all classroom teachers or specialists such as speech-language pathologists, special educators, or counselors receive adequate training in how to teach these concepts. Hence the challenges the students with social learning weaknesses bring to the school environment require specialized attention.

Across our classroom curricula, the demand placed on effective use of these concepts increases dramatically from third grade on, as children are expected to develop more socially abstract thinking in order to navigate their way towards developing independence in adulthood. Socially, by third grade, most students have started to selectively choose who they want to hang out with during free time – talk or play in cliques. Cliques are groups that are defined by common thoughts and actions. As such, social cliques can lead to children teasing other children who are not perceived as fitting in because of the way they act or look. Thus, in early elementary school, many of our students do a reasonably good job with understanding and applying their skills as they pertain to the curriculum – they may even have some basic friendships. However, as they approach fourth and fifth grade, the demands evolve such that more abstract thinking is required, and these same students often start to lose more and more footing, both academically and socially.

Academically, as students move up in the elementary and secondary school curriculum, the curriculum itself moves away from rote-based teaching to more socially abstract teachings. In kindergarten, first, and second grade, we often teach students the skills for learning by teaching them the alphabet, basic math, and penmanship. In third grade, however, we make a transition away from learning basic skills to applying what you have learned by using the basic skills. For example, now that students know how to decode a written passage (many call this reading), we begin to expect them to show that they are interpreting the reading by making more active predictions and interpretations. We also expect students to write longer and longer passages, explaining their personal point of view about the world or the text they read, whereas when they were younger, they were only required to copy the text to practice writing.

These increasingly abstract curriculum demands spiral higher and higher across middle school, high school, and postsecondary education. At the same time, the social environment becomes increasingly complex as students "leave the cocoon" where they had one teacher as their primary teacher on campus. As a result, in secondary schools they are expected to transition seamlessly between teachers with varying personalities, expectations, and applications of the school's rules, while also having to adjust to all the different students who share their space in each of their different classes. When recognizing all these changing demands, it is no surprise that many students with social cognitive learning challenges do not outgrow their problems, but rather grow into them. Thus, it is common for students who are included in mainstream classroom language arts programs to appear to get worse as they age, both in their ability to stay with the curriculum demands and in their ability to navigate the social world, which is evolving steadily in nuance and sophistication.

Unfortunately, the age when our students need the most help is often when the least help is available. This is because most public funding goes into early intervention based on the mistaken belief that, with the right interventions, all young students should outgrow their problems prior to adolescence. There are also relatively few private practice service providers in education, mental health, speech and language, or occupational therapy who have the skills to understand the far more complex needs of the adolescent and adult.

We all have to do more to help students with social cognitive deficits face very real and, at times, extreme problems dealing with the challenges and abstract demands of the adult world. If school is to help students learn to develop into adults who can work collaboratively, contribute to society, problem solve, live independently, and develop meaningful relations, we must continue to explore how to infuse the teaching of social thinking and related skills into the curriculum, both within academic lessons and within the social curriculum.

The ILAUGH Model of Social Cognition helps us learn how to explore these challenges in students and offers ideas for how to help teach more socially abstract thinking. The ILAUGH acronym is described in a nutshell below. A more detailed description is offered in Winner (2000).

I = Initiation of Language   *Initiating Communication*

Initiation of language is the ability to use one's language and communication skills to seek assistance or information. A student's ability to talk about her own interests may be in sharp contrast to how she communicates when she needs assistance. Many of our students do not ask for help or clarification. While a student may talk a lot in class about his own knowledge and ideas, he is not proficient at using his sizeable language skills to help him communicate effectively with others when he doesn't know the answer. Rao, Beidel, and Murray (2008), in their exploration of social skills teachings, found that by elementary school our students have significant social relational problems; the majority experience great difficulty initiating and maintaining friendships with same-aged peers.

Based on clinical experience working with adults, it is critical that we understand that children don't outgrow these challenges once they become adults. It is also important to realize that junior colleges or four-year universities depend heavily on students' ability to fend for themselves (e.g., let people know when you have a question or need clarification about an assignment). Further, social networking requires initiation of communication both to problem solve and to socialize.

As a result, students' ability to initiate communication for a range of purposes (prosocial, problem solving, conflict resolution) should be developed and explored in more detail as they age and the demands on them to be responsible for themselves and others increase. Developing treatments that specifically target working on initiation of communication from the early years of development is key (Paul, 2005). Research supports treatment approaches that have targeted this concept through video modeling (Murdock, 2007), pivotal response training (Koegel, Koegel, Harrower, & Carter, 1999), and specific teachings related to the development of joint attention (Whalen, Schreibman, & Ingersoll, 2006).

L = Listening With Eyes and Brain

Most persons with social cognitive deficits have difficulty with **auditory comprehension**. However, listening requires more than just taking in the auditory information. It also requires the listener to integrate information he sees with what he hears to understand the deeper concept of the message, or to make an educated guess about what is being said when you cannot clearly hear it. This may also be referred to as "active listening" or "whole-body listening," a concept developed by Poulette Trusdale in 1990. However, the ability to listen with one's eye begins with joint attention (Jones & Carr, 2004) and related neurobiological mechanisms (Marshall & Fox, 2006).

A = Abstract and Inferential Language/Communication

Communicative comprehension also depends on the ability to recognize that most language or communication is not intended for literal interpretation. To interpret adequately, one must be flexible enough to make smart guesses about the intended meaning of the message. At times, one must analyze language or communication to seek the intended meaning. Abstract and inferential meaning is often conveyed subtly through verbal and nonverbal means of communication combined with the need to analyze the language in context (Loukusa et al., 2007; Norbury & Bishop, 2002; Rapin & Dunn, 2003; Saalasti et al., 2008).

This skill begins to develop in the preschool years and continues across the school years as the messages we are to interpret, both socially and academically, become more abstract. Interpretation depends in part on our ability to "make a guess"; it also depends on the ability to take the perspective of another.

U = Understanding Perspective

Social thinking requires that everybody considers their own and others' emotions, imagination, thoughts, beliefs, prior experiences, shared knowledge, motives, intentions, and personalities (Baron-Cohen, 2000). Considering the mental states of oneself and others is what researchers refer to as theory of mind (ToM), and is considered a core feature of human psychology. Typically developing children between 3 and 4 years old intuitively develop a sense of self versus others and can talk about the fact that the brain allows us to dream, want, think, and keep secrets (Wellman & Estes, 1986). "We not only live socially, we think socially," as Wellman and Lagattuta (2000) state in their chapter "Developing Understandings of the Mind." As our interest in autASD and related disorders has increased with the steady increase in the number of individuals being diagnosed, the interest in the development of the social mind has also blossomed.

We now have a basic understanding of the core social learning abilities needed to advance into a more sophisticated ToM. In a nutshell, across infancy and early childhood, children learn that their thoughts are different from others' thoughts (Leslie, 1994), and by 4 years old they can use language to talk about how their thoughts are different from others'. Wimmer and Perner (1983) designed tasks to assess children's ability in this area called "First Order Theory of Mind." They also designed "False Belief" tasks to assess children's higher-level ability to conceal the truth or manipulate others' minds, referred to as "Second Order Theory of Mind." As students evolve through the elementary and middle school years, great advances are made in the neurotypical child's ability to interpret other people's perspective at a level of increasing nuance and sophistication. This development continues throughout adulthood.

To date, professionals are limited in testing of ToM to very basic tasks developed for children younger than 5 or 6 years old. Yet both researchers and professionals know that their older and more sophisticated clients with social learning challenges have subtle but significant issues in perspective taking that have yet to be easily defined for the purposes of formal assessment. Furthermore, the use of ToM is not limited to our social interactions but is also required when using our social thinking to interpret and respond when engaged in reading comprehension, written expression, working as part of a group, and so on. Researchers are intrigued by the complexity of this concept and continue to offer us new insights.

Perspective taking is not the only factor related to ToM. In recent years, executive functioning and central coherence have come to be regarded as playing key roles in the emergence of ToM (Pellicano, 2010). If you observe yourself in a conversation, you will begin to notice that you not only think about your own and others' thoughts, emotions, beliefs, intentions, and so on (ToM), you also consider the gist or gestalt of the communicative exchange. Within milliseconds, you then use all this information to help you shape or inhibit a response according to how you want to be perceived, which calls on your executive functioning. It can also be argued that the only way you could consider all the different elements in order to have a functional ToM is to have an executive functioning system that provides access to this social cognitive juggling and prioritizing of information.

G = Gestalt Processing/Getting the Big Picture   "Getting the gist"

Central coherence is the term used to describe the ability to think conceptually – to form gestalts, which we then deconstruct to arrive at the related details. Frith (1989) introduced this term to describe neurotypical children and adults' ability to derive meaning from more global information in contrast to persons with ASD, who appeared to have a stronger tendency to attend to and remember the details and surface structure but demonstrated weaker central coherence. Through her descriptions of weak central coherence theory (CCT), Frith hypothesized that this lack of conceptualization of information was at the heart of the social issues experienced by persons with ASD.

CCT has gained a lot of attention and sparked related research, which Happé and Frith (2006) reviewed to explain their more current thinking in which they explore central coherence as a perceptual process that may be seen as both a weakness and a strength for persons with ASD – the strength being possibly superior local or detailed focused processing, which leads directly to the weakness of poor global/conceptual processing. This type of processing suggests that individuals with ASD have a processing bias or cognitive style that is more detail focused, which can be overcome, to some extent, when information is presented in a manner than helps them to explicitly see the connections between the details and related core concepts. Some neurotypical people also demonstrate this processing bias (e.g., some engineers, scientists, doctors) but without the larger presentation of social cognitive learning challenges. Hence, more recently weak central coherence is not seen as a primary cause of symptoms related to ASD but more as a secondary factor.

Weak central coherence also impacts academic learning. Those with social learning challenges who have weak central coherence struggle with critical thinking and problem solving, also referred to as "higher-order thinking." This becomes evident when the core academic curriculum shifts from a focus on completing detailed work assignments to thinking more conceptually about the information students are learning. Typically, in the first years of schooling, students "learn to read," but then in third grade and beyond they are expected to "read to learn." Those who struggle to "read to learn" due to weak central coherence or conceptual learning challenges not only have difficulty with reading comprehension but often have related difficulties involving organizing their thoughts for written expression and organizing how to approach their homework assignments, aside from challenges related to managing their time and materials across the school and home day.

As mentioned earlier, students with weak central coherence also find it difficult to generalize what they learn in one situation and apply it in another situation. Students who learn skills by memorizing details without understanding the core concepts of what they have learned are able to apply their detailed knowledge in the specific situation in which it was taught but are not able to easily transfer this knowledge to similar but different situations (Happé & Frith, 2006; Hume, Loftin, & Lantz, 2009; Plaisted, 2001). For example, a student with an average IQ but weak ability to "get the big picture" was able to learn to work independently to complete specific tasks when working in a public library. However, when he was transferred to work in a different library doing similar tasks, he was unable to figure out what to do because the books were not organized in exactly the same rows as in the library where he was initially taught the skills.

H = Humor and Human Relatedness

The educational mandate No Child Left Behind (2002) encourages that educational practices, to the greatest extent possible, arise from scientifically based research (SBR), more commonly known as "evidence-based practices." But as the insistence on the use of SBR for treatment approaches used in the schools has grown, a countervoice has emerged emphasizing the importance of relating to our students, patients, or clients from a social emotional perspective. Simply put, this means that we as educators/caregivers listen and relate directly to the person(s) we are teaching or guiding. Those who are gifted teachers know they cannot simply apply a set of scientific rules to effectively teach. Instead, successful teachers engage in relationships, which seek to value and appreciate the people we are teaching, and through this social emotional relationship students may learn more effectively in the classroom setting (Durlak, Weissberg, Dymnicki, Taylor, & Schelllinger, 2011).

As we attempt to define how and what we need to teach to students with social learning challenges to encourage their more effective social communication skills, it is relatively easy to recognize that we have to teach them to greet others, use eye contact, and converse. What is more challenging is to teach them how to use these newly formed skills in a manner that is perceived as relating well not only to adults but also their peers (see Chapter 8). The subtleties through which we relate physically, emotionally, and through our language are as difficult to measure as they are important to the foundation of social success.

Treatment programs such as Development Relationship Intervention (Greenspan & Weider, 2006) – also known as *floor time* – and the Social Communication Emotional Regulation and Transactional Supports Model or SCERTS Model® (Prizant et al., 2006a, 2006b) seek to promote social skills specifically with a focus on relationship development.

Humor is a tool through which we establish and maintain social relations. We use humor to relate to each other from the earliest point in our social emotional development. All parents of newborns excitedly await the day when their child will smile at them, laugh with them, and then begin active forms of play. But the use of humor can be tricky. Persons with social learning challenges, particularly those with ASD, may have significant challenges comprehending the abstract concepts conveyed through humor (Lyons & Fitzgerald, 2004; Ozonoff & Miller, 1996).

Strategies to encourage human relations and age-appropriate humor dovetail with many of the other concepts discussed through the ILAUGH model as all of them overlap in many ways. The factors identified through the ILAUGH model are not only evidence based but are central in developing personal problem solving and critical thinking skills. The ILAUGH model also helps to demonstrate how the social mind is active not only on the playground but in the classroom, vocational settings, home, and community.

So Let's Just Teach These Kids Social Skills, Right? Wrong? Well, It Depends ...

Persons with ASD and like disorders (such as attention deficit hyperactivity disorder or social communication disorders) may be said to have similar social learning challenges according to the ILAUGH model, but they can differ greatly in their social functioning and social learning abilities. We observed through our clinical experience that students with similar diagnostic labels and similar measured IQs may have significantly different social learning aptitudes. Furthermore, when we studied our students' social-academic, social-leisure learning abilities and related performance skills over years, we found that a person's diagnostic label was not as predictive of his or her long-term overall prognosis as was the social learning abilities the student presented with by third grade. In a nutshell, we observed that those who were more able social learners by 9 years old produced more sophisticated social skills, adapting them based on sudden shifts with people in context, than those with more limited social learning.

Many of us who have experience working with a range of people with social learning challenges naturally define a subset of students with ASD and related diagnoses as functioning at a higher level than others similarly labeled. What is less clear is how we define the differences and needs of these individuals when comparing them to what we refer to as neurotypical social communicators. The often-used term "higher functioning" as it relates to those with ASD has a significantly different meaning than when we use a similar term to talk about typically developing students. These types of queries have pushed us to recognize that there is a lack of objective descriptors to define our students' social learning abilities. Our vague categorization of these students is likely to result in poorly defined treatment objectives and treatment planning. In short, what this means is that social skill type treatments are often inefficient and at times ineffective.

To address this issue, I began to develop what became known as the *Perspective Taking Scale* (Winner, 2007a). This has since evolved into what we refer to as Social Thinking-Social Communication Profile (ST-SCP) (Winner, Crooke, & Madrigal, 2011). Through the ST-SCP we have defined five different levels of the social mind along with related treatment recommendations for each category.

According to our model, the various categories of the ST-SCP collectively represent a spectrum of social cognitive functioning, meaning there is not a hard stop between the end of the functioning level in one category and the start of the next category. Instead, the line differentiating these groups is fuzzy. General academic IQ is not strongly considered on this scale; however, some individuals who function as Significantly Challenged Social Communicators and Challenged Social Communicators may have significant intellectual impairments in addition to significant social learning challenges. Our experience is that once students reach third grade, their social learning abilities are somewhat set within these categories. Students will continue to make progress compared to themselves over time, but the goal of treatment is not to advance a student across these categories. We believe that how a person functions – what places him or her into a category – is related to basic social cognitive learning abilities that have a neurological basis.

The general categories are listed below. (A detailed article about the social learning abilities of persons and treatment recommendations as they relate to these categorical descriptions may be found on our website, www.socialthinking.com.)

Five Categories of the ST-SCP

1. Significantly Challenged Social Communicator (SCSC)

2. Challenged Social Communicator (CSC)

3. Emerging Social Communicator (ESC)

4. Nuance Challenged Social Communicator (NCSC)

5. Neurotypical Social Communicator (NSC)

Key Factors That Tend to Help Distinguish Between the Levels of the Social Mind

When developing the categories, we explored what we perceived to be core distinguishing variables based on our clinical experience. The summary that follows introduces the reader to the idea that we cannot plan treatment based on a student's diagnostic label but need to look more deeply at his or her social learning abilities. Our summary is not intended to be comprehensive nor instructive about how to determine the different levels of the social mind but to encourage the reader to recognize a systematic way to explore social learning differences between people with similar diagnostic labels.

From our clinical experiences, we found that the most compelling factors that appear to distinguish the different levels of the social mind include, but are not limited to:

Social attention to people in context. We observed that those with the highest level of social awareness of others in context were the most likely to function as NSCs and NCSCs. Those with the lowest ability to attend were SCSCs. Logically, this makes sense given that the more one attends to critical social information such as the context and what one knows about the people in the situation, the better one is able to adapt one's social behavior within the situation. Social thinking leads to the ability to more accurately adapt one's social skills. The more a person adapts to the hidden social expectations, the more he is perceived as having good social skills. In addition, we observed that a person's core social attention span influences other related factors described below.

Self-awareness of one's social abilities. Accurate observation and judgment about others' social behavior in context provides each of us with internal social metrics for how we then perceive ourselves through others' eyes within that same situation. This is what we refer to as our own social self-awareness. There appears to be a direct link, at a very basic level, between the ability to be aware of others and the ability to develop more accurate or less accurate self-awareness. The weaker a student's self-awareness, the more difficult it is to teach the student core social skills as well as more sophisticated social thinking concepts since the student is lacking awareness of this level of social sophistication.

Literal vs. abstract ability to interpret information. A student's ability to interpret information abstractly seems to be related to social attention to others as well as his or her self. The ability to observe others and self is related to the ability to interpret the meaning of others' verbal and nonverbal cues. Since these relationships have not yet been investigated, we explore the connections we observe through logic. It makes sense to us that if a student is not good at observing the situation and what he knows about others in the situation, he will struggle to abstract the meaning of the communication of others since he is not considering all the variables needed to interpret information. Instead, he is more likely to hear what someone is saying and literally interpret the meaning of the language because interpreting through abstract or inferential means requires him to consider the context in which the message was stated.

For example, a Challenged Social Communicator (with average IQ and strong music skills) was at my house for a high school marching band party. I was attempting to converse with him, saying, "I hear you are in the school choir." This 17-year-old looked at me and said, "No, I am in your house." His literal interpretation appeared to stem from his over-focus on the language itself while he was located in my house without understanding the context in which the language was used, which was simply to talk to him about his life. For him to process the context of the language would require him to observe the situation and what he knew about people in that situation (for example, he could have presumed I knew he was in my house and, therefore, would have to infer a different reason for my making the statement).

Level of central coherence. The more literal students are with respect to interpreting language tends to dovetail with how focused they are when processing detailed vs. conceptual information. The stronger a student's social observational skills of self and others, the stronger she is at interpreting meaning and developing critical thinking skills as she tends to absorb the gist of what is going on around her. The stronger she is at getting the big picture, the stronger her central coherence skills. The weaker a student's social observational skills, the more literally she interprets information, and the more focused she is on the details the weaker she is at seeking coherence in the world around her. Parents of these students who have a solid to strong academic IQ often describe their children as "smart but clueless."

Different types of anxiety mesh with different levels of the social mind. The number of studies on anxiety as it relates to those on the autism spectrum has skyrocketed since around 2005. The research confirms that people with ASD experience higher rates of anxiety than typical populations (see, for example, Simonoff, et al., 2008; Van Steensel, Bogels, & Perrin, 2011). However, from our clinical experience, our students have different types of anxiety that warrant different types of anxiety treatments based on the level of their social mind. By the time our students with higher level social awareness of self and others (i.e., ESCs and NCSCs) reach middle school, the majority have compelling social anxiety. Their social anxiety appears to be a direct result of their higher level of social awareness paired with their inability to keep up with their peers' level of social sophistication. As these students age, their social anxiety can also co-mingle with related depression. Treatment for this group's social anxiety needs to marry teaching social competencies with treatments designed by the mental health community to combat social anxiety. This field of study is just emerging.

Students with less social awareness of self and others (i.e., solid ESCs, CSCs, and SCSCs) also tend to have high levels of anxiety, but instead of being based on how people perceive them, their anxiety is more based on their own inability to predict and infer what is happening around them in their day-to-day lives. Therefore, this group tends to have what we refer to as "world-based anxiety" – difficulty interpreting how the world works at a conceptual level. Many strategies are already designed to help persons with ASD cope with this type of anxiety (see Chapter 10).

ST-SCP category levels and social and academic functioning. Given the above information, in Social Thinking we connect the dots to demonstrate how their social learning challenges impact the way students relate to others or process and respond to core socially based academic curriculum. Table 9.1 provides a brief summary of a much larger body of work discussed in the article posted on our website about the ST-SCP (www. socialthinking.com).

Table 9.1
ST-SCP Category Levels and Social and Academic Functioning

Levels of the ST-SCP	Social awareness of self and others	Ability to interpret and conceptualize	Reading comprehension of literature	Actively paying attention to peers in unstructured social leisure settings
Significantly Challenged Social Communicator (SCSC)	Exceptionally limited	Very literal and detailed in attention	Cannot process and respond to literature at or near age group. Need to practice reading daily living information	Exceptionally limited; even with cuing are not able to accomplish this
Challenged Social Communicator (CSC)	Very limited	Very literal and detailed in their attention	Tremendous difficulty understanding how to interpret and conceptualize stories read in mainstream classrooms; good at reading the facts but miss the main ideas and inferences	Very limited; need frequent cueing to function in a group. Often space out or wander away from the group without realizing it
Emerging Social Communicator (ESC)	Emerging: weak to fair	Literal tendencies; apply detail-focused and rule-based learning to curriculum and social situations	Sluggish in developing skills for interpreting and conceptualizing. Typically find English language arts a very difficult class across the school years	Desire group participation but once in group not sure of how to sustain interactions. Need direct teaching and struggle to apply information in unstructured settings
Nuance Challenged Social Communicator (NCSC).	Fair to solid, but aware of not being included	Understand the concept of inferring and conceptualizing but may be weaker in complex situations	Better at interpreting passages read in novels than interpreting how people are thinking and feeling in real-time conversations. Executive function challenges make it difficult to stay on top of workload but can typically learn the core concepts	Want to be included in the group but may have compelling social anxiety that discourages joining the group. Need to work on addressing anxiety in addition to learning social competencies for relating in a sophisticated manner in the group
Neurotypical Social Communicator (NSC)	Considered typical for all	Considered typical in ability; that is, won't do things perfectly but usually do pretty well	Demonstrate range of abilities, but most can naturally infer and conceptualize	Demonstrate a range of abilities to participate in a group based on temperament, but almost everyone wants to feel like they belong in some type of group even if it is a small group

The purpose of developing the ILAUGH model of Social Cognition and the ST-SCP was to provide a more logical base for developing treatment plans (long- and short-term goals and objectives as well as transition to adulthood plans) that are grounded in reality. In short, we are encouraging teams to develop treatment programs that are effective and efficient since they recognize core social cognitive strengths and weakness and attempt to provide treatment within a student's zone of learning.

Teaching Students Who Function as SCSCs or CSCs

Students who function as SCSCs through CSCs are consistent with descriptions of ASD Levels 2 or 3 in the DSM-5. In terms of social learning, they have limited intuitive understanding of the social world and tend to be delayed in developing functional communication systems. Thus, we need to focus on helping them develop functional communication systems, which may include the use of augmentative communication since many are nonverbal or minimally verbal. They also need to be taught clear social behavioral expectations for school, home, and community. When teaching these lessons, information must be explicit and be consistently applied and expected. The social teaching is often rote and explicit, using clear visual supports to encourage students to produce the responses more consistently (see Chapter 11). Given that this group of learners does not easily predict what may come next in their day, even when told, we need to focus on skillfully drafted transition plans, which may be created through the use of sequenced pictures or a simple list of instructions. For this type of learner, Carol Gray's (1994a, 1994b) Social Stories™ have been very effective in providing explicit information about the situation and others' perspectives while teaching students how to direct their behavior.

To summarize, key considerations for helping these students acquire new skills include (a) establishing a **functional communication system** that helps them to communicate wants and needs and also to recognize their own emotions and, ultimately, some basic emotions of others; (b) using visual supports; (c) clearly listing expectations using explicit pictures or words; (d) consistently stating and adhering to expectations; (e) using positive praise and reinforcement; and (f) providing functional academic lessons that the student can use across environments (classroom, lunchroom, community, home, and playground).

Teaching Students Who Are Emerging in Their Awareness of Other People's Thoughts and Emotions

Our Emerging Social Communicators (ESCs) may align with the DSM-5's description of ASD Level 1. ESCs typically have near-normal to above-normal academic intelligence, and have developed more spontaneous verbal language-based communication systems. But they still have great difficulty figuring out the perspectives of those around them. They struggle with deciphering implied meaning from their classroom lessons, both within the text and from the group dynamics. They are often perceived as "friendly" but lack strong friendships with peers, preferring to be with people who are significantly older or younger. They are perceived as "quirky," and their peer group immediately identifies that they are lacking in social understanding.

For these students, we can slowly introduce lessons about social thinking, helping them to understand that other people have thoughts and feelings, but we want to do much of the teaching described above as well. These students may require lengthy lessons to help them understand the motive behind a person's actions, which the NSC and even the NCSC peer deciphers on the spot without any discussion or prompting.

Learning the lessons of social thinking can be a slow process. From our experience, it can take students one to two years to really think about how these lessons apply across environments, start to modify their behavior, and accommodate to the social needs of others. Just as with any type of learning, we all have to learn to think about or process information before we can react to it. Ultimately, these lessons are rewarding, as the student begins to understand people's thoughts and intentions in a way that more completely supports friendships, helps decipher lessons of the academic curriculum, and provides important information about people who may want to take advantage of them.

Doug in the opening vignette of this chapter is a student who functions as a very weak ESC or higher-level CSC. When teaching students like Doug, and all students, it is critical that both educators and parents understand that they are working to facilitate new learning to promote increased social understanding and related social skills without having a goal to "fix" or "cure" the student's problems. Those working with these students feel the joy of helping teach concepts to students, but they also experience the reality that these abstract social lessons move very slowly and will likely not be "mastered." Thus, the concrete, explicit lessons of clear expectations consistently applied in a positive environment, along with academic lessons that the student can engage in without tremendous stress, are also critical.

Teaching Students Who Are Very Aware That Others Have Thoughts and Emotions But Get Overwhelmed by the Information: Higher-Level ESCs and NCSCs

In a nutshell, the NCSC student presents with compelling challenges for parents, teachers, and other professionals. We often describe this group as having "mild social skill" challenges, and on the DSM-5 we are predicting that many in this group will now be referred to as having a social communication disorder rather than ASD. However, we think that identifying this group as having "mild social skill" challenges does it a disservice as most typically developing peers can quickly and efficiently recognize those with mild social issues but are not able to understand that these students have social learning weaknesses. Peers who lack this understanding may treat those who function as NCSCs quite badly as this type of student is not identified as having a learning problem based on social cognitive weaknesses; peers are more likely to make fun of them, bully, or reject them from social group inclusion (see Chapter 8).

When teaching the NCSC, we use visual strategies to help highlight how others may think and feel, but the lessons focus on interpreting and responding to complex social information rather than the more basic lessons of the ESCs. We also explore any concerns related to self-regulation, social anxiety, and depression, making referrals to counselors as necessary. Where treatment for the ESC involves learning basic social skills from a more mindful but rule-based learning system, the NCSC learns to analyze social information at a greater level of complexity and recognize and work through the executive function skills required for social adaptation.

Using Social Thinking as a Paradigm Shift and to Develop Treatment Lessons

The difference between teaching "social skills" and teaching "social thinking and related skills" can be enormous. Take the teaching of the skill of eye contact, for example. Students who lack consistent eye contact when interacting with others can be taught eye contact using a "social skills" approach. To do this, we simply cue the student to "look at me" or "look at the speaker" in teachable moments and then respond with praise or a token reward, as appropriate.

However, when teaching the child the skill of eye contact through teaching "social thinking and related skills," we assume that the student may not understand the intuitive purpose of eye contact (remember this is a skill that emerges intuitively for most people by 12 months old). Thus, we teach students that we all "think with our eyes," playing games to help them recognize that by looking at people's eyes they can figure out what others may be thinking about. As our lessons progress, we help students learn to be "social detectives," who can observe other people's thoughts even when they are not directly talking to them, in large part by watching another person's eye gaze direction combined with his or her physical actions. We can cue students to use more eye contact by helping them to think not only about what they see but also about what we see from their eyes. For example, if we see a student who is distractedly looking away at a toy in the room, we can say to her, "I see you are looking at the toy, which means you are probably thinking about the toy. What do I expect you to think about?" The students usually respond by immediately looking at the person addressing them. Through this type of technique, we are helping students to see how social thinking is active throughout the day and not just a skill that is expected because someone said to do it.

One of my teenaged students, Erin, who functions as high ESC-low NCSC, when asked to reflect on what she had learned in our program said, "I learned what eyes are for. Prior to coming here, I was always just told to look at things but I never knew why." Teaching social thinking helps us to focus on explaining why we engage in producing social skills rather than simply focusing on the social skill production itself. For our ESCs and NCSCs, social thinking provides them a platform for problem solving social situations to help them learn how they can adapt their behavior based on what is happening. This is a very different treatment model than one that teaches all students to memorize a script when relating to others.

One of the challenges in teaching social thinking is deciding where to begin, given the incredibly complex array of information that underlies all social cognitive activities. I have found that a good starting place is teaching students that interpersonal communication unfolds in a highly predictable manner. To speak to somebody in person means that one must first think about the person, then establish a physical presence, then use one's eyes to think about the person, and, finally, use language to relate to the other person.

This sequence of events, described as the "four steps of communication," teaches that communication is not one thing, but a synergistic, dynamic process. We first need to take students through the individual steps; then we can slowly increase the complexity of the lessons by combining steps and working towards more "social competence." More information about teaching social thinking and related skills may be gained from studying techniques such as those noted below.

 Social Stories™ (Gray, 1994b). These provide concrete information about social expectations in specific contexts. A **Social Story**™ encourages us to concretely describe the expectations of a setting, the perspective of people who share space in that setting, and then the direct instructions to the student about what he or she can do to create a more positive or expected outcome in that setting. Carol Gray has developed, refined, and elaborated on this technique over the past couple of decades. For more information on her latest work, please go to her website (www.thegraycenter.org).

Comic Strip Conversations™. By using comic strip-type characters' thought bubbles and talking bubbles, we can help students to better understand why someone said or did something in a specific context. **Comic Strip**

226

Conversations™ help students to interpret social thinking. This technique has been discussed by a number of people over the years; for example, Carol Gray (1994a) has written a booklet that helps to understand how to use this tool.

Social Behavior Mapping (Winner, 2007b). I created this social behavioral tool to help teachers and students explore how our behaviors, expected or unexpected, impact the feelings of people around us. It also teaches that people's reactions (natural consequences) to our behaviors are often based on how they feel about us in a given environment. We then realize that how we feel about ourselves is in part a byproduct of how people react to us. Therefore, our own production of social behaviors (expected or unexpected) affects others and can ultimately impact how we feel about ourselves.

The Incredible 5-Point Scale, 2ⁿᵈ edition (Buron & Curtis, 2012). Buron and Curtis developed this tool to help students better understand social and emotional concepts. It is another social behavioral tool. One of the uses of the 5-Point Scale is to teach students to identify their own levels of anxiety. Numbers 1-3 would define their "in control" levels (low levels), whereas 4 and 5 would be used to describe out-of-control (high) levels of anxiety. Strategies are then taught to help students self-manage their behaviors while building their self-awareness to assist in this process. The Incredible 5-Point Scale and Social Behavior Mapping can be used well in tandem.

Zones of Regulation (Kuypers, 2011). Largely left out of the discussion in this chapter is the very important role of sensory and emotional regulation needed for one's mind and body to be available for full participation. Leah Kuypers, mentored under both Kari Dunn Buron and myself to develop the Zones of Regulation, teaches students to develop deeper awareness of their sensory and emotional systems to help them understand the type of zone in which they are functioning at any given point in time. Sensory and social emotional learning strategies are then provided to help students shift their physical and emotional responses as a way of moving them into a zone that helps them to better function in their current situation, as needed (see Chapters 6 and 10).

Summary and Conclusions

Social cognition or social thinking underlies the interpretation of all social behavior and tasks that require social interpretation. Some of these tasks include comprehending literature beyond understanding the facts, using written expression to help people understand the writer's point of view, and working as part of a group in the classroom. Social cognitive development unfolds intuitively across our lifetimes, while simultaneously increasing in complexity. The ILAUGH Model of Social Cognition was described in the hope that it can provide a clearer lens through which to observe our students' strengths and weaknesses.

Our ability to use social skills with nuance and sophistication depends heavily upon our social cognition. Students with ASD and similar disorders have a clear learning disability in their development of social thinking and related skills. The *Social Thinking-Social Communication Profile* was introduced to illuminate more objective ways by which we can explore different levels of the social mind. Its intention is to facilitate treatment planning that is both efficient and effective for a specific student while remaining grounded in understanding the core social and social-academic issues with which a student presents.

As parents and educators, we can continue to facilitate the development of social thinking and related skills for all students; however, the way in which we apply these lessons will vary, depending on the student's initial functional level. The latter part of this chapter has provided a cursory glance at treatment options, ranging from rote teachings to help students establish functional basic communication and social skills to helping students who are working more at the level of acquiring social nuance and sophistication by teaching them social thinking and related skills.

It is important to remember that while the public is now more familiar with the concept of ASD, as a field we are still in our infancy. There is still much that needs to be learned and explored to help our students, who vary tremendously in learning strengths and weaknesses, gain critical information to support them throughout their adult years as productively and meaningfully as possible as members of our society.

Tips for Practical Application

The following strategies for working through issues relate to the ILAUGH Model of Social Cognition.

Sample of Strategies to Facilitate Initiation of Communication

✓ Define strategies the student can use to ask for help that may be more creative than raising his hand (e.g., showing the teacher an index card with "I need help" written on it or having the child establish physical proximity to the teacher's desk).

✓ Practice having the student ask for help; reward attempts at seeking information from others.

✓ Create an expectation. Work with all educators to encourage the child to ask for help, which means that the educators avoid offering unsolicited help.

✓ Work with the student to understand that asking for help or clarification is important for everybody, since no one can possibly know everything.

Sample of Strategies to Facilitate Listening With Eyes and Brain

✓ Work with students to learn the concept that we "listen with our eyes" by playing games that help them see that when we focus our eye gaze on someone, we are often seeking their attention or asking them to answer our questions.

✓ Help students recognize that they understand an auditory message better when they can interpret the related body language and facial expression.

✓ Work with younger students on "whole-body listening;" that is, helping them to understand explicitly that listening is far more than just hearing.

Sample of Strategies to Facilitate Abstracting and Inferencing

✓ Work with students on making "smart" or "educated" guesses. Teach students that a smart guess is when you know a part of the information and then make a small guess based on what you know. In early elementary school, we call this "prediction." We need to explicitly teach students that they are expected to make smart guesses at school and reward them for this more flexible (rather than literal/concrete) thinking.

✓ Help students learn to "code switch" more efficiently, making them recognize that the two codes of language are "literal" and "figurative." Once they have clearly understood that language can also be figurative, provide opportunities to practice switching between these two codes.

✓ Help students to explore that not only do we provide auditory messages, facial expressions, body language, tone of voice, and so on, but all of this is interpreted in a specific context.

✓ Help students learn to expand their abstract meaning of vocabulary words by encouraging them to explore semantic or word maps. These are graphic illustrations of how one word relates to other words and how these other words relate to even more words. This tool helps students develop more associations between words, thus interpreting meanings more easily.

✓ Encourage students to explore social scenario pictures, interpreting the meaning of these faces, gestures, and contexts when the information is "frozen" in the picture and can be studied. This level of interpretation explores meaning without having to involve language, since the pictures require only a visual interpretation.

Sample of Strategies to Facilitate Perspective Taking

✓ Continue the lessons offered in the "listening actively" section to help students learn to think with their eyes; this helps them learn more actively about the concept of joint attention.

✓ Work with children to learn that each person has different thoughts, and that when we are part of a group, our job is to try to think through other people's thoughts as well as our own. Only then can we begin to regulate ourselves around other people's desires or needs.

✓ Explore with students how we can predict what people will do next based on what they are looking at or on their physical movement through the environment. Also continue to explore language-based intentions.

✓ Explore how we think about people whom we just share space with, even if we are not directly interacting with them.

✓ Work with students on problem solving conflicts with others, based on understanding other people's intentions, thoughts, emotions, and so on.

✓ Explore with students their own emotions as well as those of others. Where do they come from? How predictably do people react emotionally to expected and unexpected behaviors produced by others? What do emotions look like on one's face or body? Can we control our emotions? Is it possible not to have emotions?

✓ Explore how we have to consider the motives, emotions, and intended language meaning of characters studied in the curriculum (literature, social studies, etc.).

Sample of Strategies to Facilitate Getting the Big Picture/Gestalt Processing

✓ Explore the difference between an idea or concept and a fact.

✓ Utilize graphic organizers or mind maps to help students explore how facts or details can help gain insight into a larger idea. They can "map" out information from a variety of sources, such as TV shows, movies, and pictures, in addition to reading material.

✓ Explore the presence of thinking about ideas or concepts in conversation, reading comprehension, and assignments where students must express themselves in writing.

✓ Help students explore organizing their ideas for written expression by using mind maps, outlining, stating an idea, and then exploring it with details or facts.

✓ Develop very explicit strategies to help students with organization of homework, their environment, and so on. Homework requires conceptualization at many levels: What is the homework assignment itself? How do I interpret it? How do I plan across time to get the project done? How do I budget time within a month, week, and day to meet multiple goals? How do I consider my assignment from my teacher's point of view? How do I lay out my ideas in a logical, coherent framework, and so on.

Sample of Strategies to Facilitate Learning About Humor

✓ Establish humor in your teaching environment. I use a rubber chicken as a prop to show that making mistakes is nothing more than a "rubber chicken moment." Students can choose to lightly tap themselves on their heads when they make a social error. Use the chicken on yourself as well. Every single person makes social errors on a regular basis. Social communication is so complex that we all mess it up.

✓ Explore relaxation and anxiety control techniques. Buron and Curtis' (2012) Incredible 5-Point Scale, and Social Stories™ (Gray, 1994b) are methods that help demystify stress, feelings, and expectations and promote the use of strategies for anxiety management.

✓ Strategies offered by occupational therapists can also help to calm the sensory system. The Alert Program (Williams & Shellenberger, 1996) helps to teach students to monitor their physical level of stress and attention.

✓ Recognize that students' social and emotional reactions to their often unsuccessful attempts at social interaction can create significant mental health problems that must be addressed as part of a treatment program. Do not treat these issues as if they are separate from the social issues.

✓ Many different types of professionals are developing strategies for anxiety management; keep an eye out for new ideas.

✓ Teach about the effectiveness of humor; not all perceived humor is humorous to others. Humor has a time and a place. People often laugh at jokes or odd behavior that they do not perceive as funny. The proof of successful humor is NOT that people laugh (we all laugh when we are nervous or uncomfortable); it is when people still want to be with us after they laugh. Thus, if people are laughing and leaving the person (meaning they don't want to stick around to socialize) who generated the humor, the humor did not work.

The Four Steps of Communication

The Four Steps of Communication are described below and in further detail, along with activities to help encourage their development, in *Thinking About You Thinking About Me* (Winner, 2007a, www.socialthinking.com).

✓ *Step 1: Thinking About Others and What They Are Thinking About Us*
We think about who we are near or who we want to talk to. If we are going to talk to others, we consider what information we may already know about them or what information we can infer based on the situation. For example, if you are in a school, you assume the other students there are fellow students. All forms of effective communication begin with thinking about the person you are about to talk to or share space with.

✓ *Step 2: Establishing a Physical Presence*

When we desire to communicate or "hang out" with someone, in addition to thinking about her, we have to establish a physical presence to show the person that we would like to talk to her or be with her. Our physical presence can include standing close (often about an arm's length away), having our shoulders turned towards the person and keeping our body relaxed to move easily to include other people, or to move away from the person, as needed. Our physical presence communicates intent, which helps to kick off communication. For example, if you are thinking about me and you want to hang out with me but you are standing about 4 feet away and looking around, wishing I would come to you, you have failed to establish a physical presence for me. That is, I would not be able to "read your intention" to communicate with me.

✓ *Step 3: "Thinking With Your Eyes"*

As we are thinking about the person we desire to communicate with and we establish physical presence, our intention to communicate is not explicitly clear until we have established eye contact with the other person. This is the third step, since it is possible to engage in the previous two steps without using eye contact. Communication or sharing space effectively is usually not functional without using our eyes, not only to show someone we are interested in talking but to also watch the physical movements and facial expressions of the other person in order to determine his intentions, feelings, and needs.

✓ *Step 4: Using Language to Relate to Others*

While language is indisputedly central to all language-based communication, it is often not effective or functional if the first three steps are not in place. For example, if a student comes up to you to tell you all the details about the *Titanic* and talks endlessly without considering what you are thinking about and without establishing eye contact, it is not true communication, even though it may be interesting to listen to (if you are an adult). It could better be described as "downloading" information. Language use in communication requires language users to constantly consider the thoughts, feelings, prior knowledge, experiences, intentions, and needs of the communicative partner. Each partner has to work to regulate his language to meet the needs of the listener while also conveying the message that helps to add his own thoughts to the interaction. Effective language-based communication requires students to ask questions about other people, produce supportive responses, and add their own thoughts by connecting their experiences or thoughts to what other people are saying, and so on.

Chapter Highlights

- "Multiple intelligences" refers to individuals having various types of cognition; social cognition is one of those types.

- Social cognition, self-regulation, and problem-solving skills are important for academic and social achievement.

- Early developmental milestones in social cognition include joint attention, early symbolic communication, and imitation of movement.

- Students with ASD Level 1 often develop strong academic cognitive skills but lack social cognitive skills.

- Cognitive behavioral interventions seem to offer social skills learning opportunities for students with ASD who can use metacognitive strategies to explore their own behavior.

- Treatment options vary in terms of how and what to teach with regard to social skills/social cognitive development based on the strengths and needs of the individual on the spectrum.

- If social skills are considered in the context of sharing space effectively, the breadth and variety of skills becomes more apparent, including unwritten rules of behavior for different settings and contexts, adjusting behavior based on circumstances, and understanding what others may be thinking.

- Perspective taking involves understanding that others may have thoughts that are different from yours about your behavior and monitoring your behavior based on those thoughts.

- Many students with ASD lack skills in perspective taking.

- The ILAUGH Model of Social Cognition was developed both from research and from studying individuals with ASD.

- The ILAUGH model serves as an acronym to represent six points to help explain what constitutes social cognitive functioning:
  - (I) initiating communication
  - (L) listening actively with eyes and brain
  - (A) abstract and inferential thinking
  - (U) understanding perspective
  - (G) getting the big picture
  - (H) humor and human relatedness

- Social thinking is not only for the purposes of socializing but is also required in interpreting socially abstract concepts such as problem solving, effective communication, and interpreting curriculum that requires socially abstract thoughts.

- From grade 3 onwards, students are required to demonstrate more socially abstract thinking, both in terms of developing successful social interactions and relationships and in terms of successful academic achievement.

- It is not uncommon for students with ASD Level 1 to appear to "get worse" as they become older.

- This reflects their difficulties in navigating an increasingly complex social and academic world.

- Different types and levels of ASD require different social skills interventions due to differences in social cognition, general intelligence, and associated language levels.

- When teaching students with ASD Level 2 or 3, using metacognitive strategies is not effective. These students require a focus on developing functional communication and academic skills with a clear understanding of behavioral expectation. This should be taught through explicit instruction, consistency, and with the use of clear visual supports.

- Students with ASD Level 1 often have near-normal or above-normal academic intelligence and have developed functional communication systems, but have great difficulty in perspective taking, causing problems with understanding implied meaning both from text and from group dynamics.

- Students with ASD Level 1 can benefit from a metacognitive approach to teaching social thinking and related skills.

- The "four steps of communication" for teaching social thinking are:
  - 1. Think about the person before speaking to them
  - 2. Establish a physical presence
  - 3. Use your eyes to think about the person
  - 4. Use language to relate to the other person

- A variety of programs have been developed to teach students with ASD social thinking and related skills.

These include:
  - *Social Stories*™, which provide concrete information about social expectations in specific contexts.
  - *Comic Strip Conversations*™, which use character thought and speaking bubbles to help students understand why someone said or did something.
  - *Social Behavior Mapping*, which shows students how our behaviors impact the feelings of people around us and how others' perceived thoughts about us impact our behavior.
  - *The Incredible 5-Point Scale*, which is used to help students understand their level of anxiety and use strategies to manage it.
  - *Zones of Regulation*, which teach students to develop deeper awareness of their sensory and emotional systems to help them understand the type of zone in which they function the best.

Chapter Review Questions

1. What is meant by "multiple intelligences"?

2. How do the skills necessary for social cognition develop?

3. What are general intervention/treatment options for assisting students with ASD in developing social skills?

4. Why are there problems in defining "social skills"?

5. What is meant by the term *sharing space effectively*?

6. Describe the four steps in perspective taking identified by the chapter author.

7. What are the challenges students with ASD face related to sharing space?

8. List and describe the components of the ILAUGH acronym.

9. Why does the demand for effective social skills increase significantly starting in grade 3?

10. How are the challenges in social thinking and related skills related to challenges in academics?

11. List key concepts for teaching social thinking and related skills to students demonstrating ASD Level 2 or 3.

12. Describe key concepts for teaching social thinking and related skills to students demonstrating ASD Level 1.

13. What are Social Stories™, Comic Strip Conversations™, Social Behavior Mapping, the Incredible 5-Point Scale, and the Zones of Regulation and how are they used to teach social thinking and related skills concepts?

References

American Psychiatric Association. (2013). *Diagnostic and statistical manual of mental disorders, 5th edition.* Washington, DC: Author.

Barnhill, G. P. (2007). Outcomes in adults with Asperger Syndrome. *Focus on Autism and Other Developmental Disabilities, 22*(2), 116-126.

Baron-Cohen, S. (1995). *Mindblindness: An essay on autism and theory of mind.* Cambridge, MA: The MIT Press.

Baron-Cohen, S. (2000). Theory of mind and autism: A fifteen-year review. In S. Baron-Cohen, H. Tager-Flusberg, & D. Cohen (Eds.), *Understanding other minds* (2nd ed., pp. 3-20). New York, NY: Oxford University Press.

Bronson, M. (2000). *Self-regulation in early childhood.* New York, NY: The Guilford Press.

Buron, K. D., & Curtis, M. (2012). *The incredible 5-point scale* (2nd ed.). Shawnee Mission, KS: AAPC Publishing.

Durlak, J., Weissberg, R., Dymnicki, A., Taylor, R., & Schellinger, K. (2011). The impact of enhancing student's social and emotional learning: A meta analysis of school-based universal interventions. *Child Development, 82*(1), 405-432.

Frith, U. (1989). *Autism: Explaining the enigma.* Oxford, UK: Basil Blackwell Ltd.

Gardner, H. (1993). *Multiple intelligences: The theory and practice.* New York, NY: Basic Books.

Gaus, V. (2007). *Cognitive behavior therapy for adult Asperger Syndrome.* New York, NY: The Guilford Press.

Gaylord-Ross, R. J., Haring, T. G., Breen, C., & Pitts-Conway, V. (1984). The training and generalization of social interaction skills with autistic youth. *Journal of Applied Behavior Analysis, 17*(2), 229-247.

Goleman, D. (2006). *Social intelligence: The new science of human relationships.* New York, NY: Bantam Books.

Gray, C. (1994a). *Comic Strip Conversations™.* Arlington, TX: Future Horizons.

Gray, C. (1994b). *The original social story book and social stories ... all new stories teaching social skills.* Arlington, TX: Future Horizons.

Greenspan, S., & Wieder, S. (2006). *Engaging autism.* Cambridge, MA: Da Capo Press.

Hale, C., & Tager-Flusberg, H. (2005). Social communication in children with autism: The relationship between theory of mind and discourse development. *Autism, 9*(2), 157-178.

Happé, F., & Frith, U. (2006). The weak coherence account: Detail focused cognitive style in autism spectrum disorders. *Journal of Autism and Developmental Disorders, 36*(1), 5-25

Hirsh-Pasek, K., Golinkoff, R., & Eyer, D. (2003). *Einstein never used flashcards: How our children really learn – and how they need to play more and memorize less.* Emmaus, PA: Rodale.

Hoffman, M. L. (1970). Conscience, personality and socialization techniques. *Human Development, 13*, 90-126.

Hume, K., Loftin, R., & Lantz, L. (2009). Increasing independence in autism spectrum disorders: A review of three focused interventions. *Journal of Autism and Developmental Disorders, 39*(9), 1329-1338.

Ihrig, K., & Wolchik, S. A. (1988). Peer versus adult models and autistic children's learning: Acquisition, generalization, and maintenance. *Journal of Autism and Developmental Disorders, 18*(1), 67-79.

Jones, E., & Carr, E. G. (2004). Joint attention in children with autism: Theory and intervention. *Focus on Autism and Other Developmental Disabilities, 19*(1), 13-26.

Klin, A., Volkmar, F., & Sparrow, S. (Eds.). (2000). *Asperger Syndrome.* New York, NY: The Guilford Press.

Koegel, L. K., Koegel, R. L., Harrower, J. K., & Carter, C. M. (1999). Pivotal response intervention 1: Overview of approach. *Journal of the Association of Individuals with Severe Handicaps, 24*, 174-185.

Kuypers, L. (2011). *The zones of regulation.* San Jose, CA: Think Social Publishing, Inc.

Leslie, A. M. (1994). ToMM, ToBy, and agency: Core architecture and domain specificity in cognition and culture. In L. Hirschfeld & S. Gelman (Eds.), *Mapping the mind: Domain specificity in cognition and culture* (pp. 119-148). New York, NY: Cambridge University Press.

Levine, M. (2002). *A mind at a time.* New York, NY: Simon and Schuster.

Lopata, C., Thomeer, M. L., Volker, M. A., & Nida, R. E. (2006). Effectiveness of a cognitive-behavioral treatment on the social behaviors of children with Asperger Disorder. *Focus on Autism and Other Developmental Disabilities, 21*(4), 237-244.

Loukusa, S., Leinonen, E., Kuusikko, S., Jussila, K., Mattila, M. L., Ryder, N., Ebeling, H., & Moilanen, I. (2007). Use of context in pragmatic language comprehension by children with Asperger Syndrome or high-functioning autism. *Journal of Autism and Developmental Disorders, 37*(6), 1049-1059.

Lyons, V., & Fitzgerald, M. (2004), Humor in autism and Asperger Syndrome. *Journal of Autism and Developmental Disorders, 34*(5), 521-531.

Marshall, P., & Fox, N. (2006). Biological approaches to the study of social engagement. In P. Marshall & N. Fox (Eds.), *The development of social engagement – Neurobiological perspectives* (pp. 3-18). New York, NY: Oxford University Press.

Murdock, L. C. (2007). *Video self-modeling to increase peer initiations in students with autism.* Paper presented at the meeting of the American Speech-Language-Hearing Association, Boston, MA.

Murray, D., Creaghead, N., Manning-Courtney, P., Shear, P., Bean, J., & Prendeville, J. A. (2008). The relationship between joint attention and language in children with autism spectrum disorders. *Focus on Autism and Other Developmental Disabilities, 23*(1), 5-14.

Myles, B. S., Trautman, M., & Schelvan, R. (2012). *The hidden curriculum for understanding unstated rules in social situations for adolescents and young adults* (2nd ed.). Shawnee Mission, KS: AAPC Publishing.

Nadel, J., & Aouka, N. (2006). Imitation: Some cues for intervention approaches in autism spectrum disorders. In T. Charman & W. Stone (Eds.), *Social communication development in autism spectrum disorders* (pp. 219-235). New York, NY: Guilford Press.

No Child Left Behind (NCLB) Act of 2001, Pub. L. No. 107-110, §115, Stat. 1425 (2002).

Norbury, C. F., & Bishop, D. (2002). Inferential processing and story recall in children with communication problems: a comparison of specific language impairment, pragmatic language impairment and high functioning autism. *International Journal of Language and Communication Disorders, 27*(3) 227-251.

Ozonoff, S., & Miller, J. N. (1996). An exploration of right hemisphere contributions to the pragmatic impairments of autism. *Brain and Language, 52*, 411-434.

Parten, M. B. (1932). Social participation among preschool children. *Journal of Abnormal and Social Psychology, 27*, 243-269.

Paul, R. (2005). Enhancing early language in children with autism spectrum disorders. In F. R. Volkmar, R. Paul, A. Klin, & D. J. Cohen (Eds.), *Handbook of autism and pervasive developmental disorders* (pp. 946-976). New York, NY: Wiley.

Pelicano, E. (2010). Individual differences in executive function and central coherence predict developmental changes in theory of mind in autism. *Developmental Psychology, 46*(2), 530-544.

Plaisted, K. C. (2001). Reduced generalization in autism: An alternative to weak central coherence. In J. A. Burack, T. Charman, N. Yirmiya, & P. R. Zelazo (Eds.), *The development of autism: Perspectives from theory and research* (pp. 149-169). Mahwah, NJ: Lawrence Erlbaum.

Prizant, B., Wetherby, A., Rubin, E., Laurent, A., & Rydell, P. (2006a). *The SCERTS model: A comprehensive educational approach for children with autism spectrum disorders. Vol. I, Assessment.* Baltimore, MD: Paul H. Brookes Publishing.

Prizant, B., Wetherby, A., Rubin, E., Laurent, A., & Rydell, P. (2006b). *The SCERTS model: A comprehensive educational approach for children with autism spectrum disorders. Vol. II, Program Planning and Intervention.* Baltimore, MD: Paul H. Brookes Publishing.

Rao, P., Beidel, D., & Murray, M. (2008). Social skills interventions for children with Asperger Syndrome or high functioning autism: A review and recommendations. *Journal of Autism and Developmental Disorders, 38*, 353-361.

Rapin, I., & Dunn, M. (2003). Update on the language disorders of individuals on the autism spectrum. *Brain and Development, 24*, 166-172.

Saalasti, S., Lepisto, T., Toppila, E., Kujala, T., Laakso, M., Nieminen-von Wendt, T., von Wendt, L., & Jansson-Verkasalo, E. (2008). Language abilities of children with Asperger Syndrome. *Journal of Autism and Developmental Disorders, 38*(8), 1574-1580.

Simonoff, E., Pickles, A., Charman, T., Chandler, S., Loucas, T., & Baird, G. (2008). Psychiatric disorders in children with autism spectrum disorders: Prevalence, comorbidity, and associated factors in a population-derived sample. *Journal of the American Academy of Child and Adolescent Psychiatry, 47*(8), 921-929.

Simpson, R. (2005). *Autism spectrum disorders: Interventions and treatments for children and youth.* Thousand Oaks, CA: Corwin Press.

Sodian, B., & Frith, U. (2008). Metacognition, theory of mind, and self-control: The relevance of high-level cognitive processes in development, neuroscience, and education. *Mind Brain Education, 2*(3), 111-113.

Tomasello, M., Carpenter, M., Call, J., Behne, T., & Moll, H. (2005). Understanding and sharing intentions: The origins of cultural cognition. *Behavior and Brain Science, 28*(5), 675-691; 691-735.

Truesdale, S. P. (1990). Whole-body listening: Developing active auditory skills. *Language Speech and Hearing Services in School, 21*(1090), 183-184.

Van Steensel, F.J.A., Bogels, S. M., & Perrin, S. (2011). Anxiety disorders in children and adolescents with autistic spectrum disorders: A meta-analysis. *Clinical Child and Family Psychology Review, 14*, 302-317.

Wellman, H. M., & Estes, D. (1986). Early understanding mental entities: A reexamination of childhood realism. *Child Development, 57*, 910-923.

Wellman, H., & Lagattuta, K. H. (2000). Developing understandings of mind. In S. Baron-Cohen, H. Tager-Flusberg, & D. Cohen (Eds.), *Understanding other minds* (2nd ed., pp. 21-49). New York, NY: Oxford University Press.

Whalen, C., Schreibman, L., & Ingersoll, B. (2006). The collateral effects of joint attention training on social initiations, positive affect, imitation and spontaneous speech for young children with autism. *Journal of Autism and Developmental Disorders, 36*(5), 655-664.

Williams, M. S., & Shellenberger, S. (1996). *How does your engine run? Leader's guide to the Alert Program for self-regulation.* Albuquerque, NM: Therapy Works Inc.

Wimmer, H., & Perner, J. (1983). Beliefs about beliefs: representation and constraining function of wrong beliefs in young children's understanding of deception. *Cognition, 13*, 103-128.

Winner, M. G. (2000). *Inside out: What makes the person with social cognitive deficits tick?* San Jose, CA: Michelle G. Winner, Think Social Publishing, Inc. www.socialthinking.com

Winner, M. G. (2007a). *Thinking about you thinking about me* (2nd ed.). San Jose, CA: Michelle G. Winner, Think SocialPublishing, Inc. www.socialthinking.com

Winner, M. G. (2007b). *Social behavior mapping.* San Jose, CA: Michelle G. Winner, Think SocialPublishing, Inc. www.socialthinking.com

Winner, M. G., Crooke, P., & Madrigal, S. (2011). *The Social Thinking-Social Communication Profile™: A practice-informed theory.* Retrieved from http://www.socialthinking.com/what-is-social-thinking/social-thinking-social-communication-profile

Wolfberg, P. J., & Schuler, A. L. (2006). Promoting social reciprocity and symbolic representation in children with ASD: Designing quality peer play interventions. In T. Charman & W. Stone (Eds.), *Early social communication in autism spectrum disorders* (pp. 180-218). New York, NY: Guilford Publications.

Learner Objectives

After reading this chapter, the learner should be able to:

- Define what is meant by emotional regulation

- Explain some of the issues associated with difficulty in emotional regulation

- Explain what is currently known about the neurology of emotional regulation

- Discuss the connection between emotional regulation and anxiety

- List several types of relaxation that can be used with students who have problems with emotional regulation

- Explain the importance of self-awareness for students who struggle with emotional regulation

- Discuss the use of a 5-point scale to teach self-awareness

- Explain the importance of social awareness in supporting a student with emotional regulation problems

- Explain the importance of relationship skills in emotional regulation

Chapter 10

Emotional Regulation

Kari Dunn Buron and Brenda Smith Myles

Andy is a second-grade student who is fully included with a 1:1 educational aide (Sharon). One day when the class was working on a math assignment, Andy stood up causing his chair to tip over. He seemed oblivious of the chair and continued doing his work standing up. Sharon approached Andy and told him to pick up his chair and sit down. Andy said that he didn't have to sit down. Sharon showed Andy his sticker chart and reminded him that he needed five stickers to earn extra computer time. Andy's face looked angry, but he picked up the chair and sat down.

Andy soon stopped working and told Sharon that he was done. In looking at his math paper, Sharon noticed that he was not finished with the assigned problems and told him that he had to finish all the problems to earn his sticker. She then continued to walk around the classroom to see if any other students needed help.

Clearly upset, Andy got out of his seat and began to walk around the classroom, occasionally flapping his arms. When Sharon approached him and told him that he had to return to his seat, he growled at her but returned to his seat. Sharon followed him and reminded him that if he wanted to earn a sticker, he would have to finish his math.

Andy started to work again but soon stopped. This time he threw his paper to the floor and screamed that he would never in one million years finish this paper! Sharon and the mainstream teacher approached Andy and told him that yelling was not appropriate. The teacher added that if he could not be quiet in class, he would have to do his work in the resource room. Finally, Sharon told him that because he yelled, he would not get a sticker for math class.

Andy screamed again, threw his chair and ran out of the classroom. Sharon ran after him, telling him to stop, but Andy just kept running. When Sharon threatened to call his mother if he did not stop, Andy turned and hit a student who happened to be walking past with her class. Feeling that she was losing control at this point, Sharon used her walky-talky to call the principal, who got hold of the social worker on the way out of the office and headed towards second grade.

When he saw the principal coming, Andy ran down the hall but was unable to outrun the staff, who promptly grabbed him and directed him to the office. Sharon subsequently called Andy's mother to ask her to come and get him. When his mother arrived, Andy was exhausted and in tears. His mother picked up her son and walked out of the building.

In this scenario, Andy's greatest obstacle to success was his inability to regulate his emotions and manage his anxiety. Another obstacle was the strategies used by Sharon, which were not a good fit for Andy's needs. The idea of losing a reward served to increase Andy's level of anxiety, making it more difficult for him to control his emotions. As he became increasingly anxious, so did Sharon, missing many of the cues indicating that Andy was no longer able to make good decisions. Unsure of what to do, Sharon began to misuse the strategies she had available, such as threatening Andy with a loss of stickers. She knew the situation was escalating but did not recognize that the way she was interacting with Andy was actually increasing the size of the emotion he was feeling rather than supporting him in his attempt at self-control.

Understanding Emotional Regulation

Emotional regulation encompasses the ability to experience, recognize, express, and regulate all emotions effectively and fluidly with respect to environmental constraints (Berthoz & Hill, 2004; Laurent & Rubin, 2004). For example, if a person were expecting to board an airplane at a certain time and at the last minute the flight was cancelled, the situation and the public nature of the airport would require him to manage strong emotions while dealing with the problem in an effective manner. This is emotional regulation. The ability to regulate emotions has been cited as one of the keys to living a healthy and productive life (Silvers, Buhle, & Ochsner, 2013). Individuals with autism spectrum disorders (ASD) have particular difficulty navigating the world of emotions, causing significant challenges in their capacity for emotional regulation. These difficulties can include inability to accurately identify one's emotions, as well as difficulty thinking clearly about where the emotions are coming from and why.

This chapter will highlight current findings related to the severity of problems involving emotional regulation and the need to support and provide intervention when necessary.

Research into challenges in **emotional regulation** varies in its conclusions but often attributes the cause to delays and/or differences in developing theory of mind and perspective taking (see Chapters 2, 3, and 13). Specifically, in addition to the difficulty individuals with ASD Level 1 have in identifying the mental states of others, a lack of theory of mind is linked to their inability to identify and differentiate their own mental states (Aspy & Grossman, 2011). Kanne and Mazurek (2011) ascribed emotional regulation challenges to inflexibility whereas Barrett, Gross, Conner, and Benvenuto (2001) and Samson, Huber, and Gross (2012) reported that adults with ASD Level 1 typically use less effective methods for emotional regulation than neurotypical adults. That is, they tend to rely on **emotional suppression** (or hiding the emotion), a less effective coping strategy, rather than employing **emotional reappraisal** (or rethinking the situation) to shift their perspective in troubling circumstances.

Problems of emotional regulation are often evidenced by the presence of anxiety, depression, anger, and self-esteem differences. Developmental difficulties in these areas can lead to strong reactions to the social demands and frustrations of everyday life. For example, difficulty regulating emotions can cause anxieties that impact a student's ability to benefit from the school environment.

Anxiety is a common condition experienced by individuals with autism. For example, 11% to 84% of individuals with autism experience anxiety (Costello, Egger, & Angold, 2005; van Steensel & Bogels, 2011; White & Roberson-Nay, 2009). According to Costello and colleagues (2005), the rates of anxiety disorders observed in children with ASD are more than two times higher than in typically developing children. Similarly, Lugnegard, Hallerback, and Gillberg (2011) found that more than one half of the adults in their study had experienced at least one anxiety disorder, with others having had a diagnosis for two or more, including social anxiety disorder, generalized anxiety disorder, and obsessive compulsive disorder.

Anxiety can impact all areas of life from school attendance to developing friendships to independent living to employment. For example, after interviewing six adults with Level 1 ASD about their job experiences, Hurlbutt and Chalmers (2004) concluded,

> The stress of not understanding the social rules of the environment, not knowing which topics are appropriate to talk about and which are not, having difficulty asking for help, and being exhausted from concentrating so hard all day to understand the world of neurotypicals can become overwhelming. (p. 219)

Depression can also impact the ability to respond effectively to emotional challenges. According to Roy, Dillo, Emrich, and Ohlmeier (2009), depression is linked to impairments in the personal and professional domains. Up to one quarter of children and adolescents with ASD experience depression (Ghaziuddin, Weidmer-Mikhail, & Ghaziuddin, 1998; Tantam, 2000) whereas 12% (Cederlund, Hagberg, & Gillberg, 2010) to 40% of adults (Balfe & Tantam, 2010) suffer from this mental health condition. In their study of adults with Level 1 ASD, Lugnegard et al. (2011) found that 70% had had at least one episode of major depression and one half experienced recurring depression. More specifically, college students with autism reported intense feelings of loneliness with fewer and shorter-term friendships and romantic relationships than their typical peers (Jobe & White, 2007). Further, Jobe and White (2007) reported that young adults with Level 1 ASD "do not necessarily prefer aloneness, as once assumed, but rather experience increased levels of loneliness related to lack of social skill and understanding" (p. 1479), which can lead to depression.

Related to depression are suicidal ideations and suicide attempts. Researchers suspect that suicidal behavior among individuals with ASD occurs more often than is recognized (Barnhill, 2007; Ghaziuddin, 2005; Ghaziuddin, Ghaziuddin, & Greden, 2002; Tantam & Prestwood, 1999). More specifically, Balfe and Tantam (2010) reported that 40% of their sample had contemplated suicide and 15% had attempted to kill themselves.

Social isolation plays a significant role in the challenges related to anxiety, self-esteem, and social resilience of individuals with Level 1 ASD as adults. As children they are often the objects of bullying and teasing by their peers, setting the stage for a state of social isolation that persists in adulthood (Balfe & Tantam, 2010). Further, their social and communication challenges complicate their ability to interact comfortably with others, especially those who are unfamiliar to them, despite a desire for social relationships.

Individuals with autism also report experiencing more negative emotions compared to positive emotions, including anger, than their neurotypical counterparts. According to Quek, Sofronoff, Sheffield, White, and Kelly (2012), 17% of young people on the autism spectrum experience clinically significant levels of anger. In their study, anxiety and depression were positively associated with anger, with depression explaining 25% of the variance in anger. Similar results were found by Matson and Nebel-Schwalm (2007) and Tantam (2000).

Not surprisingly, the difficulties experienced in these areas can lead to lowered self-esteem (Barnhill, 2007; Hurlbutt & Chalmers, 2004). This is significant because self-esteem is positively correlated to quality of life (Burgess & Gutstein, 2007). For example, Montgomery, Stoesz, and McCrimmon (2013) and others (Palmer, Donaldson, & Stough, 2002; Saklofske, Austin, & Minski, 2003), in their investigation of self-esteem and related characteristics (e.g., optimism, self-awareness, and self-actualization), found that these traits predict life satisfaction, social network quality, loneliness, and depression. Eugene, an adult with Asperger Syndrome, reported,

> I have to struggle so hard to achieve what NTs take for granted, and I was a little envious of their ease in socializing. It would be good to understand socialization completely, but, with the developing autistic society, these feelings of envy are beginning to go away in my mind. (Hurlbutt & Chalmers, 2004, p. 219)

As suggested above, the issue of emotional regulation for individuals with ASD is multifaceted. Problems originating in cognitive social confusion caused by failure to understand another person's perspective, emotional state of mind, or intentions, can lead to anxiety, feelings of low self-worth, and depression. Educators and parents need to consider all of these issues as they relate to an individual student.

The Neuroscience of Emotional Regulation

ASD is a whole-brain condition; that is, there is not a singular area of brain dysfunction specific to autism (see Figure 10.1). Several areas of the brain, including brainstem, cerebellum, frontal lobe, and limbic structures, have been implicated as abnormal in persons with ASD (Bachevalier & Loveland, 2006). Similarly, research has revealed that emotional regulation challenges are not limited to one section of the brain (cf. Minshew & Keller, 2010; Pelphrey, Shultz, Hudac, & Vander Wyk, 2011). For example, an enlarged amygdala and hippocampus have been implicated in problems of emotional perception and regulation (cf. Groen, Teluj, Buitelaar, & Tendolkar, 2010).

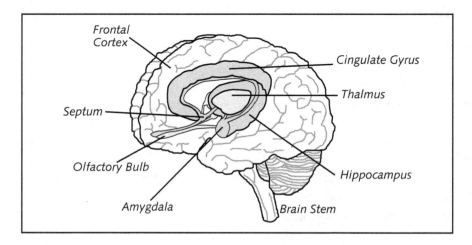

Figure 10.1. Outline of typical brain.

With regard to the amygdala, Davidson (2012) discussed what he calls a "hair-trigger amygdala," which refers to a dysfunctional emotional regulation system whereby a person gets upset very quickly and has difficulty regaining control. Individuals with ASD have high levels of worry, stress, and anxiety, which can lead to an almost constant state of amygdala arousal (Van Steensel & Bogels, 2011) and, consequently, lead to a loss of emotional control. Bachevalier and Loveland (2006) reported that the orbitofrontal-amygdala circuit, which is involved with the cognitive processing of emotional feelings, is a critical factor in the development of ASD and that some of the behaviors associated with self-regulation difficulties are attributed to this neurological circuit. This finding is significant because inherent in ASD is a difficulty understanding or correctly interpreting social information, which could lead to difficulties in accurately assessing an emotional situation and effectively using cognitive processing to guide one's behavioral responses.

Other studies have found differences in the brain's default-mode network (i.e., a network of brain regions that are active when an individual is daydreaming or not otherwise engaged in a demanding task) to be related to emotional processing and regulation. Thus, reduced activity in the default-mode network has been associated with ASD (Zielinski et al., 2012).

Lacking emotional regulation skills can lead to disruptive emotional responses, aggressive behavior, and inflexible responses to disappointments and unexpected changes, among others. Traditionally, educators have responded to challenges in these areas with a primary goal of eliminating the behaviors, but with new information documenting the cognitive nature of emotional regulation, educators are changing the focus to one of teaching new skills as exemplified in the remainder of this chapter.

Instruction and Supports

Goleman (2011) cited the following skill areas as necessary for one individual to have a positive impact on another: self-awareness, social awareness, self-management, and relationship management. As illustrated in the previous section, these cognitive areas are also essential to the development of emotional regulation, and can be utilized when framing a discussion of how to effectively support a person who lacks the skills needed to successfully regulate their emotional responses.

Due to the inherent characteristics and learning styles of individuals with ASD, any approach to teaching should include elements of self-management, visual supports and routines, and opportunities for practice.

- **Self-management.** Self-management may be defined as the ability to regulate one's behavior, including monitoring. As such, it involves learning the skills needed to reduce unwanted responses and increasing adaptive responses. The National Professional Development Center on Autism Spectrum Disorders (2010), the National Autism Center (2009), and the Centers for Medicare and Medicaid Services (2010) cite a number of evidence-based practices for ASD in the United States, including self-management.

- **Visual supports and routines.** Visual supports may be defined as visually presented tools that support increased understanding for a student. Visual supports are supported by research and may include, but are not limited to, pictures, scales, written words, flow charts, symbols, and scripts.

- **Practice in real-life situations.** This includes practicing newly acquired emotional regulation skills in a variety of natural settings and across environments. This is critical as individuals with ASD often have difficulty maintaining and generalizing skills to new contexts (Dawson & Osterling, 1997).

These three important approaches to teaching students on the autism spectrum are often understood and practiced when the focus is on teaching areas such as math, reading, and work skills, but are all to often forgotten when teaching social and emotional information. It is helpful to keep them in mind as you review the following individual strategies.

Teaching Relationship-Building Skills

Building Friendships

Friendships are integral to the development of the flexible thinking and social resilience needed for effective emotional regulation. Specifically, friendships can increase a child's ability to think through and effectively negotiate difficult social situations, and having friends makes it possible for children to practice controlling their emotions and responding to the emotions of others (Ferrer-Chancy & Fugate, 2002). Indeed, friendships have been cited as the most important relationships in the emotional life of adolescents (Conger & Galambos, 1997).

Special Interests

By the very nature of their disability, students on the autism spectrum have difficulty forming or maintaining friendships and relationships (Bellini, 2007). Our relationships with others are typically based on mutual respect and shared interests, so to help students with ASD form friendships, it makes sense to help them find others who love and value the same things as they do. An example might be to support a special interest group after school where the student can discuss and share information with other students about their particular area of interest. Such groups might include a Science Club, Chess Club, or Zoology Club where students have an opportunity to discuss their interest and showcase their knowledge of the topic (see Chapter 12).

Further, as an added benefit, many adults with ASD have reported using thoughts about their special interest as a way of reducing social anxiety and increasing the ability to remain calm during social frustration (personal interview, AuSM Adult Group, 2013).

Use of Humor

Humor and laughter and their role in relationships have been widely studied (Martin, 2010; Provine & Fischer, 1989). Findings indicate that laughter connects people in a very emotional way. Laughter can be thought of as a nonverbal expression of joy that can help individuals cope with issues of emotional regulation, rather than being overwhelmed by them.

Students who lack friendships also tend to lack opportunities for laughter and, therefore, can benefit from strategies specifically designed to elicit laughter. Creative ways of bringing humor and laughter into the classroom include video modeling, comedy improv games, cartoons, and studying jokes (Getlen, 2006).

Video modeling, which will be discussed at more length later in this chapter, is a method of using video to teach social behavior. One fun way of using this strategy is to help students write and create stand-up comedy acts. Usually, it is necessary to establish guidelines for respectful standup before starting a unit on stand-up comedy. Such guidelines set up parameters regarding subject matter and respectful behavior towards the comic, while outlining more technical topics such as time constraints and responding to the audience.

Watching pre-approved stand-up acts on Youtube is a good place to start. Examples of comics who have G-rated acts include Bill Cosby, Jerry Seinfeld, Rodney Dangerfield, Ellen Degeneres, and Bob Newhart. After becoming familiar with the rhythm and nature of stand-up comedy, educators can support each student in writing personal accounts of funny stories. The final step is to video tape the acts and watching them together as a class.

Improv games are repetitive and involve following rules so that the interactions are successful. Improv comedy games can help build camaraderie, social self-confidence, and conversation skills. Again, Youtube offers many examples of improv games for both children and older students. In addition, the website www.improvencylopedia.org has dozens of excellent and easy game ideas for the classroom.

10 Factors That Affect Relationships

It is important that strategies used to support relationship building fully appreciate the complexity of social interactions. Too often strategies target only one element of the social process. Loomis (2008) approaches social interactions in a more comprehensive manner, listing 10 factors that should be considered when programming for social situations (see Figure 10.2). These factors provide the first step in recognizing that social skills are more than the sum of their parts (Koenig, De Los Reyes, Cicchetti, Scahill, & Klin, 2009). For example, they vary across events, people, time, space, and so on, thus creating challenges that differ dependent on the social event. A brief review of these factors is provided in Table 10.1. (For a more in-depth discussion, please refer to *Staying in the Game: Providing Social Opportunities for Children and Adolescents with Autism Spectrum Disorders and Other Developmental Disabilities,* Loomis, 2008.)

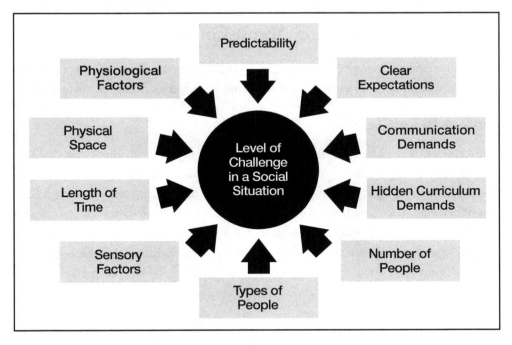

Figure 10.2. Loomis' factors that make social situations challenging.

Loomis, J. W. (2008). *Staying in the game: Providing social opportunities for children and adolescents with autism spectrum disorders and other developmental disabilities.* Shawnee Mission, KS: AAPC Publishing. Used with permission. www.aapcpublishing.net.

Table 10.1
Overview of Loomis' 10 Factors That Impact Social Interactions

Factor	Brief Description
Predictability	Routines and regular activities facilitate social success. Activities that are less than predictable can cause anxiety and the learner's focus is on personal stress experiences rather than social exchanges.
Clear Expectations	Answers to these questions must be provided: Who do you approach? How do you join the activity? When can you talk, sing, yell, etc?
Communication Demands	Verbal and nonverbal communication, emotions, opinions, jokes, and metaphors relative to an activity must be understood by the learner with ASD.
Hidden Curriculum Demands	Unstated rules, assumptions, and expectations can serve as a roadblock to successful social experiences.
Number of People	The fewer people involved, the lower the social challenge.
Types of People	Some individuals are easier to socialize with than others. It is important, especially in new social situations, to ensure that people who are easy to socialize with are included in activities.
Sensory Demands	All environments have sensory demands and the majority of individuals with ASD have sensory challenges. A mismatch between the two can cause regulation problems.
Length of Time	Social processing can be exhausting for learners with ASD. The longer a social event, the more taxing it is.
Physical Space	Crowded spaces, large open areas, noisy environments, and echoing environments can be difficult and/or exhausting for the individual with ASD.
Physiological Factors	Physiological factors, including fatigue, hunger, thirst, and illness can influence social interactions.

Teaching About Emotions

Because emotional understanding is integral to interpreting and reacting to the actions of others and self, it is essential that direct instructional techniques, such as the Incredible 5-Point Scale and modeling, be intentionally used.

The Incredible 5-Point Scale

Buron and Curtis (2003, 2012) created the Incredible 5-Point Scale to help individuals with ASD understand social and emotional concepts as well as to enhance their self-understanding. The 1-5 scale system is applicable for a variety of social and self-regulation behaviors and responses to those behaviors, including feelings of anxiety, concepts of personal space, and feelings of anger. The scale is unique in that it can be used for a variety of purposes, including an obsessional index, a stress scale, and a meltdown monitor, etc. Children and youth with ASD are taught to recognize the stages of their emotions or social challenges and methods to self-calm or "rethink" at each level. Figures 10.3 and 10.4 illustrate how the Incredible 5-Point Scale can be used to teach about emotions.

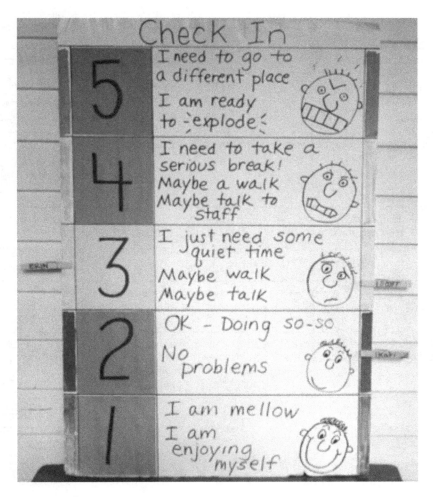

Figure 10.3. Sample Incredible 5-Point Scale. This is an example of a "check-in" scale that can be used in multiple environments by multiple students. In this model, clothespins with the student's names on them are used for each person to "check in" regarding their level of emotional tolerance throughout the day.

Danny's Self-Awareness Scale

Rating	What might make me feel this way?	How does my body or brain look?	What can I do now?
5	Nothing is working! I am out of control! I can't think!	Like being in a tidal wave. Screaming and maybe throwing things. I don't hear people talking to me.	Shut my eyes. Try to close mouth. Try to slow down my breathing.
4	Someone says something that makes me angry. This is usually about politics or history facts.	Swearing. I sometimes shake. I feel mean.	Stop talking. Slow down your breathing to slow down your brain. Try to walk to a safe place.
3	There is a change I am not expecting. Someone tells me I am wrong.	Stomach starts to hurt. I start to have negative thoughts about someone or something. I feel mistreated.	Excuse myself and go to a safe place. Maybe go get a drink of water. Look through my photos.
2	Things are going along as planned. I am getting my work completed.	My body is where it should be. I am in control of what I say. I prefer to be alone.	Hang in there. This is good. I can get some work done. I don't need to be social.
1	This is almost perfect. I got a good grade. Someone complimented me.	I am very calm and happy. I feel like being with other people. My brain is full of good thoughts about people and things.	Relax. Smile. Enjoy the moment. Compliment people back.

Figure 10.4. Sample Incredible 5-Point Scale. This scale is used like a worksheet with a student to work out how he feels in certain social situations, how he might typically respond, and how he can try to handle those thoughts and emotions in the future.

Modeling

As mentioned above, modeling involves learning skills either in real time or through video observations (Stahmer, Suhrheinrich, Reed, Bolduc, & Schreibman, 2010). Based on Bandura's (1977) concept of social learning, which posits that individuals learn from watching each other, modeling may be divided into three types: "***direct modeling*** (simply copying the model), ***synthesized modeling*** (combining several observations to create a new behavior), and ***symbolic modeling*** (copying fictional characters from television, books, etc.)" (Aspy & Grossman, 2011, p. 205).

An advantage of video modeling over live modeling is that it can be studied over and over. In addition, it is time and cost effective since, once it has been developed, the student or several students can watch it multiple times, usually without significant adult support.

Recent research on video modeling has focused on the type of model used. The strategy has been reported as successful in the formats of (a) self as model, (b) adult as model, and (c) visual point of view. When the student himself performs in the video, it is called **video self-modeling**. Buggey (2009) recommended showing only positive outcomes when using self-modeling videos so that students can watch themselves performing the skill at the level of competence. Self-modeling has the added benefit of showing a person how he looks performing the desired behavior; in this case, the video might show him handling the frustration experienced due to an unexpected schedule change. Watching oneself succeeding in this way can add to the concrete nature of the experience.

A meta-analysis found that video modeling was successful in teaching a variety of skills, including self-help, social, transition behaviors, play, on-task, and speech and language skills (Bellini & Akullian, 2007). In addition, McCoy and Hermansen (2007) found that participants, regardless of type of video modeling used, were successful in learning new skills. In addition to the video modeling mentioned here, the Mind Reading software (University of Cambridge, 2003; discussed in Chapter 13), Animal Agentz (Jones, 2008), YouTube, and eHow are all excellent examples of using video to address issues related to regulation.

Teaching Self-Regulation

There are several ways to teach self-regulation through the use of self-management. The approaches to be discussed here include relaxation, yoga, and 5 Stars.

Relaxation

Examples of relaxation include meditation, visualization, progressive muscle relaxation, deep breathing, stretching and balance exercises, and yoga. The key to successfully teaching relaxation is to make it a strong habit. When emotional deregulation has become a strong, well-learned response to stress, any new response has to be over-learned and over-practiced in order to replace it.

Progressive muscle relaxation is a method of teaching how to discriminate between muscles that are tense and those that are not. The training involves alternating between tightening and relaxing large-muscle groups such as arms, legs, and hands. Using visual picture cards illustrating the sequence of muscles to work on is an example of visual support mentioned earlier.

Imagery is another way to teach relaxation. Two ideas for teaching imagery are cognitive picture rehearsal (Groden & LeVasseur, 1995) and using photographs of people, places, and things the person loves, perhaps organized into a photo album.

Cognitive picture rehearsal is a type of social narrative that involves the repeated practice of a sequence of behaviors to teach a calm response to stressful situations. The sequence is presented in a cartoon-panel format illustrating a predictably stressful situation, and includes a script for successfully navigating that situation. If the person experiences stress when recess is canceled due to bad weather, the drawing and script might look like the example in Figure 10.5.

Figure 10.5. Sample cognitive picture rehearsal.

The photo album idea is based on the premise that many learners on the autism spectrum experience stress throughout their school day. The goal is to create a small photo album of approximately six pictures that help to make the child feel happy and calm. The photos might include a parent, a family pet, a favorite vacation spot, or the child's bedroom. The photo album can be included in the student's daily routine at least once and possibly several times throughout the day. When introducing the album, the educator can calmly recite a script while looking at the photos. For example, "Here is my dog, Eddie. I love my dog Eddie. Eddie helps me to feel calm and happy." A similar script can be repeated with each of the other photographs. (The words to the script can also be included at the bottom of each photo.) After an initial period of direct support from the teacher, the learner can then look at the photos independently.

Yoga

Yoga is a generic term for a set of practices that address the physical, mental, and spiritual elements of one's state of being (Serwacki & Cook-Cottone, 2013). This health and wellness approach is designed to (a) emphasize personal change, such as decreases in stress and anxiety and increases in self-confidence; (b) increase opportunities to lead healthful lifestyles; (c) increase responsibility and empowerment; and (d) focus on enjoyment rather than competiveness (Ellery, 2007).

Studies on yoga used with learners with autism have found decreased (a) stress and anxiety (Goldberg, 2004; Rosenblatt et al., 2011); (b) attention and hyperactivity problems; (c) depression; (c) aggression; and (d) withdrawal (Rosenblatt et al.). Similarly, Koenig, Buckley-Reen, and Garg (2012) reported a general decrease in off-task behavior and behavior challenges.

5 Stars

Another strategy for teaching self-regulation is a method called 5 Stars (Buron & Curtis, 2012). Shifting from one activity to another is difficult for many learners with ASD, and the resulting anxiety can contribute to an inability to control emotions. 5 Stars is a visual representation of the passage of time used to help students better understand when it is time to stop one thing and go on to another. The concrete, visual, and systematic nature of 5 Stars can assist the learner in maintaining self-control over a difficult situation.

The 5 Star system consists of a cardboard strip with 5 or 6 squares (with Velcro® on each square) and 5 separate stars (also with Velcro on each star). The adult hands the student the cardboard strip accompanied by a verbal prompt such as, "We'll be in group for 5 stars and then we can go for a walk." The adult has control of how quickly or slowly the stars are given to the learner, making it a more flexible system than a traditional timer. This is not a reward system. It is designed to be a concrete representation of the passage of time. The learner does not "earn" or "lose" a star. Instead of staying in a group indefinitely or for "5 minutes," the expectation is "stay in group for 5 stars" (see Figure 10.6).

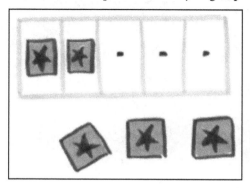

Figure 10.6. Graphic of 5 Stars.

Several adaptations can increase the uses of this strategy and increase the learner's motivation to use it. One modification involves including more squares on the strip so that you can add a picture of what comes next (such as walk, recess, drink of water, etc.). Another idea is to use an image symbolizing a learner's high-interest area to mark off the time rather than the stars. For example, use pictures of five dinosaurs, five planets, or five water towers. Finally, you can use a picture of the actual activity. For example, if the learner is working at the computer and the computer is a highly preferred activity, you can use five different pictures of a computer, handing the student a picture randomly until she has all five computers indicating it is time to end computer time and move to another activity (King, YouTube demonstration, 2012). This activity can be practiced as an "add-on" system (educator gives the learner a star or picture to fill up the strip) or as a "take-off" system (educator randomly takes off a star or picture). Hint: This strategy should be relaxing for the student. If you choose to use the "take-off" method and the student appears to become increasingly nervous as you take the stars off, try the "add-on" approach instead.

Teaching Self- and Social Awareness

Self-awareness or the ability to detect and understand one's emotions, movement, behavior, and social interactions, is impaired in learners on the autism spectrum (cf. Aspy & Grossman, 2011). For example, a student with ASD might be unaware that he is standing too close to somebody and then become confused when the other person gets upset or asks him to "back off." Healthy skills in the area of self- and social awareness can lead to increased self-confidence and lower levels of anxiety in social environments. A variety of interventions can be used to teach self- and social awareness, including (a) the Incredible 5-Point Scale (Buron & Curtis, 2012; discussed in the Teaching About Emotions section of this chapter); (b) modeling (discussed in the Teaching About Emotions section of this chapter); (c) narratives; (d) the hidden curriculum; and (e) problem-solving.

Narratives

Social narratives, which include **cartooning** (Gray, 1995; Kerr & Durkin, 2004; Pierson & Glaeser, 2005, 2007; Rogers & Myles, 2001); the **Power Card strategy** (Angell, Nicholson, Watts, & Blum, 2011; Campbell & Tincani, 2011; Davis, Boon, Cihak, & Fore, 2010; Gagnon, 2001; Keeling, Myles, Gagnon, & Simpson, 2003; Myles, Keeling, & Van Horn, 2001); **social autopsies** (Bieber, 1994); **social scripts** (Ganz, Kaylor, Bourgeois, & Hadden, 2008; Wichnick, Vener, Keating, & Poulson, 2009); **Social Stories™** (Chan et al., 2011; Gray, 1995; Kokina & Kern, 2010; Test, Richter, Knight, & Spooner, 2010); and SOCCSS (Situation, Options, Consequences, Choices, Strategies, Simulation; Roosa, 1995) were designed to help learners understand social situations. Some are to be used prior to a situation to facilitate social success (i.e., cartooning, Power Cards, social scripts, Social Stories™). Specifically, they provide information about what may occur/what to expect, how others might think about what is happening, when something may occur, what the learner can do in a given situation, what the learner should try not to do in a given situation, and so forth. Others, such as SOCCSS and social autopsies, occur after an event to help the learner understand a previous interaction to support future success. Social narratives also emphasize problem-solving skills, brainstorming, and generalization. Typically they (a) are written in the first person; (b) provide for flexibility and the possibility of change using words such as *may, probably, usually, will try to,* and *might;* and (c) are developed and presented in a manner appropriate to the learner, whether through the use of words only, pictures only, or a combination of the two.

Another type of social narrative is the **Nurturing Narrative** (Botting, Faragher, Know, Simkin, & Conti-Ramsden, 2001; Chong & Carr, 2005; Franke & Durbin, 2011; Lyle, 2000). A primary goal of these stories is to increase social problem-solving skills as well as the perspective-taking skills needed to increase social and self-awareness. This intervention " … involves systematically facilitating mastery of new language skills during engaging, interactive story-based activities" (Franke & Durbin, 2011, p. 12). They target (a) social communication and conversation; (b) grammar, syntax, and vocabulary; (c) story comprehension and retelling; (d) interactive symbolic play; and (e) theory of mind. Table 10.2 describes the various social narratives and identifies the evidence-based practices to which they are related.

Table 10.2
Descriptions of Types of Social Narratives

Type	Brief Description
Cartooning	This intervention uses thought bubbles, conversation bubbles, and cartoon or stick figures to illustrate people's thoughts and words during interactions in a comic-strip format. Gray (1995) developed guidelines for Comic Strip Conversations™, including colors to illustrate emotions.
Nurturing Narratives	This story-based language intervention approach embeds building language skills into the context of sharing personal narratives and retelling fictional stories using a blending of applied behavior analysis and social pragmatics. Narrative understanding is the primary tool through which people make sense of the world and is the best predictor of outcomes in preschool and elementary school.
Power Card Strategy	Based on a student's special interest, the Power Card Strategy contains two components: (a) a text-based scenario that describes a target behavior associated with a person of special interest and how that individual addresses the target behavior, and encourages the student to use the strategy employed by the person of special interest; and (b) a small card that synthesizes the text-based scenario (Gagnon, 2001).
Social Autopsies	In this adult-directed exchange between a student and a mentor, a social error is defined and methods of (a) making amends and/or (b) interacting successfully in future events are discussed (Bieber, 1994).
Social Scripts	Written sentences or paragraphs contain brief descriptions and text that can be used verbatim in academic and/or nonacademic settings.
Social Stories™	Developed by Gray and Garand (1993), these written stories inform or describe an activity and the anticipated behavior associated with it. They also provide information to teach appropriate social behaviors. Gray developed specific guidelines regarding types of sentences, language level, audience, and use.
Situations, Options, Consequences, Choices, Strategies and Simulation (SOCCSS)	SOCCSS provides an extensive analysis of social interactions by helping individuals with ASD learn choice-making, cause-effect relationship, and problem solving. This adult-directed strategy helps children and youth logically work through the situations by defining (a) the problem situation, (b) options the child may have in how to respond to the situation, and (c) consequences that would logically follow each option. The youth is then supported in making a choice among the options that were generated and developing a strategy to implement that choice. Finally, the child practices or simulates the strategy to ensure that he could actually carry out his choice in a social setting (Roosa, 1995).

Hidden Curriculum

The hidden curriculum refers to assumed knowledge, and includes the expectations, rules, or guidelines for successful social interactions that are not directly taught because they are universally known by most children and adults. It also addresses the incongruities of how skills are executed across communicative partners and environments, making it an essential set of skills for individuals with ASD who often do not detect the subtleties of situations and tend to be routine-bound and literal thinkers. The absence of instruction in the hidden curriculum should not belie its importance. It is significant, and if a person lacks this core social information it will not only lead to problems of social interactions, school performance, and safety, but also self- and social awareness. Despite its considerable value, little information on the hidden curriculum has been published because it has been largely considered "common sense" and is often only recognized after a hidden curriculum error has occurred (Endow, 2012; Myles, Endow, & Mayfield, 2013; Myles & Kolar, 2013; Myles, Trautman, & Schelvan, 2013). Table 10.3 contains sample hidden curriculum items that address self-awareness.

Table 10.3
Sample List of Hidden Curriculum Items Related to Emotional Regulation

1. People may not automatically recognize that you are upset, concerned or overwhelmed. If you are feeling one of these emotions and someone is not giving you space or helping you calm down, they might need you to tell them how you are feeling.

2. Sometimes your behavior can tell you how you are feeling. For example, some people will start to tap their feet or drum their fingers when they are beginning to feel upset.

3. People find it easiest to be around people who know how to recognize and control their emotions.

4. It is okay to tell someone that you are upset, overwhelmed, and confused and that you need (a) to be left alone or (b) help from someone you trust.

5. Even though you make plans and have routines, things will not always go as planned. Most of the time, we should try to accept the changes and realize that everything will be okay.

6. Almost all people need to take time for themselves throughout the day to keep calm. Some people do this by exercising, meditating, taking a walk, or going to a quiet place.

7. It is normal not to have the answers for all situations and it is almost always okay to ask a trusted friend or adult to help you figure out what you should do. Sometimes you will be asked to help a friend who is having difficulty.

Problem-Solving Interventions

Problem-solving skills are highly valued in home (cf. Dawson et al., 2012), community (Renzaglia, Karvonen, Drasgow, & Stoxen, 2003), school (cf. Cheng, Chiang, & Cheng, 2010), and employment settings (cf. Mat, Zhang, & Pacha, 2012).

Mataya and Owens' problem-solving paradigm (Mataya & Owens, 2013) is designed to help learners understand cause and effect, problem solving, and decision-making. Created for use at home, school, and community, this comprehensive and easy-to-use model is suitable for learners across the spectrum.

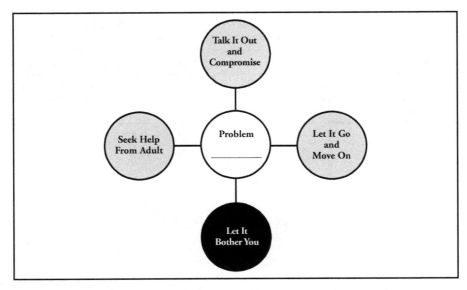

Figure 10.7. Sample Mataya and Owens problem-solving graphic.

Stop Observe Deliberate Act (SODA) is a visual, problem-solving rubric that children and youth with ASD can use to navigate unfamiliar social situations (Bock, 2001, 2002). Designed as a multipurpose strategy that individuals with ASD can use in almost any social gathering, SODA attempts to develop a schema for the child to understand novel environments and be an active decision-maker in determining how she will fit in. Bock created the following series of questions about salient environmental factors that learners with ASD should ask themselves at each stage of SODA.

Stop: What is the room arrangement? What is the activity or routine? Where should I go to observe?

Observe: What are the people doing? What are the people saying? What is the length of a typical conversation? What do the people do after they've visited?

Deliberate: What would I like to do? What would I like to say? How will I know when others would like to visit longer **or** would like to end this conversation?

Act: Approach person(s) with whom I'd like to visit and say, "Hello, how are you?" Listen to person(s) and ask related questions. Look for cues that this person would like to visit longer or would like to end the conversation. End the conversation and walk away (see Table 10.4 for an elaboration on these steps).

This strategy can be successful but relies heavily on good social skills instruction. That is, the students using SODA should have the social skills required to execute each of the stages of the strategy.

Table 10.4
SODA Strategy Steps

Stop	During this step, the child with ASD attempts to define the activities, their order, and a location near the activities from which he can observe the scene. The selected location should be one in which the child or youth can observe and learn information that will help him participate in the activity successfully.
Observe	The observation period includes facets that help the individual with ASD create a schema: length of conversations, number of individuals involved in conversations, tone of conversations (i.e., formal, casual), strategies used to begin and end conversations, nonverbal language, and any routines that may be in place.
Deliberate	Deliberation helps the learner develop an action plan. Depending on the situation, he may decide on a topic of conversation, quickly review social skills etiquette that would facilitate success (i.e., nonverbal cues, posture, social distance). Also included in this step is thoughtful deliberation on what others will think of him if he does or does not follow the social protocol he has observed.
Act	The final stage of SODA includes participation in the social event using the strategies identified during the deliberation stage. The Act stage also allows the individual to generalize skills that he may have learned in another setting.

Summary and Conclusions

Emotional regulation involves the ability to respond to the everyday demands of life. This includes not only a person's ability to control his own emotions but also the ability to monitor, modify, and accurately identify emotions in oneself and the expression of emotion of others. A lack of functional emotional regulation skills impacts a person's success across all social environments and relationships.

Competence in the area of emotional regulation for students on the autism spectrum can take years to achieve, and success will require direct teaching, repetitive practice and successful experiences.

Learning how to control emotions is a lifelong goal for most humans, and the path to that goal can be filled with obstacles, depending on one's ability to handle the life stressors encountered. In *The Autistic Brain: Thinking Across the Spectrum* (2013), Temple Grandin and Richard Panek stress the importance of controlling one's own emotions:

> If you want to keep a job, you have to learn how to turn anger into frustration. I saw in a magazine article that Steve Jobs would cry in frustration. That's why Steve Jobs still had a job. He could be verbally abusive to his employees, but as far as I know, he didn't go around throwing things at them or slugging them. (p. 194)

Tips for Practical Application

✓ Recognize emotional regulation as a skill area in need of attention, intervention, goals, and objectives.

✓ Remember to incorporate elements of self-management into your emotional regulation teaching.

✓ Remember a student's preferred learning style (visual, repetitive, routines, etc.) when developing a social and emotional training curriculum.

✓ Recognize relaxation and relationship-building skills as valid goal areas on an educational plan.

✓ Assume that a loss of emotional control is directly related to a demand that has surpassed the person's ability to cope.

✓ Address a student's ability to control his emotions in a functional behavior assessment, particularly if the behaviors being observed look like the "out-of-control" behaviors one might observe in a young child's tantrum.

Chapter Highlights

- Emotional regulation is the ability to experience, recognize, express, and regulate all emotions effectively and fluidly with respect to environmental constraints (Berthoz & Hill, 2004; Laurent & Rubin, 2004).

- Individuals with ASD often have significant challenges in their capacity for emotional regulation.

- Problems of emotional regulation are often evidenced by the presence of anxiety, depression, anger, and self-esteem differences.

- Emotional regulation challenges are related to differences in the structure and function of the brain.

- There is not a singular area of brain dysfunction specific to ASD. Several areas of the brain, including brain stem, cerebellum, frontal lobe, and limbic structures, have been implicated as abnormal in persons with ASD (Bachevalier & Loveland, 2006).

- Research has revealed that emotional regulation challenges are not limited to one section of the brain (cf. Minshew & Keller, 2010; Pelphrey, Shultz, Hudac, & Vander Wyk, 2011).

- An enlarged amygdala and hippocampus have been implicated in problems of emotional perception and regulation (cf. Groen, Teluj, Buitelaar, & Tendolkar, 2010).

- Anxiety is a common condition experienced by individuals with ASD. For example, 11% to 84% of individuals with autism experience anxiety (Costello, Egger, & Angold, 2005; van Steensel & Bogels, 2011; White & Roberson-Nay, 2009).

- Anxiety can impact all areas of life, from school attendance to developing friendships to independent living to employment.

- Individuals with ASD often have difficulty understanding the social rules, knowing which topics are appropriate to talk about and asking for help.

- An approach to teaching social and emotional information to students on the autism spectrum is to teach self-management, the ability to regulate one's behavior, including monitoring.

- An approach to teaching social and emotional information to students on the autism spectrum is to use visual supports. Visual supports are visually presented tools that support increased understanding for a student.

- Practice in real-life situations is a strategy for teaching social and emotional information to students on the autism spectrum. This includes practicing newly acquired emotional regulation skills in a variety of natural settings and across environments. This is critical as individuals with ASD often have difficulty maintaining and generalizing skills to new contexts (Dawson & Osterling, 1997).

- Adults with ASD have reported using thoughts about their special interest as a way of reducing social anxiety and increasing the ability to remain calm during social frustration.

- Students who lack friends tend to lack opportunities for laughter and, therefore, can benefit from strategies specifically designed to elicit laughter.

- Creative ways of bringing humor and laughter into the classroom include video modeling, comedy improv games, cartoons, and jokes (Getlen, 2006).

- The Incredible 5-Point Scale is a strategy for teaching students with ASD about emotions. Buron and Curtis (2012) created the Incredible 5-Point Scale to help individuals with ASD understand social and emotional concepts as well as to enhance their self-understanding. The 1-5 scale system is applicable to a variety of social and self-regulation behaviors and responses to those behaviors, including feelings of anxiety, concepts of personal space, and feelings of anger. Children and youth with ASD are taught to recognize the stages of their emotions or social challenges and methods to self-calm or "rethink" at each level.

- Modeling is a strategy for teaching students with ASD about emotions. Modeling involves learning skills either in real time or through video observations.

- Social narratives are a strategy for teaching students with ASD about emotions. Some social narratives are designed to be used prior to a situation to facilitate social success (i.e., cartooning, Power Cards, social scripts, Social Stories™). Specifically, they provide information about what may occur/what to expect, how others might think about what is happening, when something may occur, what the learner can do in a given situation, and what the learner should try not to do in a given situation. Others, such as SOCCSS and social autopsies, occur after an event to help the learner understand a previous interaction to support future success.

- Social narratives also emphasize problem-solving skills, brainstorming, and generalization.

- Mataya and Owens' problem-solving paradigm (Mataya & Owens, 2013) is designed to help learners understand cause and effect, problem solving, and decision-making.

Chapter Review Questions

1. Explain the relationship between anxiety and ASD. What is the prevalence of anxiety disorders among individuals with ASD? Which experiences are likely more anxiety provoking for individuals with ASD than for their neurotypical peers?

2. List and explain the possible causes of the challenges in emotional regulation experienced by individuals with ASD Level 1.

3. List and describe three important approaches to teaching social and emotional information to students on the autism spectrum.

4. Explain the statement "ASD is a whole-brain condition." What areas of the brain have been identified as different from typical in individuals with ASD?

5. Describe the importance of special interests and humor to helping students with ASD to build relationships.

6. Name and describe at least three strategies for teaching students with ASD about emotions.

References

Angell, M. E., Nicholson, J. K., Watts, E. H., & Blum, C. (2011). Using a multicomponent adapted power card strategy to decrease latency during interactivity transitions for three children with developmental disabilities. *Focus on Autism and Other Developmental Disabilities, 26*, 206-217.

Aspy, R., & Grossman, B. G. (2011). *The Ziggurat model: A framework for designing comprehensive interventions for individuals with high-functioning autism and Asperger Syndrome* (Release 2.0). Shawnee Mission, KS: AAPC Publishing.

Bachevalier, J., & Loveland, K. A. (2006). The orbitofrontal-amygdala circuit and self-regulation of social-emotional behavior in autism. *Neuroscience and Biobehavioral Reviews, 30*, 97-117.

Balfe, M., & Tantam, D. (2010). A descriptive social and health profile of a community sample of adults and adolescents with Asperger syndrome. *BMC Research Notes, 3*, 300-307.

Bandura, A. (1977). *Social learning theory.* Englewood Cliffs, NJ: Prentice Hall.

Barnhill, G. P. (2007). Outcomes in adults with Asperger syndrome. *Focus on Autism and Other Developmental Disabilities, 22*, 116-126.

Barrett, L. F., Gross, J., Conner, T., & Benvenuto, M. (2001). Emotion differentiation and regulation. *Cognition and Emotion, 15*, 713-724.

Bellini, S. (2007). *Building social relationships: A systematic approach to teaching social interaction skills to children and adolescents with autism spectrum disorders and other social difficulties.* Shawnee Mission, KS: AAPC Publishing.

Bellini, S., & Akullian, J. (2007). A meta-analysis of video modeling and video self-modeling interventions for children and adolescents with autism spectrum disorders. *Exceptional Children, 73*, 264-287.

Berthoz, S., & Hill, E. L. (2004). The validity of using self-reports to assess emotion regulation abilities. *European Psychiatry, 20*, 291-298.

Bieber, J. (1994) *Learning disabilities and social skills with Richard LaVoie: Last one picked ... first one picked on.* Washington, DC: Public Broadcasting Service.

Bock, M. A. (2001). SODA strategy: Enhancing the social interaction skills of youngsters with Asperger Syndrome. *Intervention in School and Clinic, 36*, 272-278.

Bock, M. A. (2002, April 30). *The impact of social behavioral learning strategy training on the social interaction skills of eight students with Asperger Syndrome.* Presentation at YAI National Institute for People With Disabilities 23rd International Conference on MR/DD, New York, NY.

Botting, N., Faragher, B., Knox, E., Simkin, Z., & Conti-Ramsden, G. (2001). Predicting path ways of SLI: What differentiates the best and the worst outcomes. *Journal of Child Psychology and Psychiatry, 42*(8), 1013-1020.

Buggey, T. (2009). Seeing is believing: *Video self-modeling for people with autism and other developmental disabilities.* Bethesda, MD: Woodbine House.

Burgess, A., & Gutstein, S. (2007). Quality of life for people with autism: Raising the standard for evaluating successful outcomes. *Child and Adolescent Mental Health, 12*(2), 80-86.

Buron, K., & Curtis, M. B. (2012). *The Incredible 5-Point Scale: The significantly improved and expanded second edition: Assisting students in understanding social interactions and controlling their emotional responses.* Shawnee Mission, KS: AAPC Publishing.

Campbell, A., & Tincani, M. (2011). The Power Card strategy: Strength-based intervention to increase direction following of children with autism spectrum disorder. *Journal of Positive Behavior Interventions,* 13(4), 240-249.

Cederlund, M., Hagberg, B., & Gillberg, C. (2010). Asperger syndrome in adolescent and young adult males: Interview and self- and parent assessment of social, emotional, and cognitive problems. *Research in Developmental Disabilities, 31,* 287-298.

Centers for Medicare and Medicaid Services. (2010). *Autism spectrum disorders services: Final report on environmental scan.* Retrieved from http://www.impaqint.com/files/4-content/1-6-publications/1-6-2-project-reports/finalasdreport.pdf

Chan, J. M., O'Reilly, M. F., Lang, R. B., Boutot, A. E., White, P. J., Pierce, N., & Baker, S. (2011). Evaluation of Social Stories™ intervention implemented by pre-service teachers for students with autism in general education settings. *Research in Autism Spectrum Disorders, 5,* 715-721.

Cheng, Y., Chiang, H., & Cheng, L. (2010). Enhancing empathy instruction using a collaborative virtual learning environment for children with autism spectrum conditions. *Computer and Education, 55,* 1449-1458.

Chong, I. M., & Carr, J. E. (2005). An investigation of the potentially adverse effects of task interspersal. *Behavioral Interventions, 20*(4), 285-300.

Conger, J., & Galambos, N. (1997). *Adolescents and youth: Psychological development in a changing world* (5th ed.). New York, NY: Longman.

Costello, E. J., Egger, H. L., & Angold, A. (2005). The developmental epidemiology of anxiety disorders: Phenomenology, prevalence, and comorbidity. *Child and Adolescent Psychiatric Clinics of North America, 14,* 631-648.

Davidson, R., & The Mind and Life Education Research Network. (2012). Contemplative practices and mental training: Prospects for American education. *Child Development Perspectives, 6*(2), 146-153.

Davis, K. M., Boon, R. T., Cihak, D. F., & Fore, C. (2010). Power cards to improve conversation skills in adolescents with Asperger Syndrome. *Focus on Autism and Developmental Disorders, 25,* 12-22.

Dawson, G., & Osterling, J. (1997). Early intervention in autism. In M. J. Guralnick (Ed.), *The effectiveness of early intervention* (pp. 307-326). Baltimore, MD: Brookes Publishing.

Dawson, G., Jones, E.J.H., Merkle, K., Venema, K., Lowy, R., Faja, S., et al. ... Webb, S. J. (2012). Early behavioral intervention is associated with normalized brain activity in young children with autism. *Journal of the American Academy of Child and Adolescent Psychiatry, 51,* 1150-1159.

Ellery, J. (2007). Integrating salutogenesis into wellness in every stage of life. *Preventing Chronic Disease, 4*(3), 79.

Endow, J. (2012). *Learning the hidden curriculum: The odyssey of one autistic adult.* Shawnee Mission, KS: AAPC Publishing.

Ferrer-Chancy, M., & Fugate, A. (2002). *The importance of friendship for school-aged children.* Tallahassee, FL: University of Florida, Dept. of Family, Youth and Community Sciences Report.

Franke, L., & Durbin, C. (2011). *Nurturing narratives: Story-based language intervention for children with language impairments that are complicated by other developmental disabilities such as autism spectrum disorders.* Shawnee Mission, KS: AAPC Publishing.

Gagnon, E. (2001). *The Power Card strategy: Using special interests to motivate children and youth with Asperger Syndrome and autism.* Shawnee Mission, KS: AAPC Publishing.

Ganz, J. B., Kaylor, M., Bourgeois, B., & Hadden, K. (2008). The impact of social scripts and visual cues on verbal communication in three children with autism spectrum disorders. *Focus on Autism and Other Developmental Disabilities, 23,* 79-94.

Getlen, L. (2006). *The complete idiot's guide to jokes.* New York, NY: Penguin Books, Inc.

Ghaziuddin, M. (2005). A family history study of Asperger syndrome. *Journal of Autism and Developmental Disorders, 35,* 177-182.

Ghaziuddin, M., Ghaziuddin, M., & Greden, J. (2002). Depression in persons with autism: Implications for research and clinical care. *Journal of Autism and Developmental Disorders, 32,* 299-305.

Ghaziuddin, M., Weidmer-Mikhail, E., & Ghaziuddin, N. (1998). Comorbidity of Asperger syndrome: a preliminary report. *Journal of Disability Research. 42,* 279-283.

Goldberg, L. (2004). Creative relaxation: A yoga-based program for regular and exceptional student education. *International Journal of Yoga Therapy, 14,* 68-78.

Goleman, D. (2011). *The brain and emotional intelligence: New insights.* Northampton, MA: More Than Sound LLC.

Grandin, T., & Panek, R. (2013). *The autistic brain: Thinking across the spectrum.* Boston, MA: Houghton Mifflin Harcourt.

Gray, C. (1995). *Social Stories™ unlimited: Social stories and comic strip conversations.* Jenison, MI: Jenison Public Schools.

Gray, C. A., & Garand, J. D. (1993). Social stories: Improving responses of students with autism with accurate social information. *Focus on Autistic Behavior, 8,* 1-10.

Groden, J., & LeVasseur, P. (1995). *Cognitive picture rehearsal: A system to teach self-control.* In K. Quill (Ed.), *Teaching children with autism: Strategies to enhance communication and socialization* (pp. 287-305). Albany, NY: Delmar Publishing, Inc.

Groen, W., Teluj, M., Buitelaar, J., & Tendolkar, I. (2010). Amygdala and hippocampus enlargement during adolescence in autism. *Journal of the American Academy of Children and Adolescent Psychiatry, 49,* 552-560.

Hurlbutt, K., & Chalmers, L. (2004). Employment and adults with Asperger syndrome. *Focus on Autism and Developmental Disabilities, 19,* 215-222.

Jobe, L. E., & White, S. W. (2007). Loneliness, social relationships, and a broader autism phenotype in college students. *Personality and Individual Differences, 42,* 1479-1489.

Jones, M. (2008). *Animal agentz.* Liverpool, UK: Animal Agentz.

Kanne, S. M., & Mazurek, M. O. (2011). Aggression in children and adolescents with ASD: Prevalence and risk factors. *Journal of Autism and Developmental Disorders, 41,* 926-937.

Keeling, K., Myles, B. S., Gagnon, E., & Simpson, R. L. (2003). Using the Power Card strategy to teach sportsmanship skills to a child with autism. *Focus on Autism and Other Developmental Disabilities, 18*(2), 105-111.

Kerr, S., & Durkin, K. (2004). Understanding of thought bubbles as mental representations in children with autism: Implications for theory of mind. *Journal of Autism and Developmental Disorders, 34*, 637-648.

Koenig, K. P., Buckley-Reen, A., & Garg, S. E. (2012). Efficacy of the Get Read to Learn Yoga program among children with autism spectrum disorders: A pretest-posttest control group design. *American Journal of Occupational Therapy, 66*, 538-546.

Koenig, K., De Los Reyes, A., Cicchetti, D., Scahill, L., & Klin, A. (2009). Group intervention to promote social skills in school-age children with pervasive developmental: Reconsidering disorder efficacy. *Journal of Autism and Developmental Disorders, 39*, 1163-1172.

Kokina, A., & Kern, L. (2010). Social Story™ interventions for students with autism spectrum disorders: A meta-analysis. *Journal of Autism and Developmental Disorders, 40*, 812-826.

Laurent, A. C., & Rubin, E. (2004). Challenges in emotional regulation in Asperger syndrome and high-functioning autism. *Topics in Language Disorders, 24*, 286-297.

Loomis, J. W. (2008). *Staying in the game: Providing social opportunities for children and adolescents with autism spectrum disorders and other developmental disabilities.* Shawnee Mission, KS: AAPC Publishing.

Lugnegard, T., Hallerback, M. U., & Gillberg, C. (2011). Psychiatric comorbidity in young adults with a clinical diagnosis of Asperger syndrome. *Research in Developmental Disabilities, 32*, 1910-1917.

Lyle, S. (2000). Narrative understanding: Developing a theoretical context for understanding how children make meaning in classroom settings. *Journal of Curriculum Studies, 1*(2), 45-63.

Martin, R. (2010). *The psychology of humor: An integrative approach.* New York, NY: Academic Press.

Mat, S. J., Zhang, D., & Pacha, J. (2012). Employability skills valued by employers as important for entry-level employees with and without disabilities. *Career Development and Transition for Exceptional Individuals, 35*, 29-38.

Mataya, K., & Owens, P. (2013). *Successful problem solving for high functioning students with autism spectrum disorders.* Shawnee Mission, KS: AAPC Publishing.

Matson, J. L., & Nebel-Schwalm, M. S. (2007). Comorbid psychopathology with autism spectrum disorder in children: An overview. *Research in Developmental Disabilities, 28*, 341–352.

McCoy, K., & Hermansen, E. (2007). Video modeling for individuals with autism: A review of model type and effects. *Education and Treatment of Children, 30*, 183-213.

Minshew, N. J., & Keller, T. A. (2010). The nature of brain dysfunction in autism: Functional brain imaging studies. *Current Opinion in Neurology, 23*(2), 124-130.

Montgomery, J. M., Stoesz, B. M., & McCrimmon, A. W. (2013). Emotional intelligence, theory of mind, and executive functions as predictors of social outcomes in young adults with Asperger syndrome. *Focus on Autism and Other Developmental Disabilities, 28*, 4-13.

Myles, B. S., Endow, J., & Mayfield, M. (2013). *The hidden curriculum of getting and keeping a job: Navigating the social landscape of employment.* Shawnee Mission, KS: AAPC Publishing.

Myles, B. S., Keeling, K., & Van Horn, C. (2001). Studies using the Power Card strategy. In E. Gagnon (Ed.), *The Power Card strategy: Using special interests to motivate children and youth with Asperger Syndrome and autism* (pp. 51-57). Shawnee Mission, KS: AAPC Publishing.

Myles, H. M., & Kolar, A. (2013). *The hidden curriculum and other everyday challenges for elementary-age children with high-functioning autism.* Shawnee Mission, KS: AAPC Publishing.

Myles, B. S., Trautman, M. L., & Schelvan, R. L. (2013). *The hidden curriculum: Practical solutions for understanding unstated rules in social situations* (2nd ed.). Shawnee Mission, KS: AAPC Publishing.

The National Autism Center. (2009). *Evidence-based practice and autism in the schools: A guide to providing appropriate interventions to students with autism spectrum disorders.* Retrieved from http://www.nationalautismcenter.org/pdf/NAC%20Ed%20Manual_FINAL.pdf

The National Professional Development Center on Autism Spectrum Disorders. (2010). *Evidence-based practice briefs.* Retrieved from http://autismpdc.fpg.unc.edu/

Palmer, B., Donaldson, C., & Stough, C. (2002). Emotional intelligence and life satisfaction. *Personality and Individual Differences, 33,* 1091-1100.

Pelphrey, K. A., Shultz, S., Hudac, C. M., & Vander Wyk, B. C. (2011). Research review: Constraining heterogeneity: The social brain and its development in autism spectrum disorder. *Journal of Child Psychology and Psychiatry, 52,* 631-644.

Pierson, M. R., & Glaeser, B. C. (2005). Extension of research on social skills training using comic strip conversations to students without autism. *Education and Training in Developmental Disabilities, 40,* 279-284.

Pierson, M. R., & Glaeser, B. C. (2007). Using comic strip conversations to increase social satisfaction and decrease loneliness in students with autism spectrum disorder. *Education and Training in Developmental Disabilities, 42,* 460-466.

Provine, R. R., & Fischer, K. R. (1989). Laughing, smiling, and talking: Relation to sleeping and social context in humans. *Ethology, 83,* 295-305.

Quek, L., Sofronoff, K., Sheffield, J., White, A., & Kelly, A. (2012). Co-occurring anger in young people with Asperger's syndrome. *Journal of Clinical Psychology, 68,* 1142-1148.

Renzaglia, A., Karvonen, M., Drasgow, E., & Stoxen, C. C. (2003). Promoting a lifetime of inclusion. *Focus on Autism and Other Developmental Disabilities, 18,* 140-149.

Rogers, M. F., & Myles, B. S. (2001). Using social stories and comic strip conversations to interpret social situations for an adolescent with Asperger Syndrome. *Intervention in School and Clinic, 36,* 310-313.

Roosa, J. B. (1995). *Men on the move: Competence and cooperation: Conflict resolution and beyond.* Kansas City, MO: Author.

Rosenblatt, L., Gorantia, S., Torres, J. A., Yamush, R. S., Rao, S., Park, E. R., et al., Levine, J. B. (2011). Relaxation response-based yoga improves functioning in young children with autism: A pilot study. *The Journal of Alternative and Complementary Medicine, 17,* 1029-1035.

Roy, M., Dillo, W., Emrich, H. M., & Ohlmeier, M. D. (2009). Asperger's syndrome in adulthood. *Deutsches Artzeblatt International, 105,* 59-64.

Saklofske, D. H., Austin, E. J., & Minski, P. S. (2003). Selfreported emotional intelligence: Factor structure and evidence for construct validity. *Personality and Individual Differences, 34*, 1091-1100.

Samson, A. C., Huber, O., & Gross, J. J. (2012). Emotion regulation in Asperger's syndrome and high-functioning autism. *Emotion, 12*, 659-665.

Serwacki, M. L., & Cook-Cottone, C. (2013). Yoga in the schools: A systematic review of the literature. *International Journal of Yoga Therapy*, 101-109.

Silvers, J., Buhle, J., & Ochsner, K. (2013). The neuroscience of emotion regulation: Basic mechanisms and their role in development, aging and psychopathology. In K. Ochsner & S. Kosslyn (Eds.), *The Oxford handbook of cognitive neuroscience* (Vol. 1). New York, NY: Oxford University Press.

Stahmer, A. C., Suhrheinrich, A., Reed, S., Bolduc, C., & Schreibman, L. (2010). Pivotal response teaching in the classroom setting. *Preventing School Failure: Alternative Education for Children and Youth, 54*, 265-274.

Tantam, D. (2000). Psychological disorder in adolescents and adults with Asperger syndrome. *Autism, 4*, 47-62.

Tantam, D., & Prestwood, S. (1999). *A mind of one's own.* London, UK: National Autistic Society.

Test, D. W., Richter, S., Knight, V., & Spooner, F. (2010). A comprehensive review and meta-analysis of the Social Stories™ literature. *Focus on Autism and Other Developmental Disabilities, 26*, 49-62.

University of Cambridge. (2003). *Mind reading.* Cambridge, UK: Author.

van Steensel, F.J.A., & Bogels, S. M. (2011). Anxiety disorders in children and adolescents with autistic spectrum disorders: A meta-analysis. *Clinical Child and Family Psychology Review, 14*, 302-317.

White, S. W., & Roberson-Nay, R. (2009). Anxiety, social deficits, and loneliness in youth with autism spectrum disorders. *Journal of Autism and Developmental Disorders, 39*, 1006-1013.

Wichnick, A. M., Vener, S. M., Keating, C., & Poulson, C. L. (2009). The effect of a script-fading procedure on unscripted social initiations and novel utterances among young children with autism. *Research in Autism Spectrum Disorders, 4*, 51-64.

Zielinski, B. A., Anderson, J. S., Froehlich, A. L., Prigge, M. B. D., Nielsen, J. A. et al., ... Lainhart, E. (2012). scMRI reveals large scale brain network abnormalities. *PLoS ONE, 7*(11), e49172. doi:10.1371/journal.pone.0049172

Learner Objectives

After reading this chapter, the learner should be able to:

- Define what is meant by "structure" in teaching

- Explain what TEACCH is

- Explain "Structured TEACCHing," including theoretical foundations, as well as implications for students with ASD and their families

- Explain what is meant by the "Culture of Autism" and provide examples of characteristics

- List the five questions that Structured TEACCHing should answer by providing the learner with visual information and organization of the environment

- Discuss the importance of spaces, schedules, task organization, activity systems, and routines in the instruction of individuals with ASD

- Provide examples of strategies to address the five questions of Structured TEACCHing

- Describe and discuss the cases presented in the text in which Structured TEACCHing strategies are used to teach individuals at different ages

Chapter 11

Structured Teaching and Environmental Supports

Gary B. Mesibov • Victoria Shea

Anthony is a 5-year-old boy with autism who is in a special education class in his local public school. This is his first year at this school. Since the age of 3, Anthony has received special education services at a child development center, where his classmates have been children with Down syndrome, physical disabilities, hearing or vision loss, or speech/ language delay.

Anthony is usually fussing when he is brought into the classroom. In fact, he is often carried into the room, crying loudly, by the assistant who meets him at the bus. He always goes immediately to the block corner, where he removes his coat and drops it on the floor. He apparently would prefer to spend the morning alone in the block corner, and he generally does not respond to his teachers' attempts to play with him or encourage him to go to a different play area. If he is physically removed from the block area, he has a tantrum. When he needs to use the bathroom (which is attached to the classroom), he generally pulls his pants down on his way across the room, and he comes out without flushing and with his pants unzipped.

Anthony willingly comes to circle time only on the days when musical instruments are passed around, but when these circle times are over, he has a tantrum when a teacher takes the instrument away. On other days, he is physically brought to circle time, but he typically gets up after a few minutes and runs back to the block corner. His two favorite activities are building tall towers and then knocking them down, and lying on his stomach watching out of the corner of his eye as he rolls a car back and forth. The teachers have found that the easiest way to interrupt him without causing a tantrum is to offer him a snack. He comes to the teacher, takes the snack, and then walks around the room eating it. Sometimes he comes to the snack table and takes food, even if it is on another child's plate. Similarly, when the other children are seated at their tables working on craft projects, he sometimes walks by and picks up some of the materials, then walks or runs around the room flapping them.

At the end of the day, Anthony does not respond when the teachers tell the children it is time to get their coats and go home, and he must often be pulled screaming from the block corner, down the hallway to the waiting school bus.

In this vignette, Anthony is not learning new skills, he is unhappy or frustrated for significant parts of the school day, and his teachers are probably also frustrated by their inability to engage or teach him. We believe that structured teaching and environmental supports based on the TEACCH model make a significant contribution to Anthony's educational plan.

In this chapter, we will explain the principles and techniques of Structured TEACCHing, and then present vignettes demonstrating its application with students of various ages and skill levels.

What Is Structure?

Most modern special education professionals indicate that structure is an important element of effective teaching, but it is not always clear what is meant by "structure" or whether the term means the same thing to all those who use it.

We describe structure for students with autism spectrum disorder (ASD) as meaning that the teacher or other caregiver decides *what* the learning activities will be, *where* they take place, and *how long* they last. These decisions should be made based on the individual student's needs (not, for example, on the basis of convenience or the student's or teacher's preferences). The purpose of structure is to organize time and space in the learning environment. Individuals with ASD tend to be disorganized or otherwise ineffective in their approach to many materials and activities, so they need external organizational support (that is, structure) in order to be meaningfully engaged in learning.

What Is Structured TEACCHing?

Structured TEACCHing is the name of the instructional strategies and environmental supports for individuals with ASD developed by the **TEACCH** Autism Program. TEACCH is the statewide autism service program in North Carolina. TEACCH, which is administratively housed in the School of Medicine at the University of North Carolina-Chapel Hill, has seven regional centers across the state that provide diagnostic evaluations, parent education, and other clinical services in addition to in-state, national, and international teacher training and consultation.

Structured TEACCHing as used within the TEACCH program has two different, equally important goals: (a) teach the individual with ASD as many skills as possible, given his developmental level; and (b) provide an environment that is as comprehensible as possible, so that the learner can understand the expectations and opportunities around him. In other words, this approach is both an educational technique and a method of organizing a supportive environment.

Structured TEACCHing can be used in all settings, including homes, schools, work sites, specialized therapy sessions, recreational activities, community errands, and so on. It can also be adapted for use with individuals with ASD of all ages and developmental levels. However, for the purposes of this chapter, we will focus on students in school from preschool to high school graduation.

Theoretical Foundations

Structured TEACCHing is a social-cognitive-behavioral approach applied to the neuropsychological characteristics of ASD. "Behavioral" indicates that the approach deals with observable behaviors and that the learning environment systematically incorporates meaningful, pleasurable consequences for productive learning and acceptable behavior. "Social-cognitive" reflects the additional importance we place on increasing the individual's understanding of his world, a broad concept that includes explaining and teaching social behaviors and interactions and broadening the individual's cognitive ideas and beliefs about the world.

We also emphasize organization of the environment and the ways activities are presented (also called antecedents to behavior) because of the distinctive ways that people with ASD think about, understand (or often, misunderstand), and then act on their environments. By including a focus on the social-cognitive perspective of the learner, Structured TEACCHing can prevent some of the misunderstanding and disorganization often demonstrated by students with ASD in typical special education and general education settings.

Structured TEACCHing and the Culture of Autism

We call the characteristic patterns of thinking and behavior of ASD the "**Culture of Autism**" (Mesibov, Shea, & Schopler, 2005). Although autism is not a culture in the traditional sense, we have found it helpful to use this metaphor to depict the shared neuropsychological patterns of thinking, communication, and behavior seen among individuals with ASD. Even though each student with ASD is a unique individual with unique skills, difficulties, interests, temperament, and personality, as a group they share a significant number of characteristics.

Table 11.1
Characteristics of the Culture of Autism

- Relative strength in and preference for processing *visual* information (compared to difficulties with auditory processing, particularly of language)
- Heightened attention to *details* but difficulty understanding the meaning of how these details fit together (sometimes called a deficit in central coherence; Frith, 2003)
- Difficulty with *combining or integrating* ideas
- Difficulty with *sequencing and organizing* ideas, materials, and activities
- Difficulties with *attention* (some individuals are very distractible, others have difficulty shifting attention efficiently)
- *Communication* problems; these vary by developmental level, but generally include impairments in the social use of language (pragmatics) and correct word usage (semantics), the understanding and use of nonverbal communication, relative difficulty with abstract or nuanced language, and for individuals with intellectual disability, delayed development of vocabulary and grammar
- Difficulty with concepts of *time*, including moving too quickly or too slowly and having problems recognizing the beginning, middle, or end of an activity
- Tendency to become *attached to routines*, so that activities may be difficult to transfer or generalize from the original learning situation, and disruptions in routines can be upsetting, confusing, or uncomfortable
- Very strong *interests and impulses* to engage in favored activities
- Marked *sensory* preferences and aversions (see Chapter 6)

The characteristics in Table 11.1 are not unique to ASD, as they overlap both with other developmental disabilities, such as intellectual disability, language disorders, and attention deficit/hyperactivity disorder, and with some mental health conditions, particularly anxiety disorders. It is the combination, severity, and pervasiveness of the characteristics of the Culture of Autism that distinguish ASD from other conditions. However, many individuals with ASD also have other, co-existing developmental disabilities or mental health problems (see Chapter 2).

The unique combination of these factors in each person means that there is no universal pattern of learning characteristics in ASD. As a result, there is no standardized curriculum that is appropriate, so the educational plan must be individualized for each student. Further, plans must be revised frequently based on learning and maturation, as well as additional observations and insights about how the student learns and think. Consequently, techniques that were effective when the student was in preschool may not be useful or necessary by first grade, much less in middle school or high school. Similarly, strategies that worked with last year's student with ASD will probably not be as effective with a different student this year.

Structured Teaching and Behavior Management

Traditional behavior management techniques may have limited effectiveness with individuals with ASD (Bregman, Zager, & Gerdtz, 2005; Schreibman & Ingersoll, 2005). Examples of traditional techniques include:

- Using tangible reward systems for good behavior (e.g., the student earns tokens for good behavior and can use the tokens for a toy or a treat at the end of the day or at the end of the week)

- Using response-cost systems in which students lose privileges or treats because of their behavior (e.g., because of misbehavior, a student is not permitted to go on a field trip or use the computer during free time)

- Praising students and expressing pride in their accomplishments and effort

- Having students observe and imitate the behavior of other students who are being praised

- Sending students to a time-out chair away from the group

The following factors frequently interfere with the effectiveness of these techniques with students with ASD:

- Reward and response-cost systems are often too language-based or too complex for students with ASD, requiring making cognitive connections among a large number of details (behaviors, rules, points or tokens, various prizes, etc.).

- Verbal praise may be meaningless or incomprehensible.

- Some individuals with ASD do not attend to, understand, or imitate the behavior of their peers.

- Time away from group activities may be desirable rather than punitive.

In thinking about how to teach and support appropriate behavior, Structured TEACCHing should be pragmatic. If a traditional technique might work, try it; if it works, use it; if something is not working, stop doing it and do something else. There is no hard and fast rule against using traditional behavior management techniques, particularly positive techniques, such as social praise and rewards. Many students with ASD can process some verbal information (particularly when not under stress), so they *may* be able to understand, enjoy, and respond to reward systems (although these are rarely sufficient to control their behavior in situations of sensory overload or intense impulses); *some* students may seek or respond to praise; and they *may* imitate another student occasionally. As a general rule, however, reward and response-cost systems are not as effective for students with ASD as they are for other students, and as a result they can be very frustrating for both students and teachers.

In particular, systems involving loss of privileges or treats are generally too abstract for students with ASD Level 2 or 3, but they may occasionally be helpful for students with ASD Level 1. An example of such a system for reducing undesirable behaviors is having a student start the day with five visual symbols. Each times she engages in the undesirable behaviors, she loses one symbol, but if she has any symbols remaining at the end of the day, she is given a treat.

Structured TEACCHing and Families

The other factor that is integral to the TEACCH Structured TEACCHing approach is respect for families. In the not-too-distant past, parents were considered to be the cause of their child's autism, but the TEACCH program was founded on the principle that parents and professionals can work together collaboratively, with parents learning to be co-therapists for their children (Schopler & Reichler, 1971).

We recommend that teachers and other school professionals communicate regularly with families and value their perspectives. As illustrated in Table 11.2, a notebook that travels with the student between home and school, with both a template of information to exchange (individualized according to the student's particular needs and challenges) and space for additional notes can be both useful and practical. The template may be completed with check marks or a few words, which is important given the time demands on both teachers and parents.

Table 11.2
Sample Home-School Communication Systems

Preschool Day_____ *(date)*

	Yes/No
Entered classroom happily?	
Ate breakfast?	
Used toilet/morning?	
Ate lunch?	
Slept at naptime?	
Used toilet/afternoon?	
Played with new toy?	
Number of crying episodes (tally marks)	

Notes:

School Day_____ *(date)*

	Yes/No
Good behavior on bus?	
Turned in homework?	
Did not argue with teacher?	
Played with others during recess?	
Raised hand before speaking during group times?	

Notes:

Home Life_____ *(date)*

	Yes/No
Any special family events last night?	
Slept typical time?	
Ate breakfast?	
Took medicine?	
Questions or problems?	

Notes:

Putting Principles Into Practice

Structured TEACCHing should provide visual information and physical organization of the environment to answer five questions for the learner:

1. Where should I be?

2. What work or activity will I do?

3. How much work will I do?/How long will the activity last?

4. How will I know that I am making progress and when I have finished?

5. What will I do next?

We have found it useful and important to answer these five questions in some form for all new learning situations. That is, Structured TEACCHing typically designs an individualized way to provide this information for all new tasks, including those focused on cognitive, language, academic, and motor skills; social engagement; and activities of daily living (such as using the school cafeteria, bathrooms, playground, and transportation system for going to and from school).

In addition, providing answers to these five questions is useful during any activity in which the individual indicates, through words or behavior, that he is confused or having difficulty staying organized or focused on the activity. Indications that a student needs the answers to the five questions to be more visually clear include:

- The student wanders or runs around the room during the activity.

- The student asks repetitive questions during the activity.

- The student often refuses to start or end the activity.

- The student often leaves an activity before completing it.

- The student often has tantrums during an activity.

In such situations, we typically try to make the structure (that is, the answers to the five questions) more clear, in addition to ensuring that the activity is within the student's ability level. Although there may be additional factors that contribute to the problematic behaviors, increasing the visual structure is almost always an important aspect of getting the student back on track.

Answering the first question, "Where should I be?" is accomplished through the use of *schedules*. In addition, because each activity takes place in a consistent and, therefore, predictable location, a student learns the association between where he is going and generally what he will do there (such as one-on-one work with a teacher, P.E., lunch, etc.), which provides some information to answer the second question, "What work or activity will I do?" Additional information is provided visually by the *task* and the *work/activity system* (for multiple tasks), which shows the student specifically what he is being asked to do once he arrives at the designated location and how many times he is going to do it (Questions 3 and 4 – "How much work will I do?" or "How long will this activity last?" and "How will I know that I have finished?"). The final question, "What will I do next?" is typically answered by indicating visually what will follow the last item on the task or work/activity system and by teaching the student *routines* (which serve other purposes as well). These elements of answering the five questions are discussed in more detail in the next section.

Schedules

A schedule of activities is a fundamental element of Structured TEACCHing. The student's day should be a series of planned activities in designated locations (typically with a few minutes in a safe play/leisure area between activities). Further, each student's schedule should be individualized in terms of both content and form so it is meaningful for the student. Rarely do two or more students have identical learning styles, communication systems, attention spans, and interests, and therefore their schedules should reflect their individuality. If all students in a class are using the same schedule, it is highly likely that their schedules are not sufficiently individualized.

Schedules should be visual, and they should be accurate. Since life is not always predictable, however, predetermined schedules must be in a form that can be changed quickly as circumstances change, so that updating is quick and easy. This means that it is not efficient to print and laminate schedules. Students may be shown, as needed, that parts of the schedule are either being crossed off or removed, or that other activities are being substituted or inserted.

For the developmentally youngest learners, schedules can take the form of objects indicating "what's next." At the simplest level, the teacher hands the student an object that will be used in the upcoming activity. There

is no symbolism involved, and the student is not required to "check his schedule." Instead, the schedule is brought to him, and he is guided toward the corresponding activity. Examples include giving the student

- A puzzle piece to get him to go to his work table, where the rest of the puzzle is waiting, along with one or more additional learning activities

- A cup that he will take to the snack table, where someone will pour a beverage into the cup

- A diaper or roll of toilet paper for use in the bathroom

- A spoon to take to the lunch table

- A carpet square to take to a group activity location

- Chalk or a bag of balls to take to the playground or gym

Although students must often be guided and assisted at first to go to the appropriate location with the object, the goal is to reduce that assistance as soon as possible, so that the student is as independent as possible in understanding where to go and what he is going to do there.

As students become more capable, we often move from the procedure of *handing them* the schedule object or picture to a procedure of *directing them to* their schedule. This skill represents increased independence on the student's part, and it enables the teacher to direct and supervise the transitions of several students at a time. Even students who use object schedules can learn to go to the location where objects are located (e.g., in a container on top of a small bookcase, or in a small row of cubbies mounted on a wall).

Learners who are somewhat more advanced developmentally can often find meaning in pictures, photographs, or symbols instead of needing concrete objects. The process of learning the association between a symbol and an activity is similar to learning the meaning of objects – that is, by repeatedly experiencing that the schedule symbol predicts the activity, many students learn the association. At all ages there are some students who can associate meaning with written words; for these students, typically, a written schedule may be used.

In addition to the individualized form of the schedule, the amount of information the schedule provides varies according to the student's ability to understand. Some students understand only "what's next," and if they see additional objects or symbols about later activities, they become confused. Other students appear to understand and make use of a series of objects or symbols, indicating the upcoming 2-3 activities. As students continue to develop, they can often use part-day or full-day schedules without becoming confused or distressed. Some students also find weekly, monthly, or yearly calendars of upcoming events to be helpful for anticipating activities they enjoy (such as vacations, holidays, special events, etc.).

Tasks and Work/Activity Systems

Tasks and work/activity systems visually show the student, from the very beginning of the activity to the finish, what items he is being asked to complete and how he will see that he is making progress toward being finished. Each task provides this information about the materials and steps *within* the task; the work/activity system provides this information about the *process* of working on a task or a series of tasks.

One way to provide this information visually is to arrange the materials or directions to specify exactly how many or how much the student must do before being finished. When the activity itself does not involve a finite amount of materials, a different way to answer the question of how long an activity will last is to make the passage of time visual (see the Practical Strategies section in this chapter for examples).

Routines

Not all activities within a student's day require work/activity systems, which are primarily used for fostering independence and for situations in which the student would otherwise be confused or disorganized. Many students can master work/activity systems to the point that they become productive, independent routines, such as entering a classroom and depositing jacket and backpack/homework in the correct location, going to a designated area to wait or play quietly between learning activities, using the bathroom, asking for help with the work, indicating that the work has been finished, and so on.

Practical Strategies for Teachers

More specific techniques for providing visual structure and answering the five questions are presented in this section.

1. **Where Should I Be?**
   The most typical way to provide this information visually is to have a designated place for the learner to sit (such as a chair, carpet square, the student's colored symbol or name, etc.) or to stand (such as on the student's symbol or name, a mark on the floor, an outline of footprints, carpet square, etc.). At times, it is helpful to have students sit down even when other students typically stand (e.g., while waiting in line or while brushing teeth), because a chair provides additional boundaries and cues for indicating where the student is expected to be.

However, some students have difficulty remaining seated, preferring to pace or move throughout the room. For those students (particularly if they are younger or concrete learners), we might begin by defining a relatively large area to indicate where the student should be. To do this, we generally find it helpful to use various physical elements of the room, including pillars, walls, corners, large pieces of furniture, screens, and so on, both to define the student's space and to reduce distractions from other activity in the room.

While more developmentally advanced, abstract learners with ASD may learn the location of activities as quickly as their typical peers, they may still benefit from structure in the form of assigned seats, a daily schedule that includes the room number for each class, a map of the route between classes, and so on.

The basic principle is that if a student has difficulty locating or staying in the "right" place, the teacher uses visual means to show her where to be.

2. **What Work or Activity Will I Do?**

Specific ways to follow this general principle also vary depending on the student's developmental level, but the fundamental approach is to organize the materials and the activity in ways that let the student *see* what he is supposed to do and for how long. The emphasis here is on showing (visually) as opposed to telling (verbally). Thus, we recommend always supplementing spoken directions or explanations with visual or physical cues, such as gestures, pictures, concrete objects, written directions, and so on.

Structured TEACCHing makes a point of organizing materials for the student so that they are available in a logical order (typically from left to right and top to bottom) and are visually clear and physically stable. To do this, we use various office supplies to keep materials organized, such as:
- Baskets
- File folders
- Clear containers
- Velcro and tape
- Clips

We also work to highlight the most important parts of the visual or physical display of materials by techniques such as:
- Making the parts larger
- Highlighting them
- Putting a colored frame around them
- Eliminating clutter on the table or desk top

3. **How Much Work Will I Do?/How Long Will This Activity Last?**

and

4. **How Will I Know That I Have Finished?**

Usually, the materials involved in the learning activity are organized and counted out (or listed) in advance, so that by looking at the materials, the student can get information about both what he is going to do and for how long. For example, for concrete learners there are containers for each of the "raw materials" involved in the task and a container for the finished product. For academic learners, there might be a set of file folders with an assignment on the left and a pocket for the finished product on the right.

When activities do not involve materials that provide information about "how much" or "how many," various forms of visual timers are available, such as hourglasses that use sand or colored water and timers that count down from a specified time (such as 10 minutes). Teachers can also devise individualized ways to make time visual; for example, the teacher puts out a set of objects (such as clothes pins) or symbols (such as clock faces or plain circles) when an activity begins, then takes one away every 5 minutes (or every minute, every 10 minutes, etc.), so that the student can *see* how much time is left.

Examples of Task Organization That Answer These Questions

- **Example #1 (Task for young or concrete learner).** The student is given a transparent basket of small objects (so he can see *how many* there are) and a container with a hole on top. Each of the small objects is to be put into the container. The student can see (and feel) that the basket of materials is getting emptier. When all the objects are gone, the task is *finished*.

- **Example #2 (Task for an older, concrete learner).** The student has a clear container of index cards, a clear container of envelopes, and a clear container of mailing labels (so he can see *how many* there are). The task is to put an index card into an envelope, put a mailing label on the envelope, and then put the envelope into a basket. Again, the student can see that the container of materials is getting emptier, and that the "finished basket" is getting fuller. When the materials are empty, the task is *finished*.

- **Example #3 (P.E. task).** The student has a container of objects and an empty container. The task is to run, skate, skip, and so on, to a finish line with one object and put it in an empty container, which shows her *how many* laps she will do. This setup can also be used for exercises such as sit-ups or stretches (objects are at the beginning position; the empty container representing "finished" is at the position reached doing the exercise). The student sees and feels that the basket of objects is getting emptier. When all the objects are in the other container, the task is *finished*.

Examples of Work/Activity Systems That Answer These Questions

- **Example #4 (Series of tasks for an academic learner).** The student has a checklist (or homework assignment book) of reading tasks: Read pages 9-11; answer questions on p. 12; write a paragraph using all of the words on p. 13. The student can see *how many* items are on the list, and by checking off each item as he completes it (or as he begins it), he can see that he is making progress. When all the activities have been checked off and performed, the work session is *finished*.

- **Example #5 (Series of tasks for an older vocational learner).** The student has a list consisting of a series of pictures of materials used in a housekeeping task: pail, water faucet, bottle of cleaning liquid, sponge mop, two bathrooms, sink, and storage closet. The student has already learned the tasks associated with each picture, so this list shows him *how many* tasks to perform (get pail, fill with water, add cleaning liquid, use mop on those bathroom floors, empty pail, and put away materials). He pulls each picture off the list and puts it into a small envelope next to the schedule before completing the task. When the list of tasks is empty and all the pictures are in the envelope, the work session is *finished*.

5. What Will I Do Next?

For some students with ASD, it appears that simply achieving "finished" is a gratifying, positively reinforcing experience (which probably explains why being interrupted can be distressing). More typical, concrete reinforcement (such as something to eat or drink, computer time, music, or time to read or play with a favorite toy) can also be helpful for making clear to students that they have successfully completed a task.

Between learning activities, we usually recommend teaching a student to engage in a productive or harmless activity in a safe, designated place in the classroom, so that the teacher can work with other students or prepare for the next activity. Sometimes the student quickly learns where to go and what is available to do during these leisure times. In other situations, an object or symbol is put in the workspace at the physical end of the work materials or at the end of the work time to show the students what to do next. This may include:

- cassette or computer disk
- picture from a box of snacks
- card that says "When you have finished your work, choose a book and read until Mrs. Smith calls you over to check your work."

Application of Structured TEACCHing at Different Ages

Any educational content can be taught using Structured TEACCHing strategies and supports, ranging from toilet training of a preschool child, to learning to read in elementary school, to college preparatory or vocational classes in high school. Presented below are some examples.

Brett – A Preschool Child With ASD Level 2

Brett attends a preschool special education classroom with four other students. None of the other children has ASD, but the teachers have put physical and programmatic adaptations in place to accommodate Brett's need for Structured TEACCHing. Brett is very active and easily distracted.

Spaces. At the entrance to the classroom, Brett has a cubby with a hook to hang up his coat and backpack. The inside of the cubby is covered with purple construction paper, because that is his favorite color, and it may serve to highlight this area for him. The teachers also put a purple beanbag chair in the play area with some of Brett's favorite toys (dinosaurs). Also in the classroom is a small table with two chairs, where the teacher works individually with Brett. When it is his turn to work there, the teacher puts a purple tablecloth on the table. There is also a larger table with enough chairs for all the students and teachers. This is where the students eat their snack and lunch, and it is also where they have group activities, because being seated at the table is a familiar and organizing experiencethat the teachers have found works better for this particular group of students than sitting in a circle on the floor. Seats at this table are assigned, using colors, symbols, or names according to each student's understanding, but the assignments are periodically changed so the children don't become too attached to a particular seating arrangement. The other main area of importance for Brett's class is the bathroom. (Each child is at a different stage of toilet training. Brett is taken to the bathroom approximately 10 minutes before the most typical times when he wets his diapers.)

Schedule. During the first week of school, Brett spent most of his time either running around the perimeter of the classroom or tapping on all the windows in sequence until he was led to an activity. Although he was reported to understand a few words in context at home, at school he did not appear to understand any verbal directions. His teachers have started a "what's next" object schedule. They began by approaching him with a cup to be used at snack and lunch, and they have noticed that he already independently takes his cup to the seat with the purple cover at the snack table. He also shows an emerging understanding that a computer disk means that he can play on the computer, and that his backpack means it is time to go home. Several times, Brett has followed the teachers to the cabinet where they keep his objects, so next week they will begin putting each upcoming object on a purple tray on top of the bookcase and will lead Brett there to find his "schedule."

Task organization. During one-on-one work sessions with a teacher, Brett works on a single task at a time. Over the course of a day, he works on many different tasks (all "put-ins" or "take-aparts"), but each is presented to him on a purple tray, with one container for the materials to put in or take apart, and one container for the results of his work. Brett has quickly mastered the routines of pulling the tray toward him, working on the task, and then, when the container of materials is empty, putting the tray into a large "finished" basket on the floor beside his chair. He has no difficulty with the actual tasks, so the teachers will begin introducing a two-task work session with a work/activity system consisting of two purple trays that he will work on in sequence. The number and developmental complexity of the tasks will also be increased over time as Brett progresses. In addition, teachers will begin using a purple tray to teach Brett to give napkins to other students at snack time and lunch time. (The tray will have a basket with a napkin for each student – when the basket is empty, and all the napkins are on the placemats, the task is finished.)

Routines. Brett does not yet have many productive routines in the classroom and must be guided through each step of his day. However, for the past three days, he has headed straight for his beanbag chair as soon as he has been assisted in hanging up his coat and backpack, suggesting that he is beginning to learn this routine. His teachers are also helping him to go to this area at the end of each activity on his schedule.

Learning activities in place or upcoming. In terms of expressive communication, Brett is being taught an object exchange system during snack and lunch (cup for beverage, plate for food). A next step will be teaching him to make choices between two beverages and between two food items. During his individual instructional sessions, the teachers will introduce an element of sorting colors. Motor development activities, each structured to show Brett how much or how many items to complete, include squeezing play dough balls, picking up small objects and depositing them into containers, finger painting, jumping off low heights, and running to a goal. Socially, he is already handing napkins to his classmates at meals; a next step will be having him sit next to another student and work on a parallel task that is already familiar to him. He is participating in the toileting routine by carrying his diaper into the bathroom, handing a wipe to the teacher, putting his soiled diaper in the trash, and washing his hands. An important play/leisure goal is staying in a designated, physically structured area (in this case, the play area) with his favorite toys (dinosaurs) until the timer sounds, at which point he will be given access to an ipad. This goal is very important to his family, because Brett's hyperactivity means that he requires constant supervision, and family life would be much improved if he could at times remain safely and happily in a designated location in the home.

Carlos – A Preschool Child With ASD Level 1

This is Carlos's second year at a typical preschool; he has only recently been diagnosed with an ASD. Based on recommendations from the diagnostic team, the teachers have added elements of Structured TEACCHing to the situations that previously caused Carlos the most difficulty.

Spaces. The preschool classroom has typical areas (play centers, small tables for snacks and lunch, a large carpeted area for group time with the teacher, etc.). The teachers have put a carpet square in the group area to provide a visual cue to show Carlos where to sit. This physical cue also serves as a boundary to keep him and the other students from intruding on each other's space during group (previously Carlos liked to touch other children's hair, but became very upset if other children bumped his knees during circle time). Another adaptation in the class is a screened-off area in one corner of the room, outfitted with a small cot and headphones for a small music player. This space is available to Carlos when he is overstimulated or distressed during classroom activities.

Schedule. Carlos has difficulty following verbal directions given to the whole class, but he is one of several children in the class who are beginning to read, so his teachers have designed a schedule using written words paired with symbols. The individual word/symbol items are on cards that have been laminated and have Velcro on the back. They are used with a strip of Velcro mounted near his cubby. The teacher puts up three pictures at a time

to indicate the upcoming activities. During transitions, before giving the other students verbal directions, a teacher tells Carlos, "check your schedule." He goes to the schedule, takes the card for the next activity, and takes the card to the appropriate location. Carrying the card to his destination helps make the transition more meaningful and, therefore, smoother for him. At each location, there is a small library pocket with a matching picture; he puts the card into the pocket and begins the activity. If plans change, a teacher takes Carlos to his schedule, shows him the card that is being removed, and puts up a different card (e.g., a card for indoor play instead of the "outside" card, if it begins to rain). The use of a visual schedule has almost eliminated Carlos's arguing and tantrums during transitions because it provides structure and predictability.

Work/activity system. Carlos participates in the same activities as the other students, but structure has been added to each activity to show him how much he should do and when he is finished. For example, instead of an indefinite period of playing with puzzles, which he loves, he is shown a digital timer that counts down from 15 minutes and then rings. This has eliminated tantrums when he is told that puzzle time is over. During craft activities (which he does not enjoy and used to resist), the materials and activity are organized for him. For example, there is an array of small baskets, each containing one item: a sheet of paper with a picture, a pair of scissors, a crayon, and a glue stick. Carlos has a list of directions such as "cut on the line, color the dog, glue the dog on the paper, write your name." When the baskets are empty and the finished product is in the "finished" basket, the task is over, and Carlos can leave the craft table. Carlos learned this work/activity system (working from left to right with baskets of materials) during individual sessions with the teacher, and he is now able to complete most tasks using this system independently and without resistance.

Routines. Carlos has learned that when he has finished required activities, he can either get a book or go to his quiet place until a teacher tells him, "check your schedule" to begin another activity. He has also learned, after individual instruction using a work/activity system, to follow verbal directions for routine activities, such as washing his hands, getting his cot for naptime, and putting his disposable snack cup and plate in the trash.

Learning activities in place or upcoming. Carlos does not have special goals in cognitive or pre-academic skills, because he is developing very well in these areas. He still needs work on personal hygiene, however, and has work/activity systems in place to assist him in wiping himself after using the toilet and in brushing his teeth after lunch. Socially, he is learning to take turns in simple board games (he used to have difficulty with this). So far, he has learned to play *Go Fish* with a teacher, and next week he will begin playing that game with another student with a teacher's supervision. Eventually, as he learns additional structured games, teacher supervision will be faded. He will also be taught some routines for less structured play, such as building with blocks, playing with small cars and trucks, and playing in a toy kitchen.

Demetrius – A Fourth-Grade Student With ASD Level 2

Demetrius spends most of his day in a special education classroom for students with autism, but he goes to music with the regular fourth grade because he is very talented in singing and playing the piano, and he participates well in that class.

Spaces. In Demetrius's classroom, there is a table for individual work with the teacher, and each student also has a private work space for practicing the skills they have learned with the teacher. There is no group space in the room, because each student's program is so different and because the students don't learn well in a group. However, there is a leisure area where two students can play or relax together (sometimes joined by a teacher).

Schedule. Demetrius has progressed from an object schedule to a schedule that uses photographs of objects and/ or activities. These photographs have been laminated and are attached by paperclips to a sheet of paper on a wall in the classroom. The sequence of photographs, running from left to right, forms a full-day schedule. When a teacher hands Demetrius a card with his name, he takes it to the schedule, slides it under a paperclip at the top of the paper, and then takes the photograph to the far left. Demetrius is still learning this system, so before he goes to look at his schedule, a teacher places a large red arrow under the picture at the far left to give Demetrius an additional cue of where to look. Eventually, the arrow will no longer be needed and will be faded out.

Work/activity system. During his individual work with his teacher, Demetrius is learning to use an advanced work/activity system that involves getting a task from a shelf near his work space, completing the task, and then getting the next task, for a total of four different tasks. Each task is contained in a large box with several smaller containers for materials inside. Demetrius knows which box to select by matching the number of the box to a series of numbers paper-clipped to his work table (e.g., 2, 1, 4, 3). Demetrius takes the containers out of the box, completes the task (such as sorting colors, shapes, sizes, objects, or plastic letters), puts the completed task back into the box, and puts the whole thing into a large "finished" basket on the floor by his work table.

Demetrius has almost learned the process of this work/activity system, which will soon be transferred to his independent work area for additional practice. He will continue to use the four-box work/activity system as he learns new tasks in individual sessions with his teacher. In the future, the work boxes will be moved to a more distant location in the room to give Demetrius experience with staying focused on his tasks even as he moves around the room to get materials.

Routines. Demetrius is quite independent in a number of school routines, including going to the leisure area after each activity, walking from the bus to his classroom, getting his home-school notebook out of his backpack and handing it to a teacher, giving the teacher a card when he wants to go to the bathroom down the hall, managing his tray after lunch in the cafeteria, and walking to the music room independently when music class is on his schedule.

Learning activities in place or upcoming. In addition to learning more complex schedules and work/activity systems, Demetrius is also working on matching sight words, writing his name, and matching quantities to written numbers. His expressive language is limited, but when he gives pictures to teachers to make requests, he is beginning to imitate some of the verbal labels they use (such as *juice, milk, outside, music*, and *ipad*). Teachers will continue to support and stimulate verbal imitation, while enabling Demetrius to use the picture communication system that is so functional for him. Other learning goals include tying his shoes, cutting his own meat and using a knife for spreading, using a variety of office tools (such as stapler, scissors, and tape), and learning to play tag with other students.

Edward – A Fourth-Grade Student With ASD Level 1

Edward has always been fully included in general education classes. He is currently in the fourth grade with Structured TEACCHing supports provided by the classroom teacher.

Spaces. Edward has a "solo" desk rather than the four-student shared work space used by his classmates, because he is distracted and occasionally annoyed when he works facing other students. He knows that he can go to a little room off the school office (where an adult is always present) for 10 minutes whenever he needs to calm down or get away from the noise in his busy classroom.

Schedule. Edward's schedule is a written list of the day's activities. At the beginning of the year, his teacher emailed his mother a template for the schedule, which Edward's mother goes over with him in the morning. If the teacher knows there will be changes, she emails that information to the mother the evening before, and the mother shows Edward what activities will be crossed out or added. She then puts the schedule in the front of Edward's notebook, where he can refer to it throughout the day. He also understands that the teacher may write in additional changes during the day. Edward likes to cross off each activity as he completes it, so that he can see that he is getting closer to computer time at the end of the day, which he loves.

Work/activity system. On Edward's desk is a set of colored folders with left and right pockets. There is one folder for each subject. The teacher puts a sheet with a written assignment (paper-clipped to additional materials as needed) on the left, and after Edward completes the work, he puts it in the right pocket and then takes the folder to a basket on the teacher's desk. Over the course of the day, he sees the pile of file folders on his desk getting smaller, and when all the folders are gone, he knows that he has completed his classwork for the day.

Edward is not yet consistent or reliable about bringing home an assignment book or the necessary materials, so most of his teachers email the assignment to his family (one teacher has a web site where all the students can check the assignment). Edward's mother prints out the assignments and puts each in a homework folder (of the same design as the classwork folder) and Edward completes his homework using the same work/activity system.

Edward also has a version of a work/activity system for recess, which had been the most challenging and frustrating part of the day for him. He used to wander along the fence for the entire recess, not interacting with any of the other students and not getting any exercise. His teacher devised a written checklist of activities for him to do, and one of the inclusion facilitators spent a few sessions with him practicing the activities privately. The activities included kicking a ball to each of the corners of the playground, running two laps around the playground, asking one child to catch a ball with him, and jumping off the jungle gym three times. At first, the teacher helped Edward mark off each activity on the checklist, but he now knows the routine and completes it without protest (although he still does not enjoy recess).

Routines. As described, Edward has learned the routine of doing his classwork, turning it in, and returning to check his schedule independently. After several months of having a written prompt in his cubby, he has also learned to turn in all his homework folders as soon as he arrives at school in the morning. He knows that during free time he can either choose a book or put his name on the waiting list for 5 minutes of computer time.

Learning activities in place or upcoming. Edward is excelling in science and math, but struggles with language arts. Reading comprehension is becoming more challenging as more inferential reading is required, but his teacher is supporting him through the use of repeated practice with a systematic approach to analyzing written material. Edward's greatest academic challenges have been handwriting and learning to write paragraphs. His teachers have supported these skills by allowing him to write about his favorite topics (Japanese animated characters), and he is now much more willing to write on a daily basis and at greater length.

Twice a week Edward eats lunch with a speech-language therapist and a group of students working on pragmatic language and social skills. These sessions have an overall goal of helping students have fun together, rather than formal instruction in specific social behaviors such as making eye contact and giving compliments. Using visual structure to help the students take turns, the speech-language therapist has helped the students learn to play several board games without squabbling over cheating and whose turn it is. She has also had students practice using the telephone to call each other to ask for information about homework assignments and to invite someone over to play. She is going to send home with Edward information about what games he has learned, how they were structured, and how to contact the families of other students in the group as a way of facilitating play dates outside of school.

Frannie – A 10th-Grade Student With ASD Level 2

Frannie spends the morning working on various tasks in the school cafeteria. She spends some afternoons in her special education classroom and some afternoons on community errands and outings (such as grocery shopping and swimming).

Spaces. For most activities, Frannie is either seated or she stands on a small piece of colored cloth – she needs these cues to keep her from drifting away from the correct location. (Several of the colored cloths come with her on community outings and are used to show her where to stand in cashier's lines, at bus stops, etc.).

Schedule. Frannie can follow a full-day sequence of symbols for her schedule. However, she tended to try to rearrange the symbols, look on the teacher's desk for symbols for her favorite activities, and in general treat her schedule like a choice board or expressive communication tool. Her teachers, therefore, added to Frannie's schedule several colored squares, representing opportunities to choose her own activities. The available choices were posted nearby on a sheet of paper of the same color as the square on the schedule. For example, "music" and "play with a teacher" were always available, and sometimes choices such as "go for a walk," "go roller skating," and "computer time" were also available. The schedule pictures were put into a frame (using the removable plastic binders from report covers) so that it was relatively difficult for Frannie to rearrange the pictures or skip over her less-preferred activities.

Work/activity system. Frannie has long since mastered work/activity systems using containers of materials while seated at a table, so now she is learning tasks that involve larger materials and tasks that require her to move around a work site. As long as her work materials are laid out from left to right, she stays organized and focused on the tasks. For each new task, her teacher or instructor plans ahead the organization of materials and sequence of steps. Then Frannie stands next to an instructor, watches one or two demonstrations of how to use the materials, and then proceeds independently. The instructor watches for mistakes, confusion, disorganization, or unanticipated problems, and modifies the work/activity system accordingly. Frannie has already learned to refill condiment containers in the cafeteria, restock the containers of eating utensils, wipe tables, sweep the floor, and put trash bags into trash cans.

Routines. Frannie enjoys structured activities more than unstructured time, so she generally works for 2-1/2 to 3 hours without a break. When she does have downtime between activities on her schedule, she works on a 1,000-piece jigsaw puzzle on her table in the classroom. With specific instruction and practice, she has also learned routines such as putting on a smock and cap to work in the kitchen and going to a supervisor with a card that says "Help, please."

Learning activities in place or upcoming. Frannie speaks in short phrases and enjoys talking with her teachers about certain topics, so a conversation time is part of her daily schedule. Although Frannie will always need some degree of supervision, she is learning several life skills, including washing dishes, doing laundry, ordering a meal in a restaurant when the available items are described to her, and assisting with grocery shopping. Leisure goals include bowling, swimming, and playing *Bingo*. She is making progress in managing menstrual hygiene independently, using a very structured system for changing and disposing of pads on a schedule.

George – A 10th-Grade Student With ASD Level 1

George is taking college preparatory classes and a study skills class. He is so advanced in math that during his senior year he will have the option of taking a class at the local college. His parents think this will provide valuable experience with aspects of college while he is still living at home.

Spaces. George's classes are scattered around a large campus, so at the beginning of each semester, a teacher walks him through the route he will take from one class to the next. The teacher points out directional signs, landmarks, and room numbers to assist George in learning and feeling comfortable with the route. (When George was in middle school, his mother used to do this, but when George moved up to high school, he said that he wanted someone else to do it, and a teacher volunteered).

Schedule and work/activity system. George is learning to use his own integrated schedule and work/activity system, which is incorporated into a notebook that also includes his class schedule, a place to list assignments and needed materials, and a calendar that shows when assignments and projects are due. This system was initially devised by his mother, and although George protested and initially resisted using it, he has seen that he is more successful when he uses it. He is becoming increasingly independent in using it, and has begun recording last-minute assignments, anticipating how long various assignments will take, and thinking about what materials to bring home at night.

Routines. George is very familiar and comfortable with all the routines at his high school; it is noticeable, however, that he is at first tense and silent in new situations. The autism specialist has encouraged school staff to provide George with written descriptions of new activities that answer the five questions (see page 271). This was successfully done prior to driver's education class and a field trip to Washington, DC. The autism specialist also provided George with a written description and explanation of the chess club and the photography club, and George is no longer protesting that he is not interested in joining any clubs.

Learning activities in place or upcoming. George is studying the driver's education manual and is on the waiting list for the driver's education class. He occasionally drops into the guidance counselor's office after frustrating experiences. He typically calms down within a few minutes and listens to advice or additional explanations of the complex social world of high school.

Summary and Conclusions

The preceding case examples demonstrate the range of cognitive and language skills, academic and vocational potential, and other personal characteristics of students with ASD. Structured TEACCHing and environmental supports provide students with lifelong, individualized arrangements that facilitate understanding, learning, and adaptive functioning in the school, home, and community.

Anthony, the kindergarten student from the beginning of this chapter, will be taught by teachers who use Structured TEACCHing principles and techniques. His teachers, having observed his interests and talked with his family about his skills and behavior at home, have designed the following initial plan:

Spaces

Anthony will have a play area on the opposite side of the room from the block area, separated by various physical and visual barriers. This was decided because it is so difficult for him to make the transition from playing in the block area to any other activity. He will also have a three-sided work table (to encourage him to stay seated), where he has brief individual work sessions with a teacher. This table is near his leisure area and also near the bathroom, so that the route to both is short and direct.

Schedule

Anthony will begin with a "what's next" object schedule that starts in the parking lot when his school bus arrives. There he will be greeted by a teacher or assistant, who will give him the object for the first activity of the day, a work session with his teacher. His day will consist of many sequences of work sessions with a teacher, alternating with free time in his leisure area, along with time on the playground, snack, lunch, nap, trips to the bathroom, and brief participation in a group activity with the other children. All transitions to new activities will be done using an object that is part of the upcoming activity. This is expected over time to reduce Anthony's confusion about what he is being asked to do and his resulting distress during transitions.

Task Organization

The object used to indicate work sessions will be a block that Anthony will bring to his work table. For this introduction to Structured TEACCHing, at the table will be a container of blocks and a container with a lid. Anthony's task will be to put each block in the container (with the teachers using the fewest number of gestures and prompts needed to help him understand the task). Once all the blocks are in the container, the work session is finished, and Anthony is guided back to his leisure area (where there are musical instruments and some toy cars, both of which were chosen based on the observation during the first week that he liked them). The task (putting blocks in a container) is very simple and well within Anthony's ability – it was chosen to capitalize on his interest in blocks while teaching him a completely new set of skills: completing a task selected by a teacher in a location determined by the teacher. Once he begins to show some emerging understanding and spontaneous participation in the activity, a similar "put-in" activity will be introduced, using some of the material from craft activities that Anthony previously grabbed and used to flap. This was decided in order to introduce him to a more productive way to use that material.

The object used to indicate snack and lunch (both of which take place in the classroom) is a small paper plate. Anthony is guided to a chair at the table with the other children during snack time, and snack foods are put on his plate. At the beginning, he will not be required to hand his plate to the teacher, but eventually she will begin to position herself slightly farther away, with snack food in her hand to encourage Anthony to extend the plate in his hand toward her. If Anthony gets up from the table, his plate and food will be removed – after several minutes, the teacher will again approach him with the plate and guide him to sit at the table. This will be done as needed, three times for each snack or meal.

To teach Anthony the first steps of participating in group time, the teachers considered having music every day and using a part of a musical instrument as the object on his schedule. However, they worried that Anthony might develop a strong attachment to this routine, making it difficult to eliminate music as the first activity of group time. So instead, they decided that Anthony's task would be to come to the group once the other children were settled and to hand each child an object from a basket that the teacher holds. When the basket is empty, Anthony's task is finished, and he is free to leave the group and go to his leisure area (although there is a chair for him if he chooses to stay with the group). The objects in the basket will vary from day to day; they will be used with the other students during a group song or activity. Sometimes musical instruments will be used; Anthony will pass those out also. When the musical activity is finished, Anthony may have the job of taking the basket around the circle to collect the instruments, putting the basket into the closet, and helping to close the closet door (which will highlight for him that the activity is finished). Eventually, Anthony will be expected to sit in his chair for another time-limited, visually based, or physical activity with the group, but for now the first step in integrating Anthony into a group activity will be a simple task in which the materials indicate how much he has to do.

During free time, Anthony sometimes is allowed to play alone in his leisure area, but sometimes a teacher comes into the area with him and sits near him, singing, imitating his play, or using "floor time" techniques (Greenspan & Wieder, 1998) to engage him in simple, playful social interactions.

Routines

Anthony's teacher will work on both establishing productive routines and on interrupting unacceptable ones. For example, after all activities are completed, he will be guided through the routine of going to his leisure area. His schedule is arranged so that he enters the class with an object that leads him to his first activity. Eventually, he will probably go to that location and activity with minimal supervision. His routines of pulling down his pants before arriving at the bathroom and leaving the bathroom before he has zipped up will be prevented through close supervision and physical guidance during these times, until he has learned more socially appropriate routines.

Tips for Practical Application

✓ Incorporating a student's special interests into learning activities makes them more interesting or palatable (for example: counting helicopters, writing about license plates, reading about computers, purchasing and preparing ingredients to make purple cookies).

✓ Many students with ASD benefit from occupational therapy (particularly with a sensory integration focus) and/or speech/language therapy (particularly with a focus on pragmatics).

✓ Parents are almost always their child's most passionate and knowledgeable caregivers. Their understanding of and love for their child can be a source of energy and support for teachers. Parents may be very busy or have additional stresses that teachers do not know about, but teachers should do everything they can to connect with parents and respect their input, their wishes, and their perspectives about their child (see Chapters 15 and 16).

✓ Incorporating choices of activities into the student's schedule can strengthen his communication and language skills, improve his mood, and increase his sense of self-worth and personal satisfaction at school.

✓ When you encounter a challenging behavior, look first at the structure. Does the student need more visual information, more physical structure, or other supports?

Chapter Highlights

- Structure for students with ASD means the teacher or caregiver decides what the learning activities will be, where they will occur, and how long they will last.

- Structured TEACCHing refers to instructionalstrategies and environmental supports for individuals with ASD developed by the TEACCH program, a statewide program for individuals with autism in North Carolina.

- Structured TEACCHing has two main goals: (a) teach the individual with ASD as many skills as possible, given his developmental level; and (b) provide an environment as comprehensible as possible, so the learner can understand the expectations and opportunities around him.

- Structured TEACCHing is a social-cognitive-behavioral approach applied to the neuropsychological aspects of ASD.

- The "Culture of Autism" refers to the shared neuropsychological patterns of thinking, communication, and behavior commonly seen among individuals with ASD.

- Integral to Structured TEACCHing is respect for families.

- Five central questions need to be considered and answered for each individual with ASD within Structured Teaching.

- Schedules, task organization, work/activity systems, and routines are integral to Structured TEACCHing.
  - Schedules are important as they allow individuals with ASD to know where they are supposed to be and what they are to be doing at a given time and allow for predictable environments with knowledge of what will come next. Schedules should be individualized, visual, accurate, and easy to alter should the need arise.
  - Task organization and work/activity systems provide visual information about what the student is to do each step of the way during a task or activity.
  - Routines are consistent daily activities for students. A student who has reached independence in an activity can be considered to have developed a routine (for example, placing completed work in a folder or washing hands before snack time).

- The authors provide multiple examples demonstrating the use of Structured Teaching at different age and ability levels.

Chapter Review Questions

1. What is meant by "structure" in teaching?

2. What is TEACCH?

3. Explain Structured TEACCHing, including theoretical foundations, as well as implications for students with ASD and their families.

4. What is meant by the "Culture of Autism" and what are some examples?

5. What are the five questions Structured TEACCHing should answer by providing the learner with visual information and organization of the environment

6. What is the importance of each of the following in the instruction of individuals with ASD: schedules, task organization, work/activity systems, and routines?

7. For each of the five questions of Structured TEACCHing, provide two or three examples of strategies.

References

Bregman, J. D., Zager, D., & Gerdtz, J. (2005). Behavioral interventions. In F. Volkmar, R. Paul, A. Klin, & D. Cohen (Eds.), *Handbook of autism and pervasive developmental disorders* (3rd ed., pp. 897-924). Hoboken, NJ: John Wiley & Sons.

Frith, U. (2003). *Autism: Explaining the enigma* (2nd ed.). Oxford, UK: Blackwell.

Greenspan, S. I., & Wieder, S. (1998). *The child with special needs.* Boston, MA: Addison-Wesley.

Mesibov, G. B., Shea, V., & Adams, L. W. (2001). *Understanding Asperger Syndrome and high-functioning autism.* New York, NY: Kluwer Academic/Plenum Press.

Mesibov, G. B., Shea, V., & Schopler, E. (with Adams, L., Burgess, S., Chapman, S. M., Merkler, E., Mosconi, M., Tanner, C., & Van Bourgondien). (2005). *The TEACCH approach to autism spectrum disorders.* New York, NY: Plenum/Kluwer Academic.

Schopler, E., & Reichler, R. J. (1971). Parents as cotherapists in the treatment of psychotic children. *Journal of Autism and Childhood Schizophrenia, 1,* 87-102.

Schreibman, L., & Ingersoll, B. (2005). Behavioral interventions to promote learning in individuals with autism. In F. Volkmar, R. Paul, A. Klin, & D. Cohen (Eds.), *Handbook of autism and pervasive developmental disorders* (3rd ed., pp. 882-896). Hoboken, NJ: John Wiley & Sons.

Learner Objectives

After reading this chapter, the learner should be able to:

- Define what is meant by a special interest area (SIA)

- Explain how an SIA of a child with ASD differs from an interest of a typically developing child

- State how SIAs relate to a person's self-esteem

- Explain how an SIA can both enhance and interfere with relationships with others

- Explain how an SIA might reflect a child's attempt to understand society

- Explain the potential emotional impact of SIAs on students with ASD

- Discuss the positive impact an SIA can have on transition planning

- Discuss SIAs and how they can be used to teach prosocial skills

- List the five most common positive effects a person's SIA may have on the whole family

- Define "learning method application" as it relates to SIAs

Chapter 12

Harnessing the Power of Special Interest Areas in the Classroom

Mary Ann Winter-Messiers

My 12-year-old son, whose passion is aviation and who was originally diagnosed with Asperger Syndrome, was lying on the floor of the family room groaning and sighing bitterly. "This assignment is mind-numbingly boring! I don't even know what I'm supposed to do! I HATE SCHOOL!" He was angry and incensed about the unconscionable injustice done to him. How dare the teacher assign a speech and poster about a family member? How dare she impose on his free time by forcing him to do something he judged to be a supreme waste of his time? Foreseeing an imminent meltdown, I was on the verge of conceding that we would try again tomorrow when an idea struck me.

"In the garage I have a box of your grandfather's WWII flight memorabilia. Would you like to look at it?" My son sat straight up, fully attentive. "Wow! That would be super!" I promptly retrieved the box, opened it, and stood back to watch what I knew was coming. "A WWII air force base flight manual! Look, his insignia and wings! Oh, cool, a canteen menu – and here are letters from his pilot buddies!" He moved quickly around the room. "I can do my speech on Papa [his grandfather]! I will have the best project in the whole class! I will write and write; my mind is racing with ideas! I can't wait to start!" In seconds, the assignment – and my son – had been transformed.

School projects were typically filled with stress, tears, anger, sensory overwhelm, and apathy, ruining countless evenings for both of us. What made the difference this time? My son's special interest area is aviation. As soon as he captured a vision for doing his project through the lens of aviation, he was fully engaged and instantly passionate about the assignment.

What Are Special Interest Areas?

Special interest areas (SIAs) have been defined as "those passions that capture the mind, heart, time, and attention of those individuals with Asperger's Syndrome, providing the lens through which they view the world" (Winter-Messiers, 2007, p. 142). In explaining SIAs, Attwood (1998) noted that they "dominate the person's time and conversation and the imposition of routines that must be completed" (p. 89). He further observed, "these pursuits are often solitary, idiosyncratic" (p. 93). We see this in the example of the elementary school girl whose SIA is toilets (Attwood, 2006), clearly not an interest that would gain her positive social status. On the playground the girl physically acted out a blocked toilet; one easily imagines how this behavior and interest would seem bizarre and unacceptable to her peers. Moreover, although some SIAs change over time, the tendency of SIAs to involve ritualistic behaviors and socially isolate the individual does not seem to change with age (Piven, Harper, Palmer, & Arndt, 1996). Professionals who serve children and youth with ASD, and certainly parents and guardians, are well aware of these all-consuming interests. *To know a person with ASD is to know his or her SIA.*

Austrian pediatrician Dr. Hans Asperger (1944/1991) was the first to record these focused interests in his young patients, noting, "a special interest enables them to achieve quite extraordinary levels of performance in a certain area" (p. 45). In describing the impact of SIAs, Attwood (1998) observed that they "dominate the person's time and conversation and the imposition of routines that must be completed" (p. 89). Typically, SIAs govern the thinking, planning, and affection of those with ASD. Their first desire is to engage in them whenever possible. Thus, SIAs consume massive amounts of time, energy, and focus – often to the exclusion of other activities, needs, or requirements, such as eating, dressing, toileting, showering, homework, and bedtime. Although the reason a child's selection of a given SIA is rarely known, he self-selects his SIA; it is not adult directed or imposed. The attraction to the SIA is strong and positive. Attwood (1998) affirmed, "the person really enjoys their interest and does not try to resist it" (p. 93).

Parents are often baffled about the source of a child's SIA, wondering how in the world their son or daughter came to be so intensely interested in dust, dead-end streets, lampposts, or frogs. An SIA is typically extremely narrow in scope and thoroughly engrossing for the child, who tends to engage in the behavior privately and has little or no idea about the degree to which the interest is socially isolating (Tantam, 1991). Most children and teens engage in their SIAs alone, although with time and support, they may learn to share their SIAs with others of like mind. In sum, SIAs are child-initiated, narrow, typically engaged in alone, and often appear to take over a child's life.

Those with ASD often hold intense, faithful, and tender affection for their SIAs, displaying not only fondness for but also the appearance of being in a relationship with their SIAs. For example, it is not unusual for children and youth to name their SIAs, carry them (or a representative object) around with them, and bring them up often, if not exclusively, in talking to others. Some possess astonishing and sophisticated professional-level knowledge about their SIAs, having researched and studied them in tremendous depth. It is often said that individuals who may have ASD Level 1 possess "encyclopedic knowledge" about their SIAs. In return, many professionals are both impressed and mystified at how these children have come to amass such knowledge and vocabulary. For example, a middle-school-aged girl whose passion is Bernese Mountain Dogs may be able to hold astute conversations about these dogs with veterinarians, trainers, pet shop owners, or breeders.

How Do SIAs Differ From the Interests of Neurotypical Children?

Many ask what the difference is between SIAs in children and youth with ASD and the hobbies and interests of neurotypical children and youth. Often the people who ask have never seen SIAs played out in a real child or youth with ASD; they cannot conceive of the power of these passions on those with ASD.

While many neurotypical children and youth have hobbies or interests, they are not engaged with them to the same extent as peers with ASD. They frequently have multiple and diverse interests at one time (e.g., sports, music, and video games), whereas those with ASD typically have one primary SIA, though they may have secondary, less dominant SIAs that can be linked to the primary ones (Myles & Simpson, 2003). Further, neurotypical individuals do not typically invest as much time, energy, commitment, or money into learning about their hobbies, or engaging in them, and it would be rare for a neurotypical child or youth to have the capacity to converse with professionals on an equal level, or have the vocabulary or insights with which to do so. Moreover, the daily activities of neurotypical children and youth are not likely to be seen as interfering with the pursuit of their hobbies, as is the case for children and youth with ASD. That is, the hobbies of neurotypical children and youth are not usually seen as the all-consuming, driving, day-and-night focus of desire and attention as are the SIAs of those with ASD.

Attwood (2006) emphasized that SIAs are far more than hobbies. Referring to Hans Asperger's highly positive perception of SIAs, Attwood observed that Asperger "considered the abilities demonstrated in the interests to be a special gift" (p. 198). This also emerged clearly from our research studies (Winter-Messiers, 2007; Winter-Messiers, Herr, et al., 2007).

The Crucial Role of SIAs in Identity and Self-Esteem

When my son was in the second grade, he was assigned to make a poster to introduce himself to parents and guests attending an interest fair. On the poster, the children were asked to answer questions about themselves, such as their favorite colors, foods, books, activities, and so on. Each child would have his or her own table on which to display favorite items, with the poster hanging behind him or her. My son selected a few cherished airplanes, aviation books, and plane models to display on his table at the fair. He also brought several planes to hang from the ceiling and insisted that we take along an electric fan so that, when it was angled properly, the air would blow on the planes and cause them to appear to be in flight.

When the day of the fair arrived, he wore his beloved orange sweatshirt with the F-15 fighter jet embroidered on the front. He carefully arranged his aviation items on the table in front of him and prepared to greet the adults who asked him about his interest. When I came to see his display, I read his poster carefully. In answer to the question, "What is something you like to do?," he had written, "I like to go to movies." I was surprised and said, "Honey, I see that you wrote that you like going to movies. Would you mind telling me why you did not talk about working with your airplanes?" My son seemed surprised by my question, clearly thinking the answer obvious, and his revealing response gave me profound insight into SIAs: "Mommy, going to movies is something I like to do, but airplanes are who I am."

In our SIA research study, we repeatedly heard in the children and teens' interviews that they defined themselves by their SIAs. Their SIAs came second only to their families and, for some, their belief in God. Some participants stated that they *were* their SIAs. SIAs are critical to their well-being and at the core of their self-image; SIAs literally are their identity. Given the importance of this concept, we entitled this theory "The Fusion of SIA With Core Self-Image." These children, who so often tragically have extremely low self-esteem, take great pride in their SIAs and in their advanced SIA-related knowledge. As one boy proudly confided, "The reason I wanna move back there [to Hollywood] is, I wanna be a composer and … just take over John Williams' job, get into that job and compose *Harry Potter, The Terminal …*" (Winter-Messiers, 2007, p. 146).

Wanting to impress and win over peers came through in participants' expressions of pride in their SIAs. One student revealed his feelings of peer rejection, as well as his desire to be the expert, when he told an interviewer, "I wish [kids at school] would accept [my interest] and, uh, not always pretend to throw up about it. I just wish they knew as much about it as I do, maybe even … no, maybe not even more." Participants clearly wanted to be recognized as experts and be accepted by their peers. As Charlie said, "Well, I first like *tell* 'em I'm talented, but then I like wanna *prove*, I mean *PROVE*, that I can do it." One participant confidently told us, "Yeah … well … apparently, like, when I make something very good, then they'll be impressed." Ryan stated, "I think I've got a *lot* more understanding on how things work than most people. I've got a corner in the back of my brain that allows me to perfectly simulate almost anything." Steve told us, "I'm the main customer at a place called Hollywood Video. I am a movie *whiz* (Winter-Messiers, 2007, p. 144)!" SIAs may also help individuals with ASD to see others' perceptions of them in a positive light. As Nate proclaimed, "My parents think I'm an unbelievable, amazing drummer!" (Winter-Messiers, 2007, p. 146).

Conversely, a sad but insightful story demonstrates the link between these objects of profound affection and a child's self-esteem. Beginning in preschool, my son had amassed an impressive collection of aviation-themed t-shirts purchased from airports, museums, fly-ins, and aviation events around the country or given to him by thoughtful friends and family. One day when he was in third grade, he walked in the house after school demanding that I take him shopping for new t-shirts for school. He told me I should buy him t-shirts displaying logos and slogans supporting our popular local university athletic team. Knowing he had no interest in this or any other sports team, or, for that matter, any sport, I asked why he wanted these new shirts. He replied, "I can't wear my airplane shirts to school any more, Mommy. They're not OK." He had finally understood that the other students did not approve of his passion for planes. In deciding to leave his airplane t-shirts at home – the evidence of his passion because they were not socially acceptable – he would also be leaving *himself* at home. His pride in sharing his knowledge of aviation at school went underground from that day on, as did much of his self-esteem.

In their SIAs, children and teens with ASD find a stable core. SIAs help them make sense of a world that can feel overwhelming and chaotic, and in that world, feel a measure of power and control. SIAs give them a focus upon which to channel their often prodigious gifts, and shape their dreams.

What Do SIAs Look Like?

SIAs can range from the expected for the age group and gender – trucks for boys and dolls for girls – to the unexpected – scabs, electrical transformers, dust, and batteries – for boys or girls. Not surprisingly, transportation is a popular SIA with boys, and animals are popular with girls. Our study of the SIAs of girls originally diagnosed with Asperger's Syndrome, aged 6-18 years ($N = 23$), supported the findings of Cohen (2003), who reported that the most popular interests among her female participants were art – primarily drawing and cartooning – and animals.

In the process of conducting interviews with our participants, we heard many insightful comments about how they felt about their SIAs. For example, Sarah firmly stated, "I'm an animal person. [People] can sense that I am an animal person" (Winter-Messiers, 2007, p. 144). Tables 12.1 (Winter-Messiers, 2007) and 12.2 list the SIAs of the male and female participants in our studies. (Two female participants were included in our first, predominantly male, study, and their SIAs are included in Table 12.2 along with the second, all-female, study.)

Table 12.1
Boys' Primary Special Interest Areas

General Interest Category	Specific Interest
Transportation	Airplanes Cars Trains Trucks
Music	Composition Drumming Rap music Saxophone
Animals	Frogs Goats
Sports	Swimming
Video Games	Role-playing games (RPGs)
Motion pictures	Disney movies *Star Wars* Vampire movies
Woodworking	
Art	Cartooning Sculpting dinosaurs in clay

Table 12.2
Girls' Primary Special Interest Areas

General Interest Category	Specific Interest
Animals	Cats Dogs Rats Goats Horses Pets
Arts	Drawing animal figures Drawing anime/manga Drawing/writing stories about penguins Painting Scriptwriting/acting
Fantasy	Literature Dragons
Gymnastics	
Video games	*Star Craft* PC game Console games
Technology	Electronic gadgets Cell phones
Mechanical	Electric fans Batteries
Medical	Midwifery Conjoined twins Anesthesia/medical issues Menstruation
Music	
Japanese language and culture	
Disney movies	

From "Toilet brushes and tarantulas: Understanding the origin and development of special interest areas in children and youth with Asperger's syndrome," by M. A. Winter-Messiers, 2007, *Journal of Remedial and Special Education, 28*(3), 140-152. Used with permission.

SIAs differ in social acceptability based on the age and gender of the individual, the age of the onlooker, the geographic location, and the interest itself. For example, a boy whose SIA is Barney, the large purple dinosaur on the *Barney and Friends* children's TV show, will find that his interest is socially acceptable – even encouraged – when he is a toddler or young child. But if he is still focused on Barney in middle school, he will likely be bullied – first, because it is not considered age appropriate, and second, because as a boy, he is expected to have outgrown stuffed animals by that age.

The role of the observer in the life of the child may also impact the level of social acceptability. If the boy shares his Barney SIA with his grandmother, she may listen kindly and patiently, but if he tries to talk to a middle school boy about Barney, the response will likely be the opposite. Social acceptability may also depend on the socio-cultural context of where the child lives. For example, the boy whose SIA is cowboy trail songs may find that his passion is socially acceptable in one part of the country but not in another. The girl whose SIA is toilets (Attwood, 2006), however, is unlikely to find support for her interest at any age, because toilets are considered socially inappropriate, unless she is speaking with a plumber.

Some SIAs seem innately socially distasteful and, therefore, inappropriate to others, such as menstruation, toilet brushes, and scabs. Other SIAs, while not distasteful or threatening to others, seem so odd to observers that they are put off by them, such as deep fat fryers, dust, elbow skin, phone books, yellow pencils (Attwood, 2003), loose threads, light bulbs, cattle skeletons, and national zip codes. Neurotypical people are often mystified as to why some SIAs would hold intense attraction for individuals with ASD. As Frith (1991) observed, "the interest may appear excessive, abstruse and sterile to others, but not to the [person with AS]" (p. 14). Further, Frith noted astutely that the response of the neurotypical world to an individual's SIA depends considerably on whether the observer perceives the SIA as acceptable or not. To illustrate, she observed that a child whose SIA is electricity pylons will be regarded as more "oddly fixated" (p. 239) than the child who talks about football.

It is critical to understand that the most socially acceptable SIAs can become socially unacceptable at any age if the child or teen talks of nothing else, imposes his interest constantly on others, uses SIA-related vocabulary that is above the heads of his peers, and/or carries the object everywhere with him. Table 12.3 demonstrates a potential progression in the continuum of acceptability to unacceptability, depending on age and sample SIAs. (The purpose of Table 12.3 is to provide examples only. It does not take into account perceived social acceptability based on gender. It also assumes that social onlookers are neurotypical school-aged peers.)

Table 12.3
Potential Progression of Social Acceptability of Sample SIAs

Socially Acceptable SIAs for Young Children	Socially Unacceptable SIAs for Older Children	Socially Acceptable SIAs for Youth	Socially Unacceptable SIAs for Youth	Socially Unaccpetable SIAs for Children or Youth at Any Age
Thomas the Tank Engine™ Trucks Flowers Dinosaurs Superman™ Legos™	Thomas the Tank Engine™ Dolls Sponge Bob™ Security blankets	Egyptian history Butterflies Solar system Flowers Drama Foreign languages	Washing machines Barney Legos™ Electrical cords Game shows Toilets School rules	Undergarments Bodily fluids Feces Automatic weapons Arson Torture Racist humor Sexual humor Sexual violence

How Do SIAs Develop?

Very little is known about how SIAs develop; their origins are one of the mysteries of SIAs. The assumption is often made that a family member has exposed a child with ASD to a particular interest, resulting in the child selecting that interest on which to build his or her SIA. However, our research did not support this idea. When queried, most parents had no knowledge or theories about the origin of their children's SIAs and were, in fact, quite surprised by them. Some parents even felt that their children's SIAs were incongruous with their family's cultures or values, such as a child interested in military war artillery who came from a family with no history of military involvement. Only one parent in our study, a professional carpenter, had an interest related to his son's woodworking SIA.

Some theorize that SIAs may originate in a pleasurable experience or represent working through a frightening experience (Attwood, 2006). Postulating on the origins of the SIAs of those with AS, Tantam (2000) stated that SIAs "may all be attempts to find a powerful quantitative clue to society" (p. 384).

What Is the Timeline for SIAs?

The timeline of a given SIA can vary widely from child to child. Some children change SIAs rather quickly, engaging, for example, in an SIA of lampposts for a few months and then suddenly wanting nothing to do with lampposts and changing to fairies. There may or may not appear to be a connection between the two interests. One girl in our study had been fascinated throughout her childhood with topics as diverse as menstruation, small forest animals, and Willie Nelson.

Other children begin with an SIA and stay with it for many years, perhaps changing only sub-categories, if anything. For example, my son has been thoroughly taken with aviation from the age of 8 months. He started with propellers and simple toy planes, then discovered commercial aircraft, next honed in on United Airlines, then learned about WWI biplanes, and ultimately progressed to jet fighter planes. Along the way, he has focused a few times on specific planes, such as the WWI Sopwith Camel and the WWII Hawker Hurricane propeller plane, but generally he has been interested in a category of planes or an aviation era for years at a time. The interest in aviation in general, however, has never waivered.

In our research study, boys tended to have one dominant SIA at a time. Some girls had more than one SIA at a time, but although the interests may appear to be related, they were distinct and narrow. For example, one girl was focused on make-up, dress-up clothes, and fashion magazines at the same time. While it may appear that this girl was focused on anything related to fashion, in reality, her interests were entirely limited to these three distinct aspects of fashion. If handed a magazine on hairstyles, for example, while a part of the fashion world, she would reject it as not being related to her specific interests.

When children and youth change SIAs, especially when the change is abrupt or the new SIA differs substantially from the previous one, the transition can be painful for parents. An SIA, particularly one that has endured for a long time, becomes an entrenched part of a family's culture and identity. Parents often invest significant time and energy in learning about a child's SIA, and even if they were not initially familiar with the topic, they develop extensive knowledge simply by hearing so much about the SIA from the child. Parents may also make a considerable financial investment in the child's SIA, purchasing SIA-related personal items, decorating a bedroom, or paying for magazine subscriptions, classes, SIA-themed camps, and SIA destination vacations. Over time an SIA becomes a major aspect of a family's personality. Parents may have difficulty letting go when the child or youth who loved trains yesterday, today wants nothing to do with them and is ready to move on to a new SIA: dead-end streets.

What Is the Emotional Impact of SIAs?

SIAs often have a relaxing, calming, and stress-reducing influence on the lives of children and youth with ASD, who may otherwise have great difficulty achieving relaxed states. They may plunge even more intensely into their SIAs (Attwood, 2006), consciously or unconsciously seeking emotional refuge. In our research study, we heard many participants reference engagement with their SIAs to self-calm. In the face of negative emotions, they had learned to focus on their SIAs, actively or in their minds, to help them cope. SIAs helped them to self-regulate stress, anxiety, and frustration, cope with depression, and self-soothe. For example, Sarah confided, "I wish that other people, especially my parents, knew that whenever I'm around horses, I don't think about anything else … like if I was stressed about one thing, and I went to see a horse or get on a horse, that thing I was stressed about, I wouldn't be stressed about anymore." Owen described what he wished other people would understand about his saxophone: "It just gives you a whole new feeling that you might have never felt before. Music is so relaxing and it just opens up your spirit, I just suppose you could say" (Winter-Messiers, 2007, p. 146).

SIAs can also be a source of great joy and happiness for individuals with ASD who may otherwise only rarely feel those emotions. Danny was bursting with joy as he announced, "I was born to like … Walt Disney. Walt Disney is my life. Disney has been my most happiest hope in my whole life. (Winter-Messiers, 2007, p. 146). Describing his warm feelings about his SIA, he further told the interviewers that seeing "Aladdin and Princess Jasmine flying on the magic carpet and singing 'A Whole New World' made me feel love in my heart" (Winter-Messiers, Herr, et al., 2007, p. 72). A most happiest hope indeed!

SIAs Are the Golden Key to the Future

It is precisely because of the passion, affection, and drive that children and youth feel for their SIAs that they should be strongly encouraged to pursue these interests, for therein lies the key to meaningful and successful futures.

Hans Asperger (1944/1991) astutely observed, "We can see in the autistic person, far more clearly than with any normal child, a predestination for a particular profession from earliest youth. A particular line of work often grows naturally out of their special abilities" (p. 88). When we inquired about their post-high school plans, all but one of our participants had solid college and career goals, firmly aligning their present SIAs to future career dreams. It was clear that they regarded their SIAs as helping them achieve their future goals. Soon after submitting her parent survey to us, Nate's mother sought me out to clarify that her son "doesn't watch DVDs for the movies, but watches all the 'behind the scenes' segments of DVDs. Actually, he knows them by heart. They help him feel like a composer, and he thinks he learns all the inside tricks. He says, 'I figure I'm saving time in the future'" (Winter-Messiers, 2007, p. 148). Nate himself resolutely informed his interviewers, "I just have to work at my hardest to be a composer and go, compose music" (Winter-Messiers, 2007, p. 148).

Temple Grandin, ASD expert and author, renowned animal sciences professor at Colorado State University, and expert in the field of cattle management, has long championed the need to encourage the development of SIAs in children and youth with ASD. She advises young people on the spectrum, "keep your career in your talent area" (Grandin & Duffy, 2009, p. 37). In her presentations across the country, Grandin constantly stresses the importance of parents, mentors, and professionals supporting an individual's SIA, so that with time, encouragement, and training, the SIA may develop into a career that will provide structure, personal reward, and a livelihood. She is especially supportive of SIAs that may not seem to others to hold promise for the future, such as video gaming. She tells of discovering her own unusual "fixation" on the tools used to retain cattle as they were injected or branded during a summer spent on her aunt's ranch in Arizona. She credits this interest for being the germ of her lifelong love for cattle and her highly successful career of 40 years in cattle management (p. 2), and observes that among those with ASD who have developed successful careers, "someone helped [them] develop [their] birthright talents." In other words, others encouraged their SIAs.

Individuals with ASD must be encouraged to choose careers in which their employment utilizes their SIAs, thereby enhancing their work product and personal satisfaction. Holding a job related to an SIA allows them to use natural talents to perform. Moreover, an individual with ASD will not require as much training to hold a job related to his SIA as he might need for another job. A job related to an SIA could mean the difference between a daily struggle to complete work-related tasks and the satisfaction of a meaningful job well done each day.

There are other benefits to having a job that relates to an SIA. Through such a job, a person with ASD may display strengths that emerge specifically in relation to working with his SIA. Our research predicts that such a person would likely demonstrate strengths in social skills, communication, emotion, sensory, and executive function in the context of SIA-related employment. For example, working as a librarian who catalogues books might be satisfying for somebody whose SIA is reading. In another case, a man in San Francisco worked for years as a street sweeper when a colleague discovered that he had drawn extensive, intricate street maps of the city from memory. When his supervisors discovered his gift, this man was promoted to the city cartography department, where his superior artistic and memorization abilities benefited the city and gave him meaningful work. As Grandin and Duffy (2009) emphasized, "For those on the autism spectrum, finding a satisfying job also provides social opportunities through shared interests" (p. ix). Attwood (2006) summarized the rich personal potential for individuals with ASD in pursuing SIAs: "The special interest can also provide a valuable source of intellectual enjoyment and can be used constructively to facilitate friendships and employment" (p. 174).

Sadly, it is not unusual for parents and educators to perceive SIAs only as annoying, socially disabling, and harmful behaviors that must be extinguished (Attwood, 1998). However, if a child's SIA is encouraged and supported by parents, mentors, and teachers, it can be key to finding meaning, purpose, and fulfillment in life as an adult. This is why it is critical to identify practical means by which to strengthen the development of SIAs and guide students to work experiences and further educational opportunities that will enhance the career prospects of their SIAs.

The Impact of SIAs on Children and Youth With ASD

SIAs have a significant and positive impact on the lives and behaviors of children and youth with autism. The type of impact may differ across individuals, but it is important to understand the critical role that SIAs can play in motivating and engaging those with autism. Further, SIAs may also result in positive impact throughout social, sensory, and other areas typically seen as challenging for those with autism.

How Do SIA Behaviors Vary Across the Autism Spectrum?

Children and youth with high-functioning ASD, who are highly verbal and approach their SIAs with a heavily intellectual drive are motivated by their profound passion and razor-sharp focus on their preferred interest. Their high level of intelligence often leads them to conduct exhaustive research through books and Internet sources. They may also seek out experts and professionals in the fields of their SIAs of whom to ask questions via Internet blogs, email, or in-person conversations. They have a tremendous capacity for memorization of endless detail concerning their SIAs and often recall these facts and figures in talking to others about their passions. They are likely to know the origin and history of their SIAs in great detail as well as every related piece of information they can find. They may be quite creative in producing items regarding their SIAs, such as displays, stories, drawings, presentations, or objects. They tend to invest vast amounts of time in studying, reflecting upon, and engaging with their SIAs, often choosing to do so alone. They may organize their SIAs according to model, genus, series, color, cost, function, production date, date of acquisition, or other categories known only to them.

In his study of SIA classification systems, Baron-Cohen (2000) identified the following categories: (a) *Patterned material*: visual (e.g., shapes); numeric (e.g., timetables); alphanumeric (e.g., license plates); and lists (e.g., cars, songs); (b) *Systems*: simple (e.g., light switches, water faucets; more complex, e.g., weather fronts); and abstract (e.g., mathematics); (c) *Collections*: categories of objects (e.g., bottle caps, train maps); and categories of information (e.g., types of lizards, rocks, or fabric). Individuals may adhere rigidly to one or more of these systems or to those of their own design. While they may be open to discussing their SIAs with others, they tend, especially as children, to hold lengthy, one-sided dialogues with hapless listeners who often become bored because they do not share their interests and may have heard the information many times before. The astonishingly copious and advanced knowledge and vocabulary of these children and youth regarding their SIAs, well beyond what would typically be expected for their ages, lead them to speak far above the heads of their peers, potentially causing peers to avoid or reject them.

Although not included in our research, children and youth with ASD who are more severely affected in their verbal capacity and may have intellectual impairments, may also engage in particular fascinations to which they feel drawn. In my observations, depending on their intellectual capacity, I have seen them memorize details regarding their fascinations. Some may speak in scripted or echolalic speech regarding their interests. They may collect and organize items related to their interests. I have also observed that they may hold lengthy, one-sided dialogues about their interests with others who do not necessarily share their interests. Creative expressions related to their interests may result in the form of drawings, stories creations, or other products. They may derive calm and comfort from engaging with their fascinations in periods of heightened stress and anxiety.

The Impact of SIAs on the Behaviors and Attitudes of Children and Youth With ASD

In our research, we found SIAs to have a highly positive impact on our participants who had been diagnosed with Asperger's Syndrome. Further research on this subject is needed to learn how others on the autism spectrum approach their interests. When discussing their SIAs, our participants with Asperger's Syndrome were unfailingly enthusiastic, passionate, engaged, and eager to tell us all they knew. Some participants who had been rather morose or reserved upon arrival came alive when asked the first interview question, "What is your favorite thing in the whole world?" Many of these children and youth were not accustomed to someone inviting them to talk about their SIAs, and they seemed to revel in our undivided attention and encouraging questions.

SIAs positively impact many abilities typically considered to be deficient in those with ASD. One of the most exciting findings of our study was that in every area in which our participants struggled (e.g., communication and social interaction), engagement in their SIAs reduced their deficits. We titled this theory the "SIA Strength-Based Model of Asperger's Syndrome" (Winter-Messiers, Herr, et al., 2007); further research is needed to learn if this model applies across the spectrum. While the classic social, communication, emotion, sensory, fine-motor, and executive function deficits describe critical and significant challenges in the ASD profile, they by no means tell the whole story of an individual with ASD. We found that in each of these traditional areas of deficit, children and youth originally classified with Asperger's Syndrome can also demonstrate surprising skills, *under one condition*: they must enter social, communication, emotion, sensory, fine-motor, and executive function skills through the door of their SIAs.

Based on our research study findings, Figure 12.1 displays the progression of engagement in the SIA to examples of strengths in each of the areas traditionally seen as deficits in our AS research population. In the trenchant words of Uta Frith, "the current theories … are more concerned with explaining the cognitive deficits of ASD than the special talents … such theories remain hopelessly incomplete" (Tréhin, 2006, p. 10). This figure displays the strengths we found in our research that emerged as the result of participants' engagement in their SIAs, based on participant and parent reports.

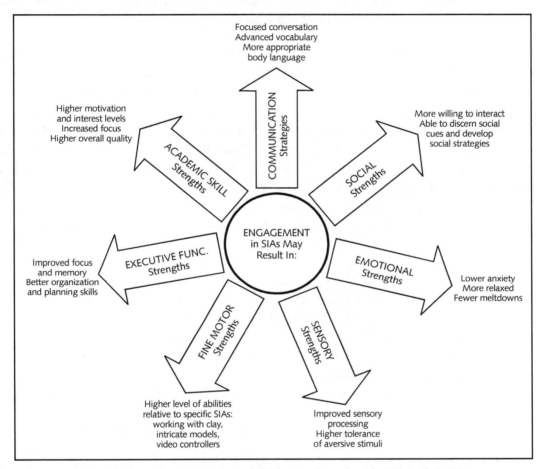

Figure 12.1. Strengths resulting from the engagement of children and youth with ASD in their SIAs.

From "How far can Brian ride the Starlight 4449 Express?," by M. A. Winter-Messiers, C. M. Herr, C. E. Wood, A. P. Brooks, M. M. Gates, T. L. Houston, & K. I. Tingstad, 2007, *Focus on Autism and Other Developmental Disabilities, 22*(2), 67-79. Used with permission.

The Impact of SIAs on the Family

In addition to impacting individuals with ASD, SIAs also impact families. Parents may have strong positive and negative feelings and concerns about their children's SIAs. SIAs can also exact quite a toll on parents, siblings, and grandparents, draining social, financial, time, and especially personal energy resources. On the positive side, however, SIAs are a powerful tool that can be used to motivate their children with autism.

Parents' Emotions and Concerns About Their Children's SIAs

SIAs can have significant impact on the family. Initially, parents may have great difficulty accepting and understanding a child's SIA, especially if it is in an area for which they have no affinity. An SIA can feel like an alien invader taking over their home and family life until it becomes woven into the family culture. The child may talk about her SIA most of the time and at great length. Over time this can become wearing for parents, who may develop resentment toward the SIA. They may even try to extinguish the SIA, typically a fruitless effort.

The majority of parents in our study, however, noted that their children's SIAs had a positive effect on their families, reporting a wide range of positive emotions concerning their children's SIA, including the five most common positive feelings in our survey data: pride, humor, fascination, pleasure, and enthusiasm. For example, Brock's mother stated, "My son inspires my respect and admiration for all he knows and his amazing brain." Marcus' mother affirmed, "It's part of what makes him special!" Justin's grandmother wrote, "I'm glad to see that if Justin has an interest, he can go far with it. If he chose a scientific study, he could be a genius." Many parents also expressed appreciation for their children's character. One parent affirmed, "He is very sweet, kind, gentle, and affectionate . . . He has a gentle soul, even when he is angry or upset, and he is very loving to us." One boy's parent wrote proudly, "I love that he is loving and caring. I love that he has a pleasant disposition. I love that he likes to spend time with us. I love his innocence. I love his lack of guile. There is so much to love about him!" One mother emphasized her son's "enthusiasm for life, his innocence, his willingness to help, kindness to others."

Nevertheless, some parents reported experiencing negative emotions regarding their children's SIAs, including boredom, frustration, and embarrassment. Justin's grandmother made clear her feelings for her grandson's SIA when she wrote in large letters, "This world is ALL ABOUT *JUSTIN!*" Justin's grandmother revealed, "I believe [my grandson] is completely unaware of how different he is from the average 17-year-old. I love him, but I dislike how this family drama around his video games is playing out." Another parent expressed her disturbance with her son's SIA, writing "It's tiring for others to listen to [him talk about his SIA] after a while; it's limiting for him, too." Many parents would identify with one mother who wrote simply, "It's obsessive and gets old."

In addition to their emotional responses to their children's SIAs, parents worried that the SIAs were socially unacceptable, not age appropriate, and not interests that would lead their children to college or careers. A grandmother bemoaned the fact that "once he is 'in' a game, there is no further participation with life in general . . . He rambles on and on about what he cares about, or things [about] himself . . . No interest shown in others." One mother worried that her son's SIA "keeps him from learning new possibilities." Another boy's mother voiced the deep concern shared by many parents for the futures of their children with ASD: "Can he really do this as a career?"

Parents also noted their frustration at having to be the public relations manager for their children, not only in explaining ASD to the outside world but also in explaining their children's SIAs to others. Thus, parents reported that they regularly interpreted their children's SIA for family, friends, and teachers, explaining why their children were so involved in their SIAs. They also reported feeling, at times, weary of this role.

The Social, Financial, and Time Impact of SIAs on Family Life

SIAs can infiltrate and dominate family and home life in ways that incur significant and varied costs to parents. Investment of patient listening, loss of space given over to the SIA, expenses for personal items, and cost of specialized vacations are but a few.

A friend once commented that I should build a hangar in the backyard to contain my son's burgeoning aviation collection, which, despite my best efforts spilled out of his bedroom into the rest of the house. (I did almost manage to maintain the living room as an "airplane-free zone.") In addition to giving up considerable space in the home to a child's SIA, parents may spend a great deal of time and money seeking out and purchasing desired SIA-related items. Depending on the general popularity of the SIA (e.g., Thomas the Tank Engine™ vs. scabs), the SIA theme may dominate across the child's possessions.

For example, during my son's childhood, in addition to his extensive collection of airplanes, he acquired an enviable personal library of aviation books, airplane pajamas, airplane t-shirts, airplane buttons, airplane socks, airplane jackets, an airplane toothbrush, an airplane-shaped nailbrush, an airplane spoon, an airplane cup and plate, airplane placemats, airplane sheets and quilts, an airplane nightlight, an airplane rug, airplane towels, an airplane shaped "rocking horse," airplane wing-shaped bookshelves, an airplane clock, an airplane desk lamp, airplane board and card games, airplane magnets, airplane Christmas ornaments, airplane notecards, airplane software, CDs of airplane takeoff sounds, airplane posters, airplane videos, and numerous stuffed soft airplanes on his bed, one of which made the loud sound of an airplane taking off. As with many families of children and youth with ASD, we also had SIA-themed birthday parties and took SIA-themed destination vacations (e.g., driving to and staying at airports for the purpose of visiting the airports, not to explore the major nearby cities and their attractions). Taking into account all SIA-related expenses, parents in our study reported that they spent between $100 and $5,000 annually on their children's SIAs. This type of overall impact of home and family life is typical of the far-reaching impact of SIAs in children and youth with ASD.

Perhaps the greatest cost to parents, however, is the energy and commitment required to enthusiastically support the child in his or her pursuit of the SIA. Parents spend countless hours listening to never-ending facts about the SIA, in the car, at the dinner table, in the bathtub, and before bed. Untold hours are invested in trying, yet again, to soothe a distraught, melting-down child when the long-awaited SIA-related item proves disappointing, other children bully him at school because of the SIA, some cherished SIA item is lost or broken, or the child cannot reach the envisioned perfection in an SIA-related creation. Journeying with the child through many years of unchanging or evolving SIAs requires phenomenal patience, dedication, and love, and parents feel at times that they cannot listen to one more word about international license plates, antique fountain pens, Sponge Bob™, or Egyptian history.

What Is the Impact of SIAs on Neurotypical Siblings?

Understandably, neurotypical siblings may have mixed feelings toward a brother or sister's SIA. If the SIA is popular and respected (e.g., the acquisition of fluency in Swahili or advanced photography skills), siblings may feel pride and their own reputations may be enhanced. If, however, a ninth-grade brother or sister is engaged in Teletubbies™, this may bring embarrassment upon siblings, who may deal with their shame by socially excluding the sibling with ASD. Siblings may also feel jealousy regarding the amount of parental time, physical space, or finances that the SIA devours. Resentment can occur if the family develops a reputation at school or among neighbor children for a socially unacceptable SIA (e.g., "that's the family with that weird girl who's always shredding paper!").

Clearly, siblings need support from their parents in understanding the SIA and the critical role it plays in the life of their brother or sister. It is also important for parents to try to share financial resources equally among children, not investing more in the SIA than they do for the other siblings' interests. When it comes to discussing vacations, from weekend camping trips to extended travel, siblings should have equal input in selecting the destination. As in all families, the ability to compromise is vital. This process can provide an excellent opportunity for the brother or sister with ASD to practice the difficult skill of flexibility – sometimes the family does what he or she would like and sometimes they do what other family members would like.

Making the Most of SIAs at Home

There are several ways in which parents can use their child's SIA to increase harmony in the home, encourage family cohesion, and manage behavior. As one mother in our study reported of her son's SIA, it "gives him an outlet … He is very happy, and it reduces the negative interactions in the house." Another parent appreciated a side benefit of SIAs in the home, writing, "It is important to have SIAs that are positive. Interests have [also] given parents a break."

As research supports, it is imperative that parents understand that engaging in the SIA provides a primary, preferred way to relax, de-stress, and cope with the outside world. As Welton (2004) noted through the voice of a child with ASD, "When I'm doing something on my computer or reading or writing about dinosaurs, I feel very happy and relaxed, and I find it really easy to concentrate and focus" (p. 18). It is extremely important that parents afford their child some free time to engage in their SIAs after non-preferred tasks, such as loading the dishwasher, mowing the lawn, or spending another taxing day at school. Allowing a child time to engage in her SIA after stressful events may reduce anxiety, and, therefore, increase her willingness to participate in these events in the future.

Free time in which the child may engage in her SIA can be offered as a reward for completing nonpreferred household chores, such as cleaning the bathroom, gathering dirty laundry, weeding, or emptying wastebaskets. A child with an SIA of horses may earn points toward a horseback riding lesson for keeping her room clean for a week, or a student who has an SIA in aviation may earn a trip to the airport after helping his parents wash the cars. Danny demonstrated that he already understood this principle when he told us, "I can think about [Disney films] when I am free, when I like to have some fun … I can think about it anywhere I want after I cooperate with work."

In order to facilitate communication and encourage interaction between the child with ASD and his family, parents could offer time spent engaging in the SIA in exchange for participation in a family outing. Parents may also wish to arrange day trips or vacations focused on the child's SIA. Family trips to a farm supply store, automobile factory, or train museum may encourage children with interests in animals, cars, or trains to engage their family members in reciprocal conversation. Furthermore, parents could invite family members or friends who share an interest in their child's SIA to participate with the family in an activity focused on the child's SIA.

Perhaps the whole family could plan a vacation centered on visiting the United States Holocaust Memorial Museum in Washington, DC, to pursue the SIA of a child whose passion is Anne Frank and her journal, *The Diary of Anne Frank* (Frank, Frank, & Pressler, 1997). The child would experience the fulfillment of her dream to see the museum, and the city offers myriad additional public attractions for the child's siblings.

Faith communities hold many possibilities for involving the child through his SIA. This may be especially relevant for children and youth with ASD who tend to be spiritual by nature, and attracted to concepts such as faith, prayer, divine power, life, and death (Isanon, 2001; Stillman, 2006). Parents belonging to religious communities may encourage their child's participation with the reward that he be allowed to participate in a church or synagogue activity related to his SIA. A child interested in musical composition, for example, could compose a musical piece for the choir to sing in a service. The SIA could also be used to motivate the student to apply himself to religious education. Preparing for religious rites of passage such as a bat mitzvah, a first communion, or confirmation may be rewarded with a special outing or trip to a place of interest related to the SIA. Parents could also invite adult members of the synagogue with an interest or professional background in the child's SIA to serve as a mentor. Perhaps the adult and child could co-teach a class or workshop to the religious community. A young person with ASD whose passion is classic literature could volunteer to read favorite passages to elderly homebound members of her mosque. A student with a special interest in photography may assist a mentor in creating a synagogue photo membership directory.

Parents can also use the child's SIA to motivate the child to participate in necessary but tedious community outings such as a trip to the dentist, pediatrician, gas station, grocery store, bank, pharmacy, hairdresser, or barber shop. Free time to engage in the SIA after the nonpreferred outing may calm the child and encourage her to behave appropriately to hasten access to the SIA.

How Teachers Can Use SIAs to Increase Student Learning

Incorporating a student's SIA in schoolwork and activities may result in positive changes in attitude, motivation, skills, engagement, compliance, and the general well-being of the student. One simple way to begin creating a bridge to the student through his SIA is to speak in respectful terms regarding the SIA. Although individuals with ASD typically demonstrate traits of obsession among their autism characteristics, and some authors and the media refer to SIAs as obsessions, using this term does not endear a teacher to her students with ASD. Few among us would appreciate our favorite pastimes being referred to as obsessions. The word *obsession* carries pejorative overtones, whereas referring to the interest as an SIA, passion, or focus honors the student and demonstrates genuine support for these fascinating topics.

Utilizing the Power of SIAs at School

Many teachers have yet to realize the power of SIAs on students' classroom behavior, academic performance, and motivation to complete assignments and tasks. The students identified with Asperger's Syndrome in our study bristled at the idea that their SIAs were mere hobbies or leisure activities; they saw them as integral to themselves. They saw no separation between their SIAs and their core beings.

There is an untapped gold mine of drive and passion living within students when they are engaged in their SIAs. The educator's challenge is discerning how best to tap into the reserve of Tom's passion about goats, Owen's love of saxophones, or Danny's zeal for Disney films. The SIA is so intensely important to a student with ASD that he is utterly compelled to be involved with it and to learn more about it. Attwood (2003) described this consuming drive as "the almost insatiable thirst for access to the interest" (p. 131).

From our study of students classified with Asperger's Syndrome, several practical ideas have emerged about how to help teachers integrate individual SIAs into the curriculum and daily practice of these students. Many of these ideas can be applied to students across the autism spectrum.

A classroom teacher may wish to set the stage for incorporating the SIA into a student's school day by interviewing the student about her SIA. This not only demonstrates the teacher's interest to the student, strengthening their connection, but the information gleaned by the teacher reduces the possibility that she arrives at premature, inaccurate conclusions about the student's SIA, otherwise a very real risk. For example, a boy may seem thoroughly invested in a local university football team. Upon talking with him, however, it becomes apparent that he is not interested in playing football or going to football games; rather, his passions are the game statistics and the players' personal achievement records. Talking with the teacher also provides the student an opportunity to converse freely about her passion, gives the teacher an opportunity to assess the student's oral language and communication skills, and ensures the teacher has an accurate understanding of the student's SIA.

Once the teacher has gathered information about the student's SIA, she has at least four ways in which to apply the strength of SIAs in everyday practice toward progress in academic, behavioral, learning methods, and school-based employment applications. In order to apply SIAs to students' daily tasks, however, the educator must first consider honestly her primary goal in assigning particular tasks to the student. Is it her ultimate goal, for example, that Kayla write about her summer vacation as assigned, or is the goal that Kayla *learn to write a well-organized essay*, even if she chooses to write about her SIA, cockroaches? If the teacher can accept that the process of learning occasionally takes priority over an assigned learning product, then she may infuse the SIA into academic tasks to enhance student motivation and progress.

Academics. Where does a teacher begin to incorporate her students' SIAs? First, the teacher must consider a student's areas of academic strength and challenge. In which subjects does a student especially need to be motivated in order to succeed? What small adjustments or adaptations could be made to the curriculum in order to incorporate the student's SIA in those challenging areas?

Incorporating the student's SIA into the math curriculum, for example, can be as easy as placing stickers on a worksheet or writing the SIA topic into story problems, something with which perhaps the child's parent or grandparent could assist. Is there a specific book to read, an Internet site to explore, an expert to consult, a presentation to prepare, or an essay to write on an SIA-related issue? Again, parents may be consulted for assignment ideas and appropriate experts to contact. Several parents reported that their children are quite proficient in Internet research, talking with experts, and sending email. Depending on the child, it may also be appropriate to ask the student for suggestions of relevant assignments that she finds appealing.

Table 12.4 displays ideas for integrating a dinosaur SIA into the typical curriculum of an elementary school student with ASD. For example, a writing lesson for an elementary school student with an SIA in dinosaurs could be to research and write a paper on the Tyrannosaurus Rex, a math lesson could be to solve story problems about how many tons of leaves a Triceratops consumes, and an art assignment could be given to build a clay model of a Stegosaurus.

Table 12.4
Examples of the Integration of Dinosaurs as SIA Into Core Elementary School Curriculum.

Academic Areas	Dinosaur-Integrated Assignments
Reading	Read *The Complete Guide to Prehistoric Life* (Haines & Chambers, 2006).
Writing	Research and write a paper on Tyrannosaurus Rex.
Spelling	Learn to spell names of dinosaurs.
History	Research the Precambrian Period.
Speech	Present life history of paleontologist George Gaylord Simpson, PhD.
Math	Story problems about tons of leaf consumption by Triceratops.
Science	The Asteroid Cretacious Extinction Theory.
Art	Design and build a clay or papier maché model of the Stegosaurus.
Internet Skills	• Research the Smithsonian paleontology wing (Washington, DC) and the American Museum of Natural History of New York. • Consult with paleontologists online.

Table 12.5 displays ideas for integrating a solar system SIA into the curriculum of an upper-elementary school student. These assignments take on the values of Copernicus, the timing of Haley's Comet, and the history of the Messier Deep Space Object.

Table 12.5
Examples of the Integration of the Solar System as SIA Into Core Upper-Elementary School Curriculum

Academic Areas	Solar System-Integrated Assignments
Reading	Read three chapters that interest you in *Astronomy: The Solar System and Beyond* by Michael A. Seeds.
Writing	Have you ever dreamed of discovering a planet or a galaxy? Imagine you found one. Name it after yourself and write a newspaper article announcing your discovery to the world! Where did you find it? How did you discover it? How will your discovery change astronomy?
Spelling	Read Chapter 3, Astronomical Tools, in *Astronomy: The Solar System and Beyond* above. List your favorite tools, such as optical telescope, and learn to spell them. You might want to draw pictures of them, too.
History	Nicolaus Copernicus, a Polish astronomer, lived in 1473-1543. He was a brilliant scientist, but he paid a high price for his belief that the earth rotated around the sun. Read *Copernicus: Founder of Modern Astronomy (Great Minds of Science)* by Catherine M. Andronik to find out what so enraged his critics. Think about this: If you had been Copernicus, do you think you would have changed your theory?
Speech	Dress and present the passion and work of Charles Messier, French astronomer born in 1730. Explain to your audience what is meant by the "Messier Number."
Math	Find out how far each of the eight planets in our solar system are from the earth. Now calculate how far they are from ech other. Which one is furthest from any other planet? Which two are closest together? What is the average distance of all the planets from the earth?
Science	Just what is Halley's Comet and who was Halley? Go to the library to find out exactly what a comet is and why Halley's Comet is so important. How do comets differ from stars? Will Halley's Comet come through again in *your* lifetime?
Art	Choose your favorite Messier Deep Space Object and make it come alive with paint, clay, fabric, recycled objects, or another medium that you choose.
Internet Skills	• Where in the world is the Kuiper Belt? When does NASA plan to go there? What do the oort cloud and some really cold bodies have in common? To find out, research NASA's amazing website at http://www.nasa.gov • Surfing NASA's site or other federal or university websites, find an astronomer and write him or her with your most burning questions about the stars!

Table 12.6 (Winter-Messiers, 2007) displays ideas for integrating a WWI biplane SIA into the typical curriculum of a middle school student with ASD. For example, students can incorporate aircraft parts into their spelling lesson, calculate biplane fuel consumption, and build a Sopwith Camel.

Table 12.6
Example of the Integration of a Special Interest Area Into Core Middle School Curriculum: World War I Biplanes

Academic Areas	Biplane-Integrated Assignments
Reading	Read *Biggles in France* (one of a classic adventure series about World War I pilot Biggles and his biplane).
Writing	Research and write a paper on the Red Baron.
Spelling	Learn aircraft parts vocabulary.
History	Study the impact of aviation on World War I.
Speech	Present the life history of Wilbur and Orville Wright.
Math	Calculate biplane fuel consumption.
Science	Study theory of aerodynamics.
Art	Design and build a balsa wood model of the Sopwith Camel.
Internet Skills	Learn to surf appropriate biplane and biplane hisory websites and positive aviation games, and correspond with pilots and biplane experts.

From "Toilet brushes and tarantulas: Understanding the origin and development of special interest areas in children and youth with Asperger's syndrome," by M. A. Winter-Messiers, 2007, *Journal of Remedial and Special Education, 28*(3), 140-152. Used with permission.

Finally, Table 12.7 (Winter-Messiers, Herr et al., 2007) presents sample ideas for integrating a first ladies SIA into the curriculum of an advanced middle or high school student. These lessons are appropriately more complex and varied, and require higher-order thinking. The purpose of these adaptations is to teach the student the concepts and skills outlined by her school's core curriculum within a context that allows her to accurately represent her knowledge and skills. Teachers can ask, is this student truly *weak* in writing or is she *unmotivated* to write? For some students, it is only by allowing a few assignments to be integrated with the SIA, as in Table 12.4, that teachers will really learn the answer and see a student's true abilities emerge. As reported previously, students with Asperger's Syndrome or high-functioning autism show improvement in communication, social, and fine-motor skills when engaged in their SIAs. Intentionally designing assignments and tasks to incorporate a student's SIA will improve the student's ability to focus on academic tasks. In return, the output produced by the student on these SIA-infused tasks will provide the teacher with the most accurate measure of the student's academic ability.

Please note that in suggesting the integration of SIAs into academic assignments, it is not our intention that a student's SIA be integrated into every academic assignment or that a student should never be required to complete a traditional assignment as originally designed by the teacher. Rather, SIA integration can be used to motivate a student to learn skills, complete particular assignments, and reward compliance with nonpreferred tasks and assignments. Individualized education program (IEP) teams can also consider the regular inclusion of a student's SIA into a student's IEP accommodations to aid in motivation and compliance with schoolwork.

Table 12.7

Examples of the Integration of First Ladies as SIA Into Advanced Middle or High School Curriculum

Academic Areas	First Ladies Integrated Assignments
Reading	Abigail Adams was a voluminous writer who championed the causes of women. Read her letters in *Abigail Adams: A Writing Life* (Gelles, 2002).
Writing	Historically, American First Ladies have chosen a humanitarian cause on which to focus their efforts while in the White House. Write an essay describing the project you would choose and how you would use your influence to bring national attention to your favorite cause.
Spelling	Choose 10 words from your books on Lincoln and Adams that are rare or no longer in use today. Investigate their etymology to learn what they meant at the time. Have they evolved into words that we use today? If not, why do you think they disappeared from use?
History	Eleanor Roosevelt held a more independent and powerful public position in the White House than any prior First Lady. Research how her influence shaped and encouraged the country during World War II.
Speech	Choose your favorite First Lady and portray her in a first-person speech about her personal values and beliefs.
Math	Find the birth and death dates of all the First Ladies, and calculate their ages at death. Plot their life spans on a computer graph. Find the average age of all the women. Did the life span of First Ladies increase over time?
Science	First Lady Mary Lincoln experienced severe depression and, some believe, chronic mental illness. Read *Mary Lincoln: Wife and Widow* (Sandburg, 1995), and consult *The Insanity File: The Case of Mary Todd Lincoln* (Neely & McMurtry, 1993). What was the view of mental illness in Mary Lincoln's day? Are American attitudes different today? Why?
Art	Construct a miniature model of your favorite First Lady's inaugural gown, or design a miniature of a White House room in her era (e.g., the Lincoln bedroom, the restored Kennedy library).
Internet Skills	Choose a First Lady and research her papers online at the National Archives (Washington, DC). Write the curator of the First Ladies exhibit at the National Museum of American History with a question you have about a First Lady. Find three Web sites that provide more information about First Ladies.

From "Dinosaurs 24/7: Understanding the special interests of children with Asperger's," by M. A. Winter-Messiers & C. M. Herr, 2013. Reproduced with permission of Kennedy Krieger Institute, Baltimore, Maryland. This information appeared originally at http://www.iancommunity.org/cs/about_asds/the_special_interests_of_children_with_aspergers.

Children and youth can also benefit from taking classes at school related to their SIAs whenever possible. This has the potential to enhance self-esteem, increase SIA-related skills, and create opportunities for friendships with students having similar interests. In our study, Nate and his mother both referred to his involvement in the school band, an offshoot of his passion for music and composition. Tom referred to wood projects he had constructed in shop class, which gave an outlet for his SIA of woodworking. One parent told of her plans "to set [Will] up in [drawing] classes in a few years."

Behavioral. A second way to apply SIAs in the classroom is by motivating the student to engage in appropriate behavior through engagement in the SIA. For example, a teacher could establish a work/play routine in which the student completes a set number of tasks to earn free time during which she may engage in an activity related to her SIA. In addition, a teacher could reward a student's appropriate behavior by allowing access to his SIA. A student with ASD could learn to self-manage his behavior by taking a sensory break from the class activity to engage in a simple form of his SIA. For example, the child who has countless models of frogs could be asked to pick one for his sensory break. A teacher could also motivate work completion by promising a student whose SIA is the work of Eleanor Roosevelt during WWII that if she writes the assigned essay on the WWII Allies, for the next essay she may write about the war time causes of First Lady Eleanor Roosevelt.

Also important to a discussion of SIAs and behavior is the challenge of working with students whose SIAs become disruptive in the classroom. A girl whose SIA is dragons, for example, may bring 10 dragon figures to school and want to display them all on her desk. We have established the fusion of SIAs and students' core beings; therefore, to remove *all* the dragons is to remove an integral part of the child's self, and is unacceptable. Further, SIAs should never be removed from a student as a punitive measure (e.g., for talking out of turn in class or speaking disrespectfully to a teacher). Teachers would never consider punishing a child who hit a classmate in anger by taking away her hearing aids or removing her braces so she could not walk. Yet the removal of a student's critical SIA-related objects is often the first method of classroom discipline for students with ASD. In the case of the girl with too many dragons at school, the teacher and parents could explain to her why it is not practical to bring so many dragons to school each day. The student could be offered a choice of one or two small dragons to bring, perhaps with a reward system in place to reinforce the desired behavior. Some students are content with a sticker placed on their desks or in their notebooks, reminding them of the beloved train, frog, cowboy hat, or saxophone. Finally, a small representative airplane, dinosaur, or fairy could be carried in a student's pocket or backpack, reassuringly available whenever contact is needed. While it is not always easy to make the transition from large or multiple objects to small or symbolic ones, it can be done with time, support, and rewards.

Learning methods. A third option for applying SIAs in the classroom is for the teacher to allow the student with ASD to use his preferred method of researching information on his SIA to learn about nonpreferred classroom topics. For example, a student who loves to look at books with photographs to learn about cars could use the same method to locate information on mammals for a science lesson. A student such as Nate, who enjoys doing Internet research on the composer John Williams, could use the same method to research explorer Meriwether Lewis for a social studies assignment.

Teachers would be wise to incorporate the student's preferred method of learning to spur work completion. In this age of easily accessible Internet resources, we were surprised when 50% of our participants told us that reading books was their preferred strategy for learning about their SIAs. Will told us, "I always like going to the library; they have really good books" (Winter-Messiers, 2007, p. 148). When asked if he learned about Disney facts from watching movies, Nate replied, "I even find them out in books, too. I have a *Disney A to Z* book that tells me everything about Disney" (Winter-Messiers, 2007, p. 148). Many participants told us they also read about their SIAs online. Sarah said, "I like to read books a lot and learn a lot about other different breeds of horses. Or, like to look on the Internet and books, magazines and all that" (Winter-Messiers, 2007, p. 148). Displaying confidence in his Internet skills, Tom asked us, "Do you know Arizona is supposed to have thunderstorms coming up soon? Some time this week actually they are supposed to have thunderstorms happening there. I read ... I saw it on Netscape" (Winter-Messiers, 2007, p. 148).

School-based employment. A final way in which SIAs may be applied directly to school is to create a school-based job related to the student's SIA. For example, if the student's interest is brooms, the teacher could arrange for the student to work with the custodian in a sweeping routine, perhaps taking responsibility for a section of the school building. A student with an interest in numbers and patterns could work in the school library shelving books. A student interested in radio broadcasting could read morning announcements over the school's public address system. A student interested in football statistics could take data for the coach during the game.

While engaging in these activities, the student learns valuable vocational skills in addition to experiencing first-hand how his SIA may translate to career opportunities after he finishes school. Formal mentoring relationships may also be structured to align the student's SIA with staff who hold expertise in that area. These could include the librarian, science teacher, nurse, custodian, cook, and technology support staff.

Students with ASD want to do well and want to please their teachers. Integrating assigned tasks with SIAs increases the possibility that the student will work hard to achieve his personal goals. Students are highly capable of investing themselves in hard work – if that investment can come through the door of their SIAs.

Dealing With Unacceptable or Harmful SIAs

While many SIAs seem odd or uninteresting to observers, thankfully, few are truly inappropriate, harmful, or illegal and, therefore, unacceptable. Occasionally, however, a child or youth develops a passion for SIAs that, for his or her own safety and sometimes that of others, cannot be permitted. Examples include undergarments, bodily fluids, feces, assault weapons, arson, torture, racist humor, sexual violence, and pornography. In speaking with parents, I have learned that they are often afraid to say "no" to their children's harmful SIAs, for fear of damaging their children in some way. Nevertheless, it is perfectly acceptable to draw boundaries at school and at home concerning SIAs that at best may result in social ostracism and at worst can lead to legal prosecution.

Some of these topics are not harmful in and of themselves. A student whose SIA is phlebotomy and who aspires to a medical career as a phlebotomist is completely appropriate in her study of blood, a bodily fluid. A student interested in fashion design, focusing on lingerie, could be appropriate in her study of undergarments. Even the study of sexual violence, examined through the lens of preventing domestic violence or child abuse, may be completely acceptable.

However, some interpretations of these SIAs are unquestionably harmful, and possibly, illegal. An SIA of child pornography, for example, can lead to arrest, as can an SIA of undergarments, if a teen is publicly displaying his own underwear or trying to touch the bra of the woman sitting next to him on the bus. Further, some SIAs, while not illegal, are not mentally healthy, such as a thorough, ongoing study of torture tactics. Especially in our present cultural climate, any child or youth who studies, purchases, or engages in the use of automatic weapons may be suspect.

In time and with abundant emotional support and a consistent reward system for compliance, some of these wrongly directed SIAs can be focused in proximal directions. For example, a child or youth whose SIA is torture could be guided in the study of The World Organization Against Torture (*Organisation Mondiale Contre la Torture*, OMCT) the largest international coalition of nongovernmental organizations working against torture and other forms of violence. A child or youth focused on automatic weapons may, with significant support and rewards, be directed toward ancient weapons, such as the swords of the legendary Knights of the Round Table, utilized within a strict code of ethics stipulating the knights' behavior. Such a dramatic shift in SIAs is not easy and may not be successful on the first attempt. It requires tremendous patience, support, and perhaps professional therapeutic intervention to help determine the draw of the harmful SIA. But it is always worth the effort to try – and try again – to direct children and youth to healthier interests, which can provide fulfillment and appropriate career opportunities.

Summary and Conclusions

We have too long seen the child with ASD through the lens of deficits, with a curious trailing shadow of special interests. But as Frith (1991) so clearly stated, this view is "hopelessly inadequate" (p. 10) in the face of manifest evidence of the many strengths that individuals with ASD demonstrate when engaged in their SIAs. The children and youth in our study profoundly moved our team as they talked about their SIAs and described their engagement with their SIAs. It was clear that SIAs, critical in their own right, also held the key to transforming our traditionally one-sided deficit view of ASD. Where once we perhaps anticipated only deficits, through the door of their SIAs, we can now anticipate strengths, as demonstrated by the children and youth with AS in our study who were able to plan social interactions, read social cues, and design strategies to deal with bullies. Their self-esteem improved, they exuded positive emotions, their distracting behaviors diminished, and they interacted with focus and clear intent. As Hans Asperger (1991/1944) comprehended long before ASD was a household term, and so eloquently expressed:

> Able autistic individuals can rise to eminent positions and perform with such outstanding success that one may even conclude that only such people are capable of certain achievements. It is as if they had compensatory abilities to counterbalance their deficiencies. Their unswerving determination and penetrating intellectual powers, part of their spontaneous and original mental activity, their narrowness and single-mindedness, as manifested in their special interests, can be immensely valuable and can lead to outstanding achievements in their chosen areas. (p. 88)

It is of prime importance that we infuse the school, home, and community environments of these individuals with opportunities for them to demonstrate their many strengths through engagement in their SIAs. We must be advocates for children and youth and their SIAs. There is no limit to what they can accomplish when they are appropriately encouraged to use their SIAs to improve their academic and social pursuits. Knowing as we do their potential, "We have the right and the duty to speak out for these children with the whole force of our personality" (Asperger, 1991/1944, p. 90). They and their futures are listening for our voices.

Tips for Practical Application

✓ Keep in mind that a special interest can be used to help a student self-calm. Thoughts about the topic are often comforting and can be used to redirect a student's negative thinking.

✓ Interview your student about her special interest. Create a time during the day to sit down and allow the student to talk about her special interest for a few minutes.

✓ Some topics might seem odd for the student's age and can open the student up to bullying. Be aware of this reality and take protective measures to avoid such negative experiences.

✓ Use the ideas from Tables 12.5-12.7 to generate your own ideas for relating a student's SIA to the general curriculum areas.

✓ Create an after-school special interest club. Either focus on one particular interest or on a more global topic. For example, if a student's SIA involves geology, create a general science club and spend time discussing each participant's favorite science topic.

✓ Have your student do an Internet search of her SIA.

✓ Help your student to expand on his SIA. If the interest is in trains, study the countries that have train systems. Find out what languages are spoken in those countries. Explore the answer to how countries decide where to put the train tracks.

✓ Recognize and respect your student's SIA as a part of his emotional self.

Chapter Highlights

- SIAs are often solitary pursuits or preoccupations that dominate the time, attention, and conversation of persons with ASD.

- SIAs are far more than hobbies.

- Some people with ASD say that they *are* their SIAs. SIAs literally are their identity.

- In their SIAs, children and teens with ASD find a stable core. SIAs help them make sense of a world that can feel overwhelming and chaotic, and in that world, feel a measure of power and control.

- SIAs give a focus upon which to channel their often prodigious gifts and shape their dreams.

- SIAs can range from the expected for the age group and gender – trucks for boys and dolls for girls – to the unexpected – scabs, electrical transformers, dust, and batteries – for boys or girls. Not surprisingly, transportation is a popular SIA with boys, and animals are popular with girls.

- SIAs differ in social acceptability based on the age and gender of the individual, the age of the onlooker, the geographic location, and the interest itself.

- The timeline of a given SIA can vary widely from child to child. Some children change SIAs rather quickly. Other children begin with an SIA and stay with it for many years.

- Strengths may emerge as the result of engagement in SIAs.

- Parents can use their child's SIA to increase harmony in the home, encourage family cohesion, and manage behavior.

- Incorporating a student's SIA in schoolwork and activities may result in positive changes in attitude, motivation, skills, engagement, compliance, and the general well-being of the student.

- Occasionally, a child or youth develops a passion for SIAs that, for his or her own safety and sometimes that of others, cannot be permitted. When this occurs, it is important to try to direct children and youth to healthier interests that can provide fulfillment and appropriate career opportunities.

Chapter Review Questions

1. Explain how an SIA of a child with ASD differs from an interest of a typically developing child.

2. What is the relationship between SIAs and self-esteem in those with ASD?

3. Explain how an SIA can both enhance and interfere with relationships with others.

4. Explain the following statement: "When children and youth change SIAs, especially when the change is abrupt or the new SIA differs substantially from the previous one, the transition can be painful for parents."

5. What is the emotional impact of SIAs?

6. How can teachers use SIAs to increase student learning?

7. What are some reasons to encourage an individual with ASD to choose a career in which his employment utilizes his SIA?

References

Andronik, C. M. (2009). *Copernicus: Founder of modern astronomy (great minds of science)*. Berkeley Heights, NJ: Enslow.

Asperger, H. (1991). Die 'Autistischen Psychopathen' im Kindesalter. In U. Frith (Ed. & Trans.), *Autism and Asperger syndrome* (pp. 37-92). New York, NY: Cambridge University Press. (Original work published in 1944)

Attwood, T. (1998). *Asperger's syndrome: A guide for parents and professionals*. Philadelphia, PA: Jessica Kingsley.

Attwood, T. (2003). Understanding and managing circumscribed interests. In M. Prior (Ed.), *Learning and behavior problems in Asperger syndrome* (pp. 126-147). New York, NY: Guilford Press.

Attwood, T. (2006). *The complete guide to Asperger's syndrome*. Philadelphia, PA: Jessica Kingsley.

Baron-Cohen, S. (2000). Is Asperger syndrome/high-functioning autism necessarily a disability? *Development and Psychopathology, 3*, 489-500.

Cohen, M. (2003). *Understanding the unique social challenges of females with Asperger syndrome*. Retrieved from www.autismsrc.org/whatsnew/ASA presentation_files/frame.htm

Frank, A., Frank, O., & Pressler, M. (1997). *The diary of Anne Frank*. New York, NY: Bantam.

Frith, U. (Ed.). (1991). *Autism and Asperger syndrome*. New York, NY: Cambridge University Press.

Frith, U. (2003). *Autism: Explaining the enigma* (2nd ed.). Oxford, UK: Blackwell.

Gelles, E. (2002). *Abigail Adams: A writing life*. New York, NY: Routledge.

Grandin, T., & Duffy, K. (2009). *Developing talents: Careers for individuals with Asperger syndrome and high-functioning autism*. Shawnee Mission, KS: AAPC Publishing.

Haines, T., & Chambers, P. (2006). *The complete guide to prehistoric life.* Richmond Hill, Ontario: Firefly.

Isanon, A. (2001). *Spirituality and the autism spectrum: Of falling sparrows.* Philadelphia, PA: Jessica Kingsley.

Johns, W. E. (1935/2009). *Biggles in France.* London, UK: Red Fox.

Myles, B. S., & Simpson, R. L. (2003). *Asperger syndrome: A guide for educators and parents* (2nd ed.). Austin, TX: PRO-ED.

Neely, M. E., & McMurtry, R. G. (1993). *The insanity file: The case of Mary Todd Lincoln.* Carbondale, IL: Southern Illinois University Press.

Piven, J., Harper, J., Palmer, P., & Arndt, S. (1996). Course of behavioral change in autism: A retrospective study of high-IQ adolescents and adults. *Journal of the American Academy of Child and Adolescent Psychiatry, 35,* 523-529.

Sandburg, C. (1995). *Mary Lincoln: Wife and widow.* Bedford, MA: Applewood Books.

Seeds, M. A. (2009). *Astronomy: The solar system and beyond.* Pacific Grove, CA: Brooks Cole.

Stillman, W. (2006). *Autism and the God connection: True stories of autism's spiritual mysteries and revelations.* Naperville, IL: Sourcebooks.

Tantam, D. (1991). Asperger syndrome in adulthood. In U. Frith (Ed.), *Autism and Asperger syndrome* (pp. 147-183). Cambridge, UK: Cambridge University Press.

Tantam, D. (2000). Adolescence and adulthood of individuals with Asperger syndrome. In A. Klin, F. R. Volkmar, & S. Sparrow (Eds.), *Asperger syndrome* (pp. 367-402). New York, NY: Guilford Press.

Tréhin, G. (2006). *Urville.* Philadelphia, PA: Jessica Kingsley.

Welton, J. (2004). *Can I tell you about Asperger syndrome? A guide for friends and family.* Philadelphia, PA: Jessica Kingsley.

Winter-Messiers, M. A. (2007). Toilet brushes and tarantulas: Understanding the origin and development of special interest areas in children and youth with Asperger's syndrome. *Journal of Remedial and Special Education, 28*(3), 140-152.

Winter-Messiers, M. A., & Herr, C. M. (2013). *Dinosaurs 24/7: Understanding the special interests of children with Asperger's.* Baltimore, MD: Interactive Autism Network (IAN), Kennedy Krieger Institute; http://www.iancommunity.org/cs/about_asds/the_special_interests_of_children_with_aspergers

Winter-Messiers, M. A., Herr, C. M., Wood, C. E., Brooks, A. P., Gates, M. M., Houston, T. L., & Tingstad, K. I. (2007). How far can Brian ride the Starlight 4449 Express? *Focus on Autism and Other Developmental Disabilities, 22*(2), 67-79.

Learner Objectives

After reading this chapter, the learner should be able to:

- List the skills needed to understand others' emotional and mental states

- Explain how difficulties in understanding mental states underlie the social interaction difficulties that are part of the ASD diagnosis

- Discuss what studies have shown regarding the ability of individuals with ASD to identify emotional states from visual, auditory, contextual, or multimodal examples

- Discuss what is meant by systemizing and how this skill in individuals with ASD Level 1 may be capitalized on when teaching individuals how to recognize emotions

- Explain how individuals with ASD are typically taught to recognize emotion

- State the advantages of using computers in teaching individuals with ASD

- Discuss how generalization difficulties related to ASD limit the effectiveness of intervention programs such as *Mind Reading* and how they are explained by the systemizing model

- Discuss what the program *Mind Reading* is and its value as a teaching tool for emotional recognition in individuals with ASD

Chapter 13

Systemizing Emotions: Using Interactive Multimedia as a Teaching Tool

Ofer Golan • Simon Baron-Cohen

During break time, Henry approached Matthew, who is 10 years old and diagnosed with ASD Level 1. Henry tried to make friends with Matthew and asked him about his favorite games. Matthew replied with a monologue about his favorite airplane models and the unique features of each. When Henry sarcastically commented, "That's sooo interesting!" and walked off in the middle of Matthew's monologue, Matthew couldn't understand why. If he found it so interesting, why had Henry walked away? Matthew couldn't interpret the look of boredom on Henry's face.

This description of one incident in the school life of a child with an autism spectrum disorder (ASD) demonstrates how many children and adults with ASD experience social interactions. The ability to use nonverbal information from **facial expressions**, **vocal intonation**, **body language**, and context to understand emotional and other mental states underlies social and communication skills (Baron-Cohen, 1995). Due to difficulties gathering, integrating, and interpreting such information, an individual with ASD can feel like a Martian on the playground (Sainsbury, 2000).

Difficulties with emotion and **mental-state recognition** (Baron-Cohen, 1995; Hobson, 1994), in turn, underlie the social difficulties that are part of the ASD diagnosis. Such difficulties have been found through cognitive, behavioral, and neuroimaging studies, and across different sensory modalities (visual and auditory) (Frith & Hill, 2004).

This chapter explores whether computer-based tailored interventions targeting emotion recognition and mental state recognition difficulties are useful methods for helping people on the autism spectrum improve their emotion recognition skills.

Recognizing Emotions

Emotion recognition difficulties in ASD may be found in different sources of emotional information. Here we review research findings from each of these channels (**facial, vocal, contextual,** and **multimodal**).

Facial Emotion Recognition in Autism

The majority of studies of emotion recognition have focused on the face and have tested recognition of six emotions (happiness, sadness, fear, anger, surprise, and disgust). These "basic" emotions are expressed and recognized universally (Ekman, 1993; Ekman & Friesen, 1971). Some studies have revealed emotion recognition deficits among individuals with ASD compared to typically developing people matched on age and IQ, or individuals with learning difficulties (e.g., Down syndrome). These studies have used both still photos (Celani, Battacchi, & Arcidiacono, 1999; Deruelle, Rondan, Gepner, & Tardif, 2004; Macdonald et al., 1989) and dynamic videos of facial expressions (Hobson, 1986a, 1986b; Yirmiya, Sigman, Kasari, & Mundy, 1992).

Other studies have found that children and adults with high-functioning autism (HFA) or Asperger Syndrome (AS) (currently known as ASD Level 1) have no difficulties in recognizing basic emotions from pictures (Adolphs, 2001; Grossman, Klin, Carter, & Volkmar, 2000) or films (Loveland et al., 1997), and that the deficit only becomes apparent when testing recognition of more "complex" emotions (such as embarrassment, insincerity, intimacy, etc.) (Baron-Cohen, Wheelwright, Hill, Raste, & Plumb, 2001; Baron-Cohen, Wheelwright, & Jolliffe, 1997; Baron-Cohen, Wheelwright, Spong, Scahill, & Lawson, 2001; Golan, Baron-Cohen, & Hill, 2006). Thus, these findings suggest that recognition of basic emotions is relatively preserved among individuals with ASD Level 1 and that they experience greater difficulties recognizing more complex emotional and mental states.

Neuroimaging studies of emotion recognition from faces reveal that people with ASD demonstrate less activation in brain regions central to face processing, such as the fusiform gyrus (Critchley et al., 2000; Pierce, Muller, Ambrose, Allen, & Courchesne, 2001; Schultz et al., 2003). Further, behavioral studies have shown that children and adults with ASD process faces differently than controls: Participants with ASD tend to process faces using a feature-based approach (i.e., attending to parts of the face, such as the mouth, nose, or the eyes), whereas typically developing individuals process faces as a whole (Hobson, Ouston, & Lee, 1988; Schultz et al., 2003; Teunisse & De Gelder, 1994; Young, 1998). Evidence has also been found of reduced activation in brain areas that play a major role in processing emotion, such as the amygdala, when individuals with ASD process social-emotional information (Ashwin, Baron-Cohen, Wheelwright, O'Riordan, & Bullmore, 2007; Baron-Cohen et al., 1999; Critchley et al., 2000).

Vocal Recognition of Emotion in Autism

Emotion recognition from voices has been studied less frequently than emotional recognition from facial recognition. As for facial recognition, the findings are inconclusive (Boucher, Lewis, & Collis, 2000; Loveland, Tunali Kotoski, Chen, & Brelsford, 1995; Loveland et al., 1997). Regarding recognition of complex emotions from voices, several studies have reported a deficit in performance of adults with ASD Level 1 compared to controls (Golan et al., 2006; Golan, Baron-Cohen, Hill, & Rutherford, 2007; Kleinman, Marciano, & Ault,

2001; Rutherford, Baron Cohen, & Wheelwright, 2002). One study measured the brain activity of participants with ASD and matched typically developing controls while they were listening to stories that require understanding other people's mental states, taken from the **Strange Stories Test** (Happé, 1994) described below. Activation in the medial frontal area of the brain, an area used for judging others' mental states, was less intensive and extensive in the ASD group compared to controls (Nieminen-von Wendt et al., 2003). This finding suggests that the difficulties individuals with ASD show in eliciting emotional and mental information in the auditory channel are also reflected in a different pattern of brain activity.

Contextual Recognition of Emotion in Autism

Studies assessing the ability of individuals with ASD to identify emotions and mental states from context have also pointed to deficits in these areas relative to the general population or to other clinical control groups (Baron-Cohen, Leslie, & Frith, 1986; Fein, Lucci, Braverman, & Waterhouse, 1992). For example, adolescents and adults with ASD had difficulties answering questions on the *Strange Stories Test* (Happé, 1994; Jolliffe & Baron-Cohen, 1999), which assesses the ability to provide context-appropriate mental state explanations for nonliteral statements made by story characters. Stories include the use of irony, lies, white lies, or jokes, all requiring the ability to understand people's mental states.

For example, one story depicted a white lie. A child wanted a rabbit for Christmas. When she got a boring encyclopedia instead, she said that was exactly what she wanted. Participants with ASD were asked to explain why the child responded like that, and whether it was a true reflection of how she felt. To answer such questions assumes an understanding of the child's consideration of other people's feelings, which made her say the opposite of what she felt. Children and adults with ASD have difficulty with such tasks. When using this task in a neuroimaging study, reduced activation of the left medial prefrontal cortex was found in people with ASD compared to matched controls (Happé et al., 1996).

Multimodal Recognition of Emotion in Autism

A few studies have assessed the recognition of complex emotion and mental states from life-like social situations (e.g., films). Such situations contain facial, vocal, body language, and contextual information, which the participant needs to process in parallel and integrate into a whole picture in order to understand what is going on. Individuals with ASD show a deficit compared to controls when performing such tasks (Golan, Baron-Cohen, Hill, & Golan, 2006; Heavey, Phillips, Baron-Cohen, & Rutter, 2000; Klin, Jones, Schultz, Volkmar, & Cohen, 2002). For example, a scene from the *Reading the Mind in Films* task (Golan, Baron-Cohen, Hill, & Golan, 2006), labeled *overcome* and shown in Figure 13.2, depicts a young woman complimenting an older woman on the way she educated the children. The older woman thanks her several times calmly, then runs towards her with tears in her eyes saying, "Oh Miss, I'm so glad you're here."

In order to tell how the older woman is feeling, information from her facial expression, tone of voice, and context must be integrated. Individuals with ASD score significantly lower on such tasks than controls. Their difficulties may be related to a failure to pick up the correct emotional cues and/or a failure to integrate them into a whole picture. The latter may stem from a cognitive style named weak central coherence, a major characteristic of ASD, and stress attention to detail instead of integration into a large, holistic, picture. At the neurobiological level, this difficulty may be manifested by under-connectivity between brain regions, which impedes integration of details in frontal brain areas (Belmonte, Allen et al., 2004; Belmonte, Cook et al., 2004; Critchley et al., 2000).

To summarize, although emotion recognition deficits in ASD are lifelong, some more capable individuals develop compensatory strategies that allow them to recognize basic emotions. However, when recognition of more complex emotions and mental states is required, either from faces, voices, context, or an integration of these, many individuals with ASD find them hard to interpret.

Systemizing in Autism

In contrast to these difficulties, individuals with ASD show good, and sometimes even superior, skills in systemizing (Baron-Cohen, 2003). "**Systemizing**" is the drive to analyze or build systems in order to understand and predict the behavior of rule-based events. Most individuals with ASD are hyper-attentive to detail and prefer predictable, rule-based environments, features that are intrinsic to systemizing. In addition, they are superior to controls on tasks that involve searching for detail, and analyzing and manipulating systems. This is reflected in improved performance on tasks such as visual scanning tasks (O'Riordan, Plaisted, Driver, & Baron-Cohen, 2001); the *Wechsler Intelligence Scale Block Design* task (Shah & Frith, 1993), which requires the ability to visualize a geometric gestalt as a combination of small constituent shapes; *Folk Physics* tasks (Baron-Cohen, Wheelwright, Spong et al., 2001; Lawson, Baron-Cohen, & Wheelwright, 2004), which include physics and mechanics questions that can be answered based on a lay person's everyday experience; and the *Embedded Figures Test* (Jolliffe & Baron-Cohen, 1997), which requires picking out a simple geometric shape from a complex pattern in which it is embedded. Individuals with ASD also report they are apt to pay more attention to and express more interest in systematic phenomena compared to the general population (Baron-Cohen, Richler, Bisarya, Gurunathan, & Wheelwright, 2003).

If individuals with ASD Level 1 possess good systemizing skills, it is possible that they will be able to use them to compensate for some of their empathizing difficulties, in this case, their difficulties recognizing emotions. This might be difficult, however, because the socio-emotional world is a context-related open system (Lawson, 2003) that is typically unpredictable and difficult to conceptualize using strict rules. Nevertheless, if provided with a *system* of emotions, it is plausible that their systemizing skills could be harnessed to help individuals with ASD learn to recognize emotions.

Next, we review past attempts to teach emotion recognition to individuals with ASD and describe a new systematic guide to emotions and its evaluation with adults with ASD.

Teaching Emotion Recognition

Past attempts to teach emotion recognition to adults and children with ASD have either focused on the basic emotions (Hadwin, Baron-Cohen, Howlin, & Hill, 1996; Howlin, Baron-Cohen, & Hadwin, 1999) or have been part of social skills training courses, usually run in groups (Barry et al., 2003; Howlin & Yates, 1999; Rydin, Drake, & Bratt, 1999). These training programs typically do not focus specifically on systematically teaching emotion recognition, but address other issues, such as conversation, reducing socially inappropriate behavior, personal hygiene, and so on. In such groups, it is difficult to target the individual's specific pace of learning. Finally, such groups are socially demanding and might, therefore, deter more socially anxious participants.

Using Computers to Teach Emotion Recognition

Other attempts to teach individuals with ASD to recognize emotions and mental states have used computer-based training (Bernard Opitz, Sriram, & Nakhoda Sapuan, 2001; Bolte et al., 2002; Hetzroni & Tannous, 2004; Rajendran & Mitchell, 2000; Silver & Oakes, 2001; Swettenham, 1996). The use of computer software has several advantages for individuals with ASD, including the following:

1. Individuals with ASD favor the computerized environment, since it is predictable, consistent, and free from social demands, which they often find stressful.

2. Users can work at their own pace and level of understanding.

3. Lessons can be repeated over and over again, until mastery is achieved.

4. Interest and motivation can be maintained through different and individually selected computerized rewards (Bishop, 2003; Moore, McGrath, & Thorpe, 2000; Parsons & Mitchell, 2002).

Previous studies have found that the use of computers can help individuals with ASD understand mental states (such as beliefs) and learn that mental states can differ from reality (such as in the case of false beliefs, when one believes something to be true, though in reality it is not) (Swettenham, 1996). Computer-based training programs have also taught individuals with ASD to recognize basic emotions from cartoons and still photographs (Bolte et al., 2002; Silver & Oakes, 2001) and to solve problems in illustrated social situations (Bernard Opitz et al., 2001). However, participants have found it difficult to generalize their knowledge from learned material to related tasks.

The computer-based interventions above used drawings or photographs for training rather than more life-like stimuli. This might have made generalization harder than if more ecologically valid or real-life stimuli had been used. In addition, the programs teaching emotion recognition have focused on basic emotions, and only on facial expressions.

No program reported to date has systematically trained complex emotion recognition in both visual and auditory channels with life-like faces and voices. In our research, summarized next, we have designed and evaluated such a program. The underlying question was: Can the good systemizing skills that individuals with ASD possess be used to teach them to improve their recognition of complex emotions?

Mind Reading – *A Systematic Guide to Emotions*

In the remainder of this chapter, we will focus on *Mind Reading* (Baron-Cohen, Golan, Wheelwright, & Hill, 2004), an interactive guide to emotions and mental states, and its value as a tailored teaching tool for emotion recognition for learners on the autism spectrum.

Mind Reading is based on a taxonomic system of 412 emotions and mental states, grouped into 24 emotion groups and 6 developmental levels (from age 4 to adulthood). The emotions and mental states are organized systematically, according to the emotion groups and developmental levels. Each emotion group is introduced and demonstrated by a short video clip giving some clues for later analysis of the emotions presented. Each emotion is defined and demonstrated by six silent films of faces, six voice recordings, and six written examples of situations that illustrate a given emotion. The resulting library of emotional "assets" (video clips, audio clips, or brief stories) comprise 412 x 18 = 7,416 units of emotion information to learn to recognize or understand, yielding a rich and systematically organized set of educational material. To facilitate generalization, the face videos and voice recordings comprise actors of both genders and of various ages and ethnicities.

Faces and voices are presented separately for each emotion (i.e., silent face films and faceless voice recordings) to encourage analysis of the emotion in each modality and to facilitate learning by avoiding overburdening the user perceptually as well as cognitively. All face video clips and voice recordings have been validated by a panel of 10 independent judges, and were included in *Mind Reading* if at least 8 judges agreed the emotional label given described the face/voice.

The Architecture of the Mind Reading *Software*

This emotions database is accessed using three applications.

The emotion library allows users to browse freely through the different emotions and emotion groups, play the faces, voices, and scenarios giving examples of the emotions, read stories, add their own notes, and compare different emotional expressions in the face and the voice using a scrapbook.

The learning center uses lessons, quizzes, and several reward collections to teach about emotions in a more structured and directive way. In addition to teaching about the 24 emotion groups, it also includes lessons and quizzes about the most common emotions, as well as a "build your own lesson/quiz" option. The various reward collections were chosen for their potential appeal to users with ASD, and were arranged systematically (e.g., pictures and information about space elements, clips of birds arranged by families, different types of trains to collect). A reward is given when a quiz question is answered correctly.

The game zone, comprised of five educational games, allows users to enjoy a game while studying about emotions. Games include a "pairs" game with emotional faces, matching thought and feeling bubbles to characters in a series of real-life situations, recognizing an emotion by gradually revealing different parts of a face, and others.

The software was created for use by children and adults of various levels of functioning. Vocal and animated helpers give instructions on every screen. Figure 13.1 shows screen shots from the software (www.jkp.com/mindreading).

A Study of Adults With ASD Using Mind Reading *Over 10-15 Weeks*

We tested for any improvement in adults with ASD Level 1 in emotion recognition (ER) skills following independent use of the software, and the extent to which these users can generalize their acquired knowledge. The intervention took place over a period of 10-15 weeks to ensure a meaningful period for training, recognizing that a longer duration might lead to some participations dropping out.

Participants were tested before and after the intervention. A no-computer-intervention control group of adults with ASD Level 1 was matched to the intervention group. The ASD Level 1 control group was also tested before and after a similar period of time, but received no intervention. The no-intervention group was included

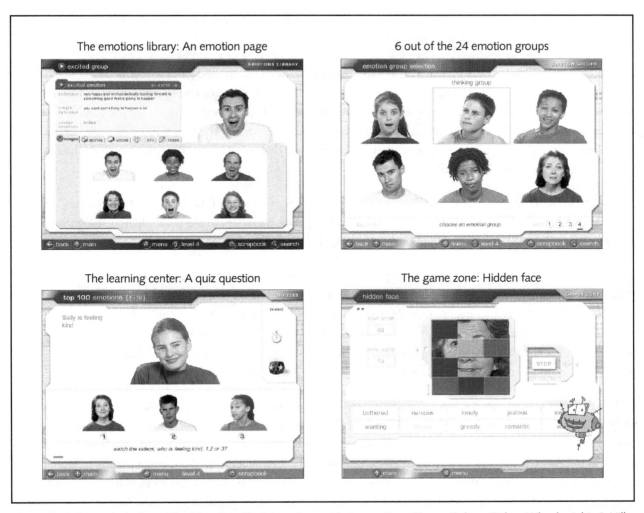

Figure 13.1. Screenshots from *Mind Reading*, the interactive guide to emotions (Baron-Cohen, Golan, Wheelwright, & Hill, 2004). Used with permission.

to assess whether any improvement was related to the intervention or merely due to taking the tasks twice or to the passage of time. Finally, a third, typical, control group from the general population was matched to the intervention groups. This group was only tested once to obtain baseline measures.

In order to test whether software users could generalize their acquired knowledge to other situations, we compared the groups' performance at three different levels of generalization, using stimuli in two perceptual modalities (visual and auditory):

Close generalization. This level tested ER from stimuli that were included in *Mind Reading*, so that participants may have been exposed to them while using the software. This was tested by playing face video clips and voice recordings that were included in *Mind Reading* on a different computer program, with more answers to choose from and with no feedback or support, as provided in *Mind Reading*. The battery used to test facial and vocal ER in this level, *The Cambridge Mindreading (CAM) Face-Voice Battery* (Golan, Baron-Cohen, & Hill, 2006), includes a face task and a voice task, with 50 items in each, to test recognition of 20 different complex emotions and mental states (e.g., intimate, insincere, nervous), all taken from *Mind Reading*.

In both tasks, four adjectives are presented after each stimulus has been played, and participants are asked which adjective best describes how the person feels. An example of the face task, showing one frame from one of the clips is shown in Figure 13. 2. The battery provides an overall facial and an overall vocal ER score, as well as individual scores for each of the 20 emotions assessed (pass/fail) and an overall number of the emotions correctly recognized. Individuals with ASD have been found to score significantly lower than controls on all three scores of the battery (Golan, Baron-Cohen, & Hill, 2006).

Feature-based distant generalization. This level tested the ability to transfer ER skills separately in faces and voices, using faces and voices that were not included in *Mind Reading*. This was tested in the visual channel using the *Reading the Mind in the Eyes* task (Revised, Adult version; Baron-Cohen et al., 2001).

The task includes 36 items. Participants are presented with a photograph of the eyes region of the face and must choose one of four adjectives or phrases to describe the mental state of the person pictured (see Figure 13.2 for an example). In the auditory channel, we used the *Reading the Mind in the Voice* task (Revised; Golan, Baron-Cohen et al., 2007), which includes 25 speech segments taken from BBC drama series. After each segment has been played, participants are asked to choose out of four adjectives the one that best describes how the speaker is feeling. Adult participants with ASD scored significantly lower than matched controls on both tasks.

Holistic distant generalization. This level comprised multimodal socio-emotional stimuli, including faces, voices, body language, and context. It used the *Reading the Mind in Films* task (Golan et al., 2006), which consisted of 22 short social scenes taken from feature films. Participants were presented with four adjectives and asked to choose the one that best describes the way a target character feels at the end of the scene. Figure 10.2 presents a screenshot from one of the task items. Participants with ASD performed significantly worse on this task compared to matched controls. This level was only tested at Time 2. Participants with ASD Level 1 were randomly allocated into the first two groups below.

Software home users. Nineteen participants (14 males and 5 females) were asked to use the software (provided free of charge) at home by themselves for 2 hours a week over a period of 10 weeks, for a total of 20 hours. Participants were included in the study if they completed a minimum of 10 hours of work with the software. If they did not complete this minimum, they were given an extension of up to 4 weeks to do more work with the software.

ASD Level 1 control group. Twenty-two participants (17 males and 5 females) attended the assessment meetings with a 10- to 15-week period between them, during which they did not take part in any intervention related to emotion recognition.

Typical control group. Twenty-eight participants were recruited for a control group from a local employment agency.

The three groups were matched on age, Verbal and Performance IQ, handedness, and gender. They spanned an equivalent range of employment and educational levels.

1. Close generalization: The CAM face task (Golan, Baron-Cohen & Hill, 2006).

2. Feature-based distant generalization: *Reading the Mind in the Eyes Test* (Baron-Cohen, Wheelwright, Hill, Raste, & Plumb, 2001).

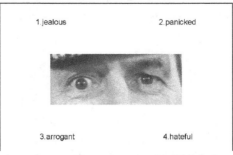

3. Holistic distant generalization: *Reading the Mind In Films* task (Golan, Baron-Cohen, Hill, & Golan, 2006). Screenshot taken from *The Turn of the Screw* (1999). Courtesy of Granada International.

Figure 13.2. Examples of visual tasks from the three generalization levels. Used with permission.

Procedure of the Study

Participants in the ASD Level 1 control group were asked to come in for two assessments, separated by 10 to 15 weeks. *Mind Reading* was introduced to the participants of the intervention group in detail. This included a presentation of the emotion taxonomy and the different areas and a demonstration of a systematic analysis of an emotion, comparing different faces and voices to identify the unique facial/intonation features of the emotion. Participants were asked to use the emotions library and learning center as they wished, but not to use the game zone for more than a third of the usage time (to ensure they focused on systematic analysis of faces and voices).

Participants were encouraged to analyze the facial and vocal stimuli systematically. For example, systematically comparing all the facial expressions of *insincere* included in *Mind Reading* reveals a conflict between the smiling mouth and the avoiding eyes. Taken together, *insincere* could be distinguished from *interested* or *intimate*, which also involve smiles, as these genuine smiles involve the mouth as well as the eyes. Similarly, a systematic analysis of *insincere* in the voice showed a conflict between the content of the verbalization (e.g., "that is very interesting") and the intonation with which it is said, which breaks the sentence to suggest insincerity (e.g., "yes ... that is very ... interesting"). If participants studied the facial and vocal expressions systematically in the various emotions covered in *Mind Reading*, it was expected that they would not only be able to recognize these emotions when played to them using examples from the software (Example #1 in Figure 10.2), but also to use this knowledge to recognize visual and auditory stimuli not included in the software, like the *Reading the Mind in the Voice* task or the *Reading the Mind in the Eyes* task (Example #2 in Figure 13.2). In addition, if participants were able to integrate their knowledge of visual and auditory expression of emotion, it was expected they would be able to recognize emotions from holistic stimuli, such as the scenes presented in *Reading the Mind in Films* (Example #3 in Figure 13.2).

Does the Intervention Help?

After 10-20 hours of using the software over a period of 10-15 weeks, users significantly improved in their ability to recognize complex emotions and mental states from both faces and voices compared to their performance before the intervention, relative to the control group. This finding is encouraging, considering the short usage time, the large number of emotions included in the software, and the fact that participants were not asked to study these particular emotions. Since no differences were found between the two ASD groups at Time 1, any difference at Time 2 can be attributed to the intervention.

The intervention group also improved significantly on close generalization measures, including faces, voices, and the emotions with which individuals with ASD Level 1 had particular difficulties (Golan et al., 2006). In the case of *insincere*, described above, participants who used *Mind Reading* improved on their ability to recognize this emotion following systematic use of the software. Improvement in the ability to recognize deception, as well as other mental states such as *intimate* or *grave*, might have a positive effect on their confidence, willingness, and functioning in interpersonal situations. This, together with participants' reports of greater attention to faces and emotions and improved eye contact, suggests that analysis of emotions using *Mind Reading* allows people with ASD to improve emotion recognition skills from both faces and voices.

Generalization Issues

Improvement following the use of the software was limited to different presentations and variations on taught stimuli (i.e., to faces and voices taken from *Mind Reading*). Participants found it difficult to generalize their knowledge to other tasks of emotion recognition from voices and eyes, and did not perform better than controls on a task involving integration of facial, vocal, and contextual cues. Similar findings of poor generalization have been noted in studies teaching understanding of mental states, emotion recognition, and social skills to individuals with ASD (Bolte et al., 2002; Hadwin et al., 1996; Swettenham, 1996, 2000). However, software usage time was positively correlated with film task scores, suggesting that using the software for a longer period assists with generalization to holistic, life-like situations. Indeed, a followup a year later has shown that participants who continued to use *Mind Reading* reported having improved friendship skills.

Generalization difficulties have been reported to be characteristic of autism spectrum conditions (Rimland, 1965). A focus on small details at the expense of being able to see the larger picture (Frith, 1989), abstraction difficulties, and insistence on sameness may make generalization a challenge for individuals with ASD. Various models have been proposed to try to explain these generalization difficulties, including adherence to rule-based categorization while failing to use prototype-based categorizations (Klinger & Dawson, 1995); an inability to recognize the similarities between stimuli (Plaisted, 2001); or the inability to deal with open systems of the social world, instead focusing on closed-system, rule-based atomic physical phenomena (Klin, Jones, Schultz, & Volkmar, 2003; Lawson, 2003).

Weak Generalization or Strong Systemizing?

Our own view is that reduced generalization is not so much a reflection of a deficit as a reflection of the strong drive to systemize in people with ASD (Baron-Cohen, 2000). Good systemizing requires that one pays attention to the small details between variables in case they are important for understanding how the system works. As such, a good systemizer resists grouping variables together until there is reliable evidence to suggest that there are no functional differences between the variables. To group them together risks losing key information.

According to this view, the ability to generalize by individuals without ASD is a sign of reduced systemizing, whereas reduced ability to generalize by individuals with ASD is a sign of their talent at systemizing, as revealed on analytic tests (such as the *Embedded Figures Test* or the *Folk Physics* tasks described above). Because the socio-emotional world is flexible, context-dependent, and often unpredictable, it is difficult (if not impossible) to systemize. Thus, attempting to systematically teach about emotions to individuals with ASD may lead to rigid application of the system, and eventually to limited generalization.

Where Do We Go From Here?

Mind Reading was used as the intervention for adults with ASD to exploit their systemizing skills. As a systematic guide to emotions, *Mind Reading* trained recognition of faces and voices separately. Results showed that this was successful. Paradoxically, this way of teaching encouraged an atomized rather than an integrative learning style. Whereas it led to improved recognition of emotions and mental states from faces and voices separately, it did not promote integration of these features into a holistic picture, which limited generalization to holistic material. Hence, we recommend that *Mind Reading* be viewed as a first step in a training program.

In this first step, *Mind Reading* could be used (on an individual basis or in a classroom setting) to provide the user with examples. The next steps would deal with the systematic introduction of context and integration of different socio-emotional cues into one (flexible) picture. To ease generalization, each step must to be explicitly connected to previous ones, and the main features must be pointed out (Ozonoff, 1995). After acquiring sufficient understanding of how emotions look and sound, using *Mind Reading*, individuals with ASD should practice integrating these and adapting them according to contextual cues. This mediation between computer-based systematic training and real-life flexibility could be led by teachers in school settings, and/or by parents at home. Suggestions for such activities appear under Tips for Practical Application at the end of the chapter.

The use of computer-based tasks to evaluate learning and generalization in this study has its limitations. Though such tasks allow for controlled and structured assessment of emotion recognition skills, testing different modalities separately, they are quite different from real-life experience. Hence, the relevance of improvement among the software users in this study to real-life functioning should be considered with care. Indeed, some participants commented that they found recognizing emotions and mental states on the computer easier than doing this in real social situations, which requires cross-modal information processing and an immediate reaction in real time. This suggests that evaluation of emotion recognition abilities via computer tasks should be backed up by observations in real-life situations, as well as feedback from parents, teachers, and the individuals with ASD themselves.

Significant correlations were found between usage time and improvement scores on some tasks. Of particular interest were the positive correlation with the holistic film task and the results of our one-year followup, suggesting that the use of the software might be associated with distant generalization measures.

Research studies indicate that individuals with ASD have both developmental delays and long-lasting difficulties in mental state recognition (Baron-Cohen, 1995; Frith & Hill, 2004). Our results suggest that learning aspects of empathizing skills (such as the emotion recognition component) is possible by people with ASD even into adulthood and that improvement in such areas is achieved when the intervention harnesses their systemizing strengths. Even greater improvement may be achieved if intervention was started at a developmentally earlier point. We are currently investigating the effectiveness of this method with children with ASD (Golan, Baron-Cohen, & Golan, 2008; Golan & Baron-Cohen, 2006; LaCava, Golan, Baron-Cohen, & Myles, 2007).

Summary and Conclusions

The results of this study, as well as the participants' reports of looking more at faces and engaging in more eye contact following the use of *Mind Reading*, call for neuroimaging studies to examine possible changes in the functioning of brain areas (in the amygdala, fusiform gyrus, or prefrontal cortex), and for gaze-tracking studies to examine subtle behavioral changes following the systematic study of emotions using *Mind Reading*. Such studies would help determine whether the observed cognitive changes reported here are arising from changes in those neural regions that are typically recruited by the non-autistic brain, or if they are due to compensatory strategies by other neural regions.

We conclude that the present experiment indicates that complex emotion-recognition can be improved over a relatively brief training period (10-15 weeks), when systematic methods such as *Mind Reading* are employed. Additional methods (possibly over a longer time period) are required to improve generalization.

Tips for Practical Application

✓ **Choose key emotions to work on that match the children's developmental stage**. With 412 different emotions and mental states included in *Mind Reading*, it is easy to lose track of the emotions and mental states that are appropriate for your students. The selected emotions should not be too challenging, but also not too easy for a given child. Use the level system of *Mind Reading* to determine which emotions are appropriate for the age group you work with.

✓ **Discuss emotion groups, emotion causes and consequences, and emotional valence and intensity with the children**. Ask questions such as the following: Which emotions belong to the same group? What are their common features? What makes some more basic than others? How does context distinguish different emotions in the same group (e.g., feeling *lonely* is feeling *sad* in the context of having no one to be with)? How do changes in the situation or in what other people say or do define the emotion we feel? Ask the children to provide their own examples of causes. Discuss consequences (e.g., what happens when I show my anger?). Sort emotions as either positive or negative. Discuss whether some of them could be positive at times and negative at other times (e.g., surprise). Could some emotions be positive to one person but negative to another? Sort different related emotions on a continuum from the most extreme to the most subtle (use the Famous Face game from *Mind Reading* as an example). Ask the student to come up with different emotion words to be placed on the continuum, with each child expressing a more extreme version of the emotions on her/his face (e.g., annoyed, angry, wild). Discuss how we can use different emotion words to describe different intensities of the same feeling.

✓ **Analyze facial expressions.** Using *Mind Reading*'s emotion library or a scrapbook, have students compare different examples of the same emotion. What are the common features in the face that tell us that different people express the same emotion? What do all (or most) people in the example do with their eyes/with the mouth? Do they move their heads or shoulders in a certain way? Can students mimic these faces? Can they guess the emotion from faces in *Mind Reading*'s quizzes or from the face of another child? Use the Hidden Face game from *Mind Reading* to emphasize the importance of certain areas in the face for emotion recognition. Can we tell how people are feeling by looking at their chin? their ears? or their eyes? Print and use worksheets available on the *Mind Reading* CD to provide the children with more opportunities to practice emotion recognition from faces.

✓ **Analyze vocal expressions of emotion with the children.** Emphasize the importance of intonation. Ask the children to listen to the "music" of speech. How is this music common to different vocal expressions of the same emotion? Use an oscilloscope to visualize sound waves to the children. Record some "sentences" in gibberish and ask the children to guess the emotion from them. Ask the children to make neutral sentences express certain emotions purely by using intonation.

✓ **Present body language to the children**. Present body language separately, as it is not covered in *Mind Reading*. A good place to do that is in the gym or outside, where different walking styles, postures, and hand gestures may be practiced and recognized.

✓ **Combine facial, vocal, and contextual expressions of emotion.** Discuss how these modalities complement each other. Use examples from electronic media to observe the different factors and how they contribute to our understanding of what a person is feeling. Ask the children to try to express contradicting emotions in their face and voice, and then to use the correct combination. Can other children tell how they are feeling in the first case/in the second?

✓ **Introduce display rules, insincerity, and mixed emotions.** After practicing emotion recognition in *Mind Reading*, discuss with the children how in real life we do not always show our emotions (e.g., why wouldn't someone show he is disgusted with the smell of his friend's new perfume?). Some emotions are not expected to be shown in certain contexts (e.g., happiness at a funeral). Ask the children to come up with examples of emotions that are hidden. Can we sometimes tell the hidden emotion by checking the different sources of information (face, voice, context)? For example, is someone who smiles happy, even though he just stepped into a puddle? Discuss how hiding one's emotions or presenting other emotions may be used to tease, lie, or conceal someone's real meaning. Analyze situations. Discuss the concept of mixed emotions. Demonstrate to students how different emotions may be felt at the same time, and how sometimes they create new emotions (e.g., *disappointment* mixes surprise over something that did not match one's expectation with sadness that it did not).

✓ **Teach degrees of emotion through the use of a system.** Use a scale, flow chart, or meter to introduce degrees of emotion to help students identify levels of emotion in themselves and others. Charting how various facial features, vocal tones, and body gestures might indicate the different levels of emotion may be added to increase understanding.

Chapter Highlights

- Individuals with ASD demonstrate difficulties gathering, integrating and interpreting the nonverbal information required to understand the emotional and mental states of others.

- The chapter offers a review of research studies regarding the abilities of individuals with ASD in terms of emotional recognition.

- Studies involving facial recognition of emotion indicate that, while some individuals with ASD Level 1 are able to recognize basic emotions (happiness, sadness, fear, anger, surprise, and disgust), they still struggle with recognition of more complex emotions.

- Neuroimaging (fMRI) and behavioral studies of facial emotional recognition demonstrate that individuals with ASD process faces differently from neurotypicals, with parts of the brain showing less activation.

- While studied less frequently, emotional recognition from voices also demonstrates less brain activation occurring in individuals with ASD. As with visual recognition, individuals with ASD demonstrate difficulties in vocal recognition of emotion.

- Similar results of reduced brain activation and difficulties with emotional recognition have been shown in studies requiring individuals to use context and those requiring use of multimodalities (such as in real-life situations).

- Individuals with ASD have been shown to be attentive to detail and to prefer a predictable, rule-based environment.

- Given the good skills in systemizing shown by individuals with ASD, the chapter authors hypothesize that individuals with ASD Level 1 may be taught a system for understanding emotions/developing better emotional recognition across modalities and complexity.

- In reviewing attempts to teach emotional recognition to individuals with ASD, the authors point out that instruction has focused primarily on social skills development rather than emotional recognition and has taken place in group settings, which make it difficult to individualize pace.

- Computer-based training has also been used to teach emotional recognition with successful outcomes, but generalization of the learning has not occurred. Additionally, the computer-based programs focused on only basic emotions and on facial expressions.

- The benefits of using computers include less potential stress for the individual with ASD, working at one's own pace, the ability to repeat lessons, and the potential for increased interest and motivation.

- The majority of the chapter focuses on the use of a computerized program to teach emotional recognition, *Mind Reading*. This program is an interactive guide to emotions and mental states and was designed to systematically train basic and complex emotional recognition in both visual and auditory channels with life-like faces and voices.

- A study using the *Mind Reading* program over a period of 10-15 weeks with adults with ASD Level 1 was described. In the study, individuals used the software independently and were assessed both in terms of their improvement in emotional recognition and in their ability to generalize the newly acquired skills.

- Results from the study indicated the intervention was successful, with significant improvement in the ability to recognize complex emotions and emotional states from both faces and voices. However, generalization remained a problem.

- The chapter authors hypothesize that, by using a program that focused on the strong systemizing skills of individuals with ASD Level 1, they were able to teach a system that improved emotional recognition but also created a limiting factor in that, by being so focused on the system or rules, individuals with ASD were unable to generalize to situations that lacked the rule-governed nature of the training tasks.

Chapter Review Questions

1. What abilities are needed in order to understand others' emotional states?

2. What did the authors mean by "an individual with ASD can feel like a Martian on the playground"?

3. What have studies shown regarding the ability of individuals with ASD to recognize emotion from visual, auditory, contextual, and multimodal examples? Why do such deficits appear to occur?

4. What is meant by the term "systemizing" in reference to individuals with ASD, and how might it be used to help teach individuals with ASD to understand emotions?

5. What are the advantages of using computers to teach individuals with ASD?

6. What is the *Mind Reading* program and how is it useful for teaching emotional recognition for individuals with ASD?

References

Adolphs, R. (2001). The neurobiology of social cognition. *Current Opinions in Neurobiology, 11*(2), 231-239.

Ashwin, C., Baron-Cohen, S., Wheelwright, S., O'Riordan, M., & Bullmore, E. T. (2007). Differential activation of the amygdala and the social brain during fearful face-processing in Asperger Syndrome. *Neuropsychologia, 45*(1), 2-14.

Baron-Cohen, S. (1995). *Mindblindness: An essay on autism and theory of mind.* Boston, MA: MIT Press/Bradford Books.

Baron-Cohen, S. (2000). Is Asperger Syndrome/high-functioning autism necessarily a disability? *Development and Psychopathology, 12*(3), 489-500.

Baron-Cohen, S. (2003). *The essential difference: Men, women and the extreme male brain.* London, UK: Penguin.

Baron-Cohen, S., Golan, O., Wheelwright, S., & Hill, J. J. (2004). *Mind reading: The interactive guide to emotions.* London, UK: Jessica Kingsley Publishing.

Baron-Cohen, S., Leslie, A. M., & Frith, U. (1986). Mechanical, behavioural and intentional understanding of picture stories in autistic children. *British Journal of Developmental Psychology, 4*(2), 113-125.

Baron-Cohen, S., Richler, J., Bisarya, D., Gurunathan, N., & Wheelwright, S. (2003). The systemising quotient (SQ): An investigation of adults with Asperger Syndrome or high functioning autism and normal sex differences. *Philosophical Transactions of the Royal Society, Series B, Special Issue on Autism: Mind and Brain, 358*, 361-374.

Baron-Cohen, S., Ring, H. A., Wheelwright, S., Bullmore, E. T., Brammer, M. J., Simmons, A., & Williams, S. C. (1999). Social intelligence in the normal and autistic brain: An fMRI study. *European Journal of Neuroscience, 11*, 1891-1898.

Baron-Cohen, S., Wheelwright, S., Hill, J. J., Raste, Y., & Plumb, I. (2001). The Reading the Mind in the Eyes Test revised version: A study with normal adults, and adults with Asperger syndrome or high-functioning autism. *Journal of Child Psychology and Psychiatry, 42*, 241-251.

Baron-Cohen, S., Wheelwright, S., & Jolliffe, T. (1997). Is there a language of the eyes? Evidence from normal adults, and adults with autism or Asperger syndrome. *Visual Cognition, 4*, 311-331.

Baron-Cohen, S., Wheelwright, S., Spong, A., Scahill, V., & Lawson, J. (2001). Are intuitive physics and intuitive psychology independent? A test with children with Asperger Syndrome. *Journal of Developmental and Learning Disorders, 5*, 47-78.

Barry, T. D., Klinger, L. G., Lee, J. M., Palardy, N., Gilmore, T., & Bodin, S. D. (2003). Examining the effectiveness of an outpatient clinic-based social skills group for high-functioning children with autism. *Journal of Autism and Developmental Disorders, 33*, 685-701.

Belmonte, M. K., Allen, G., Beckel-Mitchener, A., Boulanger, L. M., Carper, R. A., & Webb, S. J. (2004). Autism and abnormal development of brain connectivity. *Journal of Neuroscience, 24*, 9228-9231.

Belmonte, M. K., Cook, E. H., Anderson, G. M., Rubenstein, J. L., Greenough, W. T., Beckel-Mitchener, A., Courchesne, E., Boulanger, L. M., Powell, S. B., Levitt, P. R., Perry, E. K., Jiang, Y. H., DeLorey, T. M., & Tierney, E. (2004). Autism as a disorder of neural information processing: directions for research and targets for therapy. *Molecular Psychiatry, 9*, 646-663.

Bernard Opitz, V., Sriram, N., & Nakhoda Sapuan, S. (2001). Enhancing social problem solving in children with autism and normal children through computer-assisted instruction. *Journal of Autism and Developmental Disorders, 31*(4), 377-398.

Bishop, J. (2003). The Internet for educating individuals with social impairments. *Journal of Computer Assisted Learning, 19*, 546-556.

Bolte, S., Feineis-Matthews, S., Leber, S., Dierks, T., Hubl, D., & Poustka, F. (2002). The development and evaluation of a computer-based program to test and to teach the recognition of facial affect. *International Journal of Circumpolar Health, 61* (Supplement 2), 61-68.

Boucher, J., Lewis, V., & Collis, G. M. (2000). Voice processing abilities in children with autism, children with specific language impairments, and young typically developing children. *Journal of Child Psychology and Psychiatry and Allied Disciplines, 41*, 847-857.

Celani, G., Battacchi, M. W., & Arcidiacono, L. (1999). The understanding of the emotional meaning of facial expressions in people with autism. *Journal Autism and Developmental Disorders, 29*, 57-66.

Critchley, H. D., Daly, E. M., Bullmore, E. T., Williams, S. C., Van Amelsvoort, T., Robertson, D. M., Rowe, A., Phillips, M., McAlonan, G., Howlin, P., & Murphy, D. G. (2000). The functional neuroanatomy of social behaviour: Changes in cerebral blood flow when people with autistic disorder process facial expressions. *Brain, 123* (Pt. 11), 2203-2212.

Deruelle, C., Rondan, C., Gepner, B., & Tardif, C. (2004). Spatial frequency and face processing in children with autism and Asperger syndrome. *Journal Autism and Developmental Disorders, 34*, 199-210.

Ekman, P. (1993). Facial expression and emotion. *American Psychologist, 48*, 384-392.

Ekman, P., & Friesen, W. (1971). Constants across cultures in the face and emotion. *Journal of Personality and Social Psychology, 17*, 124-129.

Fein, D., Lucci, D., Braverman, M., & Waterhouse, L. (1992). Comprehension of affect in context in children with pervasive developmental disorders. *Journal of Child Psychology and Psychiatry, 33*, 1157-1167.

Frith, U. (1989). *Autism: Explaining the enigma.* Oxford, UK: Blackwell.

Frith, U., & Hill, E. (2004). *Autism: Mind and brain.* Oxford, UK: Oxford University Press.

Golan, O., & Baron-Cohen, S. (2006) Systemizing empathy: Teaching adults with Asperger syndrome or high-functioning autism to recognize complex emotions using interactive multimedia *Development and Psychopathology, 18*(2), 591-617.

Golan, O., Baron-Cohen, S., & Hill, J. (2006). The Cambridge Mindreading (CAM) Face-Voice Battery: Testing complex emotion recognition in adults with and without Asperger syndrome. *Journal of Autism and Developmental Disorders, 36,* 169-183.

Golan, O., Baron-Cohen, S., Hill, J. J., & Golan, Y. (2006). Reading the mind in films: Testing recognition of complex emotions and mental states in adults with and without autism spectrum conditions. *Social Neuroscience, 1*(2), 111-123.

Golan, O., Baron-Cohen, S., & Golan, Y. (2008). The 'Reading the Mind in Films' task (child version): Complex emotion and mental state recognition in children with and without autism spectrum conditions. *Journal of Autism and Developmental Disorders, 38,* 1534-1541.

Golan, O., Baron-Cohen, S., Hill, J. J., & Rutherford, M. D. (2007). Reading the Mind in the Voice-Revised. A study of adults with and without autism spectrum conditions. *Journal of Autism and Developmental Disorders, 37*(6), 1096-1106.

Grossman, J. B., Klin, A., Carter, A. S., & Volkmar, F. R. (2000). Verbal bias in recognition of facial emotions in children with Asperger syndrome. *Journal of Child Psychology and Psychiatry and Allied Disciplines, 41,* 369-379.

Hadwin, J., Baron-Cohen, S., Howlin, P., & Hill, K. (1996). Can we teach children with autism to understand emotions, belief, or pretence? *Development and Psychopathology, 8,* 345-365.

Happé, F. (1994). An advanced test of theory of mind: Understanding of story characters' thoughts and feelings by able autistic, mentally handicapped, and normal children and adults. *Journal of Autism and Developmental Disorders, 24,* 129-154.

Happé, F., Ehlers, S., Fletcher, P., Frith, U., Johansson, M., Gillberg, C., Dolan, R., Frackowiak, R., & Frith, C. (1996). Theory of mind in the brain. Evidence from a PET scan study of Asperger syndrome. *Neuroreport, 8*(1), 197-201.

Heavey, L., Phillips, W., Baron-Cohen, S., & Rutter, M. (2000). The Awkward Moments Test: A naturalistic measure of social understanding in autism. *Journal of Autism and Developmental Disorders, 30,* 225-236.

Hetzroni, O. E., & Tannous, J. (2004). Effects of a computer-based intervention program on the communicative functions of children with autism. *Journal of Autism and Developmental Disorders, 34,* 95-113.

Hobson, P. (1994). Understanding persons: The role of affect. In S. Baron-Cohen, H. Tager-Flusberg, & D. Cohen (Eds.), *Understanding other minds* (pp. 204-227). London, UK: Oxford University Press.

Hobson, R. P. (1986a). The autistic child's appraisal of expressions of emotion. *Journal of Child Psychology and Psychiatry, 27,* 321-342.

Hobson, R. P. (1986b). The autistic child's appraisal of expressions of emotion: A further study. *Journal of Child Psychology and Psychiatry, 27,* 671-680.

Hobson, R. P., Ouston, J., & Lee, A. (1988). What's in a face? The case of autism. *British Journal of Psychology, 79,* 441-453.

Howlin, P., Baron-Cohen, S., & Hadwin, J. (1999). *Teaching children with autism to mind-read: A practical guide for teachers and parents.* Chichester, UK: B. J. Wiley.

Howlin, P., & Yates, P. (1999). The potential effectiveness of social skills groups for adults with autism. *Autism, 3*, 299-307.

Jolliffe, T., & Baron-Cohen, S. (1997). Are people with autism and Asperger Syndrome faster than normal on the Embedded Figures Test? *Journal of Child Psychology and Psychiatry and Allied Disciplines, 38*, 527-534.

Jolliffe, T., & Baron-Cohen, S. (1999). The Strange Stories Test: A replication with high-functioning adults with autism or Asperger Syndrome. *Journal of Autism and Developmental Disorders, 29*, 395-406.

Kleinman, J., Marciano, P. L., & Ault, R. L. (2001). Advanced theory of mind in high-functioning adults with autism. *Journal of Autism and Developmental Disorders, 31*, 29-36.

Klin, A., Jones, W., Schultz, R., & Volkmar, F. (2003). The enactive mind, or from actions to cognition: Lessons from autism. *Philosophical Transactions of the Royal Society, Series B, 358*, 345-360.

Klin, A., Jones, W., Schultz, R., Volkmar, F., & Cohen, D. (2002). Visual fixation patterns during viewing of naturalistic social situations as predictors of social competence in individuals with autism. *Archives of General Psychiatry, 59*, 809-816.

Klinger, L. G., & Dawson, G. (1995). A fresh look at categorization abilities in persons with autism. In E. Schopler & G. B. Mesibov (Eds.), *Learning and cognition in autism* (pp. 119-136). New York, NY: Plenum Press.

LaCava, P., Golan, O., Baron-Cohen, S., & Myles, B. S. (2007). Using assistive technology to teach emotion recognition to students with Asperger Syndrome. *Remedial and Special Education, 28*, 174-181.

Lawson, J. (2003). Depth accessibility difficulties: An alternative conceptualization of autism spectrum conditions. *Journal for the Theory of Social Behaviour, 33*, 189-202.

Lawson, J., Baron-Cohen, S., & Wheelwright, S. (2004). Empathizing and systemizing in adults with and without Asperger Syndrome. *Journal of Autism and Developmental Disorders, 34*, 301-310.

Loveland, K. A., Tunali Kotoski, B., Chen, R., & Brelsford, K. A. (1995). Intermodal perception of affect in persons with autism or Down syndrome. *Development and Psychopathology, 7*, 409-418.

Loveland, K. A., Tunali Kotoski, B., Chen, Y. R., Ortegon, J., Pearson, D. A., Brelsford, K. A., & Gibes, M. C. (1997). Emotion recognition in autism: Verbal and non-verbal information. *Development and Psychopathology, 9*, 579-593.

Macdonald, H., Rutter, M., Howlin, P., Rios, P., Le Conteur, A., Evered, C., & Folstein, S. (1989). Recognition and expression of emotional cues by autistic and normal adults. *Journal of Child Psychology and Psychiatry, 30*, 865-877.

Moore, D., McGrath, P., & Thorpe, J. (2000). Computer-aided learning for people with autism – A framework for research and development. *Innovations in Education and Training International, 37*, 218-228.

Nieminen-von Wendt, T., Metsahonkala, L., Kulomaki, T., Alto, S., Autti, T., Vanhala, R., & von Wendt, L. (2003). Changes in cerebral blood flow in Asperger syndrome during theory of mind tasks presented by the auditory route. *European Child and Adolescent Psychiatry, 12*, 178-189.

O'Riordan, M. A., Plaisted, K. C., Driver, J., & Baron-Cohen, S. (2001). Superior visual search in autism. *Journal of Experimental Psychology: Human Perception and Performance, 27,* 719-730.

Ozonoff, S. (1995). Executive functions in autism. In E. Schopler & G. B. Mesibov (Eds.), *Learning and cognition in autism* (pp. 199-219). New York, NY: Plenum Press.

Parsons, S., & Mitchell, P. (2002). The potential of virtual reality in social skills training for people with autistic spectrum disorders. *Journal of Intellectual Disability Research, 46,* 430-443.

Pierce, K., Muller, R. A., Ambrose, J., Allen, G., & Courchesne, E. (2001). Face processing occurs outside the fusiform face area in autism: Evidence from functional MRI. *Brain, 124*(Pt 10), 2059-2073.

Plaisted, K. C. (2001). Reduced generalization in autism: An alternative to weak central coherence. In J. A. Burack (Ed.), *The development of autism: Perspectives from theory and research* (pp. 149-169). Mahwah, NJ: Lawrence Erlbaum Associates Publishers.

Rajendran, G., & Mitchell, P. (2000). Computer-mediated interaction in Asperger's syndrome: The Bubble Dialogue program. *Computers and Education, 35,* 189-207.

Rimland, B. (1965). *Infantile autism: The syndrome and its implications for a neural theory of behavior.* London, UK: Methuen. Rutherford, M. D., Baron-Cohen, S., & Wheelwright, S. (2002). Reading the mind in the voice: A study with Normal adults and adults with Asperger syndrome and high functioning autism. *Journal Autism and Developmental Disorders, 32,* 189-194.

Rydin, O. T., Drake, J., & Bratt, A. (1999). The effects of training on emotion recognition skills for adults with an intellectual disability. *Journal of Applied Research in Intellectual Disabilities, 12,* 253-262.

Sainsbury, C. (2000). *Martian in the playground: Understanding the schoolchild with Asperger's Syndrome.* London, UK: Lucky Duck Publishing.

Schultz, R. T., Grelotti, D. J., Klin, A., Kleinman, J., Van der Gaag, C., Marois, R., & Skudlarski, P. (2003). The role of the fusiform face area in social cognition: Implications for the pathobiology of autism. *Philosophical Transactions of the Royal Society, Series B, Biological Sciences, 358,* 415-427.

Shah, A., & Frith, U. (1993). Why do autistic individuals show superior performance on the block design task? *Journal of Child Psychology and Psychiatry and Allied Disciplines, 34,* 1351-1364.

Silver, M., & Oakes, P. (2001). Evaluation of a new computer intervention to teach people with autism or Asperger syndrome to recognize and predict emotions in others. *Autism, 5,* 299-316.

Swettenham, J. (1996). Can children with autism be taught to understand false belief using computers? *Journal of Child Psychology and Psychiatry, 37,* 157-165.

Swettenham, J. (2000). Teaching theory of mind to individuals with autism. In S. Baron-Cohen, H. Tager-Flusberg, & D. J. Cohen (Eds.), *Understanding other minds: Perspectives from developmental cognitive neuroscience* (2nd ed., pp. 442-456). Oxford, UK: Oxford University Press.

Teunisse, J. P., & De Gelder, B. (1994). Do autistics have a generalized face processing deficit? *International Journal of Neuroscience, 77*(1-2), 1-10.

Yirmiya, N., Sigman, M. D., Kasari, C., & Mundy, P. (1992). Empathy and cognition in high-functioning children with autism. *Child Development, 63,* 150-160.

Young, A. W. (1998). *Face and mind.* Oxford, UK: Oxford University Press.

Acknowledgments

Ofer Golan was supported by the National Alliance for Autism Research (NAAR), the Corob Charitable Trust, the Cambridge Overseas Trust and B'nai B'rith Leo Baeck scholarships. Simon Baron-Cohen was supported by the Shirley Foundation, the Medical Research Council, and the Three Guineas Trust. Parts of this chapter appear in Golan and Baron-Cohen (2006).

Learner Objectives

After reading this chapter, the learner should be able to:

- Explain what is meant by "transition planning"

- Discuss why planning the transition from school is a critical aspect of the IEP process in the middle and high school years

- Name the members of a typical transition team

- State what students with ASD should know about transition planning

- State the elements of a well-designed individual transition plan (ITP) and the federally mandated requirements of transition planning for persons with disabilities

- Explain why it is important to address career, self-advocacy, and independent living goals in the ITP

- Explain the use of the Underlying Characteristics Checklist in planning for individuals with ASD

- Discuss the types of assessment that may be used in transition planning

- List and describe the components of successful planning for and support of the transition process

- Discuss the considerations that affect job placement and retention for persons with ASD

- Explain why social skills aspects should be an important part of the ITP process

- State how services at the postsecondary level differ from those available to school-aged individuals

Chapter 14

Supporting the Transition Years

Brenda Smith Myles • Sheila M. Smith • Terri Cooper Swanson

*Treat people as if they were what they ought to be,
and you help them become what they are capable of being. ~ Goethe*

———————————

Joseph is a 19-year-old student with ASD Level 1. He is working on an advanced diploma and has a GPA of 3.2. His career goal is to be a robotics engineer. His IEP team agreed that it would be in Joseph's best interest to extend his stay in high school to five years to give him more time to develop his independent living skills and social skills, and to "allow for maturation."

Joseph is outgoing, very bright, and has an excellent sense of humor. At times, his judgment and comments have caused difficulty in interpersonal interactions, however. He excels in science and math, but English and writing are more difficult for him. He has difficulty staying on task, unless it is something of interest to him (robotics, creating video games).

———————————

Doug is an 18-year-old enrolled in a self-contained class for students with ASD at Levels 2 and 3. He is working towards a diploma that requires successful completion of IEP goals. Through a picture interest inventory, Doug indicated that he liked stock work and data entry jobs.

Doug is a strong young man who enjoys listening to the Oldies, watching the television show Stargate SG-1, and playing video games. Although he is able to speak, he does not initiate communication. He has no sense of boundaries or of danger. He will not always stay with the group. Over the last year, he has begun touching others on private parts of their bodies.

———————————

The **transition** to post-school options is a complex and critical part of any student's life. There are changes at many levels: environmentally, academically, and socially. During this time, students begin to focus on what they would like to do when they leave school and transition to life outside of school. They are beginning to learn their strengths, interests, and skills through their interactions with family, peers, and school personnel – an initial step in identifying future goals.

Students with autism spectrum disorders (ASD) are no different than their neurotypical peers in this aspect of their lives. However, their areas of skill deficit require support, not only in preparation for employment but also in preparation for success in all aspects of adult life. Regrettably, research indicates that individuals with ASD leave school programs ill equipped with the social and communication skills necessary for life success (Müller, Schuler, Burton, & Yates, 2003), despite legislation that mandates **transition planning** as part of the individualized education program (IEP) starting at age 16, or younger if determined by the IEP team (see Table 14.1). As a result, they have difficulties obtaining and sustaining employment as adults (Engström, Ekström, & Emilsson, 2003; Howlin, Alcock, & Burkin, 2005; Hurlbutt & Chalmers, 2004; Jennes-Coussens, Magill-Evans, & Koning, 2006).

Table 14.1
IDEA 2004 Transition Services Legislation

The Individuals with Disabilities Education Improvement Act (United States Department of Education [IDEA], 2004) defines transition services as follows:

A coordinated set of activities for a child with a disability that

- is designed to be within a results-oriented process that is focused on improving the academic and functional achievement of the child with a disability to facilitate the child's movement from school to post-school activities, including postsecondary education, vocational education, integrated employment (including supported employment), continuing and adult education, adult services, independent living, or community participation;

- is based upon the individual child's needs, taking into account the child's strengths, preferences, and interests;

- includes instruction, related services, community experiences, the development of employment and other post-school adult living objectives, and if appropriate, acquisition of daily living skills and functional vocational evaluation [Part A, Section 602(34)].

Transition planning is a critical component of each IEP for students with ASD. IDEA 2004 requires the following:

Beginning not later than the first IEP to be in effect when the child turns 16, or younger, if determined appropriate by the IEP Team, and updated annually thereafter, the IEP must include:

1. appropriate measurable postsecondary goals based upon age-appropriate transition assessments related to training, education, employment, and, where appropriate, independent living skills; and

2. the transition services (including courses of study) needed to assist the child in reaching these goals [Section 614(d)(1)(A)(VIII)]. In addition, IDEA 2004 requires that students be notified of their rights:

Beginning not later than one year before the child reaches the age of majority under state law, a statement that the child has been informed of the child's rights under IDEA, if any, that will transfer to the child on reaching the age of majority under Section 615(m).

Adapted from United States Department of Education. (2004). http://frwebgate.access.gpo.gov/cgi-bin/getdoc.cgi?dbname=108_cong_public_laws&docid=f:publ446.108

Planning students' transition from school to post-school is a critical part of the IEP process in the middle and high school years (Smith, 2001). Transition planning is ongoing and outcome-oriented, based on collaboration between students, their families, school and adult service personnel, and the community. Further, emphasis must be placed on acquisition of the skills necessary for **independent living** during these transition years. Research has shown that for students with disabilities opportunities for employment during their school years lead to increased success for employment after they leave school (Rogan, Banks, & Herbein, 2003). While job-related skills are typically identified as priorities for transition planning, preparing for successful employment is only one aspect of the transition to adult life. In addition to the focus on employment, schools must equip students with ASD with social skills, safety skills, and information on appropriate sexual behavior, if they are going to reach their potential as productive members of society.

This chapter offers an introduction to supporting individuals with ASD through the transition years. A major focus is on effectively preparing educators and related professionals, parents, as well as the individual with ASD him/herself, to navigate all the steps involved in a successful transition to postsecondary life. The chapter begins with an overview of transition services, touching on legal aspects that interface with the **individualized transition planning (ITP)** process. The importance of assessment in the ITP process is also addressed. The chapter concludes with a discussion of how to effectively support the transition process through implementation of the young adult's ITP.

Transition Services

When Should Transition Planning Begin?

According to the Individuals with Disabilities Education Act 2004 (IDEA 2004), an ITP, a required piece of an IEP designed to prepare a youth for adult success, must be in place by the student's 16th birthday. This is required practice; however, some professionals recommend that students start the transition process by the age of 14, if not earlier (Holtz, Owings, & Ziegert, 2006; Myles & Adreon, 2001; Schelvan, Swanson, & Smith, 2005). Planning should be results-oriented with a clear focus toward the future. Parents and professionals are responsible for collaborating on the most effective means of involving students in transition planning while taking into account their strengths and areas of challenge. Best practice is to involve the student in the process as early as possible.

Various state departments of education, local school districts, and community agencies have developed resources for parents and professionals working through the transition process. In many cases, specific personnel at a school or school district are designated as **transition coordinators/specialists**. Their role usually includes tasks such as recommending a timeline of activities during middle and high school to prepare for the transition beyond high school, connecting parents and school personnel to community agencies and resources, or working directly with students as they move through the transition process. Even if a transition specialist is not available, teachers and parents must ensure that the ITP focuses not only on the student's strengths and interests but also includes opportunities to learn missing skills. In that connection, team members need to take responsibility to educate themselves with regard to the student's disability as well as the transition process.

A typical transition planning team begins with the members of the student's IEP team and may include members from vocational options within the school system, agencies that focus on vocational support, and representatives from local universities, if appropriate. Holtz et al.(2006) identified the following as key members of the transition planning team:

- Parent and student/young adult with ASD and any other interested family member(s)
- Transition coordinator (or school personnel designated to assist with the transition planning process)
- General education teacher (may not be included in the entire process, but should be part of it)
- Special education teacher(s) working with the student/young adult
- Department of Vocational Rehabilitation (DVR) or other appropriate agency representative
- School-based administrator
- Psychologist

Other optional, helpful members include:

- Advocacy organization representative
- Business education partnership representative
- Guidance counselor, when appropriate
- Residential services representative, when appropriate
- Mental health agency representative
- Postsecondary education representative, when applicable

As noted, the team should be tailored for each youth's specific needs, and students should be participating in their transition plan to the best of their ability (IDEA, 2004). Depending upon their needs, students may need extra time to learn about the transition process and what career options are available to them, and may need visuals to help them follow the process or communicate more effectively with others. Students should (a) know who are involved in their ITP, (b) know their rights as a student receiving services under IDEA, and (c) know what their rights are after graduation under Section 504 and the **Americans with Disabilities Act (ADA)**. Figure 14.1 outlines students' rights under IDEA as well as the rights of individuals over age 21 years under Section 504 and ADA.

Regardless of when planning starts or who comprises the transition team, certain activities should occur during the planning process. For individuals with ASD, priming students for upcoming activities has proven to be a successful strategy throughout their daily routine (Aspy & Grossman, 2011). Figure 14.2, adapted from the Virginia Department of Education's web site, provides a timeline of activities that students might engage in throughout their high school years and as they transition to postsecondary options. A more comprehensive form of this list may be found at http://www.fcps.edu. In its current version, this tool might be used as a checklist for developing the ITP or to discuss goals for students.

Americans With Disabilities Act (ADA), 1990	Individuals with Disabilities Education Act (IDEA),1997/2004s	Section 504 of the Rehabilitation Act, 1973
TYPE/PURPOSE		
Civil rights law to prohibit discrimination	An education act that guarantees free and appropriate public education	Civil rights law to prohibit discrimination
ELIGIBILITY REQUIREMENTS		
• Documented diagnosis of ASD • Qualified for the program, service, or job	• Documented diagnosis of ASD • Aged 3 to 21	• Documented diagnosis of ASD • Qualified for the program, service, or job
RESPONSIBILITY TO PROVIDE A FREE, APPROPRIATE PUBLIC EDUCATION (FAPE)		
• Not directly • Provides additional protection in combination with Section 504 and IDEA	• Yes	• Yes
PROTECTIONS PROVIDED		
• Details the administrative requirements, complaint procedures, and consequences for noncompliance related to both services and employment • Individuals discriminated against may file a complaint with the relevant federal agency or sue in federal court	• Provides for procedural safeguards and due process rights to parents in the identification, evaluation, and educational placement of their child • Disputes may be resolved through mediation, impartial due process hearings, appeal of hearing decisions, and/or civil action	• Requires notice to parents regarding identification, evaluation, placement, and before a "significant change" in placement • Local education agencies are required to provide impartial hearings for parents who disagree with the identification, evaluation, or placement of a student
STEPS/ACTIONS		
• Specifies provision of reasonable accommodations for eligible students across educational activities and settings • Reasonable accommodations may include, but are not limited to, redesigning equipment, assigning aides, providing written communication in alternative formats, modifying tests, reassigning services to accessible locations, altering existing facilities, and building new facilities	• With parental consent, an individualized evaluation must be conducted using a variety of technically sound, unbiased assessment tools • Reevaluations are conducted at least every 3 years • Results are used to develop an IEP that specifies the special education, related services, and supplemental aids and services to be provided to address the child's goals	• Provides for a placement evaluation that must involve multiple assessment tools tailored to assess specific areas of educational need • Placement decisions must be made by a tem of persons familiar with the student on the basis of his evaluation information and placement options • Provides for periodic reevaluation • Parental consent is not required for evaluation or placement

Condensed from Henderson, K. (2001, March). The ERIC Clearinghouse on Disability and Gifted Education (ERIC EC), ERIC EC Digest #E606. Available online at http://ericec.org/digests/e606/html

Figure 14.1. Comparison of ADA, IDEA, and Section 504 legislation.

During the High School Years	High School to Postsecondary Transition
• Develop study skills and strategies that work for the individual across settings, including time management, stress management, and test-taking skills • Work to remediate deficit skills • Identify accommodations and/or modifications that are required • Identify tentative postsecondary career and personal goals • Plan a course of study to meet graduation requirements, investigating diploma options • Explore special interests and try to develop schedule to support these interests • If students are able, they can meet with the case manager to plan the IEP meeting and decide on their role; if they are not able, staff should meet and decide for them, but include them as much as possible in the meeting • Meet annually to develop ITP with case manager • Attend IEP meetings • Consider whether extending high school graduation by one to three years will help reach postsecondary goals • If career plans will require a college degree, register and take the Preliminary Scholastic Aptitude Test (PSAT) in the fall of the sophomore year, considering test adjustments and auxiliary aids • Explore opportunities for employment experiences, whether independently or with a job coach or mentor • During the junior year, if the career plan dictates, plan for participation in the SAT or ACT depending on which assessment best matches the chosen career path (remember to investigate all accommodations options with either instrument) • During the junior year, work with transition planning specialists in the local district to make contact with vocational rehabilitative services and community service agencies to investigate support available during and after graduation. • Invite appropriate representatives from adult service agencies to the IEP meeting • Meet with the transition specialist to identify appropriate and available career/vocational assessment options, and to make referrals as appropriate	• Identify ways that accommodations provided in high school will translate to postsecondary education, employment, and community settings • Meet with the transition specialist to identify appropriate and available career/vocational assessment options, and to make referrals as appropriate • Work with transition planning specialists in the local district to make contact with vocational rehabilitative services and community service agencies to investigate support available during and after graduation • Invite appropriate representatives from adult service agencies to the IEP meeting • Focus on matching interests and abilities to the appropriate postsecondary goals • Visit schools, colleges, or training programs early in the year • Evaluate the disability services, service provider, and staff of any schools in which the individual with ASD is interested • Obtain copies of all school records that document the disability to obtain accommodations in the postsecondary environments • Take the SAT or ACT if appropriate • Make sure to investigate supports other than vocational – focus on social and independent living as well

Adapted with permission from Fairfax County Public Schools, VA, Department of Special Services, Office of Special Education, Career and Transition Services section.

Figure 14.2. Transition timeline for student activities.

What Does an Appropriate Transition Plan Address?

IDEA 2004 specifies that transition planning is a coordinated set of activities for a student with a disability that is:

- **Outcome-oriented** – a process with clear goals and measurable outcomes

- **Student-centered** – based on the specific skills that the student needs and reflective of the young adult's interests and preferences

- **Broad-based** – includes instruction and related services, community experiences, development of employment and post-school living objectives, and acquisition of daily living skills and vocational evaluation

- **A working document** – outlines current and future goals, along with specific strategies for achieving these goals, and changes over time. (United States Department of Education, 2004)

Although sustained employment is a goal for all, school prepares students for so much more. It prepares them to address social issues, to communicate and advocate for themselves, to become independent thinkers, and supports many other skills necessary for success in the adult world. Thus, when planning for individuals with ASD, ITPs should include (a) career goals, (b) **self-advocacy goals**, and (c) independent living goals, while keeping in mind the unique characteristics and strengths specific to individuals with ASD. Career goals might include academics, career awareness, career development, and work habits and behaviors. Self-advocacy goals might include decision making and self-awareness, while independent living goals might include taking care of personal needs, community participation, household responsibilities, leisure activities, and managing finances. Table 11.2 provides a list of goals that might be included in an ITP in each of these areas.

In their transition guide for individuals with ASD, the Organization for Autism Research (OAR) outlines information that might also be included in the ITP, such as vocational training and job sampling, employment goals with a timeline for achieving them, community participation goals, including social and leisure skills, travel training, purchasing skills, and personal care, and goals relevant to postsecondary education. A young adult's transition plan is customized based on his/her needs. In particular, a solid transition plan includes many of the following elements (Holtz et al., 2006):

- Assessment of young adult's needs, interests, and abilities
- Statement of preferences for education, employment, and adult living
- Steps to be taken to support achievement of these goals
- Specific methods and resources to meet these goals, including accommodations, services, and/or skills related to the transition goals
- Instruction on academic, vocational, and living skills
- Identification of community experiences and skills related to future goals
- Exploration of service organizations or agencies to provide services and support
- Methods for evaluating success of transition activities (e.g., a video portfolio)

Table 14.2
Examples of Career, Self-Advocacy, and Independence Goals

Academic	Career Awareness	Career Development	Work Habits and Behaviors
• Identify high school course offerings related to career goals • Identify postsecondary schools that provide training in career field • Explore support services available at postsecondary schools/programs of interest • Learn about the wide variety of careers that exist • Identify training needs and effective strategies to address deficits • Enroll in test preparation courses if the career path necessitates taking the SAT or ACT	• Take part in vocational assessment activities • Identify several careers that match interests and abilities • Observe/job shadow employee at business site • Participate in on-the-job training opportunities • Explore interests through elective courses • Utilize the career supports available in the school building to investigate career options	• Develop a resumé; obtain a work permit • Participate in school-based work experiences • Obtain a summer or after-school job • Enroll in career-related courses • Participate in community-based work training program • Attend seminars about college, employment, or other postsecondary services	• Identify appropriate action to take if late or absent from school • Identify when assistance is needed and how to obtain it • Learn to respond to all types of directions or statements, including critical statements • Perform a series of tasks in response to instructions (both oral and written) • Identify appropriate dress code for a variety of work situations • Use planner to organize school work and home-work assignments

Adapted with permission from Fairfax County Public Schools, VA, Department of Special Services, Office of Special Education, Career and Transition Services section.

In addition to stating the goals for the young adult, the transition plan should include logistical information on how the plan will be implemented and monitored, such as a timeline for achieving goals, people or agencies responsible for helping with these goals, clarification of how roles will be coordinated, and a plan for identifying post-graduation services and supports and obtaining the necessary funding. In short, the ITP should address all aspects of the individual's life after high school.

Assessment

Services and supports preparing students with ASD for employment and adult life should match their characteristics. Aspy and Grossman (2007) have developed a tool that teams might utilize when planning for components of the ITP. The **Underlying Characteristics Checklist (UCC**; Aspy & Grossman, 2011) provides a framework for discussing and planning for the characteristics specific to this population, including (a) socialization differences, (b) restricted patterns of behavior, interests, and activities, (c) communication differences, (d) cognitive differences, (e) sensory differences, (f) motor differences, (g) emotional vulnerability, and (h) known medical or other biological factors. The UCC (see Figure 14.3) addresses each of the domains, providing a checklist format to facilitate team conversations and planning that thoroughly address all of the student's needs. When developing an IEP, ITP, or working with employers or institutes of higher education, the UCC provides a means for communication and assessment.

The UCC is just one informal assessment tool; other options are available. Assessments can range from simple questioning techniques to specific psychometric instruments. For example, Sitlington and Clark (2001) stressed that the focus of the assessment should be on the "individual's current and future roles as a worker, lifelong learner, family member, community citizen, and participant in social and interpersonal networks" (p. 7). As adapted from Holtz et al. (2006), questions that parents, teachers, and community members might consider when conducting assessments for transition planning include the following:

- Are there topics or activities of particular interest to the student/young adult?

- Are there certain topics, activities, or environmental conditions that the student/young adult does not like or has difficulty tolerating?

- What are the student/young adult's current academic or related strengths or talents?

- To what extent does the student/young adult's current skill set match the demands of desirable activities or environments?

- What are the student/young adult's dreams?

- What kind of support will the student/young adult require to achieve his/her goals after graduation?

In order to develop an appropriate ITP for individuals with ASD, further questions need to be addressed:

- Where does the team see the student in 5, 10, and 20 years?

- What does the team (and the student) want the student's life to be like?

- What needs to be put in place to move from now to then?

These questions should be addressed keeping in mind the knowledge, skills, strengths, and challenges the student exhibits. Special interests are inherent in this population and should be taken into consideration during the assessment process. Each planning team should utilize assessment as part of the transition process from beginning to end.

<table>
<tr><td colspan="5" align="center">**UCC-CL**
UNDERLYING CHARACTERISTICS CHECKLIST-CLASSIC
Ruth Aspy, Ph.D., and Barry G. Grossman, Ph.D.

NAME: _____ DATE: _____ COMPLETED BY: _____

FOLLOW-UP DATE: _____ COMPLETED BY: _____</td></tr>
</table>

DIRECTIONS: Place check beside all items that apply and describe behaviors observed.

Area	Item	✔	Notes	Follow-Up
	1. Has difficulty recognizing the feelings and thoughts of others (mindblindness)			
	2. Uses poor eye contact or fails to orient to others			
	3. Shows little interest in or response to praise			
	4. Does not seek others' attention in order to share an experience (e.g., bring an object to show, or point out an item or person)			
	5. Interacts with others as if they were objects (e.g., cause and effect)			
	6. Has difficulty maintaining personal space, physically intrudes on others			
	7. Has difficulty taking turns in social interactions or activities			
	8. Has difficulty imitating the actions or words of others			
	9. Fails to respond to the eye gaze or pointing of others – does not orient to the object or person			
	10. Has difficulty making or keeping friends			
	11. Has difficulty joining an activity			

Figure 14.3. Underlying characteristics checklist.

Effectively Planning for and Supporting the Transition Process

The following section highlights some areas specific to ASD where support and guidance is particularly necessary for effectively implementing the ITP. References at the end of this chapter may be consulted for a more in-depth study of transition planning, employment supports, institutes of higher education that provide support for individuals with ASD, and life as an adult with ASD.

Self-Advocacy, Self-Determination, and Person-Centered Planning

Discussions of **self-determination** and self-advocacy for individuals with disabilities are prevalent in the literature (Field & Hoffman, 1999; Fullerton & Coyne, 1999; Izzo, Hertzfeld, & Aaron, 2001; Ward & Meyer, 1999; Wehman, 2002; Wehmeyer, 1999). Socialization, communication, and relationship building skills are vital to most work environments. According to the literature, individuals with ASD have significant difficulty with the social aspects of maintaining employment (Howlin et al., 2005; Hurlbutt & Chalmers, 2004). Indeed, challenges with communication and social deficits make the task of advocating and participating fully in the transition process particularly difficult for individuals with ASD.

Held, Thoma, and Thomas (2004) conducted a single-subject design study in which they wanted students to understand themselves and be able to speak up for themselves. "I want them to understand their disability and support needs. I want them to be able to use this information to make choices, decisions, problem solve, to write their own goals and to create their vision for the future, and to direct their own message" (p. 181).

The study was successful by implementing a combination of strategies, including **person-centered planning** methods, a self-determination curriculum, and technology, that enabled the student, who was nonverbal, to have a voice in the process. The advantage for all involved was that they got a chance to get to know this young man.

Resources such as **Making Action Plans (MAPS**; Falvey, Forest, Pearpoint, & Rosenberg, 2000) and **Planning Alternative Tomorrows with Hope (PATH**; Pearpoint, O'Brien, & Forest, 1998) were utilized to assist with the person-centered planning (see Figure 14.4). The PATH and MAPS provide a platform for team planning with the future in mind. Both are designed to assess where the student is, focus on strengths and challenges, develop goals for the future and prioritize them, and allow teams to plan for maximizing student involvement.

Strategies to increase self-determination skills must be specifically taught to individuals with ASD. Scripting dialogue, video modeling appropriate advocacy strategies, and printing out a list of needed accommodations or modifications are some solutions. Further, teaching students about their disability, strengths, and challenges empowers them to advocate. Some might require pictorial representations of where they are now, and where they are going. Various graphic organizers can offer support in developing these "webs" of pictures. Baker (2005) has produced a complete guide that includes lessons designed specifically for individuals with ASD. The key to increasing self-determination and self-advocacy is developing a person-centered plan, involving the individual with use of concrete terms, and discussions that are begun early.

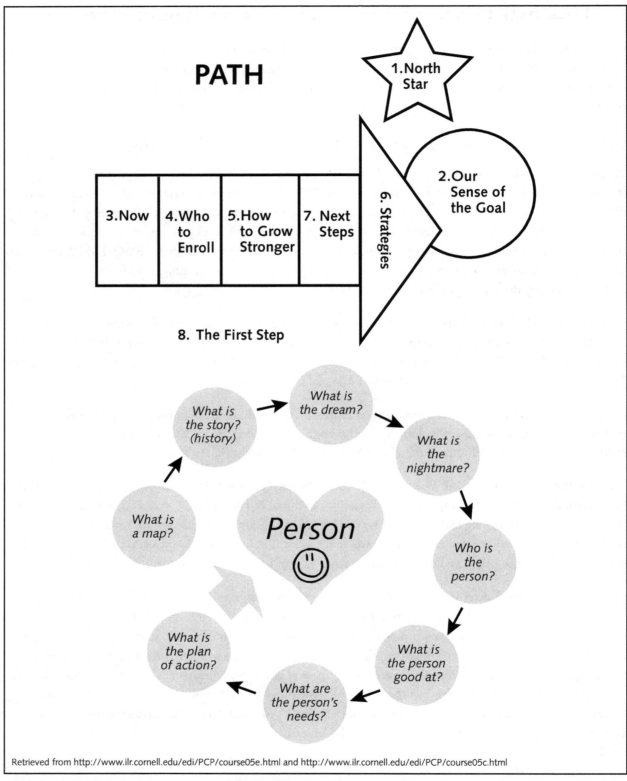

Figure 14.4. Planning Alternative Tomorrows with Hope (PATH) and Making Action Plans (MAPS).

Selecting Meaningful Coursework

The importance of involving students' special interests in planning for their future has already been mentioned. Having an open mind when approaching how a student can receive instruction at the secondary level is critical to individualizing the transition process. Incorporating special interests into career planning and coursework infuses motivation within the student's day.

The key to success is tailoring coursework that addresses skills in need of remediation and skills necessary to pursue future planning. The ITP should guide the course selection process. Course options are now more plentiful than ever before, offered with face-to-face components, in virtual environments, and in both large and small-group settings. Course selection should begin with the end in mind and take into consideration such questions as:

- How will this course provide experiences that build on prior knowledge, remediate skill deficits, and provide opportunities for continued learning of new skills needed for life after high school?

- What types of accommodations or modifications are needed for the student to derive the most benefit from this course?

- What type of learning environment best enables the student to generalize learned skills for future use?

- How do special interests fit in with specific course requirements, so that the student is getting the most "bang for the buck" with his/her course experience?

- Again, selecting coursework guided by the ITP and with the end in mind is key to success for individuals with ASD.

Increasing Job Placement Opportunities

Although IDEA mandates that students receive specific programs and services while they are in secondary school, no such mandate exists after they leave that environment (see Table 14.2). Teams need to take advantage of the resources available within school districts for student employment experiences prior to graduation. Employment is a central aspect of adult life. Finding a job that matches the individual's needs in terms of challenge, interests, comfort, camaraderie, status, hours, pay, and benefits is extremely important (Holtz et al., 2006).

Mawhood and Howlin (1999) found that a critical factor in maintaining long-term employment for individuals with ASD was assessing the job site for a match between skills and the abilities of the individual with ASD. Research on employment for individuals with ASD documents difficulties with

- sustaining employment

- social success

- appropriate job skills

- communicating with supervisors and colleagues

- level of income

(Garcia-Villamisar, Ross, & Wehman, 2000; Garcia-Villamisar, Wehman, & Navarro, 2002; Hagner & Cooney, 2005; Henn & Henn, 2005; Howlin et al., 2005; Hurlbutt & Chalmers, 2004; Mawhood & Howlin, 1999;

Müller et al., 2003; Nesbitt, 2000; Unger, 1999, 2002). Providing appropriate experiences at the secondary level could help lessen these challenges as individuals transition to adult life.

Grandin and Duffy (2009) recommend that when looking at job placement opportunities and planning for future success, teams keep in mind that the individual with ASD should do what he does best. Thus, matching requirements with strengths, skills, and interests becomes important.

According to Grandin (1999), three types of thinking are unique to individuals with ASD and should be taken into consideration: (a) visual thinking, (b) music and higher math, and (c) verbal lists and language translator brains (see Table 14.3). Understanding which type of thinking relates to a specific student will help teams develop a job match.

Table 14.3
Job Ideas for Adults With ASD

Jobs Ideas for Visual Thinkers	
• Architectural and engineering drafter • Photographer • Animal trainer • Graphic artist • Jewelry maker and other crafts • Web designer • Veterinarian technician	• Auto mechanic • Machine maintenance technician • Computer trouble shooter • Theater lighting director • Industrial automation programmer • Landscape designer • Biology teacher

Job Ideas for Music and Math Brains	
• Computer programmer • Engineer • Physicist • Musician/composer • Statistician	• Math teacher • Chemist • Electronics technician • Music teacher • Scientific researcher

Ideas for Nonvisual Thinkers with More Verbal Brains	
• Journalist • Translator • Librarian • Stock and bonds analyst • Copy editor • Accountant	• Budget analyst • Bookkeeper and record keeper • Special education teacher • Book indexer • Speech therapist • Inventory control specialist

From *Developing Talents – Careers for Individuals With Asperger Syndrome and High-Functioning Autism* (2nd ed.) by T. Grandin & K. Duffy, 2009, Shawnee Mission, KS: AAPC Publishing. Adapted with permission.

As for most of us, but even more so, the motivation of individuals with ASD to work is directly related to the extent to which they enjoy what they are doing. Holtz et al. (2006) recommend addressing the physical and social aspects of the job when determining an appropriate match. Components of the physical job match include:

- Hours of employment
- Acceptable noise levels at the job site
- Pay, leave, and other benefits
- Acceptable activity levels
- Physical requirements of the job (e.g., lifting)
- Acceptable margin of error (quality control)
- Production requirements

Components of the social job match include:
- Acceptable level of interaction with coworkers and supervisors
- Clear job expectations
- Grooming and hygiene requirements
- Demands on communication skills
- Personal space available
- Phone/vending machine/cafeteria
- Coworker training and support
- Community status

The ITP should guide the team in developing job experiences. Experiences, talents, and interests should match the plan for the future. Generally, jobs may be categorized as follows: **competitive employment**, **supported employment**, and **secured or segregated employment**. Much of the research related to employment of individuals with ASD focuses on supported and secured or segregated employment. Individuals with ASD have typically been placed within the more structured work settings. Current trends continue this pattern, and at this time only approximately 12% of adults with ASD requiring less substantial support and approximately 6% of adults with ASD requiring more substantial support are in paid employment situations (Howlin et al., 2005; Keel, Mesibov, & Woods,1997; Mawhood & Howlin, 1999; Müller et al., 2003; Rogan et al., 2003; Rogan, Banks, & Howard, 2000; Unger, 1999). These are grim statistics, considering the considerable talents of this group of individuals.

Competitive employment is generally unsupported, and individuals suited for this kind of employment are usually skilled, such as an individual with ASD Level 1. Competitive jobs include all types, from working in the computer industry to waiting tables, teaching, doing landscaping, and more.

Supported employment, on the other hand, allows individuals with disabilities to work alongside neurotypical coworkers while receiving ongoing support on the job. The amount of support may be reduced over time as the individual becomes familiar with the expectations of the position. Job environments within this sector often include hotels, restaurants, office buildings, and schools/universities.

Finally, secured or segregated employment provides a separate work environment that is usually self-contained, and where employees are not integrated with neurotypical workers. Typical tasks may include collating, packaging, and assembly. By the nature of their role requirements, such options are usually selected for individuals with ASD Levels 2 and 3.

The team should take time to investigate the options that best match the needs and capabilities of the student. Concentrate on carving out a niche, possibly breaking larger, more complex jobs into smaller components. By careful planning and exploration, a range of jobs will likely emerge that meet the needs of the individual with ASD.

Preparing Employers

Employers' management practices, such as flexibility in adapting tasks and a willingness to provide accommodations, have been noted as being important to success for individuals with ASD in the workplace (Hagner & Cooney, 2005). Supervisors who establish an atmosphere of mutual support and develop a worker-friendly environment create a "win-win" situation that benefits both the employer and the individual with ASD (Rogan et al., 2000).

How do employers get the knowledge and skill to accommodate the needs of their employee with ASD? Transition teams must establish what information will be necessary to teach future employers and coworkers about each individual with ASD. They must also emphasize where the individual will need help and anticipate what training might have to be provided to the employer and coworkers, in addition to basic information on ASD. Providing a list of accommodations that the worker might need is beneficial (see Figure 14.5).

ADA guarantees that your young adult may request certain accommodations in the workplace. Your young adult may need others, depending on his needs and where he is working. These accommodations may include:

- Pictures or drawings of the task
- Templates of forms or documents
- A note taker
- A voice recorder
- Written instructions
- Daily checklists
- Written or verbal reminders
- Written or picture instructions next to machines, such as postage machine, copier, printer
- Minimal clutter in the work environment
- Minimal noise in the work environment (such as no radios or music)
- Large tasks broken down into small steps
- A "Where to" guide for resources or coworkers
- A timer or alarm as a reminder
- Additional hands-on training
- Headset for telephone or a speaker phone
- Multiple breaks
- Performance feedback presented visually (charts, diagrams)
- Mentor or job coach
- Information for coworkers about ASD
- His own desk or workspace
- Checklist for completing task
- Timelines for completion of task
- Assignment of one task at a time
- Training on appropriate workplace behaviors (e.g., interacting with customers)
- Notice before changes (such as rearranging supply closet or change in job-related work)
- Consistent supervision by one person
- Prioritization of tasks
- Regular feedback on performance (positive and constructive)

From *Life Journey Through Autism: A Transition Guide*, by K. D. Holtz, N. M. Owings, & A. K. Ziegart, 2006. Alexandria, VA: Organization for Autism Research. Adapted with permission.

Figure 14.5. List of reasonable and common job accommodations.

Hagner and Cooney (2005) interviewed the supervisors of 14 successfully employed individuals with ASD and found that some key supervisory strategies were utilized with this population. As suggested in Table 14.4, it might be helpful to share a list of strategies to supervisors of working adults with ASD.

Table 14.4
Key Supervision Strategies

Area	Strategy
Job modification	• Maintain a consistent schedule and job duties • Keep the social demands of the job manageable and predictable • Provide organizers to help structure and keep track of work • Add activities to reduce or eliminate unstructured time
Supervision	• Be direct and specific when giving directions • Verify that communications are correctly understood • Assist the employee in learning social rules and interpreting social cues encountered on the job • Explain and help the employee deal with changes on the job
Coworker relationships and social interactions	• Encourage coworkers to initiate interactions • Ensure that one or two coworkers play a role in helping to give job related suggestions and "keep an eye out" for the employee
Support services	• Provide a sense of familiarity and reassurance until the employee and company staff get to know one another • Transfer relationships and supports to company employees • Check in and remain on-call in case problems arise • Maintain a liaison role for nonwork issues that affect the job

From "'I Do That for Everybody': Supervising Employees with Autism," by D. Hagner & B. F. Cooney, 2005, *Focus on Autism and Other Developmental Disabilities, 20*(2), 91-97. Adapted with permission.

Developing a Social Network

In addition to life at work, the individual with ASD needs to achieve success at play/leisure. This has often been overlooked. Thus, research indicates that students with ASD leave school programs ill equipped with the social and communication skills necessary for life success (Müller, Schuler, Burton, & Yates, 2003). High school is the perfect time to address social issues and build social skills. Specific guides are available for teaching social skills, but teachers may need guidance regarding exactly what skills are important to teach at this age level. Although not all jobs or postsecondary experiences have high social demands, certain skills are vital for establishing a social network.

People make judgments about a person based on appearance and conduct in public. Therefore, it is important that individuals with ASD are taught skills in the areas of (a) general cleanliness and hygiene, (b) grooming, (c) age-appropriate clothing options, (d) social greetings, and (e) issues related to sexuality, including sexual orientation and safety.

Adults have lives outside of work where effective communication is required to express their wants, needs, likes, and dislikes. Transition planning must address the vast array of communication skills, from greetings to voice modulation to obtaining help when necessary. In addition, social behaviors, including table manners, personal space awareness, what to do on a break, the difference between private and public behavior, and so on, must be specifically taught. To ensure that is done, the ITP should address all of these social needs.

Further, individuals with ASD will need to gain experience in accessing community resources if they are effectively going to establish a social network for themselves. Therefore, community resources such as church, clubs, sports, transportation, and so on, should be addressed by the ITP team.

Planning for College/University Attendance

Depending on the ability and interests of the student with ASD, further education may also be something the ITP team will need to consider. For instance, the ITP should include activities that prepare the individual for completing the required paperwork and assessments necessary for acceptance in the school of his/her choice.

Choosing the right postsecondary program is key to success. Options include vocational schools, community colleges, technical schools, liberal arts universities, as well as some that offer specialized programs geared to students with ASD. Two-year programs or certificate programs are the best choice for many on the autism spectrum. Virtual colleges may be appropriate options for some individuals. The transition timeline provided in Figure 14.2 may be used as a resource as the team plans for further education.

If career plans include obtaining a college degree, once the student decides on a university, self-advocacy becomes vitally important. Colleges or universities offer different services, so the student should check ahead of time to make sure that the necessary services are available.

A main difference from high school is that at the postsecondary level students are responsible for requesting the help they need. Disability offices typically do not track down students to see what help they need, as they are now considered adults and must advocate for themselves. To qualify for services through a college's disability office, students generally must (a) present documentation of their disability prior to arranging accommodations and (b) meet with staff to arrange accommodations. In addition, students must talk with each of their professors to let them know what their specific needs for a given class are.

While services vary, below you will find a list and description of some basic services that may be provided to eligible students. Keep in mind that when the student qualifies for services, the official documentation will specifically state what accommodations he or she requires.

- **Tutoring services:** typically provided in a group setting at the disability service office for core requirement classes (e.g., English 101)
- **Test-taking:** for students who qualify to take tests in a quiet area, need a longer test time, or need the test to be given in a different format (e.g., oral instead of written)
- **Note-taking:** typically a note taker is solicited in class
- **Alternative print:** often needs to be requested one to two months prior to the start of the semester
- **Other resources:** may include large-screen computers, scanners, and audio or video recorders

At the postsecondary level, it is important to keep in mind that students must show proper documentation to receive services under ADA or Section 504. It is also very important that they talk with each of their professors about their needs and how the professor can best assist.

Summary and Conclusions

Planning students' transition from school to post-school settings is a critical part of the IEP process in the middle and high school years (Smith, 2001). To be effective, transition planning must be ongoing and outcome-oriented, based on collaboration between students and their families, school and adult service personnel, and the community. Research has shown that for students with disabilities, opportunities for employment during their school years lead to increased success for employment after they leave school (Rogan et al., 2003). Finally, while job-related skills are typically identified as priorities for transition planning, preparing for successful employment is only one aspect of transition to adult life. Emphasis must also be placed on acquisition of the skills necessary for independent living. Thus, schools must equip students with ASD with social skills, safety skills, information on appropriate sexual behavior, and so on, if they are going to reach their potential as satisfied and productive members of society.

Tips for Practical Application

✓ Consult some of the books that focus on the characteristics of individuals with ASD, such as *This Is Asperger Syndrome* by Gagnon and Myles (1999), which provides simple visuals depicting the unique characteristics of this population. Books such as these assist teams in developing an understanding of the student. They also assist students in understanding their own characteristics.

✓ Adapt forms and worksheets to promote independence and participation in the transition process. Mayer-Johnson's Boardmaker™ (Mayer-Johnson LLC,1981-2005) may be utilized to adapt the ITP questions so that students who need extra visual supports can participate in the ITP planning process to their full potential.

✓ Some schools have developed units to teach students skills to increase their involvement in the transition process. Units might target developing a goals chart or checklist that includes (a) where they want to live, (b) how they want to get around, (c) where they would like to work, (d) what they would like to do in their leisure time, (e) and new skills they would like to learn. Units might also focus on identifying roadblocks to accomplishing goals and strategies to get around roadblocks, as well as identifying gifts and talents, and communicating those.

✓ Technology provides tools for transition planning. Web sites are available to assist professionals and families in extending questions and themes that this chapter discusses to specifically tailor planning for the needs of the individual students in your charge. An example is Mapping Your Future (http://www.mapping-your-future.org/).

✓ Develop relationships with school and community staff knowledgeable about and involved with transition early on. These resource personnel can help parents and professionals navigate the system. Relationships built with knowledgeable collaborators can make for a smooth transition.

✓ Utilize special interests when envisioning future employment opportunities or social situations for individuals with ASD. Remember it is their life the team is planning for.

✓ One of the primary obstacles to success in the workplace for individuals with ASD is a lack of social skills. Make social skill instruction a definite part of the curriculum and work with parents to provide opportunities for practice. Arm the individual with ASD with coping strategies for many social situations. Explore the *Hidden Curriculum* (Myles, Trautman, & Schelvan, 2012) of social skills that make or break a social situation.

Chapter Highlights

- Many individuals with ASD leave high school with inadequate social and communication skills for life success, often leading to difficulties in obtaining and sustaining employment as adults.

- IDEA 2004 mandates that transition services be implemented at age 16, or as early as age 14 if deemed necessary.

- Transition services include an individual transition plan (ITP) in which a coordinated set of activities is specified for the individual student. These activities are to be outcome-oriented; based on individual needs; and include instruction, community experiences, and the development of employment and other postschool living objectives.

- Transition teams include the individuals who are part of the IEP team but may also involve members of vocational services, agencies that focus on vocational support, representatives of postsecondary educational options and residential services, as well as others as appropriate.

- Students should be involved in the transition team to the best of their ability. Students should also be made aware of who transition team members are, as well as their rights under the law. Additionally, students need to be taught skills to enhance their participation in their own transition to post-school life.

- ITPs should be individualized and include assessment; the student's preferences; career goals such as academics, career awareness and development, as well as work habits and behaviors; self-advocacy goals such as decision making and self-awareness; and independent living goals, such as taking care of personal needs, community participation, household responsibilities, leisure activities, and managing finances; the steps, instructional methods, and resources to achieve these goals; and methods for evaluating success of transition activities.

- Services and supports for preparing students with ASD for employment and adult life should be based on an assessment of their characteristics and needs. The Underlying Characteristic Checklist (UCC) is an informal assessment tool designed to look at patterns of characteristics specific to individuals with ASD; it can be used to assess and then help in planning intervention based on the results.

- It is important to take into account the student's interests, strengths, skills, tolerance for various stimuli, and supports when creating transition plans.

- Effective planning for and support of the transition process needs to include self-advocacy, self-determination, and person-centered planning.

- Making Action Plans (MAPS) and Planning Alternative Tomorrows with Hope (PATH) are two resources that assist in person-centered planning by looking at hopes for the future as well as the student's current skill level related to those hopes and using that information to develop strategies that will lead to success.

- Strategies for self-determination and self-advocacy must be directly taught to students with ASD. This can be achieved through a variety of means, including scripting dialogue, video modeling, and teaching students about their disability.

- Using the ITP to assist in selecting meaningful coursework based on students' special interests, goals, skills and needs as related to those goals, and requirements for generalization is a critical use of the ITP.

- Students with ASD have documented difficulties in the area of employment, including issues with sustaining employment, social success, job skills, communication with employers and colleagues, and level of income.

- Increasing job placement opportunities for students with ASD should be addressed in secondary school through appropriate experiences; matching the student's interests, skills, and needs with job placement; and matching the type of job to the type of thinking unique to that individual.

- Physical and social aspects of the job need to be considered in matching the individual to a particular job.

- Jobs may be categorized as competitive employment, supported employment, and secured or segregated employment. Most research related to employment of individuals with ASD focuses on the latter two forms of employment.

- It is important to prepare employers to work with individuals with ASD. Such preparation may include strategies for job modification, supervision, coworker relationships, and support services.

- Teaching social behaviors necessary for work and for community involvement should be part of the ITP considerations.

- Students with ASD may consider pursuing postsecondary schooling as an option. If so, the ITP must include information about the student's strengths and needs in terms of self-advocacy and independency.

- Students with disabilities, including ASD, can obtain specialized services and accommodations at the postsecondary level. However, they are responsible for requesting the services and providing documentation of need.

Chapter Review Questions

1. What is meant by "transition planning"?
2. Why is planning the transition from school a critical aspect of the IEP process in the middle and high school years?
3. Who are the members of a typical transition team?
4. What should students with ASD know about transition planning?
5. What are the federally mandated requirements of transition planning for persons with disabilities?
6. Why is it important to address career, self-advocacy, and independent living goals in the ITP?
7. What are the elements of a well-designed ITP?
8. Why is the Underlying Characteristics Checklist (UCC) useful in planning for individuals with ASD?
9. What types of assessment might be used in transition planning?
10. What are the components of successful planning for and support of the transition process?
11. What are the considerations that affect job placement and retention for persons with ASD?
12. Why should social skills development be an important part of the ITP process?
13. How do services at the postsecondary level differ from those for school-aged individuals?

References

Americans with Disabilities Act, 42 U. S. C. §§ 12101-12213 (1990).

Aspy, R., & Grossman, B. (2011). *The ziggurat model: A framework for designing comprehensive interventions for individuals with high-functioning autism and Asperger Syndrome. Updated and expanded edition.* Shawnee Mission, KS: AAPC Publishing.

Baker, J. (2005). *Preparing for life: The complete guide for transitioning to adulthood for those with autism and Asperger Syndrome.* Arlington, TX: Future Horizons.

Engström, I., Ekström, L., & Emilsson, B. (2003). Psychosocial functioning in a group of Swedish adults with Asperger Syndrome or high-functioning autism. *Autism: The International Journal of Research and Practice, 7*(1), 99-110.

Field, S., & Hoffman, A. (1999). The importance of family involvement for promoting self-determination in adolescents with autism and other developmental disabilities. *Focus on Autism and Other Developmental Disabilities, 14*(1), 36-41.

Falvey, M. A., Forest, M., Pearpoint, J., & Rosenberg, R. (2000). *All my life's a circle: Using the tools: Circles, MAPS, and PATH.* Toronto, Canada: Inclusion Press.

Fairfax County Public Schools. (2006). *Transition toolkit for parents.* Fairfax, VA: Fairfax County Public Schools, Department of Special Services, Office of Special Education, Career and Transition Services Section.

Fullerton, A., & Coyne, P. (1999). Developing skills and concepts for self-determination in young adults with autism. *Focus on Autism and Other Developmental Disabilities, 14*(1), 42-53, 63.

Gagnon, E., & Myles, B. S. (1999). *This is Asperger Syndrome.* Shawnee Mission, KS: AAPC Publishing.

Garcia-Villamisar, D., Ross, D., & Wehman, P. (2000). Clinical differential analysis of persons with autism in a work setting: A follow-up study. *Journal of Vocational Rehabilitation, 14,* 183-185.

Garcia-Villamisar, D., Wehman, P., & Navarro, M. D. (2002). Changes in the quality of autistic people's life that work in supported and sheltered employment. A 5-year follow-up study. *Journal of Vocational Rehabilitation, 17,* 309-312.

Grandin, T. (1999). *Choosing the right job for people with autism and Asperger's Syndrome.* Center for Study of Autism. Retrieved from http://www.autism.org/temple/jobs.html

Grandin, T., & Duffy, K. (2009). *Developing talents: Careers for individuals with Asperger Syndrome and high-functioning autism* (2nd ed.). Shawnee Mission, KS: AAPC Publishing.

Hagner, D., & Cooney, B. F. (2005). "I do that for everybody": Supervising employees with autism. *Focus on Autism and Other Developmental Disabilities, 20*(2), 91-97.

Held, M. F., Thoma, C. A., & Thomas, K. (2004). "The John Jones show": How one teacher facilitated self-determined transition planning for a young man with autism. *Focus on Autism and Other Developmental Disabilities, 19*(3), 177-188.

Henn, J., & Henn, M. (2005). Defying the odds: You can't put a square peg in a round hole no matter how hard you try. *Journal of Vocational Rehabilitation, 22,* 129-130.

Holtz, K. D., Owings, N. M., & Ziegart, A. K. (2006). *Life journey through autism: A transition guide.* Alexandria, VA: Organization for Autism Research.

Howlin, P., Alcock, J., & Burkin, C. (2005). An eight-year follow-up of a specialist supported employment service for high-ability adults with autism or Asperger Syndrome. *Autism: The International Journal of Research and Practice, 9*(5), 533-549.

Hurlbutt, K., & Chalmers, L. (2004). Employment and adults with Asperger Syndrome. *Focus on Autism and Other Developmental Disabilities, 19*(4), 215-222.

Izzo, M. V., Hertzfeld, J. E., & Aaron, J. H. (2001). Raising the bar: Student self-determination + good teaching = success. *Journal for Vocational Special Needs Education, 24*(1), 26-36.

Jennes-Coussens, M., Magill-Evans, J., & Koning, C. (2006). The quality of life of young men with Asperger Syndrome: A brief report. *Autism: The International Journal of Research and Practice, 10*(4), 403-414.

Keel, J. H., Mesibov, G. B., & Woods, A. V. (1997). TEACCH-supported employment program. *Journal of Autism and Developmental Disorders, 27*(1), 3-9.

Mapping Your Future. (2002). *Welcome to mapping your future.* Retrieved from www.mapping-your-future.org. http://www.mapping-your-future.org/

Mawhood, L., & Howlin, P. (1999). The outcome of a supported employment scheme for high-functioning adults with autism or Asperger Syndrome. *Autism, 3*(3), 229-254.

Mayer-Johnson LLC. (1981-2005). *Boardmaker: The picture communication symbols.* Solana Beach, CA: Author.

Müller, E., Schuler, A., Burton, B. A., & Yates, G. B. (2003). Meeting the vocational support needs of individuals with Asperger syndrome and other autism spectrum disabilities. *Journal of Vocational Rehabilitation, 18,* 163-175.

Myles, B. S., & Adreon, D. (2001). *Asperger Syndrome and adolescence: Practical solutions for school success.* Shawnee Mission, KS: AAPC Publishing.

Myles, B. S., Trautman, M., & Schelvan, R. (2012). *The hidden curriculum for understanding unstated rule in social situations for adolescents and young adults* (2nd ed.). Shawnee Mission, KS: AAPC Publishing.

Nesbitt, S. (2000). Why and why not? Factors influencing employment for individuals with Asperger Syndrome. *Autism, 4*(4),357-369.

Pearpoint, J., O'Brien, J., & Forest, M. (1998). *PATH: A workbook for planning alternative tomorrows and hope for schools, organizations, businesses and families.* Toronto, Canada: Inclusion Press.

Rogan, P., Banks, B., & Herbein, M. H. (2003). Supported employment and workplace supports: A qualitative study. *Journal of Vocational Rehabilitation, 19,* 5-18.

Rogan, P., Banks, B., & Howard, M. (2000). Workplace supports in practice: As little as possible, as much as necessary. *Focus on Autism and Other Developmental Disabilities, 15*(1), 2-11.

Schelvan, R. L., Swanson, T. C., & Smith, S. M. (2005). Making each year successful: Issues in transition. In B. S. Myles (Ed.), *Children and youth with Asperger Syndrome: Strategies for success in inclusive settings* (pp. 127-157). Thousand Oaks, CA: Corwin Press.

Sitlington, P. L., & Clark, G. M. (2001). Career/vocational assessment: A critical component of transition planning. *Assessment for Effective Intervention, 26*(4), 5-22.

Smith, T.E.C. (2001). Section 504, the ADA, and public schools: What educators need to know. *Remedial and Special Education,22*(6), 335-343.

Unger, D. D. (1999). Workplace supports: A view from employers who have hired supported employees. *Focus on Autism and Other Developmental Disabilities, 14*(3), 167-169.

Unger, D. D. (2002). Employers' attitudes toward persons with disabilities in the workforce: Myths or realities? *Focus on Autism and Other Developmental Disabilities, 17*(1), 2-10.

United States Department of Education. (2004). *Individuals with disabilities education improvement act.* Retrieved from http://frwebgate.access.gpo.gov/cgibin/getdoc.cgi?dbname=108_cong_public_laws&docid=f:publ446.108

Ward, M., & Meyer, R. (1999). Self-determination for people with developmental disabilities and autism: Two self-advocates' perspectives. *Focus on Autism and Other Developmental Disabilities, 14*(3), 133-139.

Wehman, P. (2002). A new era: Revitalizing special education for children and their families. *Focus on Autism and Other Developmental Disabilities, 17*(4), 194-197.

Wehmeyer, M. (1999). A functional model of self-determination: Describing development and implementing instruction. *Focus on Autism and Other Developmental Disabilities, 14*(1), 53-61.

Learner Objectives

After reading this chapter, the learner should be able to:

- List the members involved in an educational support and intervention team

- Discuss the importance of collaboration among team members

- Differentiate between an IEP and a 504 Plan

- Discuss what is needed in terms of planning and preparation for effective team meetings

- Discuss the importance of preparing students for team meetings

- Discuss the factors that contribute to positive and effective collaboration

- Demonstrate an understanding of how students with ASD think and learn, based on the scenarios given in the chapter

Chapter 15

The Education Team: Positive, Effective Interdisciplinary Collaboration

Paula Jacobsen

Sam, now 10, was diagnosed with ASD Level 1 before he was 3. He could talk, but primarily repeated things he had memorized, such as parts of videos or educational TV programs. He did not use language for communication. He became easily overwhelmed by sensory stimuli, especially sounds, and demonstrated self-regulatory behaviors (body movements), poor eye contact, and poor attention. From the age of 3, Sam received intensive speech and language therapy, behavior therapy, and occupational therapy through his public school district, as well as privately. As mandated by law, his IEP team met annually to determine continuing concerns and progress, and to write goals.

After several years, Sam had a larger vocabulary and used more eye contact (briefly stared, but did not use eye contact to regulate interactions to indicate meaningful attention or communication). His gross-motor planning improved, but fine-motor continued to be poor. Sam had rote knowledge of some "appropriate" behaviors, such as sitting in a circle with his legs crossed and his hands in his lap. He had learned number facts so well that he scored above grade level when tested orally, but he did not grasp math concepts or even appear to understand number value beyond the number 3. He could attend to an adult who was working with him individually, but did not seem to follow the same basic communication and expectations in a small group (even when led by the same adult). He raised his hand and waited to be called on in class, but then made comments that were tangential or completely off topic. Medication reduced his anxiety and decreased his sensory overload somewhat, but it did not increase meaningful attention. By second grade, Sam had developed some skills but was unable to function adequately in school, even with an aide beside him.

Sam's parents invited all the specialists who had worked with him (from his public school and privately) to attend the next IEP, with the understanding and agreement of all that this would be an opportunity to share information and problem solve. Each participant spoke and was heard. Each described efforts, challenges, and concerns. Although the individual skills they worked on with Sam varied, there were similarities in their experience of Sam, and there were concerns about him that they all recognized. Each described instances in which they felt he could understand and learn, and then presented evidence that he could not apply what he seemed to know. The skills that were the focus of their goals and work seemed splintered, perhaps reflecting Sam's inability to integrate and use much of what he mastered.

As they spoke and listened, most recognized that Sam was not aware of his own behaviors or the point of their interventions, although he seemed to have a positive and comfortable relationship with each participant; most appreciated his efforts, regardless of how clueless he was about what he was doing. His math tutor had begun working with him on the most basic number concepts, utilizing concrete materials and verbal descriptions of concrete concepts, which he could understand and then express himself. This seemed like such a good idea that the school occupational therapist said she would begin describing concretely what he was doing or saying, using some of the specific language that was suggested by the language therapist. His teacher and aide would try to incorporate mirroring language, at least some of the time (pointing out the "obvious" that was occurring, not just redirecting), as would most of his school-based and private therapists.

This subsequently became an ongoing topic in formal team meetings and interim consultation between team members. Sam developed an awareness of and ability to describe what he and others were doing and sometimes why. Most team members saw this happening, as each recognized the effectiveness of articulating the obvious. As Sam became able to recognize what he was doing and what was expected, he did and continues to do more of what is expected.

At 10, Sam is close to grade level in many subjects, but he cannot learn in a classroom of 20 students. He is in a small special education class without an individual aide and, although he moves around a lot, he attends adequately for this setting (sometimes with reminders), participates on topic (with reminders), and is learning and producing grade-level work (with extra time and a reduced workload). He still has difficulty with pencil-paper tasks, but uses larger spaces for math problems and can now type his other written work. Over three years, there have been several meetings and many briefer collaborations between team members to address concerns as they arose. This team focus on understanding Sam, and then working with him in similar ways based on a mutual understanding, supports the work of team members and the tremendous growth that Sam has made.

Individuals with all levels of autism spectrum disorders (ASD) live in a world where most people around them think and communicate quite differently than they do. They often have specific strengths (some are gifted), and they also have cognitive, communication, and social challenges (Attwood, 1998; Klin, Volkmar, & Sparrow, 2000; Siegel, 1996). These students benefit from many therapies and supportive interventions (Bate, 2004; Leventhal-Belfer, 2004; Wiss, 2004). Each service may have a unique focus, such as language, gross- and fine-motor development, behavior modification, and assessing appropriate learning strategies, and services may be provided in a variety of locations. Yet, everyone's work with and on behalf of the child can be enriched, and the benefit to the child enhanced, when providers collaborate. In addition to each unique contribution, team members often develop a shared focus and a shared language that is meaningful to the individual child.

Once the student begins to receive special education services, teachers and classroom aides, administrators, other service providers at school and in the community, parents, and the students themselves, all become a part of an **educational support and intervention team**, as mandated by the law that provides access to education for students with disabilities. For those who work with these students, collaboration can be a supportive and a very rewarding aspect of that work (Jacobsen, 2003, 2005). Specifically, **collaboration** generally results in a better understanding of what students can and cannot understand, what they can and cannot be expected to do successfully, and what supports or scaffolding they require to learn and function at school.

This chapter addresses how knowledge of the factors that support **resiliency** can inform a collaborative team approach and the contributions each member on the student's team can make. Opportunities for collaboration, topics of importance or concern to the student's team, as well as how to prepare and plan for effective team meetings are explored. The final section clarifies and further explores the factors that contribute to positive, effective collaboration.

Understanding, Supporting, and Enhancing Resiliency Can Inform the Collaborative Process

Research has clearly demonstrated that children can succeed in school and in life if they feel that someone knows who they are (sees their challenges *and* their strengths), and if we have *appropriately* high (clear, manageable, and attainable) expectations for them. An interested, caring approach supports **school connectedness** (McNeely, Nonnemaker, & Blum, 2002; Noddings, 1992), and school success enhances resiliency and the likelihood of future success (Benard, 1991, 2004; Werner & Smith, 1992).

Students with ASD, even the most capable with ASD Level 1, have very different ways of processing information, of understanding language, and of communicating, than typical students. As a result, knowing who they are (their challenges and their strengths) and determining appropriate, clear, manageable, and attainable expectations is not always easy. However, the likelihood of success is greater when team members work together with a shared desire to understand the student. Team members with varying degrees of knowledge about ASD can contribute and learn when they collaborate.

Education Team Members

Teachers

With the exception of parents, no adult spends more time with a student than his teacher(s) and classroom aide(s). General education teachers are responsible for many students, some with special needs and others with the range of abilities and learning styles that can occur in all classes. Special education teachers (including resource teachers) generally are responsible for fewer students, each with special needs and an individual plan. The challenge for the special education teacher is to know each student, his abilities, and special needs, and to provide a manageable environment in which he can function and learn.

Even teachers who are very familiar with ASD sometimes become frustrated or discouraged by their students' behavior and learning difficulties. Teachers' openness to knowing and supporting a manageable environment for their students is important. The power of a patient, positive, and collaborative relationship between teachers and their students with ASD, and the value of a supportive, collaborative relationship between the teacher and other team members, cannot be overstated. Such relationships can change situations in which challenges are something to avoid or eliminate to situations where challenges are to be expected and to be addressed as part of a problem-solving process.

Other School Professionals

School psychologists, speech-language therapists, occupational therapists (OTs), administrators, behavior specialists, counselors, and others, may also be part of the student's team. They provide observations and assessments that determine eligibility for services, and they participate in planning goals. Finally, they may also provide direct interventions to students or consultation to teachers and each other. Often they have varying levels of experience and understanding about the behavior and learning style of a particular student.

For example, speech-language therapists generally work with pragmatic language, including translating and processing language issues as they occur. They may work with students individually, with small groups of students, and with classroom teachers. Occupational therapists primarily address sensory needs. They can observe and explain certain behaviors (such as mouthing objects, covering ears, bouncing, pacing) as a student's attempt to manage internal and external sensory stimulation. They may recommend that such behaviors be allowed or suggest alternatives that better meet the student's need (such as sitting or kneeling on a special pillow or ball instead of a regular classroom chair, or chewing gum to calm).

When we identify a student's actions as "inappropriate," we focus on what we think must change. When we recognize that we do not understand the benefit of the student's actions or words, we can attend to who the student is and what he needs … and we can recognize the necessity of meeting the student's needs as we try to bridge the gap between those needs and our own.

Outside Professionals

In addition to services provided by the school, parents may obtain private assessments and services, such as **neuropsychological** assessment, occupational therapy, speech-language therapy, social skills groups, individual **psychotherapy**, specific educational and/or behavioral therapies, and **psycho-pharmacological interventions** (medications). Collaboration between school personnel and outside professionals can benefit everyone's work with the student.

Outside professionals and school personnel can add to and learn from each other's understanding of the student when collaboration is informed by an effort to understand the student's perspective and make the school experience manageable for him. This is possible if the collaboration is one in which school and outside professionals listen to each other's concerns about and for the student … when all are open to seeing the positive contributions as well as the challenges of others, thus supporting the development of goals, plans, and specific interventions that support a student's success.

Parents

Parents have varying degrees of understanding of ASD. Some parents of children with ASD Level 1 may have first learned of their child's issues through the school. Others may have had concerns about their child's development long before anyone else did, including their pediatrician. Often parents have had a range of experiences with professionals whom they have consulted before and after their child started school. These can vary in their usefulness. At worst, professionals who do not adequately understand ASD may be well meaning, but they may be reassuring that everything is fine (when intervention is needed) or critical of the parents' concerns (even when such concerns are realistic and relevant). Others may understand the child's challenges and offer direction that supports the parents and provides early intervention.

Parents sometimes develop responses that support their children that appear to others to be over-involvement or to foster dependence. For example, a parent may be facilitating and supporting a child with ASD by oversight, guidance, and direction that enables that child to function but that would be inappropriate for a more typical child. Just as it is most productive to understand the child's behavior as an attempt to master, it is most productive to attempt to understand what *is* supportive and effective about parents' behavior toward their child, as well as their understanding and interpretation of the child's needs and behavior. The support may be what is needed and, therefore, should be continued for as long as it is needed. In this kind of problem-solving atmosphere, it is also possible to consider and evaluate alternative or additional supports and interventions. Unfortunately, some parents have not had an opportunity to participate in a positive meeting in which they have felt heard. Indeed, many have even felt blamed and criticized by professionals and by family members.

Parents also can share information or provide support in very concrete ways, such as helping out in the classroom. For grade-school children, parents may be interested in talking to the class about ASD. More capable students on the autism spectrum may also want to talk to others about having ASD. This can be very supportive to the student and to the entire class. Giving this type of information can facilitate understanding and a more positive relationship between classmates (Jacobsen, 2005) (see Chapter 8).

The Student

When a student with ASD is able to be a member of his team, he is more likely to know his strengths and be able to ask for and accept help. Maintaining positive, accepting, respectful, problem-solving relationships with adults engages the student as a member of his team. When it is difficult and energy-consuming for the team to understand the student's perspective, it can be instructive to remember how difficult and energy-consuming it is for the student to understand the rest of us.

Students are less likely to engage when they believe that adults are primarily interested in gaining compliance. By contrast, they view communication with and between adults as a support when they see adults as being interested in knowing them as well as wanting them to learn and to get along with others. Students with ASD Level 1 can become aware of being part of a team when team members describe their work with the student as a team approach. Students can be informed about team meetings, and as they become older and more aware, students can develop lists of issues and concerns that they would like addressed and participate towards the end of the meeting or hear the team's responses later. Older students who can articulate their issues or concerns, perhaps with the prior help of a team member, and can listen as well as speak can be effective participants in team meetings.

Opportunities for Collaboration

Teachers and other professionals who work with students with ASD face many challenges. At times their work may not feel like part of a team effort, and remembering that they are part of a team may not be easy. In fact, collaborating with team members may not come to mind or may seem like an additional burden. The reality is that supportive, effective collaboration makes our work easier. Formal and informal collaboration, even if infrequent, can facilitate a team approach. Team members can share their perceptions and how each is responding to the student. The most helpful and meaningful collaboration addresses the student's perspective as well as the questions and dilemmas that perspective may present.

Formal and Informal Team Collaboration

Public schools must hold mandated team meetings as well as abide by district procedures for communicating about students of concern. School personnel must understand these procedures and requirements and inform parents about them when appropriate. Private schools, although not obligated by law, may also hold formal meetings. Understanding the differences between formal team meetings and informal collaboration can help team members remain aware of and better utilize the team, and thus support an effective team approach.

Formal Team Meetings

When parents, teachers, or other school personnel are concerned about a student who has not yet been evaluated or formally identified as having special education needs, they may request a team meeting, sometimes called a **student study team meeting (SST)**. Students who have been evaluated and identified as needing special services or support have an individualized education program (IEP) or a **504 Plan**.

Students who are eligible for an IEP receive services (such as special education placements, language therapy, occupational therapy, etc.), specific goals are developed and monitored, and accommodations and/or modifications are identified that may help meet their needs and support their abilities. A 504 Plan, on the other hand, is for students who can function adequately in the mainstream with accommodations, such as assistive technology for writing, reduced homework, longer time for tests and assignments, and so on.

Students with an IEP or a 504 Plan are assigned a team that is responsible for planning and monitoring progress Other students may have a less formal team, which may include teachers, parents, the student, and outside tutors or therapists who work with and support them after school or through informal school support. Regardless of their specific purpose, teams meet to develop a shared understanding of the student and exchange ideas for supporting the student.

The perspective of the person who facilitates a team meeting can set the tone and greatly influence the effectiveness of the team. When there is a desire to know, to understand, and to support the student, this position of advocacy supports the efforts of all team members. Goals, benchmarks, accommodations, and modifications must be clearly stated so they make sense to the student and the adults. Recommendations should make it easier, not more complicated, for students to be successful.

Informal Collaboration

Whether or not a student has a formal team, informal collaboration between the teacher, the parents, and others who work with the student can facilitate understanding and enhance communication. Collaboration provides an opportunity for the teacher, other professionals, the parents, and the student to share information and address concerns and can be an opportunity to support strengths and respond to the student's needs and challenges. On occasion, when a student is experiencing difficulty with a particular situation or with an intervention, a telephone call or a brief meeting is enough to resolve the problem.

Andrew

Andrew is a fifth-grade student with ASD Level 1. He was upset because he would not be able to complete his report on time. This was a major, long-term assignment, and he was convinced the report would not be accepted, because his teacher told the class that there would be no time extensions. Andrew knew that extra time was provided in his IEP but could not consider the possibility that the teacher did not mean him when she said that there would be no extensions. He refused to ask her about it, because she had been perfectly clear.

Andrew's teacher and counselor discussed the situation, with Andrew listening quietly, but attentively. The teacher said that Andrew could have extra time if he needed it, as was always true, as stated in his IEP. When the teacher says "no exceptions," she does not mean him, she explained. Andrew does not understand why someone says "no exceptions" when there are exceptions. It is this inaccurate way of speaking, this assumption that people should just "know" what applies to them and what doesn't, that he has never been able to understand.

This brief collaboration between the teacher and the counselor meant the difference between Andrew accepting help and completing this assignment late or refusing to complete it and giving up. Andrew understood then that he was allowed more time, but he may never understand why someone would say "no exceptions" when there truly are exceptions.

The inexact communication of others can be difficult for students with ASD to understand and even difficult to accept when fully explained. This kind of overt clarification of assignments and other expectations often helps the student to move on, especially when he sees that he will be expected to do what he actually can do.

Addressing Areas of Importance or Concern

Language and Communication

Communication is an essential ingredient of every team function. Although the communication and comprehension difficulties of students with ASD Levels 2 or 3 are often apparent, even those who know them well sometimes misunderstand. This can occur when students understand something they are unable to convey, as well as when they make a rote statement that coincidentally fits a circumstance that they do not understand.

For students with ASD Level 1, it is especially important for the team to remain aware of the pragmatic challenges that affect learning, communication, and relationships. Pragmatic language assumes shared meanings and recognition of what is relevant to others. Pragmatics cannot be easily taught. Keeping this in mind helps team members avoid setting unreasonable expectations for the student and other team members (see Chapters 5 and 10).

Joey

Joey is a sixth-grade student with ASD Level 1. He recently began middle school. Joey's teachers saw him as bright, disorganized, inattentive, unmotivated, oblivious, and sometimes rude. His test grades were excellent, because he knew a great deal of the information already, yet he was failing. A student study team meeting was arranged. His English teacher told the team that Joey often did not listen when she explained an assignment to the class and subsequently asked her what to do. On one occasion he was to look up the definitions of the vocabulary and spelling list, write them down, and write a sentence using each word. "Well, that's a waste of time," Joey said, turning around and walking away, as though he were announcing this to the other students. His teacher saw this as an example of the very dismissive and rude way Joey sometimes speaks to her. From Joey's perspective, however, this was a statement of fact. He was talking aloud (not to the other students) as he turned away. This assignment was a waste of time for him: He knew the spelling and definitions of the words and was already using them. He intended to state a fact, and he did not understand why the teacher was upset when he gave her this factual information.

A brief follow-up: In this scenario, it would be important for the teacher to understand that Joey's language disorder impairs his ability to understand how his tone affects others. His teacher thought she would feel supported by a language clinician's recommendation that Joey's IEP include a goal related to nonverbal social communication skills.

Social-Emotional Issues

Social skills are dependent on understanding the experience of others, including our effect on them. When team members collaborate about social skills, even in schools in which social skill groups and Social Stories™ (Gray, 2000, 2002) are used to help the student anticipate and respond to a situation, it helps to remember that it is difficult to teach social skills that can be generalized. We can prepare a student for a specific situation or for many specific situations that occur regularly and are easily recognized, but even small changes in routine situations can be difficult for the student. Similarly, presented with a problem, the student may learn the expected answer, but in real-life situations, it is necessary to recognize what is relevant, to generate the questions, not just the answers, and that can prove problematic. Rules for very specific behaviors in very specific circumstances (manners) can be taught. These may help in those specific circumstances, but do not solve the problem of pragmatic communication in many situations.

Collaboration can address social-emotional issues by considering the level of the student's awareness of himself and others, as well as his needs. For example, recess is a time to relax and play, because socializing for most students is often a break from structure and assigned work. If working on socialization is important, the team can plan structured, supervised instructional opportunities. If a break is important as an opportunity to relax, a school can allow alternatives to interactive playground recess in addition to opportunities to engage in interactive play with adult support (see Chapter 8 on peer play and friendships).

George

George, an 11-year-old fourth-grade student with ASD Level 1, did not like to miss anything that he saw as required, including school. The most difficult time for him was recess, which he understood as being a time when he was supposed to play with others. But there were too many people, too much activity, and too much noise for him. He walked around the periphery of the play area trying to keep away from others until he could return to the relative calm and predictability of the classroom. When George was informed that recess should be a break, a rest from class work, and a time to relax, he told his mother that he had decided to lie down on one of the benches after lunch. "What will you say if other kids ask you why you are doing that?" she asked. "I'll just tell them I'm resting," he answered. "They can rest their way. I'm going to rest my way."

George had participated in individual and group OT and speech-language therapy, as well as social skills groups, on and off since he was in preschool. He had gained a great deal, but it was hard work and could be exhausting for him. When George's team understood his perspective, they provided alternative choices instead of playground recess for him. They explained to him that this was to address his needs and ensure his comfort, not to manage his behavior or teach him to be different. He was relieved to have his perspective understood and his needs accepted.

Behavior

When team members collaborate to understand a student's behaviors, they have an opportunity to meet her needs as well as address the needs of others. Some behaviors, such as pacing, standing up to work, and so on, can be accepted. Standing or pacing may not distract the student or indicate avoidance of work. Instead, these behaviors may enable a particular student to attend longer to a task or to think more clearly and productively. At other times, a behavior may be acknowledged as meeting a need, but a substitute may be suggested, such as allowing the student to chew gum, use an object to fidget, sit on a special cushion, or take time-out.

Some students have little awareness of their emotional and behavioral escalation. They may not even recognize their loss of control when or after it occurs. Sometimes teams develop specific behavior plans for students with clearly stated expectations and prearranged cues. A team can ensure that the plan addresses the student's needs and abilities *as well as* the school environment. When collaboration focuses on developing awareness, recognizing the student's arousal state becomes more important than any expectation of teaching or compliance at that time (Buron & Curtis, 2012).

Teachable times are only those in which the student can maintain self-control. Cody (below) provides a vivid example of this. Some students, like Cody, become extremely angry or tantrum at more predictable times, such as when there is an expectation to work on a group project or to learn a new concept. When we know that, we can prepare for or avoid some of the situations that are particularly anxiety-producing for a student.

Cody

Cody, a student who had received special education services throughout his schooling, had academic strengths and challenges. He also had severe sensory and mood-regulation challenges. Cody understood and enjoyed math, but dreaded learning new concepts. He could learn from a computer lesson (when that was available), but did not expect to be able to learn from the teacher. He became frustrated, overwhelmed, and sometimes had a full-blown tantrum (screaming, crying, destroying papers, throwing things off his desk, etc.). Perhaps Cody anticipated more difficulty learning the new material than he would actually have encountered, but that was not relevant, given his inability to tolerate the process involved in learning new concepts or procedures. This was observed when he attended a selfcontained special education day class for students with autism in kindergarten and first grade and also when he attended a higher-level special day class. He was also observed in mainstream classes (which he was able to attend for part of the day in fourth through sixth grade, after which he attended a special day school for students with ASD and other significant learning and behavior challenges).

Trying to force him to do what he was not ready for alienated Cody. Working to understand his needs let him know that the adults were trying to understand his experience and eventually engaged his cooperation in a problem-solving process. The team considered alternatives. Cody could observe the lesson without the expec-

370

tation that he would demonstrate anything afterwards. He could observe the general education or resource teacher or another adult describe the concept and work on solving the problems (talking them through out loud), a first step in making him more comfortable. For Cody, that was somewhat like watching a video, but live, and it enabled him to watch without an expectation that he would participate or even fully understand. As a result, it reduced his anxiety and gave him a chance to recognize what he did understand – and later to do assignments based on what he had learned by observing. Cody later benefited from being exposed to material before it was taught in class. Currently, computer programs are available that provide the kind of opportunity to observe and understand without learning in the classroom. This kind of "prelearning" would have benefited Cody if it had been available at the time.

Academics and Learning

"The problem with school," a middle school student with ASD Level 1 told his parents, teachers, and anyone else who would listen, "is that everything is either too easy or too hard." Schoolwork is supposed to support learning. Yet, the usual expectations for schoolwork may be a poor fit for a particular student's way of thinking and learning. Team members are often concerned about the discrepancy between students' knowledge and apparent abilities and their performance.

Collaboration can support understanding and accepting what a student knows *and* how he learns. Modifying assignments or providing **accommodations** that reflect the student's needs and abilities makes school less overwhelming and learning more possible for more students. Discussing accommodations or **modifications** (what they are and why they are used) develops awareness in the teacher and the student.

Team members often worry that the student will not be prepared for the future … the next grade, the next school experience, or independent adult life … and, therefore, are resistant to changing their expectations. However, a stance that the student "must" learn to do what is expected of others can be overwhelming to everyone and, ultimately, be ineffective, or worse, detrimental to the student. The most effective way to prepare for the future is to keep the student from being too overwhelmed to function in the present. And the best way to help students in the present is to ask or require of them what they can do. While this sounds simple, knowing what the student can or cannot do is complicated by the appearance, at times, that a student is able to understand and do more than she can consistently sustain.

A collaborative process that begins with and addresses the student's subjective experience can allow the team the flexibility and creativity necessary to support the student's learning and management of academics. For example, students who have difficulty imagining what others mean often have difficulty understanding literature. They can be told in advance what is relevant (not be expected to discover it on their own), and then try to find it in the text. When writing fiction is difficult, students can write about a true event and, with help when needed, fictionalize it. Teams can address these issues, and many others, in a way that provides a more manageable school experience for the student.

Trevor

Trevor is a bright high school student whose social cognitive challenges were identified early. He had struggled in classrooms that were not a good match for his needs but responded more positively with formal and informal support. In addition to school support, he had benefited from early occupational therapy, language therapy (that addressed reading comprehension and paragraph composition), and individual psychotherapy that helped him learn about his own mind and the minds of others. When he started high school, Trevor had an IEP with goals that addressed organization and pragmatic language. The study skills teacher was helping him with organization (other teachers kept her informed when he was missing assignments), and he was given extra time when he needed it. However, even with this level of support, he was overwhelmed and depressed by the work required in high school.

Trevor had been interested in science for a long time. In addition to reading and watching educational TV programs on science, he had participated in hands-on enrichment programs at science museums, specialized summer school programs, and science camps. In his high school biology class, he was bored with the material and overwhelmed with the work. When Trevor was allowed to take several chapter tests (before reading the chapters), he scored from 80 to 90%. Because he had had adequate lab experience prior to high school, the team agreed that he could take a self-paced, teacher-supervised independent study using the textbook instead of doing the regular class work. After six weeks, Trevor was halfway through the book, because much of it was review for him. His school and his IEP team recognized how stressful and exhausting school could be for Trevor and wanted to support his success in the mainstream. He was trying to keep up on his assignments in many classes. Requiring less for a subject he knew well already (such as providing an alternative to the freshman biology class and allowing him to reduce his math homework when he clearly understood the concepts) was one way to support him.

Preparation and Planning for Effective Team Meetings

Formal meetings (including, but not limited to, IEP meetings) provide opportunities to develop meaningful goals and accommodations for students. Test assessments and observations of the student, as well as suggested goals and benchmarks, are usually prepared in advance by school personnel, sometimes in collaboration with outside consultants. These can be shared ahead of time so that team members can give thought to them (in light of their own observations) in preparation for a meaningful, problem-solving process. The student can also be prepared in advance to have his concerns addressed, or to participate actively when he is able to do this.

Formal Assessments

Test results may be used for determining eligibility and may also be helpful in assessing strengths and challenges. Results should be an accurate reflection of the student; they should be consistent with and help explain what team members experience with the student. If not, every effort should be made to understand the inconsistency. We know that some students do better on a test than in a classroom. Others who do well in the classroom may not do well in the test situation. This is as true of students across all levels of ASD. Some have difficulty answering if they are not sure of the answer, or if the tester does not tell them immediately whether their answer is correct (which is not possible in a formal assessment). Some students who have difficulty comprehending less concrete material may score well on some reading comprehension tests, because they attend to and remember factual details. Students who have had social skills or pragmatic language interventions may answer appropriately on a test of pragmatic language. They know the rules and the correct answers when presented with a situation, but may not recognize the relevant factors in real-life situations. On the other hand, a nonverbal student with autism may have learned a skill through a system using a visual cue, but cannot perform in a test situation, because the prompts are unfamiliar.

A neuropsychologist or skilled clinical child and adolescent psychologist, one who uses neuropsychological instruments, may understand and explain the way the student thinks and processes information. Specifically, he or she can explain the way that a child arrives at an answer, or the reason why the child is unable to generate an answer. Knowing these aspects of the child's thinking and processing can often result in meaningful recommendations about what is reasonable to expect and what methods to consider when working with and teaching the child.

Adam

Adam is a fifth-grade boy with ASD Level 1 who has difficulty knowing what to write even when he knows the information. He has difficulty summarizing, often because he does not understand what the teacher has in mind, and he cannot generate ideas for an open-ended topic. Adam worked with an educational therapist and learned to write an acceptable three- or four-paragraph essay using a formula that sometimes worked. In a test situation, one of the stimulus pictures coincidentally reminded him of a topic he had previously written about, and he wrote an excellent short essay that was supposed to be based on the picture. Unfortunately, this rarely happened in schoolwork and homework situations, when he often spent hours unable to generate ideas, even with help. His educational therapist was at the team meeting, and she helped the team understand what had happened – Adam's testing seemed to demonstrate an ability that he had not really mastered.

Stephen

Stephen, a middle school student with ASD Level 1, did poorly on math homework and standardized tests although he could answer word problems that required an understanding of concepts when they were presented one at a time. When asked about his poor performance, he said the work was too hard because there were too many problems and they were crowded on the page. The student felt overwhelmed when he saw the number of problems on the page and how little space was provided for the work.

Understanding this difficulty helped the team develop accommodations. Stephen needed math problems that were spread out on each page. He could demonstrate an ability to do each kind of problem, but not long assignments that require "practicing" similar problems over and over (something that may help other students become more proficient). Standardized testing seemed to demonstrate a math weakness that he does not have. Based on this understanding, his math teacher and resource specialist decided to provide less work in a format that enabled him to demonstrate his competence.

Formal and Informal Observations of the Student

Any team member may observe a student in the classroom, at lunch, or on the school grounds. All participants discuss their observations at a team meeting, but sometimes a written observation report is prepared, by itself or as part of a larger assessment. As with formal assessments, reported observations should be consistent with the observations and experience of other team members. Because it is natural to draw conclusions from our own perspectives, as well as our training and experience, our impressions may not be accurate for a student with ASD. However, even when impressions and conclusions are accurate, it serves the team better if the presentation develops in a way that team members can reconcile with their own experience of the student.

The following is one way to organize written observations (or even those given orally) that facilitates this.

1. **Descriptions** are clearly stated (in a way that would have been observable to anyone present).

2. **Impressions** are an attempt to make sense of observations by considering what the observable behavior might mean about *and* mean to the student.

3. **Suggestions, recommendations, and questions** (for the team to address) follow in an understandable way from the descriptions and impressions.

It can be a challenge, even for an experienced observer, to differentiate objective observations from impressions of what observations mean. One strategy that can help when writing notes is to develop a list of what is observable and a separate column (perhaps even drawing a vertical line on the note paper) for thoughts, reactions, and impressions that occur to the observer at the time, such as the brief examples in Table 15.1 that were part of an hour-long observation of an 8-year-old, second-grade student with ASD Level 1.

Table 15.1
Sample Observation Form

Sample Observations (S = student, T = teacher)	Impressions
S reads at desk, chewing shirt. T tells class to take out workbooks and begin page 25. Class responds. S still reading.	S doesn't listen; does not respond to directions.
S reads for a couple of minutes. W/o looking up, S closes book, then takes out workbook and turns to correct page.	Delayed, but correct response; no indication that S has heard and understood, although he has.
Later: S sits outside group of students listening to T, who reads a story, stopping to show illustrations, make comments, or ask questions. S chews shirt, raises hand after some questions.	S not willing to join group, not attending to meaning of story, responses to questions are inappropriate. S willing to participate but seems to need physical distance from other students (who are sitting close to each other). Seems to chew constantly when listening or concentrating. Wants to participate, but does not understand the main points of the story or T's questions.
S comments on a detail of a picture on the page three times. Once, the detail was relevant to the question, and the other two times it was not.	T does not correct S or direct to join group (perhaps understanding his need for physical distance, chewing).
T commented on what was relevant and repeated it for the class. T had questioning expression and called on another child w/o comment when S's response was not relevant.	T responds in a positive way when S says something relevant, does not comment on tangential or incorrect responses. T shows that she is confused (other students may recognize this more easily than S) and moves on to another child's more relevant response, clarifying the correct response, and modeling a respectful handling of the inappropriate response for the other students.

Detailed observations enable us to better understand both the problematic and the successful aspects of the student's school experience. They should include examples of when the student is doing well and what the teacher may be doing to support that success. Noting when unusual behaviors, such as mouthing objects, kneeling when writing, or rocking, occur in conjunction with desired behaviors may help the team understand these as problem solving as opposed to problematic behaviors. Further, noting supports (cueing, direction, redirection, etc.) that are successful helps the team recognize what is effective. When we explore a breakdown in a student's school functioning, we sometimes find that supportive interventions used earlier have been withdrawn. The student may have been doing better, but only because the interventions, modifications, accommodations, or supports were in place.

Independent functioning is desirable when it is possible on a consistent basis, but sometimes supports are essential for a student to function adequately and should therefore be maintained. In addition, we can establish a goal, with and for the student, that he learns what helps him. Knowing his needs will eventually help him to advocate for himself, to ask for support that helps him succeed.

Goals and Benchmarks

There are specific legal requirements for writing IEPs, such as stating measurable goals and specifying benchmarks to work towards the success of those goals. The most meaningful and useful goals and benchmarks are based on an understanding of what the student does and does not understand – not just what he can or cannot do. For students who are capable of achieving them, academic goals and benchmarks must be aligned with **content standards** in general education. If benchmarks address the very smallest steps that come next (considering the student's current level of understanding), they address the possible. Just as with assessment reports and observation reports, when team members have an opportunity to look over suggested goals in advance, it allows for a more efficient and productive meeting.

Brandon

Brandon was an 8-year-old boy with ASD Level 1 who was well ahead of other students in his third-grade class in reading (decoding and comprehension of facts) and basic math, but he had significant difficulty participating in school and often read books unrelated to the lesson. He stood an open book on his desk in a way that formed a barrier between him and the class. At times, when attempts were made to engage him, he became so overwhelmed that he cried, pushed, or tried to withdraw, particularly when someone came close to him. He was unable to participate in any effort to resolve a problem that arose with a classmate, even with the assistance of an adult. At these times, he occasionally ran out of the class or even away from the school, resulting in concerns for his safety. Although he liked to listen to books that were read aloud, he was confused and upset when discussion questions were raised unless they were about specific details or concrete facts. Brandon was eligible for an IEP based on his poor pragmatic language skills. The following (see Table 15.2) were suggested pragmatic language and abstract language goals that team members previewed prior to the meeting, along with the revised goals that the team adopted.

Table 15.2
Sample Pragmatic Language and Abstract Language Goals for Brandon

Suggested Goals (Previewed by team)	**Revised Goals** (Approved by team)
Social Pragmatics Goal. Increase awareness and use of strategies to assist with problem solving.	**Social Pragmatics Goal.** Increase awareness and use of strategies to assist with problem solving.
Given that a problem occurred, Brandon will accurately identify the cause of the problem with one prompt 50% of the time.	When an adult has identified a problematic situation, Brandon will be able to answer the question, "What has happened here?" descriptively from his point of view. If he cannot, the adult will describe her observation in the most specific, concrete language. Brandon will listen and say if he agrees 50% of the time.
Given that Brandon identified the cause of the problem, Brandon will generate two possible solutions and the consequences of each with minimal adult cueing 80% of the time.	Brandon will listen to the adult's view. If it is different from his own, Brandon will accept that it is a different perspective (tolerate hearing, and be able to stay with the class or go to an acceptable alternative place) 50% of the time. Brandon will be able to choose from solutions that are offered, solutions intended to meet his needs, and obey classroom and safety rules 80% of the time (e.g., Brandon may need a break. He does not want to stay with the class. The teacher says it is not safe or permitted to go outside, because there is no adult supervision. Brandon can go to a safe corner in the class or to another location in the school to rest, read, bounce).
Abstract Language Goal. Increase awareness of and use of abstract language and thought.	**Abstract Language Goal.** Brandon will differentiate questions of fact and opinion.
During discussion of a story, Brandon will answer questions such as "What might happen next?" "What do you think about ...?" with one prompt 50% of the time.	Brandon will identify questions of fact (Is it a who, what, where, or when question?) as questions about facts one out of three attempts.
Brandon will state if a question has a correct factual answer or if it asks for his thoughts or opinions with one cue 50% of the time.	Brandon will identify questions of opinion, possibility, or personal preference as questions that do not have a right or wrong answer, one out of four attempts.

It would be wonderful if Brandon were able to accomplish the suggested goals, but unfortunately, they were far beyond anything he could understand. Brandon did not know why his behavior was a problem for others. He rarely noticed other children, unless they were trying to engage him or interfered with what he was doing. He did not understand the consequences of his behavior. He did know when someone thought he was bad or angry, but not why. Also, Brandon did not understand questions that were not factual. To him, "What might [a character in a story] do next?" was a factual question with a right answer, and he did not know the answer. He did not fully understand this question because it required attention to the mind of others.

The revised goals addressed this student's needs in a way that matched the team members' experience of his functioning. The team agreed that if Brandon could recognize a situation (as an adult described it) and learn to describe what happened, that would be a good beginning. Knowing the difference between questions that have a right or wrong answer and questions that do not have a right or wrong answer would also be a good start. If Brandon could do that, he might begin to identify his preference for factual questions and difficulty answering opinion, possibility, or personal-preference questions, and eventually communicate that. The team members also felt they could adequately assess if this plan was working. If Brandon did not respond, it might be that the steps were too big and that new steps closer to his current abilities could be considered. It is the problem-solving process that is important, not a particular solution.

Long-Term Goals and Future Planning

At IEP meetings, parents are asked to state their long-term goals for their child. These are subsequently recorded, sometimes without discussion. To address long-term goals meaningfully and realistically, teams should examine them in the context of the student's current functioning, considering maladaptive functioning and missing skills. The small steps leading to improved skills and functioning can become the more short-term goals and benchmarks, meaningful benchmarks that consider current abilities and develop the foundation for functioning in school and in life. This also allows for re-evaluation and adjustment of meaningful short- and long-term goals as part of an ongoing team problem-solving process.

Tom, described below, is clearly engaged in a process that can lead to achieving his long-term goals. This was made possible because the team understands his strengths and his challenges and has set short-term goals and benchmarks that he can achieve and that develop the skills and help him to utilize supports that make the long-term goals possible.

Tom

Tom is a student with ASD Level 2, who attended public school special education classes since preschool and recently graduated from high school. After many early interventions, step-by-step remediation, and therapies to address his language and other learning issues, attention, and behavior issues, the IEP team had a good understanding of Tom's ability to learn rote material and behavior, as well as his ability to use an interest in clear, straightforward computer games, computer programs, and other assistive technology. At the same time, team members understood his poor comprehension and his inability to solve or even identify problems accurately in the moment. Tom learned information and routines anew for each situation, even when the situation was similar to one he had mastered.

The transition-to-high-school IEP team addressed Tom's long-term goals. These were: to hold a job, to get himself safely to and from work, and to live as independently as possible, perhaps in a group home or apartment facility with a resident supervisor. Many aspects of his high school plan were structured to help him develop the skills he would need. For example, for two years, Tom participated in ROTC with mainstream students. This program did not require planning, problem solving, or much coordination. The rules were clear and exact, and the activities were repeated many times in the same way. The adult officer was understanding and appreciated Tom's enthusiasm and compliance with many repetitive drills. As a result, Tom did well.

In his junior and senior years, Tom attended a county-run, part-day vocational school for high school students. He took a school bus to the program with other high school students. One day he got on the wrong bus (one returning students to another high school). The driver kindly drove Tom to his school. After that Tom always checked the bus number and name (not only the spot where the bus was generally parked). This was important, because he now knew that the number and the words on the bus told him where it would take him. The location of the bus was also important, but it was not enough, and for this particular situation he had all the information he needed to successfully return to the school.

The first year he took the most basic course for office help. The second year he took managerial accounting, a computer-based bookkeeping course. He did not finish the course material, but his teacher created a special Introduction to Managerial Accounting certificate to give him. This was important to Tom. He saw getting a certificate at the end of the year (something he knew that the other students were earning) as meaning that a student had done what he was supposed to do, and not getting one would have meant he had not done the right thing. He was happy with his certificate, and his family was very appreciative of the teacher's understanding and sensitivity to Tom's way of seeing the world.

By his final high school IEP meeting, Tom's team members were very experienced at being flexible and open to creating or changing programs so that they would support Tom's best functioning. He could benefit from continuing the vocational school another year to finish the course and from attending a special education program at a community college that is designed to prepare students with developmental delays for work. He has started the college course. Although he is eligible for transportation, his family declined, so they could help him learn to use public transportation. After practicing with a family member several times, Tom takes a bus from the school to the light rail station, and then takes the light rail to meet his mother. Tom prepares his own lunch. He assembles and takes his school supplies, his cell phone, his wallet, and his bag lunch.

One day he forgot to make his lunch. He was very hungry when he met his mother outside the light rail station at 3 p.m., so she took him out for a late lunch. Another day Tom missed his bus stop and got off the bus on 2nd Street instead of 1st Street. He called his mother, told her the street names (by checking the sign at the corner) and a landmark, and she picked him up. She showed him that he could walk one block from 2nd to 1st Street if it happened again. (Everyone is quite confident that Tom will remember and follow his mother's suggestion if he gets out on 2nd Street again, but they are equally confident that he will call if he gets out on 3rd Street.)

Next year, Tom will return to the half-day vocational program to refresh his knowledge, complete the program, and begin a job or internship. After he is settled in a job, his family will work with community support services to find an appropriate supported, but more independent, living situation nearby. The collaboration of many people who were providing services and educational opportunities for Tom resulted in an understanding of the need for and benefit of adapting the programs and expectations to support as high a level of independence and functioning for Tom as he could manage. He will always need support and some supervision, but perhaps considerably less than he would have needed without the benefit of these ongoing efforts to understand him and the flexible problem-solving efforts of members of his team.

Preparing the Student

With all but very seriously challenged or very young children, someone can prepare for team meetings or conferences with the student, whether or not he attends the meeting in person. This may entail as little as making the student aware of the meeting and its purpose in making school a more comfortable place for him to be.

It can include exploring issues of concern to him. Preparing with him in advance enables the student and the adult to clarify the student's perspective and articulate his concerns. It also allows them to examine together what has improved, as well as what is still difficult or problematic. They can decide who will present the information, if the student attends all or part of the meeting.

Andrew

Andrew, described earlier, was preparing to enter sixth grade. He had learned to help his therapist, his mother, and his teacher prepare for his IEP meetings. He and an adult discussed what would be included. The list included any information that he felt the team should know, and was organized into positives and concerns.

Andrew's Preparation for the IEP Meeting

1. *A list of positives and improvements:*
   a. *Does more work in class, cooperates more with what the teacher wants done, concentrates more during lecture and demonstration*

b. *Still doesn't like how other kids act, but this does not bother him as much as it used to*

c. *Likes playground volunteer; sometimes plays in supervised team activities during recess; contact more O.K. in this situation (pushing with pressure, as part of a supervised game, is more comfortable than light touching)*

d. *Has one friend who lives near him and also goes to the resource specialist's class (Andrew says that he can't make more friends because you can't say "Hi" to be friendly, you have to say "Hey, dude," and he does not want to do that)*

2. *Issues, concerns, and things that are hard:*

a. *Homework:*

- *Forgets or loses homework*

- *Mom may tell him to do the assignment the wrong way (not the way the teacher wants)*

- *The teacher said homework could be reduced to half plus one. For an odd number, that would be the "larger half" plus one. If there are five questions, the larger "half" is three (two and a half rounds up to three) plus one is four. Four out of five is too much.*

b. *Math word problems: assignment is to solve, explain reasoning, and describe a three-step solution for each problem. Andrew can find the answer. He can generally explain how he gets it, although that is harder. He cannot find three steps and does not see that there are three steps for all the problems. That may be how the teacher solves the problem; it is not how he does it.*

c. *Group project: Everyone loses 5 points if anyone forgets or loses work. Everyone is mad at him if he forgets. Answering comprehension questions can make up points, but he does not always know the answers. Other group members should not be punished; he is willing to take his punishment if he forgets his work.*

d. *The teacher said that if there is cheating on tests, both the students whose work is copied and those who copy get a zero. Andrew cannot concentrate if he has to keep looking up to see if anyone is looking at his paper. (Andrew was asked if the teacher meant that students should not purposely show their work to someone. He was sure she meant more than this. "This teacher means exactly what she says," he explained. Even if he were unaware that someone was copying his work, he was sure he would get a zero.)*

The team considered Andrew's list. It was an excellent reminder of how Andrew thinks and why school is so exhausting for him. Everyone recognized how disturbed Andrew was by the results of his disorganization. His IEP had included organizational goals, which he did not achieve. It was modified to include organizational support. For now, an adult (the aide from the resource room) would check his backpack before he left school to be sure that he had his assignments and the materials he needed to complete them at home.

Andrew's list helped the team understand how overwhelmed he was by his need to do what he thought was "right." His teacher and mother agreed that he was to do assignments, as his mother understood them. Even if she were wrong, he would get full credit. The "half plus one" modification was changed to read: "If there were an odd number of problems, perhaps five, seven or, nine, he could do the 'larger half' and not add one." The purpose was for him to do every kind of problem, but that was too difficult for him to deal with at this time. He needed a concrete formula. Although his teacher had thought that the students in the class were well aware of opportunities to make up points lost by a group, this was not clear to Andrew. He needed to know that the team would not be punished for anything he did wrong, and the teacher agreed to talk to his team about that. The teacher was surprised at his response to her rule about cheating. (It is easy to continue to be surprised by the thinking of students with ASD, even for those who know them well.) She did not want him to watch out for other students who were trying to cheat. She wanted him to concentrate on his test.

Although all Andrew's issues were not fully addressed (his difficulty explaining his reasons in math was acknowledged, but without time for discussion), the team was becoming much more aware of and accepting of the fact that Andrew often has his own way of understanding. His list was very clear evidence of that; it was also evidence that he cared and tried. Andrew saw that people were trying to understand his perspective. He was satisfied with the process, and the team members were pleased with his increasing ability to advocate for himself and with his level of participation.

Factors That Contribute to Positive, Effective Collaboration

It can be helpful to articulate the factors that support effective collaboration. This enables us to know what is working as well as what to address to improve team efforts. Utilizing the example of a specific student's team, we can examine some of the most important factors that contribute to functional and successful team collaboration.

Team members are open to hearing, reflecting on, and trying to understand each participant's observations and concerns.

Edward is mainstreamed with supports and accommodations. He has had an IEP since preschool, at which time he was unable to participate or attend without individual assistance, since he was unaware of what was expected or even what was happening around him. By third grade, Edward's team recognized significant improvement in his ability to respond to directions, complete many assignments, attend to the teacher, at least some of the time, and raise his hand to answer questions. These skills all corresponded to goals that had been articulated and agreed upon the year before. However, Edward continued to require and benefit from frequent cueing and redirection.

Some team members were concerned that Edward did not function independently, something that would be required in the higher grades. This could have developed into tension and polarization between those expressing "the need for support" and team members pressing for "expectations of independence." Instead, it led to agreement that the future was worrisome, but that providing what this student needed had slowly been resulting in less need. Perhaps more important, it was agreed that trying to make something happen before a student is ready can make it less likely to happen.

Team members make an effort to understand the student, to understand his strengths and challenges and how these impact his learning, as well as his responses to academic, social, and behavioral expectations at school.

Edward had an excellent memory. He wrote slowly, but learned vocabulary, spelling, and math facts easily. He had difficulty learning new math concepts (was overwhelmed by the new language, especially during class explanations and demonstrations), but could do new math problems once he understood the concepts. The team learned to recognize that Edward wanted to do well and often seemed stressed and exhausted by his efforts. At these and other times, sensory stimuli (internal and external) could be difficult or even overwhelming for him. He engaged in several behaviors (chewing, kneeling in his chair, standing up and pacing) that could have been seen as problematic, but the OT helped the team understand that many of Edward's physical movements were his way of managing his sensory overload, and in that sense were a solution rather than a problem. They enabled him to work or to stay in or near his seat, rather than distracting him from his work. Explaining this to him and the other students made him more aware and others more tolerant.

Many decisions were made based on an understanding of Edward's strengths and challenges. He was allowed to chew gum and take breaks. His teacher shortened his spelling assignments (since he knew most of the words or easily learned them). Edward was also allowed to prelearn new math concepts with his tutor or his parents (utilizing concrete materials and vocabulary that was consistent with his own experiences and led to true comprehension of concepts). He was allowed more time for short-answer written work and to dictate longer writing assignments to his aide or parents.

Edward wanted to run around the field during recess, but the team wanted him to develop peer skills. It was decided that he could use his recess to run, but the language therapist facilitated a social/communication group for him and two peers once a week. In addition, his teacher placed him with a kind and supportive peer for small-group assignments. To make it easier for others to accept and support him, his mother explained his autism diagnosis to the class, pointing out how it accounted for Edward's strengths and challenges.

Team members work to understand and show respect for the student's perspective (his view of his experience), whether or not it conforms to that of the team members or the student's classmates, and work to help the student learn about the perspectives of others.

Although Edward could be aware of and attentive to the teacher, he had appeared completely oblivious of other students until recently. Everyone was encouraged that Edward sometimes responded appropriately to a question or comment directed to him by a peer, although this was only likely to occur if the classmate was physically close and got his attention first (such as by saying his name or touching his shoulder, which is what the teacher or classroom aide sometimes did to get his attention).

More recently, some team members noted that Edward approached other children to engage them. He might start talking about something in great detail without determining interest or recognizing what the other child was doing. He might not give the other child enough information to make his reference clear. In addition, he sometimes moved in a kind of dancing motion, very close to another child. When the child backed away, Edward was likely to move closer and increase his motion. Team members were concerned for Edward and the other child. This was not the kind of peer interaction they wanted to see. Some children who had ignored or tolerated Edward before, and even some who were especially kind to him, now backed away from him. Explaining about personal space or providing redirection might be effective for the moment, but it did not have any real meaning to Edward and did not result in permanent change. That is, the pragmatic language/social skills group lessons did not carry over to these real-life situations. Several team members recognized that children like Edward often do not generalize, because they do not recognize the essential similarities in somewhat different situations.

Those who had observed Edward felt that in those situations he did recognize that the other child was near and did want to engage the child (have that child notice or respond to him). However, he was not aware enough of himself and others to understand what was happening. Strategies for heading off troublesome interactions were considered.

Explaining rules of engagement in a way that would make sense to Edward was not possible, considering his lack of understanding of other people. Raising Edward's awareness seemed to be a good first step. The prior year the team had developed a goal to raise Edward's awareness of the teacher's role in explaining and giving directions by directing his attention to what she said and what other students were doing as a result. He became more observant and responsive. The team decided to develop a response strategy that would raise Edward's awareness of his own behavior towards peers as well as their responses. Once or twice a day, when possible, an observing adult would tell Edward very concretely what she observed. (For example, she might note aloud: He is twisting and turning very close to a specific child. Does he want the other child to notice, to like what he is doing, and so on? The other child is backing away or telling him to stop. Does the other child want Edward to see that he is uncomfortable? Edward is moving even closer. He wants the child to play this way, and the other child does not. This is a dilemma.) Just articulating these observations can raise awareness and engage both children in a problem-solving process. If Edward continues, he might have to be separated, but what happened would be easier for all to understand as a dilemma. Edward, the other child, and the adult would be aware of Edward's intent (to be physically closer, to be watched, to be friends, to play with the other child), as well as the discomfort of the other child. This is a dilemma that can be articulated by or with the help of the adult.

Team members are interested and willing to provide support and develop expectations that the student can meet (a manageable environment).

In an ongoing collaborative process that includes relevant team members at various times, Edward's team continues to engage in problem solving. Team members try to understand Edward and to develop modifications, accommodations, and alternative learning options that support him at school. This, in turn, helps team members to understand and support each other's efforts on his behalf. The following are just a few of the supports and expectations that have served Edward's growth and mastery.

- *Since participating in class is such an effort for Edward, and he can relax and relieve his stress by pacing or running, he is allowed to run around the perimeter of the school yard and is not expected to participate in peer activities during recess.*

- *For unfamiliar assignments, he may not understand what is most relevant and has difficultly following multiple-step assignments when directions are given to the entire class. He is often given a sample or a list of sequential directions to keep beside him, even for familiar assignments. When the assignment is not familiar, he is given an opportunity to pre-learn or observe before participating.*

- *Edward is allowed to dictate, and later will be allowed to type. Students in Edward's school learn to type in a computer lab that utilizes a typing program that he has found very difficult and frustrating. It begins with the "home keys." Edward finds it easier to learn the location of the letters on the keyboard utilizing a program that teaches the letters in alphabetical order (King, 1986). He began at home during the summer and then was allowed to practice his own program during typing instruction class at school.*

If we truly are all here to understand and plan for the student in as meaningful a way as possible, each participant in the education team both learns and contributes, and small steps for the immediate future can be achieved. As the team works to know a student, the plan can make sense in light of this knowledge, and team members often develop a common language. The shared language becomes familiar to the team and to the student.

Summary and Conclusions

Members of the most successful teams know that they have much to learn from the student – about the student's mind and his subjective experience. With greater understanding, meaningful long-term outcomes (competence, comfort, and independence) may be achieved. The student can see this as possible, because he sees that we value understanding his perspective as we try to meet his needs, as well as help him consider and respond to the reactions and expectations of others. It helps to keep in mind that "independence" does not have to mean doing something the way most other people do, or doing something without help. Independence may mean knowing our own strengths and challenges and asking for and accepting help when we need it. The objective is to problem--solve and develop plans for cognitive, social, emotional, behavioral, and communication issues. Such plans must allow a student with ASD to be who he is, to experience an educational environment that he can manage, and (step by small step) to learn to live and function adequately in the world as it is.

Tips for Practical Application

✓ Recognize that each member of the team has something to contribute. There is no one answer to the questions faced by educational teams, and no one person is equipped to make all the decisions.

✓ Make an effort to include the student's perspective whenever possible. This may be done through direct interview or an interest survey or by gathering data about the student's preferences.

✓ Educate yourself about all levels of the autism spectrum. Biographies of people with ASD Level 1 can be very helpful. Educate yourself about the impact ASD has on how the student thinks. Her thinking directly influences her ability to make good decisions.

✓ Reach out to other professionals involved with the student's life and invite them to the IEP meetings. These could include child care workers, extended family members, recreational supervisors, doctors, social workers, or therapists.

✓ Realize that parents can be terribly outnumbered and consequently overwhelmed at typical IEP meetings. Encourage parents to bring support people.

✓ Avoid falling into the "defensive" position. To work in the field of ASD, it helps to be humble. If people question your program ideas, accept the questions as opportunities to discuss the long-term goals and get added input for how to reach those goals.

✓ If there are obstacles to the process, address them. The teaming process should make life easier for everyone, not harder. When the team has difficulties, the focus should always return to the student's needs as identified in the evaluation, as well as previous goals and objectives and the levels of success.

✓ Keep in mind that futures planning involves identifying long-term life goals for the student and addressing any obstacles that may be keeping her from reaching those goals. Current levels of performance can be identified in each goal area, followed by a team discussion about how to systematically reach the goals.

✓ Task analyze goals when writing attainable objectives. For example, if team members have agreed that they would like the student to learn to do her own laundry, they can first break the task of doing laundry into steps (sorting colors, white and dark, measuring detergent, turning the knob, etc.). The team can then write objectives for each step, which provides a systematic way of addressing goals together.

Chapter Highlights

- It is important that all those working with a student with ASD communicate with one another and share information about what they know of how the student learns, the student's strengths and challenges, and how they meet the student's needs.

- Educational support and intervention teams are mandated by law. They are comprised of teachers, paraprofessionals, administrators, other service providers (such as speech-language therapists, occupational therapists, and behavior specialists), both in and outside of school, family members, and the student him/ herself.

- Collaboration among team members can benefit all members of the team. When collaboration is based on a shared focus and shared knowledge of the student's challenges and strengths, the chances for student resiliency and school success are increased.

- Each team member brings different perspectives and knowledge to the collaboration, leading to opportunities for discussion that can result in greater opportunities for student success.

- Collaboration can be either formal or informal.

- The purpose of formal team meetings can be to initiate evaluations for a student not receiving services, to review progress for a student already being served, or to develop goals and objectives/benchmarks.

- Students can receive special educational services either through an individualized education program (IEP) if they meet eligibility requirements as a student with disabilities under federal law or through a 504 Plan if they are able to function adequately in the general education classroom with accommodations.

- Informal collaboration, which can occur at any time, gives all participants on the team the opportunity to address concerns and issues as they happen.

- Areas of importance or concern on behalf of a student may include language and communication, social-emotional issues, behavior, and academics and learning.

- Modifying assignments and providing accommodations can help keep the student from becoming too overwhelmed by school.

- Effective planning and preparation for team meetings may involve any and all of the following: formal assessments; observations of the student; developing goals and benchmarks; examining progress in terms of long-term, adult-outcome goals; future planning to reach long-term goals; and preparing the student to be actively involved in the meeting.

- Factors that contribute to positive and effective communication include (a) openness among team members as well as a desire for mutual understanding; (b) awareness of the student's strengths and challenges and how they impact learning; (c) respect for the student's perspective and a desire to help the student understand the perspectives of others; and (d) a desire to create a manageable environment for the student.

Chapter Review Questions

1. Who might be members of an educational support and intervention team?

2. Why is collaboration important?

3. What is an IEP? What is a 504 Plan? How do they differ?

4. What are some components necessary for successful team meetings?

5. Why might you want to plan with a student prior to a team meeting?

6. List some of the factors that contribute to effective collaboration.

7. Based on the scenarios in the chapter, give three examples of how individuals with ASD may think and learn.

References

Attwood, T. (1998). *Asperger's syndrome: A guide for parents and professionals*. London, UK: Jessica Kingsley Publishers.

Bate, C. (2004). Enhancing relationships through speech and language intervention. In L. C. Levental-Belfer (Ed.), *Asperger's syndrome in young children* (pp. 190-210). London, UK: Jessica Kingsley Publishers.

Benard, B. (1991, August). *Fostering resiliency in kids: Protective factors in the family, school, and community*. Portland, OR: Western Center for Drug Free Schools and Communities.

Benard, B. (2004). *Resiliency: What we have learned*. San Francisco, CA: West Ed.

Buron, K. D., & Curtis, M. (2012). *The incredible 5-point scale* (2nd ed.). Shawnee Mission, KS: AAPC Publishing.

Gray, C. (2000). *The original social story™ book: Illustrated edition*. Arlington, TX: Future Horizons.

Gray, C. (2002). *The sixth sense II*. Arlington, TX: Future Horizons

Jacobsen, P. (2003). *Asperger syndrome & psychotherapy: Understanding Asperger perspectives*. London, UK: Jessica Kingsley Publishers.

Jacobsen, P. (2005). *Understanding how Asperger children and adolescents think and learn: Creating manageable environments for AS students*. London, UK: Jessica Kingsley Publishers.

King, D. H. (1986). *Keyboarding skills*. Cambridge, MA: Educators Publishing Service.

Klin, A., Volkmar, F. R., & Sparrow, S. S. (Ed.). (2000). *Asperger syndrome*. New York, NY: Guilford Press.

Levental-Belfer, L.C. (2004). *Asperger's syndrome in young children: A developmental guide for parents and professionals*. London: Jessica Kingsley Publishers.

McNeely, C., Nonnemaker, J., & Blum, W. (2002). Promoting school connectedness: Evidence from the national longitudinal study of adolescent health. *Journal of School Health, 72*(4), 138-146.

Noddings, N. (1992). *The challenge to care in schools: An alternative approach to education*. New York, NY: Teachers College Press.

Siegel, B. (1996). *The world of the autistic child: Understanding and treating autism spectrum disorders*. New York, NY: Oxford University Press.

Werner, E. E., & Smith, R. S. (1992). *Overcoming the odds: High risk children from birth to adulthood*. London, UK: Cornell University Press.

Wiss, T. (2004). Building connections through sensory and motor pathways: Occupational therapy. In L. C. Levental-Belfer (Ed.), *Asperger's syndrome in young children* (pp. 211-237). London, UK: Jessica Kingsley Publisher.

Learner Objectives

After reading this chapter, the learner should be able to:

- Discuss the impact of early theories of autism on a family

- Discuss the options available for educating persons with disabilities prior to the passage of PL 94-142 (now known as IDEIA or IDEA 2004)

- Describe the educational experience of an individual with ASD through the eyes of a mother

- Discuss the impact of PL 94-142

- Discuss the importance of teacher acceptance of the unique strengths and needs of individuals with ASD

Chapter 16

Growing up With Autism:
One Parent's Perspective

Julie A. Donnelly

Jean-Paul was in the same school from kindergarten to second grade. In 1975, he moved to a different state, a different home, and a different school. When he entered his new third-grade class, he felt overwhelmed, so he walked to the shelf of books at the back of the room. He began reading volume A of the encyclopedias and continued reading through the rest of the volumes for the next three days. He did not respond to requests that he go to his desk or participate in activities. Jean-Paul heard the call for lunch and the announcement to get on the bus to go home. Otherwise, he hid himself in the books.

On the third day, a letter was sent home telling me, his mother, that Jean-Paul was being placed in the class for the mentally retarded. There was no request for a meeting to discuss concerns. They did not require my signature for an evaluation. There was no evaluation or diagnosis. I was not asked my opinion about placement. There was no individualized education program (IEP) with goals and beginning and ending dates of services. I was not given a list of procedural rights. Jean-Paul and I apparently had no rights. The decision was made without us.

I cried for the rest of the day. However, the next morning, I went to the school and told the principal that they would not put my son in the special class. I then walked to the back of his third-grade room and told Jean-Paul to get to his desk and do what the teacher asked. He was on the final volume of the encyclopedias by then, but put it down and did what I asked.

Today, as an over-25-year veteran of special education teaching under the Individuals with Disabilities Education Act (IDEA), I complain about the paperwork load and the complexity of the ever-changing law. At the same time, I never stop giving thanks for the legislation that prevents the kind of injustice that happened before Public Law 94-142 – the first law to guarantee a free and appropriate education to children identified with special needs.

During the first 20 years of my life, I was unaware of autism, but I heard the word pronounced over my son when he was 3 and I was 23. The year 1971 was not a good one to have autism. Bruno Bettelheim was still director of the Orthogenic School in Chicago and considered the leading theorist on autism. Bettelheim (1967) described mothers of children with autism as "rejecting mothers" and compared them to the "devouring witch" of *Hansel and Gretel* with destructive intents (p. 71). Bettelheim claimed that autism resulted from psychological damage to the child by cold, aloof parents, and referred to the mothers of children with autism as "refrigerator mothers."

It wasn't until after his death that the public became aware that Bettelheim had lied about his history, did not have a doctorate in psychology, was Freudian and psychoanalytic in his treatment methods without being trained in either, and was often cruel to and hit the children under his care. Bettelheim also falsified records about his experiences with children with autism and exaggerated the "cures" he supposedly effected (Pollack, 1997). Yet, most medical professionals of that period agreed with Bettelheim that autism was an emotional problem with no known cure.

In 1964, Bernard Rimland published *Infantile Autism,* the first work to present evidence for a physical, not psychological, cause for autism. But it took a long time for these ideas about autism to penetrate the medical establishment. Although Bettelheim's theories have been disproven, many are still misinformed about the cause of autism. Unfortunately for families of children with autism, many still do not understand that autism is a neurological difference. The people who blame the parents may be your neighbors or relatives, and their judgments can cause great personal misery.

This chapter gives a personal account of raising a child with autism at a time when little was known about the disorder. It reviews the early history of legal and educational services and how they affected the life of my son. Lessons are drawn from my experience as both a parent and an educational specialist in an effort to enhance parent-professional collaboration.

Early Childhood

In 1971, when my son, Jean-Paul, was first diagnosed, the medical recommendation was to put him in a mental hospital for an indefinite length of time. Instead, we chose to work with Jean-Paul in our home. In 1972, when my son was 4, I found a pamphlet from the National Society for Autistic Children (NSAC; later became the Autism Society of America). We were making progress with Jean-Paul in our home program, but were thrilled to know that there were others out there. We felt so alone and misunderstood by friends, family, and others, who had never heard of autism.

The pamphlet included a checklist entitled *Could Your Child Be Autistic?* As I read down the list, I noted that JeanPaul met most of the criteria. He had been severely impaired in speech development, but after a year of work, he could communicate a little, although it was mostly echolalia. He was also impaired in his relatedness to others. While he was close to me, he mostly used me as an object to take care of his needs. He did not have difficulty with change; in fact, he seemed oblivious to it. He had no sense of himself and did not respond to his name when called. Further, he did not seem to have a feeling of ownership, and his belongings could all be taken from him with no protest.

The checklist also mentioned "Lack of intellectual development or retardation in certain areas, sometimes accompanied by normal or superior abilities in other areas." The schools tested Jean-Paul as retarded, but he knew his numbers and ABCs, and at 4 years of age was already reading. He showed no interest in other children or toys and chose to sit staring into space, listening to music or reading books. He often acted as if he was deaf. He did not seem to feel temperature or pain. He did not look at us, was poorly coordinated, and under- or hypoactive. The checklist from the National Society for Autistic Children was describing my son.

I was frustrated with doctors who said that autism was incurable by definition and then told me that I had caused it. Even if it had been true, it was not helpful. With no programs or books to guide us, Jean-Paul's stepdad, Mike Donnelly, and I devised a plan for him in our own home. Mike had some experience working in a residential placement with children with autism. He had ideas, and I was the chief implementer of the program. We had never heard of Lovaas or applied behavior analysis or any other model. However, we came up with some basic principles that turned out to be important aspects of autism programming.

Our home program was centered on communication, keeping Jean-Paul focused and engaged in our world, and teaching him to do age-appropriate self-care. We insisted that he try to use words instead of screaming to get his needs met. The first months were terrible, as Jean-Paul increased his screaming to try to get us to respond. We insisted he try to form words. He resisted, because this was difficult for him. His first communications were lines he had memorized from songs and a sound that resembled a yes and that we continuously shaped into a clear response. Jean-Paul loved to eat, so we used food reinforcement to encourage him to try these difficult skills. As Jean-Paul became used to the highly structured routine and expectations, he resisted less and began to make progress.

Jean-Paul did not like to move. Many years later we would find out that he had a neurological difference in the motor skill area of his brain that made it difficult for him to control his movements. In addition, he had an eye muscle problem that caused him to see double. Visual-motor coordination was a challenge. However, we insisted that he participate in family activities and chores. He was taught to take care of his body: brush his teeth, wash, dress, and make his bed. He screamed and resisted, so it sometimes took all morning to complete these basic activities.

Jean-Paul's love for music was obsessive. We had noticed as early as when he was 2 weeks old that when music was playing, he would stop crying and look entranced and happy. Since his father was a musician, and we were almost constantly surrounded by live or recorded music, this worked out well. By the time he was 3, we became aware that Jean-Paul's need for music was out of control. When there was an album on the record player, he would be watching the record spin around and be lost in a trance. When there was no music, he would scream. As we began trying to bring him back into our world, we decided that music took him too far away from us. We put away the record player and radio and only allowed live music that was participatory. This resulted in more screaming, but we endured.

His two sisters and brother were a tremendous help to Jean-Paul. They felt that he should play with them and they made him play by group force. They taught him to be a kid, often against his will. In addition, these three siblings kept him engaged in our world. Jean-Paul would have chosen to listen to music, read books, eat, or just space out. His siblings would not let him be off to himself. Sometimes it seemed cruel, but it was the greatest gift they could have given him. Jean-Paul gradually learned to focus and participate in the world of our family.

When he was 4-1/2, I took him to the University of Minnesota to see Dr. Uwe Stuecher and Sheila Merzer at the program for autistic-type children. Dr. Stuecher confirmed the diagnosis of early infantile autism. He was pleased with the progress that we had made in our home and agreed to advise us on our home program. When he left the University of Minnesota, Sheila Merzer became our advisor. Under Dr. Stuecher's advice and with a letter of explanation, we placed Jean-Paul in the rural community school at Orr, Minnesota, for his kindergarten year in 1973.

In 1974, the TEACCH (Treatment and Education of Autistic and related Communication-handicapped CHildren) program was started in North Carolina by Dr. Eric Schopler (Schopler, 1994). The program was remarkable for its acceptance of parents not as the problem, but as part of the solution. Schopler had studied under Bettelheim at the University of Chicago, but came to see him as a "negative role model." When I visited the TEACCH program, I found that they treated parents with respect. I was so moved by their willingness to listen and their considerate responses that I cried. It was a complete contrast to what I experienced with most professionals up to that point. For this alone, I am grateful to TEACCH.

Rather than being based on one technique or philosophy, the TEACCH center trained teachers and parents to support the individual with ASD in a wide variety of ways. They promoted structure and organization to help the individual with autism understand his environment and taught the use of visual schedules and supports. They also developed functional and community-based programming. Communication skills were stressed at TEACCH as were social and leisure skills. While the TEACCH program did not invent all these methods, it became a national and international model promoting what have now become standard aspects of good autism programming.

Elementary School Years

Orr is a very small community 50 miles south of International Falls, Minnesota, and the Canadian border. No one in Orr schools had heard of autism when we moved there. Although some special services were available, **Public Law 94-142** would not be in place for another three years. The public schools were not required to take a student with autism, but since two of our children already attended, they took their brother. The school attempted to give Jean-Paul an intelligence test and decided that he was "untestable" because of his lack of language.

The speech therapist was able to give him a *Peabody Picture Vocabulary Test* (PPVT; Dunn, Dunn, Robertson, & Eisenberg, 1959), a test of receptive language. The test page shows four line drawings. The evaluator names one, and the child is asked to point at that picture out of the four. I am amazed that Jean-Paul scored at all on a test that required pointing, but his score was 2.8, which equated to an IQ of about 55 (average is 100).

Jean-Paul did not understand most of the social skills needed for kindergarten, but he was already reading and knew his numbers and letters well. I came in to assist his teacher every other day. The speech therapist recognized that Jean-Paul needed a lot of help and saw him an hour a day. His first speech/language goals included increasing attention span, reducing echolalic responses, improving eye contact, making communication a pleasant and necessary experience, using speech to make his needs known, using gesture and facial expression, responding to outside stimuli, and developing social skills.

In second grade, Jean-Paul received remedial reading instruction for comprehension and help completing his workbooks and ditto sheets. A note from the second-grade teacher said, "The main reason Jean-Paul's grades are low is that he loses his work, so I have no grades for him. I try to keep a watch on him so this won't happen, but it is just about impossible to do this constantly with all the other students I have to attend to." This is so typical for kids with autism that I can probably find the equivalent of this note in most students' files. In addition, we continued working with Jean-Paul at home, where our goals were adaptive and social rather than academic. Over his first three years of school, Jean-Paul made dramatic progress. When he was 7 years and 3 months old, he was retested with the PPVT. He now had a receptive language age level of 8-2, which equated to an intelligence score of 112. His tested receptive language ability had doubled.

Orr was a rural school with few resources; yet, they tried to make a difference with an unusual student. During his first-grade year, the school sent Jean-Paul to the Mayo Clinic for an in-depth evaluation. When the results said that Jean-Paul was retarded and his mother was hostile, the school ignored the results and went on working with the child they knew was bright but different. Were things perfect? Definitely not. After a good kindergarten teacher, his first grade teacher was intolerant and tended to raise her voice at the students. Jean-Paul was unable to differentiate whom she was yelling at and always came home anxious. His second-grade teacher was kind, but I remember her saying, "What is it with Jean-Paul?" She never did have a clue about his autism, but a good teacher is a good teacher.

Public Law 94-142 was passed in 1975 and trickled down into the schools through 1976 and 1977. In my life, Public Law 94-142 and its reauthorizations as IDEA are THE LAW. According to this law, the public schools would provide an education for ALL students (no matter how severe their disability). Every child had a right to a free, appropriate public education. Orr School District took my son out of kindness, but many children with autism and other disabilities were turned away from their neighborhood schools. If they did not fit the classrooms the school had, if they were not toilet trained, if they could not communicate or had difficult behaviors, the school could turn them away. No longer!! The law promised all students the right to an education.

Years later, I had an experience while traveling in Asia that reminded me of the importance of THE LAW. I was presenting an autism workshop in Kuala Lumpur, the capital city of Malaysia. People had traveled from all over Asia to attend. On my first day in the huge city, I had visited their one and only special education class. I had also visited the American School, where people who could pay sent their children with disabilities. Needless to say, these two classes provided services for only a tiny percentage of students with disabilities. During my workshop, I told the attendees about our law, which says that our government is required to educate every child, no matter what their disability is. People gasped. One woman cried and asked, "How did you get your country to pass a law like that?" One mother was trying to educate her daughter with autism in her home because no school would take her. I had to admit to these people that our law is still a work in progress. It is an enormous commitment and is still not an actuality, but we are attempting to fulfill it.

I think many parents and professionals take the law for granted. They don't have a good sense of the past or a sense of our society compared to most of the world. They don't see what a new and different attitude this piece of legislation represents. It is also easy to lose sight of the enormity of the task. *All* children, no matter what their disability is, will have their educational needs met. Many of us know in the day to day that this is no small chore. And, certainly, some of our children with autism are major challenges.

By the time Jean-Paul entered third grade, he was what we then called a child with high-functioning autism or Asperger Syndrome (now called ASD Level 1). But in 1976, I had never heard those terms; it was just autism. That year we moved out of the cold north woods to the south-central midwest. THE LAW was in effect, but it had not reached the schools in Winona, a small southern-Missouri town. As described in the opening vignette, Jean-Paul spent the first three days in his new school reading volume after volume of the encyclopedia while largely ignoring his teacher's directions.

Puzzled about their new student, the school sent a letter home with Jean-Paul, informing me that he was being put in the class for the mentally retarded (the catch-all special education class at the time. The only one they had.). There was no request that I come in and discuss concerns. There was no paper to sign for evaluation – and no evaluation. There was no permission for placement or individualized education program. Before IDEA was in effect, all decisions were made by the school, and parents did not even have to be informed.

At home, I progressed from a feeling of devastation to anger. I went to the school the next day to remedy the situation. I told the principal that my son was not going to the MR class. I told Jean-Paul to listen to his teacher and do what she said, which he tried to do. I talked to his teacher, a sweet person, who had never had a student like Jean-Paul and had no idea what to do. I gave her suggestions, and she was glad to keep him in her class and follow through with my ideas.

By the next year, 1977, THE LAW landed in Winona, and a teacher for students with learning disabilities (LD was hired. Jean-Paul was served under LD, as autism was not put on the list of educational disabilities until 1990. He also continued to receive language services. In the rural schools, the speech-language pathologists (SLP) had more training than most of the staff members. They were the ones who had a clue about how to approach autism. I now realize that Jean-Paul desperately needed help from an occupational therapist for both fine- and gross-motor skills as well as sensory differences. However, he was out of high school before we even knew that such services existed. He might have benefited from additional adult support in the classroom, but we didn't realize that was possible. He received pullout language and LD support through his fifth-grade year.

During that period, his grades were poor. His handwriting was almost illegible. He lost his worksheet ditto pages, did not complete his workbooks, and ignored a lot of his math class in favor of reading his own books on history and geography. He was "spaced out" and had no friends. His teachers had a sense that he was bright but did not have much hope that he would be able to graduate from high school. In the meantime, Jean-Paul was happy with his own interests and seemed unaware that he was different and friendless.

Sixth grade was a watershed year for my son in many ways. His sixth-grade teacher had taught for 40 years, many of them in special education. She asked if we could stop the pullouts for language and LD and just have Jean-Paul in her class full time. I was willing to let her try. She sat Jean-Paul front and center in her crowded classroom with his desk touching hers. When Jean-Paul was spacing out, she cracked her paddle across his desk, and he would jump and refocus on the classroom. Sometimes she would send Jean-Paul out of class on an errand and talk to the other students about how we all are different and how Jean-Paul was just different in more obvious ways. Most of the students were supportive. However, a few boys teased and tormented him. They picked on him verbally and physically in the bathroom and the hall when teachers were not around. Twice that year, they pulled his pants down in the hallway. Jean-Paul, who had begun to be aware of his differences, was humiliated by their actions and his inability to defend himself. For the next five years, he would continue to endure the torment of these bullies and become more and more depressed.

During his sixth-grade year, we also found out that Jean-Paul had an eye muscle problem that caused him to see double. His eyes had adapted and learned to work one at a time so he could read. However, other than for words, most of his vision was barely functional. He had never told us that he saw differently than others, because he did not know what typical vision was. With the prism glasses that were prescribed, his eyes slowly and painfully changed and began working together.

Secondary School Years

For seventh grade, in 1980, Jean-Paul was in the junior high/high school building and had to change classes every 50 minutes. We discussed the supports he would need with an educational resource teacher, who promised to talk to all his teachers and inform them about his differences and support needs. I assumed that she would do this before school started. When nothing had been done two weeks into the school year, I went in and talked to all Jean-Paul's teachers. I supplied them with pencils to give him, because he showed up without his materials. We got him a big backpack, and he carried all his books with him so that he would have what he needed. Some time in November, the educational resource teacher finally showed up, but did little or nothing to help.

Jean-Paul received virtually no services through junior high and high school. He only got the adaptations that I wrestled out of the school through my own advocacy. The only special education service available at the secondary level was a self-contained classroom. Students in that room were labeled MR and LD; however, they all worked as a group on the same materials and at the same level. The teacher was working on a master's thesis at a nearby university on individualized curriculum in special education. When I asked why she was not individualizing in this classroom, she laughed. That was only research to get her degree, she said; it was not possible to individualize in a real special education classroom.

With this person as the only special education resource, I realized there would be no support for my son, who was struggling through mainstream classes. Special education, despite what the law said, was an all-or-nothing business in most rural schools at the time. A push for inclusion and inclusive support practices would not come until the 1990s, and my son graduated in 1986.

There are some benefits to having a pushy mother. With his visual-motor problems, art was torture for Jean-Paul. After one particularly bad event where he destroyed his art project, I requested – no – insisted, that he be taken out of art class and allowed to substitute music class for that requirement. That removed a major source of stress.

Jean-Paul wanted to go on to college, but his handwriting was still barely legible. I knew he would have to learn to type, but I remembered speed-typing drills from my high school typing class. I could visualize Jean-Paul falling apart under the pressure to make his fingers move faster and faster. I demanded that he be graded only on accuracy, not speed. The business teacher said, "We have never done that before," to which I retorted, "There is always a first time for everything." Jean-Paul learned to type.

I did not rescue him from physical education (P.E.), and that is where the bullies antagonized him the most. I have now learned that it is O.K. to take some students out of typical physical education classes and allow them to earn P.E. credit in another way. Sometimes, they need this adaptation because of poor motor skills, poor social skills, emotional sensitivity, and/or vulnerability.

Another source of anxiety was algebra. Jean-Paul had learned basic math skills, but he could not understand abstract math. He had a particularly good teacher who got him through, just barely, and did not allow his algebra difficulties to keep him out of the Honor Society. Being chosen for Beta club (Honor Society) raised Jean-Paul's self-esteem, and was one of the first steps in pulling him out of a deep depression.

At age 14, everything began piling up on Jean-Paul: The bullies, his anger at his inability to deal with the bullies, his lack of friends or girlfriends – in contrast to his brother and sisters who had many – his inability to be an athlete – in contrast to his brother and sisters who were – the world situations (he took the nightly news personally); and then there was algebra, which he could not seem to understand. Jean-Paul talked of feeling that he would be better off dead, but despised himself for not having the courage to commit suicide. It was a frightening time.

At this point, the school tested his IQ, resulting in a verbal score of 145 and a performance score of 77. A neurologist found an unusual EEG reading in the motor area of his brain and said that Jean-Paul was not depressed; he was extremely frustrated. As we had always thought, he was a bright young man with difficulty showing all he knew.

Several factors helped to pull him out of the depression. Jean-Paul began receiving personal counseling. He took the neurologist's advice and gave up on his hope to play team sports and instead began competing against himself at long-distance running. He was also given the job of manager for the basketball team. Although this mainly consisted of carrying the balls and towels, he got to go on the bus with the team to games. He was such a loyal fan that one year he was allowed to dress in the tiger suit and be the team mascot. Despite his poor coordination, he developed a dance style that resembled break dancing, and he attended all the dances. People would circle around and clap for his unique and totally enthusiastic dance performances. Some of his teachers were so taken with his knowledge of the history and lyrics of rock music that they asked him to sing during class. This acceptance of his strengths by his teachers encouraged student acceptance, but it was all too unusual for the girls to choose him as a boyfriend. He had a shallow level of acceptance, but no true friends.

While many teachers were good to Jean-Paul, his history teacher realized that he had a prodigy on his hands. This teacher organized a history bowl team and invited Jean-Paul to be a member. There were five students on the team, including one of Jean-Paul's sisters. The other members just sat and watched while Jean-Paul answered the questions. The team won the district title and went on to compete at a university history bowl in a nearby city. When they defeated most of the big-city schools, Jean-Paul became a hometown hero. He ran for vice president of the student council against the principal's daughter, a popular cheerleader. While his opponent took victory for granted, Jean-Paul worked to win the vote, and when it was counted, he had won. He remained as vice president of the student council for his junior and senior years. He was captain of the history bowl team and won a history and a leadership scholarship to college.

Transition to College and Beyond

During his senior year, rather than special education classes, Jean-Paul was taking college courses and passing advanced placement tests for college. The month of his graduation, he was ready to tell his schoolmates and community about his disability. The newspaper in the nearby city interviewed Jean-Paul and our family and did a full-page Sunday special on this young man with autism who was graduating with honors and going on to college. It was something very new in 1986.

Was he ready for college? Was the university ready for him? Well, no; there was no special education support in college, and his struggles continued. Jean-Paul learned and grew, and after a B.A., two master's degrees, a job, and a marriage, I am sure he would say it was a hard road, but he would do it all again if he had to.

Summary and Conclusions

I frequently hear parents and professionals say there are so many choices of therapies and methods that they do not know which to select. It is unfortunate that we do not yet know which techniques work best for which profiles of children. However, we know so much more than we used to. And we actually have choices!

We know that our children function best in highly structured environments. We know that we have to ease their anxiety by creating patterns and routines and then teach them how to function more flexibly in real-life situations. We know that communication is extremely important, whether that means finding an alternative type of communication system or teaching pragmatic language in real-life situations. We know that play is the work of children, and we must help our children learn the many lessons of typical play in order to build a bridge to their peers. We know that our students should be included with typical peers at the level and amount that they can benefit from. We know how to help individuals with sensory and motor differences. We know that they need a wide range of services, varying from early intensive one-to-one teaching to support services for those in the mainstream with college as a goal. We know that social skills make the difference in a successful life for all the diverse individuals labeled with autism. We realize that many behavior differences have a function, and we can find positive supports that prevent difficult behaviors while we teach these individuals to understand the rules for functioning in the home, school, and community. We know that functioning in school is not an end in itself but a preparation for being an independent and interdependent human being.

The basic principles of good education for students on the autism spectrum are available on the Internet, in books, through conferences, and trainings. Universities are beginning to realize that autism is no longer a low-incidence disability and are starting to train teachers in these skills. The gap between our need for well-trained teachers and those ready to teach is huge, but the necessary skills are not rocket science. My first question to a prospective teacher is: Do you like individuals with autism? Are you interested in teaching and learning from the most unique individuals on the planet? None of Jean-Paul's teachers were trained in autism; yet, some were excellent, just because they were good teachers. I send them my heartfelt thanks.

When parents ask me, as they frequently do, where to move to get good educational services for their child with autism, I recommend that they stay in the area where they have the best personal support system. Don't move away from family, friends, church, or support groups expecting that being in a new location will solve the problem. Each child's needs are so unique that we cannot name one area that is excellent at every level for every student. It comes down to individuals, each particular administrator, teacher, parent, and child working out the best possible program in their own way.

It seems to me that we have come a long way, and yet I know that we have a long way to go. We parents and professionals still have the opportunity and the obligation to be trailblazers in autism education. Good educational services are not some lofty goal but what we work at every day as a team, together.

Tips for Practical Application

✓ It is important for professionals to understand the history of autism and its impact on the family. Although we know today that autism is a result of brain function, previous beliefs can still impact how the general public views autism and, as a result, affect the struggles a family may have to endure.

✓ An educational team must always include the child's parents. Parents have valuable input regarding their child's functioning at home and in the community and are the only members of the team who will go on to be lifelong advocates for that child.

✓ Formal testing has limitations in its ability to predict lifelong success for students with ASD. IQ scores can change over time and do not necessarily determine academic success.

✓ It is important for special educators to work in an advocacy role by training general educators in the nature and implications of autism.

✓ Educators need to be aware of the impact of bullying and recognize that children with autism are likely targets for such behavior.

✓ A teacher's acceptance and appreciation of a student's unique strengths can influence the perspective of peers and lead to greater acceptance.

✓ A good advocate for a student with ASD in the general ed. classroom might be a teacher or mentor whose content area matches the special interest of the student with autism.

✓ Finding a role for a student with autism within the school setting, such as score keeper for an athletic team, can go a long way in alleviating depression and isolation in adolescence.

✓ It is crucial that educational teams determine the purpose of behaviors demonstrated by students with autism rather than dismissing them simply as noncompliance.

Chapter Highlights

• In the early 1970s doctors often told parents of children identified with ASD to institutionalize their children and that autism was incurable. At that time, the cause of autism was still seen as based on a reaction of children to cold, non-loving mothers.

• Siblings can be very important to the positive development of individuals with ASD.

• Pre-PL 94-142, options for schooling for individuals with ASD were limited, and the public schools did not have to even accept students with disabilities.

• PL 94-142 was essentially the civil rights law for individuals with disabilities.

• Families and teachers need to serve as advocates for children with ASD.

Chapter Review Questions

1. How did early theories of autism impact this family?

2. What were the choices for the family described in this chapter regarding educational options prior to the enactment of PL 94-142?

3. List and describe three things you learned about the educational experience of the child discussed in this chapter.

4. State why PL 94-142 was so important.

5. Why is it important that teachers and others within the school community accept and work with the strengths and need areas of individuals with ASD?

References

Bettelheim, B. (1967). *The empty fortress*, Toronto, CA: Collier-Macmillan.

Dunn, L. M., Dunn, L. M., Robertson, G. J., & Eisenberg, J. L. (1959). *Peabody Picture Vocabulary Test*. Circle Pines, MN: American Guidance Service.

Pollack, R. (1997). *The creation of Dr. B*. New York, NY: Touchstone.

Rimland, B. (1964). *Infantile autism*. New York, NY: Appleton-Century-Crofts.

Schopler, E. A. (1994). A statewide program for the Treatment and Education of Autistic and related Communication-handicapped CHildren (TEACCH). *Psychoses and Pervasive Developmental Disorders, 3,* 91-103.

Learner Objectives

After reading this chapter, the learner should be able to:

- Describe the experiences of one individual on the autism spectrum

- Explain what narration is and why the chapter author believes it is important

- Discuss the importance of understanding the "hidden curriculum"

- Discuss the importance of using special interests to engage students in learning

Chapter 17

Educational Experiences Across the Lifespan: A Personal Perspective

Stephen Shore

It may seem humorous now, but it wasn't when it happened …

It's homeroom time in high school, and the secretary from the principal's office walks in the door. From my vantage point at the opposite corner of the room, I hear her mention to the homeroom teacher that "the principal has just lost his mother" and that she would like to have an announcement made to that effect. As the homeroom teacher started to tell the class about this unfortunate situation, my unflappable comments to my classmates went something like this: "Mr. Brown can probably find his mother in the last place he left her, and if he only concentrates on where he last saw his mother, he might just relocate her."

Well, the homeroom teacher heard my remarks, and the events that followed were not pretty.

Due to a lack of awareness of the hidden curriculum (Endow, 2012; Myles & Kolar, 2013; Myles, Trautman, & Schelvan, 2012) (see Chapter 10), I was unaware of the rules that everyone seemed to know, but that nobody ever talks about. As a result, like so many people with ASD Level 1, I became a social outcast. In addition to social challenges, there were many academic obstacles to overcome along the way.

This chapter will use an autobiographical framework to highlight some of the challenges in educating people on the autism spectrum, along with some practical suggestions for solutions from a personal standpoint.

Preparing for the Educational Experience

After typical development for the first 18 months, I suddenly lost functional communication, withdrew from my environment, got involved in self-stimulatory activities, and exhibited many other autistic behaviors. After spending a year seeking a diagnosis for my change in behavior, my parents were told by a team of professionals at a child clinic that they had never seen a child "so sick" and that an institution could take better care of me than my own family. Going against medical advice, my parents took me home to provide their own version of early intervention.

Many young children with autism demonstrate an inability to imitate others, and my parents' initial attempts to get me to imitate them failed as well. Despite having no formal schooling in psychology or child development, my parents figured out that imitating me would create a response from me. As a result of this approach, I became aware of their presence, and they could then begin the process of teaching me verbal interaction.

The important educational implication here is that before any significant teaching is to occur, a relationship must be developed with the learner. If that means getting on the floor and flapping with a child, that's where you start before you move on to teaching social, academic, and other skills.

Based on my experiences, ranging from teaching young nonverbal children with autism to adult students in doctoral programs, a personal connection must be made before any significant teaching will occur.

Another strategy my parents used during my nonverbal days was to talk through what I was doing in the style of an excited sportscaster. This technique, known as "**narration**," and used extensively in the Miller Method (Miller, 2007), sets the conditions for a child to attach meaning to words he hears. In my opinion, this technique is far superior to uttering "good job" every time a child succeeds on a task. For children who tend to live in the present, "good job" may be far too abstract to yield any useful meaning.

Preschool

By the time I entered the school that initially rejected me and was enrolled in a class with three other students, my speech was starting to return. The teacher often thought of the four of us as making up one whole child (Shore, 2003). One of us had verbal skills, another could emote and share feelings, the third child seemed to be more challenged than the rest of us, and I seemed to have the ability to engage in play.

Psychologically oriented, this school prohibited teachers from sharing the events in the classroom with the children's parents, based on the director's view that the teachers did not have the extensive psychological background necessary to be able to answer parental questions such as "Did my child eat lunch today?" This lack of communication with the parents was common in my early years. Parents were presumed to be part of the problem, and so were not often treated as "team members" like today. My teacher was and continues to be horrified by having been forced to deprive parents of vital information about their children and the lost opportunities for parent-school collaboration we see today.

In order to set the stage for interaction between the four of us, the teacher began by engaging us individually with our own train and set of tracks, all arranged as segments of a circle. Gradually, our tracks became longer and connected with the lengths from the other children. Connected tracks led into trains stopping at each other's stations, which led to social interaction. The teacher successfully engaged our interests and used them to encourage social interaction.

Elementary School

At age 6, I entered regular public school kindergarten. Even though my verbal skills were at least age-appropriate, school was a social and academic disaster for me. Unable to understand the hidden curriculum of interacting with others at school, I quickly became a social outcast (Myles et al., 2012) – with all the bullying and teasing that came along with it. Sometimes when the bullying got to be too much, there would be meltdowns – which I now suspect was what the bullies were looking for.

In those days, bullying was thought of as a developmental phase that all children went through. According to Heinrichs (2004), over 90% of children on the autism spectrum report having been bullied in grade school. Fortunately, we have authors such as Heinrichs to help us identify and eliminate this problem at the individual, classroom, and schoolwide levels.

Mathematics and Other Subjects

Academically, things were difficult as well. All through my elementary days, I spent hours at my desk reading my favorite books on meteorology, geology, natural history, dinosaurs, cats, astronomy, and other interests. Although sometimes I wondered if there was more to school than just reading my favorite books, I was happy to continue to isolate myself.

Some time in first or second grade, as I was happily reading a book on astronomy, I remember a teacher telling me that I would never learn to do math. Fortunately, these days, an educator would probably have noticed the stack of astronomy books on my desk and built lessons around what was clearly a topic of interest for me. Just about everyone learns faster and better when they are interested in the content. The same holds true for those of us on the autism spectrum, maybe even more so. See Chapter 12.

This comment about not being able to do math stuck with me, which may be part of the reason why it was very hard for me to learn my multiplication tables. One day I noticed a slide ruler-like device called a multiplier pencil box and knew instinctively it was the answer to my troubles. In those days, using this device might have been called cheating. These days it might be referred to as a low-tech assistive device.

The multiplier pencil box got a lot of use at school and at home as I spent hours in my bedroom using it for multiplication problems. While multiplication presented challenges, long division was even harder. But one day I figured out that by using this assistive device backwards, I could work out division. Slowly, and in the low-stress environment of my bedroom, I began to memorize the multiplication tables and no longer needed the multiplier pencil box.

An important implication of this experience is that it is often preferable to give people access to a skill using an assistive device if it is not possible to for them to do it on their own. For example, being able to perform arithmetic tasks with an assistive device (these days a calculator) is decidedly better than not having access to these skills because the operations cannot be done in one's head. There is another important lesson to be learned here. Eventually, I learned the multiplication and division tables as well as did my classmates. It just took longer. People with autism and other developmental delays do learn. Sometimes it takes more time. That is why conditions such as autism and intellectual disability are referred to as "delays." Assistive technology and accommodations are hand-ups, not hand-outs.

Later on, this teacher's remarks haunted me as I avoided all college majors that had a math requirement. Yet, I decided to add a bachelor's in accounting and information systems to my music education degree and had to face the math monster in a series of prerequisite math courses. Initially, the work was very hard, and I spent a lot of time trying the patience of the instructors as I received extra help in their offices. However, by the time I took the statistics class, math had become a close friend and even a sort of special interest to me. At this time, one of my passions is teaching statistics at the college level and making sure that it is taught well.

Reading Comprehension and Literal Thinking

Reading comprehension was another challenge for me during my elementary school years. Catalogues of all kinds, the encyclopedia in our home, and the daily newspaper were fascinating reads for me. However, answering questions from reading assignments in class proved difficult. Many class periods would be spent reading a short passage in preparation for answering multiple-choice, fill-in-the-blank, and short-answer questions, usually with poor results.

I remember one time refusing to answer questions related to a passage containing an Indian legend on how the earth was formed. After learning from science books about the solar system and the formation of the planets, I was not about to accept that the ground was actually the carapace of a large turtle. Like many on the autism spectrum, I was literal-minded. If there had been mention that this passage was actually an Indian legend, I might have been able to get through the questions, even with the realization that American Indians had a lot more to learn about the science of nature – that is, until I learned more about other perspectives.

Social Interaction and Physical Education

As mentioned, appropriate social interaction and making friends did not come easily for me. I spent most, of my social time at school trying to avoid and navigate around bullies. Fortunately, people are beginning to realize the damage bullying can have on victims, and tolerance for this activity is decreasing rapidly (Dubin, 2007; Heinrichs, 2004).

Most bullying takes place during times of less structure, such as on the school bus and during recess. My special interest in bicycles paid off handsomely in avoiding bullying situations on the school bus since I rode my bicycle to school most of the time. When I did take the bus, I would sit close to the front to be near the bus driver, who was trying to keep an eye on the other passengers. Recess, however, could not be avoided, and was a time of anxiety as I kept an eagle eye out for bullies and Velcroed™ myself to the "lunch ladies" for safety.

One day, one of these ladies suggested that if I just "did my own thing" and didn't look at the bullies, they would ignore me as well. I followed her advice, and much to my surprise, it worked! Nevertheless, knowing what I now know about bullies, I would rarely recommend a solution of essentially ignoring the presence of bullies in hopes they would go away, but instead would advocate for a more direct approach focused on the bullies themselves (Dubin, 2007; Heinrichs, 2004). It doesn't make sense to ask the person who is least empowered to take the most responsibility in these situations. However, perhaps in some very limited situations, if bullies know that you are not concerned about their presence, they may ignore you.

Sports was another challenge, made worse by the fact that engaging in and talking about sports plays a major role socially in our society, especially for males. Talking about science and other topics was much more interesting to me than talking about sports. Due to poor motor control and perception, baseball was a very scary activity.

Catching a ball hit by a batter or even just tossed over by another person was impossible for me because it looked like the ball was going to hit me; so I'd run away out of fear of being hit.

One day, while at an overnight camp, my central nervous system must have matured to a point where I could hit a ball with a bat if it was tossed from close by. I caught my first ball at that same camp. Standing in the outfield, I noticed a fly ball headed my way. Unable to focus on the ball as it made its way to my glove, I focused on trees swaying in the breeze instead. The ball thumped into my glove, and the team switched sides. On the way from the field, a counselor remarked, "Steve, you made a great catch, but you really should keep your eye on the ball when you are catching it." What the counselor did not understand was that not looking at the ball was exactly what had enabled me to concentrate and catch it. Tracking the ball would have been overstimulating, resulting in my ducking from it. The implication is that, for people with autism, eye contact or looking at what one is attending to is not always necessary or even desirable for attending to a task or talking with another person.

Middle School

Middle school can be a very challenging time for students both on and off the autism spectrum. Schoolwork becomes more conceptual, and nightly homework becomes a reality. Additionally, there is a lot more physical transitioning between classes, and the entire social schema among the students begins to change. Finally, middle school is also a time of puberty with great changes taking place within the bodies of the students themselves. However, there are many positive things about middle school as well.

I was much more successful in social interactions and academics once I reached middle school. Below I take a look at how some of the elements of middle school can have a positive effect, based on the characteristics of children with ASD Level 1 in terms of social interaction and academics.

Social Interaction and Academics

Possibly due to greater awareness of my impact on the environment and on others around me, middle school was actually easier for me than elementary school. First, interaction with my classmates became easier when I figured out that communicating using words rather than sound effects from the environment, as I had done in the elementary grades, went a long way towards making friends. Second, I began to realize what teachers wanted in order to properly evaluate my work. Since I was in general education classes from kindergarten, there was no thought of employing an aide or other person to help me understand the **hidden curriculum** (Myles et al., 2012) of the school classroom. Direct instruction, even as early as kindergarten, in proper interaction with my classmates and providing teachers what they needed would have helped ensure a more productive elementary school experience for me.

Between elementary and middle school, something must have "clicked," and teachers began to consider me better than average at mathematics and put me into an accelerated class. This worked well until we got to algebra and word problems. Navigating the differences between the letters and numbers, combined with having to keep two or more intermediary answers in mind while solving a problem, was too difficult for me. As a result, I was soon moved down to remedial math class – where the bullies were.

An administrator, who was also my math teacher, noticed the bullying and called me into his office for a discussion one day. He asked me if certain classmates were bothering me and whether I would like them to stop. I told him that, of course, I would like them to stop but that I was afraid of the repercussions from tattling on them. His plan was to bring each of the bullies into his office for a three-way discussion between them and me to inform them that their behavior was not acceptable and that it had to stop immediately. With much trepidation, I agreed to the process, and I am happy to say that it turned out well. Former bullies seemed much friendlier and would even talk with me.

The Role of Structure in Academic and Social Success

Another important reason why middle school was more successful than elementary school for me was that I was able to explore my special interests. Electronics was a passion of mine at that time, so I enrolled in an electronics shop class. I enjoyed making an electric motor as well as other devices run by electricity and finished the coursework about 3 weeks into a 15-week semester. However, in the school I attended, this and other shop classes, such as woodworking, drafting, and metalwork, were infested with bully-type students. Fortunately, the instructor saw the problem and, after finding out that I was a musician, had me transferred into band.

Socially, band was a much more successful experience for me for the following reasons. As with electronics, music was a special interest of mine. Further, in contrast to the electronics class, students in the fine arts were a bit different, making it easier for me to fit in. Finally, I had a structured activity that could be used to mediate my interactions with other students. In other words, there was predictability to the ensemble rehearsals, and there was always something about the band director or the music that I could use as the subject of conversation with my classmates. People on the autism spectrum need structure to be successful.

Social interaction is much more successful for individuals on the autism spectrum when gatherings are activity-based rather than socially oriented. Examples of activity-based gatherings include musical ensembles, computer clubs, bicycle clubs, and other events focused on a particular interest. Some socially oriented events include the senior prom, most class parties, and holiday dinners at a relative's house. However, non-structured events are a part of life, and it may be necessary to help a person with autism add structure to such situations. For example, a student with an autism spectrum disorder could be helped in getting through a classroom holiday party by giving her a job arranging drinks, food, or other items related to the event.

Probably due to sensory challenges, along with differences in perception and thought processes (Myles et al., 2012), for children on the autism spectrum the world often seems to be a confusing and disorderly place with rules that do not make sense (Miller, 2007). Anything that can be done to make life more predictable will reduce anxiety and position the child better for academic and social success. In addition to helping all children plot how they will spend their time in school, it is important to use the schedule to announce changes in advance. For example, children may carry a text or picture-based schedule in their notebooks. If it is known that a change is going to occur, the teacher and student can modify the schedule together in preparation for the new event. Failure to do so can result in a catastrophic meltdown, as seen below.

Lack of Structure Resulting in a Meltdown

Robert, who has ASD Level 1, asked his teacher when math class was later that day. Usually, this class was scheduled for 1:00 p.m., right after lunch, but today there was going to be a schoolwide assembly. Instead of telling Robert of the schedule change, the teacher thought she could put off the difficulty of dealing with the change of routine a little longer while she completed some work. Therefore, Robert's repeated queries were met with indefinite answers such as "later today" or "this afternoon."

Robert's anxiety continued to rise – his high voice became more and more strident, and he began to pace about the classroom. Soon his mother had to be called in because he had bitten a teacher and was in the throes of a full-scale meltdown.

Waiting quietly until Robert calmed down, his mother gently produced a 3 x 5 inch index card with the word "Oops" written on it and told her son how sorry she was that somebody had not told him of the change in plans. "Adults make mistakes, too," she added. Robert got up, and the two of them walked silently out of the room, went outside, and walked around the field as a way of calming Robert before returning to class.

What happened to Robert, and what was the significance of the "oops" card? Robert went through a rage cycle – he experienced increased anxiety to the point that he had a full-blown tantrum, followed by a period of calming down with his mother (Myles & Southwick, 2005; Shore & Rastelli, 2006). The "oops" card Robert's mother produced was part of a teaching tool she used to help her son deal with frustration in a systematic way. Because he has a very low tolerance for change and adult errors, his mother also wrote him a story about why these things might happen. She let him know that she understood how hard such things are for him and then introduced the oops card as a way to visually reassure him that she understood. The oops card can also remind Robert that changes sometimes happen and that adults sometimes make mistakes.

The Role of Sensory Issues

The inclusion of sensory challenges in the recently released DSM-5 (American Psychiatric Association, 2013) squares with my experience of having yet to meet a person on the autism spectrum who does not have challenges in sensory integration and modulation.

One way to conceive of sensory modulation is to think of a graphic equalizer with a slider representing each of the outer senses of sight, touch, taste, hearing, and sound, along with additional controls for the inner senses of proprioception and the vestibular and gustatory senses. Most people would have their sliders on or near 0 Db, close to the center. However, many people on the autism spectrum have some of these "sensory sliders" set too high, resulting in sensory overload due to hypersensitivity. For others, they are set too low, making those senses hyposensitive, thereby preventing sufficient data from being input to the brain. Additionally, data from the senses tend to be distorted. As a result, people on the autism spectrum depend on unreliable information from their senses as they attempt to make order out of what is often a confusing world.

Sensory issues were not taken into consideration throughout my time in grade school. However, that did not lessen their effect. Often I found unstructured time such as classroom parties, recess, and physical education overwhelming and causing me to withdraw from the environment. Sometimes even attending to my coursework in a room full of students was sensorially overwhelming, and I would have to leave the class. One teacher must have realized this intuitively, as she helped me tremendously by putting a three-part cardboard divider on my desk.

Sensory challenges may be responsible for the need of people with autism to prefer sameness of routine and careful attention to transitions. It is much harder to interact successfully with the environment using new information from the senses than it is to do something tried and true that allows you to predict the outcome.

Typical Autism Spectrum Relationships

In middle school, it suddenly occurred to me that all my friends were older than me. For example, I seemed to have more in common with my teachers than with my classmates. This fact did not trouble me, but I did find it curious. Upon graduation and entering the world of work, I found that all my friends were from other cultures. My sense is that the reason is cultural. People of a given culture intimately know how others are "supposed to behave." Those with differences often get bullied in grade school and shunned as adults. On the other hand, people of another culture may not perceive as many of those differences or may attribute them to local culture and, therefore, are more accepting. Finally, having their own challenges integrating into a new society, people from other countries may be more tolerant or even appreciative of differences from a societal norm.

As I continue to meet more and more people on the autism spectrum, I find that many of us have long-term relationships with individuals who also have "differences," be it racial, age, neurocognitive, physical, religious, or in other dimensions. The following are examples of my making friends with teachers and staff at school.

Shortly after my father had his first heart attack, I was called out of Spanish class to meet with a guidance counselor. The only thing I knew about these people was that they had a reputation among students in the school of being strange or weird. However, upon entering the guidance counselor's office, I found a friendly man who seemed interested in what I had to say. Later I found that he was always available for good conversation on short notice. We would trade stories of childhood experiences, and soon we became friends.

My time with him opened up a whole world of friendly counselors in the guidance office, as well as administrators. Having these relationships work properly was important to me, so upon finding malfunctioning fixtures around the school, I would be right in the principal's office making sure he was aware of what needed repair in the school. He was open-minded and interesting to be around as well.

My brother, Martin, two years my senior, was diagnosed with mild to moderate intellectual disability. I believe he has also some autistic characteristics. In contrast to me, almost all of his schooling took place in a special education room. When I realized my brother's classroom was just down the hall from my homeroom, I began to spend time in that classroom as well. There I found a teacher accepting of differences and students who seemed to know more about life than my general education classmates.

Physical Education

Physical education was always a difficult class for me. In elementary school, I was the last one chosen for any team sport, and my coordination (or lack of same) made me a liability to the team. Bombardment, sometimes referred to as dodgeball, was a particularly heinous game to me that violated the senses – you had to simultaneously avoid being smacked by a dozen or more balls while trying to hit someone on the other team. Middle school brought about more complexity in different team sports, and my participation continued to be poor.

However, just as the diversity in course and club options can be a boon to a person on the autism spectrum, so can carefully thought-out choices for physical education. My initial experiences in middle school physical education involved the challenges and anxiety of the boys' locker room and competitive team sports. One day, the gym teacher told our class to run around a track for 10 minutes. Having ridden my bicycle extensively the previous summer, I was in better shape than most of the other students for endurance activities. As I would do when bicycle racing, I stayed behind the lead people and then zoomed past them as we got close to the end. Upon seeing my performance, the coach invited me to join the track team; however, the ever-growing collection of negative experiences in gym kept me away.

In retrospect, joining the track team would have been good for me, since it was a sport that could be done individually as well as on a team. I have had good experiences with other similar sports, such as rock climbing and, of course, bicycling. Other people with autism report success with similar types of sports.

What that experience of running around a track taught me was that walking or running could be fun, or at least not as onerous as standard gym class. I had noticed a poster listing the names of people who had joined the "100-mile club." A student's name was placed there if he or she completed 100 circuits around the field, to make up 100 miles. One day, I asked the gym teacher if I could join the club and if it might be possible to start right then, instead of joining my classmates for gym. Emboldened by his positive answer, I ventured further by asking if I could work on my goal in "civilian clothes." His consent solved two major problems I had with physical education. First, I could continue to get my exercise through alternative means instead of through team sports. Second, I bypassed the locker-room scene by not having to change clothes.

In today's educational world, such a modification would have required a team meeting and the signing of documents attesting that my being on the autism spectrum required an accommodation of alternate or adaptive physical education. In those days, all that was needed was a physical education instructor who perhaps intuitively sensed that walking or running around a track to reach a goal was better for me than engaging in standard gym activities. However, while the latter was less formal, it was by no means standard practice.

High School

Middle school was better than elementary for me, and high school was in some ways even better. One reason was that my special interests led me to meet some interesting teachers and administrators. Although I now got along better with most of my classmates, there was nobody, with the exception of a student from elementary school, whom I could really call my friend. Sometimes I would arrange to do something with a classmate, but most of my time outside of school was spent reading books, conducting experiments with my chemistry set, and feeding my bicycle interests by working as a bicycle mechanic and riding my bike.

Music

While mathematics remained a challenge, things were much better in the music room. Since music was a special interest of mine, I spent as much time in the band room as possible, practicing and learning new instruments. It became a passion of mine to learn as many of the band and orchestral instruments as possible. For example, I bartered trombone lessons for instruction in string bass from a student music teacher. In fact, one of the main reasons I chose music education as an undergraduate major was that learning all the instruments was a requirement.

Since I was interested in classical music, I made friends with a kindly older music teacher who conducted the orchestra. I also enjoyed his courses in music theory. Not many students seemed to like him, possibly because they thought he was old-fashioned. Music also made a good common interest with one of the guidance counselors at the high school. When he learned that I played the flute, he asked if I would be willing to teach him to play.

Counselors

My positive experiences with guidance counselors opened me to the possibility of making friends with the counselor mentioned above. In addition to learning how to play the flute, he was also interested in learning music theory. Perhaps this person saw my way of interacting through music as a way to address other issues. He was successful in doing this, as illustrated in the following.

Since I had good relationships with most of my teachers, I was puzzled about my difficulty in relating to my homeroom teacher. He seemed cold and distant and looked like a cat. I wanted to change my classroom so I could be with a friendlier teacher. Even if this meant that the teacher was boring, at least he or she would be friendly and comfortable to be with.

In responding to the counselor's queries about why I wanted to switch teachers, I mentioned that my current homeroom teacher was cold and unfriendly and that I had nothing in common with him. The counselor answered that he could change my homeroom assignment but that he wanted me to try something first. "See if you can strike up a conversation with your homeroom teacher about music. Maybe you could show him your flute."

I was willing to give it a try, and to my surprise it worked! The formerly cold, unfeeling homeroom teacher asked me to play my flute, and soon we were talking about music. We became friends, and I visited him at his home a number of times to fix his bicycles. Later on, I took a course from him, which I found enjoyable. As a result, I ended up adding him to the list of teachers that I kept in touch with after my graduation.

From this vantage point, I suspect that my counselor knew my homeroom teacher had an interest in music and saw that as a common point of interest. I am grateful to him for encouraging me to reach out and make the first step towards developing relationships with others. Without his suggestion, it might never have occurred to me to initiate contact in this manner.

Employment in High School

Employment is usually something that takes place out of school. However, since many, if not most, students begin their work careers while in school, it merits some mention. First, it is important to make sure employment does not interfere with time needed for school, family life, and other important matters. When work can be fit into a student's schedule, many benefits can accrue, such as learning the value of money and gaining additional experience with social interaction. Common employment paths for young people, such as working in a restaurant, being a cashier, or other situations where there is high sensory input, are not suitable for people on the autism spectrum. As with education, it is important to take the person's interests into account.

My first two jobs in high school were serving as a busboy in a restaurant. Now that I understand more about sensory overload, I realize that my working slowly, even during busy times, was a form of shutdown due to overstimulation. Needless to say, I did not last long in those jobs. At that time, bicycles were a special interest, and with the help of a job counselor at school, I drafted a letter to managers of bicycle shops, introducing myself as a candidate for a bicycle mechanic position.

After sending the letter to local bike shops, I made followup calls, which netted me several interviews. I had a customized bike, which I rode to the interviews. My bicycle served as a sort of portfolio that could be used to start a conversation. After talking about the construction of my bicycle, right down to building the wheels, I would ask for a job.

At that time, building a bicycle wheel from scratch was a valued skill. In fact, I got hired for one job by completing an assignment of building 10 bicycle wheels in short order. I stayed with this shop for four years, eventually rising to the role of shop manager.

This experience proved invaluable to me in college, as I ran my own bicycle repair shop to earn a good portion of my tuition. When asked by a financial aid officer why I did not use my work study funds, I told her that I could make much more money faster and be much happier fixing bicycles than serving as a security guard or working in the dining commons as part of the work study program.

Bicycle repair was much more suited to me than a standard job for the following reasons. First, it was an area of special interest, so I was motivated to do a good job. Second, it made use of my considerable mechanical ability. Third, fixing bicycles in the shop at the back of the store involved relatively low sensory input. As with teaching curriculum, it is important and often vital to match a student's interest and strengths with employment possibilities. Everyone learns better and faster the things he or she is interested in. For those on the autism spectrum, this fact is particularly true.

Learning Self-Advocacy Through Educational Planning

A topic that is getting more and more recognition is the importance of teaching children how to advocate for themselves, along with disclosure. Every person with a disability will arrive at a point when he or she has to advocate for him or herself in an effort to achieve better mutual understanding. For example, a person might need to ask for changes in the environment to help him focus or relax. It is important that the person be clear about the reason for the requested change so that others are able to empathize with the need (Shore, 2004).

These valuable skills can be taught by involving children in their own educational plan to the extent of their ability. For example, a more severely affected child who is nonverbal and hyperactive might be involved in an educational planning meeting by initially interacting with a couple of the IEP team members whom she already knows and then leave. In addition to introducing the child to the educational planning process, the team members – who may work with dozens of children – get a quick reminder of the specific child's strengths and needs.

Another child may be able to communicate through pictures, sign language, written words, or verbally that he likes and/or dislikes certain classes. Yet another child may state that she likes English class but the scratching of other students' pencils drives her to distraction. Students may get to a point where they can research different accommodations and lead portions of the IEP meeting under the watchful eye of the team leader.

For example, suppose a third grader with ASD Level 1 needs to have an accommodation written into her IEP for a visual sensitivity to fluorescent lights. Like many people on the autism spectrum, this young student perceives fluorescent lights like most others see a strobe light – fun for holidays and special effects but a serious distraction while doing work in class. Possible accommodations include placing her near a window, allowing her to wear a baseball cap in class, unscrewing the fluorescent bulb above her head and using an incandescent lamp, or perhaps a combination of these suggestions. While it may be faster to just write these accommodations into the plan at a team meeting, it will be much more helpful to the student to bring her into the planning process.

Perhaps the first thing to do would be to have a discussion with the student to validate her feelings of frustration and anxiety in having to deal with this type of lighting in the first place. During this discussion, the teacher or other person supporting the student clearly indicates that together they will work to resolve the problem. By brainstorming and using familiar visual systems to review social situations, the student and supporting person develop a plan for resolving the challenge and meet with the IEP team, or even just the teacher of the class, in the advocacy effort.

Children with little or no experience in advocating for themselves may need to see the process modeled for them, whereas students with greater experience can take on more and more responsibility and may even learn to complete the entire advocacy effort entirely on their own (Sibley, 2004).

Perhaps later in life in a work situation, this same person is placed in an office illuminated with fluorescent light. The education in advocating for herself that she received in school will pay handsome dividends as she now has to request her supervisor for change in lighting and explain the reason why in a way the supervisor can understand and act on.

Summary and Conclusions

As for many children with different ways of learning and interacting with others, for me grade school was a time of anxiety, misunderstandings, and confusion. However, I was lucky for several reasons. First, the structure of the school day and my desire to learn new things attracted me to education in general. Second, I had some good teachers and school administrators along the way, who intuitively understood and accommodated for my needs. Even though there is now a special education law with the IEP as a vehicle of advocacy and provision of a free and appropriate public education, the best results occur when teachers combine an intuitive sense of the needs of a child with an educational background in providing for those needs. Third, no matter how difficult school was for me for academic and social reasons, my parents supported me in my efforts while at the same time working with the school to make sure I got the best education possible.

My wish is that this book allows readers to combine their desire and love for educating children who have differences with the plethora of easy-to-implement, practical solutions available today to address the educational and social needs of children with ASD in the school setting.

Tips for Practical Application

✓ Developing a relationship between you and the learner is vital to success in education. Sometimes this can be done with simple imitation.

✓ Narrate the activities of a child as he is doing them. This deposits the words into a sort of "bank," allowing for future retrieval to think about and describe what he is doing.

✓ Parents are the experts on their children. Seek to collaborate with them whenever possible.

✓ Engage a child through an interest as a launching pad for teaching social interaction skills and other areas.

✓ Bullying is a form of harassment and should not be tolerated.

✓ Assistive technology and accommodation are hand-ups and not hand-outs.

✓ Tell children what they *can* do; not what they can't.

✓ A common characteristic of people on the autism spectrum is literal-mindedness. It is important to be aware of this when using idioms or studying mythology, for example.

✓ Eye contact does not give people with autism the kind of information that those not on the autism spectrum receive. In fact, it may detract from paying attention. Just because we are looking away doesn't mean we are not listening, perceiving, or paying attention.

✓ Sensory challenges are a characteristic common to just about all children on the autism spectrum. Such challenges, if not addressed, can lead to challenging behavior.

✓ Direct instruction in the hidden curriculum of the classroom and school in general may mean the difference between failure and success for children on the autism spectrum during their school time.

✓ Many people on the autism spectrum desperately want to make friends. Unlike others, we may need direct instruction on how to do so.

✓ Involving students in their own educational planning will pay dividends after graduation, as adults with autism will have learned how to advocate and disclose for themselves at home, at work, in continuing education, in relationships, and in the community.

Chapter Highlights

- The chapter author describes experiences from pre-K through high school.

- Some of the areas the chapter author stresses as being of particular importance include:

  o Developing a relationship between instructor and learner

  o Engaging students through use of their special interests

  o Teaching the "hidden curriculum"

  o Realizing that individuals with ASD tend to be very literal in their thinking and taking this into account when teaching

  o Making use of assistive technology as appropriate

  o Understanding that many individuals with ASD are victims of bullying. It is important that school personnel are aware of this and take steps to deal with it.

  o Being aware that structure is an important part of a comfortable environment for persons with ASD

  o Understanding that persons with ASD have sensory integration and modulation challenges

  o Involving students in educational planning so self-knowledge and self-advocacy skills are developed

Chapter Review Questions

1. List and describe three experiences discussed by the chapter author.

2. Define narration and explain why the chapter author believes it is important for children with ASD.

3. What is the "hidden curriculum" and why does the chapter author believe it is crucial to directly teach it to students with ASD?

4. How did using his special interests assist the chapter author in being successful?

References

American Psychiatric Association. (2013). *Diagnostic and statistical manual of mental disorders, 5th edition.* Washington, DC: Author.

Dubin, N. (2007). *Asperger syndrome and bullying: Strategies and solutions.* London, UK: Jessica Kingsley Publishers.

Endow, J. (2012). *Learning the hidden curriculum: The odyssey of one autistic adult.* Shawnee Mission, KS: AAPC Publishing.

Heinrichs, R. (2004). *Perfect targets: Asperger Syndrome and bullying – Practical solutions for surviving the social world.* Shawnee Mission, KS: AAPC Publishing.

Miller, M. (2007). *The Miller method: Developing the capacities of children on the autism spectrum.* London, UK: Jessica Kingsley Publishers.

Myles, H., & Kolar, A. (2013). *The hidden curriculum and other everyday challenges for elementary-age children with high functioning autism.* Shawnee Mission, KS: AAPC Publishing.

Myles, B. S., & Southwick, J. (2005). *Asperger Syndrome and difficult moments: Practical solutions for tantrums, rage, and meltdown* (rev. ed.). Shawnee Mission, KS: AAPC Publishing.

Myles, B. S., Trautman, M., & Schelvan, R. (2012). *The hidden curriculum for understanding unstated rules in social situations for adolescents and young adults* (2nd ed.). Shawnee Mission, KS: AAPC Publishing.

Shore, S. (2003). *Beyond the wall: Personal experiences with autism and Asperger syndrome* (2nd ed.). Shawnee Mission, KS: AAPC Publishing.

Shore, S. (2004). Using the IEP to build skills in self-advocacy and disclosure. In S. Shore (Ed.), *Ask and tell: Self-advocacy and disclosure for people on the autism spectrum* (pp. 65-105). Shawnee Mission, KS: AAPC Publishing.

Shore, S., & Rastelli, L. (2006). *Understanding autism for dummies.* New York, NY: Wiley & Sons.

Sibley, K. (2004). Help me help myself: Teaching and learning. In S. Shore (Ed.), *Ask and tell: Self-advocacy and disclosure for people on the autism spectrum* (pp. 33-63). Shawnee Mission, KS: AAPC Publishing.

Index

Making Action Plans (MAPS), 347, 348
Manual signs, 121, 125
Mapping Your Future, 355
MAPS. *See* Making Action Plans
Marks, D. F., 26
Mataya, K., 253
Mathematics
    abilities of ASD individuals, 350
    assistive devices, 403
    learning, 403–404, 405
Mawhood, L., 349
Maxims, conversational, 116, 119
Mayer-Johnson's Boardmaker, 355
Mayo Clinic, 393
Mazurek, M. O., 240
McCoy, K., 249
Medications, 45, 162, 364
Meltdowns, 43, 406–407
Memory
    impairments, 62, 71–72
    working, 64, 69
Mental-state recognition
    computer-based training, 319, 326
    difficulties, 315
    See also Emotion recognition
Merzer, Sheila, 391–392
Metabolism, errors of, 46
Metacognitive strategies, 209–210
Middle school, 395–396, 405–406, 409
    See also Secondary schools
Miller Method, 402
Mind blindness, 47
    See also Theory of mind
Mind Reading software
    adult use, 320–324
    architecture, 320
    description, 319–320
    emotion taxonomy, 319–320
    generalization issues, 324–325
    screenshots, 321, 323
    studies of, 320–324, 325
    use of, 249
    visual tasks, 323
Minshew, N. J., 71, 120
Mirenda, P., 121
Mirroring, 190
Modeling, 180, 244–245, 248–249
Modifications, academic, 371
Mood disorders, secondary, 48
Mothers. *See* Parents
Motivation
    of preschoolers, 96–97
    special interests and, 297
Motivation Assessment Scale, 160, 163
Motor skills impairments, 62
Movement abilities, 38
MRI. *See* Magnetic resonance imaging
Multitasking, 63, 74
Murray, D., 216
Muscular dystrophy, 48
Music, 350, 391, 406, 409–410
Myles, B. S., 212

N

Narration, 402
Narratives, social, 251–252

National Autism Center, 22, 88, 243
National Council for the Accreditation of
    Teacher Education (NCATE), 24
National Professional Development Center
    on Autism Spectrum Disorders (NPDC),
    23, 88, 243
National Research Council (NRC), 21, 86,
    88, 89, 176
National Society for Autistic Children
    (NSAC), 390–391
National Standards Project (NSP), 22–23
Naturalistic contexts, 119
Natural reinforcers, 97
NCATE. *See* National Council for the
    Accreditation of Teacher Education
NCLB. *See* No Child Left Behind Act
Neurochemistry, 45
Neurodevelopmental disorders, autism as, 41,
    44, 45–46, 60
Neuroimaging
    emotion recognition studies, 316
    functional, 45, 46, 68–70
    studies of autism, 45, 46, 71
Neurological disorders, 37
Neurons, 109–110
Neuropathology, 45
Neuropsychological assessment, 364
Neurotypical infants, 110
    See also Typical peers
Newhart, Bob, 245
No Child Left Behind (NCLB) Act, 21, 218
Nonverbal communication, 124, 125, 216,
    315
Normalizing, 181
Notebooks, home-school communication,
    269–270
Nouns, 118, 122
    See also Words
NPDC. *See* National Professional
    Development Center
NRC. *See* National Research Council
NSAC. *See* National Society for Autistic
    Children
NSP. *See* National Standards Project
Nurturing Narratives, 252

O

OAR. *See* Organization for Autism Research
Observations
    of behaviors, 157–158
    of play, 195
    of students, 374–375
Obsessions, use of term, 303
    See also Special interest areas
Occupational therapists, 364, 394
Occupational therapy (OT)
    benefits, 285
    sensory processing interventions, 139
    stress reduction, 230
Odom, S. L., 87
Ohlmeier, M. D., 241
Olfactory system, 135
    See also Sensory perception
O'Neill, R. E., 160
Oppositional behavior, 48
Organization for Autism Research (OAR),

343
Orienting, 190
OT. *See* Occupational therapy
Outcome-oriented framework, 92
Owens, P., 253

P

Panek, Richard, 255
Parallel play, 190, 208
Parents
    blamed for autism in children, 44, 390
    early intervention by, 90, 391, 402
    goals for child, 377
    perspective of, 389–398
    reactions to ASD diagnosis, 86, 90
    recognition of autism signs, 39
    relations with professionals, 365, 385, 402
    school involvement, 365
    as team members, 365, 385, 398
    transition planning roles, 339, 340
    See also Families
PATH. *See* Planning Alternative Tomorrows
    with Hope
Pathophysiology, 72
Paul, R., 120
PDD. *See* Pervasive developmental disorder
PDD-NOS. *See* Pervasive developmental
    disorder-not otherwise specified
Peabody Picture Vocabulary Test (PPVT), 392,
    393
PECS. *See* Picture Exchange Communication
    System
Pedantic speech, 41
Peer culture, 177, 179
Peers. *See* Bullying; Friendships; Typical peers
Perner, J., 217
Perra, O., 112
Perrett, D., 112
Personal experiences
    parent, 389–398
    student, 401–413
Person-centered planning, 347
Perspective-taking
    learning, 217, 229, 252
    pragmatic language and, 116
    in sharing space, 212
    skills, 216–217
    steps, 213
    See also Theory of mind
Perspective Taking Scale, 220
Pervasive developmental disorder (PDD), 37
Pervasive developmental disorder-not
    otherwise specified (PDD-NOS), 37
PET. *See* Positron emission tomography
Phenylketonuria (PKN), 46
Physical education classes, 395, 404–405,
    408–409
Picture Exchange Communication System
    (PECS), 95–96, 154
Pictures. *See* Visual aids
PKN. *See* Phenylketonuria
Planning Alternative Tomorrows with Hope
    (PATH), 347, 348
Play
    of ASD individuals, 176, 178–179
    development stages, 208–209

Appendix A: Chapter Review Answers

Chapter 1

1. Three factors that have contributed to the evolution of EBP as applied to learners on the autism spectrum:

   ✓ ASD is the fastest growing special education eligibility category in the public schools in the United States.

   ✓ As the incidence of autism has risen, schools have faced chronic shortages of competent educators and related service providers.

   ✓ The Elementary and Secondary Education Act (ESEA), known as No Child Left Behind (NCLB), requires states to ensure that educators at the elementary and secondary school levels: demonstrate accountability, provide scientifically based instruction, and are highly qualified.

2. A major challenge has been the lack of university-level special education and clinical preparation programs that include a specialization in ASD (Baker, 2012; Barnhill, Polloway, & Sumutka, 2011; Scheuermann et al., 2003). An initial reason was that autism was not included as an eligibility category for special education until the reauthorization of the Individuals with Disabilities Education Act (IDEA) in 1990. Moreover, it took more than a decade before autism became identified as a distinct category by the Council for Exceptional Children (CEC), which designates standards (i.e., professional competencies) for teacher training that are aligned with state teacher credentialing agencies (CEC, 2009).

   With the influx of students with ASD into the system, school districts have had to carry much of the burden of compensating for the gap in the knowledge and skill of teachers and related staff. To deal with this challenge, many districts hired outside contractors to provide services at premium costs. In addition, they often went to great lengths to patch together their own inservice training programs.

3. With respect to ASD, there is an overrepresentation of EBP based on applied behavior analysis (ABA) compared to practices that are developmentally or socio-culturally based. This is largely because ABA is rooted in reductionist scientific principles that easily allow for the measurement of observable behavior using research methodologies that are more heavily weighted. By contrast, interventions rooted in scientific traditions that address the process and nature of development in a broader cultural context are more difficult to study using the same methodologies.

   Similarly, there are drawbacks to determining the validity of interventions that reduce development and socio-cultural experience to a discrete set of skills or behaviors in an effort to apply the dominant research paradigm. For instance, interventions designed to foster developmental capacities such as spontaneous initiation, imitation, mutual engagement, play, and imagination are not readily assessed using common measures such as percentage of correct responses.

Chapter 2

1. Early-onset autism is characterized by sleep disturbances, feeding problems, inability to be comforted, withdrawal from social objects, lack of pointing to objects wanted, poor or no eye contact, fascination with sensory experiences, lack of imitation, limited language development, delayed self-care skills, lack of response to conversation or direction, and general developmental delay. Children who exhibit late-onset autism achieve the typical developmental milestones until late into their second year, demonstrate interaction skills and interest in others, and show early symbolic and imaginary play. However, over a short period of time, these skills begin to deteriorate and, by age 3, there may be no clear distinction between a child with early-onset and a child with late-onset autism.

2. The following specifiers relevant to ASD are included in the DSM-5:
   - ✓ With or without accompanying intellectual and/or language impairment
   - ✓ Association with a known medical, genetic condition, or environmental factor
   - ✓ Association with another neurodevelopmental, mental, or behavior disorder or catatonia
   - ✓ Severity of expression from Level 1 to Level 3 based on the level of support needed for social communication and restricted, repetitive behaviors

3. Deficits in social communication and restricted and repetitive behavior.

4. Six aspects of ASD:
   - ✓ *Social reasoning:* including relating to others, social understanding, and social maturity.
   - ✓ *Language abilities:* including verbal and nonverbal language usage and understanding.
   - ✓ *Cognition:* intellectual abilities, as well as organization, memory, and time management.
   - ✓ *Special interests:* demonstrating an extremely strong interest in an object or part of an object, collecting objects, acquiring large amounts of information on a particular topic.
   - ✓ *Sensory sensitivity:* response to various things that affect the senses (e.g., sight, taste, smell, sound, touch, or body awareness).
   - ✓ *Expression and management of emotions:* the ability to express reciprocal emotions as well as to label and describe emotions in others and himself and to express and manage intense emotions.

5. The term *refrigerator mother* was coined by Leo Kanner and used extensively by Bruno Bettelheim to refer to mothers of children with autistic disorder. Until the 1970s, the cause of autism was believed to be the response of children to mothers who lacked the ability to appropriately interact with their children and were seen as cold and unloving.

6. Currently, possible causes of autism include genetics, such as chromosomal abnormalities; neurological dysfunction; possible errors of metabolism; and infections in pregnancy.

7. Three psychological theories of autism:

   Theory of mind: the ability to understand others' mental states (e.g., beliefs, thoughts, desires, perceptions, and feelings) and apply this understanding to their actions. Theorists believe that individuals with ASD may lack abilities in this area, resulting in "mind blindness," or the inability to make sense of others' behavior.

   Central coherence: the ability to integrate information into a meaningful whole. Theorists believe individuals with ASD have weak central coherence in that they process information by tending to focus on the parts and lose sight of the whole.

Executive function: the ability to properly use a group of mental processes, including organizational and planning abilities, working memory, inhibition and impulse control, time management and prioritizing, and using new strategies. It is believed that individuals with ASD have deficits in executive functioning.

8. ASD is diagnosed four times more often in males than in females. However, the ratio can be two to one when comparing boys and girls with ASD Level 1. Girls have the same clinical profile and depth of ASD characteristics but are often more creative in camouflaging social confusion by strategies such as imitation, and may have less conspicuous restricted and repetitive patterns of behavior.

9. There are several possible explanations. These include a broader definition of ASD, realization that ASD may co-occur with other disorders, and better diagnostic procedures.

Chapter 3

1. A spectrum disorder is one in which children receiving the diagnosis can differ considerably in terms of abilities, needs, preferences, and areas of delay.

2. Early intervention is crucial for children diagnosed with ASD because research has unanimously demonstrated that the earlier the intervention, the better the potential outcomes in terms of independence, cognitive functioning, and communication.

3. Some of the major issues surrounding early identification of ASD include (a) a problem with early and accurate detection and diagnosis, particularly with regard to individuals who are culturally and linguistically diverse; (b) the fact that the diagnosis of ASD is complex and cannot be tied to any individual behavior at any age; (c) the need for improvement in the accuracy of screening and diagnostic tools; (d) the need for educating pediatricians and others about ASD; and (e) the need to influence policy and practice to ensure proper implementation of appropriate assessment tools.

4. The developmental red flags that may indicate ASD in infants and toddlers include:
    ✓ No big smiles, or other warm, joyous expressions by 6 months or thereafter
    ✓ No back-and-forth sharing of sounds, smiles, or other facial expressions by 9 months or thereafter
    ✓ No babbling by 12 months
    ✓ No back-and-forth gestures, such as pointing, showing, reaching, or waving by 12 months
    ✓ No words by 16 months
    ✓ No two-word meaningful phrases by 24 months
    ✓ A loss of speech or babbling or social skills at any age

5. It is important to provide families with information on intervention services and community supports because families are often left scared and confused by the diagnosis of an ASD. Helping families identify service providers, supplying information on the characteristics of effective intervention, resources such as books, websites and parent support groups, and providing families with temporary support until they can obtain support and assistance is crucial. Following up with a phone call or visit within two weeks to answer any additional questions is recommended.

6. The key elements of effective programs for young children with ASD include:
   ✓ Sufficient hours and intensity of services
   ✓ Comprehensible environments with access to typical peers
   ✓ Specialized curriculum with an appropriate scope and sequence
   ✓ Family involvement
   ✓ Problem-solving approach to challenging behaviors
   ✓ Appropriate evaluation tools for monitoring progress

7. The types of questions families should consider when selecting an intervention program include:
   ✓ What are the primary concerns for the child?
   ✓ Does the considered intervention(s) address those concerns?
   ✓ Are the procedures of the intervention acceptable?
   ✓ Are the interventions a good match for the child and family?
   ✓ What types of evidence of effectiveness of the intervention exist, and is it convincing?
   ✓ How will the interventionists communicate with the family and demonstrate the child's progress, and is that acceptable?

8. The term *outcome-oriented framework* refers to looking at desired outcomes for the child from the beginning and ensuring intervention strategies focus on achieving those outcomes.

9. In deciding on meaningful outcomes for their child, families need to look at the strengths and needs of the individual child, the family's priorities, and existing data.

10. Curriculum-based assessment (CBA) identifies functional skills across multiple domains (i.e., adaptive, social, cognitive, communication, and motor) that are common in early childhood. A CBA is useful by giving a starting point of where the child is functioning and what he or she needs to learn.

11. The five components of Project DATA are:
    ✓ Integrated early childhood experience
    ✓ Extended intensive instruction
    ✓ Technical and social support
    ✓ Collaboration and coordination of services
    ✓ Transition planning and support

12. The areas to which Project DATA preschool environments pay particular attention are:
    ✓ Structuring the classroom environment to promote independence, participation, and successful interactions with typically developing peers
    ✓ Developing a consistent schedule and following it
    ✓ Creating the need to communicate with adults and peers
    ✓ Using preferred materials and activities to promote engagement
    ✓ Providing embedded and explicit instruction on valued skills
    ✓ Providing frequent reinforcement and developing effective motivation systems

13. Based on studies involving learning and memory, the chapter authors believe that the effects of autism go beyond problems with social interaction and restricted and repetitive behaviors to involve other interactive brain systems, particularly those involving language and reasoning.

Chapter 4

1. A spectrum disorder is one in which children receiving the diagnosis can differ considerably in terms of abilities, needs, preferences, and areas of delay.

2. Early intervention is crucial for children diagnosed with ASD because research has unanimously demonstrated that the earlier the intervention, the better the potential outcomes in terms of independence, cognitive functioning, and communication.

3. Some of the major issues surrounding early identification of ASD include (a) a problem with early and accurate detection and diagnosis, particularly with regard to individuals who are culturally and linguistically diverse; (b) the fact that the diagnosis of ASD is complex and cannot be tied to any individual behavior at any age; (c) the need for improvement in the accuracy of screening and diagnostic tools; (d) the need for educating pediatricians and others about ASD; and (e) the need to influence policy and practice to ensure proper implementation of appropriate assessment tools.

4. The developmental red flags that may indicate ASD in early childhood include:

Social
- ✓ Has poor eye contact
- ✓ Lacks sharing interest and enjoyment with others
- ✓ Fails to respond to his or her name
- ✓ Appears disinterested in or unaware of others

Communication
- ✓ Lacks gestures – pointing, reaching, waving, showing
- ✓ Doesn't appear to understand simple questions or directions
- ✓ Speaks in an abnormal tone of voice or with an odd rhythm
- ✓ May repeat words or phrases exactly as heard but doesn't understand how to use them

Behavior
- ✓ Repeats the same actions or movements over and over again
- ✓ Develops specific routines and rituals and becomes upset at the slightest change
- ✓ Is preoccupied with a narrow topic of interest

5. It is important to provide families with information on intervention services and community supports because families are often left scared and confused by the diagnosis of an ASD. Helping families identify service providers, supplying information on the characteristics of effective intervention, resources such as books, websites and parent support groups, and providing families with temporary support until they can obtain support and assistance is crucial. Following up with a phone call or visit within two weeks to answer any additional questions is recommended.

6. The key features of effective programs for young children with ASD include:
   ✓ Sufficient hours and intensity of services
   ✓ Comprehensible environments with access to typical peers
   ✓ Specialized curriculum with an appropriate scope and sequence
   ✓ Family involvement
   ✓ Problem-solving approach to challenging behaviors
   ✓ Appropriate evaluation tools for monitoring progress

7. Families need to ask the following types of questions when selecting intervention programs for their young children with ASD:
   ✓ What are the primary concerns for the child?
   ✓ Does the considered intervention(s) address those concerns?
   ✓ Are the procedures of the intervention acceptable?
   ✓ Are the interventions a good match for the child and family?
   ✓ What types of evidence of effectiveness of the intervention exist, and is it convincing?
   ✓ How will the interventionists communicate with the family and demonstrate the child's progress, and is that acceptable?

8. The term *outcome-oriented framework* refers to looking at desired outcomes for the child from the beginning and ensuring intervention strategies focus on achieving those outcomes.

9. In deciding on meaningful outcomes for their child, families need to look at the strengths and needs of the individual child, the family's priorities, and existing data.

10. Curriculum-based assessment (CBA) identifies functional skills across multiple domains (i.e., adaptive, social, cognitive, communication, and motor) that are common in early childhood. A CBA is useful by giving a starting point of where the child is functioning and what he or she needs to learn.

11. The five components of Project DATA are as follows:
    ✓ Integrated early childhood experience
    ✓ Extended intensive instruction
    ✓ Technical and social support
    ✓ Collaboration and coordination of services
    ✓ A quality of life-influenced curriculum

12. Project DATA preschool environments pay particular attention to:
    ✓ Structuring the classroom environment to promote independence, participation, and successful interactions with typically developing peers
    ✓ Developing a consistent schedule and following it
    ✓ Creating the need to communicate with adults and peers
    ✓ Using preferred materials and activities to promote engagement
    ✓ Providing embedded and explicit instruction on valued skills
    ✓ Providing frequent reinforcement and developing effective motivation systems

Chapter 5

1. Social communication involves the ability to use words to interact with others in order to affect their behavior and/or thoughts.

2. Theory of mind and social language learning are intertwined with the processes underlying language learning, including understanding what is in another person's mind.

3. Autism can be described as a deficit in communication because it leads to an inability to share feelings, beliefs, and knowledge with others. Individuals with autism may have the words but fail to understand how to use them based on others' perspectives.

4. A student with autism might have a large vocabulary but fail to understand how to use the words to communicate because he lacks knowledge of how to affect others, or even an awareness of the need to do so in order to communicate effectively.

5. The chapter authors describe ineffective language intervention with individuals with autism as being based on interventionists' lack of understanding of (a) the language learning process and (b) the effect of abnormalities in interpersonal relatedness and social cognition demonstrated by individuals with autism.

6. Interactive games assist infants in developing social communication because they provide opportunities for attention and affect sharing and social reciprocity, which helps the infant develop the interpersonal relatedness needed for later social communication.

7. Experiential learning is critical in brain development based on research showing an increase in brain activity when infants are actively involved, thus providing neuron development and increased brain connectivity.

8. Babies with autism do not engage in games as do their neurotypical peers and, therefore, miss out on opportunities for emotional regulation, attention sharing, anticipation, and reciprocity with their caregivers. Additionally, as infants with autism tend to engage in repetitive behaviors, their lack of opportunity to develop connectivity and the failure of neurons to be "pruned" may lead to less capacity for social-cognitive behaviors and brain development.

9. Joint attention refers to behaviors suggestive of an increasing understanding of the need to engage other minds, such as gaze following, pointing, and showing/offering gestures. It is important in the development of communication because social communication is based on a shared awareness and engagement, which is absent or less developed in children with autism. Additionally, research shows joint attention impacts both typically developing children and those with autism in a similar way in that the amount of joint attention engaged in is highly correlated with vocabulary development and sets the stage for intention reading.

10. Intention reading is central to social-pragmatic theory in that the development of language is based on an understanding of symbols and the development of social cognition.

11. Understanding social-pragmatic theory can provide a basis for understanding what goes wrong in the language acquisition process in autism; specifically, impairments in social cognition in terms of joint attention, affect sharing, and intention reading are seen as likely causes of the pragmatic deficits demonstrated by individuals with autism.

12. Pragmatics is important to the development of language because it is integral to the communication process, including understanding what others might be thinking (intention reading) and feeling, and using that knowledge to adequately convey thoughts and information.

13. Social-pragmatic theory might be considered the "rule" in typical language development as it seems to best account for why children develop words at certain times, the social-cognitive elements that underpin communication, and the way in which children typically learn language

14. Presuppositional knowledge refers to having an understanding of the listener's needs in terms of information content and communication style. For example, one would probably recount an experience differently to a friend than to a policeman.

15. Presuppositional knowledge refers to having an understanding of the listener's needs in terms of information content and communication style. For example, one would probably recount an experience differently to a friend than to a policeman.

16. The four conversational maxims related to understanding the rules of spoken interactions are as follows:
    ✓ Quantity: using only what is needed to convey information
    ✓ Quality: understanding what is true and what is not
    ✓ Relevance: staying on topic
    ✓ Clarity: conveying information in a way that is clear to the listener

17. Research indicates that word learning depends on context, knowledge of the underlying concept, the communicative goal of the speaker, word class, and level of novelty

18. From a social-pragmatic perspective, the general considerations related to assessment of language for individuals with autism include (a) the use of situated pragmatics and naturalistic contexts, (b) evaluating conversational maxims and presuppositional knowledge, and (c) evaluating comprehension at both the literal and the discourse level.

19. The general principles of intervention include:
    a. Intervention must begin where the learner is
    b. Intervention should be experiential
    c. It is important to use augmentative means for communication
    d. Emphasis should be placed on comprehension
    e. Active student engagement is important
    f. Vocabulary targets should be within the individual's conceptual understanding
    g. Different classes of words need to be taught differently
    h. Intervention should take place in context in order to support learning of meaning
    i. Theory-of-mind activities should be included within language intervention
    j. Intervention that promotes generalization of language occurs in contextually relevant routines

Chapter 6

1. Sensory processing is a person's way of noticing and responding to sensory events that occur during daily life.

2. Sensory processing systems include touch (somatosensory), body position (proprioceptive), sight (visual), hearing (auditory), smell (olfactory), taste (gustatory), and movement (vestibular).

3. The accumulation of inputs increases the chances that the student will reach thresholds and become more responsive.

4. Dunn proposed a conceptual model for understanding patterns of sensory processing. Figure 6.1 contains a diagram of this model; the vertical axis shows the **brain thresholds** and the horizontal axis shows the **self-regulation** continuum. High thresholds require a lot of sensory input, and low thresholds require very little sensory input to react.

   Dunn's conceptual model for understanding patterns of sensory processing combines brain thresholds with self-regulation to create four patterns: registration, sensitivity, seeking, and avoiding. The model proposes four patterns of sensory processing: registration, sensitivity, seeking, and avoiding.

5. Children with ASD are more likely to be sensitive to touch, as well as auditory and oral senses. They also have significantly different scores on registration and avoiding. For example, they may have differences in both registration (i.e., fails to notice stimuli that others notice) and avoiding (i.e., detects and withdraws from stimuli) at the same time. As with the other *Sensory Profile* measures, students with ASD exhibit significantly different patterns of sensory processing and school behaviors than peers (i.e., they engage in behaviors more frequently than peers).

6. A sensory processing framework is used for intervention to improve participation, not change the sensory processing patterns.

7. Examples of sensory processing interventions that address each type of pattern and that support student learning are as follows:
   - ✓ *Registration*: The plan for students whose registration interferes at school is to provide enough continuous and intense sensory input so that they can persist in their work. Construct a flow chart for more complex tasks that students like Bradley can check off as they complete task components.

     To address registration needs, increase the contrast and reduce the predictability of events as this creates more opportunities for the sensory systems to meet high thresholds. Make objects weigh more, change an item's color or the background color, or add a movement to the assignment. For example, if a student is lethargic, we might break his seatwork assignments into smaller parts so he has to get up and turn in the parts several times during the seatwork period. We might also give the student construction paper to write on (increasing the texture) and scented markers for certain assignments. Each change adds sensory input to the seatwork task (i.e., movement, touch, smell, visual inputs, respectively), and the accumulation of inputs increases the chances that the student will reach thresholds and become more responsive.
   - ✓ *Seeking*: As students with a seeking pattern enjoy sensory experiences, providing more experiences as part of schoolwork can be helpful so they don't stop working to obtain the extra sensory input they desire.
   - ✓ *Sensitivity*: As students with sensitivity tend to notice everything, it can interfere with schoolwork. Providing such students with more structured patterns of sensory experiences can be helpful.
   - ✓ *Avoiding*: As students with an avoiding pattern notice and are bothered by things in the environment much more than peers, reducing sensory input is effective. When the environment is "quiet," these students can continue daily life activities for a longer period of time. Additionally, increased sensory experiences should be introduced gradually.

Chapter 7

1. Crisis management is designed to have an immediate impact on behavior, with the intention of diffusing or interrupting a potentially dangerous situation. While the approach may be effective in the short term, crisis management is not designed to effect sustained behavior change; additionally, in some cases, it may serve to be reinforcing to the individual.

2. Behavioral perspectives are shifting from focusing primarily on changing consequences in order to change behavior to designing support plans intended to teach prosocial ways of responding to situations. The set of assumptions that come with this shift in perspective include:

    Behavior is influenced by context.

    Behavior is functional, purposeful, and meaningful.

    Behavior is affected by external events, including emotional and biological conditions.

    Behavior is influenced by factors outside the immediate environment.

    Behaviors change as people mature and develop new competencies.

    · Behavioral supports are guided by a strong base.

3. The members of the behavioral support team may include family members, educators, paraprofessionals, therapists, and the students themselves. Ideally, the team is composed of individuals from all environments in which the student interacts. The team's role is to problem-solve, support, and guide the process of the functional behavioral assessment.

4. The components of a functional behavioral assessment and intervention plan are:

    Defining the behavior

    Gathering behavioral information

    Developing hypothesis statements

    The information is then used in:

    Creating a behavior support plan

    Implementing intervention

    The final stage is:

    Monitoring implementation and outcomes

5. Major issues involved in defining behaviors of concern include the need for the behavior to be clearly specified so that it is observable and measurable.

6. The goal of a functional behavioral assessment is to identify the underlying causes of the behavior exhibited by the student.

7. *Antecedents* occur prior to the behavior being exhibited; they are sometimes referred to as triggers for the behavior. Typically, the focus has been on immediate antecedents (fast triggers); however, slow triggers or setting events (e.g., changes in health, schedule, how well the student slept) are also being considered as they may affect the student's ability to cope.

    Consequences are responses that occur after the behavior and can either serve to maintain the behavior or end it.

8. The types of questions that need to be asked include those related to the history of the behavior, strengths of the student, reinforcement history, conditions under which the student does well, type of curriculum and whether it is a match for the student, amount of structure in the student's day, types of instructional approaches, occasions when the problem behavior is more likely to be exhibited, the apparent purpose served by the behavior, communication skills of the student, any medical/sleeping/nutritional concerns, and special conditions affecting the student outside the school setting.

9. Collecting information is an ongoing process because as a student's life and educational circumstances change, conditions surrounding the behavior may also change.

10. Hypothesis statements are informed guesses about the potential underlying cause(s) of a behavior based on the information gathered in the functional analysis.

11. Problem behavior pathways are important because they allow the interventionist to view the behavior in terms of antecedents (both slow and fast triggers) and consequences, which can lead to looking at various approaches to intervention, including antecedent control, changing consequences, and teaching alternative behaviors.

12. Positive behavior support approaches focus on creating positive learning environments and teaching students alternate ways of behaving.

13. Curriculum considerations in implementing interventions focus on ensuring the curriculum matches student goals, skills, and needs and include looking at teaching alternative and prosocial behaviors to replace those that may be problematic.

    Classroom management and instructional considerations focus on ensuring the classroom environment is structured in a positive way that creates opportunities for engagement, includes systematic instruction and clearly articulated expectations, allows for rehearsal, and supports student chances for success. Included are the use of routines, consideration of the student's learning style, and teaching strategies for coping with the stresses of daily demands.

14. Applied behavior analysis serves as the basis for positive behavior supports. Additionally, specific techniques within applied behavior analysis such as shaping of behavior, creating behavior chains, reinforcing successive approximations, prompting, extinction, and planned ignoring have been used successfully to effect behavior change in individuals with ASD.

15. Behavior support plans may be unsuccessful for several reasons, including lack of implementation across environments, lack of adequate information collecting in terms of monitoring (thus leading to either ending the plan early or continuing for too long), and inadequately planned interventions.

16. Implementation and outcomes of support plans must be monitored to determine if they are working and, if not, possible reasons why not. Additionally, even if the plan is effective, it is important to gain information as to why it works and how it might be changed or improved.

Chapter 8

1. Play is considered a primary social activity through which children develop symbolic capacities, interpersonal skills, and social knowledge. Learning and development are seen as being mediated through social experiences with others. Friendships, like play, occupy a central place in children's social lives and are considered to be associated with social, emotional, and cognitive development, as well as being a determining factor for social adaptation and adjustment.

2. Children with ASD face challenges in how they express play interests and how they make social overtures, leading often to isolation, bullying, neglect, and lack of friendships. Many children with ASD (a) demonstrate play skills that are detached, isolated, and repetitive; and (b) have unique fascinations or are attracted to toys, activities, or themes that reflect the preferences of younger children. In terms of developing friendships, children with ASD often have difficulties in both verbal and nonverbal communication and lack skills in joint attention and emotional responsiveness in social play.

3. Peer culture involves active participation in the social activities that are most valued by the peer group. It consists of shared understandings, values, beliefs, and associated behaviors, activities, and relationship patterns children construct out of their everyday experiences with one another. Many students with ASD are excluded from their peer culture because of behavior that does not fit perceptions of what is "normal. " As a result, a social void is likely to exist between children with ASD and their typically developing peers.

4. Play culture reflects the unique social and imaginary worlds that children create together, apart from adults. It refers to jointly constructed activity through which children acquire interrelated skills necessary for achieving social competence, mutual friendships, social communication strategies, resolving conflicts, problem solving, building trust, and developing other foundational social skills.

5. The Friend 2 Friend Autism Demystification (F2F) model is designed to foster mutual friendships for children with ASD by building understanding, acceptance and, empathy in their peers, siblings, and classmates. The model provides a framework for designing autism demystification programs for children ages 3 and up.

6. F2F is implemented through a four-step teaching process of modeling, labeling, explaining, and normalizing.
   - ✓ Modeling: a visual model of the characteristics of ASD is presented to help peers understand puzzling behaviors they may see in children on the spectrum.
   - ✓ Labeling: after presenting the characteristics through modeling, children are helped in accepting them by giving each a name or label to make it easier to accept the characteristics or behaviors as real.
   - ✓ Explaining: the meaning or purpose behind the behavior or characteristic is explained to help answer the question of "Why does my friend do that?"
   - ✓ Normalizing: the characteristics and behaviors of children with ASD and their differences are linked to differences and commonalities all children exhibit, allowing typically developing peers to empathize with children on the spectrum.

   The program uses puppet shows for children aged 3-8 to teach characteristics associated with ASD through a six-step process; for children aged 9 and above, a simulation game is used for the same purposes.

7. The five key learning goals of F2F are:

   ✓ Recognize and accept differences in themselves and others by identifying and labeling their own affinities (strengths or gifts) and their own challenges (weaknesses or disabilities)

   ✓ Recognize individuals with autism as individuals and valuable friends through the use of "people-first language"

   ✓ Recognize that it is important to ask questions and express feelings as a means of learning new things about themselves and others

   ✓ Empathize with what it feels like to have autism by providing an experiential learning opportunity and by modeling, labeling, explaining, and normalizing the characteristics of autism

   ✓ Embrace all types of diversity by supporting participants to recognize the importance of peer relationships, play, and friendships

8. The seven friendship tips offer prosocial communication strategies that enhance social interactions between individuals on the autism spectrum and their peers. When peers know how to communicate or interact with somebody on the spectrum they are more than willing to do so.

   ✓ **Get your friend's attention.** Move closer to your friend and say his or her name to get your friend's attention before you start talking.

   ✓ **Use short sentences**. Use fewer words or shorten your sentence when speaking to your friend.

   ✓ **Use gestures or visuals.** Use a gesture like pointing to something or a visual (i.e., picture communication symbols) to help your friend understand what you are communicating.

   ✓ **Wait.** Give your friend extra time to think about what you are saying and then answer you.

   ✓ **Watch your friend.** Watch your friend to learn your friend's affinities (things your friend is good at or likes to do).

   ✓ **Give your friend choices.** When you want to play, offer your friend choices of things your friend likes to do.

   ✓ **Use friendly words.** Use friendly words when speaking with your friend like "hi."

9. The IPG model is designed to support children with ASD in play experiences with typical peers/siblings as playmates through a system of careful guidance and support.

10. Through a carefully tailored system of support, emphasis is placed on maximizing children's developmental potential as well as intrinsic desire to play, socialize, and form meaningful relationships with peers.

    Included in the considerations are:

    ✓ Form IPG parent-professional team.

    ✓ Determine if IPG program is appropriate for a child.

    ✓ Identify qualified IPG Provider.

    ✓ Develop an IPG program schedule.

    ✓ Choose play space and materials.

    ✓ Develop session structure and supports.

11. Assessments in the IPG model include evaluating the symbolic dimensions of play, the social dimensions of play, the communicative functions and means used by the children, and the play preferences and diversity of play exhibited.

    ✓ Symbolic dimensions of play: refer to play acts the child directs toward objects, self, or others to signify events, including manipulation, functional and symbolic-pretend play

    ✓ Social dimensions of play: involve a focus on the child's proximity and involvement with one or more peers, including isolate, onlooker-orientation, parallel-proximity, common focus and common goal

    ✓ Communicative functions and means used by the children: address both how and in what ways the child communicates within the play experience

    ✓ Play preferences and diversity of play exhibited: evaluate what the child and peers like to do to identify and match play interests

12. Guided participation refers to an adult guiding novice and expert players to engage in mutually enjoyed activities that encourage social interaction, communication, pretending, and interactive games. It is used to implement a carefully tailored and intensive system of supports appropriate to each child's needs and abilities. Key components include:

    ✓ Nurturing play initiations focuses on discovering and supporting novice players' meaningful attempts to socialize and play by recognizing, interpreting, and responding to the way they express their intentions.

    ✓ Scaffolding play involves building on the child's play initiations by systemically adjusting assistance to match or slightly exceed the level at which the child is independently able to engage in play with peers through support structures.

    ✓ Guiding social communication involves using cues to facilitate social exchanges between children.

    ✓ Play guidance provides strategies to support children in engaging in experiences slightly beyond their capacity and include orienting, mirroring, parallel play, joint focus, joint actions, role enactment, and role playing.

Chapter 9

1. The term *multiple intelligences* refers to individuals having various types of cognition, including athletics, music, art, math, and social.

2. Skills necessary for social cognition, including joint attention, early symbolic communication, and imitation of movement, develop through interactions with caregivers and others.

3. Treatment options vary in terms of how and what to teach with regard to social skills/social cognitive development based on the strengths and needs of the individual on the spectrum. The purpose of developing the ILAUGH model of Social Cognition and the ST-SCP was to provide a more logical base for developing treatment plans (long- and short-term goals and objectives as well as transition to adulthood plans) that are grounded in reality.

4. "Social skills" are defined as social behaviors we produce based upon our related social thinking. Social skills vary with circumstances. Producing the expected behavior depends on using the given situation and who is present in it and what we know about them to help figure out how we are expected to behave to encourage them to have normal if not good thoughts about us. When teaching more advanced students on the autism spectrum, those who are language-based learners (i.e., they comprehend and use language spontaneously in order to continue to learn about the world), we teach them about social thinking.

5. The term *sharing space effectively* refers to having the skills and abilities to understand the rules of behavior (verbal and nonverbal) in different settings and contexts.

6. The four steps in perspective taking identified by the chapter author are as follows:

    1. When you come into my space, I think about you and you think about me.

    2. I wonder why you are there, what your intentions are, and what your purpose is, in order to predict what will happen next and to keep safe.

    3. I wonder what you are thinking about me.

    4. To keep you thinking about me in the way I would like, I monitor and possibly modify my behavior.

7. Students with ASD often have challenges related to sharing space due to deficits in perspective taking, as well as failure to understand the rules of the environment.

8. The components of the ILAUGH acronym:

    ✓ ***I = Initiation of Language***
    Initiation of language is the ability to use one's language and communication skills to seek assistance or information.

    ✓ ***L = Listening With Eyes and Brain***
    Listening requires more than just taking in the auditory information. It also requires the listener to integrate information he sees with what he hears to understand the deeper concept of the message.

    ✓ ***A = Abstract and Inferential Language/Communication***
    Communicative comprehension also depends on the ability to recognize that most language or communication is not intended for literal interpretation.

    ✓ ***U = Understanding Perspective***
    Social thinking requires that everybody considers their own and others' emotions, imagination, thoughts, beliefs, prior experiences, shared knowledge, motives, intentions, and personalities.

    ✓ ***G = Gestalt Processing/Getting the Big Picture***
    Central coherence is the term used to describe the ability to think conceptually – to form gestalts, which we then deconstruct to arrive at the related details.

    ✓ ***H = Humor and Human Relatedness***
    Successful teachers engage in relationships, which seek to value and appreciate the people we are teaching, and through this social emotional relationship students may learn more effectively in the classroom setting. Strategies to encourage human relations and age-appropriate humor dovetail with many of the other concepts discussed through the ILAUGH model as all of them overlap in many ways.

9. From third grade on children are expected to develop more socially abstract thinking in order to navigate their way towards developing independence in adulthood. In early elementary school, many of our students do a reasonably good job with understanding and applying their skills as they pertain to the curriculum – they may even have some basic friendships. However, as they approach fourth and fifth grade, the demands evolve such that more abstract thinking is required, and these same students often start to lose more and more footing, both academically and socially.

10. Academically, as students move up in the elementary and secondary school curriculum, the curriculum itself moves away from rote-based teaching to more socially abstract teachings. In kindergarten, first, and second grade, we often teach students the skills for learning by teaching them the alphabet, basic math, and penmanship. In

third grade, however, we make a transition away from learning basic skills to applying what you have learned by using the basic skills. For example, now that students know how to decode a written passage (many call this reading), we begin to expect them to show that they are interpreting the reading by making more active predictions and interpretations. We also expect students to write longer and longer passages, explaining their personal point of view about the world or the text they read, whereas when they were younger, they were only required to copy the text to practice writing.

11. We need to focus on helping them develop functional communication systems, which may include the use of augmentative communication since many are nonverbal or minimally verbal. They also need to be taught clear social behavioral expectations for school, home, and community. When teaching these lessons, information must be explicit and be consistently applied and expected. The social teaching is often rote and explicit, using clear visual supports to encourage students to produce the responses more consistently.

12. These students are often near-normal or above-normal in academic intelligence and have developed functional communication systems, but have great difficulty in perspective taking, causing problems with understanding implied meaning both from text and group dynamics. For these students, we can slowly introduce lessons about social thinking, helping them to understand that other people have thoughts and feelings, but we want to do much of the teaching described above as well. These students may require lengthy lessons to help them understand the motive behind a person's actions, which the NSC and even the NCSC peer deciphers on the spot without any discussion or prompting.

13. These are programs developed to teach various types of social skills to individuals on the autism spectrum. While addressing different areas of social skills training, the programs share the use of concrete, consistent, and predictable elements.

Chapter 10

1. Anxiety is a common condition experienced by individuals with autism. For example, 11% to 84% of individuals with autism experience anxiety (Costello, Egger, & Angold, 2005; van Steensel & Bogels, 2011; White & Roberson-Nay, 2009). According to Costello and colleagues (2005), the rates of anxiety disorders observed in children with ASD are more than two times higher than in typically developing children. Similarly, Lugnegard, Hallerback, and Gillberg (2011) found that more than one half of the adults in their study had experienced at least one anxiety disorder, with others having had a diagnosis for two or more, including social anxiety disorder, generalized anxiety disorder, and obsessive compulsive disorder.

   Anxiety can impact all areas of life, from school attendance to developing friendships to independent living to employment. Individuals with ASD often have difficulty understanding the social rules, knowing which topics are appropriate to talk about, and asking for help.

2. A lack of theory of mind in individuals with ASD is linked to the inability to identify and differentiate their own mental states (Aspy & Grossman, 2011). Kanne and Mazurek (2011) ascribed emotional regulation challenges to inflexibility. Barrett, Gross, Conner, and Benvenuto (2001) and Samson, Huber, and Gross (2012) reported that adults with ASD Level 1 typically use less effective methods for emotional regulation than neurotypical adults. That is, they tend to rely on emotional suppression (or hiding the emotion), a less effective coping strategy, rather than employing emotional reappraisal (or rethinking the situation) to shift their perspective in troubling circumstances.

3. **Self-management.** Self-management may be defined as the ability to regulate one's behavior, including monitoring. As such, it involves learning the skills needed to reduce unwanted responses and increasing adaptive responses.

    Visual supports and routines. Visual supports may be defined as visually presented tools that support increased understanding for a student. Visual supports are backed by research and can include, but are not limited to, pictures, scales, written words, flow charts, symbols, and scripts.

    Practice in real-life situations. This includes practicing newly acquired emotional regulation skills in a variety of natural settings and across environments. This is critical as individuals with autism often have difficulty maintaining and generalizing skills to new contexts (Dawson & Osterling, 1997).

4. There is not a singular area of brain dysfunction specific to autism. Several areas of the brain, including brainstem, cerebellum, frontal lobe, and limbic structures, have been implicated as abnormal in persons with ASD (Bachevalier & Loveland, 2006). Similarly, research has revealed that emotional regulation challenges are not limited to one section of the brain (cf. Minshew & Keller, 2010; Pelphrey, Shultz, Hudac, & Vander Wyk, 2011). For example, an enlarged amygdala and hippocampus have been implicated in problems of emotional perception and regulation (cf. Groen, Teluj, Buitelaar, & Tendolkar, 2010).

5. To help students with ASD form friendships, it makes sense to help them to find other people who love and value the same things as they do. In addition, many adults with ASD have reported using thoughts about their special interest as a way of reducing social anxiety and increasing the ability to remain calm during social frustration.

    Findings indicate that laughter connects people in a very emotional way. Students who lack friends also tend to lack opportunities for laughter and, therefore, can benefit from strategies specifically designed to elicit laughter. Creative ways of bringing humor and laughter into the classroom include video modeling, comedy improv games, cartoons, and jokes (Getlen, 2006).

6. **The Incredible 5-Point Scale.** Buron and Curtis (2012) created the Incredible 5-Point Scale to help individuals with ASD understand social and emotional concepts as well as to enhance their self-understanding. The 1-5 scale system is applicable to a variety of social and self-regulation behaviors and responses to those behaviors, including feelings of anxiety, concepts of personal space, and feelings of anger. Children and youth with ASD are taught to recognize the stages of their emotions or social challenges and methods to self-calm or "rethink" at each level.

    Modeling. Modeling involves learning skills either in real time or through video observations. Based on Bandura's (1977) concept of social learning, which posits that individuals learn from watching each other, modeling may be divided into three types: "*direct modeling* (simply copying the model), *synthesized modeling* (combining several observations to create a new behavior), and *symbolic modeling* (copying fictional characters from television, books, etc.)" (Aspy & Grossman, 2011, p. 205). A meta-analysis found that video modeling was successful in teaching a variety of skills, including self-help, social, transition behaviors, play, on-task, and speech and language skills (Bellini & Akullian, 2007).

    Narratives. Some social narratives are designed to be used prior to a situation to facilitate social success (i.e., cartooning, Power Cards, social scripts, Social Stories™). Specifically, they provide information about what may occur/what to expect, how others might think about what is happening, when something may occur, what the learner can do in a given situation, what the learner should try not to do in a given situation, and so forth. Others, such as SOCCSS and social autopsies, occur after an event to help the learner understand a previous interaction to support future success. Social Narratives also emphasize problem solving skills, brainstorming, and generalization.

    Mataya and Owens' problem-solving paradigm (Mataya & Owens, 2013) is designed to help learners understand cause and effect, problem solving, and decision-making. Created for use at home, school, and community, this comprehensive and easy-to-use model is suitable for learners across the spectrum.

Chapter 11

1. Structure for students with ASD involves the teacher or caregiver deciding what the learning activities will be, where they will occur, and how long they will last.

2. Structured TEACCHing refers to environmental strategies and environmental supports for individuals with ASD developed by the TEACCH program, a statewide program for individuals with autism in North Carolina.

3. Structured TEACCHing has two main goals: (a) teach the individual with ASD as many skills as possible, given his developmental level; and (b) provide an environment as comprehensible as possible, so the learner can understand the expectations and opportunities around him.

4. The "Culture of Autism" refers to the shared neuropsychological patterns of thinking, communication, and behavior commonly seen among individuals with ASD.

5. The five questions Structured TEACCHing should answer by providing the learner with visual information and organization of the environment are as follows:

    1. Where should I be?
    2. What work or activity will I do?
    3. How much work will I do?/How long will the activity last?
    4. How will I know that I am making progress and when I have finished?
    5. What will I do next?

6. The importance of schedules, task organization, work/activity systems, and routines for individuals with ASD:

    ✓ Schedules are important as they allow individuals with ASD to know where they are supposed to be and what they are to be doing at a given time and allow for predictable environments with knowledge of what will come next. Schedules should be individualized, visual, accurate, and easy to alter should the need arise.

    ✓ Task organization and work/activity systems provide a visual representation of what the student is to do each step of the way during a task or activity.

    ✓ Routines are consistent daily activities for students. A student who has reached independence or mastery on an activity can be considered to have developed a routine (for example, placing completed work in a folder or washing hands before snack time).

7. Practical strategies for teachers, including providing visual structure, organizing materials, sharing information, and creating schedules, are integral to Structured Teaching. The authors provide multiple examples demonstrating the use of Structured Teaching at different age and ability levels.

Chapter 12

1. While many neurotypical children and youth have hobbies or interests, they are not engaged with them to the same extent as peers with ASD. They frequently have multiple and diverse interests at one time (e.g., sports, music, and video games), whereas those with ASD typically have one primary SIA, though they may have secondary, less dominant SIAs that can be linked to the primary ones (Myles & Simpson, 2003). Further, neurotypical individuals do not typically invest as much time, energy, commitment, or money into learning

about their hobbies, or engaging in them, and it would be rare for a neurotypical child or youth to have the capacity to converse with professionals on an equal level, or have the vocabulary or insights with which to do so. Moreover, the daily activities of neurotypical children and youth are not likely to be seen as interfering with the pursuit of their hobbies, as is the case for children and youth with ASD. That is, the hobbies of neurotypical children and youth are not usually seen as the all-consuming, driving, day-and-night focus of desire and attention as are the SIAs of those with ASD.

2. According to the author, SIAs are critical to the well-being of individuals with ASD and are at the core of their self-image; SIAs literally are their identity. Because of the importance of this concept, the author of the chapter and others developed the theory called "The Fusion of SIA With Core Self-Image." These children, who so often tragically have extremely low self-esteem, take great pride in their SIAs and in their advanced SIA-related knowledge.

   In their SIAs, children and teens with ASD find a stable core. SIAs help them make sense of a world that can feel overwhelming and chaotic, and in that world, feel a measure of power and control. SIAs give them a focus upon which to channel their often prodigious gifts, and shape their dreams.

3. SIAs differ in social acceptability based on the age and gender of the individual, the age of the onlooker, the geographic location, and the interest itself. Neurotypical people are often mystified as to why some SIAs would hold intense attraction for individuals with ASD. The most socially acceptable SIAs can become socially unacceptable at any age if the child or teen talks of nothing else, imposes his interest constantly on others, uses SIA-related vocabulary that is above the heads of his peers, and/or carries the object everywhere with him.

4. "When children and youth change SIAs, especially when the change is abrupt or the new SIA differs substantially from the previous one, the transition can be painful for parents." This means that an SIA, particularly one that has endured for a long time, becomes an entrenched part of a family's culture and identity. Parents often invest significant time and energy in learning about a child's SIA, and even if they were not initially familiar with the topic, they develop extensive knowledge simply by hearing so much about the SIA from the child. Parents may also make a considerable financial investment in the child's SIA, purchasing SIA-related personal items, decorating a bedroom, or paying for magazine subscriptions, classes, SIA-themed camps, and SIA destination vacations. Over time an SIA becomes a major aspect of a family's personality.

5. SIAs often have a relaxing, calming, and stress-reducing influence on the lives of children and youth with ASD, who may otherwise have great difficulty achieving relaxed states. SIAs can also be a source of great joy and happiness for individuals with ASD, who may otherwise only rarely feel those emotions.

6. A classroom teacher may wish to set the stage for incorporating the SIA into a student's school day by interviewing the student about the SIA. SIA integration can be used to motivate a student to learn skills, complete particular assignments, and reward compliance with nonpreferred tasks and assignments. IEP teams can also consider the regular inclusion of a student's SIA into a student's IEP accommodations to aid in motivation and compliance with schoolwork. A second way to apply SIAs in the classroom is by motivating the student to engage in appropriate behavior through engagement in the SIA. A third option for applying SIAs in the classroom is for the teacher to allow the student with ASD to use his preferred method of researching information on his SIA to learn about nonpreferred classroom topics. A final way in which SIAs may be applied directly to school is to create a school-based job related to the student's SIA.

7. Individuals with ASD must be encouraged to choose careers in which their employment utilizes their SIAs, thereby enhancing their work product and personal satisfaction. Holding a job related to an SIA allows a person to use natural talents to perform. Moreover, an individual with ASD will not require as much training to hold a job related to his SIA as he might need for another job. A job related to an SIA could mean the difference

between a daily struggle to complete work-related tasks and the satisfaction of a meaningful job well done each day. There are other benefits to having a job that relates to an SIA. Through such a job, a person with ASD may display strengths that emerge specifically in relation to working with his SIA.

Chapter 13

1. In order to understand others' emotional and mental states, one needs to be able to read nonverbal information from facial expressions, vocal intonation, and body language. One also needs to integrate information from all these channels in context in order to get a coherent picture of other people's emotions.

2. The authors were referring to the difficulties persons with ASD often face in gathering, integrating, and interpreting others' emotional states, which can leave them with no idea of what is going on socially.

3. Individuals with ASD demonstrate deficits in the ability to recognize emotion from examples. While findings related to determining a reason are inconclusive, theories link the problems to difficulties in empathy or theory of mind, to differences in how information is processed (feature by feature rather than holistically), also known as weak central coherence. Based on fMRI studies, there appears to be under-activity of brain regions in individuals with ASD compared to neurotypical peers.

4. "Systemizing" refers to the drive to analyze or build systems to understand and predict the behavior of rule-based events. Most individuals with ASD are hyper-attentive to detail and prefer predictable, rule-based environments, both of which assist in systemizing. As a result, it may be possible to teach high-functioning individuals with ASD a system for understanding emotions.

5. Individuals with ASD often prefer a computerized environment as it is predictable, consistent, and free from social demands. Additionally, one can work on computers at one's own pace and level of understanding, repeating lessons as necessary to reach mastery. Last, interest and motivation can be maintained through computerized rewards.

6. Capitalizing on the systemizing strengths exhibited by persons with ASD, *Mind Reading* is an interactive software program designed to systematically train complex emotional recognition in visual and auditory channels using life-like faces and voices. Early research has shown the program is successful in improving emotional recognition skills in isolation; however, generalization has proven problematic.

Chapter 14

1. Transition planning is a federally mandated part of the IEP of students with disabilities and includes the skills necessary for success in postsecondary life. Starting at age 16 (or 14 if considered necessary), each student is required to have an individual transition plan (ITP), which is defined as a coordinated set of activities based on individual needs and designed to focus on improving academic and functional achievement to facilitate success in postschool activities.

2. Planning the transition from school is a critical aspect in the middle and high school years because it requires the team to focus on the skills necessary for independent living, including job-related skills, safety skills, social skills, self-advocacy, and so on.

3. The members of a transition team typically include the individuals who are part of the student's IEP team but may also involve members of vocational services, agencies that focus on vocational support, representatives of postsecondary educational options and residential services, as well as others as appropriate.

4. Students with ASD should know who is on the ITP team, as well as their rights both while in school and in the post-school world.

5. The federal mandate stipulates that the ITP must be a coordinated set of activities that are outcome-oriented, student-centered, and broad-based. Additionally, the ITP should be a working document that changes over time as needed and appropriate.

6. It is important to address career, self-advocacy, and independent living goals as part of the ITP because school is supposed to prepare students to function in the adult world and, for individuals with ASD, direct instruction in the areas noted is critical.

7. A well-designed ITP should include assessment; statements of individual preferences for education, employment, and adult living; specific steps, methods, and resources needed to meet goals; instruction in academic, vocational, and living skills; identification of community experiences and skills related to future goals; exploration of service organizations; and methods for evaluating the success of transition activities.

8. The UCC is useful because it is a framework for discussing and planning for the characteristics specific to individuals with ASD. A completed UCC yields an evaluation of an individual's specific characteristics in each of several domains that allows for team discussion and planning to meet that individual's specific and unique needs.

9. Types of assessments in transition planning can include everything from informal observation and checklists to formal assessment and asking questions. Regardless of the method used, it is important that the student's current and future roles in adult life be addressed.

10. The components of successful planning for and support of the transition process include (a) self-determination, self-advocacy, and person-centered planning; (b) selecting meaningful coursework; (c) increasing job placement opportunities; (d) preparing employers; (e) developing a social network; and (f) planning for college/university experiences.

11. Considerations affecting job placement and retention for persons with ASD include ensuring the job is a good match in terms of challenges and interests as well as in terms of a physical (hours, noise level, activity level, etc.) and a social match (e.g., communication demands, level of interaction required, coworker training and support, etc.); creating experiences at the secondary level in the areas of job skills, communication with employers, and social skills to help lessen the challenges that might be faced in adult life; matching the job with the type of thinking (visual, music and higher math, verbal) demonstrated by the individual with ASD; and category of employment (supported, segregated, or competitive)

12. Social skills development should be an important part of the ITP process because research shows that students with ASD often leave school with inadequate social and communication skills for life success. These skills include social behaviors such as table manners, personal space awareness, and so on, as well as grooming, hygiene, and issues related to sexuality, including sexual orientation and safety.

13. For school-aged individuals, IDEA mandates that services are received and students themselves are not responsible for requesting help. In post-school settings, individuals with disabilities can continue to receive assistance, but are responsible for requesting it and for providing documentation of their disabilities.

Chapter 15

1. Members of the educational support and intervention team include, at a minimum, the teachers who work with the student, the parents, the student, school administrators assigned to lead the teams, and various professionals both inside and outside of school (e.g., speech and language pathologists, occupational therapists, physical therapists, counselors, behavior specialists) who might work with the students with ASD.

2. Collaboration is important as it provides mutual support, usually results in better understanding of the student, ensures that everyone working with the student is focusing on the same outcomes using a consistent approach, and provides the opportunity to share perceptions and effective interventions.

3. An IEP, or individualized education program, is a federally mandated requirement for students found eligible for special education services. The IEP includes a statement of functioning, measurable goals, benchmarks or objectives to meet the goals, accommodations and modifications, persons responsible for services, and amount of services, among other requirements. 504 Plans, on the other hand, are used for students who may not meet eligibility requirements for special education services but who need accommodations or modifications to be successful in school. 504 Plans are also used in post-school settings as the IEP is only mandated for school-aged children.

4. Components necessary for successful team meetings may include:
   ✓ Discussion of findings from formal and informal assessments
   ✓ Development of goals and benchmarks and sharing them with team members for evaluation and modification
   ✓ Observation of the student and sharing among team members of the findings

5. Planning with a student prior to a meeting can serve a number of purposes, including gaining the student's perspective on goals and objectives; understanding the student's perception of challenges and strengths; exploring issues of concern to the student; and assisting the student in developing skills to work as a productive member of the team.

6. Factors that contribute to effective collaboration may include:
   ✓ Team members being willing to consider each other's perspectives, including the student's
   ✓ Team members working together to understand the student's strengths and challenges
   ✓ Team members who are willing to provide needed support

7. Three examples of how individuals with ASD may think and learn include:
   ✓ They may lack awareness of social situations.
   ✓ They may not be able to integrate information from various sources into a meaningful whole.
   ✓ They may need narration of their actions in order to develop an awareness of what they are doing and how that behavior affects others.
   ✓ They may be very literal in their thinking.

Chapter 16

1. The mother who authored this chapter describes being thought of as the cause of her child's autism and also writes about the fact that she was told autism was incurable. Both these aspects were hurtful and unhelpful.

2. Prior to the passage of PL 94-142, schools were not required to provide educational services for individuals with disabilities, including those on the autism spectrum. Therefore, placement options ranged from institutionalization to home teaching to the general education class with the hope that teachers would be supportive.

3. Three things related to the educational experience of the child:
   ✓ Formal testing has limitations: IQ scores can change over time.
   ✓ In many cases occupational therapy support is needed: Individuals with ASD have sensory and coordination difficulties.
   ✓ Lack of understanding and support can lead to frustration and depression; individuals with ASD may not interact socially as do other children, nor may they demonstrate the same level of academic and physical skills. Failure to understand these differences and support alternative ways of completing tasks can lead to frustration on the part of the individual with ASD.

4. PL 94-142 was important because it mandated public school services for all children with disabilities. Additionally, the law required that schools involve parents in all aspects of their child's schooling, from permission to conduct assessment, to placement decisions, to development of educational plans.

5. It is important that teachers and others within the school community accept and work with the strengths and need areas of individuals with ASD not only because it can affect the educational experience and outcomes for the person with ASD, but also because it can affect the perception of and acceptance by peers.

Chapter 17

1. Three experiences discussed by the chapter author:
   ✓ Using a multiplier box to help in solving multiplication and division problems, essentially creating a low-tech assistive device.
   ✓ Literal thinking, which led to misunderstanding and academic difficulties as the author experienced difficulty answering questions involving more abstract thinking.
   ✓ Spending most of his social time at school trying to avoid and navigate around bullies.

2. Narration is the technique of someone talking through the actions of the person with ASD. This may help the individual with ASD to attach meaning to words as those words describe actions she/he is doing.

3. The "hidden curriculum" refers to the set of rules in school (and in the world) that are learned by neurotypical individuals without instruction but that need to be directly taught to individuals with ASD. Some examples include teacher-pleasing behaviors, the meaning of body language and personal space, and appropriate responses when asked questions (such as when a "white lie" is appropriate). It is crucial to teach these skills directly to individuals with ASD as doing so will allow for more successful social interactions.

4. The chapter author's special interests provided him with a vehicle for interacting with others (such as in band class) and also in job development (working at a bike shop).

Appendix B: Glossary

504 Plan. A formal plan for the school to provide appropriate accommodations to a student with a qualifying disability, as required by Section 504 of the federal Rehabilitation Act of 1973. (Does not include special education services.)

A

Accommodations. Alterations to the environment, equipment, or format of a curriculum to allow equal access to the content. Unlike modifications, accommodations do not alter the actual content of the material being taught.

Adaptive behavior. An individual's manner of dealing with the demands of daily life, including self-care skills, organizational skills, basic interpersonal skills, and conformance to community standards (obeying rules, taking responsibility, etc.).

Affect sharing. A mutual sharing of emotional states.

Americans with Disabilities Act (ADA). A federal law protecting the civil rights of individuals with disabilities.

Antecedent. An event that precedes a behavior.

Applied behavior analysis (ABA). An approach to intervention, rooted in behavioral psychology, that emphasizes a systematic approach of understanding, evaluating, and modifying behavior.

ASD (see autism spectrum disorder).

Asperger, Hans (1906-1980). Austrian pediatrician, whose 1944 paper "Autistic psychopathy in childhood" described four patients with severely impaired social skills, poor pragmatic speech, all-encompassing special interests, emotional immaturity, unusual use of language, sensory sensitivities, insistence on sameness, difficulty making friends, below-average self-help skills, and poor motor coordination. This set of characteristics later came to be called "Asperger Syndrome."

Asperger's Disorder (also known as Asperger Syndrome or Asperger's Syndrome). Currently defined in DSM-5 as Level I ASD, characterized by average-to-high intelligence, significantly impaired social interaction, and repetitive behaviors or interests (most often, circumscribed interests about which they spend an inordinate amount of time gathering facts).

Attribution. Assignment of some characteristic or quality to a person or thing.

Auditory comprehension. Receptive language skills; understanding of spoken language.

Auditory discrimination. The ability to differentiate among similar sounds in words (e.g. "chair" and "share").

Auditory processing. How the brain processes and interprets what is heard through the ear.

Augmentative communication (also referred to as augmentative alternative communication, or AAC). Any communication system designed to supplement an individual's existing mode of communication.

Autism Diagnostic Interview-Revised (ADI-R). A standardized parent interview designed to identify children with autism.

Autism Diagnostic Observation Scale (ADOS). A standardized assessment tool that uses structured activities and materials to assess social interaction, communication, and play behaviors. The ADOS is considered the "gold standard" for assessing and diagnosing autism and pervasive developmental disorder (PDD) across ages, developmental levels, and language skills.

Autism spectrum disorder (ASD). Current umbrella category used to define all levels of autism across a broad spectrum. The current DSM-5 groups the spectrum in three levels based on an individuals need for support.

Autistic disorder. Previously known as "infantile autism" or "Kanner's syndrome." First described by Leo Kanner in 1943, autistic disorder is characterized by severe impairment in social interaction and communication, as well as restrictive, repetitive behaviors and/or interests. May include delay in or total lack of development of spoken language. Individuals with autistic disorder may or may not have comorbid intellectual disability.

B

Behavior support plan. Based on a functional behavioral assessment, a written plan for changing a child's problem behavior(s), utilizing multiple intervention strategies to teach alternative behaviors and create a supportive learning environment.

Body language. Information about a person's thoughts or feelings that is unconsciously conveyed through physical mannerisms.

Brain connectivity. The rich array of neural pathways that carry signals to various areas of the brain.

Brain synchrony. Various regions of the brain increasing or decreasing their activity simultaneously.

Brain thresholds. The points at which the brain recognizes/responds to sensory input.

C

Cartooning. A type of social narrative that uses thought bubbles, conversation bubbles, cartoon or stick figures to illustrate people's thoughts and words during interactions in a comic strip format.

Central coherence. The brain's ability to process multiple chunks of information in a global way, connecting them and viewing them in context, in order to determine a higher level of meaning. Poor central coherence can make it difficult to generalize.

Chaining. A method of teaching in which a task is broken down into several smaller steps, which are then taught in order. The student must master a step before the next one in the sequence is added.

Childhood disintegrative disorder. A rare pervasive developmental disorder in which a child develops normally for at least two years and then experiences severe regression in two or more areas of previously acquired skills (language, social skills or adaptive behavior, bowel or bladder control, play, motor skills). Typically occurring between ages 3 and 4, the regression is more severe than the regression that is sometimes seen with autistic disorder.

Cognition. Conscious mental activity, including thinking, perceiving, reasoning, and learning.

Cognitive behavioral interventions. Interventions that change a child's behavior by altering or enhancing his understanding of a problem situation.

Cognitive delay. A deficit in intellectual abilities beyond typical variations for the child's age and background. Sometimes used synonymously with "mental retardation."

Collaboration. Individuals working together for a common goal.

Comic Strip Conversation™. An intervention technique developed by Carol Gray that uses cartooning to help students interpret the reasons behind others' behavior.

Communication. The deliberate conveying of information to another person.

Communication deficit. A difficulty in expressing ideas or intentions (expressive communication deficit) and/or interpreting the language, thoughts, or intentions of others (receptive communication deficit).

Communicative function. The idea that a student is trying to convey through his behavior. For example, the communicative function of throwing a pencil on the floor may be that he doesn't want to work, that he wants a pen instead of a pencil, that he finds the process of handwriting physically painful, or a number of other possibilities.

Compensatory strategy. An unusual problem-solving tactic used to compensate for some sort of deficit.

Competitive employment. Employment in the community, at a competitive wage, without supports.

Complex language: Higher-level language, such as complex sentences, inferences, metaphors, or idioms.

Complex memory. Memory for complex material or for a large amount of similar material, such as word lists.

Complex motor abilities. Skilled motor abilities requiring coordination or precision, such as handwriting, typing, or skipping.

Complex sentences. Sentences consisting of multiple clauses.

Computerized axial tomography (CAT or CT) scan. A technique that uses a rotating x-ray machine and a computer to produce cross-sectional images of the body's internal structures.

Concept development/formation. Problem solving in the absence of set rules; understanding meaning/significance.

Concept identification. Recognizing a concept, although not necessarily understanding it. For example, a child might be able to read the word *cat* without understanding that the word represented the animal.

Connectivity. How well different regions are connected to one another, allowing signals/information to pass among them.

Consequence. The response (positive or negative) to a behavior.

Content standards. The state's expectations for what every student should know, understand, and be able to do at a given grade level.

Contextual recognition of emotion. The ability to infer another person's emotions and mind-set, based on situational clues.

Conversational maxims. The unspoken rules of conversation, relating to the quantity, quality, and relevance of a person's remarks.

Cooperative play. Interactive play with one or more peers, which is structured for the purpose of attaining a common goal or making a product. Child and peers explicitly plan and carry out a common agenda by defining specific rules and roles, negotiating behavior exchanges, and compromising around divergent interests.

Core deficit. A primary, underlying problem common to everyone with the same disorder. May result in a cascade of varying symptoms.

Crisis management. Finding a short-term solution to a dangerous or potentially dangerous situation.

Cueing. Providing prompts to indicate what a person should do next.

Culture of autism. Characteristic strengths, challenges, and patterns of thinking and behavior associated with ASD.

Curriculum-based assessment (CBA). An assessment of student performance in the local curriculum that is used to make instructional decisions.

D

Data collection. Any method of recording behavioral data for subsequent analysis.

Detroit Tests of Learning Aptitude (DTLA-2). A series of norm-referenced tests of specific mental abilities.

Developmental disorder. A disorder that typically develops during childhood.

Direct modeling. A type of modeling that requires simply copying the model.

Duration. The period of time from the beginning to the end of a single instance of a behavior.

E

Echolalia. The repetition of words or phrases used by another person.

Educational support and intervention team. Under IDEA, a mandated team for any student receiving special education services, consisting of teachers, paraprofessionals, administrators, service providers, parents, and the students themselves.

Electroencephalographic (EEG). A recording of electrical activity in the brain by means of electrodes attached to the scalp.

Elementary motor abilities. Simple motor skills requiring little coordination or precision.

Emotional reappraisal. Rethinking a situation that resulted in an emotional response in order to shift perspective in troubling circumstances.

Emotion recognition. The ability to recognize emotional states in another person or in oneself.

Emotional regulation. The ability to experience, recognize, express, and regulate all emotions effectively and fluidly with respect to environmental constraints.

Emotional suppression. Hiding of emotions.

Empathy. The ability to understand how another person feels or what he/she may be thinking. Sometimes referred to as "putting yourself in another person's shoes."

Evidence-based practice (EBP). Any practice that has been established as effective through scientific research following an explicit set of criteria.

Executive functions. Higher-order cognitive skills that include organization, planning, problem solving, self-regulation, and inhibitory control.

Experiential learning. Learning through experience. "Learning by doing."

Extinction. Weakening an undesirable behavior by withholding the reinforcer previously associated with it.

F

Facial emotion recognition. The ability to discern a person's emotional state based on their facial expression (e.g., a furrowed brow meaning that they are worried or a smile meaning that they are happy).

Facial expressions. Positioning of the facial muscles to convey emotions.

Fast triggers. One of two types of antecedents; also called "immediate antecedents."

First Signs. A national not-for-profit organization dedicated to teaching parents and pediatricians how to recognize the early signs of autism

Frequency. Common way of measuring behavior (along with duration and intensity).

Friend 2 Friend model. Social facilitation model that fosters mutual friends for children with ASD by building awareness, understanding, acceptance, and empathy in their peers through demystification programs comprising specially designed puppet presentations and simulation games developed by Heather McCracken.

Functional behavioral assessment. A method of identifying the underlying cause of a behavior by analyzing the behavior's antecedents and consequences.

Functional communication system. A communication system that is meaningful to the student and helps him participate in his environment

Functional magnetic resonance imaging (fMRI). A relatively new procedure that uses MRI technology to map tiny metabolic changes in active areas of the brain.

Functional neuroimaging. Technology that measures brain function. It is often used to understand the activity in certain areas of the brain.

G

Generalization. Using a skill/behavior learned in one environment and/or with one person in other environments and with other persons.

Gestalt processing. The ability to understand overall concepts, rather than just a collection of individual facts.

Grandin, Temple (1947). Considered one of the highest achieving adults with autism in the world. A professor at Colorado State University, international expert on livestock handling equipment and popular speaker/author on autism spectrum disorders.

Guided participation. A customized system of supports designed to help children with ASD socialize and play with their peers while participating in mutually engaging experiences. See also Integrated Play Groups.

H

Hidden curriculum. Unspoken social rules or norms that are often missed by individuals with ASD.

High-functioning autism (HFA). Currently defined as ASD Level 1 in DSM-5, autistic disorder generally accompanied by average or above average intelligence.

Highly qualified teachers. A term used in No Child Left Behind (NCLB) to indicate teachers who demonstrate knowledge and skill-based competencies in the design and delivery of effective educational programs and who understand and apply core elements of effective educational practice.

I

ICD-10. International Statistical Classification of Diseases and Related Health Problems, 10ᵗʰ Revision. The international coding system used to classify diseases and disorders.

IDEA (see Individuals with Disabilities Education Act).

Idiosyncratic language. Unique, unusual, personalized use of language.

ILAUGH. A model developed by Michelle Garcia Winner for understanding social thinking. The acronym stands for (I) initiating communication, (L) listening actively with the eyes and brain, (A) abstract and inferential thinking, (U) understanding perspective, (G) getting the big picture, and (H) humor.

Imitative learning. Learning by watching someone else perform an activity.

Incredible 5-Point Scale. A highly systemized cognitive tool developed by Kari Dunn Buron and Mitzi Curtis for helping individuals to understand social and emotional concepts and ideas including self-awareness, self-management, emotional identification, and social expectations.

Independent living. Being in charge of one's own life, including personal care, housing, community responsibility, and social relationships. Does not preclude the use of community resources, assistive technology, etc.

Individual family service plan (IFSP). A written plan specifying the services a child will receive through an infant-toddler (early intervention) program.

Individualized education program (IEP). A written plan specifying the services and accommodations the school will provide to a child with a disability, as well as related goals.

Individualized transition plan (ITP). A written plan addressing the post-secondary needs of a student receiving special education services. A required section of the IEP for students age 16 and over.

Individuals with Disabilities Education Act (IDEA). A federal law guaranteeing students with qualifying disabilities the right to a free appropriate public education.

Integrated Play Groups (IPG). A model developed by Pamela Wolfberg, in which children with ASD participate in mutually enjoyable, reciprocal play activities with neurotypical peers while being supported by an adult play group guide.

Intellectual disability. A disability characterized by a significantly below-average score on an intelligence test and limitations in functional abilities. Also referred to as mental retardation.

Intensity. Common way of measuring behavior (along with duration and frequency).

Intentional communication. The deliberate conveyance of information to another person.

Interpersonal relatedness. Interest in other people and skillfulness in interacting with them.

Intersubjective engagement. The ability to share the emotional states of others.

J

Joint action. Attending to and establishing shared attention with a social partner about an object, event or another person using nonverbal means, including eye gaze alteration, emotional expression and gestures.

Joint attention. Actively attending to and establishing shared attention with a social partner about an object, event, or other person using nonverbal means, including eye gaze alteration, emotional expression, and gestures.

K

Kanner, Leo (1894-1981). Austrian-born child psychiatrist at Johns Hopkins Medical School, whose 1943 paper "Autistic disturbances of affective content" described the case histories of 11 children, all of whom exhibited extreme social isolation or withdrawal, ritualistic behaviors, and communication difficulties. These characteristics are now termed autism or autistic disorder.

L

Labeling. Giving a name to a characteristic.

Lexicon. Vocabulary; word bank.

Linguistic. Relating to language.

Lovaas model. An intensive early intervention ABA program emphasizing discrete trial training. Developed by UCLA clinical psychologist O. Ivaar Lovaas.

Low registration. High thresholds and passive self-regulation.

M

Magnetic resonance imaging (MRI). A noninvasive, painless medical procedure that uses magnetic fields, radio waves, and a computer to produce detailed pictures of organs, soft tissues, and bones.

Making Action Plans (MAP). A student-centered transition planning process.

Mental-state recognition. The ability to recognize others' intentions, emotions, desires, etc.

Metacognitive strategies. Intervention strategies that involve "thinking about thinking."

Microcephaly. Head circumference more than two standard deviations below the mean.

Mind blindness. Difficulty inferring another person's thoughts or feelings.

Mind reading. Empathy. Being able to tell what another person is thinking or feeling.

Mind Reading. A computer program for teaching recognition of emotions.

Mirroring. Mimicking the actions of another.

Modeling. Teaching a skill through demonstration.

Modifications. Changes to the curriculum and/or instruction to meet a student's needs. As opposed to accommodations, when using modifications students are not expected to master the same content as others in the classroom.

Motor skills. Purposeful movements of the body or limbs.

Multimodal recognition of emotion. Recognizing emotion based on a variety of clues, including facial expression, voice, body language, and context.

Multitasking. Doing several activities at once.

N

Narration. Verbally describing what a child is doing, in the manner of a sportscaster, to help him attach meaning to words.

Natural reinforcers. Reinforcers that are logically related to the task at hand. For example, if the student points at a book and says "book," handing him the book is the natural reinforcer.

Naturalistic context. A typical environment/typically occurring situation for the student.

Neurochemistry. The study of chemicals and chemical changes in the brain.

Neuro-developmental. Relating to brain development.

Neuroimaging. Advanced technologies that take x-ray-type pictures of the brain and nervous system, such as CT scans or MRIs.

Neurons. Cells of the brain/nervous system.

Neuropathology. Brain or nervous system abnormalities.

Neuropsychological. Related to how the structure and function of the brain affect cognitive processes and behaviors.

Neurotypical. A term to indicate that an individual does not have autism (i.e., the brain works in the "typical" way).

Nonverbal behaviors. Deliberate behaviors other than speech/vocalizing.

Normalizing. In the Friend 2 Friend model, explaining autism characteristics to peers by linking them to characteristics all children exhibit.

Nurturing Narratives. A story-based language intervention approach that embeds building language skills into the context of sharing personal narratives and retelling fictional stories using a blending of applied behavior analysis and social pragmatics.

O

Orienting. Watching peers and activities.

Outcome-oriented framework. Identifying the desired results before intervention begins and then building in the methods or strategies that are most likely to produce those results.

P

Parallel play. Children playing side-by-side simultaneously using the same play space or similar materials, but not with each other.

Pathophysiology. Abnormalities in brain function.

Pedantic speech. Lecture-like or overly formal speech.

Peer culture. The unique set of values, beliefs, understandings, and relationship patterns that is shared by a group of peers, based on their common experience.

Person-centered planning. A process for planning for the future of a person with a disability based on their own desires/interests/dreams, rather than based on the systems and resources that may or may not be available to them.

Perspective taking. Looking at something from another person's point of view and, if necessary, changing one's behavior accordingly.

Pervasive developmental disorder-not otherwise specified (PDD-NOS). The terminology previously used in the DSM-IV to define an autism spectrum disorder characterized by severe impairment in social skills, plus impairment in communications skills *or* repetitive behaviors or interests, but that does not meet criteria for another more specific ASD.

Pervasive developmental disorders (PDDs). Previously used to define the category of autism spectrum disorders in the DSM-IV.

Phenylketonuria (PKU). A genetic disorder that prevents the body from metabolizing phenylalanine, an amino acid found in meat and dairy products. Can lead to brain damage and intellectual disability.

Picture Exchange Communication System (PECS). A "low-tech" functional communication system utilizing picture symbols.

PL (Public Law) 94-142. The Education of All Handicapped Children Act of 1975, renamed the Individuals with Disabilities Education Act (IDEA) when it was reauthorized in 1990. The first law to guarantee a free and appropriate education to children with disabilities.

Planned ignoring. Deliberately ignoring a problem behavior that is reinforced by attention. A type of extinction.

Planning Alternative Tomorrows with Hope (PATH). An eight-step person-centered planning process.

Plasticity. The ability of the brain to adapt or change in response to experience.

Play culture. A central aspect of children's peer culture involving the co-creation of social and imaginary worlds apart from adults.

Positive behavior supports. Based on behavioral observations, strategies designed to change the student's problem behaviors by altering the environment and/or teaching alternative behaviors.

Positron emission tomography (PET) scan. A procedure in which a small amount of radioactive glucose is injected into a vein. An imaging scan then measures the activity level of the brain by measuring its use of glucose.

Power Card Strategy. A type of social narrative that contains two components: (a) a text-based scenario that describes a target behavior associated with a special interest area and how that individual addresses the target behavior, and that encourages the student to use the strategy employed by the person of special interest; and (b) a small card that synthesizes the text-based scenario.

Pragmatics. The social aspects of language.

Presuppositional knowledge. In communication, the speaker's understanding of what his listeners already know, what they need to know in order to understand the information being communicated, and the style in which they would like the information to be communicated.

Problem behavior pathway. The sequence of events that typically precede and follow a problem behavior.

Proprioceptive. Relating to the sensory processes that inform the brain of body parts' movements and location.

Prosody. The intonation, rhythm, and pitch of spoken language.

Proto-declarative. Indicating an intent to communicate, share interest.

Proto-imperative. Communicating a desire to obtain something.

Psychogenic. Having a psychological, rather than physiological, cause.

Psycho-pharmacological interventions. Medications that affect the mind and behavior.

Psychotherapy. The treatment of emotional or behavioral problems through psychological counseling.

Q

Quality of life. Subjective well-being, including safety, health, happiness, autonomy, etc.

R

Reciprocity. Give-and-take.

Refrigerator mother. A theory, popular in the mid-20th century but later disproved, that autism was the result of a cold, unfeeling mother.

Reinforcement. Any response to an individual's behavior that maintains or increases the likelihood that they will perform that same behavior again.

Representational. Referring to something else; depicting something in another form. In children's play: pretend play.

Resiliency. Ability to overcome adversities and achieve success.

Rett's disorder. A pervasive developmental disorder, occurring primarily in females, that is characterized by normal development for at least 5 months, followed by sudden deceleration of head growth, loss of previously acquired hand skills and development of stereotyped "hand-wringing" movements, loss of social engagement, severely impaired receptive and expressive language development, and the appearance of poorly coordinated gait or trunk movements.

Role enactment. In play, imitating real-life activities such as making dinner or driving a car.

S

Savant. A person with an ability that far exceeds his overall level of development and may exceed those of most neurotypical individuals. Examples include photographic memory, ability to do complex math in the head, unusual calendar abilities, or perfect pitch.

Scaffolding play. In play interactions with peers, systematically adjusting the level of support offered a child to match or slightly exceed the level at which the child can independently perform.

Scatter plot. A simple two-dimensional chart used to track the occurrence of a behavior.

School connectedness. A student's belief that adults in the school care about his learning and about him as an individual.

Scientifically based instruction. A requirement of No Child Left Behind (NCLB) stating that educators must demonstrate knowledge and skill in applying "evidence-based practices" supported by research that applies rigorous, systematic, and objective procedures to obtain relevant knowledge.

Secured/segregated employment. A job in which individuals with disabilities work in a separate environment from neurotypical employees. Usually involves simple, repetitive work.

Seizure. A symptom of sudden, abnormal electrical activity in the brain. In *tonic-clonic seizures* (formerly referred to as "grand mal" seizures), the child loses consciousness and becomes rigid, then experiences convulsions with severe muscle spasms and jerking of the limbs. In *absence seizures* (formerly referred to as "petit mal" seizures), the child abruptly stops what he is doing, stares into space for a few seconds with his eyelids fluttering, unaware of his surroundings, then just as abruptly resumes normal activity, unaware that a seizure has occurred.

Self-advocacy. Speaking up for oneself; asking for what one needs.

Self-determination. Deciding one's own fate/future.

Self-management. The ability to regulate one's own behavior, including monitoring (see also self-regulation).

Self-regulation. Ability to recognize and regulate one's own emotional or sensory responses (see also self-regulatory behaviors).

Self-regulatory behaviors. (Previously referred to as self-stimulatory behaviors or stimming) Repetitive or idiosyncratic physical movements, vocalizations, or actions that function as an attempt to regulate one's own emotional or sensory responses (see self-regulation).

Semantic. Relating to the meaning of a word or phrase.

Sensitivity. Level of reaction to sensory input.

Sensory meltdown. A tantrum in response to overwhelming, unavoidable sensory experiences (e.g., the noise and smells of a lunchroom).

Sensory needs. The necessary types/amounts of sensory input required for an individual to be comfortable.

Sensory perception. The brain's recognition and interpretation of sensory input.

Sensory processing. The brain's perception of and response to sensory input.

Sensory Profile. A norm-referenced questionnaire developed by Winnie Dunn for assessing an individual's sensory processing patterns.

Shaping. Teaching a new behavior by reinforcing successive approximations of it.

Shared focus. Two or more people paying attention to the same activity, object, or issue.

Simple memory. Basic memory for straightforward information.

Slow triggers (setting events). Situations that cause stress and make a student less able to cope with demands; indirect triggers.

Social autopsies. An adult-directed exchange between a student and a mentor in which a social error is defined and methods of (a) making amends and/or (b) interacting successfully in future events are discussed.

Social Behavior Mapping. A cognitive behavioral strategy for teaching the connections among emotions, behaviors, others' perspectives, and consequences.

Social cognition. Social thinking. How a person processes and interprets information about other people and their interactions.

Social communication. Communication that has a deliberate effect on another person's concentration, thought processes, or emotions.

Social dimensions of play. The quality of a child's interactions with others during play.

Social interaction. Individuals modifying their behavior in response to one another.

Social learning. Learning to understand others' perspectives and to behave in ways that others will consider socially appropriate.

Social motivation. When the desire to have some interaction with others is an incentive.

Social-pragmatic theory. The theory that a child's language development is highly dependent on joint attention, affect and attention sharing, and intention reading.

Social referencing. Looking to others (especially parents) for clues as to how to behave, react, or interpret a situation.

Social scripts. Written sentences or paragraphs that contain brief descriptions and text that can be used verbatim in academic and/or nonacademic settings.

Social stimuli. Stimuli involving human interaction.

Social Stories™. A cognitive intervention developed by Carol Gray that uses short, individualized narratives to explain social situations and appropriate behaviors.

Social thinking. (see Social Cognition).

Social validation. Evaluation of intervention outcomes pertaining to social relevance and importance based on feedback from key stakeholders, including family members and the individuals themselves as well as others who serve and care for them.

Somatosensory. Relating to the sensory signals from the skin, muscles, and joints.

Special interest areas (SIAs). Often solitary pursuits or preoccupations that dominate the person's time, attention, and conversation.

Specifiers. A term used in the DSM-5 to describe additional information relevant to the diagnosis.

Speed of processing. The rate at which the brain is able to take in information, sort it, analyze it, and respond to it.

Standardized tests. Tests that are administered and scored in a uniform manner, after which an individual's results are compared to large group norms.

Strange Stories Test. A theory-of-mind assessment in which individuals are asked to interpret nonliteral statements (e.g., sarcasm) made by characters in stories developed by Francesca Happé.

Structured teaching. An educational approach to teaching children with autism that emphasizes physical organization of the environment, schedules, work systems, and visual structure. See also TEACCH.

Student-centered. Based on the individual student's needs, preferences, and interests.

Student study team (SST) meeting/Child study team (CST) meeting. A formal meeting of teachers, professionals, and parents, when there is concern about a child who has not yet been evaluated or formally identified as having special education needs.

Subjective states. The ability to share others' attitudes and feelings.

Successive approximations. In shaping, incremental changes in behavior that increasingly resemble the desired behavior.

Supported employment. Jobs in which individuals with disabilities work alongside neurotypical individuals but receive ongoing support.

Symbol. An abstract representation that communicates an idea. Symbols can range from pointing to pictures to written and spoken language.

Symbolic communication. Use of symbols of any sort to communicate meaning..

Symbolic currency. An abstract way of exchanging ideas — usually language.

Symbolic dimension of play (simple and advanced). Play acts directed by the child toward objects, self, or others to signify events, exploratory play, and/or conventional object use.

Symbolic modeling. A type of modeling that involves copying fictional characters from television, books, etc.

Syntactic. Relating to the grammatical arranging of words into sentences.

Synthesized modeling. A type of modeling that requires combining several observations to create a new behavior.

Systemizing. Creating and utilizing concrete systems to understand social information and predict events.

T

Tabula rasa. Latin term meaning "blank slate." Refers to the belief that an infant is born with no innate mental content, and that a person's entire resource of knowledge will be based on his or her experience of the world.

TEACCH (Treatment and Education of Autistic and related Communication handicapped CHildren). Statewide autism services program in North Carolina, where the Structured Teaching method was developed.

Theory of mind. The ability to recognize and understand other people's thoughts, feelings, desires, and intentions in order to make sense of their behavior and be able to predict what they will do next.

Threshold. The point at which the brain notices/responds to stimuli.

Transition. 1. Any environmental change, such as a change of location, activity, or support personnel. Transitions can be minor, such as changing activities within the classroom, or major, such as moving from elementary school to middle school. 2. The change from school to post-school life.

Transition coordinator/specialist. An individual who specializes in transition planning and coordination of resources.

Transition planning. The collaborative process of planning for a student's transition from school to post-school life.

U

Underlying Characteristics Checklist (UCC). Developed by Ruth Aspy and Barry Grossman, an informal assessment tool used to identify an individual's ASD-related characteristics for the purpose of intervention.

V

Vestibular system. The parts of the inner ear and nervous system that control balance and movement.

Video self-modeling. A type of modeling that involves the individual who is learning a skill performing the skill on video.

Visual thinking. Thinking via mental imagery.

Visuospatial processing. The brain's interpretation of spatial relationships among objects, based on information sent from the eyes.

Vocal intonation. Tone and pitch of voice.

Vocal recognition of emotion. The ability to recognize another person's mental state based on their voice.

W

Working memory. Short-term memory used for temporarily storing information while simultaneously processing additional material.

Z

Zones of Regulation. A strategy for teaching students to develop deeper awareness of their sensory and emotional systems to help them understand the type of zone in which they are functioning at any given point in time. Sensory and social emotional learning strategies are then provided to help students shift their physical and emotional responses as a way of moving them into a zone that helps them to better function in their current situation, as needed.

Advance Praise ...

"It is rare to see such a comprehensive guide to research and theory in autism that at the same time uses exemplars to make it all accessible and addresses the question that parents and educators most want to know – what does it all mean, and how can I use it to make a difference? This book will be a wonderful resource for all those seeking to understand (and value) people with autism spectrum disorders."
  – Professor Rita Jordan, Autism Centre for Education & Research, University of Birmingham, United Kingdom

"How much easier my life would have been if I had read this book during my teacher education classes years ago! This material bridges the gap between theory and practice for those who work with children on the autism spectrum, saving much trial and error. The Tips for Practical Application are especially helpful."
  – Mary Schlieder, special educator and author, *With Open Arms – Creating School Communities of Support for Kids with Social Challenges*

"From the perspective of a parent of a child with autism, a former special education teacher, and a teacher educator, this book is terrific! The editors and authors did a great job of explaining the subtleties and the challenges of teaching children on the spectrum; and, all of them are highly respected leaders in the field. When I teach courses on autism, I will definitely use this book as my core textbook."
  – Pamela LePage, Ph.D., San Francisco State University

P.O. Box 23173
Shawnee Mission, Kansas 66283-0173
www.aapcpublishing.net

CPSIA information can be obtained
at www.ICGtesting.com
Printed in the USA
LVHW050843070521
686670LV00001B/6